WE'LL SEE THE CUCKOO

We'll see the Cuckoo

JEAN BROWN

Illustrated by

Pauline Walters, Joe Walters and Jennifer Sharp

We'll see the Cuckoo
Copyright © Jean Brown, 1993, 2004, 2008

First published in 1994
Reprinted in 1995
Second edition published in 2004

This edition published in 2008 by Palatine Books,
an imprint of Carnegie Publishing Ltd
Carnegie House, Chatsworth Road, Lancaster LA1 4SL

British Library Cataloguing-in-Publication data
A catalogue record for this book is available from the British Library

ISBN 978–1–874181–56–9

Typeset by Carnegie Book Production, Lancaster
Printed and bound by Biddles Ltd, King's Lynn

For Mother, of course

This is an autobiography about ordinary people getting the maximum of fun out of ordinary things. If it has any value at all on a bookshelf it is to say to other ordinary people that life isn't ordinary at all. It's a miracle from first to last and if you don't know how to find it so you have missed the most important truth of all.

We'll see the Cuckoo, p. 420

Dear Folks who live on a Hill,

Last night I watched the moon as it tried to make its presence known from behind a church tower and a myriad of chimney pots and TV aerials, and I thought how different from the unobstructed and effortless path it travelled last week.

It goes without saying we thoroughly enjoyed our stay, the atmosphere, the company and the exceptional fare.

Margaret, thanks for those little chats that convinced me there really was a 'once upon a time'.

I wouldn't like to think we won't be able to come and see you again.

Our sincere wishes to you and yours,

Lily & Phillie.

Introduction

I t is one song of a morning. There is nothing like a downpour to green the countryside. God is in his Heaven this morning, that's for sure.

We are travelling gently northwards towards Oban where, because it is Sunday, the mail boat to Tiree lies anchored against the quay, waiting for us, for we have left The Currer. The present is a wonderful anodyne, a blissful in-between. I am not even driving, for Margaret is doing this lap of the journey we know so well. We need no map and the A6 is empty. Occasionally, when the old road brushes the new too closely, we hear the M6 roar of traffic and see people in a hurry but we can no longer identify with them.

Do not mistake me. Thirty-five to forty m.p.h. is the speed at which we travel in the Range Rover and not the speed at which we lead our busy lives. Perhaps that is what is different about other people who saunter more sedately and sensibly through life but punctuate their less energetic activity with fast driving along the highroads. We career from one big job to the next, without pausing to take a breath, but, having left The Currer behind, having exchanged two legs for four wheels, we gently meander northwards as relaxed as if yesterday, the last month, year, lifetime, has never been.

Why bother to think about what is behind us? The present is enough, climbing Shap Fell on a simply glorious day. I should be dreaming about the holiday ahead, for Scotland will call us for just as long as we can take our ageing family. On the western horizon Tiree is bathed in sunlight, I am sure, and most of our friends are waiting. Sadly, this year there will be no Auntie Chrissie and no John Lachie. The flowers for his funeral will hardly have withered. Tiree without John Lachie cannot be imagined.

There are five of us in the fifteen-year-old, white Range Rover, and two collies, Lusky brought from Luskentyre, on Harris, five years ago and Jess, a pup we brought from Hubbersty, in the Lakeland hills. Mother, an incredible ninety-one, sits in the middle back seat between our handicapped brother Harry and me. Beside Margaret is the fifth member of the family, Auntie Mary, our almost permanent resident.

To think forward to our holiday in the Hebrides is bliss and normally I would be sitting anticipating the joys I know lie ahead. I love the together-ness of family in the Range Rover, with nothing to do but find the emptiest road, and all our needs within arm's length. There is a comfortable silence, even more so than usual, and it could be that the others are thinking back-wards, too. A few days ago we reached an important milestone in our joint history with The Currer and it is understandable if our thoughts are not on the present journey, beautiful though it is with the sun streaming down the fells and falling hotly on our starboard windows, but on the journey we have all made together for more than half a century. It's been an uphill climb and the milestone is a pinnacle on a hilltop.

Just leaving The Currer for a fortnight is an experience which all our guests profess to share. Pre-holiday activity everyone knows, but leaving The Currer must be a unique experience known only to my sister Margaret and me. If we were to define ourselves, my diminutive, fifty-year-old sister would say she is a farmer and I would say I am a retired village school headmistress, nine years her senior, but the definition would be too simple, in the same way that to describe the past month as pre-holiday activity is an understatement.

The marathon task begins with the annual spring clean of the two dozen rooms within our converted seventeenth-century barn. Endlessly, like some bizarre Florence Nightingale, Margaret dodges the continual flow of guests and, with Paint-Mate in one hand and the pad oozing white emulsion in the other, she goes from room to room, often in the small hours, until every one is Persil white.

I begin getting up at five to do an hour a day of year-end accounts and fill in VAT and income tax forms before the first breakfasts are needed. On fine days, two by two, bedspreads and curtains take their turn in the washer and dance on the line with the normal, huge, daily wash which has become our lot.

Spring-cleaning annually becomes an obsession. Every door and wash boarding, every window frame and cupboard, receives a once-over with the gloss paint brush. I lay the paperwork aside and hang a few rolls instead. The room looks fresh; I get the bug and paper another one. Margaret puts the white paint away and gets out the varnish.

We ponder, occasionally, on what it would be like to tidy a small house, pack a bag, lock a door and go, leaving ordinary life to stand still. Our life cannot be halted. Supply staff must come in and the show must go on.

We must not allow spring-cleaning mania to make us forget to send for the boat tickets, order more coke and wood and corn and bread. We must make sure the tractor man knows he must take the two feet of bedding muck out of the cattle sheds and that the man who delivers the straw knows that the next load must come before we leave. Deliveries are not simple. It is our job to restack the straw, throw two tons of logs under the barn steps, prepare the corn bin, collect the bread. Four hundred pounds' worth of food must be bought at the Cash and Carry and the four freezers emptied, cleaned and restocked.

But the leaving of food, fuel and fodder and a maze of clean rooms and tidy cupboards is as nothing compared with the leaving of the herd of one hundred cattle, the pigs, the goats and donkeys. The whole herd of yearling heifers must be driven, one by one, into the crush and given a spring copper injection, for Pennine hillsides are short of it and a deficiency means death. Strong animals are potential back or leg breakers. We are crushed, trampled on, indecently assaulted with manure and skin is ripped from our knuckles before the last animal is taken away by Jess. We have heifers which think they are show jumpers, to whom a gate is nothing, others who try to climb out of the crush on hind legs like dancing bears and those who prefer to pray, kneel down in the crush and refuse to budge. We win, of course. Margaret sees to that.

The three hour job is completed without interval for on one occasion we did break for coffee and found that the waiting half of the herd had let themselves out and mingled with their contemporaries! We had been worming on that occasion. As a double dose will not kill, we had to begin the job all over again the next morning and our negligence cost us £40.

The donkeys' feet need a manicure. Both donkeys are friendly until the blacksmith comes. The concrete round the house keeps their hooves trim most of the time but after the snow melts and if the earth retains too much water and the pastures abound with mud, the blacksmith must be sent for.

I remember the first time. Aware that Jasper had never been haltered, Margaret had set about breaking him in. Each day she became more confident that he was becoming tame and biddable but when the blacksmith came Jasper went berserk. He was deaf to all Margaret's endearments. She tried to calm him with gentleness, muttering reassuring, female extravagancies. 'Good boy, good boy,' she said to the raving lunatic. 'Gently now,' she begged the maniac. I was leaning, with the blacksmith, over the shed gate expecting, every minute, to see my sister trampled underfoot.

Suddenly the blacksmith began to climb over the securely tied gate. 'O'd on yer bluddy bastard,' he shouted. 'Wot the bluddy 'ell d' yer think yer at?' and Jasper stopped in his tracks. The swearing continued whilst the mesmerised donkey allowed himself to be haltered and tethered. It continued whilst each hoof was cut and filed and we were as flabbergasted as the donkeys. After that the brown donkey, Chocolate, behaved sensibly. Each year, just before we go on holiday, the performance is repeated. For days Margaret halters and woos Jasper into docility. He gently tolerates her lifting each foot in turn and, with quiet eyes, listens to her explanations. But can she catch him in the shed, when the blacksmith comes, not she! The amused man waits a little longer, each time, before he makes his dramatic entrance. He does not need to speak, let alone swear. Jasper knows when he is beaten.

With a few exceptions, nearly all our pre-holiday activity is replay. Our annual appointment at the vet's comes in the week before we leave and both dogs must have their booster injections. Our dogs know how to drive cattle, pen geese, bark at passing joggers, nip guests who embrace us in the farmyard and, to their shame, how to chase cars up the road. They also know how to behave very badly in the surgery waiting room, holding unpleasant conversations with the other dogs, in the same way that they become monsters when they are in the back of the Range Rover, barking at every dog that comes in sight. We are ashamed. We behave much better in the dentist's waiting room, a few days later, for our six monthly inspection lands close to departure date and we always forget to change it. We would forget to go but Harry reminds us. There is no aggression in our behaviour. If we have to wait more than a few minutes we fall asleep and the reclining dentist's chair puts me out without any anaesthetic.

Each year it is the same. The corn traveller comes for his upwards of a thousand pounds a month. As the cheque book is still on the table, beside his empty coffee mug, I sit down and pay all the bills and the overdraft soars. So I write to the bank manager and tell him that the spring calves will be bought on our return and that the hundred bulling heifers will not be sold until August. No doubt he grins widely at the amount of interest we'll have to pay!

Margaret rings the man who sells us a hundred weaned calves and learns that the delivery date is on our immediate return. She also learns that the cost of each will be considerably higher than the year before!

During this week of panic and the two weeks of our absence, no cattle, pigs or donkeys must stray over the boundary. Margaret walks the three-mile enclosing drystone wall, older even than the farmhouses which perch on our untouched medieval hillside. Weather and seasons, frost and hot sun ensure their constant need of repair. She rebuilds where stones have fallen, secures the stiles and notes the fences which will need both of us and a hefty mallet. At the first opportunity we take sledgehammer, bar, staples and barbed wire and sometimes a bale of straw to stand on to do this, the least attractive of the many lousy jobs we do. Barbed wire is evil and alive and we always return from fencing with torn flesh and black thumbnails. It is not easy to bake cakes and pastries with hands decorated with sticking plasters. Mother is our chief cake baker, and Auntie Mary will also be busy making shortbread and ginger biscuits for us to take on holiday.

Three months before it pleased us to receive pre-holiday bookings from those dear guests who come every year. 'The last week will be easy,' we said. When the time comes we remember that frequent guests are also frequently in our kitchen, or chatting with Mother in our sitting room. In fact we fall over regular guests all the time. They come from Canada and Glasgow, Kent, France and Australia and think they belong to the family.

Without Harry to keep reminding us, prompting us and finding numbers in the telephone directory, many things would be forgotten. We dash into town, buy the only new pairs of trousers we get each year, Harry a shirt and Mother some stockings. Piles begin to grow on the dressing table and the bathroom window ledge and cases are lifted from the spare room cupboard. Lusky knows what is happening. Jess is bewildered, never having been on holiday before.

The load of ordered straw is delivered and with it comes a mischievous wind which blows it all over the yard and through open windows into the newly spring cleaned bedrooms. The last bale is thrown into the shed. Jack says, 'That's the one I've been looking for,' and sweeps the floor of his lorry. The air is full of flying straw and little drifts of it settle at the front door. A good wind should, in all fairness, blow debris away but a wind, from any direction at all, circles in the yard and everything comes to rest on our door-step. When the tractor man comes to take the manure out of the cattle sheds, it is invariably raining. The spreader dribbles its load all the way up the road, time and time again. The huge wheels drag manure and mud into the yard and the rain continues.

When the two days of muck spreading and rain are over I put on my wellies, take the muck pusher and remove the black mess from the yard and road. The sticking plasters on my fingers soak up the smelly wetness. I walk into the duck pond, clean my gumboots and tear off the revolting Elastoplast.

Margaret takes spring head nails and secures the corrugated tins on the Dutch barn. We are out too long and Mother begins to have a nervous break-down, once again declaring that this is absolutely the very last time we are going on holiday. I scrub up with nailbrush and Vim for I must start yet another evening meal. People have just booked in from Germany, or Cambridge, Austria or Aberdeen. I am ashamed of the discoloured yard and beg the cleansing rain to continue.

Harry reminds us that he wants a bath, needs shaving, must go to the barber's, and that we must ring for his prescription and collect his Gaviscon. Just as the evening meal is about to be served the phone rings. Someone, who knows we serve at seven, rings to re-book for the summer!

At last the large family round the extended dining room table is fed and it is the turn of the hundred heifers. So help me, one will be lame. 'I've got a heifer with foul!' Margaret will tell me. It is never too lame to refuse to go meekly into the crush for a dose of Streptopen.

'We'd better put the whole herd through a foot bath!' Margaret decides. So next morning she fills the crush well with innumerable buckets of water and half a gallon of formalin and we persuade the herd to walk through and not be put off by the strange smell. Having steered a hundred Hereford heifers through the crush, Margaret guides Mother into the kitchen for a hair wash and holiday perm. The front room begins to smell heavily of lotion.

Guests returning early say, 'Is this a good time to go in and chat with Mother?' but Mother's head is still under the kitchen tap so the guests are given a cup of tea and the visit everyone so enjoys is postponed. A family friend from the village, who has walked three quarters of a mile to get here, cannot be turned away. Her dog and ours disagree and Lusky and Jess are shoved into the Range Rover whilst the canine stranger swaggers into their house.

Someone from the Min. of Ag. appears, a neighbour with a query about a right of way, a rambler grumbling about the mud winter has left on the footpaths, some children wanting to look at the donkeys, a man from the Ordnance Survey. If Margaret and I are both at home, only one of us will stop work. If one of us is out there is no alternative but to down tools. Unexpected visitors are prepared to wait even two hours for our return and when the Range Rover spills out its people and groceries they are still here. Our callers are quite happy to ignore the fact that we have not eaten, happily accept an invitation to join the family lunch and do not seem to notice that Margaret and I have stopped eating altogether. Before a holiday it, like sleeping, is something that other people do.

The Range Rover must have a service before we make the long, lovely trip north. The Land Rover specialists are six miles of country lanes away. Margaret asks a friend to follow her there and bring her home. When the vehicle is to be collected we dare not ask again. In the days before bed-and-breakfast we thought nothing of walking the six miles, but now the 'unforgiving minute' is so full we take a taxi, reluctantly and critically. Harry, of course, comes too. We sit on the back seat, holding on, whilst the driver speeds along narrow country lanes at 60 m.p.h. and his radio loudly pours out pop music. We are both trembling when we arrive at the garage. I tell the young man he drives too quickly and he is not one bit pleased. Harry and I get into our own vehicle and drive gently home.

Once through the gate into The Currer, to say the view is splendid is an understatement. Why have we been given so little time to stand in quiet worship?

A guest in a wheelchair has arrived. A bed must be raised, lowered, or moved to accommodate his winch. The phone is ringing. Some firm wants me to advertise with them, put in payphones, sell me a computer, put TVs in the bedrooms. 'We are farmers,' I say. 'I'm sorry but we do not need your services.'

Margaret is outside unblocking a drain. Always, before we go, there is a foreign body blocking a pipe. We bring out the drain rods and poke first from one manhole and then from another until there is a glug somewhere and a torrent of water and you-know-what plus the foreign body. We heave a sigh of relief if there are no guest spectators and helpful, interfering men!

Days hurtle by at a frightening speed. We must go to the bank, find our driving licences, include the boat tickets, pack the groceries for self-catering. The last day comes with its steady downpour. I drive the Range Rover into the yard, take a bucket of soapy water and a soft, long handled brush and lather the old friend well. The cloudburst rinses it better than I could. Whilst the rain bounces off the yard I take the stiff brush and sweep it clean. 'Thank God for rain,' I sing, wiping the river running from my drenched hair. Inside it is a different story with the day's washing hanging from the kitchen ceiling.

At the last minute things have a habit of going wrong, the washer begins to leak, the vacuum won't work. We send for the electrician and fall over him all day. Someone forgets to draw the shower curtain; there is flood on the bathroom floor and water seeps into the dining room. I mop it up and tidy the linen cupboard. Margaret rolls up her sleeves and cleans the ovens. I guide Mother upstairs where the old lady is still capable of doing her own packing and Harry struggles on alone with the washing-up.

I follow Mother upstairs determined to be on call should she dissolve into tears because she cannot see well enough to find something she has lost. She cannot accept that to be packing a suitcase at all is no mean feat and that not many people of ninety-one are heading for the Hebrides. I sweep the pile from the dressing table and the towels from the window-ledge.

One of us takes the empty vehicle for Auntie Mary, throws her suitcase in with Harry on the back seat, turns off her water and electricity and then leaves her tidy house to return to ours which is in turmoil. But the rain has ceased and the clouds are breaking. Margaret climbs onto the Range Rover roof rack and I begin throwing up the luggage peculiar to all those heading for self-catering cottages with the disabled and elderly. Finally up go the wheelchairs which make it possible for Margaret and me still to walk briskly on the hard, Hebridean sands. On goes our excellent, Bowness-made roof rack cover.

We begin to wonder if we told our stalwart friends everything when they came to be briefed a few days ago, if our written instructions are clear and adequate. They have been our supply staff for years but every time is different. To explain feeding and bedding and numbers and when to call a vet is Margaret's responsibility. Mine is to detail who will come, when they will come and when they will go, where they will sleep and how much they will pay.

But there is no time to agonize for we must turn all our attention to making and serving the last evening meal for a fortnight. I peep at the roast beef in the oven and make the soup. Margaret prepares the vegetables and I mix the Yorkshire puddings. That we are five minutes late taking out the soup and still have the fruit to put on the flans and the cream to whip, is normal for us. There is the usual cheer from the dozen or more guests at the table when the Yorkshire puddings are taken out, the usual argument as to who will carve the roast beef, the usual relaxed and friendly atmosphere.

Then bedding must be put down, cattle counted and fed, ducks and hens locked up for the night and the nanny goat milked. Long before we have finished it is time to take out the hot chocolate and Horlicks and time for three members of the family to have a bath. A new day begins and we are still checking and re-checking. It is one o'clock before Margaret fetches up the last hod of coke for the Aga.

Exhausted, we crawl under a blanket on the sitting room floor, for our beds are already made for our supply staff. This is no hardship. We sleep equally well on the ground but know we have succumbed to sleep before there is complete order and that we must rise long before dawn. That, too, is no hardship. We are asleep simultaneously as heads touch pillows, remain so for three hours, and wake in the coldness of four o'clock to finish doing what has to be done.

It seemed to me, when we rose at that early hour this morning, that we must have been on a great many holidays for the feeling was familiar. The morning of departure had arrived, like all its predecessors. In the last minutes before dawn Margaret ran out to catch the billy goat and pare his over-grown hooves, a struggle she was too tired to make last night.

I filled the freezer bag, simplified the notice board, loaded and started the washer, filled the flasks and put stamps on my letters. Outside, a new day was dawning 'silver and green and gold'. Yesterday's rain had left a clean and empty sky and a mist followed the river and filled the floor of the valley. Eight car windscreens caught and reflected the rising sun. Behind them waited the Range Rover with its blue PVC roof rack cover.

We roused our sleeping, elderly family quietly so as not to wake our recumbent guests and all had a cup of tea. Of course, we were not absolutely ready when Dorothy and George came at six o'clock. The table needed the first of the many wipes it gets each day and our tea mugs were not washed, but there comes a time when what is not done remains so and we had to leave Dorothy and her daughter Joy to begin the early breakfasts. There will come a time too, when life itself is done and our work may not be quite finished but we will have to go and let someone else get on with it at The Currer.

Three hours ago we pulled out of the yard with hair undone, faces unwashed and shoe laces untied. The dogs were barking enough to wake our sleeping guests and we were a little shamefaced because all was not perfect as we left. We climbed the hill to the cattle grid and began the descent, first into the village and then into town.

Mother was asking innumerable questions and our answers were not being heard. Three-quarters of a mile from home Margaret said, 'She's not got her hearing aid,' and we turned round and went back to The Currer. On the other side of the cattle grid, on the steep hillside a quarter of a mile above home, Mother said, 'Stop. Don't let's go down. Just run down and get it.'

'Yes Jean, just run down and get it,' said Margaret who was driving and we all had hysterics. We were still laughing when we drove into the yard to the amazement of the breakfast makers and still laughing when we drove out. We had already relaxed.

Again at the cattle grid we turned to look at the place in which we will always live, God willing. Yesterday's rain had washed and glorified our Yorkshire hillside. The mist had already climbed out of the valley and lost itself on our moor top. On the distant horizon, fifty miles away, stood the table top of Ingleborough. What a place to live, this Pennine hill farm that we fell in love with as soon as we were able to walk and married as soon as we were able to work.

But now we have left it well behind and are gently travelling northwards on the empty A6, not thinking about our holiday but about our history because of the incredible milestone we reached a few days ago when our joint signatures preserved, in perpetuity, our four-hundred-year-old farmhouse and the 170 acres which surround it. Behind us, in the immediate past, lies the rush to get away. But there is so much more than that, packing our memory with happiness.

I see it all, better, perhaps, because of the hour's sleep we gave ourselves, after breakfast, outside Kirkby Lonsdale. If behind us there lies a saga worth telling it must surely be part of the history of ordinary people. The things we have done, and still do, are part of a past that may never return. The slow, poor, get-there-by-walking, do-it-yourself-by-hand, self-supporting real-life will soon be unknown and this account of our lives at The Currer will indeed read as history.

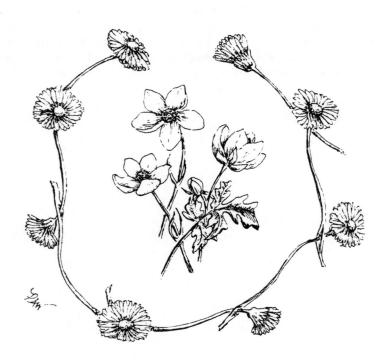

Part One

Here hath been dawning
Another new day,
Think, wilt thou let it
Slip useless away?

Out of Eternity
This new day is born.
Into Eternity
At night will return.

(*Author Unknown*)

Chapter One

O n the night that I was born my almost three-year-old brother slept all night for the first time. It was as if Someone up there said, 'Enough is enough,' as if a successful birth took away some of the trauma of the painful one, as if the handicapped child felt instinctively the security of having another baby in the family. Whereas it is generally supposed that toddlers are jealous of new siblings, my birth acted as an anodyne for my agitated and frustrated brother and from then onwards his dreadful, sleepless nights were infrequent.

Contentedly sleeping in an adjacent cot, I was unaware of the fact that I had already reached the point of no return, that one road only lay ahead and that great joy would be in developing the technique of loving what I had to do. To do only what one pleases seldom brings happiness. Liking what one has to do is a philosophy worth adopting, for happiness is not then a risk but a certainty.

My birth was normal and there was a great relief within our extended family. The night that Harry was born had been very different. His birth had required forceps and both mother and baby had been in danger. Grandma Brown was a competent, untrained midwife, often giving her services in the neighbourhood. She and a well loved family doctor, Dr Tom Spencer, delivered the baby alive but the difficult birth had resulted in a handicapped child. The condition was known as birth paralysis but now it is called cerebral palsy.

When I was old enough to understand, Father talked to me of the morning after the night that Harry was born. Delivering milk in a fast, preoccupied silence, he had only been worried about his wife. Suddenly, with his last call and the prospect of a long hill home ahead of him, he realised that he could not bear to lose his son either. He was a gentle man and it wasn't his custom to harass the staid, black horse pulling the milk float up the steep and mile-long hill. The cobbles gave the hooves plenty of grip but made the empty cans rattle and bounce. Always, on the homeward trek, Father walked beside his horse, lightening the load but that morning, he told me, he had jumped aboard and urged the horse quickly up the hill.

His brother Percy's only child was a girl so the arrival of a son called for the carrying on of a family name. The baby was named Harry after his paternal grandfather and Booth after his maternal grandmother's family. To rear such a fragile baby in those days was no small achievement. He had big brown eyes and a beautiful face but the nerve-shattering experience had made him fretful and demanding.

For two years and nine months my parents had not had one night of uninterrupted sleep. Hour after hour they had taken turns pacing the floor, hushing their restless baby. He could neither walk nor talk but the big, brown eyes proclaimed intelligence and his frustrated screams cried out for help. Totally worn out, my parents learned to sleep at the touch of a pillow but I never heard one grumble. The experience had only brought tiredness.

But on the night of my arrival, Harry slept all night. My parents felt as if some turning point had been reached. Mother told me, years later, how they all said, 'This baby has come for a place.'

There is a great acceptance in our family of the inevitable.

Contentedly sleeping in my cot I was unaware of Grandfather Brown's recent visit to the sale of the nearby St Ives Estate. Death duties necessitated that many farms and acres should be sold in small lots. Grandfather went to the auction and made a successful bid of £1,050 for a sixteenth-century farmhouse and 170 acres of poor pasture and moorland. He was a very uncommunicative man who never knew how to relate to either of his sons or to his grandchildren but we owe everything to him for having had the courage to make that successful bid.

His intention had been that Father, his youngest son, would live at The Currer, the newly acquired farmhouse. The beamed and mullioned house was as it had been built. The only approach was a deeply rutted cart track, walled and very steep and the only supply of water came from a well in the cellar. There was no sanitation and no electricity and even Grandfather must have realised he could not expect Mother, with a handicapped son and a new baby, to accept such primitive isolation.

Father refused, and the house was let to a succession of tenants who were prepared to put up with the inconveniences, for a very small rent. The barn and pigsties we used and the land was grazed and hay harvested from the intakes but the potential of the 1929 acquisition was never realised. No money was spent on the house and its condition deteriorated. Grandfather collected the rents and, I have been recently told by a lady who was born there, he took sweets for the children. I liked to hear that, for I can never remember one time when my grandfather gave us anything but I do not bear him any grudge, for he left us The Currer. Throughout my child-hood the house was always avoided and to me, 'T' Currer' was simply an expanse of moorland, some fields and a wooded glen. The Currer was land, not house, isolated land where the wind blew us in front of it and where, at hay-making time, the sun beat down on us and our hand-rakes and pitch-forks. The extra land put more work on Father's shoulders but there was no mistaking his deep love of the newly bought hillside with its unparalleled view of the dale.

My progress was normal. Pessimistic neighbours peered into the pram expecting to see another maimed child but they saw only an ordinary baby whose needs must inevitably come second. As I began to talk, so Harry followed suit. Others could not initially tell what he said but I always could and if there had been speech therapists in those days I am sure Harry's speech would not have proved his prime handicap. It was never a problem within the family but everyone, and Harry in particular, likes to extend his conversation to other people. Soon after I began to run sturdily around, Harry began to take his first tottering steps and he has been on his feet ever since. Mother bought gallons of liniment and olive oil to massage his spindly legs, I began to drag him around with a normal child's enthusiasm and muscles began to develop on the thin limbs. The doctor used to say, 'Just farmhouse food, Mrs Brown.'

My first real recollection is of being awakened on a dark night at the beginning of the calendar year in which I was three. I was wrapped in a blanket and carried through falling snow to my uncle's house. I remember that I felt unco-operative and I am told that I protested quite loudly. My brother had been taken ill, but not at home. Once a week he spent a night with Grandma Smith and the aunts in town. On this particular night, his attack was frightening enough for my parents to be sent for and Auntie Mary braved one of the worst snowstorms of the century to climb the long hill to fetch them. So I was carried through the driving snow to spend the rest of the night in my cousin Freda's bed.

I was miserable. There was no affinity between my father and his brother and, though Uncle's family lived next door, they were comparative strangers. Their house was a place I did not know well and I was very unhappy.

My Aunt Bertha was kind and nine-year-old Freda coaxed me to eat my breakfast and to play but I know my sulkiness remained until my father came. Two feet of snow had fallen and it was over a mile to Grandma Smith's house but I know that the struggle through the snow with Father would be all I needed to restore my good humour. When we reached my grandmother's house, he lifted me to peer, red-cheeked and frosted, through the window and all the ladies cried. I remember none of this, only the fear of being left behind in the night. The walk through the snow was to be repeated so many hundreds of times that the first has been forgotten.

I haven't forgotten Grandmother Smith's house. It was a very familiar place until 1970. When we were only knee high, Harry and I knew all about Mother's family for story telling was our entertainment and Mother can talk better than anyone I know. She is never at a loss for a subject to raise, and will still talk until morning if we let her. So often now, more than half a century later, we gather round her to hear the fascinating stories of when she was a girl.

When we were small, of course, Father worked late, milking cows and foddering the herd. Harry went to bed when they did and so did I. Whilst waiting for Father to come in from the farm Mother would talk to us, telling us all she'd done, all she knew and how we should always behave.

She told us all about Great-grandfather Smith. She was so proud of him and repeatedly told us how the doctor had feared he had TB and advised him to give up his job as a mill mechanic and find an outdoor life. The young man had bought himself a couple of baskets and begun hawking fruit and vegetables. Some kind friend had loaned him a donkey but later he had bought his own, and a cart, and eventually he had opened a market stall. Great-grandfather sold greengroceries for forty years but will not be remembered for that. Mother proudly told us how he had branched out into the livery stable business, eventually owning twenty-two horses and all the coaches and horse-drawn vehicles necessary to provide a service for almost the whole town. Her father Tom, one of the younger sons, had driven horses, sometimes four in hand, pulling carriages and the hearse. He had also skated on Redcar Tarn, selling oranges during frosty winters. No one else, it seemed to Harry and me, had such an interesting family.

Mother's childhood fascinated us. She had been born in 1896, two years after Great-grandfather had built the Town Hall Livery Stables, the first of five children. Grandfather reared them on 18s. a week which must have been barely adequate. Business does not prosper if sons get well paid! There were, however, many compensations for if customers did not require his services, he could take his family out in the governess cart, to visit relatives or to picnic in the Dales. Harry and I could picture the happy family outings, the long dresses, starched sailor collars, laced boots and big bonnets. 'Tell us again,' we would say and Mother would repeat the story of a return from Leeds, when the horses had shied, throwing Grandfather from the driving seat and terrifying the children. After any outing, Mother remembered, Grandmother seated the children, in their coats and leggings, in a row on the sofa whilst she, still wearing her bonnet, bent to re-light the fire. She remembered the clip-clop of horses' hooves growing fainter as Grandfather took the governess cart back to the stables.

I remember that whatever local town or village or hamlet anyone mentioned, Grandfather would always say, 'Ah took a corpse from theer.'

Mother would take out the photographs of him perched on the outside seat of the carriage and of the funerals of gentry and tell us that it was Grandfather driving the hearse. She would tell us of the twenty-two horses stabled on the first floor of the Town Hall Livery Stables, above the tack room and underneath the living quarters of Great-grandfather's family. She would tell us how Grandfather smelled of the polish used on the harness and of wet carriage blankets. The Aunts would let us handle the polished carriage horn and we would make feeble attempts to blow it. Mother told us they always knew when Grandfather was coming by his whistle as he came over the railway bridge and turned into the street. She told us of the first horse-drawn penny bus, of the charabanc taking picnic parties and all the rich variety of coaches and carriages.

What a blessing it was for parents before the age of soap operas. Children could be taught from real life family history. We didn't know anything about how other people lived, what were their values and priorities. We only knew what was acceptable in our family until we were old enough not to be influenced by that which, outside our lives, would not be tolerated. Mother made sure that we knew all about our background and that we mirrored it.

In our sewing box was a tin of trouser buttons, metal and engraved with the name, William Booth. All our clothes were homemade and, when a garment was done, the buttons were kept for future use. The button box was our counting apparatus, our toy and our history book. Sometimes Mother would thread a large one on a piece of string and we would make it spin. Sometimes we would ask about Great-grandfather Booth, the tailor, who sewed these buttons on the trousers he made.

William Booth had also been landlord of The Royal in a hilltop village six miles out of town. His wife died suddenly after a short illness, probably Bright's disease, and soon afterwards William died too, people said of a broken heart. He left six orphans. My Grandmother, Jane, after whom I was named (with a slight variation of the letters) was second youngest and only eleven. Immediately she joined an elder sister, Annie, who was in service at the doctor's house.

There was an extraordinary bond between the five sisters and one brother which was never broken. It was this example of a caring family which Grandmother brought into her own marriage to influence Mother and directly affect us.

Maybe it was the glamour of the horse-drawn limousine and its handsome young cabby which excited Jane to fall in love with Tom Smith. When they married she lived in town but she remained a country girl and her children spent a great deal of their childhood in the countryside. The youngest of the Booth sisters became a teacher. Although she married and brought up five children in Scotland they were frequently back in the village or staying with Grandmother in town.

Clara married a farmer and Annie's husband, who originally kept a drug store and was the local, untrained dentist, acquired the post as landlord of the Black Bull. With them lived the unmarried sister Julia and bachelor brother Jimmy. There were cousins all over the place, all of them christened, often several at a time, in the village church. The vicar there had christened Grandmother, married her and he christened all her children.

Mother's childhood was far more familiar to us than that of Milly-Molly-Mandy or Ameliaranne Stiggins. The five children had such fun. Four were named after grandparents: William and Sarah, Jane and Joseph, and Mary after a great-aunt. There were modest holidays in digs at Morecambe and the joy lasted all year. Mother told us that the children, on Friday night, bath night, using the tub on the kitchen floor, used to stand on the table in their nightshirts and put a finger in their mouths shouting, 'Yoodleoodleooo, I'm Tonio the diver,' before jumping off onto the hearth rug.

One story she told us again and again. The All Blacks were to play in the nearby football field. All the children from the street climbed onto a shed to watch the team go down the lane for they were sure they would all be black. More and more children climbed on the old shed and the roof gave way. To climb up they had found it necessary to take off their clogs and, when the roof gave way, a score of children and forty clogs plummeted into darkness. People ran out of their houses for the screams of the children could be heard throughout the area. Splintered and bruised, they were all pulled out alive and the almost identical clogs paired. Mother said that when she next went to the clogger he said, 'Do you know you're wearing odd clogs?' So, possibly, were all of them!

The impression Harry and I got of Mother's family was always that it was a happy one. The children had quarrelled only about who had the best nose. They were not gifted singers but on winter evenings they entertained themselves singing the catchy tunes they had learned from the Pierrot Troupe on Morecambe Pier. Auntie Janie could recite long poems. Her skill fascinated us when we were small. Auntie Mary would say, 'Two little kittens, one stormy night, Began to quarrel and then to fight,' over and over again but from Auntie Janie's repertoire came a new one every time.

At the turn of the century childhood was not long. Mother told us that she did all the family shopping before she was tall enough to see over the top of the counter so the manager used to lift her onto it. Sometimes, she said, there was just sixpence left for the rest of the week. She used to stagger home with a stone of flour in the family flour sack.

My school days were imminent. The Education Authority had refused Harry entry, which was a great trouble to Mother and she hoped they would allow him to go when I was five. She talked a lot about her own school days. Grandfather had been the first little boy on the new school steps, she said, and when she went, twenty-five years later, it was the same headmaster. She told us he'd been a friend of Great-grandfather Joseph Smith and that, one day, Grandfather had been given a note to take home to his father. It contained details of a fishing expedition but Grandfather thought it was an unfavourable report on his not exactly model behaviour. Consequently he had dropped it down one of the street drains. We could well believe it. Grandfather always had that mischievous look in his eye.

Mother admitted that, when she was at school, she was often getting the cane for talking in the lines. I don't think Mother has stopped talking since she was born. When the headmaster found out whose granddaughter she was he began to scold her instead of caning. When Mother was eleven she went into the advanced class. She was very proud about that, telling us she did 'algebra'. She wasn't preparing me for the same school. I was to go to the village one a quarter of a mile away.

One of our constant visitors was our lame Uncle Joe who practically lived in our spare room. He was twelve years younger than Mother, being eighteen when she married. The birth of Joe, the last baby in the family, meant that

Mother had had to leave school. She was the eldest and was needed at home. Mother talked a lot about when Uncle Joe was a baby because he was a real favourite of ours. One leg was much shorter than the other and very thin. He wore a built-up shoe and a legging and when he ran his lameness was very pronounced.

I don't know why children like sad stories. Uncle Willie, we were always told, used to say, 'Sing something sad,' and Grandmother would oblige with, 'Don't go down in the mine, Dad.'

We liked the story of active baby Joe who was forever dashing out into the street where horse-drawn vehicles were constantly passing. It had been a terrible shock, one morning, to find the normally mobile toddler, not yet eighteen months old, lying paralysed in bed. One leg had no movement at all. Grandmother and her thirteen-year-old daughter had swept the baby into a blanket and rushed him to Great-grandmother's house. The anxious trio of ladies had sent for a doctor but there was nothing anyone could do against polio. 'Only quietness,' the doctor said, so the younger children were sent to Aunt Annie's and Mother kept at home to nurse the sick baby through the fever. Most polio victims spent the rest of their lives in wheelchairs but Mother and Grandmother were determined that Joe should walk. Illness had weakened the other leg but they massaged and oiled both until, with a special shoe, he re-learned to walk. Everybody loved him, the Tiny Tim of the family.

So, at thirteen, Mother's life of caring for a handicapped person had begun. Nearly eighty years later she is still going strong in that capacity. Some people live a life without any responsibility for the disabled but Mother never knew a life without it, and she agrees she was not the loser. It is not good fortune to have escaped or evaded caring for the less able or the elderly, for they are fun and a joy to be with if you learn how to like doing what there is to do. Harry once said, 'Would you be better without me?' We were indignant. 'Well, it would be rather boring, wouldn't it?' he laughed. It would indeed!

After a while, when the little boy began to cope with his lameness, Grandmother felt she could do without Mother. They were comparatively poor and a few more shillings a week would be appreciated. Mother got a job at the local printers and like all the other workers she went to work in a shawl. It hasn't been used since Mother married but it still lies folded in one of our drawers. We could imagine Mother skipping up Lawkholme Lane to her work at the printers, overjoyed at being able to contribute to the family purse.

Mother did not work there long, for a better job became vacant at the local laundry. The wage was a shilling a week more and the day off was Monday. Mother thought this was a real joke because Monday was always the family washday and it enabled her to help Grandmother do the full day's work. The clothes were put to steep the night before then possed in hot water in the dolly tub. They were soaped and rubbed on the zinc rubbing board, wrung out by hand, dipped in the dolly blue, if white, and starched to make them crisp. Then they were pegged onto the line. Everyone washed on Mondays and lines crossed the cobbled yard between the two streets, and sheets and garments danced in the wind. There was a rivalry amongst the housewives to hang out the cleanest wash. In the evening the flat irons were put to heat and the starched things were wetted. Everything was folded and mangled once more to make the final ironing easier.

All these things Mother also did every day at work. There was more skill needed for the delicate lace and finery of the well to do for there was the usual industrial town abundance of mill owners. The laundry was behind the theatre and each week there was an interesting assortment from the travelling players' wardrobe. It was a backbreaking job amongst constant steam and wet floors and Mother worked a long and arduous day.

Grandmother's closest sister, with whom she had been in service at the doctor's, was courageously coping with illness amongst her children. Tuberculosis, in those days, was a nightmare for many families. Grandmother willingly devoted herself to helping and involved all her children in doing so. Harry and I listened to Mother with wide open eyes as she told us of the terrible illness of her cousins, of Mabel and Lily who were so beautiful and Harry, eleven, who said, 'Don't cry, Mother.' She told us that other workers at the laundry had scoffed at her because she had no social life.

Grandmother did not isolate her children from disease or spare them from the deaths, or the funerals. It was all part of life and they had to help each other. Mother told us that after one funeral, at which she had been a pallbearer, Aunt Annie had set the table and begged them all to eat. 'Come,' she had said, 'we've uther childer t' care fer.'

Grandfather's brother George became ill and needed help and a home. Mother told us that he had said, 'Ah Tommy'll hev me.' It's one of the things I most like to remember for much of the family's benevolence seemed to stem from Grandmother and her daughters whilst Grandfather just smiled and let it happen. That George knew his brother Tom would make room for him in his busy home, tells me all I need to know. George lived with them until he died. He was an enormously fat man and had been too heavy a drinker. Grandmother told George he could come providing there was no more drinking and the bargain was honoured.

The small house must have bulged with people. When Aunt Minnie came from Scotland, for the birth of her children and for their christenings, they often stayed there, too. Several in each bed was a frequent occurrence.

We knew the street house very well indeed, and the enclosed, communal backyard. Standards of cleanliness were high. People not only scoured their front door steps, they scrubbed the pavement in front of the house as well. The twenty householders of the yard passed a bobbin from one house to the next. If the bobbin was hanging on your door you were responsible, that week, for sweeping the passage between the row of toilets and the matching row of dustbin cubicles.

Mother was eighteen when the First World War broke out. Her brothers were too young for conscription and her father too old but the railway passed in front of their house and they saw the carriages going south full of soldiers and north full of wounded. They heard the daily cries of the newspaper vendors telling of massacres and mourned when the Bradford Pals were almost wiped out. They cried when the army conscripted several of their best horses. They saw them being led down to the station, innocent victims of Man's inhumanity to Man. Her friends and neighbours went to war. Many never came back. It was a time of shortages, of queuing for food and making-do. Mother never glamorised war but we listened intently.

Harry's memory is infinitely better than mine. He has retained the detail of our early years together and we accuse him of being able to remember things which happened before he was born. I don't think Mother ever stopped talking to him. He remembers places and names and dates, shop owners, street names, hawkers, recipes, the lot.

I suppose there was plenty of work during the war. All but Uncle Joe were wage earners so the family decided to pay for their youngest to go to the local Grammar School. There were a few scholarship winners in those days but a substantial number of boys were paid for and Joe would never have fared well with a manual job. He had terrific determination to overcome his lameness and never let it interfere if he could help it. He came home soaked to the skin one day, having fallen into the river whilst at play.

At some point, halfway through the war, Grandmother simply could not cope alone with all the family chores and visitors, Uncle George, Annie's family and all the extra washing and baking it entailed. So Mother gave in her notice and stayed at home. She was no less busy but (and Mother used to laugh), if there was a shortage of rations Grandmother used to say, 'Let the workers have it.'

A neighbour, who knew Grandmother's outstanding ability to help others, warned her not to loan out her stay-at-home daughter all the time. Such was the neighbourliness in the street that when the husband of one of them died, Mother was sent to sleep with the widow who was afraid to be alone.

Every morning and again in the evening in summer time, for there were no refrigerators, milk was delivered by Henry Brown. His milk float, with its four ten-gallon milk cans, rattled along the cobbles and he entered houses, one after the other, measuring out the milk into whatever receptacle was provided. During the war the younger of his two sons was in Glasgow, ship-building, but when the young man came home he took over the delivery. He had acquired a Scottish accent and his visits were a novelty. It must have taken him two or three years before he dared ask Mother out, for his home circumstances left him no time or money to go courting or think of marriage.

When we were little, Harry and I, I don't think we heard many stories of Father's childhood. I think they did not come spontaneously. That we know anything is due to the fact that when we were much older we wanted to know. Fragments of his experiences excited us to ask for more. Mother happily told us about her home life because she was totally satisfied that it had been good.

Father talked to us endlessly but about the present, his philosophy, his beliefs about right and wrong, good and bad in people and politics and religion. He talked about animals and flowers, about the countryside and how to enjoy all weathers. He didn't think that stories of a somewhat lonely little boy were all that necessary.

Mother's marriage to him meant that we were farmer's children with our paternal grandparents living in the farmhouse just a few yards away. There seemed fewer members of Father's family and his relationship with them was different but his loyalty to them was no less so there must have been some similarities.

Grandfather Brown, for instance, would dearly have loved to be the self-made man that Great-grandfather Joseph Smith was. Ironically, his more feeble attempts were more lasting for he aspired to be a landowner. When the age of the horse and carriage gave way to the motor car, the stables became a picture palace and all we have left are a few photographs, a horn and some horse brasses. Grandfather Brown's legacy has perpetuity. No one can deny that.

We learned little about him during the twenty-two years we lived so close because he was unable to relate to either of his sons and stubbornly wanted to make all the decisions himself. I would love to know why he wanted to be a farmer. He was a moulder with no history of farming in his blood. He wasn't a countryman or an animal lover, neither was he addicted to working round the clock all the days of the week. It must have been that he aspired to be a landowner. Anyway his blundering efforts gave us the opportunity we so value and we are only full of gratitude.

He had married a young and lovely mill-worker who stood by him devotedly throughout their marriage. She was the mental strength and maybe the muscle, and we acknowledge a great admiration for her. She was not a country girl but she became a good farmer's wife. She was never a farmer. Her place was in the dairy and not in the cowshed, in the hen-run not on the milk round and in the garden not on the fields. In the house she was not the needlewoman, cook, or homemaker that Grandmother Smith was but the neighbours valued her help as a midwife, her skill when they were bereaved and when they were sick or depressed she was an able counsellor.

Father's birth, thirteen months after his brother, was a blow, for Grandmother Brown had wanted a girl. Mother told us this with more than a hint of disapproval. Father was not very communicative about his childhood. He thought there were more interesting things to talk about than a lonely little boy, whose elder brother received all the praise and was excused all faults. Children know when another is favourite and treatment is unfair. The couple could not find any fault in their first-born and did not seem to notice that it was the younger boy they really relied upon. When Grandfather bought his first allotment and began what is commonly called backyard farming, it was always Percy who had his head in a book and Father who was feeding the goats and the donkey. The fact that he was undisputedly needed compensated for the fact that he was ignored. If you are needed, someday you hope you will be recognised and if what you are needed for is what you most want to do, life is not so bad after all. Father wanted to farm, and the allotment, though it meant rising early and working hard, was almost all joy. Strangely it did not provide any closeness between him and his father.

So Father's childhood was spent working and his brother became a bookworm and they were both happy to go their own ways. Both won scholarships to the Grammar School; Percy did excellently but Herbert struggled along and was glad when the bell rang. Grandfather should have recognised his firstborn's academic potential and allowed him to stay at school and go forward to university but instead he was intent on buying land and the sooner both boys were earning money the better. So both became apprenticed engineers, a ten-acre farm was bought on the hill top and a brilliant mathematician was lost.

At the beginning of the war Father had completed his apprenticeship but was just too young for the army. He lied twice about his age but to no avail. Skilled engineers were needed in Glasgow, shipbuilding, and Father was sent there. His brother reluctantly left his job for the security of being exempt from conscription as a farmer. Father sent all his wages home hoping that the business would survive his absence. If it did he planned to emigrate to Australia. Father often talked about his workmates together building big ships on the Clyde. He did not join them after work for he had no money and he was a country lad who did not drink or swear. He had dreadful lodgings, dirty and flea-ridden and the other occupant was a drunkard.

As the war progressed and Father's generation was being slaughtered, revulsion for war grew in him. He began to acknowledge that shipbuilding was preferable to the trenches and to dream of Australia. His engineering qualifications would get him there and once he had found his feet he would find a job on an Australian farm. He had no eagerness to return to the loneliness of his family.

When the Armistice was declared he found, to his dismay, that the farm had not prospered. It was not really surprising because he was the only farmer amongst them. He was forced to shelve the Australian idea for a time and buckle in. He took the reins again on the milk float, his Scottish accent captivated Mother and the Australian idea fled out of the window.

I am pretty sure that Father had had no real fun until he met Mother. She was the best thing that ever happened to him. He was shy and had no money or house or any prospects of either but he knew what he wanted. Mother told us he never asked her to marry him. She just knew he loved her and had never had any doubts about her affection for him. She used to laugh about how he had turned from confident milkman, walking vigorously into the kitchen with his 'livering can, to shy suitor sitting uncomfortably at the back of the room waiting for her to put on her coat.

Grandfather had said, 'Nay, cum up t' fire, lad,' and Father had embarrassed Mother by saying, 'Ah'm all right. Ah'm hot stuff.' Whatever he was,

Father was not hot stuff. He was a most correct and honourable young man. Grandfather knew, but Mother never ceased teasing him.

Father liked everything about Cabby Tom's family. He found Mother's parents comfortable to be with. He loved Grandmother. She set a more appetising table and everyone laughed a lot. He used to look at Grandmother and say, 'That'll be what Sarah will be like in another twenty-five years' time' but he never thought that he would be like his father. Nor was he.

Given the opportunity, Father could make a decision but he seldom got the chance. He had no wage or bank account or property; farmers did not pay their sons a wage until they married. Fortunately Percy had married already so Father knew it could be done. He knew, too, that though his parents treated him differently from his elder brother in many ways, he wasn't treated differently where money was concerned. Though he did not get a wage he could take what was absolutely necessary from the family purse. He could use this privilege to buy Mother a box of chocolates or take her to the local theatre.

And, of course, to buy her an engagement ring. They went to Bradford for this important occasion and the ring they chose was too big for Mother's small finger and had to be left for adjustment. It was Mother's idea that they should go to Woolworth's and buy a sixpenny one to show, teasingly, to the family. Father would never have thought that one up but he loved the fun in Mother. We often call her our Fun Mum even now. In the warmth of her gaiety, Father would sit back smiling.

He slipped comfortably into her family like a loved son. It was a new experience, and as was going on holiday with them in the summer. Grandmother's code of behaviour was very positive. Mother always said she would rather face the river than her Mother's disapproval. But, somewhere, perhaps from an excellent Sunday School teacher, Father already had a code of behaviour which remained unshakable for over eighty years.

The young milkman found an affinity with the cabby. A generation separated them but they were both sons of businessmen, both had a more favoured brother, both were deprived of any say in how the business was run. They understood each other's problems. Father slipped into the habit of sharing Mother's extended family responsibilities, helping Joe with his homework and spending long hours tabbing at the rug frame.

He thoroughly enjoyed popularity for the first time. Other members of the family were quick to comment when he received preferential treatment. One day Mother admonished her Aunt Julia for stepping on the newly scrubbed step. Hearing the clip-clop of the milk horse coming up the street, Aunt Julia had said, 'Here's someone who will be allowed!'

Incredibly, this penniless young man was about to present his bride with a brand new house. Unable to extend his land with the money accumulating now Father was home, Grandfather Brown was speculating in property. He bought three small cottages adjacent to the farmhouse. In the field across the road, part of his ten acres, there was a quarry and Grandfather employed a stonemason to cut stone for the building of two sets of semi-detached houses.

Father ferried the stone with the horse and cart and builders put up four double-fronted houses close to the farmhouse. It was 1926 and most of the country was in deep depression but Grandfather was using his money in the most attractive way possible for the young couple. The ladies in Mother's household began to sew and tab and the bottom drawer began to fill. The four years prior to the wedding, on Easter Monday 1926, were incredibly busy.

My uncle and his family were to live in the semi with the smaller garden. Father's had a garden right to the chapel wall. Grandfather must have thought he had enough money from the sum from the building society, raised by the two mortgages, so he let the two remaining ones and, for twenty years or more, collected 10s. a week from each of them.

It was a simple, early morning wedding in Holy Trinity Church on Easter Monday with breakfast in Mother's family home. Mother had always daydreamed that she would drive to the church in a horse-drawn carriage. Sadly those days had gone. The young couple caught a morning train to Llandudno for their honeymoon. Mother remembers that the Welsh seaside resort was crowded on their arrival with singing rows of people enjoying the last night of their Easter holiday on the promenade and that, next morning, everyone had gone and the place was deserted.

The return to the new house must have been exciting. Father began to receive a small wage. Twenty-four years later, when I went to college, it had risen to £4 5s. 0d. We never had money but we had everything that mattered. We were country children, living on a hilltop and both parents wanted for us the childhood each had had. Mother wanted us to have fun in a family, closeness with grandparents and aunts and uncles, laughter with cousins, a sharing of household chores and an annual holiday by the sea. Father wanted us to love the out-of-doors, to understand and work with animals, to build and make and work for a common good. Both wanted us to work, to know how to and to enjoy doing so. They wanted us to work for no other reward than that of knowing we were needed.

The village school was just a quarter of a mile away. After the chapel, which was only parted from our house by a high wall, and the row of terrace houses opposite, there were only fields between us and school. One dirt track left the road on the left leading beyond two farm cottages to Fortie's place and another track disappeared over the hill and was called The Private. In front of the school a few old houses hid with dignity behind a screen of trees. At the school there was a crossroads and the through road ran steeply down into the village and became a cobbled, precipitating snake leading to another part of the valley town. The left turn at the crossroads was unsurfaced and fell dangerously down to the church and the network of snickets and ginnels and the footpath, through Park Wood back into town. The narrow road, right at the crossroads, continued a gradual ascent for another quarter of a mile to the Moor Gate, through which was The Currer. Our twenty dairy cows were grazed there and collected and driven through the village to be milked at the home farm. In summer they did this journey twice a day and the road was perpetually coloured with splattered manure.

During the pre-war years we led a sheltered life. We seldom went over to the farm buildings. Animals were dangerous where wobbly children are concerned and farms are places of work, not play. So we played in the garden. It was big and because of Harry's physical handicap our garden was the playground of other children in the village. He could not go far afield and it never occurred to me to leave him behind so we opened the gate and other children came in. Helped occasionally by my cousin Freda but more often just the gang from the village, we did all the things normal kids should do. Around the garden was a fairly high wall. The top stones had been cemented and were reasonably safe so that walking along the top could progress to a run. A wobble and you were rolling with laughter in the garden. The brave and difficult bit was to cross the narrow, wooden traverse of the gate. Having reached the privet hedge which separated our garden from Uncle's, we leapt over the rockery and catapulted onto the lawn.

There was a tree just right for climbing and a well to scramble down and to hide secret gardens. There was a lawn to roll on and a hedge to jump. We had a lean-to coal 'ole at the corner of the house to get really mucky in, to make dens and tell secrets, and the ash-tub cubby holes had roofs to climb on and jump from; they collected a bun of snow in winter that we could measure and gloat over. At the rear of the house was a hen cote and behind that two sloping meadows which, in spring, were a carpet of daisies, buttercups and milkmaids.

I suppose we did cross the few yards of field path to the farmyard in those eight early years of my childhood but I cannot remember. To me it seems that we were always at play in the garden with Harry wobbling along behind or leaning on the wall watching, or sitting on the lip of the path where it stepped onto the lawn. I remember that the weather seemed always fine or deep in snow. We made huge snowmen on the lawn and had hilarious snowball fights with the village children. We hurtled down Harden Road, risking life and limb on homemade sledges for, in those days, it was single track and the snow plough never opened it and we could claim it as ours. This was a sport Harry could not enjoy. He stayed cold and wet when we were glowing so I would take him home and return to continue my dangerous activity without responsibility.

Our play was unbelievably varied. We made houses and secret gardens, wrote books and plays, performed concerts, held societies, and conducted sports days; we led processions through the village dolled up in curtains and ribbons; and had a regular milk bar mixing all manner of dubious milkshakes in empty shrimp pots. We constructed assault courses and made swings and seesaws that could have been responsible for many a fatality. Mud pies were made by the dozen, decorated with ferns and cow parsley and bedstraws. Harry was my constant companion and I did not mind at all.

The village children never came inside the house but we had a regular visitor. Mother's eldest brother's daughter, two and a half years younger than I, was often at our house, staying weekends and holidays. My mother received into our house all the cousins and fed them without a word about the added workload. Nor did Father mind the extra children. He was good with them. When you work sixteen hours a day, amusing other people's children can be wearisome but I never heard him grumble.

There were activities that took us outside the garden. The chapel was our next door neighbour and everything happened there. Everything about the chapel was exciting, even the love/hate relationship we had with the caretaker's children who alternated from roles of intimacy to those of stone throwers from the chapel wall.

The chapel was the venue for Shrovetide and November teas when Mother would make butterfly buns and all and sundry would come along with a basket of homemade cakes for a Faith Tea. Afterwards there would be the Romp during which there would be a lot of cavorting about, sliding on the polished floor and bumping into each other. No occasion was more fun than the Harvest Romp. The smell of the Chapel Harvest! There was nothing anywhere to compare with it.

The concerts, which punctuated each year with such fun, gave us an opportunity to recite and sing and really enjoy ourselves. I remember one role of mine at the end of a train of children with their arms encircling the child in front. We were infants and the song was an action one. The boys in front became over-enthusiastic. The end of the train left the lines and I was hurtled into the audience. I was always smaller than everyone else.

Every year, at the beginning of haytime, the chapel would hold its Sunday School Anniversary in the adjoining field. For this momentous occasion we would have new clothes and I was bought another straw bonnet. Auntie Janie was the lady in our lives responsible for new clothes. She was a skilled needlewoman and tailoress and made beautiful things. We were definitely the best-dressed poor children in the area.

On the Friday before the Sunday School Anniversary there would be great activity over the chapel wall. From some mysterious dungeon, under the chapel, came the poles and planks with which the miniature grandstand was erected. We used to sit on the wall listening to the men.

'O'd this, lad. Tha's dun it afore!'

On completion the wooden masterpiece was encircled with a roll of dark material which gave it a regal look and minimised the draughts. On the front row a lectern was placed behind which the visiting preacher would stand and on the tiers behind would sit the choir and the musicians. One of the violinists was my friend Violet's Auntie Maggie. A little bowlegged lady she was and her appearance did not suggest natural talent. I was always amazed by the annual performance of musical skill by this otherwise insignificant villager.

The congregation sat on plank seats in the field in front of this masterpiece of craftsmanship. People came from far to join the villagers and all the ladies sported their new summer clothes and the children their straw bonnets. The singing was lusty and the day almost always fine. A hay day, in fact! I know that because I frequently saw my Mother's face, red with embarrassment as Father and the horse and cart rattled up the road empty of hay heading for The Currer or, squeaking and groaning, returning with the full load. He made a serious effort to avoid passing whilst the service was in progress but he never wore a watch and it was impossible to judge correctly. Father was not a religious man. He did not join the other farmers in the locality obeying the Sabbath. If God sent a fine day for the hay then Father gave thanks and went out to make it. He was not a church-going man but his faith was as firm and as unshakable as the Altar Rock, a prominence at the far corner of The Currer. It was impossible to live with him and not know and be affected.

We were, in the 1930s, more influenced by season than children are today. I remember the excitement of coming down to dress by the fire, and seeing, in October, my winter clothes hanging on the rail above the Yorkist Range and in May my summer dress. Apart from Christmas and November 5th, there is now a dearth of annual activities. Recognising the importance to children of a known and expected calendar of events is wisdom that parents, teachers and youth leaders should know.

We kept the New Year with Mummers and First Footers. I remember sixpences being given to children who came to the door to wish us a Happy New Year. I remember the bringing of a piece of coal and the sweeping of the hearth. We kept Shrovetide with slave-like regularity. It was a two-day holiday from school. On the Tuesday we had pancakes and we went to the Shrovetide Tea and we brought out the shuttlecocks. It was a ritual. 'Betsy Baker, shuttlecock laker,' we sang. 'How many days can you play? One, two, three ...'

On Ash Wednesday Auntie Janie made fritters. We never referred to the day by any other name than Fritter Wednesday. Then came Winking Thursday. By this time children were back at school and could wink and blink to their heart's content. Further up the valley it was called Petticoat Thursday and girls wore their prettiest and the boys tried, usually unsuccessfully, to lift skirts and take a peep. Only one day could follow winking and petticoat peeping and that was Kissing Friday. Some wise sage had put a time limit on the day and kissing had to end at noon. The girls, of course, resisted the attentions of the boys in a most unladylike manner with feet and fists and giggles.

One of these days of traditional festivity has continued. The town Hospital Gala and Procession and Fair is still held though it is over fifty years since I attended.

The route of the procession passed my grandparents' doorstep so we had a royal box. My cousin and Harry and I would be on our stools at the pavement edge long before the first strains of the band in the distance proclaimed the start of the floats and jesters, the mayoral cavalcade and all the tradesmen's vans and horse drawn vehicles. The procession seemed to take hours to pass and we hurled pennies and streamers into the street and shouted and cheered like nobody's business. After tea we would wait impatiently to be taken into the park where the gypsy caravans were stationed, and all the carousels and sideshows and brandy snap stalls. I did not particularly want to go on the swings and roundabouts though Mother quite liked to accompany us. We had few pennies to spend. Harry loved to use them on the Roll a Penny stalls. I would have loved to stay late and watch the fireworks but Harry had a thing about the time and could tell it from an early age. He became very fractious if we were out late when he was small.

There was one day which was the Sunday School Walk when currant buns were eaten on the hilltops and the Sunday School Trip when we went to play on the swings at Newsholme Dene. Mischief Night never went uncelebrated and the local lads guarded the huge bonfire for which we had progged for weeks, lest some foreign mischief-makers should come and set it alight. Individual bonfires were unheard of. There was one bonfire up in the Delph and that belonged to everybody.

There were special times when we began to play taws and cheggies. By unspoken invitation out would come the taw bags full of clay marbles and the occasional glass ally. Similarly it would undoubtedly be the season for skipping ropes and next, the only possible play was whip and top. We carried sponges and, with a little spit, we could clean the top and rechalk the pattern so that, spinning, the rotating disc was lovely. The time of the year would come to put a piece of string in your pocket and play cat's cradle, or a piece of folded paper to tell fortunes, or a big coat button threaded with a circle of thin string to twist and then keep spinning. There was a time when everyone played hopscotch with a broken tile, or sevens with a ball against the wall, or kick-can or just tipply-top-tails over the ladder rest on the nearby gas lamp.

Christmas was a family time. The closeness of Mother's family was more obvious than ever at the end of December for aunts and uncles' wives all individually invited everyone to a party and we went from one house to another eating well and playing games. All the ladies in our family were excellent pastry cooks and cake makers and the Christmas spreads of the pre-war days were a sight to behold. In our family the tradition of plentiful hospitality goes back several generations. A letter to my great-grandparents, replying to an invitation to the christening of one of their children, comments on my great-grandmother's table.

> Her hospitality so full and free,
> Her table, when set out, is grand to see
> And yet she shyly will pretend to say,
> 'My friends, Ah'm sorry, I hev nowt t'day.'
> This often would my good wife's mother tickle.
> She'd say, 'Now lass, th'art in a bonnie pickle.
> Think on, nah, don't forget tha axes me
> When tha hez summat, then let's see.
> There really isn't room nah, on the tabletop
> For thee t' cram another cake or pot!'

That was written more than a hundred years ago but could well describe my mother's table and those laid by my aunts at Christmas.

My separate life from Harry began when I went to school and he did not. This was a great trouble to my mother who knew he was intelligent enough and capable of being taught but in the mid 1930s there was, in this locality, no provision made for spastic children. Every effort to get him into school failed. Mother wanted him to go with me, to learn beside me as he had always done, but no one would listen and I went to school alone. It was a great pity for at school he would have learned to read before it was too late. Educated as a normal child his life would have been richer and his nerves steadier but it was, at that time, still an unlightened education system.

In the school cloakroom I would struggle, with the small buttonhook kept in my pocket, to fasten the many buttons up the side of my leggings, knowing that Harry's envious face would be peering through the railings, waiting for me. His dependence on me did not frighten or annoy me and I was unaware that it fettered me at all. His possessiveness and his demands were all part of his affection for me and I found nothing unusual in that. I am told that I occasionally reacted by seeking extra attention from my father, pretending that I could not walk and must be carried. It was obviously just a little attention seeking on my part and Father always understood. The problem arose mostly when we were on holiday. On one occasion Mother took me aside to scold me in no uncertain terms but her reprimand was thwarted by an interruption from a do-gooder who insisted that I must not be spanked. As corporal punishment was never used in our household Mother was very annoyed. I have no recollection of the scolding but I have many, many memories of those pre-war holidays in a small boarding house down St Chad's Road in Blackpool.

In spite of our limited income we always had two weeks' holiday every summer. For a ridiculously small amount we could secure lodgings with two elderly ladies who were willing to rent us the use of their sitting room. Other boarders used the dining room with the bay window on the front but we had our meals sitting on horsehair seats round a table in their private sitting room. Each morning we would go out and buy the food we wanted the Misses Spencer to cook. A dozen other people in the dining room would do the same and it staggers me to speculate on how those two old ladies managed to cope with so many different things.

What a wonderful companion my mother was on holiday in those fondly remembered days. She loved the sea and the shore and knew how to have fun. Harry knew the names of all the hotels on the promenade, all the shops, the post offices, newsagents and fish and chip restaurants. The smell of the ozone, the comfortable boarding house, rubber wading shoes and waffles being cooked in the Pleasure Beach lasted long after we came home. I can still hear the voice of Miss Nancy shouting to make her deaf sister hear. I remember Miss Lily taking an order for a second helping and Miss Nancy's loud kitchen reply, 'It's a tale!' The phrase became a household answer far more emphatic than a mere 'No.'

I loved going to school. The lessons posed no problem, and the three teachers were kind. Each of the three classrooms was heated with an open fire. The desks were all fixtures and the iron pedestal seats were rather uncomfortable. Many a time I have fleetingly longed for their re-institution when confronted with a fidgety class.

In wintertime the teachers often arrived late because they had to walk to the village, impeded by deep snow. On those occasions we would hope that they never arrived and we would have great fun in the playground. We were never waiting long before the headmaster and the two elderly spinsters arrived and lessons began.

It grieves me to realise that I remember little of my primary school days, few of the songs and stories and poems we must have been taught. I remember nothing of the morning assemblies, the religious education, the lessons on social behaviour and conduct which must have come my way. I do not remember learning anything of the world around me, the flora and fauna, the social predicaments of my neighbours or the industries in the town. I recollect only the pleasant process of learning to read and write and calculate. I remember putting a gusset in a pair of homemade knickers in needlework and the tobacco boxes in which were kept the too-small balls of plasticine with which we were allowed to play when work was done well.

Yet I have taught primary school children for over thirty years in the hope and belief that they will remember my words, my philosophy, my ideals; the stories and situations, the projects and experiences we shared. I have said, 'This remember always.' 'Never forget.' 'Some day when you are old, you will remember what I have just told you,' and I have believed that the lesson I have pressed home so emphatically will have been heard. Now, trying to remember my own childhood, I wonder! In retrospect it seems to me that all I have ever learned of life was out of school, at home and at work and at play.

There must be a fundamental truth hereabout, some lesson to learn. Was it this which prompted me instinctively to meet my children so often in out-of-school situations, in the evening, at weekends, in the holidays, at home, in the locality, travelling and camping in the Dales and the Highlands and the islands of the Hebrides?

Chapter Two

W ork came to me early when I was eight years old. All too soon the carefree days of my childhood were gone. They disappeared overnight, on
my eighth birthday. As a family we do not celebrate anniversaries, and there
is but one of my many birthdays which I remember as different from the
everyday. This one fell on a Sunday and we went to The Currer.

The aunts and my grandparents came to tea every Sunday and we used to
go for an afternoon walk. Normally we got as far as the Moor Gate but on this
particular day, glorious spring sunshine tempted us down Currer Lane, that
walled cart track plunging down the hillside to the farmhouse. Arriving at
the spring, we took off into the Dyke Field to avoid the farmhouse and went
to gather bluebells in Jimmy's Wood. It is a long, narrow dell, lined with trees
and floored with blackberry bushes, and it hides the quarry from which stone
had been taken to build the house and laithe of The Currer. It was my first
visit to the bluebell bank. We did not often go so far afield with Harry.

On our return up the Five Acre we saw Father beckoning us into the farmyard. Maggie, the brown mare, was stabled there and Father kept some sows
in the steadings. He was waving, so we went straight up to the farmyard and
entered it, which was not our common practice. I don't think I had ever been
in the laithe before. This is the huge, dry stone building at right angles to the
house, which would be called a barn elsewhere in the country.

The memory of my first entry seems vivid enough. I went inside with
curiosity, as children do. They dash in with a rush of interest and an urge to
explore. I know that the sinister house, with its unknown occupants, was too
near for my liking and that I followed Father in eagerly to get out of sight.
With our arms full of bluebells we hurried up the cobbled incline and entered
the empty dimness. In autumn there would be a store of hay to take away the

echoes but in spring it was empty and when our eyes grew accustomed to the lack of light I saw the gnarled beams and cobwebs, and the eight cow stalls, greasy and worn with centuries of use. Though open, this part was inevitably called the mistal and it had its own entrance sheltered from the north wind by the lean-to stable. It had its own window, too, and this provided what little light there was in the whole building.

Within the laithe was a rich smell of pig and we followed Father through a narrow door and up an unlit passage into a low, dark room, with heavy beams supporting worm-eaten floorboards. Holes had been chiselled in the one wall the room shared with the laithe and wooden partitions separated the sows. One had littered and was the reason my father had called us. Amid the straw, she lay, huge and sleeping and away from her, against the up-sweep of the nest she had made, lay her heap of piglets.

I have often wondered why, though photographs show us with calves and hens, I have no recollection of a life with animals until I was eight. Perhaps it was that they were too rough for Harry. When Father was in the house he was playing with us but when he was at the farm he was working and a wobbly son was a responsibility where danger was ever present. It amazes me that so many people think that farms are places where children can play. Farmers' children work. We made haycocks, we did not leap over them; we built haystacks, not houses amid the hay; we cleared the dykes and ditches, we never made dams.

From my eighth birthday my life seemed to change. I was given a small gosling to rear on the lawn and Harry was given three piglets by a neighbouring farmer. Previous to this we had no animal in the house other than a dying one, a chicken or piglet brought onto the hearth in Father's flat cap. The gosling was a great thrill but anyone who is knowledgeable about geese knows how quickly goslings grow. Mine was little for too short a time but the pigs had arrived so it didn't matter.

Our next-door-farm neighbour was a man called Jack. That year his sow littered twenty-one pigs. The little runts were being trodden on and no sow has teats for such a number so Jack put three of the smallest in a box and brought them round to our house. They were really too small to be reared away from their mother for baby pigs have no body temperature and need a maternal radiator. To succeed we had to rear the pigs in the house which was tremendous fun.

We had a large, rectangular fireguard which protected us from danger and provided Father and Uncle Joe with a warm seat. When they came in from the farm with frozen rears, this was an ideal perch on which to thaw. Had they been muck-spreading the heat stirred the rich smell of their clothes and filled the house with the breath of warm manure.

I was eight and Harry nearing eleven and so the fireguard could be spared to use as a pen for our three orphans. Mother visited the chemist to buy teats and the good man was full of advice about the right ones a mother should use for a baby. He was understandably amused when Mother confessed she wanted the teats to feed three pigs. These delightful pink babies were the first pets we had. They gave Father many sleepless nights for every few hours they began to scream and could only be silenced with food.

The living room, in this locality, is always called the 'House'. The best room we called the 'Room' but where we lived was the 'House'. We had our dining table in the House and the Yorkist Range with its shining black-leaded grate and hot-air oven and the atmosphere was perpetually warm.

Because they had every attention possible those little pigs survived and when we could no longer keep them indoors they were removed to the shed in the back garden. We loved to feel their warm, clean bodies between our bare legs as we sat to bottle feed them. Healthy pigs are rough when hungry and frequently they pulled off the weakening teats and wasted milk all over themselves and us. It was not out of character that, when the three fat animals must be sold, my grandparents assumed ownership. The milk and corn had been theirs and so, therefore, must be the profit. There was no good in objecting or arguing. That was the way things were and the way things stayed throughout my grandfather's life.

Quite soon after this my mother was expecting her third child. We were not told, for babies did not always come right in our house. Imperceptibly the days of play were over and there were responsible jobs to be done. A helping hand had to be given in the house and if I went with Father it shortened the time it took to deliver the milk. Suddenly I was in at the deep end. My play-mates stopped coming for I was always at the farm, cleaning and washing the cattle ready for milking, standing on a stool in the dairy, feeding the calves, getting Old Dick ready and harnessed for the milk round. Then we were off in the milk float on the two-hour milk delivery and the man in my life was my father. Neither wind nor rain nor snow, neither Christmas nor birthdays nor Gala would prevent me from 'livering milk as a working member of the one-man, one-horse, one-child team.

'Keep changing hands,' my Grandmother Brown used to say when she saw me carrying the two-gallon delivering can which had been bought for me because I was only eight and the normal two and a half-gallon ones were too big.

'Keep changing hands and you won't grow lopsided,' she'd often call when Father clicked his reins and muttered, 'Gee up,' and the horses and milk float clattered down the walled fold. Hard work and arthritis had crippled Grandmother but she insisted on walking across the cobbled yard to the dairy and washhouse. I never heard her complain. She did not spare herself or Father or me. She was not troubled that at eight I was doing serious work, only that it was backbending and prevention was better than cure. With my shoe-blacked clogs and my knee breeches and my khaki smock I thought I looked wonderful and school and chapel and everything else took second place.

Every weekend and holiday I would be out early helping with the pre-round chores. I learned to climb the cat steps into the loft where loose hay was stored. There were trap doors and hay could be thrown down in front of the mangers. I learned an easy way of throwing back the hinged door and found the smallest fork to let down the required amount. My diminutive size did not prevent me from sweeping the mangers in front of the cattle nor risking a tumble head first into the corn bin to scoop out the daily rations. I knew all the cows by name. They knew their stalls and never made a mistake when they were brought home. We had progressed from a cotton halter to an iron collar, somewhat like a giant safety pin, and I nimbly ran between their bulging bellies, for they were always in calf. As they entered the stalls I noisily clicked the collars fast. It was great fun.

There are many eight-year-old children who now deliver milk, I am sure. I have taught some of them and seen them running happily between the delivery van and the doorsteps with the familiar pinta. Mine was a different profession. We delivered milk from a shiny metal 'livering can. Inside, on a steel bracket, hung the half-pint and full-pint measures. Delivering milk for me meant first the catching of the milk from the cooler until the ten- and twelve-gallon churns were full. Then came the harnessing of Old Dick into the milk float. The churns had to be rolled from the dairy and out of the laithe porch and heaved into the float. This was not difficult once the knack was acquired for the churn lids were tight fitting and the rim at the foot of each churn made rolling easy. Milk floats were low, too and the back step nearly touched the ground. Then came the two 'livering cans and a box of eggs and we were almost ready. The last job was to go into the farmhouse kitchen for a handful of small change from the bread tins in the top drawer of the dresser. Though I never recollect ever being given one penny reward for all the hours of labour I saved during the next ten years neither can I remember ever once having my loose change checked out or my paper notes and silver scrutinised on return. There was a lack of trust shown by my grandparents in that they would not delegate management but there was no lack of trust where money was concerned. We knew what the customers owed; we made sure that they paid and turned in the morning's takings with the same regularity that Father turned in every last penny of his Glasgow earnings. The trust my grandparents placed in me was something I valued and it made up, in part, for the lack of affection where Father was concerned. During the milk round I had money in my pocket. At other times I had none. I never had any spending money like other children who didn't work, not even in my teens. Come to think of it, I've never had any money in my life which didn't belong to all of us.

With our pockets thus prepared Father would step up beside me into the float and click the reins, and the horse would pick his way carefully down the fold. Out in the road Dick began to trot and the music from his metalled shoes on the road was the theme song to our daily adventure.

All too soon we reached the first house on the round and thereafter we walked and delivered and Dick, who knew his part excellently, timed his precise movements perfectly with ours, drawing forward and stopping at exactly the right time and place. He knew those houses where kindly ladies fed him with crusts of bread and every so often he would mount the pavement and wait patiently with his twitching nose breathing moisture onto the benevolent door.

There was always someone at home in those days. Our standard practice was to open the door, call, 'Milk!' and walk inside. Receptacles reflected the character of the home and owner and ranged from china jugs to earthenware bowls, cans and pans and jam jars, and in cleanliness from spotless through 'much to be desired' to positively filthy. There were some homes where I could have eaten from the scrubbed floor, where I stepped carefully on the newspaper intended for that purpose and where the smell of delicious cooking made me realise I was hungry. But there were houses overcrowded with children and the aged, depressed by poverty and ignorance, where the smell of drying, unwashed nappies fouled the air. The cellar cotts and apartments and back-to-back houses where these people were forced to live have been pulled down. Slum clearance was already under way before the war and we also delivered to people who lived on the new council estate on the hillside. However, re-housing has to be accompanied with re-education and full pay packets and sadly these new houses were no longer salubrious. Surrounded by a neglected garden littered with broken furniture, rusty old prams and bicycles, they often looked worse than those of the town.

Coming before the days of mechanised transport, the industrial revolution had piled the houses of the mill workers in a chaos of narrow streets, back-to-back houses, attic dwellings and cellar cottages; a jigsaw of yards and steps, squares and balconies. Where the streets began to climb out of the town they looked like some child's immature drawing. Sandwiched between the houses or at the end of the yard, the closets and ash tub kennels stood side by side. Behind each kitchen door hung the privvy key, a monstrous thing identified by a wooden bobbin.

I remember the town when people lived close together in the centre, over and under the shops, in the mill yards, up the steps and down the back alleys, when neighbour inevitably brushed shoulder with neighbour and so many people lived in each house that they spilled out to clutter up the street. Out came the chairs on a summer evening, out came the snow shovellers in the winter when the unemployed made a pauper's fortune. There were Lowry people everywhere. No matter how early you were up, the mill workers, in clogs and shawls, were clattering along the cobbles to 'clockin'. The streets were never empty of the horse-drawn vehicles of the brewers, the milkmen, the rag-and-bone men and the greengrocers. The music of horseshoes on the setts was accompanied by cries of, 'Apples to eat', 'Sweet pears' and 'Rags'an'bones'. A hurdy-gurdy was rattling in the street, a brass band could be heard playing on the stand in the park and a busker was singing outside the theatre.

Buses were on the streets replacing the trams, but the terminus was so small and queues so big it was a miracle that no one was killed. Houses crowded round it so that buses came close to their windows and to the little café on the corner. We used to hold our breath and wait for the bump which seemed inevitable.

To me, a moor child delivering milk, the town seemed to hold all the people in the world. Before the war there were railings everywhere. Railings round the chapels, the parish church, the schools and the Town Hall Square. There were railings beside the steps leading to the cellar cottages and almost every public place from the dignity of the parks to the almost embarrassingly numerous urinals.

Steam trains frequented the station sending clouds of smoke up the valley. House and mill chimneys puffed away happily creating a pall of smog to blacken walls and dowdy people irrespective of class. But there was colour in the streets. There were flower vendors with tulips and daffodils and scores of small bunches of wild primroses and the familiar lady with her basket of celery sticks. There was Spud Mick, and Pie Tom with his hot pies and brown peas and occasionally a scissor grinder trotting from door to door.

I can remember when Low Street, extremely narrow and lined with shops, was so crowded that a car on the road crawled and stopped and waited and tried again to proceed. I remember that the queue at Redman's went right round the shop and out into the street and that the manager never stopped advertising his bacon and butter and cheeses. To progress round Woolworths, when nothing in the shop cost more than 6*d*., was well nigh impossible. Small children were grabbed by the hand by determined mothers and dragged through the mêlée. A fearsome feeling it was to be hauled through a crowd of skirts and legs, pushing and being pulled and trodden upon.

In the market there was Lancashire Arthur who sold cheap fents and whose wife had sometimes left the stall to go for 'er 'erdo'. The Accrington man sold apples and oranges wrapped in blue papers which escaped and littered the alleys. There were the fishmongers in front and the butchers, with hanging poultry and rabbits at the back, beside the church. There was the boiled sweet shop, the corn and pet food store and Teddy Roper's interesting collection of second hand furniture. A large man had a stall in what we called 'bottom o' t' market' and he sold toiletries and advertised in the local bus as Jerry's Bottom Market. It tickled us. Bob Smith sold boots and shoes and Sam Scaife carpets and oilcloth.

Was there a cloud hanging perpetually over the market or was it our imagination that it was always raining, that water was forever dripping from the awnings, becoming a steady stream underfoot and making a lake out of every hollow?

The winter darkness fell long before the shops closed. The gas lamps were lighted and people gathered under the dim lights, adults gossiping, children playing. There was crime. A pickpocket can work in a crowd but not a mugger. Today's nightly deserted town centre and empty avenues and groves are as big a temptation to violence as are the hundreds of old people living alone instead of with their families as they used to do.

I have never regretted the broad education I received dragging my heavy can from door to door. I heard the frustrated shouting of despairing parents and felt sorry for their barefooted and often bare-bottomed offspring. It was a life so different from mine. We were poor financially but they were poor in opportunity.

I soon discovered that the job of the milkman, in those days, was not merely to measure out the right amount and add that extra drop so that the measure should be good and public relations happy. The milkman of the pre-war days was also a social worker whose role it was to check that the elderly were not in any need or distress. No one feared that days might pass and no neighbour come. The postman passed and the paperboy but not the milkman. He would open the door and step inside and if help was needed he would give it. Here and there I would fill a coal scuttle, light an old man a pipe and put the overflowing bowl in the larder away from the cat. There were old people who were bedfast and alone. I heard coughing, saw sickness, respected age, smelled filth and squalor I had never known existed. I had my first encounter with senility and death. I saw children with bug bites and heads shaved by authority, who slept on mattresses on the floor and covered themselves with rags. I learned that there were those who were open to ridicule because of low intelligence and mental handicap.

Walking the streets with a milk can I found that there were many at the mercy of children's laughter and adult derision. There were town characters known by everyone, hawking and begging. One such character was Freddie Gramophone who pushed his hurdy-gurdy round the streets, playing to the people waiting in bus and theatre queues. Another was Old Mothballs who shuffled his way round the shopping area smelling strongly of the camphor he persistently tried to sell. My favourite fear was an encounter with Emily Matchbox. It was one thing to know these odd people but it was quite another thing to be known by one and she knew me. She lived in a cellar cott, though those close by were condemned and empty, their windows broken and their doors unhinged. For a long time we delivered a gill bottle of milk to this famous lady. At school I learned that the bottle I took wasn't a gill at all. All children quite enjoy being afraid and I scuttled down those steps half hoping, half fearing that she would be in. She was notorious and meeting her was always a colourful experience. She sold matches in the streets and sang in the theatre queue. Her language was rich and her temper noisy but she brought out a sense of humour in people and went her way unharmed. She was quite unpredictable, never paid for the daily bottle and I was agreeably petrified of her. Whenever she saw me in the town she would draw attention to me by calling out, 'Little Milk Girl!'

I remember being in Woolworths, self-conscious because of my new school uniform, when her grating voice called out the phrase which so aptly described me. Everyone in the emporium turned to look at me. There, in beret and fur collar, Emily Matchbox was coming straight towards me, jerkily on spindly legs in their perpetually wrinkled lisle stockings. I was embarrassed but there seemed no place to escape. Then, to everyone's astonishment, she was giving me humbugs.

I became known as 'The Little Milk Girl' by everyone. We were on the streets when the mill workers sat on the walls eating lunchtime sandwiches, and daily the horse and float could be seen galloping through the town, for our last call was always at Grandmother's. Now, when I am asked if people will know me, I answer, 'More than likely.' I've either delivered their milk or taught them or taken them to the Hebrides.

Occasionally we had to call at the blacksmith's. Sometimes we had to visit the clogger's on Brunswick Street. I sat with Father on the shiny leather bench which followed two sides of the tiny workshop. It was too wide for me and my stockinged feet stuck out at right angles not far over the edge. I would sit there watching the leather-aproned old man ply his trade and enjoying the distinctive smells of his materials and tackle. When my turn came he would release the right-sized irons from a bunch hanging on the wall and fit my clogs over the most suitable last. The worn out irons would be discarded and the new ones secured with rectangular clog iron nails. The old irons had been rattling for days and, when the new ones were fixed and my clogs re-buttoned on my feet, they would make a new sound on the pavement, a firm sound that told everyone I was coming. Unless, of course, there was snow in which case they silently gathered a pad and I would teeter along on my snow stilts for as long as I could without spraining an ankle. At last I would have to kick the toes firmly against a wall and the pad of compressed snow would fall off whole.

Every day we delivered milk at Mrs Crabtree's shop; 'Mrs Crabapple Tree', I used to call her. She had a pronounced goitre and very bowed legs. She sold groceries and she baked bread and teacakes, sweet loaves and sponges. The smell of her warm shop was tantalising because I knew that one of the hot, delicious teacakes would be mine. I would receive it in a small piece of tissue paper to protect my hands from its direct-from-the-oven heat and did I love that daily currant teacake. It acted as a hot water bottle for my fingers and filled my small inside with warmth.

Delivering milk was fun and the companionship between my father and me was all joy. I didn't mind the wind and rain, the frost and snow. It was all part of the game. I whiled away time waiting for Father by picking up broken tiles from the gutter and playing an impromptu game of hopscotch on the causeway. I became a bright-eyed jackdaw finding all manner of things in the pavement leaves or the melting snow. I often found money dropped by cold fingers and reappearing with the thaw. I learned to disapprove of the zealous souls who shovelled away the snow leaving icy, treacherous paths and to walk in safety in the deep, undisturbed blanket at the side. I learned to be alone, to think profound thoughts and to imagine wonderful things. 'Tread on a nick, you'll be buried in a brick,' I muttered, meandering along the pavement with my can, avoiding all the crannies between the pavement flags. I made up plays predicting things. If Mrs Smith's gate is open it will snow tomorrow. If the Tanners' dog barks my mother will have bought me a Lucky Bag. Lucky Bags were bought for a ha'penny at Mrs Holmes' shop and contained sweets and a toy.

There was one house whose milk I loved to deliver. I thought it was a mansion. Indeed it was so big that most of it was occupied by billeted soldiers during the war. There was a long drive with a tunnel in it, eerie, damp and bone-chilling. The garden, except for the lawn in front of the house, was wooded and tangled with ivy. I liked it and I liked the people who at Christmas gave us presents.

There was one house I would not deliver. It belonged to a man with the peculiar name of Minnikin and he had a monkey which could never be let out because it was so savage. The story was that the monkey had frightened away a burglar whilst the dog had cowered under the dresser. The monkey created noisily whenever any caller came but although I am perfectly sure it was safely imprisoned, I didn't believe it. I stood rigid in the milk float praying that it wouldn't get out and kill my father. I never saw that monkey and it was years later, when visiting a zoo, that I found out how small monkeys usually are. I had imagined that Minnikin monkey was enormous.

With the last pint poured we would jump onto the float and Dick would begin to trot enthusiastically home. He knew the routine so well he needed little encouragement. At the foot of the cobbled hillside we dismounted and walked beside him, leaning companionably on the shafts, talking. The smell of horse and harness and wet clothes was as familiar as the smell of Mrs Crabapple Tree's newly baked bread. At the top of the hill, where the road levelled out for the last quarter of a mile home, we had to jump quickly into the float for now the faithful horse was in a hurry, as ready for his dinner as we were for ours. The chore of taking off the harness and hanging it up in the laithe porch was always irksome, a discipline we had to accept however tired, hungry and wet we were.

A week before my ninth birthday something exciting and quite unexpected happened. Father came into the bedroom Harry and I shared, awakened us and told us to get up for Mother was ill and a nurse was taking care of her. He helped Harry into his clothes and I cried as I struggled for mine for I was unused to parents being ill. Father had prepared our breakfast; it was Tuesday and I had to go to school. My agony did not last long before turning to joy. We had barely begun eating when a tall, buxom woman put her head round the door and said to us, 'Well! you've got a baby sister.'

It amazes me, knowing that nowadays parents feel it essential to prepare siblings for a birth in the family, that we accepted the announcement as matter of factly as we did. I remember Father crying and that we were all told to, 'Come an' look,' and that it was just eight o'clock on a normal school morning. I'd seen new born babies before. I'd never questioned their origin and neither was I curious about the arrival of my sister. We accepted that addition to the family as we accepted a sudden family treat or an overnight fall of snow. We had no jealousy, no inhibitions.

Just as I had had to assume an adult role on the milk round so now I accepted a maternal role in the house. Some time earlier my grandmother in the town had suffered a crippling stroke. My aunts were almost fully occupied taking care of her and Father was working all hours on the farm. Mother's eldest brother's wife came to stay for the first couple of weeks but after that we were alone and it wasn't as easy coping in those days. Now handicapped children can go to school or day centre but there was no such provision for Harry. We had no washing machine and no vacuum cleaner. The installation of a wireless a few months ago had been our first step into the new world of technical miracles.

Our progress was slower than most people's for there were no allowances for children or disabled people and we had no money for luxuries.

I remember that baking day was always on a Thursday and that my mother baked all day. When I came home for lunch the bowl of white dough for the bread would be rising in front of the range and the hearth would be covered with baking sheets on which the week's supply of currant teacakes would be rising. When I came back at home time the newly baked miracles would be stacked on the cooling trays and Mother and I would have to tackle the washing up.

They were wonderful days, the summer that Margaret was born. When I was not at school and not on the milk round, I was too busy with household chores to be much company for my friends. I, who had played with such intensity and imagination, now only did things for real. If I baked, gone were the days of thimble cakes and diddy pies and gingerbread men. What I made had to be eaten. Floors had to be scrubbed and windows washed. When I hung out the washing it was no longer a play line with dollies' clothes but the family line with sheets and tablecloths and I loved it. Who says children do not like to work!

One evening my grandmother came over from the farm to teach me how to crochet. She did so with determination, did not heed my frustrated tears or give up until success was achieved. Thereafter I crocheted madly in my spare time making matinee coats for my small sister.

The old fashioned tub of a pram, which had been used nine years ago, was unearthed from somewhere and sometimes we would push the pram into town to visit Grandmother who was confined to a wheelchair. The return journey up the hill was so arduous that more often than not we would struggle onto the bus instead. That was a palaver! Well known as the 'Little Milk Girl' I became conspicuous as part of the family which was always struggling onto the bus with a handicapped boy, a baby and far too many bags.

The family had become quite a comedy act. Mother usually set us all off laughing. She loved a silly half hour and sometimes Father would look on, frowning and saying the silliness would end in tears. There was a togetherness of tremendous value in our family relationships which should have been the example of all, but no one would have exchanged her role for mine then any more than anyone would now.

There was no holiday in Blackpool that year. The aunts took Grandmother to Morecambe for a month in a self-catering bungalow and we visited them for one day only, the baby being so small, and there were to be no more holidays until after the war.

I thought that the declaration of war, on 3rd September, was very exciting and the tears of my mother and aunts did not make me change my mind. We did not envisage six years of conflict but neither did we expect to get off so lightly. Tucked away in this Pennine valley the bombers never found our town and, though the siren gave warnings, we only heard our planes go out to intercept. We heard the wireless bulletins and wondered how long our safety would last. The Army brought tanks to The Currer, and our moor became mutilated with caterpillar wheels and dangerously unsafe because unexploded hand grenades were lost in the heather. There was a dreadful accident when a group of children found some explosive device and threw it against a wall. During the first year soldiers were being billeted and trained in the locality and The Currer still bears the scars of the heavy tanks which made such a mess. Mines were being laid, the Home Guard and Air Raid Wardens briefed and at school the shelter was dug and gas masks distributed.

But when all this was over and activity moved to the Continent we were left to get on with the school collections of aluminium; our playground lost its railings to the war effort and we learned to cope with rationing and the blackout and the evacuees. Because of home pressures we were not considered for fostering, but there were plenty in the locality and my last year in the village school saw the classes swollen to bursting point. Air raid practices were held and my parents opted for the choice of having me at home instead of in the shelter. So, every time the siren went, for real or for practice, I must run like mad, home, where there was no real safety but where we would all be together. There was never any need for alarm for the nearest bomb fell ten miles away.

At school and home we began to Dig for Victory. The small, childish plots we worked at school, instead of doing handwork, were handkerchief-sized compared with the enormous garden at home. Much of the digging fell on me. Fodder and provender became rationed and it was a case of all hands on deck. My help in the mistal became essential. Grandfather, who had given up his part-share in the milking and more or less retired, came back to the task with three-legged stool and piggin and I began to join him milking the drying-off cows whilst Father slaved away at those heavy in milk.

Increasingly often the job of collecting the cows from The Currer became mine. On returning from school I would take the dog Peter (Floss, my father's dog, would not come with me), and together, child and dog we would pass through the village, turn right at the school and along the narrow road to the Moor Gate. Thereafter we would hunt for cattle on the 170 acres. Because their journey was regular and routine, herding the cattle was no problem. At sight and sound of the dog they would head towards the gate onto the road and the liggers-off seemed to know they hadn't to come and continued grazing undisturbed by the moving milk herd. The scattered formation became a single line as they neared the gate and passed through onto the road. Happy, happy days, on my own, driving cattle, singing and leaping. I used to think, 'I'm as agile as a mountain goat,' and the feeling made me light-headed and giddy with health and energy.

Eventually the single line of the herd would reach the fold and each cow would enter the right mistal and step into the right stall. Then would come the grooming, the washing of the udders and finally the milking. The three of us would hand-milk up the line and from mistal to mistal. Each frothy piggin of milk would be emptied into the cooler. Auntie Janie made me a milking cap like Father's but Grandfather always wore a white-knotted handkerchief. He did not talk to me.

I knew all about my father, his ideals and principles and priorities. From him I learned a code of conduct, a compassion, a sense of responsibility and a faith. He and Mother continually told me what to do and how to do it and whilst they taught me to tolerate hardships and imperfections in others they never spared me. I was never told to, 'Leave it,' or, 'Give ower.' At least, if I were advised to 'give ower' it was always with the addition of, 'Fer t'night.' Other people might give up but my father and his family 'kept right on to the end of the road.'

I knew nothing of Grandfather. He never told me anything. I might just as well never have been there, and Grandmother's loyalty to him was a barrier between us.

One would have thought that my life was so packed with positive activity

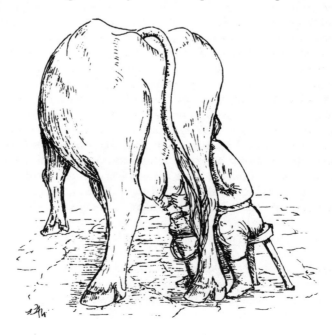

that it could absorb no more. I was to learn that you can do practically everything you want to, that time is elastic and twenty-four hours can be stretched, and that the speed at which jobs are done can be accelerated and work output doubled. As my tenth birthday approached I wanted to join the local Guide Company which met in the schoolroom of St Barnabas' Church.

My mother and her family were, however, against it. They did not want me to wear uniform. It was unfeminine enough to do so much work on the farm without my becoming military and banner-carrying. But the thought of camp-fires and tracking and perhaps camping was like a magnet. Father came to my rescue. He realised that I must have some life of my own. All work and no play was not altogether a good thing so he came down heavily on my side and Auntie Mary, my godmother, bought my uniform.

So my birthday heralded a new and adventurous future. Little did I know then that permission for me to become a Guide opened the door for hundreds of children, for over a quarter of a century, to roam the Yorkshire Dales and the isolated beaches, wild moors and rocky mountains of the Hebrides.

Strange as it may seem, it was as a Guide that I became really familiar with The Currer. I had, during the last twelve months, collected cattle almost daily from the moor but now I began to explore it in detail. There were other farms in the area but the Guide Captain nearly always took us to spend summer evenings on our land. It had more variety than the land of our neighbours and infinitely more footpaths. We had moor and pasture, meadow and woodland. The ground was a treasure trove of wild flowers to be identified, the air was full of birdsong. Blackbirds nested in the hawthorn thickets, the flutter of bats and the whirr of snipe wings stirred the first fall of darkness. Peewits screamed over the moorland diverting our attention from their vulnerable chicks by unashamedly acting lame ahead of us. Wood pigeons rose in scores from feeding on the bilberry bushes, an owl hooted and we searched for pellets and displayed their contents in the church schoolroom. In April the cuckoo sang to us as we learned to follow trails across the pastures, through the bracken to the heather and the path to the Druids' Altar, and as we went we gathered birch bark and kindling twigs from the spinney to light fires, beneath the sacrificial rocks, to cook sausages and bread roll dampers. We learned to identify trees for their burning suitability, to know where to find the best punk and how to cut sods neatly. We collected our water from the spring at The Currer and from the stream which rushes out of the hillside at Lovers' Leap. I was in my element. Life was full. I did not want it to change.

Chapter Three

W hen the opportunity came for those in the top year of the primary school to sit the examination for the County Minor Scholarship to Grammar School, I had no hesitation in refusing. There was no incentive for me to look for an academic career. I believed that the farm would need me and that I would work there. No one from my village school had won a scholarship for years. The only pupils I knew who went to the Grammar School were fee-paying. I knew that Father and Uncle had been scholarship winners but Father hadn't enjoyed it and Uncle, though he lived next door, was an enigma.

So when the headmaster asked me to sit the examination I said, 'No!' I fully expected my parents to agree and was rather taken aback when they insisted that I tried.

I was a practical child, not a studious one. I wasn't a reader. In my home we did not read, we talked. I was never to be found with my head in a book or a pen in my hand. I was the least likely candidate for an academic career.

However, one March morning, I accompanied some of my classmates to a school in town where the examination was to be taken. There were scores of children wandering apprehensively round the playground waiting for the ordeal. I was more concerned with wondering how to refuse a bottle of milk. I could see the crates stacked high and knew we would be expected to take one at playtime and I only liked our own milk. I remember the examination room with single desks, the awful silence and the two invigilators, one in the front desk and one sitting glaring at us from behind. I think I felt a little truculent. I wasn't going to pass. Everything was perfectly all right as it was.

I don't remember much about the exam papers. One was arithmetic, one an intelligence test the like of which I'd never seen before, and one was an essay. Over this I lost my patience completely.

'Write about who you would like to change places with and why.'

I stared at the black print, frowning at the empty page for a long time. What a daft question!

Quickly and without hesitation I wrote one short paragraph informing the reader that a little more money in the house would greatly help my parents and that to have a car would be nice for my handicapped brother but that I didn't want to change places with anyone and I wasn't going to say I did when it wasn't true. I wanted to remain, and here I wrote my name in block capitals and put down my pen.

My behaviour was apparently being monitored by the rear invigilator. She rose from her seat and came to look over my shoulder. The paragraph amused her and she went to the front teacher's desk and whispered the co-ordinates to fix my position in the examination room. Having identified me she made an amused comment and they both laughed silently. I was deeply embarrassed and for the rest of my school days the fear of teachers looking over my shoulder and reading my work remained.

I count that day as all-important. The way that I must go was surely pre-ordained for I certainly did not choose my future on that awful March day. It took us thirty years to buy a car for Harry, an Austin Gypsy which cost £80. Ten years were to pass before my modest earnings could swell the kitty and the relative affluence they brought lasted only a year. I never regretted, however, my childish declaration of contentment with my lot nor the fact that I never changed my name.

After the exam, I went cheerfully home to get on with my life the way I wanted. Many years later a farmer's five-year-old daughter told me confidently, whilst clearing the school dinner tables, 'Ve ovvers won't clear ve tables, Miss Brown, bu' ah don't grumble. Ah jus' ge' on wiv it.' She understood the secret of being happy. As a child, I had known it, too.

It was a terrible shock to me, later in the spring, to collect from the school letterbox a long brown envelope and find that its contents concerned me. The headmaster used to call me Big Jean though I was small. When he saw the village postman he used to nod at me and, lip-reading the word 'post', I would scamper to the cloakroom to empty the box. On this particular morning there was only one letter and when the headmaster opened it he called the class to attention, beamed with pleasure and told me to stand up. Without preamble he announced that I had won a County Minor Scholarship to the Grammar School. I was stunned! This being his first scholarship success since his appointment the headmaster was obviously over the moon, 'Put on your coat,' he said. 'Go home and tell your parents before your father sets off on the milk round.'

Blindly fighting back tears I left the classroom. Alone in the cold cloakroom I let them run freely. Disaster had befallen. Many of my friends had prayed for a place at the Grammar School and I had been aggressively against it. I was to learn that nothing hurts children more than unfairness and I was to teach them to accept it as unavoidable and to take what comes with a chin up. But that morning, I was hurt and angry because, in my eyes, the whole business was unfair. I probably wiped my tears and my nose on the sleeve of my coat. Despite my adult role I was only a child.

Opposite the school, owing to blocked drains or maybe a hidden spring, there was always water running in the gutter, water on which to sail boats made out of bits of paper, feathers and twigs, water to wade along in shoes or clogs or wellies. On this particular morning I waded along the whole length of the ditch careless of being wet, thoroughly and hopelessly miserable. I don't think I was ever a cry-baby because tears and sobs always hurt and once started would not stop. Kicking stones and dawdling I tried, unsuccessfully, to control my distress. I must have looked a pathetic sight sauntering down the long garden path at ten o'clock in the morning. Mother was horrified. She thought immediately that I had run away from school and presumed I had been beaten.

'What 'ave yer done?' she demanded.

'Ah've passed me scholarship,' I stormed. Mother sent for my father who was just preparing for the milk round. They both cried and not one word was said about my not accepting. I didn't expect them to. Eventually I went back to school feeling better. I knew that it would mean a parting from all my classmates but the break had already been made when work took me away from their play circle. I wasn't really afraid of going it alone any more than I was afraid of being different. Secretly I couldn't believe that I'd earned the enviable place and wondered if a mistake had been made. Even I knew the essay was a write-off.

One of the Guides had passed a Transfer Scholarship to the second form of the Grammar School. During the long summer holidays, obeying the Dig for Victory campaign, students had to take their turn at holiday gardening. She collected me on her allocated day and I went along with her to weed the cabbages and saw the enormous school I would have to attend. It looked like some grand palace with its laid-out gardens, tennis and netball courts and well-kept hockey field.

Shortly before the new term began Mother and I had an interview with the grey-haired headmistress in her flowing black gown and met the sixth form prefects in their gymslips and long black stockings. After the interview we were ushered into a room where orders were being taken for school uniform and Mother explained that an aunt would be making mine. I felt foolish at the time but later found that my gymslip was of a much better serge than the Utility ones, that the pleats were deeper and the hem heavier. Mine was quality. Being poor was an advantage if you had an Auntie Janie like mine.

My first day at school was preceded by two lonely bus journeys, one into and one out of town. My satchel was a discarded one given to me by one of the milk customers and my gas mask had a bag specially designed by my clever aunt. My journey was free, for the scholarship also provided a bus pass. I found I was the smallest child in the class and as such had to stand first in the form line for Assembly. It was a position of absolute exposure but preferable to suffering the claustrophobia of being somewhere in the middle of 450 pupils. The bells and books and homework timetables had me baffled and I got lost when lessons and classrooms changed. I frequently used the wrong book for homework and one day Margaret quietly shredded one with a pair of scissors.

However, I coped. Father helped me with my homework and gradually the transition was made. School dinners had been introduced with war-time but it was decided that, as my new school was only a mile out of town, it would be easy for me to walk to Grandmother's and Auntie Janie would make my meals. This meant that when the mid-day bell rang I left promptly and walked briskly into town. I loved those two miles every day, whatever the weather, although they cheated me of having many close friends for I shared no lunchtime gossip. I could not stay after school to join any of the societies for I had to bring home the cows and milk before my homework, and I could not watch or take part in any Saturday games because there was milk to deliver.

I loved my mid-day meal. It was wartime and food was rationed but I never heard a grumble. Likewise not one grumble ever left my lips. I never refused anything or asked for more or said I didn't like or didn't want or had too much. I was alone with older people, Grandma was in a wheelchair, mentally and physically handicapped by the stroke, it was wartime and there was no payment agreement.

It was about this time that we suddenly didn't want to go to Chapel Sunday School, Harry and I. As Primary pupils we'd been together. Now we were separated and the boys did a lot of larking around and Harry could not cope. As a Guide, one Sunday every month was Church Parade at St Barnabas' Church and I liked it and wanted to go every week. Harry could walk better and the distance was good for him so we changed our denomination and I was confirmed. Had I waited until I went to college I would have been confirmed in the Chapel of St Margaret, Ripon, and the ceremony may have been more meaningful. I cannot say why, but just as my real education seemed to be out of school so my religious education was out of church. I found an affinity with a Creator far more meaningfully on the milk round with Father or on The Currer with cattle or in the fields with the Guide Company.

It was during my initial year at the Grammar School that I first went to Steeton Hall to a County Pageant of Guiding. I went with a few members of the Guide Company but for some reason I left alone. I was leaving the grounds after the scores of other girls had gone and reached the pavement outside the Hall gates when the county dignitaries drove through. I stood on the pavement and saluted as they passed, believing that to be correct, and when they drew away I suddenly realised I was using the wrong hand. The County Commissioner remembered this years later when together we buzzed round the capital in a London taxi.

Whether it was the era, or the war, or the influence of the Guide Movement but those days seemed alive with idealism and courage and I was as eager to accept the discipline of Guide Law and the dedication of the Promise as I was to run and jump. It was on this sort of food that I was fed in those busy wartime days and my formative years were in the hands of fine people.

Many things I did learn within the grounds of Steeton Hall: good things, happy things. That first visit, on the day of the County Pageant, was a milestone in my life. Through the massive gates there was a wonderland for me. In 1941 I felt the magic instantly. Here was a large and beautiful house peopled with those who loved to explore and camp and follow the Woodcraft Trail. Here were places to light fires, and stalk and create. There was a large beamed loft above the stables where we all gathered for a campfire and I sang without anyone complaining. At school I was always told to open my mouth but let no sound out but at Steeton Hall nobody minded.

I remember a girl called Beryl Robinson who was sitting near to me and she pointed to a short-haired woman with an elaborate hearing aid and said, 'That's the lady who owns the house.' I had no premonition that her influence would be greater than any other in the future pattern of my life. She was 'Cloughie' to thousands of Guides.

The following summer I went to camp for the first time. Because of the war the tents were all sprayed with camouflage and we had to take our gas masks. In the event of a siren we all went down into the dungeon-like cellar of the house and sang,

> We're awl dahn in t'cella 'oyle weer muck splarts on t'winders,
> Wi've bunt awl ah coil and agate burning cinders.
> If ole 'Itler cums, 'e nivver will find us
> Cos we're awl dahn in t'cella 'oyle weer muck splarts on t'winders.

This first experience of camping was to infect me for all time. I loved the discipline, the laughter, the challenge, the joy of the open air. I loved the smell of woodland and wood smoke and the cheerful noise of the stream rushing through the orchard. Later, we were able to camp in the open fields but during the war years we had to pitch among the trees. We were as happy as sand boys learning so many skills and having such glorious fun as I'd never believed possible. We often had permission to go into the big house with its wonderful smell of polish and old age, its gilt edged pictures and beautiful furniture. But there were Cloughie's wellies in the cloakroom, maps and compasses galore, a union flag, tent pegs and numerous bird and flower books, star charts, rope and string and I loved it.

Quite early in the war my Guide Captain left to join the Land Army and our Lieutenant married and left the area. Everywhere Guiders were being called for service and it was necessary for the Cloughies of this world, whose hearing, or sight or health was impaired, to train Patrol Leaders to run the companies themselves. On Saturday afternoons, at least once a month and in the winter-time at indoor weekend trainings, I learned how to pass on the fun to the other girls in the Guide Company. The weekend indoor trainings were the best. We used to play treasure hunt and Kim's Game with the pictures on the wall. One was a favourite, of poultry causing chaos in the kitchen. I saw this former plaything sold for £36,000 at the auction in 1981. We used to crawl about the house in darkness. Under the beds night-light candles would represent campfires and illuminate scenes of battle and villages and the jungle. We had to scout the area, creep up the stairs, find the tableaux and report in detail. Those lead soldiers, Zulu warriors and miniature houses were sold for hundreds of pounds and I'm sure Cloughie never knew the value of the bric-à-brac with which we trained.

The huge kitchen where the meals for thirty were cooked fascinated me. I used to daydream what I would do with a house like that. We all ate in the impressive dining room, thirty hungry children all on our best behaviour. All had individual serviette rings and starched linen napkins. It was a different world from the milk round and the muck spreading and milking cows.

Now, a long time and many experiences away, I look back on my childhood with such gratitude. Yet when I try to analyse it there are contradictions to the recommended ideals I was taught. Give praise, I was instructed. I was never given praise. Mother always thought our capers were 'ridic'lous' and she criticised us, more than other parents I know. The wall I was building was never 'plumb' according to Father and when helping with cattle I was invariably 'in t' wrong place'. We were never paid or rewarded and never kissed and fondled. Similarly Cloughie, my mentor, was the most abrupt of women. Only once did she say I was 'a grand lass'. Her voice was deep and often accusing, her eye sharp enough to find fault; a mistake was never made but what she saw.

We were not commended, Margaret and I, we were trusted. We were given responsibility and hard and dirty work and we were told the truth even if it hurt. We never got away with negligence and we were continually being told how to do things right. We were given responsible tasks and we did not need to be told whether or not we'd made a good job. If it wasn't right we pulled out the six-inch nails and started again for if it went wrong we'd have to cope with it.

Now I was organising my patrol, taking them firelighting in the low pastures of The Currer, cooking with and without utensils, tracking and stalking, climbing trees and building bridges in Jimmy's Wood. Occasionally I failed to pass a badge test and I had many a tumble from my pedestal. Like my father I wasn't awfully clever. Perhaps if I'd been more studious I'd have shone more in school. As it was I continued mid-stream, a not very interested pupil, one who was always ready for the final bell.

But I was finding I had a love other than farming. I was, it appeared, an organiser. As the war progressed and clothing became rationed we had to improvise uniforms. I was forever cutting up flour sacks and dyeing them and making ties and triangular bandages. I lengthened and shortened and improvised in a way that only war-time can teach. Auntie Janie made it her responsibility to teach me the right way to sew and adapt; she disapproved of the standard of the First Form dress I made at school and forced me to undo the seams and start again. Auntie Janie is another on my list of very important educators who did not shower praise. Children know when they've done well and they are not impressed by an adult who says it's 'luvly' when it's 'nowt o' t' sort'.

More and more I was going to The Currer. For a month and more in the summer we took hay from The Currer intakes, first turning the swaithe with hand rakes and later leaving little heaps all over the field in case the weather deteriorated. We had no weather forecasts to help us make decisions, and changes come abruptly in the Pennines. The prevailing wind is a westerly and at the home farm we used to say, 'It's tekkin up. It's breetning up ower 'Oworth 'oil.' As quickly as possible we used to cock the hay into big pikes which would withstand even torrential rain and could be led in the autumn if necessary. Cutting and sweeping the hay was done by horses, all except the headings which were cut by scythe, for not one bit of hay must be lost. The sweep was a wooden pronged affair with tubular, iron hand-shafts and was pulled by the horse with ropes. When enough hay had been swept onto the prongs, the wind row was left and the moving hayrick taken to a suitable site for loading or piking. The horse was brought to a standstill, backed a couple of steps and then the iron handles were given a hefty jerk forward and the sweep did a somersault over the heap. If the weather looked like holding, the swept hay was pitchforked onto the wagon. The load was roped and led through the village and thrown through the fork holes into the loft at the home farm. A few loads were taken up the cobbles of the laithe porch at The Currer and stored there in the loft above the mistal.

Mother and Harry and Baby Margaret would come laden with picnic baskets and bottles of home-brewed herb beer, a delicious drink Mother made in the earthenware bread bowl. I can see it now, the yeast all frothing on the top.

I loved the novelty of the haymaking. I longed for it to begin and got excited when Father began to sharpen the teeth of the machine. You knew the hay had been cut just by the smell in the air. That at least has not changed with the years. The smell of the newly laid swaithe is a perennial joy.

Haymaking interrupted the monotony of milking and delivering but the daily chores could not be escaped. I very much resented the fact that I was sent from the field, away from the banter of the hired help, to call my dog, take home the cows and begin the milking. It seemed totally unfair that Father and the men should have the fun and that I, with Grandfather, should have to do the routine jobs. I used to wish that I could stay at the hay until dark, that the call to leave the field with Peter would not come, but it always did.

Choking back tears of resentment I would go without one backward look at the cheery workers and make my lonely way over the moor. We would gather up the cattle together, Peter and I, and drive them through the village.

Some thought I was far too young for such responsibility and that Father was a slave driver like his father, expecting and demanding that his daughter worked too hard. They were wrong. I worked because he did and Mother did. That was the sort of family we were.

Father was no taskmaster, no employer of an unpaid daughter. He was a friend and whilst he worked so did I. The hired haymakers could not be sent to milk the cattle and he could not leave them at the hay so either I went without grumbling, or it would be still there for Father to do after dark. By thinking rationally, the tears would be gone for another day before I shut the collars on the milking herd.

Grandfather began leaving the harder drawn or more nervous cows to me. Perhaps I was never as fearless as my much younger sister turned out to be. I was more than a little afraid of some of the more wilful of the bovine species. I cannot count the number of times I have been kicked into the groop, that two-foot wide channel behind the cattle which collects the manure and urine and leaves the sleeping stall dry. To be suddenly kicked from a three-legged stool with a too-full piggin of frothy milk is bad enough but to land in the muck in the groop is to add insult to injury. The secret was to press so hard against the flank that there was a chance that the splather-footed cow might miss so small a milker. If I missed the kick I had an even chance of receiving a stinging swish of the tail across my face. Most people think that cows are placid animals that like to be milked. Experience contradicts any such idea.

I took pride in being as near finished as possible before the arrival of the last load. Father would leave the men to unload and come to help me. There was no word of commendation or thanks. His smile was reward enough.

I don't think it ever occurred to me that we were working often from dawn to dark for a business over which we had no control. The hiring of help, the buying and selling of cattle, the ordering of provender was all none of our business. Till the day he died Grandfather ruled. Father's wage, though not impossible, was low. Mine was nil but still I expected to make my career farming. It was my life.

Margaret stood up in her pram at six months old and fell out of it. At nine months she was running all over the place. Unlike my early childhood spent in the garden, Margaret's was spent in the mistals and calf sheds. Nimble and athletic, she could climb the rope ladder at Steeton Hall when she was only three. I've never seen anyone so small walk on her hands and no one could climb the cat-steps as quickly. In my dolls' pram there had been Connie, bought from Mrs Lunny's cheap emporium up the High Street. In the same pram, nine years later, Margaret pushed a kitten.

I was always scared of Billy, tethered in the bull stall close to the milking machine motor. This we did not use, for the new acquisition, Grandfather's pride and joy, was blamed for an increase in mastitis. Much later, improvements to the milking unit made it possible for us to reintroduce mechanical milking successfully. When Billy was turned out for the very reason that he was kept. I was off home like a shot, dashing upstairs to look out of the bedroom window. I could just see the backs of the animals and the mistal door, so I knew when the bull and Father went back into the mistal and I waited in fear for Father to reappear alive. Margaret was never afraid.

Over the years I had never really become acquainted with our relatives next door. My cousin was now in her late teens and out with her friends. My uncle returned home from the milk round very late at night and my aunt, whose health was poor, I hardly ever saw. She died suddenly after a few days' illness and I was deeply shocked. I was digging in the garden in front of our house, when I saw the curtains being drawn and the implication of this began to dawn. I was quite unmoved by the news, ate my tea without any feeling of sadness and put on my uniform to go to the Guide meeting. The house next door was full of activity but it didn't seem to affect us. My aunt's family came and there was nothing for us to do.

I called for a friend who always came to the Guide meeting. She wasn't quite ready and I sat on the chair near the door, just beside the sideboard. My friend's mother came in and she asked me how my aunt was.

'She's dead,' I said and suddenly I was weeping tears I couldn't control and did not understand. (How often I've seen children do that in recent years. They have arrived at school as if the day were like any other and suddenly they've been in tears and blurted out some loss. Neal came to school outwardly relaxed and sunny. Two hours later, just before lunch, he was sobbing and choking with his head on his desk buried among his gangling eleven-year-old arms, tears blotching his exercise book. I put my arm across his shoulders and whispered, 'What's matter, Neal. What's wrong?'

'My best friend's dead, Miss Brown. 'E was runned over last night,' he said. Sooner or later it comes to everyone.)

Not long afterwards my Grandmother Smith died. The news was brought to my father and me in the mistal. We had a part-time helper called Edgar. I remember his look of understanding and his Yorkshire expression, 'Ee, hez she deed?'

When Father and I delivered the milk that morning we were both taken into the sitting room to see her. It was the first time I had seen anyone dead and I was amazed not to feel afraid. We were not taken to the funeral. Harry and Margaret and I were left alone for the very first time.

A few months before Margaret was four my cousin Freda married and she and her husband lived with her father next door. Consequently the cousin we had hardly known suddenly became almost part of the family. She was dependent on our neighbourly help when her first baby was born. A second one was born thirteen months later and there seemed to be babies all over the place. The young couple were struggling on the bottom rung of a ladder which was eventually to take them to exceptional success.

An independent little girl was Margaret. She was given a lot of attention for she had almost two mothers in the house. Before she started school she could recite most of the stories in her storybooks and thought she could read. She began school happily enough but changed her mind when she found out that she couldn't read after all. Leaving her protesting inside the cloakroom, Mother could hear her screaming nearly all the way home. We tease her, saying that she has shouted ever since.

Six months later she contracted scarlet fever and was extremely ill. We'd all willingly have died for her. When Mother urged her to eat a little food she refused and said, 'I could just eat you,' and we all cried. The ambulance came and she was wrapped in a blanket and taken to the isolation hospital. Outside, men waited to come in and stove the bedroom in which she had been ill and my father was very angry and accused them of intruding on our grief. But they pushed their way in, lit a sulphur flare in the bedroom and sealed the windows and the door. We felt visited by the plague.

We didn't see our little five-year-old again for a month. At first I hoped to catch the infection so that I could go along to take care of her as she would have to be in hospital over Christmas but as the first week passed with no deterioration in my health I began to hope I would escape. Several days later I awoke with a sore throat. Some old wife told Mother that scarlet fever could be prevented if brimstone were blown into the throat so Mother creased an envelope and emptied a teaspoon onto it. I was commanded to open my mouth and Mother put one end of the crease on my tongue and took a deep breath at the other end ready to blow the yellow powder down my throat. She was so near to me I burst out laughing and whoops, she was covered. She had yellow eyes and hair and nostrils and I got a sharp flat hand against my cheek. We did not try again. I never got scarlet fever and Margaret was more than capable of coping alone.

Each of the four Saturdays in that month found us walking over the canal bridge and up to the gates of the hospital with a bag containing letters and homemade toys and fruit. We left it at the lodge and returned without even a glimpse of our invalid. Auntie Mary started knitting and by the end of the month a new suit was ready for her. A pillowcase with Santa's toys was placed at the foot of the bed and a taxi ordered. It came late and Mother and I were impatient and worried. So was Margaret, waiting in the room set aside for those to be discharged. When we arrived the case containing her clothes was taken from us and she was dressed to leave. She looked very thin and pale.

Scarlet fever used to be a killer and the log book in my village school bears witness to many deaths. Now however the disease is so mild that a child will have a sore throat and be a bit off colour but continue school; the only significant sign will be a tell-tale peeling of the finger tips.

The end of the war came with bonfires and everyone in festive mood. There was one at the Druids' Altar. We didn't attend. Fireworks and bonfires are dangerous where animals are concerned. We got a cat, once, on the day after a bonfire, which was badly burned and blinded. We called it Nelson and it decided to stay with us and lived a long time.

One of the few good things to come out of the war was the Government institution we called the War Ag. The production of food was second only to the production of armaments. All hilltop farmers were bribed with grants and forced into reclaiming moorland, re-seeding and even growing corn at grossly unsuitable altitudes. I remember stooking sheaves at 1000 feet.

At The Currer we only took hay from the Intakes, the Eightacre, the Footpath field and the meadow adjacent to the house and steadings. When loose hay had to be taken home by the horse and when the carts had wooden wheels, easy access to the road was important. The eight fields at the Altar, to which there was not even a cart track, showed decades of neglect. The moor had crept in on them with a carpet of bilberry and crowberry and bracken round the headings. If they had once grown an arable crop they must have been farmed from the estate for they had gates into the green lane to the Altar and the big gate into St Ives.

Grandfather had periodically made somewhat feeble attempts to plough strips of the moor with horse and a single share. The War Ag made it obliga-tory to reclaim the far fields. A caterpillar-wheeled tractor blazed a track across the moor and ploughed in the bilberry and crowberry. Father cleared the stones and boulders away, spread manure with a muck fork and mowed the headings with a scythe. Oats and rape were sown but the altitude was too high for corn and the seasons unsuitable for ripening. Nevertheless we harvested oats during the war and brought home the sheaves, and from somewhere came an old threshing machine which toured the neighbour-hood. It pulled up behind the home farm buildings and, with a great deal of noise, performed its yearly task.

The War Ag, like food rationing, lasted quite some time after the war was over. We used its services to plough a few stretches of the moor and we reverted to grass, ploughing and re-ploughing and using kibble lime and basic slag. Father's hopes of a green and pleasant land began to grow. It is with pride we look back on the post-war activities of one man and the joy those meadows gave him when the wind stirred the long grass in June, before the horse-drawn mower laid the swaithes.

The end of the war brought the opening up of the concentration camps and thousands of displaced persons. The Guide Association began to train teams of workers which were eventually sent into the chaos of Displaced Person camps in Germany. One team was trained at Steeton Hall where I was a frequent visitor. Cloughie had what was called a trike cart, a one bicycle-wheeled affair with long shafts behind and a rope in front. With it camp equipment could be carried up mountains and down ravines and over walls. My gallant friend put the team through their paces on the Pennine Hills knowing that she would never be chosen to accompany them to Germany because, even with a hearing aid, she was almost totally deaf.

That year I became a First Class Guide and as a reward, during the Easter holidays, Cloughie took a friend and me round the Dales with our camping gear strapped onto the trike cart. I packed my homemade rucksack with the sleeping bag I'd made from the Christmas plucking. Our cooking utensils were tinned food tins with wire handles. We set off on a frosty morning for

what was one of the most memorable holidays of my teens. We pushed that
funny cart up hill and down dale to the amusement of passing traffic and
Easter ramblers. We slept in lightweight Itiza tents and it was so cold we had
to break the ice on the water in the canvas carrier every morning. I remember
waking early on Easter Sunday to find the world was white and rabbits were
scuttering everywhere.

In the summer I sat my Matriculation Certificate in a veritable heatwave.
It encouraged Father to make hay and all my swotting time was stolen to
help him. It is difficult to say if the sudden haymaking demand on my time
affected my examination results. Perhaps entering the silent gymnasium with
sore hands but a clear head counterbalanced the lack of recent revision. It is
enough to say that I had never hoped for Distinction and was surprised and
satisfied with Credit results. I did not collect them with the other students on
that August Saturday for we had been able to return to our digs at Blackpool
for a wonderful post-war holiday with the Aunts and Grandfather and a
cousin of Mother's.

Margaret had looked forward to going to Blackpool for a long time. She
had absolutely no idea of the sea. From the tree-line at The Currer, the town
sewage works are seen as square, artificial lakes and I remember the first day
she saw so much water in the valley she shouted, 'I can see Blackpool.'

The old magic had not been lost. Indeed it was more fun than ever having
a seven-year-old to play with. Margaret would play with a ball all day and
must have been a more satisfying daughter for Dad who liked to kick a football about and play cricket more than potter about looking for shells and
flotsam and jetsam brought in by the tide.

There was now the problem of my future. I could legitimately leave school
and start earning a much-needed wage for the family. Students with eight
School Certificate credits invariably went into the sixth form and on to college.
My subjects were maths and biology and for seven years I had believed that
one day I would work full-time on the farm. I had assumed that I was needed
and that it would be my career but it was obvious that there was really no
future for me there. I was sixteen; my brother who was nineteen would never
work. My sister was just seven years old. We had no social benefits for my
brother, no child allowance, no earnings supplement. My father's £4 5s. 0d.
a week must be helped by some contribution from me and although a job
might await me on my grandfather's farm I was absolutely sure that a wage
did not.

I was also under an obligation to a number of people. Five years at Grammar
School must be justified. Contemporaries from the village school would have
given their eye teeth for the place I had taken. The aunts had sacrificed to
clothe and feed me in wartime and I couldn't throw it all away. There was
only a week to decide and September found me entering the sixth form with
an uncertain future. I took an after-school job as laboratory assistant at 1s. an
hour just to put a few pennies into the purse and at Christmas I signed on
with the Post Office. Students were always needed to deliver the Christmas

post. Trudging the streets in the chill of a cold December was no new experience. I woke when it was dark and walked into town. I delivered so quickly that I could take out two deliveries a day, often putting the last envelopes through the letterboxes by teatime torchlight. That Christmas, with the bonus of working Christmas Day as well, I put £3 into the kitty at the expense of my father having to deliver the milk alone.

I had something new to think about as I tramped the streets. Just before the village school closed for the holiday Mother, Harry and I had attended the Carol Service, primarily because Margaret was taking part and secondarily because I often went back to my old school to see the headmaster and present my report. I loved to feel the familiar smallness. It was an environment I knew, so much more personal than the airy classrooms and wide corridors of the Grammar School.

The Carol Service moved me strangely. I felt an affinity with the teachers and I knew that just as I was happy teaching and organising Guides, so I would be happy teaching children. Walking the cold streets with only my own thoughts for company I went over and over in my mind the problem I must soon solve.

I had to admit that farming was not my only love. Had the farm been ours there would have been no decision to make. But it wasn't. It might never be! Things were getting more difficult, for a stubborn man does not mellow with old age. Indeed, the whole set-up was impossible. There was no working together, no equal sharing of the work between the brothers, no delegating of responsibility and, quite obviously, less and less money to play with. Equipment was never replaced, repairs could not be afforded, mismanagement was obvious and there wasn't one thing we could do. Father became more and more frustrated, less confident that something would turn up.

Grandmother was becoming more crippled with arthritis and there was no one but us to help. Father was not favoured but his family was needed. Since Margaret's birth, when we bought a washing machine, Mother had taken the grandparents' washing. We did a lot of their baking and shopping and I did a weekly clean of the house, scrubbing the flagged floor and scouring the edges and the steps with white stone.

All these thoughts occupied my posting. I thought about the village school and I decided that if I couldn't farm then I'd like to teach. It was a selfish decision. It meant long years of training during which I would contribute no money and little help. I do not remember discussing it with my parents. They must have feared four years with insufficient wage and no prospects. They must have wondered how they'd manage without me, with Harry and the old folks. If they did worry they need not have done for Margaret was to grow up suddenly, as I had done at nine, and Freda and her children were to be a source of comfort no further away than next door.

Changes had been made in the Guide Movement and a new Award Scheme inaugurated. It was called The Queen's Guide Award and I suddenly had little thought for anything else. The final of a group of three challenges presented itself to my friend Audrey and me on a cold February Saturday. We were told to go to Rylstone, three bus journeys away, twenty miles up the valley. Our instructions said we were to go to the rather awe-inspiring home of one of Cloughie's relatives where, on arrival, I was told that guests were expected: a bedroom must be prepared and a meal must be ready at a frighteningly early hour. Whereupon the good lady promptly 'fell' down the stairs, needed immediate first aid, went to bed and left me to cope.

It was extremely cold and I remember that it was the 1st of February 1947. Days of frost had hardened the earth and frozen the ponds. No ducks swam on the small lake in the centre of Rylstone. On Sunday snow fell and fell and fell. It fell until it was deeper and more drifted and sculptured than I have seen it before or since. The people in the terraced houses in front of the chapel found a drift which buried the ground floor, doors and windows alike, and half-covered the bedroom sashes. In this Pennine area of black stone walls and small intakes the patchwork of the hillside was obliterated. Walls completely disappeared and roads became so filled with drifted snow that we, who knew the locality blindfold, could find no recognisable landmarks. All wheeled traffic came to a three-week halt in our locality. Nothing like it could be remembered. Drifted snow by the village school so effectively blocked the through road and was so deep that a tunnel was dug through it and Margaret and her school friends could run backwards and forwards over the snow bridge.

On the Monday morning I did not go to school. When snow had closed the roads in previous years I had got up earlier than usual and walked the two miles to the Grammar School. Snow was always fun and the early walkers I joined on the downward journey were always cheerful, ready to laugh and careless of being late for hadn't we all the best excuse ever. Pedestrians in the snow are warm, happy people. It is the car drivers who are cold and complaining and thoroughly miserable.

Three feet of snow would not normally prevent me from going to school or doing whatever I wanted. In 1947 school was not even contemplated. The wind had played havoc with the fallen snow, scraping parts of the road clear and heaping drifts mountain-high. Snow shovelling was a waste of time. There was a steady stream of people walking the hill out of town, clambering over and round the drifts. The only possible way of delivering milk was by nailing a box on my sledge, dragging two full chums of milk down the hill and walking to and from it endlessly until the chums were empty. Then back we went to the farm for the remaining ones, dragged them further from home and started the carrying all over again. The effort required to carry the brimming delivering cans was sufficient to generate a false feeling of warmth.

Every time we entered a house we were delayed by kindly good wishes, enquiries and commiserations. Each time we departed we left a tell-tale pool of melting snow in the doorway. I cannot say that I did not enjoy it all but it was extremely cold and measured milk cannot be delivered with gloves.

I was allowed three days away from school without sending an excuse note, but on the Thursday it was decided that I'd have to go back. In my pocket was an absence note saying that I had been ill. It was a blatant lie and I was ashamed of it but anything else sounded like truancy. After the early mile into town, through the new covering of snow which seemed to fall every night in that memorable February, I found that there was a bus going up the valley. I noticed my maths teacher, Miss Freeman, sitting just inside the doorway. I knew her well for she taught advanced maths to a group of four of us. I was the least intelligent of the group and it was a struggle to keep up, so I was more than a little in awe of her and a bit apprehensive when she motioned me to sit beside her.

'We've heard all about you,' she said. 'How ever is your father managing without you?'

I crumpled up the excuse note and, on arrival at school, I went straight to the headmistress and confessed. Unexpectedly, she told me to go straight home and not to come back until after the snow had gone. Halfway home I met Father and his smile of relief was a picture.

Things were bad in 1947. Rationing was worse that it had ever been, and corn for the cattle was rationed too. Everything seemed to be deteriorating. We had too much work and no money was being spent. The buildings were ancient and draughty and windows here and there were broken. Many of the cows were old, the calf pens were dilapidated and there was a feeling of despair. Grandfather's bronchitis troubled him and Grandmother was increasingly infirm. There was a lack of tackle, an absence of tools, a shortage of hay and the allocation of corn, though due, could not be delivered.

The struggle to deliver milk in those arctic conditions was clean and pleasant compared with the havoc the weather was causing in the cowsheds. We stuffed up the cracks with hay, for snow comes into buildings like magic. The minutest draught hole lets it in. We boarded up the broken windows and threw manure against the draught coming under the doors, but we fought a losing battle. Urine froze in the groop and blocked the drains. We managed to remove the manure daily from the mistals but the drifts outside in the cobbled yard made it impossible for us to reach the midden. So we had to make a temporary pile just outside the door. Hardened with the well-below-zero temperatures and daily re-covered with snow it was no eyesore but we dreaded to think what mess the thaw would bring.

Normally the tied cattle created such warmth inside that it was a comfortable pleasure to be in the mistal. In 1947 their heat failed to warm the concrete or melt the icicles on the window ledges and sores appeared on their knees and shins. We could spare insufficient straw in the calf pens. One calf died, then another and we could not bury them or send for the remover. Their stiff carcasses were thrown out onto the snow.

By the end of the first week we had run out of corn and had hardly any hay left at all. If we had ceased to farm and were now employed in comfortable office jobs I would be condemning my grandfather for his failure to keep enough food in store. I would say, 'What fool would enter February with so little hay on the loft and so many mouths to feed?' But we have been in that predicament ourselves, many times, always because of a shortage of money. Feed bills are high, cattle always eat more than even the most experienced expect and one is often caught napping.

There was no let-up in the weather, and it became all too apparent that a miracle would have to happen or the herd would starve. Perhaps it was in 1947 that I really began to believe life to be full of small miracles. The one which saved the day was an unwanted store of loose hay in a barn about a mile and a half away. The owner of Heather Lodge had no cattle and a barn full of hay and, another small miracle, he also had a horse sled, a very light one which he thought we would be able to pull manually, for the journey home would be downhill and there was so much snow that the walls had disappeared.

We were able to approach the farm by climbing the steep fields belonging to the home farm. They led, eventually, to a walled and stony snicket which had completely disappeared and which joined the cart track leading to Heather Lodge. The track would have been impassable without the snow but the white covering made things easy. All things are relative and the snow which necessitated the ordeal of the next two weeks and more, also made the expedition possible. The last half mile of the cart track, through three or four fields, was more or less level and we left the sled on the hill above the home-stead, preferring to carry the bales to it, one by one, rather than struggle to pull a laden sledge uphill.

We were helped by Jack Clay, a young boy from the next-door farm, and we could not have managed without him. Each afternoon, after we had delivered the milk and after a brief hot meal before the fire, we exchanged our wet clothes for yesterday's, unwashed and stiff. The house smelt of new bread and drying farm clothes. Stiff woollen gloves and socks littered the hearth. Mother's supportive role was unique, as it usually is in an emergency. 'My Super Mum,' Harry calls her. Margaret was too small to be of much help. Her days of struggle, which now far outnumber mine, were still to come.

Sunshine during the day and severe frost at night resulted in a partial melting of the snow and then an icing of the crust. The snow became so hard we could walk on it with only infrequent, rather sudden, wallowings in a new drift. With heads down against the wind and without talking, for the air was thin, Jack, Father and I would tow the sled up the hill and across the level until we could see the oil lamp welcome of the little farm, almost buried in snow. Sometimes we tried to follow yesterday's semi-obliterated track but the wind at play altered the landscape overnight as it does the sand dunes of Hebridean Luskentyre.

Our sled turned and left ready for the return, the three of us slithered down the hillside to the quiet warmth of the barn with its life-saving store of hay. It was as solid as if it had been stacked out of doors and each day, with a hay knife, Father cut eight bales. Each was originally a 6 foot by 4 inch rectangle which we rolled and roped. Today the baler compresses hay so expertly that a half-hundredweight bale is relatively small and manageable but a hand-cut one is as big as a bale of wool and weighs no more. It was sheer size rather than weight which made us stagger up the hill to the waiting sledge. Meeting or following each other we saw only a moving haystack without any human bearer. 'Ah'm on t' wrong side o' fifty for this,' my father said.

Having overloaded our snow raft we each took a tow rope and began the journey home. Some of the way we were in front dragging and straining in the traces. Sometimes we had to walk behind holding the moving stack back lest it complete the downward trail alone.

After new falls of snow the sledge would sometimes bury itself and we had to dig it out with our hands and re-route our way. Sometimes the ground gave way under us and we were floundering. Always we arrived home after dark. Always we were exhausted. Blistered and weary, with frost sores on our lips, we would long to go inside and shake off the balls of snow adhering to gloves and hoods and the tops of knee socks overlapping our wellingtons. Instead there were hungry cattle waiting to be fed and the milking which must be done and it was nearly midnight when we finished. By that time, and in that state of coldness and dirt and fatigue, we were quite happy to go to bed without a bath. There were times when we thought we'd never see the end, when we wondered if our endurance was really an indestructible thing, but the relationship between my father and me was always magic.

There were times when I thought I knew how men must feel who have gone the limit in arctic temperatures, who give up and lie down and sleep. We were never at 'the band end' as Mother would say. There was always one or other of us with a little spurt of energy, gathered from somewhere, to haul the sled on when the others suddenly floundered. It was an experience!

There were days when snow fell all the way and there were no tracks or landmarks or distance and we would pray that there was no change of wind for it was on this that we then had to rely to find our way safely. But there were days when the sun shone and we screwed up our eyes against the glare, days when the wind whipped roses into our cheeks and there were moments of great beauty when the moon illuminated the strange landscape and the stars were near.

It was over three weeks before I returned to school. The aftermath of the snow lasted for weeks. The manure heap outside the mistal door became a slick of liquid muck that had to be attacked daily. The dead calves had to be disposed of, drains unblocked and frozen pipes mended. Slabs of snow appeared in the midden when muck was taken out to spread on the meadows, long after the cuckoo had returned to Jimmy's Wood.

A new excitement filled my mind. Cloughie called on my parents one morning to tell them I had been chosen to represent the county at the unveiling of the memorial to Lord Baden-Powell in Westminster Abbey. My mother had never been anywhere alone and she needed more than a little persuasion to agree to my going to London, of all places. I am still amazed that at eleven she let me go to camp. I think if she'd really known what we did she'd have fainted. Being a farmer's wife in the true sense of the word and never a farmer she really had no idea what I did with animals and as for knowing what Margaret has had to do! Well ...!

There was a field in which I was, still am, uneducated. I knew nothing at all about dancing and evenings out with boy friends, nothing of the application of make-up, of the art of buying clothes, or the almost universal habits of smoking, drinking and eating-out. Now if I am asked what I will drink I say, 'A small sherry, please,' because I haven't a clue what anything else tastes like. I knew how to entertain friends to farmhouse cooking and, thanks to Cloughie, I could behave properly in more elegant surroundings but of the pursuits of my teenage friends I knew nothing. I was friendly with everyone in general and two in particular. Kathleen was my school friend and Audrey shared the Guiding that I did at Steeton Hall. Neither of them knew anything about my farming activities. Neither really knew me at all.

The visit to London was a new experience. I loved the ceremony, the service in the Abbey, the night in the YWCA Hostel, the London taxis and Tube and the buffet meals in a Lyons Corner House.

I returned ready to meet anything with that confidence only youth can command; the 'Anything you can do, I can do' attitude. I've seen it again and again in my Guides and Rangers. It's an excess of self-confidence which is soon knocked for six after college. Whilst it lasts anybody can do anything.

So, to prove this, Audrey and I passed the exacting final of our Queen's Guide Awards one rather dull day in unknown Harrogate, and earned an invitation to the International Scout and Guide Folk Dance Festival in the grounds of Hampton Court Palace in the summer. From this memorable camp I wrote letters home to my handicapped brother and eight-year-old sister, telling of our guard of honour for the Princesses Elizabeth and Margaret along the Mall, and our private visits to the Grace and Favour rooms which were the home of the Chief Guide. I told of the thrill of sitting on her bedroom carpet listening to her talking to us and I described the camp activities and the folk dancing by the Scouts and Guides from so many different nations.

Immediately on returning, into the Upper Sixth, applications for college had to be filled in. I was interviewed at my first choice, Ripon, on 13th of October. I went alone. The college, red brick and old, appealed to me. I was in no doubt about my choice of career, just a little worried that they wouldn't be able to manage at home without me. No one is indispensable, I was to find.

We formed a very small Cadet Company with Ada Mann as our Guider and met in the billiard room at Steeton Hall. We were frequently orderlies at County Trainings of Commissioners and Secretaries, Guiders and Patrol Leaders, sleeping weekend after weekend in the Nursery. The milk round became somewhat easier as Old Dick finally had to go and was replaced with an old-fashioned Austin. So old and decrepit was the poor vehicle that the passenger door was tied with string. We were delivering more and more bottled pints and, old though she was, Grandmother insisted on washing up. A steriliser had to be bought for this purpose. Harry helped her with ours in the afternoon and she worked alone on Uncle's bottles late at night. He came home very tardily but she would not complain. The eldest son could still do no wrong.

There was tension on the farm. There was no progress. Without it there could be no prosperity. One thing only kept Father from breaking loose and saying, 'Enough is enough.' It wasn't because of me. I had decided to free myself and could soon be independent of the farm. Nor was it for our eight-year-old, for all she loved animals and had a way with them. No, I think Father held his tongue, kept an uneasy peace and stayed the course for Harry, his disabled son, who could never hope to manage the farm. Strange as it may seem the farm was a vital opportunity for Harry to find a niche, a job to do. Every day the lad could be seen sweeping up the manure which littered the yard when the cows were turned out. He was more upright then than he is today and the picture of him methodically sweeping the pats into little heaps, for us to lift onto the midden, is a vivid one. The yard was cobbled and the fold solid with a century of animal traffic and Harry kept both clean. Father knew that to give up now, whatever the provocation, was to deprive Harry of a purposeful life.

This maimed, laughing brother of mine was completely uncomplaining and did not resent his disability. He was utterly devoted to me. He could so easily have been jealous of my strength and opportunities. From boyhood most of his anxieties had been on my behalf, where was I, was I all right, wasn't it time I was home? He was exceptionally healthy and tough and his sense of humour was unique but his right arm and leg were of little use. He never went to school and he never learned to read. That was a great pity and caused many frustrations. He became very agitated if we did not agree so quarrelling within the family was a mistake not to be indulged in often. It is to be remembered that seventy per cent of handicapped people are looked after at home and it is not a thing one can do alone. Our help came from the aunts, God bless them.

We grew used to people staring, especially when we were on holiday. I used to resent it in the same way an eleven-year-old did who came for a holiday here with his parents and spastic brother. 'We get fed up of them staring,' he smiled with the wickedest of twinkles in his eye, 'so Nick and me, we just stare back.' He leered menacingly at us to demonstrate his point.

Nick, in the wheelchair, went into fits of laughter. 'Last time,' he spluttered, 'you put up two fingers!'

But I have a word to say for those who stare. At least they see. Most people walk by on the other side with their eyes closed.

In March came the letter of acceptance at my chosen Teacher Training

College. It was the cue for Auntie Janie and me to get busy on my humble wardrobe. I needed a trunk, the letter said. However would I fill it! I was also told that I must have a tailored suit and an umbrella. One of my Guides went to university a short while ago and came to see me before leaving the area. 'Have you got your trunk?' I asked.

'No,' she smiled. 'I'm a right plastic bag person!' The old days are gone for ever.

I remember the day we went to Knaresborough market, Auntie Janie and I, to buy cheap materials for my college debut. Together we made everything, even the ball dress which was also on the list. Me! in a ball dress! Whatever was the world coming to!

Leaving home was not easy. I felt I was deserting the ship but I was swept along by the current and there was nothing I could do to change direction. I think leaving The Currer hurt me most. I remember herding the cattle on the day before my departure and singing, 'I love the place, O God, wherein thine honour dwells.' I didn't mean the church but the broad acres my grandfather bought for £1,050 when I was born.

The environment I found so rewarding at Steeton Hall I now found in Ripon. The college way of life was just a magnification of the indoor week-ends. The college Principal was another Cloughie, abrupt, wise, awe-inspiring and I liked her. I thrived on the companionship of my contemporaries, the strict discipline and routine. I loved tradition and ceremony and service and I found them all at Ripon. I didn't love school, as Margaret eventually did, but I loved college and there followed two of the happiest years of my life.

Some resented the 8 p.m. roll call of the first weeks and the lights out rule at 10.30 p.m., and a few had boy friends and slipped quietly home at weekends to escape what they called 'the imprisoning walls of college'.

I couldn't have afforded weekend visits home, even if I'd wanted, but I was happy for them to do so for it left me free, Saturday afternoons and Sundays, to wander the countryside alone. I'd had plenty of prac-tice walking without companions and at Ripon I wandered hundreds of weekend miles, becoming intimate with the surrounding villages and the parkland of Studley Royal and Fountains Abbey. After the last lecture on Saturday morning, I would be up and away, rain or shine. My bed-sit cubicle was always fragrant with wild flowers and my walking shoes all muddied. Sometimes I borrowed a friend's bicycle and went further up Wensleydale to West Tanfield and Masham.

Both my college years were spent resident in the main building. The first bed-sit was a cubicle on Byland corridor. The cubicle walls did not reach the ceiling. Each had a 2 foot 6 inch bed, a marble-topped dressing table, a desk and a chair. Until a small unit wardrobe was added, later in the year, all our clothes hung behind a curtain in the corner. Food, clothes and soap were still rationed.

Because the walls did not completely enclose each small room it was easy to talk to our next-door neighbours and friendships grew fast. Every small community needs a jester, and we had such a person on Byland. Betty, her name was, but everyone used surnames for even the staff called us 'Miss'. Betty went through college as Dalby. She ensured however that I should not be labelled Brown for on the same corridor was a student called Joy and another who was often sick so our fun-loving friend named them Joyous and Bilious and it followed, for no logical reason, that I should be Jeanius.

There were those who complained unnecessarily about the food. Nothing was returned to the kitchen which could possibly be purloined for further use. Every slice of bread was taken, every pat of butter, spoonful of sugar and every drop of milk. I was as clever as the next at surreptitiously removing food to my cubicle and, with a can of beans and a cake from home, a feast could be enjoyed.

It was amazing how much fun could be had with so few luxuries, so little freedom and so few entertainments. Once again I found I learned more about teaching children from college social life than in the lecture theatre, but without the lessons and the lectures it is possible that I would not have been taught by my environment. It is on this supposition that I based my own teaching. I must teach children, I argued, how to learn from the life outside.

Incredible as this may seem my parents spared me 10s. from the £4 5s. Father earned each week. I never used it all. Others more affluent often borrowed from me. With this, my first ever spending money, I paid for my return fares at holiday times, bought books, school practice equipment, soap, toothpaste, stamps and stationery. What was left I took home. I dared not spend it on sweets and gave away my coupons. I seldom went to the cinema, although a Saturday night seat was only a shilling.

In college the prig in me was, I hope, efficiently dealt with. When I was unbearable Dalby would change my name to Bumptious and I'd take the hint. Very occasionally I would join the cinema queue on a Saturday night and wait for a seat to become vacant. They were good days before television, when the cinemas were crowded. The Ripon one was full of soldiers from the nearby camp, and the air was thick with cigarette smoke. There in the fug of smoke and people we wallowed in escape stories. The epics of courage and romance glorified war unforgivably and, like everyone else, I was patriotic and proud.

My first half-term holiday brought mixed blessings. I was enjoying college and the folks at home were struggling for survival. Just as I had begun serious work at eight so now did the full load fall on Margaret. She stepped straight into my shoes and found they fitted her better than they did me. There was a suspense hanging over the farm, an uneasy atmosphere, a feeling that something was wrong. Mother had taken over Grandmother's cleaning and she, too, was at a rather low ebb. I was eternally grateful that Freda was next door. The children were a joy and Freda a good friend to Mother. I went home for half term on a chartered bus taking students to Manchester and I left them at Skipton.

It was a pleasure to be back on the milk round and helping in the mistals but the greatest joy was in bringing home the cattle and feeling the good earth of The Currer once again under my feet. There was something so special about the place, even in the fog of my last day. There was time to collect the cows before dashing to Skipton to rejoin the special bus. A smelly smog was filling the valley and obscuring everything. Returning through the village a small boy, Jim Smith, ran out to help me drive the animals. His face was rather dirty and he said, 'Ah ampt sin yer fer ages.' Suddenly I was in tears and mortified.

It was a perilous journey back over Blubberhouse Moor. That day remains one of the very few memories I have of bad weather during my Ripon days. Even when there was snow the sun shone and lent sparkle to the ice crystals hanging in millions from the trees surrounding college and the great, ancient oaks and beeches and horse chestnuts in Studley Royal and Fountains. In summer it was always weather for tennis and sitting sunbathing on the terrace. Maybe it was because I was free of the necessity to fight the weather and could view it from behind glass instead of having to cope with its inter-ference with chores which must be done. Be that as it may, the feeling that the weather will be fine in Ripon has remained. The sun shines benevolently on all our Reunions and should we set off for Studley on a school trip and it be raining when we left, we could be assured that it would be fine when we got there.

We were not in college just to play tennis and sit on the terrace. It was a place of great industry and we were there to learn how to teach. We returned from the mid-term break to School Practice and I was sent to a school in Harrogate. It was overflowing and another student and I taught classes at opposite ends of a Sunday School hall, quite a distance away from the school. Teaching against the background noise of another class was frustrating. We used to spend dinner break in a poky little vestry, sweating round a gas fire. It was there, on 14 November, that we heard on the wireless of the birth of Prince Charles.

I was a nature enthusiast and had told the children to bring some leaves back when they returned from dinner. The news about the new baby was suddenly interrupted by a din in the schoolroom. The children were bringing in armfuls of crisp leaves, dropping them, losing control and dignity and having a hilarious time kicking them all over the place. There was absolute bedlam. 'Off you go,' said my class teacher, 'You started it. You must finish it.'

'What did I do wrong?' I groaned.

'Next time ask for three leaves each,' was the wise reply.

By Christmas I was settled to the new life. Compared with student days today mine were very staid and proper. Our Christian names were never used by the lecturers until we left. College Chapel services took a prominent place in every day and some thought a nunnery could be no more restricting. Male visitors had to be announced and were not allowed on the dormitory corridors, stockings and skirts must be worn and no trousers. Our predecessors had had to wear a hat for chapel. Some thoroughly modern Millie had relaxed this rule and we could enter chapel bareheaded. Such were the degenerate post-war days in which we were living!

On the morning of our departure for the Christmas holiday I was awakened by what I thought must surely be an angel choir. It was very dark. I lay listening and heard someone else stir on Byland. One by one we were all out on the corridor listening to the eighty voices of our seniors on their traditional pilgrimage the length and breadth of the college, carolling. As the college 'mothers' passed the cubicles of their 'daughters' they dropped their Christmas gifts. It was a tradition which really appealed to me.

I had only been posting two days when I slipped and badly sprained my ankle. In agony I finished the delivery and I limped home to apply some simple first aid. There was no way I was going to forfeit our Christmas bonus so I was back on the job next morning, biting my lips and looking hale and hearty in front of the post office staff and limping rather badly when out of sight. I had a very bad ankle over the festive period and Margaret did the milk delivery and helped with the milking, but Mother had the extra £4 in her purse and we were all satisfied.

I began helping the Guider of the city Guide Company, Miriam Smith. This gave me friends outside college and a colleague, Barbara, and I used to cycle up to her house for tea.

My summer school practice was in York. It was very grand going daily to the walled city and I became familiar with the ancient streets and buildings. The school was old but without grandeur, in a depressed locality outside the walls. The children were poor and some were dirty. The school was under-equipped — I remember buying skipping ropes — but I loved it and suffered it under a blistering heatwave.

I had been criticised on my first teaching practice for over-stimulating children and then having insufficient material to feed their enthusiasm. I have found no difficulty in stimulating children. That is a gift but the ability to feed their interest must be learned. It is painstaking work and needs hours of preparation and planning. At my school in York I introduced a project on the market. There was a spare classroom and in it we built a market square. We erected awning over the stalls with broomsticks and ample square lashing. I spent hours of extra work and only ever caught the college bus by running along Fossgate in a most undignified manner. My efforts pleased my tutors. 'Now you are getting the idea,' my 'infant' lecturer said. I wonder if she'd still have thought this if she'd seen my tactics to induce those forty children to sit in a circle at story-time.

'Look,' I whispered with all the dramatic art of a magician, 'see this chair.' I held high a chair made for a five-year-old. 'W ... e ... ll, when you are sitting in a circle I'm going to sit on it and tell you a story! Shh! I'll just close my eyes. Don't let me hear you.' Having got them seated I was aware my story had better be good. Forty pairs of eyes watched me tiptoe to the small chair

I had claimed as mine. There was absolute silence. 'I'm really quite clever,' I thought. I lowered myself dramatically onto the flimsy piece of furniture and all four legs splayed in different directions. I sat ignominiously on the floor amid the hysterical laughter of a delighted class.

My popularity at that down-at-heel school was no more than that of any lively young student but it fell foul of the class teacher. She did not understand that, when I left, I'd soon be forgotten or seem aware that when hurt or ill they always went to her. She was just annoyed because the children were enjoying the novelty of a new voice. It was unfortunate and embarrassing and I was sorry but her role was my role hundreds of times in the future. Her attitude taught me a lesson I needed to learn as a teacher and Guider and it is a lesson all parents have to learn sooner or later. Children take the familiar for granted but love no less when someone new is exciting and all-important for a little while. I have risen early to feed fifty hungry children in camp and watched the adoration of those who depended on me for everything focused on a new colleague, a popular senior or a natural joker. It is normal.

I returned home a little high and mighty for the summer holiday. Fortunately I had a three week Vacation Practice to do in a local nursery school to keep me out of the way until some of my haughtiness had been blown off. There had been a noticeable improvement in my speech. I had changed my vowel sounds and Mother didn't approve. Coming out of the church hall I spoke to some old friends and Mother was embarrassed and whispered, 'Speak prop'ly.'

My home seemed drab after the highly polished corridors of college, the carpets were threadbare and the matting in the living room was worn. I am still accused of entering home critically and causing an upheaval by noisily hoovering and shaking out the rugs. I spring-cleaned vigorously, turning carpets to hide the holes. I went mad with a paintbrush in the kitchen, earned the nickname Hell-Fire-Jack and was probably quite objectionable. No doubt I was well and truly ticked off by Mother which would be very good for me and my inflated ego.

Back on my old job milking cows, delivering milk and haymaking I gradually calmed down and began to behave myself. I got rid of my energy digging the garden and mowing the lawn. I think they were all quite glad when I returned to college and the whirlwind I caused subsided.

I returned to college with mixed feelings, for the community on Byland was dispersed to senior accommodation. One of my friends went to Hostel, Dalby to Jervaulx, which was a convenient headquarters for all our midmorning cuppas and I went to Back Alley on the new wing, above the gymnasium and too isolated to get much student traffic.

During the holiday I was amused to receive the name and address of my college 'daughter' and to find she was another Jean Brown. What joy that friendship has brought to both our families.

I applied myself seriously to my studies for there was a well-founded rumour that not everyone passed the finals and I dreaded the thought that I might fail and let the family down so near to safety. I needed a job for it was time I started paying my parents back. There were two great debts I owed, one to the family and one to the Guide Movement. I was twenty and it was time I was doing something about it. So many parents deceive themselves into a belief that their children owe them nothing. Fiddlesticks! Life is one continual effort to pay off debts we owe and so it should be.

I spent long hours in the biology lab dissecting dead birds for a Long Study of Flight and I worked into the night making apparatus for Teaching Practice. There were a few distractions. Our production of Gordon Daviot's *Richard of Bordeaux* occupied a big slice of our time. Then I was sent once more to an important Guide occasion. I was a member of the County Colour Party at the dedication of the English standard belonging to HRH The Princess Royal at St George's Chapel, Windsor. I remember little of the great occasion, the long hours preparing for the ceremonial and the service itself. I remember that I stayed with a Windsor Guider who had a sister living in Slough who had a television. One evening I was taken to see this very magic box. It was ten years before we rented one and the little Slough box was a poor relation.

There were a number of students who had been Guides and, in the second year, we formed a cadet company with the headmistress of the Grammar School as Guider.

Our biology lecturer was a bee-keeping fanatic. Bee-keeping and gardening were considered obligatory and all students had to do one or the other. Food production in those very rationed days was a preoccupation and everyone was expected to lend a hand. Our apiary was presided over by a lady we secretly called Dickie Bee. Tall, beautiful, with naturally waving grey hair swept into a neat bun in the nape of her neck, she managed to put the fear of death into everyone. She was always mysteriously there when crime was being committed, when the forbidden staircase, called Golden, was being climbed in a hurry by someone taking a short cut, when a careless bather had left the tap running on Byland and the resulting overflow ran down the steps onto Jervaulx and through some crack to cascade onto Main Corridor or when two day-old chicks were being secretly kept in the sink room for a School Practice project. This lecturer was capable of reducing the hardest criminal to tears. I was frightened of her too, but she was my advanced subject lecturer and I had to learn to cope. That she chose me to be there as chaperone when she invited the chairman of the City Bee-Keeping Society to tea, my colleagues considered hilarious.

Characters like this elderly lecturer fascinated me. I never had teenage crushes on PE mistresses or new young members of staff but I did love an eccentric and this erect lady was one of my favourites. She called all men 'man', and the story went round that when she took the bees to the heather, one late summer, an old shepherd had commented on her unusual headgear with the black, protective veil. 'Aye, missus,' he'd said, 'ez t' getten tha Sund'y bonnit on?'

'Man,' she had replied with her usual dignity, 'This is my bee-keeping habit.'

There was a supposition, even in those enlightened days after the war, that teacher-pupil relationships must be formal in the interest of discipline. Time was to prove them not always right. One of my nicest memories is of Bryan. I knew him before he came to school because I taught his brother. He first spoke to me one day when I was going to the bread shop in town and he was waiting outside whilst his mother collected their order. His face was a bit of a mess for he'd had a spill from his bicycle. Meeting him was unexpected and he was rather unrecognisable. He grabbed my sleeve, exhibited his mangled lips and with four-year-old pride said, 'Wot d'yer think abou' that then, eh?'

Seven years later he was a tubby clever boy in my top group and it was a maths lesson. I had the younger children round me learning a new skill. Suddenly the broad mass of Bryan was leaning over my desk and he was interrupting me with a totally unexpected question. 'How old are you, Miss Brown?' he asked.

I had a wicked vision of Dickie Bee and her withering reply but the most important thing ever to teach children is the truth. So, in the same ordinary way that I would have answered a query about the product of eight and five, I said, 'Forty.' He went to his desk and no one appeared interested.

A few minutes later he reappeared to ask my date of birth. I never told children when it was my birthday. I didn't want a class of children who knew. So I told Bryan that teachers didn't tell children their birthdays and he said, 'S OK, Miss Brown,' and turned away.

'Just a minute,' I detained him, for I was curious. 'Why do you want to know?'

'It sez so in me maths book.'

'Never,' I laughed. 'Modern maths books say all sorts of funny things but never are you told to go and ask your headmistress how old she is.'

'Aw noh,' he gave me an exasperated sigh. 'It says ask six o' me frien's.' I kept laughing and was happy all day.

My college days were far behind me when that happened. They were all too few and my time at Ripon was shortened by a month, for fifteen of us were sent to Bridlington on Final School Practice. It came as a surprise and we were all annoyed for friends had been split and we resented being isolated at a time of examination stress. Even the thought of a month by the sea did not tempt us. We were, however, to have a wonderful time. The early walk, from hotel to school, was along the shore and, although it was only March, that year must have held a record for mildness. Throughout the month I don't think we had any rain and at weekends we were able to sunbathe on the promenade. How I love the salty breath of sea. The other students thought I was crazy but they hadn't had a mother who'd sprinted with me to lean over the railings on the Blackpool promenade just to drink deeply of the ozone.

One incident stands out in my memory. My class teacher lost her register, that most sacred of all records. It had a special folder and was surrounded by ritual. It must be marked at the same time each morning by children calling out their number in the class list. It was closed at 9.30 a.m. and after that a late scholar was not marked. Upon its accuracy, it would seem, depended your job. At term end it was checked vertically and horizontally and at year-end, for some reason, it was sent to the Education Office. At night it had to be kept under lock and key in the headmaster's room. At the home-time bell the registers were ceremoniously taken to this holy-of-holies and one day, my class teacher's register was missing and neither she nor I could go until it was found. We searched everywhere, she in near panic and I inwardly critical of a piece of red tape so unconnected with what really mattered in teaching. I wasn't a Yes Man, agreeing implicitly with the so-called wisdom of the older generation. No young person should be. I try not to worry if my teenagers are critical of the system and question accepted beliefs and customs. They eventually have the strongest faith and the clearest understanding.

The missing register was eventually found under a pile of art paper we had returned to the store and we both went home. Somewhere in my teaching history this reverence for registers was lost and I have often marked mine after school. Perhaps relaxation came with smaller classes when it was easier to spot an empty chair. I had forty-six children in my first year out of college.

One weekend, sitting on the shore, I picked up a soft white pebble and found it could be carved so I crudely fashioned a fish and sent it to college for my 'daughter's' 1st April birthday. Thus began a tradition which has lasted nearly forty years. Each year there is a search for a different fish. Although it be only December, next year's offering may have already been found.

Things were going rapidly wrong at home. Obviously there was some financial crisis. Without consulting Father, my grandfather sold the two milk rounds. Just like that! They were saleable assets which did not reduce property but they should have been profit-making for the dairy price of milk is negligible compared to the retail. In selling the rounds he sold my uncle's job and he sent my grandmother to tell Mother that they wanted my uncle to take over the cattle. It was the most cruel thing they could do to Father; Mother knew it and cried. Father loved his herd. They were good milk producers, those twenty or so Ayrshires and the odd Friesian to add colour as they filed through the village. Father went to the labour exchange to hunt for another job but there was nothing for a fifty-three-year-old man to do who had recently been a farmer. We learned later that Grandfather had tried to sell the farmhouse at The Currer to a boy who often did part-time work for us at the beginning of the war. But he wouldn't sell land and without land a farmhouse is not much good.

Terrible weeks lay ahead for my father. He need not have worried but just let things take their course, for a man who has seldom farmed, and doesn't want to, can't simply take over from an experienced one. It wasn't long before the milk yield was down and the calves dying. Margaret was incredibly angry and when things went very wrong, which they did, the two brothers trod on each other's toes, sparks flew and tempers were lost. It was such a stupid situation, hurting everyone. Of course, things cannot go on in that vein and eventually Father had to take over again and, with Margaret, sort out the mess. The atmosphere was bearable only because I would soon be home and more money would come and, as Father always said, something would turn up.

There was never any argument about where I should live and teach. There were plenty of vacancies in those days because a generation of would-be teachers had been lost in the war and Emergency Training Colleges were turning out teachers after one year of study.

I was needed at home on every count. Margaret was doing an incredible job but she was only eleven. My cousin Freda was an excellent neighbour and indispensable but she had two children to rear. Although Harry was busy sweeping the yard, shopping and washing up he was always a care. So it never crossed my mind that I might leave home where I could live free and have all my salary to put in the kitty.

I applied to two Local Authorities and both interviews were during the Easter break. The first was for a job in my own locality and I was accepted. I didn't want to leave Ripon and could have happily stayed another year. Some were eager to escape the petty restrictions of a Church of England College but I liked it. I was lucky to be with a group of friends who all laughed at the same things. To have the same sense of humour is everything in a relationship. We were like Eskimos in college: laughing people. I think I learned to teach there. I certainly learned to laugh! For me college was a good thing and when it ended I wept, quietly, alone, in chapel, not for the future and the hazards it might bring but for the happy days of friendship and laughter which were over. In college there had been an abundance of time for an infinite number of friends and leaving I felt bereft.

Father used to say we were allowed just so long to cry when things went wrong and then 'ger on wi' it.' When a calf died and Margaret felt a failure he used to say, 'Cum on. We'll buy another o' Munday.' I was lucky. There was a valuable link left with college for I was appointed year correspondent and would be obliged to keep in touch with students and visit college for the annual general meeting of the Past Students' Association. This link remains unbroken.

Desperate to make money I went straight to the Local Education Authority and begged for a July supply job. They obliged and I was sent to an Infant School in the centre of town to replace a sick teacher. There I got cold feet about whether I wanted to teach at all. The responsibility seemed alarming. It is not wise to taste the cake until you have to eat it all. Parents used to beg me to let pre-school children have a preview, but I refused. Even a pre-entry visit to Secondary School could ruin a child's summer holiday. I tried real teaching for a fortnight and panicked.

In a Slough of Despair I escaped to The Currer. Why hadn't I pursued my first love? If I'd gone to Agricultural College it would have been more sense. Something was about to turn up any time, for Grandfather was failing and the partnership between the two brothers was simmering. I walked miserably across The Currer moor. It was bilberry time but I had no receptacle and no inclination to pick. I climbed the stile onto the rough and took the path to the Druids' Altar. The silver birch trees shimmered in the breeze which always blows at this altitude. It was very hot and I paused before the house slipped out of sight. It held no memories; meant nothing. There was no promise in the dry stone walls of the barn and the sinister farmhouse that I had never been in. It was as if the land was ours but the house wasn't. Because it warranted a condemnation order, owing to its lack of basic amenities and crumbling deterioration, tenants seldom stayed long. We did not know who they were or what they paid. The fortress round my grandfather was impregnable.

Gone were the lovely carefree days when the only thing that mattered was eventually to pass an examination. Gone were my close and amusing friends. There didn't seem anything to look forward to and I lay down on the bent grass and cried until my face was a shocking tear-stained mess. Then my nose, that part of me so capable of enjoyment, caught the smell of the good brown earth of my home and I could identify bracken and bilberry. I could smell the myriads of wild flowers in the meadows over the wall. Above, a lark was singing, peewits called from the pasture and a bumble bee buzzed among the heather. Suddenly I could cope. I began to laugh. Not hysterical laughter. Just the laughter of common sense and I knew that whenever winter came we'd live to see the cuckoo.

Chapter Four

N ow it was Margaret's turn to go to the aunts' for dinner. As I began teaching so she began Senior School. She had failed to get a Grammar School entrance, which, at the time, upset us all. We can only say that perhaps it was for the best. Someone up there knows better than we do and plans accordingly.

It was a time of change. Village schools, up to then, had kept their senior pupils. Now all children over eleven must attend Senior Schools. It was called Reorganisation. With it came some headteacher redundancies and, until everything was sorted, some headteachers were in temporary posts. I was appointed to a village four-teacher school and we had a headteacher who was only staying one term. At Christmas she was to become head of a big Junior School in town and we were to have a permanent appointment. She came and went as a competent friend whom the children liked and we respected. I liked my children, enjoyed my job and didn't miss my college friends half so much as I'd expected.

The doubling of the wage packet was terrific. To father's £4 5s. 0d. a week was added my take-home pay of just over £16 a month. We felt rich. I find it intriguing to look back on this period of my life when there was no call on our purse other than food for the family, electricity, and so forth. Most people live all their lives earning a wage which they spend totally on housekeeping and personal luxuries. The period that we could do this was so brief it was hardly any time at all.

The newness of my job and Margaret's new school made us forget the stalemate at the farm. I remember that Christmas at school was great fun with concerts and parties and all the multitude of seasonal activities. Then the new term began and our permanent headmistress joined us. She was friendly and we thought everything was going to be fine until we realised that she was ill.

The infants' teacher was a small, emergency-trained spinster who loved her unexpected chance to teach. The teacher of the lower juniors was one of the 'old school', an incredibly strict disciplinarian whose shouts frightened me as well as the children. Like all noisy people her bark was worse than her bite and beneath the surface she was really quite gentle. There were a lot of spinster teachers at the time who had done little else but go to school. Excellent though they may have been at teaching the basic skills or academic subjects, they were quite unqualified to teach children how to live.

Rightly or wrongly I thought I had already done more in my short life than they who were my seniors by thirty years. I felt older. Andrew thought I was and asked me a question he should have put to the infant teacher. 'Why are you asking me?' I said.

"Cos yer knaw t' best,' he replied. 'Yer t' oldest.' Tallest maybe, but surely I didn't look older!

Even the little infant teacher acknowledged that there were some things I might know more than she did. Peter had had a bad fall from his bicycle and his face was skinned with gravel. His teacher brought him to me, showed me his face and whispered, 'He's got a lump in his groin. I'm rather worried about it. Will you look? You've got a brother.'

Peter certainly had a very big lump in his groin. I touched it and asked, 'What's this, Peter?' I saw a startled look come into the little teacher's eyes at my indelicate question.

Peter looked straight at me and said, 'Miss, it's me 'ankie.'

Surprisingly the children soon got used to the noisy sarcasm of the junior teacher and learned the basic subjects extremely well and were grateful. She had been at the school a long time and many pupils came back to see her out of affection and respect. The three of us were soon to be bound together facing a storm we never expected.

No one could fail to see that our new Head was ill. The junior teacher showed surprising compassion which endeared her to me. When the Head sought refuge in her room the junior teacher coped with the extra class but when the Head stayed away from school I was amazed to find that our disciplinarian was afraid of the responsibility of headship and I was flabbergasted that she came straight to me for help. She wouldn't sign a form or add up a column that I didn't check.

It all happened very quickly. None of us could even guess the mental agony our new Head was suffering. She taught very little and spent long hours in the office with her head in her hands. One day she did not come to school and when the junior teacher went across to the canteen to phone there was no reply. We left the infant teacher in sole charge of the school and begged a lift from the School Welfare Officer.

He took us to the Head's home and we could not make her hear. So we went for the Methodist minister who was her friend and finally we roused her. She was in her nightgown, distraught and unkempt. The minister promised to get a doctor and we went back to school. A few days later came the news that she had been found dead with her head in the gas oven. The subject was all over the newspaper placards when I went home that evening.

To say we were shocked is an understatement. We had been afraid when we had failed to rouse her at once but we thought we had left her in the safe hands of a doctor. For some people there is no haven from the torment of their minds. It was a gruelling experience to have to cope with explanations to the children. They could not be spared the awesome facts for the newspapers supplied them in detail. We bought flowers to decorate the chapel and were completing the job when the coffin was brought in to its overnight resting place beside the altar. We were a little unnerved by this because we had the supply teacher's two children with us and Eleanor, who was only five and rather tired, found it a good place to lean. The trolley rocked alarmingly. We were very glad to collect the spare leaves and scissors and go out into the street and home.

I cannot remember which came first, my headteacher's death or my grandfather's. I mention the first because it placed the burden of headship on our junior teacher who wouldn't carry it alone and I found myself an apprentice Head within the first half year of my career. It was a high price to pay for such an opportunity but during the next six months I learned the clerical side of headship pretty thoroughly. I am eternally grateful that our noisy disciplinarian had a weakness where responsibility lay and turned to me for help.

My grandfather's death altered the course of our lives considerably. At the beginning of March his bronchitis was much worse but Grandmother would not admit it or send for a doctor. She was as tough as old rope, that arthritic old lady, wearing clogs and sitting always on a hard stool. She had seen many people die and laid them out ready for burial and she must have known that Grandfather was really ill but she blinded herself to the truth and nursed him with loving care. He could not go to bed so we carried our sofa across the field to put by the fire in the kitchen. One Saturday she agreed to send for the doctor and allowed Mother to help her wash and prepare the old man in readiness.

I was in Bridlington for the weekend, visiting my college 'daughter' who was doing final School Practice and living in the same hotel we had pioneered the year before. Grandfather died before my return and, coming home in the dark of Sunday evening, I found Mother, Harry and my uncle at the farm and Margaret and Father milking in the mistal. It was sad to see Grandmother allowing others to attend to things and make the funeral plans. She had given up and she looked very old and alone. It was decided that I should stay overnight and I spent the rest of the week before the funeral sleeping beside the little old lady, my arm around her. Grandfather lay in state in the damp, unused parlour with its large, gilt-framed pictures, its ornaments and stuffed birds in their glass bell-jar prisons. The coffin on the fringed velvet table cloth must have almost filled the room. I did not go in to see.

Yes, I felt very sorry for the bent old lady in her clogs and apron from whom, surely, we must have inherited our physical strength and dogged determination. Her life had been spartan from choice. She had not asked for, nor wanted, luxuries but had followed her man and done it his way. That way hurt both sons, but she thought she was doing the right thing and that is all any of us can ever do.

She liked me with her in the big brass bedstead above the kitchen. There was a bath in the bedroom but the toilet was outside. Each night when I walked across the field to join her, I found my pyjamas warming on the shelf of the Yorkist Range and I knew this state of affairs was likely to continue.

I had the afternoon off school to attend the funeral. The coffin was open and I saw a beautiful old man, looking just like George V with his short beard and moustache neatly clipped. He didn't look a bit stubborn or uncommunicative. Mother made a tea, for those who came to the funeral, in our house and when everyone had gone my father told Grandmother that she had better stay with us. Quietly, without a qualm, that independent old lady accepted his authority and settled herself in the comfortable rocking chair, too lost and numb and lonely to fight any more.

With my salary we had just bought twin divans for the room Margaret and I shared. They were very new and we were proud of the new look of our bedroom. From that night, however, Grandmother had mine and Margaret and I shared the other, top and tail. The old lady discarded her clogs, accepted a pair of slippers and relaxed in comfort. She mellowed and became 'Granny Brown' and we grew to love her. What a silly woman she had been to hold herself away from her youngest son and his family for so long.

For six weeks she was content. Mother was incredible. She knew, more than we did, the second place Father had always had to take and she had wondered if she could ever forget and love. She knew the closed door which had always kept Father outside. She knew how I, and now Margaret, worked endlessly, for nothing, without praise or comment and she could have been bitter.

Then some of the old lady's spunk returned. The will left her still in command. She put on her clogs, took her stick and walked slowly back to the farmhouse. There were problems she must solve. From then on my first morning job was to unlock the door and see that she was all right.

About this time Cloughie sent for me to go to Steeton Hall. The old friendship was as green as ever and I knew that sooner or later I would be drawn back into the great Game. Just as I had a debt to repay my family and the aunts so also had I an outstanding overdraft from the Guide Movement. When we were both sitting in the lovely drawing room which brought back so many happy memories of campfires and Guides' Own services, she said a leader was needed to take over a Methodist Guide Company in the centre of town. I was hesitant about accepting the job for recently my experiences had been wholly Anglican. The 'creed and the colour and the name don't matter' to me but I thought the Methodist minister might prefer a member of his own congregation. One, it seemed, was not forthcoming and beggars cannot choose so I joined a unit which was to keep me very busy for the next thirty

years and bring me more joy than anyone has a right to expect. I joined it with
all the unique enthusiasm of youth, giving everything I knew how to give, to
the three dozen girls meeting every Thursday evening in the Temple Street
Guide Headquarters, a room too small for all the paraphernalia of Guiding.
There were patrol corners filled with books and scout poles, maps and billy
cans. The walls were decorated with colourful posters and charts. Two standards leaned against the mantelpiece. There had been a caretaker Guider for
twelve months, a very popular gym mistress from the Grammar School. She
was prepared to stay as my lieutenant but unwilling to carry on with full
responsibility because she was about to marry and would eventually leave
the district.

This very attractive and likeable young woman had, as is usually the case,
a following of hero-worshippers from the Grammar School. They adored
her and wouldn't accept that she wanted to hand over to me. I learned very
quickly that one cannot fight another's popularity. It must be accepted and to
win one must join the club; to oppose children's loyalties is openly to declare
war. I learned to do most of the work practically ignored. Very good for my
ego.

There was no new appointment at school until September. The supply
teacher stayed with us until midsummer and I continued to stay long after
school checking and re-checking forms for my timid deputy head. If I was
surprised by the lack of confidence, I was too aware of the benefit it brought
me to complain.

My tutor was indeed a strange mixture of disciplinarian and recluse and
in retrospect I walked a good many precarious tightropes in my first year out
of college. I learned that the difference between harmony and chaos is just
one false step. I learned, that first year, to be a bit of a doormat at school and
in the Guide Company. My grandfather, Cabby Tom, always used to say, 'Be
reight wi' fowk,' and it's the best way. An even wiser man than he had said
there was no loss of dignity in being a servant. One way and another the
school year drew to a close and I felt a lot older.

My grandmother had been so close to my grandfather in the running of
the business that, had it not been on the rocks, I think she would have been
almost impossible to depose. As it was she gave in without much fuss when,
several months after Grandfather died, my father asked to see the books and
the bank statement. He was unprepared for the fact that finances were four
figures in the red. The sale of the herd would only have reduced it minimally
and outstanding bills could only have been met by sale of land or property.

Father was shocked. It is not unusual for farmers to be well in the red but
a business must be capable of paying interest without adding it to capital
overdraft. If assets cannot be sold to cover any loan then land is at stake and,
to a farmer, land is home and work and kingdom. Since the sale of the milk
rounds, two wages had to be found out of the farm and that was impossible.
The only sensible thing to do appeared to be to sell. I had a wage coming so
the family could live.

But it wasn't ours to sell and had we persuaded Grandmother to do so, what then? She would have had no home, the sons would have no work and no money, and what of Harry? The farm was his passport to a semi-ordinary life. There had to be another solution. It amazes me that a man who for fifty-four years of his life worked as a poorly paid employee could, when the necessity presented itself, cope so well and assume responsibility so confidently. My uncle had no interest in the continuation of the farm. He wasn't a farmer. His potential had never been reached. When I was struggling to keep up with my more intelligent classmates I had occasionally taken a difficult applied maths or calculus problem to him. He could always solve it. If any child brought me such a problem now I wouldn't even know how to begin. But he wasn't a farmer.

My father was and it was therefore up to him to solve this problem. He laid a plan before them and they accepted. There really was no alternative in the hopeless financial mess. It was a gamble and my father had never gambled before. While Grandmother lived the two farms could not be used as property against which a bank loan could be obtained. The only thing Father had was his house. The mortgage payments had just ended and the house was his. It wasn't worth the amount he needed to borrow to buy the cattle and pay off the farm overdraft but it was a start. He said he would pay a rent and the existing farm debts could be met from that. The cattle would then be his, the financial problem would be shifted and he would 'go it alone'.

Uncle seemed relieved. He went back to his original job as an engineer, re-married and went to live in the town, leaving his house next door to his daughter.

Whilst all this was happening I was being noisily persuaded to take the Guides to camp. My Ripon Guider friend offered to take us when she took her company to camp beside Gouthwaite, that beautiful reservoir up above Pateley Bridge. My ability to excite enthusiasm was a liability. Feeding it was extremely time-consuming and there were not enough hours in the day. My assistant, the much-loved gym mistress, remained the most popular but I was needed. Without me they could not take badges or go to camp so they tolerated me. The camp at Gouthwaite was a huge success and I began to relax and enjoy myself.

On 1 September 1951 I opened our business account with the four-figure overdraft and we rolled up our sleeves and got on with the job. We had no car, no tractor, no horse, a few broken down bits of haymaking machinery, a two-unit milking machine, the milking herd of about twenty, half a dozen yearlings and a few calves. We had to pay someone to take the milk to dairy each morning until the days of churn collection. It was an inauspicious start!

For one year the doubling of our income had seemed affluence. Now Father's wage was gone and we began to live frugally on a fraction of mine and put the rest into the business. I began walking into town rather than spend the bus fare. We sold a cow on 15th October for £43 16s. 6d. and one in November for £25 15s. 0d. and knew what the herd was worth against the overdraft. The monthly milk cheque disappeared in corn and overheads and we knew we were going to have to work like the dickens. We became jacks-of-all-trades, experts in making ends meet, finding secondhand bargains, and craftily using whatever resources we had. They were lean days and it didn't matter at all because for the first time we were working for our own business and, sink or swim, we were all in it together.

We began the autumn term with a permanent headmistress. I remember our first meeting. We all wore overalls in those days and hers was made of pretty pink cotton with a pattern of very small flowers. It made her look tall and severe but she sat on a desk in the deputy head's classroom to talk to us informally and we knew things were going to be all right. The traumatic year was over and for the eight and a half years that she was our headmistress we were happy. She was younger than the other assistant teachers but she had authority and the school retained its good reputation. She offered to teach my six- to seven-year-olds singing if I would take the PE and games of the top juniors. I was very grateful because the piano lessons I had recently begun to take were failing to make a musician out of me and everyone seemed to agree that my singing was out of tune. I loved the top class. The girls joined my Guide Company and I began to meet my children out of school.

At this time I know I left a good deal of the farm chores that had been mine to Margaret who was quickly proving herself more capable in that field than I would ever have been. In farming I was an employee, doing the job I was told to do, adequately and happily but Margaret knew what to do without being told. She could handle any animal and was extraordinarily conscientious about their welfare. I gave Father and her my money and my physical help but it was their expertise which brought us from the brink of disaster.

Sadly one cannot farm without money and there was nothing for it but to borrow as much as the bank manager would allow. It became an unpleasant annual ritual to go to the bank, lay our finances on the table and beg him to continue the loan.

When we took over in 1951 we had no dog. At half term I caught the bus to Wooler to stay a few days with my college 'daughter's' parents and Jean's brother bought me one, Jed, from one of the Cheviot hill shepherds. The bitch followed me home by train and we collected her from the station a few days after my return. She was very frightened and it took over a month of careful handling by Margaret to win her confidence and affection. Thereafter she was Margaret's dog, faithful, loyal and intelligent to the extreme. She never lost her wildness and would only litter in secret places, regurgitating food for her pups.

Christmas, for most of my life, had spelled more hard work than usual. Milk had to be delivered on Christmas Day as on any other. Poultry was to pluck and dress and after festivities and family parties we always had to come home and milk the cows. It takes discipline to come home from the warmth of an aunt's sitting room, over-full of cream cakes and fancies, take off clean, best clothes, replace them with dirty trousers and cow-hairy sweaters and go out to the cattle sheds to do the milking. It was a discipline I had learned from the age of nine. We were always glad when the family parties were all over but we would never have been allowed to miss one. Harry enjoys everything to do with family. I have found this to be a common trait in all handicapped people. I have listened to those in wheelchairs talk at great, affectionate length about relatives who never come to see them. Harry knows all about his family, all the distant relatives, where they lived, who they married, just as he knows every shop in the town, past and present, every birthday, anniversary, name and number. No matter how unpleasant the task of late milking we would never have deprived Harry of a family get-together.

Christmas started early for Mother with the making of the cake, the puddings and the mincemeat and after I began teaching it came even earlier for me. Three weeks before the end of term we began in earnest and now, bereft of all the activity and fun, no Christmas will come but what I mourn the loss of the good old days.

Each year our jovial, cigarette smoking caretaker went to collect a tree from The Laveracks. It was always big and, as the youngest member of staff, mine was always the high climbing job. Our party meal was ordered from the local baker and paid for by the deceased mill owner's widow. Even when Mrs Pigott left the area a cheque came annually.

Added to all of this were Guide parties, service projects and carol singing. From the cold night air, muffled in gloves and scarves and hoods, we would troop into the intense warmth of the Blind Home, there to de-coat and de-sweater and still begin to perspire before the programme of carols was over. From our ranks there was always a pianist, always a choir and several soloists. Most of the residents would sing, a few would fall asleep and some would make irrelevant comments and set the youngsters giggling. After our hoarseness prevented any further warbling the Guides would talk individually to the old people, kneel at their feet to touch and be touched by those who could not see and finally we would all go our separate ways, quietly happy.

During the first years of my teaching my maternal grandfather was rapidly becoming as revered as royalty. Although as untalkative as my farm grand-father, there was nothing withdrawn about him. We all loved him. He was always good humoured, always smiling, petted and pampered by his two daughters, warm, comfortable and outrageously important to us all. Was this soft old man really the same fellow as the young cabby who'd braved all weathers with his team of horses, sodden in rain, frozen in blizzard, blistered in sun? Was this gentle octogenarian really the young man who'd taken out picnic parties in the charabanc, brought corpses from the outlying villages for burial in the home cemetery, waited long hours in the dark and cold for his passengers? Did this clean old man once muck out the stables, groom and handle twenty-two horses, clean and polish the harness, joke with the stable boys in the tack room and trim and light the lanterns? It was difficult to believe, but Mother was witness.

Now our old man lived a cosseted life with his two unmarried daughters, setting the table for meals and washing up the dishes. 'Ah'm noan freetened o' deeing,' he told Father, 'Ah've nivver dun owt wrong. Not reet wrong.' It became a slogan in the house and a motto at my school. What better advice can you give to children than, 'Don't do anything right wrong.' It is impossible not to make mistakes and those who do most make most. It is more easy for others to forget than for you to do so, if you know you've done something 'right wrong'.

I have childhood memories of Grandfather being allowed first choice from the celery jar. He always chose the hearts for he was a little bit selfish. He then waited for an opportune moment to tweak my ear with the wet leaves still attached. No one could then look more innocent than my grandfather. He was a man of few words. He always greeted me with, 'Ah nivver saw yer. Wheer wo' yer sat?' We always laughed. If we sulked for any reason he scolded, 'Be reet wi' fowk.' Just once he gave me something. He had always left generosity to his wife and daughters, remaining uncomplaining when this left him the poorer. I don't think he ever had more than a little small change in his pocket but once, when I was home from college, he gave me half a crown. 'Yer mo'ant tell 'em,' he said, and I never did.

In the spring of our first taking over the farm business we bought a tractor. It cost £85 and we thought we had bought a Rolls. With it Margaret and Father began to reclaim The Currer. Those neglected 170 acres took every penny we earned and borrowed. Father was so confident of ultimate success that he was willing to take risks and spend not just the money he made but borrow on the money he expected to make next season and he used it all on improving and cultivating the land. The monthly milk cheque was already spent before it came and my salary spoken for. Father was not a young man and time was short for the big job that had to be done.

It was time for us to think seriously about whether we could afford holidays and we came to the conclusion that we could not afford not to take a holiday. Working a sixteen-hour day, seven days a week, every week, all the year would not end in ultimate success but mental and physical disaster. Nonsense, some will say! Holidays are not that important! Well, there were two people in our household who must have a holiday. Mother and Harry. We could afford the time to take a holiday during my long school vacations and we could share the workload. Mother, Father and Harry could take a week in Blackpool while Margaret and I did the daily farm work and then we could hand over to Father so that we could slip away for a change. The important thing was cost and holidays can cost very little. There is a Czech doctor in Nevil Shute's *A Far Country* who says, 'I am older than you and I know that if you really want something you can sometimes make it happen', and what we have really wanted from life we have 'made happen'.

Our old ladies in Blackpool charged the ridiculous sum of 5s. a day. That would not break the bank. The wanderlust was bugging me. I wrote to a cousin of Mother's who lived in Glasgow and who always spent holidays on

Scottish islands. She wrote by return that she and her husband were going to Mull and Tiree, on cycles, and we could go with them if we wished.

Whilst plans were being finalised I was rejoicing over our first Queen's Guide Award in the company. There were so few successful finalists that this was, indeed, cause for celebration and I invited our County Commissioner to come from Harrogate to make the presentation.

One morning, just before playtime, I saw the caretaker cross the hall and beckon the headmistress from her classroom. Teachers had high seat desks at the time. We towered over the children and the glass partitions made it possible for us to see anyone cross the hall. We were all similarly summoned. The caretaker's news was obviously of some importance.

'The King is dead,' he told us. The shocking news stunned us and took us by surprise. I felt an overwhelming compassion for the young couple at Tree Tops, in Africa, for the Princess I had so recently seen in Sea Ranger uniform when I had been part of her Guard of Honour lining The Mall. I remember the cancellations of programmes on the radio and the continuous, sad music all day. I gathered the children round me to tell them of the good man who had just died leaving his daughter a Queen.

This was the second time I had had to talk to my children about death. It is not such a familiar experience to children as it used to be. No one wants to return to the days of diphtheria and polio, of death at childbirth or in early infancy. The horrors of TB, typhoid and smallpox are best a thing of the past. Still, I think it sad that so many of the elderly die in hospital or old people's homes and that children are denied the sorrow and beauty which destroy fear. They are left totally unprepared for the inevitable when, sooner or later, they have to cope with it.

With the prospect of a cycling holiday in the Hebrides and a Blackpool holiday for my parents and Harry there was unusual urgency to take in the hay. We bought a brand new side delivery rake for £31 15s., the only new piece of machinery I think we have ever bought. We had an old mowing machine and the tractor and my cousin's husband made us a trailer to lead home the hay. A very strong relationship was being cemented between us and the young couple next door. None of us had any money at all. We were all on the bottom rung struggling to get up the ladder. Father cleared one half of the loft for Howard to install an electric saw and the young fellow worked daily until midnight, making field gates. Father recognised extraordinary potential in that practical young man and did not grumble that when the hay came in, the loft space was halved and a stack had to be built. Nor did he grumble when, in the winter, the stack had to be cut with a knife, instead of thrown through the trap doors within the mistal complex.

That first year of going it alone we worked frantically to get in the hay. Margaret milked before she went to school and we both hurried back at 4 p.m. to dash straight into the hayfield. Often we were still bringing in hay after dark. We could afford no hired help, so gone were the days of leaving the hayfield and doing the milking. We all did one job then we all did the other, always after dark, always jiggered. It became an annual anxiety to bring home the hay before we went on holiday, an annual miracle that we always managed to do so, an annual ritual to sing, 'Come ye thankful people, come … All is safely gathered in,' as the last load came home.

Little did we know, as we sped north to Oban, that we would go so many times with so many children. Mother's cousin Minnie and I had single cycles. Thirteen-year-old Margaret and David shared a tandem. We sailed from Oban to Craignure, on Mull, in watery sunshine and took the road over Glen More to a small hotel on Loch Scridain. The days we spent there were full of exploration and activity. We cycled along the Ross of Mull to Bunessan and further to Fionnphort. We sailed from there across the transparent Sound of Iona to that most lovely of islands. We took a small boat trip to the island of Staffa, landed on the basalt, walked to Fingal's Cave to hear the Atlantic crashing in and listened to the music of the receding waves shifting the sands, the same sound which inspired Mendelssohn.

Halfway through the week we left the hotel and cycled along Loch na Keal, beneath the towering Griban Rocks, to Salen to have bed and breakfast with the MacAlisters. Then we followed the Sound of Mull, to the attractive township of Tobermory. We loved it and had no difficulty imagining the Spanish galleon which sank so conveniently in the harbour providing many generations with speculation and sport for many a treasure hunter.

The RMS *Loch Earn* called on its way out to Coll and Tiree and we embarked about coffee time and sailed to Tiree. We spent a week in Catriona MacKinnon's cottage, Rhum View, at the end of the Upper Vaul road. The view of Rhum, Eigg, Canna and Muck and the distant Cuillins of Skye, is quite something. On clear days we saw the archipelago of the Barra Islands and the Uists and we caught an island fever which has excited us ever since. The Gaelic-speaking islanders were so friendly we felt immediately at home. Cycling round the island is no problem for the roads are flat and the presence of the RAF during the war ensured that they were well surfaced. The island is so small that within the week we had toured every road, often on foot and we had made friends to last a lifetime, among them Calum MacLean of Salum and his neighbours the MacInnes family and the MacLeans.

We spent a couple of days, finally, on the island of Seil crossing to it via the Clachan Bridge and staying with an old lady we affectionately called Auntie Bess. On our last morning we sailed across the narrows which separate Seil from its neighbour Easdale and then our island hopping was ended — or begun.

Our return released Father and he went to Blackpool with Mother and Harry. Jean and her fiancé came to stay. They were planning an Easter wedding and scoured the town and the local mill shops for bedding and curtain bargains. Cousin David came, too. He loved the farm and he and Margaret did practically all the work. Neither she nor David could milk by hand and, fearing mastitis if the udders were not fully emptied by the machine, we used to strip out the last half pint by hand. For this I was needed and on the first morning that Jean and Peter were staying, young David came across the field and into the house. 'Will yer cum an' strip?' was his somewhat ambiguous request.

The autumn came bringing, as always, the joys of blackberry picking at weekends and the purpling of Ilkley Moor. Of the 170 acres, over 100 were moorland, rock and boulder strewn, covered with bilberry, cotton grass, crowberry, rushes and bracken. Four acres gave us Jimmy's Wood, a dry valley, sparsely wooded with a few ancient oaks, ash, beech and elm, a holly or two and a tangle of hawthorn and briar. Several birch saplings provided the invaluable punk for our hike fires and blackberry bushes climbed over the drystone walls. East of the valley lay the low pasture with a hollow overhung with giant ash trees to which the cuckoo returned each April. Little has changed except that now there is green pasture where the bent and bracken were and the moorland feeds the herd as adequately as the pastures.

Within the boundary wall of Jimmy's Wood, close to the footpath, is the quarry from which Arthur Currer took stone to build the farmhouse in 1571. The distance from the home farm to the Moor Gate was a Sabbath day's journey, a pleasant half-mile Sunday walk. Driving cattle through the village was only a problem when there was a calf to bring home. Then the road was long and the little thing would weary and have to be carried and the mother would be protective and every dog was a danger. The half-mile, too, was a nightmare when there was an emergency and it had to be run in a frantic lather of sweat. I remember a heifer falling over the quarry and breaking its back on the rubble at the foot. When Father and four-year-old Margaret did not return, on that evening I remember, we were worried. Suddenly the child came running home alone saying that she had been left at the Moor Gate whilst Father had checked the yearlings and liggers-off in the bottom corner of the land. He hadn't come back and she had run home heartbroken. In a panic I ran that long half mile to meet Father hurrying up Currer Lane for help. The heifer was too badly injured to save.

That must have been Margaret's first experience of accidental death and she was badly shaken. It is always an ordeal searching for a lost animal. If several cattle are missing then they have broken the boundary wall and gone astray. If one is missing it is either calving or dead or going to die. One sees in every rock and boulder a blown carcass. The financial loss can be great but that is never our first concern. Sudden death is always glassy-eyed, nearly always distended and blown. Death after illness, in the barn or sheds, is peaceful and acceptable but death in the field is sudden and grotesque.

As the land began slowly to improve so did the hay harvest. It became necessary to stack some of the hay in the far meadows. One year we misjudged the amount and added an extension to the stack. The cattle broke through the fence we put round it and the easiest place to eat was where the two stacks were joined. In autumn, when grazing was thin and the warm mistals a temptation, the herd would be awaiting collection at the Moor Gate and so their break-through into the stack was not noticed. Days of stealing from it had resulted in a tunnel where the two stacks joined and one evening, when Margaret went for the herd, one was missing. A search wasn't immediately successful and darkness comes early. What had happened was disastrous. The animal had entered the tunnel and the stack had fallen and buried it. That it had floundered before suffocation was obvious. It was only found by the incredible smell. The flesh decayed immediately with the heat of the struggle and then the heat of the hay. After that Howard put us a shed in the corner of the first five-acre.

Jean and Peter were married in Wooler at Easter. We gathered masses of daffodils to decorate the church. I sat with her mother, wearing a new suit Auntie Janie had helped me to make. We were very young, full of romantic dreams, so sure that the future would be good.

School was a hive of industry for the Coronation. Local schools were to provide floats for a grand procession through the town: historical floats depicting our glorious or infamous past. We chose to portray Florence Nightingale at Scutari. Whilst those who had had television sets installed for the great day packed all their friends and neighbours into their sitting rooms, my headmistress and I put bandages on our wounded, added some blood from the red paint jar and assembled the tableaux on the lorry. It was pouring down when the procession wended its slow way through the town. We dashed into the crowds to watch and when our float passed all our brave soldier boys had taken refuge under the nursery blankets. Not a gory bandage was in sight. Amused but disappointed I went to tea at the aunts' and we all watched the Queen and her family come out onto the balcony on a neighbour's television.

In the summer Margaret and I travelled to Ireland alone, found a small hotel at Letterfrack in the heart of the Connemara and knew that it suited us perfectly. For a week we enjoyed the blessed peace of the hills west of Galway, explored deserted shores, climbed Tully and Diamond mountains with only sheep for company and swam when we felt like it. Gypsies there were along the country roads, women washing in crystal streams and donkeys bringing home peat in wicker paniers. It was just the sort of holiday we wanted. Full board accommodation at the hotel was only £1 per day. Even then it was an extravagance not to be indulged in often in the years ahead. We spent no more, the whole week, for we were content just to walk the fuchsia-lined roads, hunting for shamrock and chatting with the inhabitants.

It seems to me that I have had far more than my share of holidays. It has been my only luxury and even so I have had only a handful without masses of children or Harry and the old folks. I need no money for make-up or hairdresser, cigarettes or drink but I love holidays.

Weddings came thick and fast at that time. I attended them, made scores of presents of crochet work, tapestry, and tatting, but there was no room in my life for envy, no time for that sort of thing for me. There was a job we all had to do together on the farm and there were thirty girls looking to me for adventure. In the fifties the Guide Movement was one of the very few channels down which a girl could find challenge. I still think it is a foremost one. Guiders give their girls much more fun on holiday than teachers do. In the fifties how else could a girl hike and climb, camp and build bridges and canoes? So, whilst all my friends married, I became a 'Pied Piper' and I was happy.

Every autumn for at least a dozen years I went to the Northumbrian coast to spend a few days with Jean. When she first married she lived in Alnwick and the October after her marriage I shared with her the joy of an expected baby. Every ha'penny of my monthly salary was contributed to the family purse but if I wanted money for a bus ticket or a camp fee or a donation I just took it. I never asked if it would be all right if I took the Guides for a weekend in the Dales or an Easter hike to Bolton Abbey. I was free in my imprisonment. I suppose that I chose suitable dates so as not to leave them in the lurch but just as they had accepted my absence during the two years' teacher training so now did they uncomplainingly suffer the continual activity of my presence. I never asked if I could invite friends home, or clutter the sitting room with patrol leaders. I continually stored equipment, was perpetually making, disrupting, coming and going. I assumed I could and I did and now, many years later, I am not unaware of their tolerance.

Margaret did not join the Guide company as, I suppose, I expected that she would. She was an individual and wanted to choose her own activities. Whereas I spent my teenage building rafts to sail on flood waters and dealing with staged first-aid accidents, Margaret spent hers playing netball and badminton with extraordinary energy. Sport was her relaxation after the farm work was done. She had no homework and she was much more involved in the farm for, without any part-time help and with Father raring to do all the things he wanted to, she was very busy.

There was never any doubt that she would be a farmer. She could choose what I had not dared to do in the uncertain climate of the early post-war years when Grandfather ruled. I wasn't jealous. Things had worked out for the best for both of us.

If we had thought that with Father in charge things would go right we would have been mistaken. An old car is perpetually in the garage for repairs; an old fishing boat breaks up in a storm; old tackle, old cattle and things are bound to go wrong. We lost one cow, I remember, with a bad attack of summer mastitis. Her bag was so rotten with the hard pus that it burst and emptied itself continually from the side. In this dreadful condition she calved. The calf was beautiful and suckled the healthy teats but the mother was weakening and began to stagger, impeded by the hard, festering udder. One night she must have got down awkwardly and unintentionally landed on the calf. Next morning we found it smothered and soon afterwards the cow died too.

With too much to do and too little equipment the manure of winter became a mountain in the yard. Muck from the top mistal was thrown out onto the field ready to be taken to The Currer and left in little heaps all over the meadows. Margaret used to spend hours, alone, over the moor, spreading muck with a hand fork. She used to take a tin of baked beans and some bread and butter and eat them cold.

We bought our first hundred pullets in 1953 and kept them in the loft above the donkey 'ole. Solid shelter is a valuable asset and increasingly we were stacking the hay outside so that we could use the buildings for animals. Stacking hay outside is all right if the hay is loose and hopeless if the hay is baled unless you have a very good sheet and can afford to lose a good many bales at the apex. The hens brought us in a flow of cash. Mother and Harry used to wash the eggs ready for the Egg Marketing Board.

Point of lay pullets were expensive so in January of 1954 Father ordered a hundred day-old pullets to be sent from a reputable breeder. We assembled enough broody hens by borrowing from neighbours and partitioned off a part of the loft to receive them. They were beautiful but we should never have bought them in January. All might have been well if the chicks, hatched in an incubator, had accepted real mums. The hens were maternal enough but the chicks didn't want to know. The maternal biddies clucked away in the necessary way, fluffing up their feathers and making all the right noises and the stupid chicks huddled together as they had done at birth in the incubator. Valiantly Margaret and Father fought to foster those chicks and pushed them repeatedly under each hen, over and over again. But whatever ploy they used, those chicks would not conform.

Whether it was prolonged messing about in the loft on that cold January day or whether there was a bug around, during the night Father suddenly threw a very high temperature and sweat poured from him. It was unheard of for my father to be ill but in the state that he was next morning, there was no hope of him doing any work, Margaret was fourteen and it was her last year at school. She had an unbroken attendance so she got up very early indeed and went out to do the milking alone. Her first job was to see to the hundred chicks and she climbed the cat steps to the loft hoping that last night's struggle had been successful.

The restrictive pen in the corner of the loft was a scene of horror. The chicks not already dead were lying on their backs, frozen balls of fluff from which little legs stuck incongruously into the air. Choking back tears of self-condemnation Margaret scooped up scores of the cold babies and put them into a cardboard box, covered them with hay and carried them down the cat steps. She hurried across the field, crying and blaming herself. When things go wrong it is nearly always the fault of those in charge, sometimes with the contribution of weather or poverty. We had been ill-prepared and the weather cannot be expected to behave. Only very occasionally is a disaster a real accident.

So Margaret pushed through the door with her burden and her tears. Poor Father was too poorly to be of much help. He got up, of course, and when he saw the chickens he said they must all be brought into the house and kept there until they were fit to return. He told Margaret to bring over two or three hens and some cardboard boxes and seal up hens and strong chickens in a nest of hay. The very weak ones were laid on the hearth before the fire. Their little hearts beat for a time and then one by one they died.

It's a mystery to us how the morning milking was done that day. Both of us went to school, Father went back to bed and Mother was left to cope. Every couple of hours there was commotion in the cardboard boxes signalling that it was a feeding time. Then Mother rolled up the matting, laid out newspapers and steeled herself to lift out the very protective biddies and investigate the babies in the nest. These she lifted gently and placed them unsteadily among the oatmeal and tipped their tiny beaks into the water. The weakest she removed to the hearth before the fire to die in peace, the more agile she continually returned to the newspaper lest droppings littered the floor. The operation successful, she returned the birds to their boxes and thanked God, whose help she had evoked throughout the ordeal with a repetition of, 'Oh Lord, do 'elp me.' Not once during that day did she caffle at her job. We can laugh now at the strange predicament in which we left Mother. It would be nice if we could report that most of the chicks survived, but once a day-old chick has looked back there is apparently a 97 per cent chance that it will die. Only three of the hundred lived.

Father had the worst bout of flu he'd ever had. Margaret was very able and dedicated but she suddenly found a bad swelling in her neck and Mother insisted that she should see the doctor. They went down to the surgery before school so that Margaret's unbroken attendance should not be in jeopardy. The doctor told her she had mumps and must go home to bed and stay there until the swelling went down. She was furious for she was convinced he was wrong. She called to tell her teacher at school and received sympathy, not because of the mumps but because of the ruined record.

Now there were two invalids and we had to find help. Father sent me to ask if a neighbour could come in and supply-milk until he was well enough to go back to work. We wondered how on earth we were going to pay him for he asked a weekly sum greater than I received. But there was nothing we could do.

Father improved only slowly and when he went back to work we kept Arnold for a while. Margaret was still in bed at the end of a fortnight. The mumps had not appeared at the other side of her neck and she was still sure the doctor was wrong. I rang him to say that the swelling was still bad and would he come at once. He did and within an hour he'd called a specialist and Margaret was in hospital. The abscess had to be lanced and drained and Margaret was away from school for a month.

It was essential that I qualify to take Guides to camp alone. The Movement is responsible for such things and Guiders must pass a test before receiving a licence. In the fifties this necessitated a weekend training at Steeton Hall. It felt good to be back in the old groove. A written examination followed and then a Whitsun Test Camp. I was sure of my ability to pass for I had had more experience with 'The Master' than anyone. Cloughie had been tutor and was now tester. In anticipation of success, on my twenty-fourth birthday, I took the patrol leaders on an overnight hike to Arncliffe in search of a campsite for the summer. All my leaders were First Class Guides and one of them was Janet who was as dedicated to her Guiding as I was. An absolutely super youngster, she was, and it was her enthusiasm and the presence of my school children which were my inspiration during the first years. Joyous years they were.

After school Janet would take something interesting to eat, stride off to The Currer and find a new way to cook it. She had an eccentricity which endeared her to everyone and life with her was always amusing. An excellent actress, extremely sensitive and compassionate, she brought out the best in me and was the rock on which I built my company. I have never been under any illusions; a good pupil makes a good teacher.

Very cold, very blue weather we had for Arncliffe. We took hot stones from the fireplace to bed with us we were so cold. We had borrowed Steeton Itiza tents and we woke early and had to get up and move or we'd have frozen as the water did in our canvas carriers.

I returned home to face increasing responsibilities. One daily task was to unlock the door of the farmhouse and see that Grandmother was all right. She was always up and preparing her breakfast. Shortly after my return from Arncliffe I opened the door and found her not in the kitchen. I called upstairs and got no answering response. In a panic I ran upstairs to her bedroom and found bloodstained towels and bedlinen strewn all over the floor. Grandmother was in bed, weak and exhausted after a severe nosebleed.

For a few hours she could not be moved. Someone had to be with her all the time and it could only be us. Mother was with her most of the day; my uncle and his wife came up in the evening and said they would stay overnight. I don't think Grandmother wanted us to leave her but we were grateful for the overnight release. Early next morning Uncle came running across the field saying that Grandmother had died on the commode. I outstripped the family and ran upstairs. I could see she wasn't dead. I lifted her bodily onto the bed and when the others arrived she was stirring.

When the doctor came again we asked if we might take her the short distance to our house and he sent for an ambulance. She was rolled in a blanket and carried down the stairs on a stretcher. We had no spare bedroom and no extra bed. We hastily bought a single one and installed it in my parents' bedroom. It was very overcrowded but it was the only space in the house. They did not want Margaret and me to share a single bed as we had done for six weeks in 1951. For one thing Margaret was bigger. Nor would they have agreed to either of us sleeping on the floor, a thing we have done so many times since.

For eighteen months Grandmother occupied that bed and I never once heard either parent complain. It seems to me rather wonderful that the less favoured son, deprived of love and consideration, hurt and unheard, should show such kindness and even more so that Mother, whose loyalty to Father made her so angry with his parents, should now, when Grandmother needed us in this new way, respond so completely without bitterness.

The end of Margaret's last term at school came too soon. When she had failed to get an entrance to Grammar School we had thought it was a disaster but it was a blessing. I believe, too, that she left school as well educated as I did. She is certainly my superior as a businesswoman, a politician and a theologian and when I want a wise answer she is the first person to whom I take my problem. I write her letters and do her accounts. If she had time she could probably do them herself.

The Arncliffe site for the July camp was cancelled and I chose a site at Rylstone. It rained all the time but for one bright hour when we all fell asleep in church. It was a test camp in more senses than one, a camp to end all camps if we'd not been as tough as old rope. It had been already pouring down as we waited in the schoolroom for the lorry. I finally went to phone the driver to see what was wrong and he said, 'The weather. I was sure you wouldn't be going in this.'

I told him he had better come quickly for there were twenty-four women who didn't care two hoots about the weather. After the gear had been slung on the lorry those twenty-four women were cheerful enough to clamber on top and were laughing when the huge tarpaulin was slung over all. The journey, in darkness, was hilarious. Sheila, my first Queen's Guide, and Jill and Foxy, all members of the PE teacher fan club, came to help. Sheila was Quarter Master and a good lass she proved to be. The week was so wet we had to pave the fireplace which had become a mud bath. Those who wore wellingtons had sore calves and when I took off my plimsolls at night my feet looked like unrisen dough. By the end of the week I'll swear they were rotting.

Haycocks stood in a foot of water in the neighbouring fields and the narrow stream at the entrance to our field became a raging torrent. I felt like Noah with a lot of dependent relatives. If we stood a few minutes a pool formed round our feet and trenches were dug round all the tents. On the fifth day I decided we must get off the site or it would become a mire. Spirits were high and we walked in a singing procession into Grassington. A kind café proprietor did not object to an invasion of dripping females; we all had hot soup and no one complained.

The condition of the site had deteriorated in our absence and the tents had, at last, begun to leak. I decided to abandon ship and seek shelter in a dry barn the farmer offered us. There was great excitement removing to this luxury hotel. I left them all planning a fancy dress party. The seniors and I inspected the site and decided we'd have to go home a day early. I made the necessary phone call to announce our decision to the parents of our big family. The news was met by strong camper opposition. No one wanted to go home. Rain continued to pour throughout the strike. Had we known that this was the last wet day we'd have waited but we didn't and battled on getting muddier by the minute. We left everything in the barn for collection next day and caught the bus home like a lot of drowned rats.

Next day I returned with the lorry to pick up the equipment. The valley was flooded all the way. The farmers' crops were ruined. Few people, passing flooded fields of hay or corn, have any idea what financial loss that means to a farmer. As I write this, inflation has meant that a flooded field of hay is a loss of thousands of pounds. We took the heavy wet tents back to Steeton Hall for hanging to dry under the glass canopy in the stable yard. By the time I was ready to catch the bus home I was pretty filthy and fed up. My clothes bore the evidence of fire-blackened billies and anything looking less like a respectable teacher never before waited in the bus queue. I tried to look invisible. When the bus came I found the least conspicuous seat and looked out of the window.

During camp I learned that Janet had unexpectedly had a holiday to Scotland cancelled. I had made arrangements to take Margaret to Skye and I asked Janet if she would like to come with us. I might have offered her the moon. She could not come for the first week for she was already a working girl but she was prepared to travel up alone to join us for the second week. We had been on the island for some days and there is an out-of-this-world feeling in the Hebrides. It did not seem possible that one of my Patrol Leaders would be on the ferry crossing from Kyle. But she arrived and together we had a wonderful holiday staying, for the most part, at Ose Farm on Loch Braccadale.

One memorable day we went, with a party of guests from the farm, by small boat to the island of Harlosh. With us was a family called Sweet. Mr Sweet took his sketchpad and paint box and began a picture of us landing from the small boat with a backcloth of Cuillins. He sent us the picture some time later; we had it framed and it now hangs in the dining room. A while ago an arriving guest said, 'That's my brother's picture.' With no difficulty at all he had recognised his deceased brother's style. For us the sudden recognition brought back memories of a hilarious holiday. To be with Janet is fun and together we laughed at the same little things.

One day we were going to the Cattle Show at Dunvegan and were walking the six miles along the single-track road. The bus carrying many of our fellow guests passed and we stepped aside to allow it to do so and there was a great waving of hands. Stupid fools that we were, we stepped back onto the road without a thought for any other vehicle. A car, on the heels of the bus, hooted a horn and our reflexes were tested. All three of us fell backwards to avoid being mown down. A ditch was behind us and like some comic film we disappeared with legs in the air. The car driver nearly followed us, such was his hysteria. So often I have grabbed a child and saved him from doing the same thing.

Such little things made us laugh. The holiday was a success and I had taken my first teenage children to the Hebrides.

On our return my parents and Harry went to Blackpool. It was one of the things for which we have been most thankful, this love that Harry has for going places and being on holiday. During the war, when we could not go on holiday, we used to have a family trip in a friend's 'chara' and all our relatives came. How Harry used to enjoy that. The need for holidays for the handicapped has been known by us, I think, since we were born.

It is incredible how many things seemed to happen of the catastrophic kind when Father was away. In 1954, Grandmother, now permanently resident with us, had another nosebleed. During the long night my cousin Freda and I caught the blood in bowls. The doctor assured us that the bleeding was a safety valve and Grandmother survived the ordeal but stayed in bed most of the week.

It grew to be expected that something would occur whilst we were alone. Things seemed to happen on the farm, after we took over, that had not previously happened. I suppose disasters had dogged Grandfather as they did us but then I hadn't been so aware. Now there seemed a million things to go wrong. One year the pigs had bowel oedema. One year Jed had pups and two fighting cocks chose to have their quarrel too near the litter. Jed flew at them and killed. That really upset Margaret.

'Something will happen,' we began to predict. David had been feeding the hens in the loft above the donkey 'ole. He had barely stepped to safety when there was a cracking of timber and suddenly the roof fell in and the hens and nesting boxes and perches were all buried under a pile of Yorkshire stone. Badly shaken, the two children waited for the dust to settle and then fought to save as many lives as they could. David was trembling. Eventually they came running across the field to fetch me. Part of the horror of extracting dead hens was offset with the relief that David was not under the pile. That roof fall was enough to give us all a fright. David was so filthy his white vest was grey and he a coloured boy. That sort of filth is hard to wash off and I remember scrubbing him with a loofah and giving him an aspirin to calm his nerves.

Grandmother's presence in the house became a pleasure. Had she died on the commode, we'd have missed seeing the old lady mellow into a lovely octogenarian. With Grandfather's death the hardness seemed to drain away and we began to love her as we had never believed possible. She enjoyed the warmth and the comfort and company of our home without grumbling. She used to talk to Harry and he was fond of her. We felt deprived that we hadn't been able to be close as children, for Margaret and I would have greatly admired Grandmother's unique character if there had not been the perpetual barrier, the chasm we were not allowed to bridge. She was capable as few people are, loyal beyond the bounds of duty, hard, determined, never giving in. Now, without Grandfather, she softened and she never interfered with the way Father was running the business. I felt sorry for her that she had missed so much. She had known her place. It was in the dairy. In my memory she never went to the hay field or The Currer. She didn't know the land or the animals other than her hens. Mother knew the land more than she did. Grandmother never went blackberry or bilberry picking or just for a Sunday walk. Poor woman. There was all this to be had and she never knew.

Even within the security of our home she still loved the first-born best but she wanted to be with us. She loved his daughter more than she did us and when she sold the two semis and had a little money she wanted to buy things for Freda. But Freda would not take unless a similar gift was offered Mother. We ignored this apparent neglect. It was something to laugh about, not be bitter over. Grandmother was content to leave her home, fully furnished, every drawer full. She never went back.

*   *   *   *   *

Memories of children were accumulating and it is sad that I had no time or thought to record.

Certain incidents stand out against a background of many children. I remember Graham saying, 'I don't mind yer scoldin' me 'cos Ah knaw yer don't mean it.' Wise child. He knew an infinitely precious truth that where there is caring there can be chastising and disapproval and it won't alter that love. He gave me the phrase I've used so often, 'It's a good job I like you because I don't like what you've done.' Scolding is ineffective where caring does not exist and caring is a lie where correction is neglected.

When the headmistress was away from school in the early years of my teaching, I began automatically to take over her class along with mine and this made my six-year-olds feel very important. They loved to pick up their books and take them to the Top Class. I remember Tony, a ten-year-old, who caused trouble when I'd more than seventy to cope with and I told him to stay in after school and not to leave until I gave permission. Three-quarters of an hour later I left the school and caught the bus into town; I was just doing some shopping when I remembered the boy. I was horrified and dashed for the next bus to take me back to school. There I found Tony still staring out of the window, very white and frightened. I was very cruel. I said, 'Right, now you can go.' I hurried out ahead of him and ran quickly to the shop behind which he lived. His father greeted me cheerfully from behind the counter. 'Don't laugh,' I said. 'I've just treated your boy abominably.' I told him what had happened, begged that he should not get into further trouble and be comforted if necessary.

'Nowt o' t' sort,' said his father. 'It'll teach him a lesson!'

It taught me one!

We recently ran out of petrol on the hill road home from a meal with friends. It was very late at night and we had to phone our hosts and beg a lift home for our OAPs and Harry. Next morning I took a petrol can to the garage and carried the full can back to the Land Rover. I poured in the petrol but the vehicle wouldn't start. There was a young mechanic not far away who was pleased to help. 'It's Jack, isn't it?' I said.

Jack loved bird watching. One afternoon he did not appear after the dinner hour and the rest of the boys were ready to lynch him for wringing a bird's neck, a crime he had apparently admitted. He crept in late and stood very close to me and there was sudden uproar. "'E's a killer, Miss Brown!' ''E murdered a bird!' ''E wrung its neck!'

Jack's eyes widened in understanding. 'Ah di'n't,' he shouted, 'Ah rung its leg. Ah fought Ah'd see it agen!'

Jack is a good mechanic. He got my Land Rover moving again.

There was the boy who had an hysterical fit in the yard, the girl who frightened me so with epilepsy and Stefania's broken arm. That was funny! We took her home, the Head and I, and she said her father worked nights and would be in bed. We all went into the house and the child called up the stairs in Polish. I had visions of Papa rushing downstairs in his night attire and getting such a shock when he landed in the midst of two teachers so I prompted her to tell him that we were there.

So, in the language of her school fellows, Stefania called up aloft, 'Miss Watson an' Miss Brown 'ev cum!' So much for my teaching of English.

There was a near-fatal accident once in the schoolyard when it was my day for playground duty. One boy was running round and round the schoolyard being an aeroplane and his football scarf, wrapped twice about his neck, was streaming behind him. I saw another boy leaning on the dividing wall reach out and grab both tails and before I could prevent it the runner was strangled. He was on the floor, still with the scarf taut around his neck, fighting for breath. I have seldom been more frightened. It was so simple. How very many times I have told that story to children! One child, I remember, opened a packet of crisps with her teeth, swallowed the corner of plastic and choked. She, too, nearly died.

I could sit all day in the yard watching children play. Watching Beresford! There were fairies, he said, down the grate which took the surface water from the yard. Sometimes they were washing their clothes, sometimes shopping, and for weeks Beresford spent playtime bending over the drain. He lived in a world of fantasy and when he came to tell me a man had fallen from the roof I did not believe him. But it was true; a young lad, working on the slates, had indeed fallen off. He had missed the spiked railings by a miracle.

One of the most frightening accidents happened after a May fall of snow which caught everyone by surprise. There was a foot of it everywhere. The morning sun melted it and caused an avalanche on the roofs. A good four feet of it blocked the guttering and the water could not get away. The first intimation we had of this was a steady drip through the ceilings of three of the five classrooms. We had to position bowls in strategic places to catch the drops. The caretaker went onto the roof and reported that all the night's fall on the roof was solid in the guttering and even May sunshine would be some time in completing the melting job. The bowls filled with alarming quickness and we knew that they would overflow during the night. Indeed the caretaker was in school all evening and back early in the morning mopping up a lake.

Our headmistress reported the state of things to the Education Office and a man was sent out to inspect the plaster ceilings. His verdict was that they were safe and we were told to carry on teaching away from the deluge. I had a student in my class at the time. I was in the staff room when the crash came. The ceiling fell above my reading corner when the children were using it.

The noise echoed through the building; classroom doors shot open and teachers ran out. Children started to scream, more plaster fell and the mess was incredible. Books were ruined, children's hair was full of plaster and poor Susan had wet her knickers and was in great distress. No one was really hurt but close on this escapade came the shocking news of a similar incident at a school in the town which resulted in the death of one child. We were trembling for days.

I was getting an overdose of children but it did not seem to do me any harm. A colleague was horrified that I could put up with them out of school. 'Don't you weary of them?' she said and gave me a look of disbelief when I said, 'No.' Every spare minute I was taking children along the Woodcraft Trail and to camp every available opportunity.

At some point I must have thought seriously in terms of a Headship. Possibly I thought about it as early as the end of my first teaching year for I was involved then and I never stopped being part of the administration. I knew I was too young and I knew I didn't want an infant school appointment. Somehow I must get more experience and more qualifications.

I had no wish to leave my present post. A two-year course, leading to a Diploma in Primary Education, was advertised at Leeds University, and the qualification for application was a minimum of five years' teaching. Early in 1955 I went to see my College Principal. Gone were the student days of being Miss Brown. I was Jean and invited to tea. For a brief half hour I was reduced to size and shut in her sitting room with a sheet of paper and instructions to write out my reasons for wanting to take the Diploma Course. Perhaps if I'd known what it entailed I'd have decided that I couldn't possibly find enough time and wasn't capable of doing the work. I knew nothing, so I blindly committed myself for the next two years and began really to burn the candle at both ends.

Apart from the farm and the Guides, the one thing that bound us all together most was Harry's disablement. It was something he could accept best if we accepted it and made it an instrument of love and family commitment. This dependent member of the family bound us together, gave us understanding, taught us unselfishness and reduced us to size. Whenever we felt superior because of some achievement, somehow or other Harry's fortitude, his lack of jealousy and his dependence put us in our place. I have heard people say a handicapped child can cause friction between parents and put too much strain on relationships. Not so with our family. Not one of us would ever walk out on Harry. No man would have stood a marriage chance with either Margaret or me if he had not accepted that we had a responsibility we would never hand over to someone else. But neither of us believe that our lives should centre round Harry alone. There is room for everything you want to put into life. It is sad that in this world some people have to go through life physically, mentally or socially crippled and we would die to give Harry normality but handicapped people have a place in society and, hard as this may seem, the world would be a poorer place without them.

Grandmother being with us took away the job of doing her chores. We were all glad to have her for it is much easier to look after someone in one's own home than to care for them in theirs. No one grumbled about the over-crowding. Something important was being put right.

I decided to take a Whitsun camp and on Easter Monday one of my Patrol Leaders and I went up to Gouthwaite looking for a campsite. It was a lovely day. No place on earth is more beautiful than the Yorkshire Dales in springtime. They are so clean and the villages nestle against the hillsides. We walked along the road which skirts the reservoir looking for somewhere right for us. I find it easy to talk to farmers and before the afternoon was far gone we had found a place with a sheltering belt of fir trees and a fast-flowing stream for drinking water. We followed it for half a mile but found no dead sheep polluting it.

Whitsuntide brought a heat wave that year. We'd christened it 'The Jungle Camp' and we all had names from Rudyard Kipling's *The Jungle Book*. I was the Elephant, Hathi, the old one. I carved an elephant out of balsa wood and suspended it on a green ribbon and embroidered a jungle motif. We presented it to the best camper and thus began a tradition which lasted thirty years. We called a Water Truce and it did not let us down until half an hour before we left a week later. We were very sunburnt and swollen. To bang in tent pegs was agony for my arms wobbled. We painted ourselves with calamine and there wasn't a grumble. Gone were all the memories of the wet camp at Rylstone. 'This is the life!' sang Eleanor, the child who had once rocked our head-teacher's coffin. Eleanor was one of my most rewarding children. During that camp she caught a baby rabbit just by sitting outside a burrow and waiting. I sincerely hope it did not die of shock.

There was the annual rush to take in the hay but now Margaret had left school there were two workers all day and three at night. Margaret never got a wage any more than Father had done before he married. Hay-time began to be a different job with the switch to baled hay. Much easier one would think. Not at all! Baled hay is a liability in the field. There is no way it can be made safe or left safe. It must lie in readiness in long windrows, fluffed up and vulnerable to any dark, rain-bringing cloud. If the cloud beats the baler the hay is spoilt. So haymaking must be fast and furious and bales are so compressed that they are heavy and the twine is tight and mutilates hands. Baled hay on a Pennine hill makes haymaking harder by the half.

Farming goes on and on. The farmer was right when his wife asked, ''Ev yer dun?' and he answered, 'Aye lass, Ah've nivver dun. Ah just gi' ower.' After the hay was in, Margaret and I 'gave over' and went north to Tiree and Barra. We took Janet because she was so much fun. We had been only an hour on the island of Tiree when we received an invitation to go to the evening wedding of Margaret MacKinnon and Duncan MacInnes. An island wedding is an experience not to be missed. There was a banquet fit for royalty. After the speeches we joined the volunteers and helped with the washing up. Dancing went on until the young couple left by the early morning boat. The céilidh went on and on, dancing, singing, dancing. The Gaelic, the pipes, the friends we knew and the new ones we made were more intoxicating to us than the bottled variety. But even we can only go on so long. The haymaking, the end of school year and the long cheap journey up by bus and slow boat finally won.

We sailed to Barra and the Minch was kind and the island of *Whisky Galore* captured our imagination. We stayed at Northbay post office, the House of the Choddie, regrettably after his recent death but his reputation as a bard and storyteller will live for a long time. So will the magic of that island. Like daffodils, Barra will 'flash upon that inward eye'. There is a lesson to be learned at Northbay, for the peace which exists on the Traigh Mhòr, that two-mile cockle strand, dazzling when bare, lagoon-like at high tide, is a fragile one. A narrow, deceiving belt of sand dunes hides the restless Atlantic. I remember the evening we first found Traigh Vais. The din of the huge breakers coming in from America can be heard from the Cockle Strand. We stood looking out over water so still the clouds were mirrored, and we could not place the direction from whence came that Atlantic pounding. We began to run the quarter of a mile across the dunes and suddenly the peace was gone, wind disturbed the marran grass and my two teenagers were shouting and pointing. The sea was white as far as the eye could see. So narrow is the dividing line between right and wrong, between calm and unrest, between harmony and discord. That is one lesson but the metaphor is ambiguous. The parable can be read another way. We all three stood there in noisy appreciation of movement and activity and strength and knew that of the two ways of life we would always choose the hard and reject the easy and we chose Traigh Vais in preference to the Traigh Mhòr.

There was, unexpectedly, a showing of the film *Whisky Galore* in the village hall at Castlebay. We sat on improvised seating in a packed and noisy hall with the people who had formed the crowd scenes. Undoubtedly we would return to Barra.

*   *   *   *   *

I began my two years at Leeds University one alarming Saturday morning when I found that, of the twenty teachers on the course, I was the only woman. It was not a pleasant discovery. I was easily the youngest. My male contemporaries had all done National Service and any man completing the five teaching years must necessarily be older. So they were all my senior, more intelligent and more widely read. On that first Saturday we were given half an hour to handle the heavy, typed and bound theses of our predecessors and a bibliography of the books we were to study in detail. Freud and Froebel, Gardener and Gesell, Piaget and Pestalozzi, Susan Isaacs, Stern and

Sturt, Jean-Jacques Rousseau and Margaret MacMillan. The man next to me leaned over and whispered, 'I don't even know how to spell "resignation".' We were taken to the library to choose two books for immediate study and told to prepare a seminar on them to deliver to the rest of the members of the course. They were shock tactics and I was shocked! I remember the day I'd cried because I'd won a scholarship and an academic career loomed ahead. Then I had had no say in the matter. This time I had filled in the application form myself and had no one else to blame.

So I read Hartley, Frank and Goldenstein's *Understanding Children's Play* all the way to Alnwick to greet my new goddaughter and have fun and games with two-and-a-half-year-old Paul. My visits to see Jean were very domesticated. We would hunt for material, either in the market or in the huge chest in which she kept fents and we would sew together all day. Whilst she made the mid-day meal I would take the children out for a walk with the pram or the pushchair and a wonderful relationship grew between us all.

Shortly after my return from Julie's christening, my grandmother was eighty-five and her health began to fail. For eighteen months she had rocked happily by the fire, only venturing out to see Freda next door. She occupied herself with small tasks Mother brought to her knee but she was no way the active woman my mother is at ninety-one. One day she began unravelling a mess of tangled wools. She was agitated; Mother noticed and enquired if something was wrong and she admitted she had a pain. Within days she was in bed, a weak old lady. The doctor came daily. The canny old Irish man had no patience with those who, although able, wanted their old folks in hospital and his approval of Mother's caring was almost affectionate. Mother tells the story of a man who was wheeling his father to the workhouse in a wheelbarrow and the old man muttered, 'Ah mind t' time, lad, when Ah pushed me Fahther t' t' wukhouse an' orl.'

His son turned round and pushed the old man home again. 'Well,' he declared, 'We're off 'oam. Ah'm noan 'avin' that 'appen t' me.'

The doctor little knew what had been so obviously missing for over twenty years but Grandmother did. Once, when Mother was lifting her towards the commode, the old lady's arms tightened round her in an affectionate grip and my mother knew she was trying to make amends. Once, just once, she turned to my father with a grateful, loving look. Silly old woman. She had been so hard and blind and had missed so much.

We were helped in the final vigil by an aunt of my father's. When she arrived to see her sister-in-law our old lady had already slipped into a coma. Aunt Maria said she would stay the night and relieve us. The November evening was cold and dark. We were just clearing away the tea things and I was going to do some university work. Margaret and Father had gone out to milk the cows. Harry and Mother were going to do the washing up together. Suddenly Aunt Maria, alone with Grandmother, became aware that her breathing had stopped. The exact moment she could not say for it had been imperceptible. We gathered round her and the children next door were brought to see Great-grandmother whilst she lay there in a sleeping position. We had done all we could for her, willingly, and there was a feeling of content.

I am glad that there is, within our family, this tradition of care for the aged for when loss and parting come there is no hysterical mourning, no self-recriminations, no feeling of guilt. We have, as yet, known no hospital death. There is a lack of parental respect these days, a haste to put the elderly into care that offends me. The older members of our family have given us real pleasure. An old person needs a family, love and security, in the same way as a child does. It is the human metamorphosis. We are born, cared for, give birth, rear children and then care for our parents. Independence is nearly always selfish. Inter-dependence, needing and needed, leads to happiness. Of course people say that it is different for us, that we can look after our parents and brother and the aunts because we are unmarried and have no children. I have had hundreds of children, Harry has been to care for now for nearly sixty years. They are unconvinced so I tell them about my mother and father whose son never became independent, who welcomed Grandmother, giving her a corner of their bedroom for eighteen months. But they still do not understand and the old people's homes are overcrowded.

The fact that the two farms were inherited by the two sons meant no change in circumstances. My uncle seemed happy with his job and his new wife and home. Like Toad he loved riding around in his car, was generous with lifts and pleased to pick up Mother and Harry from the aunts on a Saturday night and bring them home. He seemed content to let his brother work the farm. He didn't want to sell but he didn't want to farm. Nor did his daughter or her husband.

There was no friction. If Uncle had any worries at all we were unaware. We had the burden of an increasing overdraft. Inflation was an enemy. The land was greedy and crying out for lime and the plough and re-seeding. Everything we had seemed old: tools, cattle, buildings, materials. They were difficult days and Margaret remembers them most because I was involved with my Guide Company and struggling to keep my head above water at the university.

On a sunny Easter Monday the following year Auntie Mary and I found a camp-site at South Stainley, near Ripon and I planned my third Guide Camp for the coming Whitsuntide. By that time the bluebells were out in profusion and the smell of them was like a dusting of talcum over everything. At night we heard the fox in the woodland. We camped as a tribal gathering of Sioux and Cherokee and Blackfeet and ceremoniously 'smoked' a peace pipe. My first camps were well and truly influenced by *Scouting for Boys* and woodcraft, fantasy and totem poles. Janet came as my QM.

Our only grandparent now left was Cabby Tom. We reverently idolised him. He could have got away with anything. We hadn't planned a summer holiday, Margaret and I, for we were struggling to make ends come somewhere near meeting. Farming eats money. A farmer, on being asked what he would do if he won a quarter of a million on the pools, is reported to have said, 'Ay lad, Ah'd just go on farming till it were orl used up.' With a dead animal can go half the year's profit but farmers send for the vet and incur more expense when they know there's little hope. Margaret fights to the last gasp and only when she fails does she think of the hole in her pocket. There is always financial risk when money is in livestock.

So we planned no holiday. I had a lot of university commitments and work to do on my thesis. I stopped having cheese on toast at Betty's Café or beans and chips in the refectory on the campus and frequented the station buffet for coffee and ate sandwiches on the train. I bought a second-hand typewriter and my cousin Freda helped me by typing sheets and sheets of records and observations. I learned an adequate two-finger skill which has improved but little. As the term drew to a close I knew I was desperately in need of a holiday. We could ill afford it but there is a limit as to how far one can go without a refuel. Margaret needed a break too for her job was seven days a week. It was as urgent as always to get in the hay and, what with the end of term and the tiredness left by travelling to Leeds twice a week and all the study it entailed, I was pretty exhausted. The year had been enjoyable. I'd loved the quiet train journey and the feeling of isolation a city can give to a country girl. To know no one and to be unknown, to receive no smiles, no greetings, can sometimes be the necessary drug. It certainly kept me going. The powers that be realised the pressure imposed by the part-time Diploma Course and ours was the last. The following year students were seconded from school for a year and the part-time course was scrapped. What a miracle for me I applied when I did. Never in a month of Sundays would I have applied for a full-time course.

By the end of haytime we were jiggered and we decided we must afford a holiday or we'd be ill and have to afford a wage for some temporary help. I phoned the delightful, inexpensive hotel in Letterfrack, with little hope that our host would have two vacancies but we are lucky people. We had only a few days in which to secure sailing tickets. We couldn't afford sleeping berths, said 'Goodbye' to dignity and slept with the other common folk on the littered floor of the boat lounge.

It was to be our last stay in an hotel. The year was 1956, the weather utterly beautiful and we were idyllically contented. We wandered happily along the fuchsia-lined roads, chatting with Romanies, inhaling peat smoke and befriending donkeys. We walked long miles, leaving after breakfast and wandering along the fjord-like inlets of the western coast of Connemara, glad to be alone, tramping round Little Killary and Killary Harbour with its dark, deep waters and not a soul in sight.

We have always meant to go back to Ireland but an opportunity has not yet come. We loved the deserted shore where there were only the two of us swimming in the clean sea. We loved the lush undergrowth of the grounds of Kylemore Abbey and we liked being with the people outside their homes or at the races on Lettergesh beach. That was a great day. One jockey fell off and the horse continued to run. Suddenly from out of the crowd came a substitute. Running alongside the riderless horse he mounted and finished the race. We were at home among the rocky outcrops and between the stone walls. We loved the peat bogs carpeted with flowers and found an affinity with the crofters' wives washing their clothes in the stream hurtling down Tully and we listened to one lady tell of her well-educated children. It is a beautiful country full of fine and gracious people whose ways are so different from those of the city dwellers of England that they should never have been expected to belong and to conform. It was a crime to ill-use and starve them into bitterness and frustration.

Grandfather was still alive on our return but failing fast. Within days he had taken to his bed. The aunts were tired out with loss of sleep so I offered to sit up and let them rest. I curled up in a chair beside the dear old man, thinking happy thoughts about our holiday and about Grandfather, dying peacefully at home amid his family, able and ready to meet his Maker, never having done anything 'reet wrong'. He had not given much from his pocket but he had allowed his womenfolk to offer a unique hospitality to others and had stood back and watched them visit the sick, fetch and carry for other people without grumbling. He had been a home bird, neither seeking nor needing the company of other men or the escape of alcohol. When he died, two days later, we could only think of good things, only proud thoughts of a truly fine gentleman.

One of the most tying jobs in the world is milking cows. Father, rapidly approaching sixty, had spent nearly all his life, twice a day, seven days a week, doing just that. Millions of gallons of milk, first by hand, more recently by machine, on and on and on. Nights out, weekends off, a change of routine were all unknown.

We began to feel the need to be in the farmhouse. Even the short field distance away was too great, but it was too small for us. A visiting Ministry of Agriculture official asked Father why he didn't live in the farmhouse at The Currer and he was told that the sixteenth-century dwelling was a write-off. He dropped a big hint that we might get a grant to build a new house and buildings at the Moor Gate. I sat for hours drawing ground plans of an ideal home and steadings. In our enthusiasm we even named it. In our imagination we furnished and decorated it and in reality we sent an application to the Ministry for a grant. A committee of men came to see Father and they all went to The Currer. They walked over the field where the new building would be and they looked down the hillside and saw the old house, a near ruin, nestling against the boundary wall. Of course they wanted to see it so Father took them down the walled cart track and into the overgrown yard with its disused pigsties and its huge, drystone barn. They wanted to see inside the house, investigate its lack of sanitation and electricity. The present tenant was at home so the committee filed inside and their verdict was that the tenants must be given notice and the house condemned. Structurally it was sound but a great deal of money would have to be spent. However, unsuitable as the house was, the fact remained. There was already a farmhouse at The Currer and therefore we were ineligible for a grant.

Father came home depressed and disappointed. Now we certainly had problems. After their report had gone to the council the farmhouse would be condemned and the tenants given notice. It rendered the barn an unsafe place to keep hay or animals, for empty houses invite vandals and squatters. In no time it was a ruin.

Life had to go on. The autumn term found me seconded from school attending the university full-time. My thesis took up long hours into the morning which suited me not at all. I am as bright as a cricket at 5.30 a.m. and good for nothing long before midnight but it was often 2 a.m. before I went to bed. Jill, now warranted as lieutenant, took most of the Guide meetings. In my guilt it seemed necessary to make it up in some way. I could think of no way that there would be time for a Whitsuntide camp. Acknowledging this, Margaret and I put our heads together and wrote to John Lachie and Effie MacInnes on Tiree, that flat, sandy island we were beginning to love so much.

After Christmas the full-time term was over and I was back behind the desk and taking the Thursday evening Guide Meeting. One early January evening I had a secret up my sleeve. As the meeting drew to a close I gathered two dozen girls round the open fire, in our poky little headquarters, to end the day singing campfire songs. I had been playing for an audience all night, pulling out of the bag, tired as I was, the choicest tit-bits. We had laughed a lot and I'd got them in the right mood for my surprise.

'I've had an idea,' I whispered and waited for interest to kindle. 'It's a good one.' Again I paused, an artist in the skill of exciting children.

'War is i'?' they chorused.

'Well ... would you like to camp on an island?' I said and Enid Blyton could not have done it better.

'Yeh, yeh,' they shouted.

'Right out at sea? A long way away?'

'Mmmmm ...'

'We'd have to go on a boat. Sleep on it. In a cabin berth.'

'Ooooooh ...'

'We'd camp on the shore. A lovely beach. No one but us.' The air was electric. To a man they were with me.

So the idea became reality and plans and bookings were made. After the submission of my thesis there was only an interview and I'd be a free agent once more. The two long, hard years would be over and I could do again the real things I wanted to do.

Somewhere about this time we had opted to have a TT test on the herd. The time was coming when these tests would be compulsory and it was wise to anticipate this voluntarily. There was, at that time, plenty of tuberculosis in cattle and eradication was slow. Cows reacted to the test if they had the disease and also if they had come in contact with it. The autumn test revealed a reactor or two but the spring test knocked us for six. So many reacted that it would virtually mean starting again. As the vet delivered the verdict Father knew he would have to sell cattle at a grave financial loss. Mother cried. She could take no more. Our vet, a Tiree man, said, 'Don't cry, Mrs Brown. It is happening everywhere. That's why compulsory testing is so slow.'

Somehow we had got to start again. The dairy herd would have to be sold. After a lifetime of milking twice a day Father was ready to give up but milk was daily income and anything else would take time before it brought return. Fortunately there was my wage. Father decided to use the pennies which the doomed milking herd would bring to buy Aberdeen Angus and Hereford calves and rear for beef. It was a two-year programme and the months ahead looked bleak financially. But it was something new to plan and there was a relief in knowing that the daily chore of milking was coming to an end. Father, at sixty, had done his share.

It was a sad time for the herd was not unhealthy. Given the same test we would all have reacted too. Contact with a disease often brings natural immunity. People relied on this in those days when cows and countesses alike could not be inoculated against nearly everything as they can today.

We began selling animals for £25–£40 and the monthly milk cheque dwindled and finally stopped. It was fortunate that I was so exhausted with the DPE course that I needed Margaret's help preparing for our Hebridean camp. It was the stimulant she needed when everything else seemed to be going wrong. Together we scrounged the ex-army stores for essential equipment light enough to send in advance 400 miles to a relatively remote island. We began to use my grandmother's house as a second headquarters and did all our serious packing in the farmhouse kitchen. The newness of the job excited us and numbed a little of the sadness and despair of diminishing the herd. We didn't know what we were going to do about that so we threw ourselves into the activity of preparing for adventure and decided we'd sort everything out when we returned.

For a surprisingly small sum of money we were away for a fortnight. In those days you could buy a meal in the McColl's cafeteria for half-a-crown and a berth for 7s. 6d. Children's meals on board were half price and well within our pocket. Twenty-five years later we couldn't afford any of these luxuries.

In 1957 a fortnight on the white beach of a small island in the sun and wind was the height of adventure for any girl. None had been abroad, few had been on a train, none so far away from home. Sleeping berths were a novel experience, Gaelic a foreign language, camping the ultimate in survival technique and it is a measure of our success that, twenty-five years later, the girls enjoyed the annual camp no less than the pioneers of 1957. They were much more experienced and travelled, but the magic, the flame that was kindled during the first camp never dimmed and it is still burning in hundreds of grown women.

This is not a saga of our camping days in the Hebrides. It is sufficient to say that the barefoot hours on beach and machair, the quiet hours round the fire of a crofter's kitchen, the joy of sea and air and friendship, the calm of nights under the starlit canopy of heaven after an hour of singing round the fire are a part of us which can never be separated from the rest of our makeup. We are what we are because of what we began on that first, very memorable experience. It, and the years that followed, influenced us so much that we say very reverently, 'Thank God for the Hebrides.'

We returned from that wonderful fortnight believing that, whatever happened in the long struggle ahead of us to salvage what we could, build a new herd and begin a new venture, we'd be able to survive. We have never looked at society and said 'them and us'. We have never differentiated between high and low, rich and poor, black and white, good and bad, boss and employee, head and assistant, but we outrageously shuffle people into two categories. There are quite distinctly those who can cope and those who cannot and those who can, do so usually because they have been to camp or had some similar experience.

We returned with our batteries recharged after long, God-given days at Salum. The Guides had left in tears. The glamour and romance of the island had affected them all. They had danced to the pipes, bathed with seals, littered the shore with a thousand bare footprints and made a multitude of friends. An era of island camping had begun which was to last a quarter of a century. But the joy in our hearts could not obliterate the knowledge that the future of the farm hung over a precipice. We dug in our heels, lowered our heads into the wind of autumn as determined as ever to 'see the cuckoo'.

Part Two

When I first came to this land
I was not a wealthy man,
But I built myself a shack.
I did what I could.
Call my shack
'Break my back'
But the land was sweet and good
I did what I could.

Chapter Five

Big decisions are usually taken with tea or morning coffee. This one was made one Friday tea-time in the middle of October. I know it was Friday because the next day was Saturday and I ought to have been able to go with everyone to The Currer but instead I was sick. Imagine that! It seems incredible that I should be sick on the day that we meant to go to the farmhouse, condemned and empty now for over a year.

We were at a crossroads and we'd got to decide at once which way to go. We have never been ones to delay decisions. Time, whatever our Hebridean friends may think, is not in plentiful supply. In our modern semi, a field away from the home farm, a dairy herd was barely possible. Living three-quarters of a mile away from a beef herd was well nigh impossible. Margaret and Father were away all day and Mother alone with Harry.

On that Friday, in late October, Father came in from a lone visit to The Currer steadings and the empty ruined house. On an impulse he had made a solitary tour. Since the condemnation order it had deteriorated fast. Every window had been broken, the first, no doubt, by troublesome children. Then, the wind having found a way in and no way out, the rest had followed suit. Father had wandered around inside the building, trampling on fallen plaster from the walls, splintered wood from the rotten, sagging window frames and a mass of broken glass. He had forced open doors whose rusted hinges protested at being disturbed and he had seen a vision of order and comfort. The walls were sound behind the crumbling cow hair plaster and the roof wouldn't fall in just yet. He became deep in thought. His handicapped son was not in a wheelchair. His two daughters were strong and game for anything and he was only sixty. But he had a wife who could never visualise potential, whose reaction to all our mad schemes was, 'It's ridic'lous!' The hardest task would be to convince her.

But Father underestimated her frustration. She had had more than she could take. Her husband had worked all hours all her married life. There had never been any money. Nothing had ever been ours. Now, after thirty years the stock was ours and Father his own master, and what had happened? The chickens had died, the herd had reacted. There was a jinx on the home farm and she was 'at the band end'.

'Sal,' said Father, that memorable Friday morning, 'We've no money. There's nowt for it. We'll 'ev t' go t' me muther's or t' Currer.'

'Then we'll go t' Currer,' my mother said. 'I don't want to go t' yer muther's!' Life is full of miracles and that one was a big one.

So when I came home from school there was a proposition on the tea table and we talked and talked excitedly and that night I was sick. I was so groggy all weekend that they decided to wait until Monday and go to The Currer without me, their number one ally!

They were a little older and a little wiser when we gathered round the tea table on Monday night. They had been shocked at the state of the farmhouse and its adjacent dry stone barn and the unhealthy, old-fashioned pig sties, but although they were rather pale and breathing a little irregularly they were unmoved. They were ready to stick to their willingness to give it a go.

After the Guide meeting on Thursday I was ready to drop. One more day to half term and a brief few days in Alnwick with Jean. I could hardly wait but that day held two major interviews. The first was for the headship of an infant school in the town. What did I want with a town infant school? Nothing at all, but even so I had applied because I had been advised to do so by the local County Council Inspector (CCI). He had been insistent that I must get my foot on the ladder. The post had been offered to a head teacher whose job was to be lost in a reorganisation programme. She had turned it down so its vacancy was advertised and the CCI thought I should apply. I went to look at the school and it didn't appeal to me but I was young and foolish and I allowed myself to be persuaded because I was a little bit flattered by the inspector's interest.

Dutifully I appeared at the Education Office at the appropriate time and found the headmistress, who had turned down the post initially, also short-listed. She had changed her mind that morning and the forthcoming interview was now only a formality. I breathed a sigh of relief and hurried to the bus for home.

I did not get off at the usual place for I had arranged that Mother, Harry and Margaret would be at The Currer and that I would go straight there from the Education Office. So I stayed on the bus until it reached the end of the field track and alighted, in my best clothes, for my interview with The Currer.

Like a ship appearing over the horizon, the roof is the first glimpse of the grey stone barn. It was as if I'd never seen the house before that cold, grey

Friday in October 1957. It seemed very short of windows. Few gazed from the north face. I'd never looked through them or even touched the grey stone of the walls. Standing on the boundary it might just as well have belonged to George's farm on the other side of Currer Lane.

Mother, Harry and Margaret were waiting for me and we went into the neglected yard, riddled with potholes and overgrown with grass and nettles. Rain during the day had filled the holes and grey skies and a wuthering wind coming straight from 't' 'Oworth 'ole' added to the eerieness of the place. Two pigsties on the eastern wall of the yard were empty and ugly in their outdatedness. The yawning laithe porch doors, rotting and paint-flaked, gave us a glimpse into the emptiness. We saw its drystone walls, incredibly thick, its three huge principals bearing the gnarled purlins and the slates of Yorkshire stone. We saw the greasy, old cow stalls and the loft with its worm-eaten floor joists supporting a flagged floor. The only door to the house was adjacent to the laithe porch so that one step out, on a wild winter's night, and the farmer could be in the barn tending his cattle, or a farrowing sow in that stalled room.

We opened the heavy house door with an enormous key but we could have climbed in at any one of the gaping windows. The hinges creaked ominously as we entered the lean-to porch, which must have been the washing kitchen for a cracked stone sink stood against the south wall, full of glass from the small window above it. The walls were crusted with tens of layers of whitewash and the floor littered with plaster, rotten bits of wood and blown-in debris from the yard. There were old tins, bottles and cans and two packets of rat poison which did not escape Mother's eye. The roof was flagged with huge slabs of Yorkshire stone and from the rafters hung curtains of dusty cobwebs.

A filthy door separated this entrance from the living kitchen. The area round the handle was deep in black grease and great nails were hammered into the wood where no doubt heavy coats had hung for centuries. Every bit of glass had gone from the four mullioned windows and fragments of it littered the floor. The window frames exposed to rain and drying sun had rotted and splintered and the plaster on the mullions had fallen, leaving the clean stone bare. The floor was of uneven stone flags and the late tenants must have padded the hollows with sawdust. It still filled the crevices, providing haunts for a multitude of beetles and silver fish.

The Yorkist Range was rusted beyond repair and the sagging doors of the kitchen cupboard swung in the wind which found such easy entry everywhere. The beams were bare and rough, bending where they had succumbed to the wind which had savaged them four centuries ago. They were studded with nails from which hams must have hung, a long time ago when the people who lived in it also farmed the land. Four doors led from the room, one to the domed, crypt-like cellar with its gaping square hole which was a well. Recently residents had carried drinking water from the spring. Another door led up two stone steps to a curing kitchen with big stone slabs along the back wall and a chimney where the hams could be smoked. The slates of this lean-to were missing in many places. A fall of chimney bricks had brought down a lot of soot making a black mess on the floor.

The door to the right of the Yorkist Range led to the parlour. This room, sheltered from the prevailing wind and still waiting the ravages of winter and the snow which the east wind would hurl through the window, was still in good condition though the decor was not to my liking and a glance upwards to the blackened beams revealed a gaping hole and a preview of the bedroom. There is a compulsion on entering the parlour to cross to the mullions and worship the view. The valley spreads out beyond the tree line of Jimmy's Wood, climbing the Pennine ridge to the wastes of Ilkley Moor. Hamlets nestle on the rising slopes and the pattern of walled fields and patches of woodland is pleasing however grey and bleak the day. The floor was evenly and cleanly flagged for the shattered panes had fallen outwards and lost themselves in the carpet of fallen leaves from the sycamore tree standing sentinel not four feet from the gable end. A Victorian fireplace in a narrow chimney breast was ugly and too small to heat the spacious room adequately. The walls had been decorated with hideous alabaster swirls and distempered sickeningly in violet but the aspect of the room was pleasing and it was absolutely free of damp.

The fourth door led up stone steps to the two large bedrooms, one over the kitchen with a matching mullion and a bigger one at the end of the passage, above the parlour and with the same window and view. The floorboards had given way but its more sheltered position had obviously been chosen by a recent tramp. It showed unmistakable signs of occupation. There was a pile of dirty rags in the corner, empty food cans in the fireplace and human excreta on the floor.

I began to laugh. Were we crazy even fleetingly to think this was the place for us? No water, no sanitation. The privy outside was empty; there was not even a bucket to suggest its utility. No electricity, no road, no neighbour! Why didn't Mother just say, 'It's ridic'lous!' and begin to cry? How did Father at sixty years old, penniless, with a substantial overdraft, think we could do anything with this rapidly deteriorating property? Margaret and I were young and it was comprehensible that we would be willing to tackle it. Youth could be expected to have a vision insane enough to look forward to a life at The Currer but it was unbelievable that Mother and Father could welcome it too. Now, nearing the age they were then, I can understand.

'Come on,' Margaret said. 'I'll show you where Dad thinks we could have the kitchen and put the extra bedrooms and bathroom.'

We went up the sloping, cobbled entrance to the barn. The setts were necessary to give the horseshoes a grip when they towed the heavy hay wains into the barn. Within the doors, on either side of the cobbles, there was a flagged wheel path but we were interested in the dark passage and the room beyond where so many pigs had farrowed. Enormous beams supported a rotting loft and old, dried manure littered the floor. Rickety, greasy stalls and a fully paned window gave it a closed in, musty atmosphere. A door, virtually draught-proof, led out into the field. Rat droppings could be seen and the laughter was creasing me again. This a kitchen! The old man must have gone mad. Where had he found the courage to approach his wife and why had she said, 'Then we'll go t' Currer'?

If she had said, 'I'll never go t' Currer', wild horses would not have dragged an alternative answer from her, but the amazing reply had been positive and remained so even though Auntie Janie cried and Uncle Joe's wife said, 'No man would take me to a place like that!' Dear Mother! She worries about little things. She will get into a state of flummox about packing a case to go on holiday and not a hair turn grey over removing to The Currer.

Early next morning I set off for Alnwick. I attempted to paint a word picture of the sixteenth-century house and explain to Jean and Peter the reasons why we were going to leave a modern semi and live in a ruin. It all sounded very much like a tale of defeat and failure, so I wasn't offended that she didn't understand. So I said little and spent a glorious few days with three-year-old Paul and Julie, who was just taking her first steps.

The miracle of Mother's acceptance preceded the second miracle by only a few days. When approached my uncle agreed very amicably to divide the property legally. He seemed quite happy that my father should have the barren land of The Currer and the condemned farmhouse with its pathetic absence of buildings, road and amenities and he have the home farm, poor in acreage but not lacking in building potential and with a better house and cottage and buildings. We never expected the legalities to be so easy. Uncle just didn't want to farm. He didn't want to do anything with his inheritance but he didn't want to sell it either. His daughter with her husband and children went into the farmhouse and used the buildings extensively for the storing of stock and equipment for the business they were responsible for, and which was growing like a mushroom. My uncle was able to sell his next-door house and everyone seemed to have got what he wanted.

And now we had to start ridding The Currer of its condemnation order. Father organised it all. He was advised to forget extending the house into the muck-encrusted section with its rotten loft and filthy stalls. 'Divide the two bedrooms,' he was told. 'They'll make three small bedrooms and a bathroom.' But Father would have none of it. We were to learn that he never did little things. His ideas were basically good; he dug in his heels and did not listen when they argued. Where the pigs had farrowed had been part of the house and should be so again. That big buttress within the barn could only be a chimney of a previous living room. He showed them a lintel in the dividing wall backing up against the house. 'There'll 'ev bin a doorway there,' he said. 'We can teck it dahn. There'll be one upstairs an' orl.' He was right.

'It'll be big,' he was warned.

'It'll need t' be,' the prophet said.

For the time being we decided to seal off the curing house, because it was too dilapidated, and the cellar because Mother had premonitions about it.

She said there would be rats and she was sure we would fall down the well. We chose to let her have her way. There was no need, just then, for a cellar and Mother was doing very well and must have her way in some things.

One day in December I took a hammer and a stone chisel and went alone to The Currer. Perched precariously on an orange box I began, not very skilfully, to carve out a motto above the door separating front porch and living kitchen. I chipped away with determination for a long time. I wrote, '*Nisi Dominus Frustra*', without God all is in vain. So, I believe, it is.

The last day of the old year closed with torrential rain which turned to snow overnight and next morning it lay twelve inches deep and Persil white. Margaret and Father had shut some yearling heifers in The Currer barn and it was a daily job to go and feed and water them. I decided to accompany Margaret and we planned to spend the day making a start on the house. The first day of January 1958 seemed the right moment to begin in earnest. The surface of the snow lay unbroken all the way from the village except for bird and rabbit tracks and the lonely trail, with its brushing of top snow, left by a hunting fox. We had food with us and yard brushes and shovels intending, at least, to sweep out the snow and to clear the debris of broken glass and plaster littering the floor.

Snow lay deep in the parlour. The east wind is a snow-bringer and a good depth had been hurled through the gaping windows. We gathered up a pile of splintered, paint flaking wood and put a match to it in the fireplace. The reflection of the flames danced round the room in friendliness. Outside the east window, the sycamore stood almost white against the blue sky for the snow clouds had passed and a weak January sun flooded the yard and threw a patten of the mullions against the west wall of the kitchen.

We shovelled out the great drifts from below the empty windows and, with stiff yard brushes, began to sweep up the mess of shattered glass. The icy cleansing air filled the house, ridding it of any smell of human occupation. We blessed the open windows. They did for us what no amount of soap and water could.

With crowbar and sledgehammer we tore out the rotted window frames and doors and stoked up the fire until we could feel the heat. With broad scrapers we began hacking off the layers and layers of whitewash down to the smoothness of the cow hair plaster. Lime is clean and sweet smelling and as we scraped the walls smooth and bare there was a freshness in the fine white dust.

Neither Margaret nor I can sing very tunefully but on that first day of January we filled our ruin with song, experiencing a new-found freedom. The sun, shining on the snow and decorating the valley with icing sugar, quite literally turned us on. 'Oh, what a beautiful morning,' we sang, 'Oh, what a beautiful day.' Our repertoire of campfire songs carolled out into the morning followed by all the joyful hymns we knew. 'Glad that I live am I, that the sky is blue.'

We had brought a large tin of soup. Puncturing the lid, we set it among the ashes and then sat, drinking it in turns from the can. We sat toasting ourselves on the hearth imagining the new life beginning at The Currer and wondering how many ups and downs the road ahead would have. Looking through the mullions we visualised the many visitors who would come. They would appear round the corner of the stable and take us unawares because the road, which was then just an overgrown cart track, cannot be seen from the house. They would surprise us into action and one of us would greet them and the other try to bring order to whatever chaos reigned at the moment just like any normal family. We imagined ourselves standing at the door waving farewell and Mother inevitably calling, 'Come again.' It was optimistic imagery, for who would come to this out of the way spot with no road to it and no streetlights to guide the way?

For three months Margaret, Father and I worked steadily throughout the spare daylight hours of every day. The place was thoroughly gutted. Manure was taken out, loose plaster chiselled from the walls, cupboards ruthlessly torn out until nothing remained within. The debris was burned or stacked or thrown into the potholes in the yard. The pigsties were dismantled and the stones pitched and sledge hammered to form the hard core of the yard. We added to this foundation every time we broke up a sink or knocked out a doorway. We levered out hundreds of nails from beams and walls and one day we completely exposed the stone of the mullions, lifting off their coats of thick cow hair plaster. The pile of wood grew outside to provide fuel for the winter.

The fireplaces and the range were torn out but we continued to light fires on the floor below the chimney. There is a different smell about old wood when burning, which is not quite pleasant. The worm-eaten timbers smell of demolition. Nowadays when an old piece reappears on the pile and is added to the logs, the distinct smell of it takes my memory back over the years to the spring when we worked alone in our beloved ruin.

Our woodpile is friend and enemy. From it can be taken a quick source of heat. From the woodpile we can always find a suitable beam of the right dimensions, a gate post exactly the required size or a duck board to make a hasty partition. It seems to be self-propagating, never growing smaller and never failing to produce the right-sized piece. It is no small miracle to find a beam which does not need to be sawn. I do not choose to labour through a 6 inch by 8 inch piece of oak and am very grateful to be so often spared.

The woodpile is also enemy for the piece we need is always underneath and, even more exasperating, the whole pile is always in the wrong place. We find it sitting just where we plan to build a new shed, or in the shed we have suddenly decided to use for an urgent purpose. To put it simply, the woodpile is always in the way and is laboriously moved several times a year. We have often imagined the effect a quickened up filmstrip of our lives would have on a viewer with a sense of humour. The record of constant activity would be punctuated regularly with a complete removal of the woodpile to another site. We would appear like ants removing their precious eggs after a disturbance of their stone. 'Oh no,' the amused audience would laugh, 'they're not moving the woodpile again!'

We were too busy to calculate whether we could afford it, too obsessed with an idea to worry about the work it would entail or the isolation it would bring. We had never had a car so what real use was a road? Sanitation we would have to have and running water, in order to lift the condemnation order, but electricity we could wait for. We had no television and we had washed without a washing machine and used a flat iron before.

For a short time we kept a change of clothes at The Currer so that we made a more dignified return through the village at night. We often scrubbed up in the stream. Eventually we were too tired to maintain decorum and dragged our weary feet homeward, mucky beyond belief. Each morning I went to school with roughened hands that no amount of Vim or Fairy Soap would whiten, no hand cream soften. My nails became broken and scratched and my children quite frequently found a flake of whitewash trapped in my hair.

The professional work on the house began in April and was completed at the beginning of June. Most of the work was done by an employee of Freda's husband. New windows had to be individually made and thirty-three panes of glass were needed. Immediately the whole aspect of the house changed. It came alive as a drawn face does when the pupils of the eyes are painted. For twelve months fresh air had flowed through the ruin. Now the windows were left open so that the spring fragrance could enter, too. New floorboards were laid in the east bedroom above the parlour and above the room which would now be wash kitchen but had previously housed cattle and farrowing pigs. A brick wall was built to lessen the area of this room from over-large to very spacious, leaving a silly room behind which could only be entered by the window. For many years it housed our coke. It became known as the Silly Room when we opened it up as a storeroom many years later. The beams were left exposed and the loft above was partitioned with stoothing and plasterboards to make two more bedrooms and a bathroom.

The house was now a sixty-foot long row of rooms and the upstairs corridor measured eighteen yards for carpet we could not possibly afford. Mother was to carpet the whole length, the staircase and the living kitchen with handmade, six-foot pieces of tabbed rug from thousands of half-inch strips of old coats and skirts looped into hessian with a rug hook.

A builder was employed to break through the enormously thick walls and put in the extra windows. He and his mate dug the septic tank which was to serve our purpose for twenty-five years. The builder found the door lintels Father had insisted would be there, and took out the stones which blocked both the downstairs and the upstairs doorways. The result was a difference in floor levels needing four steps to the kitchen and two to the bedrooms.

The plumber was now able to put in the utility bathroom suite and the double sink unit Father had bought for fifteen shillings. He and Harry had gone to the sale and Harry had been adamant that Father should bid for a particular lot. Unable to ask what it was, in the middle of an auction room,

Father had bid and secured an unknown lot, for the princely sum of fifteen shillings. He found Harry's insistent advice had been worth taking for he now owned two porcelain sinks of enormous dimensions set in a teak framework which would look very much at home in our sixteenth-century farmhouse.

A neighbouring farmer hired a mole digger and laid a polythene pipe from the water main a quarter of a mile away. There was suddenly a water supply and we could have had a bath if we'd settled for cold water. New doors were hung, two with eight panes of glass which brought brightness into the house. Finally the plasterer came; he renewed the old and plastered the new and everything looked good. This craftsman, Les Smith, was to become a friend who eventually found us timber for sheds. The 170 acres had a potential for well over a hundred cattle but there was nowhere to house them. The barn, though enormous, would not store all the hay we would need to harvest and the straw we would have to buy.

Of course we'd spent too much money. I always find it difficult to believe that, after a succession of lucky second-hand finds, our own free labour, our skimping and saving, our lack of personal basic needs, let alone luxuries, we have always spent one pound and sixpence against Mr Micawber's recommended nineteen and sixpence.

Margaret joined the Guide company as lieutenant after the Hebridean camp and this opened more possibilities. Frequently we began to hold the meetings at The Currer. The girls were incredulous when they first saw the shell of a building we proposed to live in and watched its rebirth with interest. After firelighting, tracking, or bridge building, they would gather round the parlour fireplace, thirty youngsters seated on the stone flags, singing camp-fire songs whilst they waited for their billy of cocoa to boil on the wood fire in the hearth. It was here, after an exciting evening's treasure hunt or wide game, that we would happily plan for summer. For all there was to be a Whitsuntide camp at High Wray on Windermere, and for the few, there was to be a Hebridean Journey, a trek with Cloughie's trike carts to Tiree, Barra, the Uists, Eigg, Rhum and Skye. What ambitious plans for us to make at this time of work overload. We always dawdled, drinking cocoa and talking ten to the dozen, and had to run like mad to the end of the field for the Guides to catch their bus. We were as fit as fiddles and believed we could do anything. One can't but it's not a bad idea to think so.

We learned the minimum time it took to dash through the fields. It was useful information for the future. Later we learned how to hide wellingtons in the wall to await our return, and how to wash muddy shoes in puddles and use long grass similarly to clean dirty hands and faces.

Somewhere around this time, our first Hereford heifers calved. One, named Paddy, nearly died. Father was a long time missing and when he returned he reported a dead calf. We decided to milk Paddy for the house and her milk was beautiful. She supplied our needs for the first year at The Currer.

Our 1926 semi proved difficult to sell for we entered the market when mortgages were hard to get and many would-be buyers were thwarted. Had we not had every minute occupied we would have been worried. So often, since, we have taken the one vital step from which there is no retraction. A phone call, a short answer, 'Yes,' a single signature on a form and the die is cast. Until the house satisfied building regulations, we could not live in it. Therefore we had no option but to go on spending the bank manager's money. He came to look at the project he was financing and did not seem unduly worried. He asked Margaret what she was going to miss most and she replied, 'My radio.' We were quite resigned to the absence of electricity but Margaret was a teenager. The manager told Mother to call in at the bank and ask for him. When Mother did, she found a battery powered wireless waiting for her. She is the only member of the family who has ever asked for the manager without the embarrassment all small business people feel when they make their annual call to report and re-negotiate their overdrafts.

For weeks we had no potential buyers for our house. One Saturday before Whitsuntide, Mother and Harry were down at the aunts' house to tea and Margaret and Father were at The Currer so I washed the camp kitchenware and arranged it all over the living room to dry thoroughly. There is a lot of equipment for thirty campers: enamelware, plastic bowls, billies and dixies galore. I decorated the table, chairs and hearthrug and then locked the house and went to The Currer to do my stint. When Mother and Harry returned there was a car parked outside the garden gate and interested people wanting to look round. 'Do come in,' Mother begged, anxious to make a sale. Returning late at night I entered a hornet's nest, for Mother was angry.

We camped for a week on the shores of Lake Windermere and left all our cares behind. We travelled by train and then by removal van and we alighted to see thunderclouds gathering fast. We pitched the dining tent in a hurry and threw personal gear inside. Thirty of us climbed on the pile and listened to the thunder and the deluge. 'Keep away from the tent poles,' I shouted. 'Sing and you won't hear the din.' So we sang lustily until it was all over. In over thirty years we never had a worse storm in camp. Free at last, we crawled out barefoot to pitch on the wet grass. My children never wore long trousers. Bare legs are easier to dry.

We had a wonderful, hilarious week perched on the hillside overlooking the lake. The water was constantly disturbed by speedboats and the air noisy with their engines but the crowds were all on the other side. A wood separated us even from the farm. We were more isolated from other people than we had been on Tiree. We liked it well enough but there was a burning desire in everyone to get back to the Islands.

We returned home to find the professional work nearly completed. The fireplaces were in but not the Aga. The plasterer was just finishing his contribution. It was a fine June evening, the nights were light and our working day getting longer. Little had been done in the reclaimed kitchen apart from the building of the reducing wall and the plumbing in of the sinks. Every other job was ours. What prompted Margaret and me to start chipping away at the wall in front of the buttress we had named a chimney escapes me, but before we knew what was happening we were making a mess in the kitchen and exposing an inglenook fireplace which had probably not seen daylight for over a century. As the beautiful arch began to appear so did our excitement grow until we were scratching at the soot-blackened stones with bare hands and hurling them into a haphazard pile. The rubble came away easily. As it did we found a perfectly preserved beehive oven. The cow plaster which had sealed the entire wall had cleaned the stone so that when we broke it away the huge, hewn pieces of the arch were clean. We had found treasure indeed. At last we were able to stand completely within the fireplace and look up an enormously wide chimney.

There was a disturbance behind us. Mother had walked over the fields from her clean semi to see how near things were to completion. When she saw the huge fireplace, the sooty pile of stones on the kitchen floor and her very mucky daughters, she just sat down and cried. We had no right at all, she said, to make more work and more mess and put a great big hole in her kitchen. The plasterer told her that we had added incalculable value to our house but that did not interest her. It matters not what something is worth if you are not going to sell it and she knew already that her daughters were in love with The Currer and there would never be a divorce. She was not to be cajoled into any admission that we had done right. Our behaviour was 'ridic'lous' and there was no way that she would approve. A quarter of a century later, at the end of a television programme called 'The Object in Question' she sat smiling, waiting for the presenter to say, 'We are indebted to Mrs Brown for allowing us to take this photograph of a beehive oven.' Onto the screen flashed our inglenook. Mother's one moment of television fame had come.

Cold water was useless to remove the soot. Margaret and I hurried home through the village, hoping that no one would see us. Our interest in the ruin was now an obsession. A local historian told us where to look for information. We asked the man in charge of the local archives at the city library to search out the deeds and any relevant information. One morning, a few days later, I spent an interesting few hours finding the bare details of the history of The Currer.

I found a record of an indenture on the 20th June in the 14th year of Elizabeth (1571), between Francis Paslewe of 'Ryddlelsden', in the County of York, esquire, Walter Paslewe, son and heir of the said Francis and John Paslewe of Wyswall, in the County of Lancashire, gentleman, of the one party and Arthur Currer, one of the sonnes of William Currer of Marley and grandson of Hugh Currer of Kildwick, within the said County of York, yeoman, of the other.

The indenture continues to say that Francis, Walter and John, in consideration of the sum of £30 sold Arthur Currer

all that one messuage or tenemente situate in Marley af/sd in the tenure and occupation of one Richard Leeche and all the edifices, howses, barnes, orchards, stables, gardens, lands, meadows, closes, pastures, leasures, woods, underwoods, wayes, waters, water courses, common rents, etc, in Marley and also all those several intakes or inclosures lately improved and inclosed of the common moors or wayste ground of Marley.

Authority was given, so the archives say,

to Arthur Currer to dig, get, break and carry away stones upon the Marley moor for walling and fencing of the said intakes and also the residue of common moor. To fell, cut down and take sufficient timber and other wood within the capital messuage of Marley Hall, for the necessary building of one house, of the payer of crocks to be crocked and builded upon one of the improvements.

There were subsequent details of a sale to the Parker family, well-known Quakers. The farm below us bears the cross of the Knights Templar. A stone bearing the initials RP and a seventeenth-century date could be found above our stable. There was record of a sale to the Ferrands, big local landowners from whom Grandfather bought the place in 1929 for the princely sum of £1,050.

I unearthed information which suggested that before the Paslewes of East Riddlesden Hall, the land had been farmed by the monks of Rievaulx Abbey. If there had been orchards and gardens they were there no longer. The house and barn stood gaunt and neglected. A pear tree had died clinging to the plain face of the south wall. What was left of it we burned early in our activity. The moor had crept up on the house. Whatever byres and buildings there had been were gone. As the incoming tide obliterates the portcullises and moats and gatehouses of a castle built in the sand, and leaves the centre mound to the last, so had gales and hot sun eroded the lesser buildings. The tide of grass and nettles and bracken had crept in until only the house and barn had been left to withstand weather and time.

On fine spring weekends there were plenty of walkers passing by on their way to the Druids' Altar. They paused to see what we were doing. They were attracted by the perpetual smell of burning, rotten wood and rubbish, by the constant hammering and the untuneful singing which came from two very dirty young women. We had become Jacks of all trades. Everything we could possibly do now, we had to do ourselves for our house was still unsold and borrowed money is always a liability.

Wallpaper was cheap. My father literally stood over me, with his make-shift plumbline, a piece of string with a nail on the end, and he did not leave me until he was sure I was hanging the lengths straight. I put on the other fifty rolls getting better every time. The old walls were thick and irregular. There were contours which resemble an upended physical map of the Pennines but wallpaper covered a multitude of sins. Everyone else painted every bit of woodwork white and the difference it made to the house was all the encouragement we needed. We knew our simple, well-worn furniture would look inadequate, but there was nothing that we could do about that.

We arranged for our one extravagance, the Aga, to be installed at the beginning of July. It cost £200 but was necessary. Completely wired throughout, not a single light would work, not a plug produce any energy. The Electricity Board was insensitive and could promise no immediate supply. We had no gas, so solid fuel cooking was the only alternative. The Aga was installed on the first Friday in July and lit by the workmen who put it in. Since then it has gone out only when we have accidentally neglected to feed it.

Feeling it was too precious to leave unsupervised, Margaret and I carried sleeping bags and put them in the empty east bedroom. We placed candles and matches at strategic places around the empty house. The oil lamps we eventually acquired were never taken upstairs. Margaret had arranged to see a film in town with an old school friend. When darkness fell Mother, Father and Harry went home and I was alone. I lit a candle in the front room, made a cup of coffee and sat on an orange box to wait. There must have been something ludicrous about the scene illuminated by the candle, for Margaret collapsed in a fit of laughter when she eventually entered after her walk home along the fields. Her laughter was infectious. 'We must be wrong in our heads!' we admitted. 'Just like Mother says.'

We lit the candle in the bedroom and took Jed with us, more for her sake than ours. Sleeping has never been a problem to either of us. We undress with unseeing weariness, crawl in and sleep until necessity demands we crawl out. But on that first night, in our relatively isolated farmhouse, we could not sleep. Perched on the hillside with nothing to muffle the sound, the prevailing wind was bringing us sounds we had not heard in the village. We could hear the constant rumble of the traffic on the A650 a mile away and we heard

every train to and from Scotland. So we lay awake and thought of those distant islands we were beginning to love so much. We heard the 3.30 a.m. Glasgow express with nostalgia and counted the days before we would be heading north again. Memories of the soft green machair and the near-white, deserted beaches and the sound of the Yorkshire dawn chorus, through the open window, eventually put us to sleep.

Chapter Six

During the week that followed we lifted our threadbare carpets and brought them on the tractor to lie like ridiculous pocket-handkerchiefs on the floors of The Currer. The real removal, on the following Friday, had all the ingredients of a first-rate cartoon. We hired a small, open lorry and prayed for a fine day. It was essential that the ground should remain firm in the First Intake and the Footpath Field for there was no way that a small lorry could come down the cart track in Currer Lane. The ruts, mutilated by the tractor wheels, were deep and wide. Stones had rolled from the parallel walls and become overgrown, and presented hidden dangers. The hillside at the bend was slipping and generously spilling its clay onto the track. In wet weather it was a quagmire and in sun the clay ruts hardened into miniature cliffs. The only possible way for any normal vehicle was through the field.

I missed the removal for there is no clause which says a teacher can have a holiday to remove her belongings less than a mile. So whilst everyone else was there to see the funny side I was teaching the three Rs. The lorry had to make two journeys; both were precarious. Mother went with the first load and was there to organise the distribution of the incredibly few contents. Conforming absolutely to character, she saw the hot oven and started to bake. When I came home from school there was a lovely smell and a batch of newly baked scones on the table. Mother has an obsession about having her cake tins full. She loves to bake and it is as good as a tonic for her to do so. Seldom would a guest arrive here and find the cupboard bare.

And so a new life began at The Currer, a life of living next to a barn and animals being our nearest neighbours; a life of trimming Tilley lamps and filling them with paraffin, of carrying all the shopping across five fields and ironing with a flat-iron. My early impressions were all olfactory. The smell of new-mown grass whilst still wet with dew, the sickliness created by the new hay stacked in the barn so close to the house that the smell penetrated the west wing bedrooms and competed with the soap and talcum in the bathroom. There was the constant fragrance of wood smoke from the sitting room fire, paraffin lamps and snuffed-out candles. Mother baked perpetually, and nothing smells nicer than newly baked bread and currant teacakes.

I began to love the early morning walk across the fields. By the time I reached the bus stop I felt so healthy I ignored it and walked down the snicket, past the church and took the steep, cobbled way through the wood.

My energy knew no bounds. There were evenings when I walked the three miles from my school over by The Gormless, John Brown's Lane and Fairfax Pinnacle. I bragged that I could do the three miles quicker that way. I loved coming home in the dark and had no fear of the fields or Currer Lane. The latter I preferred for it afforded a better view of the valley lights, a truly wonderful display.

More especially I learned to love the dawn. The early morning is my time. Margaret is difficult to move in the morning and can stay up till long after midnight. This makes us a very good partnership for one or other of us is about for eighteen hours of each day. At dawn there is often a mist which lies in the valley like a huge, white lake. It creeps up the hillside and escapes through the funnel of Jimmy's Wood, follows the stream in the Dyke Field and misses the house. It is a friend, for it brings a beautiful day. The early morning is alive with the song of lark, peewit and blackbird, wrens hunt for insects in the stable wall and only the north wind picks up the metallic sounds of the twentieth century. Mother became vocal that first sun-filled July. Making her beds with heat shimmering on the counterpane she would open the mullioned windows and sing.

My father's part in the installing of his family in the farmhouse was the major one. He was the pillar of strength which kept us all going and to whom we all turned for advice. He had a fantastic optimism, was always sure that, 'Summat 'ud turn up,' and he worked like a young man to achieve a green and pleasant land. Now other people do not know, or have forgotten, what these acres looked like: fields carpeted with crowberry, the bent turf full of rushes and cotton grass, the moor patched with bracken and bilberry. Others do not remember the ruin at the foot of Currer Lane but we do and that is why I write.

Where did we find all the hours to use in those early days? It was the summer term and time for the annual School Trip. My headmistress always had a tin of 'Quickies', those damp, sweet-smelling discs which bring miracle freshness. John asked, 'Can ah 'ev one o' them there wot make yer smell as if yer've bin courting?' Sports Day came in July, nature walks and Year End celebrations, equipment to pack for our Hebridean Trek and the haymaking to be done.

On the Friday night, two weeks after our removal to The Currer, I took a cheap night return on the Glasgow bus. I slept all the way and walked blearily from Port Dundas Street to Buchanan Street station for the Oban train. Quite possibly I slept all that journey, too. My errand was to collect one of the Macinnes girls from Salum, Tiree who was coming out on the morning boat for her first mainland holiday. She was arriving in Oban before me and was being met by her auntie. Fifteen-year-old Mary and I then caught the teatime train back to Glasgow for the long bus journey home. I had originally intended to pick up all three MacInnes girls and their friend, Mary Ann, but at the last minute only Mary had been brave enough.

We arrived home in the early morning. One of the most beautiful journeys on earth is from Kendal to Skipton when the early morning dews and mists add more whiteness to the limestone and the newly risen sun gilds the crags and reflects in the windows of the compact hill farms dotted everywhere on the hillside.

Mary gave no sign that she was a stranger to trains and towns and all the paraphernalia of the mainland. Only I knew she would not cross the jerking passages between two railway carriages and fumbled when she had to put a penny in a slot. She appeared composed in the ordered chaos of busy streets and the high tenements of Glasgow. I was amazed that she could accept it all with so few hesitations. But I was glad to be taking this beautiful, island child to our old farmhouse with its paraffin lamps and candles and its isolation. We returned to hay making, bilberry picking and, for me, another week at school. The hay was important. We could not afford to lose a bale and every bilberry was needed.

Our young visitor from the Hebrides spent a fortnight with us before returning with the lucky seven at the beginning of our Island Trek. She accompanied us to Steeton Hall to pick up the Itiza tents and the trike carts. Having no transport of our own we were dependent on a friend who, because of illness, had bought Heather Lodge. Mr Ainley was the proud and useful owner of an ex-army jeep. What we would have done without him to ferry our equipment from Steeton to home to station, I just do not know!

The last load of hay came into the barn on the eve of our departure. Appropriately we sang, 'Oh the wanderlust is o'er me and tonight I strike the trail.' The trek had been planned for a year. Our feet will always itch to return to the islands, our backs ache to feel again the bending wind of the Hebrides. We have a great deal of work to do and it is necessary for us to recharge our batteries on the wild, beautiful beaches and communicate with the crofting people with whom we have found such an affinity. No more did we want to stay in hotels. We had breathed the morning freshness from a tent door, heard the dawn chorus on the shore and felt the machair beneath our sleeping bags. Canvas was to excite us for many, many years.

The story of that wonderful island trek is dealt with adequately elsewhere and is only mentioned here because it seems important to put it into the calendar in its rightful place just four weeks after our hectic removal, at a time when we were bubbling with enthusiasm and cramming more than seemed possible into every day. To our list of islands we added the Uists and Eigg and Rhum; to our wealth of friends we added the Campbells of Tangasdale and many more. It is a great pity that we were never able to repeat it with a chosen few. Thereafter every Guide demanded the right to come and numbers increased each year until we were journeying north with approaching sixty boys and girls.

Immediately on our return Mother, Father and Harry were to set off for their annual week in Blackpool. Jean, Peter and the two children came to stay with us in their absence and arrived on the night before they left. We have an amusing memory of that night. Perhaps it was because we spent such outdoor lives or perhaps it was just that she was such a master of her craft but Mother never expected us to know about cooking or baking. 'Sum day, when Ah've time,' she'd say, 'Ah'll stand over you.' In the meantime she thought that cooking for thirty in a Guide camp was different and that the culinary art was hers alone. Before going on a holiday, therefore, she would make sure that all the tins were full and that the weekend roast was cooked.

On the eve of their departure for Blackpool in 1958 she put the precious joint in the oven and forgot it. She finished her packing late and we had all gone to bed before she and Father had their pre-holiday bath. They carried up their candle into the bathroom and the house was almost in darkness. Father had extinguished the Tilley lamps and the only sound was Mother in the bath. She got out and completed the exercise by placing her dentures in their overnight dish and was just climbing into bed when she remembered the meat. It is easy to forget for cooking in the Aga does not increase the heat in the kitchen. There is no pilot light, no smell, nothing to remind you that you have something cremating.

Together the little old man and the little old woman, in their nightgowns, toothless and very clean, descended the stone steps with their small candle. Re-telling it sounds like a story from *Beacon Book Four*. Opening the oven door they lifted out tomorrow's very overcooked joint. Mother expects miracles. She cannot see when the impossible is obvious. 'Fetch a bowl and a plate,' she said. 'It'll press.' The hard brown joint made a metallic sound as it fell into the bowl. The plate, when pressed above it, broke not only itself but the bowl, too.

Margaret heard the unusual noises and hurried downstairs thinking to surprise burglars. She found the vision, illuminated by the candle, hysterically funny. There was a little old woman in curlers and a little, bald old man in a nightshirt, his legs white and thin, his bare feet already cold. He could have been Gandhi himself. There they were, staring and toothlessly grinning at a piece of cindered meat and a mess of broken crockery.

These candlelight and paraffin lamp days were very dear to us. They accentuated, more than anything, the difference there was between life in the village and life at the foot of the moor. The lamplight was infinitely more comfortable and warm than the hardness of electricity and because the light was local we drew near to it and to each other to laugh over the events of the day and plan the tomorrows.

More and more children were coming to The Currer. On Saturdays when I didn't have some Guides about the place learning knots and camp craft, there was always Ann, the first of many Saturday children. She would appear each Saturday afternoon, help with the farm chores and then sit knitting all evening. We would walk with her to the end of the fields to catch the bus. She was wholly dedicated to becoming a Queen's Guide, very much in love with camping and Scotland and she was always singing folk songs. She wore her hair in two dark plaits and whilst she remained a happy youngster and later became a friend, she was a loner, an individual we learned to respect but never quite to know. She always gave more than we expected. Her apparent indolence hid a source of extraordinary energy. When needed she could pull out of the bag resources we did not anticipate. A sensitive teenager was Ann. I remember the day when she came with a new song. 'Listen to this,' she said, 'it's got beautiful words.' She was right. The words of 'Blowin' in the wind' have beauty and meaning. I have known a lot of children who have loved and recognised lovely things and the truth when they have heard it.

The sale of our 1926 semi took place at the end of August, just before I returned to school. The price was shockingly low. We received a mere £1,400 for a house which, thirty years later, is worth more than fifty times as much. The proceeds only partially covered what we had been forced to spend on The Currer, to satisfy the Council, so we were even more deeply in debt to our long-suffering bank manager.

Our first gamble was on forty Hereford and Aberdeen Angus calves. Father had never had to buy and sell before but he proved himself a brave bidder, unafraid of taking a risk and not screaming if things went wrong. We had nowhere to house the calves except the sixteenth-century barn which was pretty hopeless at feeding time. The only way was to let four calves out at a time. Once they got the idea, forty wanted to come out at once and the rotten old doors bowed against their weight. To let out just four was a test of human strength against healthy determination. Margaret and Father were bruised and trodden on but there was pride and joy in seeing the calves grow, admiring their shiny coats and watching their exaggerated gambolling round the yard when feeding time was over. Exhausted but triumphant, Margaret and Dad would lean on the gate watching their big family have a good time. This was a new experience, this buying of week-old calves in great numbers from markets in the locality. Most of our calves had previously been home bred and numbers small.

A newly fed calf shivers with satisfaction. These super calves had to be chased away from the bucket. A gate had to be tied on the outside of the laithe porch to prevent them returning for seconds. Having failed to stay with the bucket they found something else to lick; another calf, a wooden door, anything. Froth and saliva drooled from them and anything tasted good.

Father and Margaret watched them career around, up and down the yard, round and round. The pile of discarded wood, rotten and paint flaking, was well out of harm's way. And still it happened. Imperceptibly, there was a deterioration in the health of the baby herd. Suddenly one or two calves were really ailing and the rest looked very shoddy. The vet was called, a calf died and the awful truth was learned. Lead poisoning. The words bring horror, a sickness to the stomach, as we remember the plague of November 1958.

A newly fed calf will lick anything, gates, wood partitions, tins. It will suck another calf's navel, a length of binder twine or a hessian sack being used as a draught excluder. Our beautiful calves licked paint from somewhere and there was nothing we could do but accuse ourselves. No veterinary skill or farmer's devotion could prevent eighteen of our calves dying and many more became weak survivors. Very little lead is needed to kill a calf and old paint had a very high percentage. Now the content is usually nil but the wood on door posts, an old cupboard, a sink bottom, was covered in peeling old paint and it was impossible to find it all. We thought we had, for we knew about lead and before the first calf was born we had checked and double-checked. The symptoms are extremely distressing. There is blindness, diarrhoea, racking cough and fits. They left such an impression on Margaret that whenever she finds a piece of painted wood on a beach or pasture, anywhere, she collects it and burns it. Daily the tractor pulled its pathetic trailer load of dead calves for burial in Jimmy's Wood. Without a road no dead animal removal van could come to us in wintertime. A terrible lesson had been learned and we were sickened.

More and more strong became the determination to survive. It wasn't merely to save face, though there were scores of pessimistic relatives and friends eagerly waiting to say, 'I told you so! An elderly man and a slip of a girl not five feet high can't reclaim 170 acres and stock them on a shoestring. Get your sums right,' they said, 'Get out whilst you can. Sell to someone who can afford it. If you don't you'll work till you drop.' But we never listened. We would survive not to prove them wrong but to prove us right. We'd work but, by golly, we would not drop.

There had been another activity on the moor that autumn which had nothing to do with us. The Electricity Board was working on the overhead supply line and re-siting pylons. Irishmen were at work on the land with huge tractors and they were making an even greater mess of Currer Lane which belonged to us and to Altar Lane which belonged to the Council. The work was completed towards Christmas and we were due a certain amount of compensation. He was full of ideas, that incredible father of ours. We used to laugh and say there was one good one in ten but that was a gross exaggeration. If an idea wasn't a good one it was a stepping-stone to one that was and this December idea was 'a stunner an' no mistak'!'

The man to negotiate with had called many times in the past few months and Father asked that, in lieu of compensation, the tractor digger should be used to lift the east wall of the lane and throw it into our mutilated cart track so that we could pitch a road. It was a huge wall, three feet thick at the base, full of sandstone and millstone grit. The Electricity Board agreed and a few hours were spent by the tractor man and his digger, lifting and dropping hundreds of tons of stone into a ribbon of a road all the way from the Moor Gate to the pond which lies at the foot. The long, chaotic tumble of rocks, two feet deep in places, looked more like the Khumba ice fall on Mount Everest than a road.

A few days later our elderly junior teacher, whose discipline was of the very noisy kind, retired after many years at our school. I could smell change in the ordered, known and much-loved environment but I was too busy making Christmas presents for Jean's children and our many Hebridean friends. School festivities ended, the Guide Party was a success and we all went to the Blind Home for the annual carols. Margaret and I walked home together. There was magic in walking home to The Currer. It was like leaving the world behind and finding a hospice on the moor.

Christmas came, our first at The Currer. The aunts were here and we went to the midnight service in our local church and then sang carols beneath the window just outside our own front door. It had given me a thrill to gather holly from the bottom of the low pasture and I thought it exciting to carry home a small Norwegian fir, on my back, all the way from the bus! We were not only used to the deprivations of our new life, we welcomed them. Not so, I'm sure, our car-rich relatives who came for the annual Boxing Day gathering. They had been used to leaving their cars outside the gate in the village and now they had to walk the last quarter of a mile on foot. Still, they came, Aunt Elsie seated herself at the piano and everyone enjoyed the singsong. The cousins were missing but Freda and Howard and their teenage children came and I believe eighteen sat down in the spacious farm kitchen. They were not as romantically enamoured by the dark return to their cars as they should have been for it was a beautiful night and we led the way with hurricane lamps. The things which excited us were cheap and easily obtainable. The smell of hawthorn embers, bending winds, early sunshine and a full moon; all extremely intoxicating.

With Christmas over and the lead poisoning a dreadful memory, we looked forward to a new year. Father had bought a few more calves. We believe in 'The king is dead, long live the king.' If a calf died Father's philosophy was always to go and buy another. If you must cry, he expected you to be dry-eyed before you reached the house.

We began the New Year with the usual burst of acceleration. On 1st January we began our marathon on the road. If this is a history of our humble love affair with The Currer then this date is one to remember for it is the date Father, Margaret and I took sledge-hammers and pick-axes and began to bring order to the boulders which had been emptied higgledy-piggledy down the hill side. There had been a satisfying weight of stone in that wall, enough to scatter the whole length, two feet deep where the ruts were cavernous and a generous eighteen inches over all. We had not expected such abundance and the task of bringing order to the random mess was quite formidable. We were asked by passing ramblers what we proposed to do. 'Now what?' said family and friends.

'We're going to bash up the surface and level it all out,' we answered, with the confidence of the bigheaded.

'Huh!' they replied in the tone used to imply that such a silly answer could only be in jest and that we must have engaged a team of workmen.

But we were not joking and quite sure that if we began at the bottom and kept going we would get to the top. So on the 1st of January 1959 we borrowed an extra sledgehammer and another pick and we began to bash away at our native stones and rocks as if heaven was our goal. We forced ourselves to keep going in spite of swollen and blistered hands and broken nails. We ignored strained muscles, tired biceps and shattered nerves and daily blasted our way ahead, yard by backbreaking yard.

'Does the road wind upward all the way?' quoted Margaret. 'Yes, to the very end.'

Broken stone will always look beautiful to us. The sandstone and the millstone grit of our black walls, when shattered, reveal a wealth of colour from deep red and brown to grey and orange, cream and white and a thousand crystals sparkle. We worked with the black avalanche ahead of us and the level colourful ribbon behind. We worked in rain and snow and ice, an hour before school and two hours after, all weekends, every possible daylight hour and often after dark. Father would sing. 'Keep right on to the end of the road,' and we'd join in like a happy band of Snow White's dwarfs.

Passers-by would say, 'What a mess!' 'What a job!' 'It's worse than being in Dartmoor,' was one opinion passed but no one paused to lend a hand. There is a dearth of helpfulness amongst ramblers in this locality. Walkers pause to comment but very few help, whatever the job. Be we walling, fencing, ditching; be we haymaking, snow-shovelling or struggling with difficult cattle, like the priest in the story of the Samaritan, most cross over to look and then pass by.

We know every inch of that road we built and we do not join the gang of critics eager to condemn a roadman when he leans a while on his shovel. On the contrary, we jump to his defence. 'Have you built a road?' we say. 'Have you shovelled and hammered from dawn to dusk? Don't dare criticise unless you have walked a mile in the roadman's moccasins!'

When we reached exhaustion point on the road we recharged with oranges, big juicy oranges eaten with no dignity, only extreme thirst. We made uninhibited noises sucking out the delicious pulp, noses and chins buried in sweetness. Just once we sought help with road construction. This was about fifteen years later when the topping of quarry bottoms had eroded and the clay from the hillside encroached on the bend. We planned to tarmac a stretch of the hill and decided that first we would use up some railway sleepers to hold back the hill. So we asked Jonathan and Stephen, both annual campers, to come and help. They were in their late teens and very strong.

It was a scorching hot day and those two fine fellows took off their shirts and we worked together for a long time. We dug deep holes to stand vertical half-sleepers and then carried whole lengths to wedge behind making a solid wall to protect the road. It was hard work and eventually our two strong helpers straightened their backs and groaned. Suddenly Jonathan came up with a very kind and thoughtful idea. He looked at Margaret and me with affection and said, 'I'll tell yer what, Skipper, I'll go and make us all a cup of tea!' We laughed as we saw the male workers go off to the kitchen.

The class of our newly retired disciplinarian began to take advantage of their newfound freedom from authority and gave the temporary helper we had rather a bad time. I was all too aware that the peaceful days at school were soon to be challenged by change. First there was the disturbance of this elderly teacher's retirement and secondly, I knew, wedding bells would ring shortly for our headmistress. The peace, whilst it lasted, must be preserved and there was an earth tremor in the juniors freed from rigid discipline. It threatened the tranquility we were used to and I was asked to leave my beloved infants for two terms and teach the nine- to ten-year-olds. The challenge was just what I needed. It could have been expected that, having always wanted to farm, I would now have lost some of my interest in the profession which had been an alternative. But familiarity did not breed contempt nor did the outdoor life I loved pull so strongly that I longed for the 3.30 p.m. bell. There was room in my life for farming, teaching and Guiding, for they all fitted together like a jigsaw. This opportunity to teach juniors was unexpected good fortune. With this experience behind me and the Diploma in Primary Education, I would be able to think seriously about a village school headship. I ordered a weekly copy of the *Times Educational Supplement* and the search was on.

But first there was the road to finish. We reached the summit of our mountain on the last day of March 1959. I know which day it was because, in anticipation of our nearness to the top, we had ordered nine loads of two-inch quarry bottoms to be brought the following day. There was a Ministry of Agriculture grant on road materials or we could never have afforded it. Harry has a real sense of humour, he always knows the date and can remember when, how and where things have happened. He is the brains behind the chronological order of this account.

On this memorable morning, very early, he walked along the passage, scraping the wallpaper with his shoulder as he always does. We have a shiny line everywhere. He came to the bedroom where Margaret and I were dead to the world and said, 'Four grit lorries are at the Moor Gate!'

We shot out of bed, reaching for working trousers and sweaters and struggling to manoeuvre aching legs and arms into the right holes. Harry leaned against the wall laughing. 'What's so funny?' we wanted to know.

'April Fool!' he said.

We were already dressed and, though it was early, there seemed no point in going back to bed. We sat quietly by the Aga, drinking coffee and preparing ourselves for the ordeal. If you have spread nine loads of two-inch quarry bottoms six inches deep over a quarter of a mile stretch of road you, too, will sympathise with the roadman leaning on his shovel.

There were two places where it was necessary to cross streams and Father and Margaret did this with the help of railway sleepers. Later in the summer we had the bridges concreted and part of the yard in front of the house. It controlled one per cent of the mud which was to become our number one enemy of the future. The road, like the one the highwayman rode was 'a ribbon of moonlight'. The final icing of small limestone chippings made it look like a clean white causeway to the mainland and we were as proud of it as the Romans surely were of Watling Street. Cattle are curious; they soon used it and manured it and before long the stark whiteness had been spoiled. The limestone greened the verges very rapidly, traffic made it smooth and few remember what Currer Lane used to look like. The road has needed a little tarmac and some widening at the bend but the foundations have never moved in more than a quarter of a century.

Now, friends who had feared the walk came in plenty. The corn lorry could come all the way and only had to drop the sacks at the Moor Gate in snow and ice. The removal wagon could come to take away animals to be sold and calves could be delivered to the barn door. Torrential rain occasionally eroded the limestone topping but a few days could put things right. The road was a blessing but it took away some of the novelty of our isolation, made us a little more normal and quite a bit more vulnerable.

We were spending too much money on non-productive things and too little on animals which would bring a return. The survivors of the lead poisoning would be a while before they could be sold. The heifers we would keep to increase the suckling herd. The first suckled calves were a long way off sale and there was a limit as to how far a teacher's salary would go. So we borrowed some more money to buy some point-of-lay pullets and put them in the all-purpose barn. The Nissen hut to house them properly we did not buy until we needed the barn for the hay. We always bought animals before accommodation.

There was no ignoring the cry of the Guides to go to the Hebrides. 'Tiree,' they chanted, 'Tiree is the place for me.' I found that scrawled in the sand a score of years later, along with the rewarding exclamation, 'Glad that I live am I!'

'All of us!' they cried. Never again were we able to get away with only taking a few, which is sad for there were possibilities in a small group which had to be forfeited because the needs of many must always come before the needs of few. It was a clamour I could not ignore, a clamour which was to beat in my ears for twenty-five years and fill our summers with a happiness few have been privileged to know.

So we planned the 1959 camp once again on Tiree and my Ripon Guider friend asked to come with us and bring her daughter Janet. They stayed one night with us before we left with our happy band. Mr Ainley's jeep, which was taking us to the station, broke down at the bend and we had hurriedly to get out the tractor, take our rucksacks and everything to the bus via the fields.

Island children flocked to the camp swelling our numbers and adding a new dimension. Gaelic songs were sung, we learned the eightsome reel and one of the MacLean boys became our resident piper. Calum Salum was our patron and we thought that surely we must be the luckiest Guide Company in the country.

The first few days left nothing to be desired. Then, midweek, a telegram was delivered to me, in the breakfast horseshoe, and I read that the father of one of our eleven-year-olds, whilst on holiday at a local resort, had suddenly died. I looked up to see the expectant faces full of curiosity. I smiled an untruthful assurance that all was well.

After breakfast Miriam, Margaret and I went to the post office at Salum and with May and Marion MacLean pored over the problem. The telegram stated briefly the death and the request that the child should be sent home. The first statement shocked. The second put us in a quandary. We were inexperienced and terribly sorry for the mother and child. In later years we stipulated that no adult could be spared to accompany a child home even for a reason such as this. The loss of one-third of the adult team was too high a price to pay when we were four hundred miles from home, on an island, with thirty and eventually nearly sixty children. But faced with the only request we were ever to have, we didn't know what to do. I rang the airport but they had only one emergency seat on the plane. They offered a police escort for the child to the Glasgow station and protection on the journey home but the mother was distraught and would not agree. I begged that her daughter be allowed to stay in camp for she was, after all, only young and it was too late to say 'Goodbye'. There was no way this was acceptable so Margaret decided to return with the eleven-year-old and Lachlan MacLean, who was returning to the south of England at the weekend, offered to make a detour and take them both home.

We kept the news secret until Friday. On a lovely afternoon we picnicked at Coales and played in the seal waters of Urvaig, one of the most beautiful places on earth. In the early evening, I asked for two volunteers to accompany me back to camp the quick way and begin making the meal. There was a show of hands and I chose Lesley and her friend. The rest of the campers walked the shore track back to Salum. Immediately we were out of earshot I told Lesley she would have to go home the following day because her father had died. I have had few worse jobs to do. Mercifully she cried, so did her friend and so did I and we wrapped our arms round each other.

The uninhibited tears acted as balm and eventually we walked back to camp hand in hand. Together we began the busy task of preparing the evening meal. The awakened campfire helped excuse the tears and work occupied our minds and hands so we were composed when the rest of the big family returned. Margaret had told them the sad news of the journey home she and Lesley would make on the morning boat. I could have cried, too, for Margaret. Camp is not a holiday when so many children are involved but it is a change from daily routine and was a holiday to us. Urvaig, on that day she prepared to go, was paradise.

Only when we left camp at 4.30 a.m. the next morning did Lesley cry again. I remember the early morning cup of tea and the boiled egg Marion

MacLean prepared for us before Lachlan took them to the boat and drove them the long journey home. I was very cold when they had gone and I felt alone. My child sister had grown up. She had become my right hand, my only hope of relaxation. Without her I would have to carry all the responsibility. We worked together in harmony and to wave her goodbye and return to so many children needed discipline. To go back ready to laugh and play and lead needed self-control and the cold, early hour was not conducive to that. I went and sat on the deserted shore, barefoot as we always were, and I felt sorry for myself for just a little while. I realised that should either of my parents die or need me, I would not be able to go. This stark truth was with me for twenty-five years, that, come hell or high water, sickness, death, disaster, my place would have to be with these children, so totally dependent on me, so far from home. But the biggest ordeal in twenty-five years was over. Nothing worse happened in my career with children on remote islands. Severe weather tested us and taught us how to survive. We learned to cope with the elements but I had to face nothing so bad as Lesley's bereavement and Margaret's going.

The cloud passed by and the sun came out again as it is perpetually wont to do if we can only have faith and patience. The spirit of laughter and freedom returned and the camp was a success everyone clamoured to repeat.

We returned home bringing Ellen MacInnes, Mary's sister, for a fortnight's holiday at The Currer. At the end of her stay I took her back to Edinburgh and put her on the Oban train to be collected by her Auntie Chrissie. I paused for a few days at Budle Bay on the Northumbrian coast with Jean and her little family. They were staying in a caravan. The children and I slept in a tent pitched behind it and it was the only time, ever, that I have slept on a camp bed, in a tent. Every other night, of all the hundreds I have spent in the open air, the earth has been my bed. Inexperienced people will not believe me that the ground is warmer than the air and that to sleep snugly there must be no air space between you and the earth. The airbed was an invention in the right direction but the earth has always been good enough for me.

*   *   *   *   *

The foundations of the deep litter hut, to house our point-of-lay pullets, were laid at the end of August. The MacAlisters from Salen, Mull, were staying with us at the time. We seemed to be never without guests. Much as we loved entertaining we knew the drain this was on our time. We were always feeding people, always inviting them to stay. 'You'll be lonely at The Currer,' friends had said!

Then the autumn calves were bought. There was no room for them in the barn so we acquired some second-hand timber from several demolition sites. We were scavengers of the rare kind. It was imperative that we should build sheds round the farmhouse and we knew we'd have to do it ourselves. The suckled herd could winter out but not the bought-in calves. I have a vivid memory of returning home from school, one Monday in September, and finding the first of the annual calves, bought that morning, running around the field whilst Margaret and Father were valiantly digging deep holes and erecting upright beams to hold roof timbers and support corrugated tin.

Just as we began to look forward to the darker nights and the subdued light and warmth of the Tilley lamps and the restrictions they would bring, the Electricity Board woke up to the fact that we had no electricity and brought us a line. We hadn't expected it, for one official had been very rude to Mother and Harry. He had laughed at our optimism in getting the house wired and Mother had been very upset. But, at last, a line was carried over half a dozen fields and we were illuminated. Suddenly every switch would work and a hard, cold light cruelly filled the farmhouse. We heralded its possibilities with the same mixture of joy and sorrow with which we had welcomed the road link. The quiet evenings in the lamplight were gone, for the good light shamed us into extending the working day. Mother set about her marathon task of carpeting the eighteen yards of upstairs corridor and the staircase. The big frame was brought out and every evening Mother pegged away. When the evening chores were done Margaret would dash across the fields to spend a couple of hours playing badminton, or Scottish country dancing or just seeing a film with a school friend. We would open the door and send Jed to meet the last bus. The dog seldom left her during the day and waited uneasily all evening for the command to 'fetch Margaret'.

Mother thought nothing of walking to the village for the bus into town and returned happily with the heavy bags. Father would go to meet the bus she was expected to catch. He was devoted to her and loved the way she had accepted The Currer and adapted herself to the changes. She baked continually, entertained graciously, criticised, nattered and developed a character which endeared her to us all. 'Let 'er 'ave 'er little natter,' Father would say.

In October we hired a television and she was able to watch the show jumping. One day she heard Father come into the yard with the tractor and she hurried out, rather floury, and placing the wooden spoon in front of his mouth in an imitation of a microphone, she asked, 'What do you feel about noise?' The Currer was good for Mother.

And Harry! He loved the novelty of it all, and he found he could walk to the village alone to do the shopping. I like to remember this freedom that he enjoyed for he is now so crippled that he can scarcely walk across the yard without help and if we want to buzz around the lanes and villages and across the beaches on holiday we pop him in a wheelchair. But we were able, twenty-five years ago, to let him wander off to the village alone. He seldom fell in those days and we rarely worried if he were out of sight as we do now if he is upstairs any longer than we expect.

Being at The Currer made an extraordinary difference to him. He had always been loved and he had been needed in a way that we could understand because he had been the root of our character training. But now he was needed in a way that he could understand. He was a full partner in the business and as such had to put his signature to all documents. For the past thirty years we have needed him to work. His contribution began with household chores, particularly the dish washing. Sweeping was left to him be it house or yard.

Every week he would walk the three-quarters of a mile to the village shop and visit Cousin Freda. He would return with the groceries and the gossip. He was unafraid of the cattle and would move among them and throw out bales of hay on the uneven surface of the fields. An animal has never knocked him down whereas we have been upskittled regularly.

He thought nothing of walking to the bus, with Mother, on a Saturday so that he could visit the aunts in town. Physically he became much stronger and was quite straight in those days. He began to take an interest in the animals. The goat Betty was often his companion, shopping with him in the village.

One does not need an engagement diary in the house with Harry. He never forgets when a dental appointment is and knows exactly when a birthday card must be sent and the name of some so-and-so which escapes us.

We no longer thought of him as handicapped because his life became full of useful activity without which we would have found the burden of work too much. All his help was positive and productive.

I who had written that I would like a car for Harry in my Grammar School entrance examination, now acknowledged that being without a car was good for Harry. During those first years at The Currer, when physical activity was survival, Harry passed the test. Psychologically that was terrific. Harry can say, along with the rest of us, that, 'Without me they couldn't have done what they did!'

Nor did he lose out on fun. There were as many laughs for him as for all of us. He was able to join in all the discussions and plans and his horizon was wider than that of most able-bodied people. We couldn't possibly have done without him then any more than we could do without him now, when, late at night, he and Margaret tackle the washing up of sometimes thirty evening meals. On the rare occasions that I have to do his 11 p.m. shift I think I will die and Margaret grumbles all the time that my help, compared with his, is most unsatisfactory.

We had acquired two goats, Betty and Rosie, for Paddy was in calf again. We had to have milk and were not prepared to fetch it from the village. Our present goats are beautiful but they haven't the character of their predecessors. Our castrated billy is our good luck charm and the two nannies have never been properly named. During the past twenty-five years thousands of animals have enjoyed the comfort and freedom of our kingdom. At first they all had names. Susan and Biddy and Guilty were three remembered sows; Cindy, Paddy, Cuckoo, Peggy, Ozzie, Craig and Joanna our bovine neighbours; Trixie, Nelson, Threelegs, Ginger but four of the many cats; Quackers, Gandhi and Susan decorated the pond; Mary and Belinda clucked in the yard. There were many dogs: Jed and Bess, Laddie and Lassie, Floss and Skye and Shep, Lusky and Jess. Squeak and Featherlegs were important pigeons, Macrae the wounded crow, Dick the Shetland pony, Jasper and Chocolate, the donkeys. Their names crowd into my memory as do the Toms and Johns and Davids, the Lindas and Julies and Jennifers of my school, the Nellies and Janets and Christines of my Guide company. Names and faces, people and animals, have washed into my life like so many pebbles on a beach, appearing and disappearing with the tide. Some have been washed away and almost forgotten. Can we be blamed, now there are sometimes two hundred cattle to check and feed and several hundred holidaymakers in the summer, if we name but a few? Will we be forgiven if we sometimes forget faces and hardly ever remember Christian names? There is a limit to what the mind can store. In a crowd or herd only some among our two- and four-footed friends stand out from the rest.

Rosie's life was brief but Betty appeared to have immortality and was devoted to her owners with whom she would have lived, given the chance. We found it very difficult to go anywhere without her. She accompanied us at blackberry time, like another dog, but would steal from the bucket which no dog would do.

We kept one of Jed's pups, the only one of the litter with mottled feet, and we called her Bess. She was with us for twenty years. Until we came to The Currer, Jed had not been kept in the house but she had been our constant friend throughout the rebirth of the farmhouse and not one of us would have turned her out when the carpets came. We did feel, however, that we ought to have a dog in the barn so we kept Bess from the litter and gave the others away.

A whistle to the dogs always alerted the goat and her ungainly but dignified gait was so different from the easy speed of the dogs as to be laughable. She was a definite nuisance when she insisted on walking in front of the tractor. At hay time, we would attempt to lock her up somewhere but she had an uncanny habit, common only to herself and Houdini, and before we had gone far she would be running after us.

I always had to check her whereabouts before going to school and make my exit by the appropriate door to deceive her. Sometimes she smelled me and I failed to make my get-away in secret. Sometimes she would be grazing just by the stile and I had no defence other than to tempt her with corn into the most secure shed we had. Try as I might I could never depend on getting all the way to the bus stop without hearing the tell-tale patter of hooves behind me. I used to hop over the highest wall, furthest away from a gate, and leave her swearing behind. The rest of the family did not mind her being a shadow quite so much as I did. Harry indeed was happy to have her accompany him to the shop, providing he could be quick enough to shut the door on her.

My headmistress announced her engagement and the end of things as they had been for eight years was in sight. I began tatting tablemats for her wedding, scores of them with fine cotton. I used to take my tatting shuttle to school with me and blindly tat whilst I supervised children in the playground. One day a nine-year-old boy came to see me and asked what the 'thing' was in my hand. 'It's a tatting shuttle,' I said.

He looked at me first with disbelief and then with amusement and with mature tolerance said, 'Ask a silly question, get a silly answer!'

I loved the easy way the children spoke to me. 'Your legs are just like my mother's!' Eileen said, 'the hairs all stick through your nylons.'

There was a day when I was marking nine-year-old Ian's sums. A quick glance showed all the answers different to the ones in the answer book. I was surprised for Ian could do maths.

'Oh dear,' I said, 'Let's see what you've done wrong.'

'I'm on Exercise 10, not 9,' he said with tempered patience.

'Sorry, Ian,' I said and ticked all the answers right. He looked up at the ceiling with a sigh and muttered, 'Women!'

One dark winter evening Margaret and I went to a meeting in a neighbouring town to hear a lecture given by a young man who had been working with refugees in the still overflowing camps in Germany. He was supported by other students and his aim was to promote local interest for the Refugee Year of 1960. He was really asking for other young people to help organise holidays away from the camps and cities of war-torn Europe, for children who had known no other all their lives. We couldn't remain unmoved and immediately promised our help. We boasted we were the right people for the job! We had experience of taking children on holiday, we had camped and, we were told, these holidays for the refugee children would be in camps in the German countryside.

So we volunteered, and there was a certain amount of correspondence; we learned a little German, made plans and put out feelers for financial support. Surely, we thought, the Girl Guide Association will help such a worthwhile project. But our plans were frustrated by the Mayor who had already committed the town to a refugee programme. They had promised to give holidays here to sixteen refugee children from Germany and had made no arrangements either for the holiday or for foster homes. They simultaneously approached the Guide Association with a plea for help and the powers that be saw a solution to both problems. I was willing to take refugee children on holiday. They needed someone to do so. What was easier than to persuade me to take the girls in the party to camp by the sea in England? The Guide Association and the town would help me to finance this scheme. There was little I could do except allow myself to be persuaded that I was needed in this local project.

With hindsight I would have been more cautious and explored the problem more deeply. Laymen, Borough Councillors and inexperienced citizens are often genuinely eager to 'do good' without any research into the right way to go about it. Almost everyone thinks he knows best and those who promoted and financed us and we who planned the whole affair thought we knew a good way of doing things when, in practice, we were proved to be so wrong.

I chose Budle Bay, in Northumberland, for the site of the camp. The Northumbrian coast is beautiful and quiet and, when responsibility was somewhat unknown, I thought it no bad thing to be near Jean.

The plan appeared workable and contributions came from generous people. Practical help was offered and many people became involved. Some were knitting sweaters and assembling wardrobes for three weeks in camp. Fool that I was, I sought to clothe these unknown children in the uniform way in which the Guides were dressed. All my knitters were given the navy blue wool of normal camp jerseys. Navy blue shorts and sky blue tee shirts were bought. We were quite wrong. These deprived children wanted orange and scarlet. They did not want sensible things; they wanted glamour and we had no idea.

The first of January 1960 was like any other day. Usually we began the year with some sudden burst of increased energy but the beginning of this momentous year was quiet. There was nothing to suggest that it heralded a year to remember, a year in which the Girl Guide Association celebrated a Golden Jubilee, the world tried to tackle the refugee problem and we learned, the hard way, that Rudyard Kipling's 'If' was 'spot on'.

My headmistress's marriage was imminent. She had come to us nearly nine years ago from a post as head of a village school further up the dale. The *Times Educational Supplement* published an advertisement in January for the same village school headship and I was immediately interested. I accompanied my friend on her preliminary visit to the vicar and afterwards we went through the churchyard to look through the windows of the little school. A beautiful tenth-century church, it is, and the little school had been built to resemble it in many ways. The classroom windows were mullioned and each topped with a window within a stone trefoil. Inside, the roof was not underdrawn so that the dark rafters were exposed and the glass partitions separating the three classrooms, when folded back, would leave the whole school open, like a nave. Children's work covered the walls and the desks and chairs were grouped informally. There were only two classes, since reorganisation had removed the senior children. The juniors were the responsibility of a teaching Head and the infant teacher had already been at the school a dozen years or more.

This was just what I wanted. I remember that the field walls kept back drifts of recent snow but that the snowdrops were out in the memorial garden at the foot of the church steps and that the daffodil shoots were already healthy in the vicarage garden.

My application for the post of headmistress was posted the following week and I attended the wedding of Margaret and Charles at the end of February. My summons to attend for interview came before Easter. This time I had to go to Wakefield for the school was in the West Riding. A college friend lived on the outskirts of the city and I arranged to go there, for lunch, after the interview. Apparently there were two Education Offices: one for the City and one for the County. I did not know and when I asked my way, I was directed to the wrong place. I gave my name to an office girl and said I had an interview at eleven o'clock and she told me to take a seat and wait.

At five to eleven no other member of a short list had appeared and I went to the desk again to re-announce my presence. I was appalled to be told I must be at the wrong Education Office. A glance at my watch warned me that I had just lost a golden opportunity of the sort of headship I wanted. I could have taken that day-dream of an office girl and dumped her in the nearest horse trough.

A young man suddenly had me by the arm and was propelling me out of the building and yelling, 'Quick, follow me!' We ran as if we were being filmed for a 'Whodunnit', dodging pedestrians and traffic and avoiding one accident after another. Every moment I expected the police to arrest the young man I was chasing. People stopped shop window gazing to stare at my far from dignified progress and when I finally arrived at the right office I looked no more like a headmistress than Eve did. At the best of times I can never be described as elegant but this was one occasion I had really made an effort.

I found that my name had already been called. Others on the short list looked at me and thought, I'm sure, 'Well, that's one rival we can eliminate.' I followed an office girl down to the interview room outside which sat the next in alphabetical order to me.

The office girl knocked on the closed door, opened it and said, 'Miss Brown has arrived after all.' Without more ado I was told to step inside. I had no time to consult a mirror. No doubt I looked flushed and out of breath and rather young. I remember my apologetic excuse for being late. There was general laughter and everyone seemed to relax. All dignity had been lost somewhere along the High Street and there seemed nothing to lose. I felt a warmth coming from the interviewers but it may have been generated by my marathon on the streets. I could feel my hands sticky and my legs trembled as I returned to the waiting room to sit, for the first time, with other members of the short list.

The embarrassment of being called from the group and asked to return to the interview room to be formally offered the post, was acute. I looked at no one and felt extremely awkward and clumsy. It seemed to me that they were all looking at me as if I had stolen something of inestimable value.

At the home of my friend I relaxed, ate lunch and talked of other things. Now, twenty-seven years later, with such a rewarding and satisfying career behind me, I can look back on the thread on which all that happiness hung and my heart beats a little quicker remembering the burst of energy it had to produce to propel me across Wakefield for the most important half hour interview of my life.

At Easter there was a change of head and another term before my headship began. I spent a little of the holiday in Northumberland, talking to Peter about his village headship and visiting the chosen site at Budle Bay. We were naive enough to think that to do good would feel good. The Guides were ready to care and share and anticipated a glow of satisfaction which was never to materialise. We were to learn to give without getting rewards, to not be hurt or disappointed, or depressed and to expect no miracles.

During the spring bank holiday the Guides, in this area, celebrated their Golden Jubilee by camping at Steeton Hall, in one great happy get-together. Ann, who after her Queen's Guide Award had become a Sea Ranger, introduced me to the small crew of SRS *Spartan*, to the Skipper and to a Danish Guide of fifteen years who was in this country as an *au pair*. Almost immediately both of them became frequent visitors at The Currer, the Danish girl literally appearing every time she had a half-day. She was full of nervous energy, adolescent, amusing and extraordinarily likeable. The new Sea Ranger Skipper was a dreamer, quiet and just a little sad. She loved to come with Ann on Saturdays and sometimes she stayed over the weekend. She had recently taken a teaching post in the area and had been asked to skipper the *Spartan* crew. Until she emigrated to New Zealand she became part of the family.

Quite a serious problem arose. For financial reasons the ground floor of the Methodist Sunday School was sold. Our headquarters were on the first floor but the sale halved the church's accommodation and we had to give up our room and remove into what could only be described as a cupboard; a small box room we could not all get into even if we stood. We stored the equipment there and held our meetings in the big hall after the Girl's Brigade had vacated it.

The situation was impossible but there was little I could do about it in the whirl of activity caused by the Refugee Year. There was too much to do on the farm with sheds to build, cattle to rear and feed, hens to tend and eggs to wash. Father bought some pigs and altogether he and Margaret were working a sixteen-hour day. Margaret went less and less to badminton or the cinema. Thoughtlessly I added to the farmers' already full day by overloading the house with people. Whenever we could we held the Guide meeting at The Currer, fire lighting, tent pitching and practising for Sports Day. I believed it was an important part of their training to help with the hay, see the animals and absorb Margaret's philosophy regarding living things. The youngsters fed calves and pigs and drooled over the kids when Betty had babies. The farm made up, in part, for the loss of our headquarters but we knew that the arrangement could only be a temporary one and that eventually we would have to move elsewhere.

*   *   *   *   *

I had to prepare to leave a school in which I had taught for ten years. Had I left after the first year I may have mourned my pupils more but a teacher quickly learns that children come and go. There is no future for a teacher who finds this distressing. 'All must count but none too much.' Any pain there was, when the final parting came, was softened by the imminent arrival of the children from Germany.

There were to be eight; Poles, Rumanians and Germans, and they came from appalling conditions. They lived in cellars, wooden shacks and single rooms. Families were separated, some by deportation to the eastern sector, some by death. One child had seen her father shoot himself. Another took her basin to the soup kitchen daily as the single room she lived in, with six brothers and sisters, was too small to prepare meals. Several families had histories of illness, TB and starvation. One family was of noble descent and their ancestral home had been taken by Germans and turned into a hospital.

It would be unrealistic to think that these conditions were unique and peculiar to the Continent in the wake of war. There are disturbed children from distressing backgrounds in our own country but there is something different about refugees and we were unprepared for it and ill equipped to deal with it. The arrival of the children coincided with the last day of the ten years at my first village school. I remember the excitement as I hurried home to finish the packing of the camp equipment in the mill skips we had acquired and which were so suitable for sending our things on trains and boats. Packing for forty-one people to spend nearly three weeks by the sea was becoming a known job. I could almost mechanically assemble the tents and kitchen equipment and catering packs of food. I became quite maternal about those full skips. I can see them now piled in the station left luggage rooms, sitting on station buggies, being lifted by the crane onto the boat. They were a part of me I will never forget.

Having signed for their journey north east, Margaret and I went to collect the children. My whole life has been short of in-between times. I have literally gone from one thing to another without a pause to take a breath. My hands were still grey with station dirt and my clothes still smelling of tent canvas when we picked up the refugees and took them home with us. I think we were more than a little tired.

From friends and neighbours we had borrowed the extra single beds we needed and, miraculously, we were ready. We had promises of shoes and raincoats, pleated skirts and anoraks and we felt rich. Yet, in everything we had chosen wrongly. In everything we had prepared for normal children. Even expecting them to live on the farm was a mistake. They had always lived in crowded conditions in cities and they feared the isolation of the farm. It was too strange. It was our constant task during the preliminary week to search the town streets for the runaways.

The children were incapable of sitting down to a meal. We had prepared a varied menu and they wouldn't eat it. They didn't want anything cooked. The contents of a bag of tomatoes disappeared. Bowls of fruit were emptied at once, sandwiches were opened and meat thrown away, then filled with salt and pepper and eaten. Puddings were wasted, plates of meat and vegetables pushed away. Poor Mother! She had never experienced anyone who didn't like her food.

They were extremely critical of the clothes we had assembled. It was my fault. Clothes have always had to have a utilitarian purpose for us. As a child I had loved my farm clothes, my school uniform and the navy and blue of the

Guide Movement. Poor little refugees, to get landed with me! They wanted colour and anything serviceable was rejected. They wanted something gaudy and frivolous; they wanted cheap, flimsy skirts and frilly blouses and we had bought quality and uniformity.

The children were highly-strung, excitable and violent in their emotions. When displeased they swore expertly in German, wept, destroyed, and fought. When pleased they loved us equally violently, strangling us with passionate embraces and covering us with kisses. Anything they wanted they clung to tenaciously. All were wilful and demanding, only one ever tried to please us and only one did any work willingly.

At first, as was expected, not one trusted us. Each seemed afraid that we would beat her and withdrew flinchingly. They were children who had never played, whose experience of the streets shocked and frightened us. They lay on their beds moody and indifferent; our only success was the purchase of some magic painting books which they found very exciting and every page was quickly used.

Certain characteristics were present in all the children but they could be then divided into three different groups. Four of them, we felt, might possibly benefit from a holiday in England. They appeared to have at least one caring parent who had tried to preserve some self-respect. The two small Rumanians curtsied sweetly when introduced and their cases had an inventory of their few contents. The little Polish girl brought nothing but the clothes she wore but she folded them neatly when she got into bed. The eldest girl was embarrassed by her dirty hair. I felt very sorry for her when all the children had to have their hair washed with Derris soap. She was the only one who would work without pressure.

Two children had been mentally disturbed by cruelty and fear. They had seen things children should never see; they were the most needy and what we could give was not enough. Their fathers had been forcibly returned to the eastern sector and all hope had disappeared. They were withdrawn, sad and weak, both physically and mentally. They offered no resistance to the remaining two twelve-year-olds who led them astray outrageously. These were hardened sinners. They had already walked the streets and learned some English from their questionable association with the British and American soldiers. They needed constant watching and gave us a great deal of anxiety.

The children were not shy. They demanded food but rejected meals. After eating they disappeared, hiding in the wardrobes to avoid washing up. We employed patience, lifted them out of the wardrobes, put tea towels in their hands and barred the kitchen door. We held out sheets at bed-making and shopping baskets when in town but we had little success. I admire those teachers of unresponsive children. If we have had success, and there are many who think we have, it is because we have always worked with good materials. To be more admired are those who have nothing and succeed. We had The Currer and though it would have defeated many it was a 'talent'.

To be commended are those who receive no 'talents' and win. Similarly we have always worked with children who have had good sparking plugs; who only need the starter pressing and they are revving up like mad. Much more was expected of the man in the parable who received ten talents. The absent Master left us with many also.

The saga of the refugees was one of keeping on to the end of that particular road and making the best of it. I thanked God for Mother and Margaret, Janet, Ann and the Danish girl whose official role in all this, she said, was to be the sun when it was raining. She kept us sane and laughing and acted as interpreter when our communication floundered. She was a tonic when we needed medicine and saved the day as far as the Guides were concerned.

To add to our problems the children were accompanied by a German student who was to act as chaperon and interpreter. She was better suited to give them what they wanted than I was. She was frivolous and gaudy and I was too practical and drab. I had planned integration with my own children, and was prepared to treat everyone the same. I was wrong but in the environment we had created her opposition made things more difficult. She spent hours with them in the bedrooms, combing hair and experimenting with make-up, loaning them clothes and adapting those we bought for them until they were unsuitable for their specific purpose. She ruined rainwear by cutting away inches; she encouraged their promiscuity by making bikinis out of ordinary swimming costumes and took inches from the accordion pleated skirts until they looked like ballerinas. She aided and abetted their refusal to help by insisting that the children were here for a holiday and disapproved when we coaxed them to wash the dishes.

We dreaded to think what was going to happen when we introduced them to the Guides and camping. We taught children that success and survival depends on everyone pulling together and everyone lending a hand. These new children had been taught that survival was an individual affair. By fair means or foul their only thought was food, of the variety which needed no preparation. They had no idea of play. They did not know how to bath or wash their clothes; they could not adapt or improvise; they did not know how to share or save but we kept on trying.

After a few days we introduced them to their Guide hostesses and foster parents but offers of friendship were all rejected. Two disappeared in the afternoon and were found in the shopping centre in town. Two more escaped after tea and were located under the village cricket pavilion drinking beer with a couple of surprised village lads. The foster parents went home, very worried, with good cause.

By the end of the week they had begun to like being warm and comfortable and fed and it seemed a great pity forcibly to take them away to an empty field on an exposed north-east coast where it might rain and blow. It was a ridiculous arrangement. Whatever had made the authorities think that these children would want to go to camp with English children! I do believe it was the last thing they wanted to do but a three-week camp cannot be cancelled. Guide parents were going on holiday. The equipment had all gone in advance and the show must go on.

The night before we left, when all the kit bags had been carefully packed, we were amazed and delighted to see the children actually at play. They were running in and out of the barn, climbing over the yard walls and running in the Dyke Field. We couldn't believe it and were ready to shed tears of relief. Much later we found out what their game had been. Article by article their kit bags had been emptied and the contents hidden in the dark recesses of the barn, in the clumps of nettles beyond the yard wall and the calf shed mangers. Some things had been stuffed into the bathroom cupboard and some under beds and in wardrobes.

We were unable to sleep! Janet, Margaret and I repacked the kit bags and then kept a worried vigil, glad to half-wake the children early and bundle them onto a train before they fully realised what was happening. Mother had cried that the camp be cancelled. Father had shaken his head and said 'nowt'.

And after all it wasn't as bad as we expected. Things seldom are as bad as anticipation would lead one to believe.

Arriving on that very bare field the refugees sat in a sulky, unco-operative group, silently watching our pitching. After an initial failure to form any relationship with the foreign children the Guides decided, wisely, to have a good time anyway and for the most part they ignored the bewildered onlookers. The Danish girl was favourite and Jean's children were enthusiastically greeted by baby-loving teenagers.

In retrospect one gets a different view. So often, in the many teaching years that followed, did I see children who were misfits or very shy, sit against the playground wall just looking at normal children. I have seen introverts lean against the back of the classroom, not ready to join in lessons, the timid hold back when the others were enjoying movement or football or swimming and I've remembered the refugees and, in later years, the island children who often sat at the tent door just watching, and I've let them be.

With forty-one mouths to feed and all the hard work and fun of camp the refugees received a healthy share of neglect so, for a lot of the time during the first few days, they just sat and watched, first with scorn and later with interest. They saw normal children having a whale of a time, working and playing and singing and gradually they left the tent door and came towards us. The very difficult twelve-year-olds were to be seen with the washing up bowl, liberally squirted with liquid soap so that froth and bubbles overflowed. They were splashing the foam over themselves, the grass and anyone in the vicinity and they were singing. Surely a miracle had happened. The two young Rumanians were noticed to have acquired the glove puppets of one of the Guides and they begged me to watch their performance. For half an hour I sat and watched, an appreciative one-man audience watching and listening to a language I could not understand and laughing. 'Don't laugh,' cried the Danish girl. 'They are saying rude things!'

Gradually the fear that they would run away left us and we slept more peacefully. In camp we were coping. In the towns our troubles returned. On Holy Island, a stranger would have found it difficult to identity our two groups of children as all searched happily on the exposed seabed for hermit crabs and starfish and collected the discarded shells of colourful crustaceans.

Edinburgh was a nightmare. We thought we had overcome some of their eating problems until we went into the Zoo café. I had ordered a meal and it had been prepared on three, long trestle tables. I was at the head of the centre one with Margaret and Janet in charge on either side. Janet was having problems. She who copes with any emergency lifted her hands in a gesture of defeat and whispered across the aisle, 'Ah can't cope!' We had arranged a visit to the Zoo and the Castle and Holyrood House. We must have been crazy. There were too many temptations in the city. Janet's inability to cope in the café is remembered every time I acknowledge a state of flummox. I look at Margaret and say, 'Ah can't cope,' and we both get hysterics.

We let time work her miracles and we let the sea do what we could not. In the sea the refugees were water babies. Right from the start they loved it. The weather was kind; we swam every day and in the water the children integrated. Splashing and shouting is a language all children understand. I was so glad we had come to the coast.

Incredibly, after three weeks, we did not want to go home. Just when success might have been imminent we had to pack up our things and go. We had to hand over our little horrors to foster parents and we knew there would be problems. What we had thought so impossibly unwise had not been so bad after all. We could not look objectively at the project until we got home and even then we came to no real conclusions as to whether what we had done had been right. Had we even begun to teach Guides to give and refugees to live? Barely. But if they had gained a little from the experience, we had gained a lot. If they had been hurt by the unusual environment then our greater understanding had cost too much. We emerged from the experience, older and wiser. It eases my conscience to think that perhaps they did, too.

I have been scoffed at, many times, for taking children to camp, frequenting isolated places and avoiding the towns. They fail to understand. I just know that I would rather be with a lot of children on an empty shore than with a few children in the city or at a seaside resort and that I would rather have coped with the refugee problem for another six weeks in camp than bring them home to distribute them in families. Most of the temporary families did an admirable job and the summer passed. It is comforting to know that it is not only good things which come to an end. Now, I am ashamed of the emphasis we placed on such a small part of the refugee problem. There has never been a time in history when there have not been sufferers from the aftermath of a war. Some people spend all their lives trying to ease the pain of it. Could it be that war is too high a price to pay for freedom?

Chapter Seven

I f my part in alleviating the refugee problem was small so also was my part in educating the young. My appointment at the small village school was the top of the professional ladder for me. I loved it and I stayed. For most ambitious head teachers a small school is just a stepping-stone to a big one but I had no such aspirations. I was a wee bit apprehensive about my new appointment for I knew perfectly well that history was going to repeat itself.

I had already had several experiences of taking charge whilst someone older, more popular, but unwilling to take full responsibility, stayed to watch. On at least two occasions I had had to drive from the back seat. I was glad of this earlier experience because I was all too aware of the fact that the well-established infants' teacher, the only other member of staff, was exceptionally popular among children and parents and was my senior in years. I knew that the former Head had taken a new appointment two terms previously and that the supply Head had leaned heavily on his assistant for leadership and decision-making. The role of this beloved teacher had been virtually that of Head since the previous Christmas and, had she wanted the permanent post, I am sure she would have been accepted by the Authority. Ultimate responsibility for the school would be mine but the affection was already firmly fixed on the favourite. This I knew I must accept, generously and without jealousy, if things were to go smoothly. The measure of understanding which was to grow between us is surely demonstrated by the duration of our happy partnership. I drove from the back seat for a little while and the rest of the twenty-one years we were side by side. I never usurped her unique place in the hearts of the village people and I don't think I ever opened a door and went through first. My respect for her grew over the years. We laughed at the same things and we laughed often. This I believe is the most important factor of any relationship: a sense of humour which is tickled by the same feather. A sense of humour is not enough, for there are many variations. A good relationship depends on the feather.

I have cherished memories of my first day at that village school. I had had to rise earlier than before, for the school was farther up the valley. Most head teachers had a car. We could not afford one and loudly proclaimed that we didn't want one. We all had good hiking legs. Even Harry did not mind the walk. It was good for the physical health of the body and surely for the soul. I loved walking the cobbled way through the wood behind other hurrying workers heading for the mills and offices of the town or the railway station.

I appeared early, that first day, but not before the first arrivals, those eager children who were always there before me, leaning over the railing ready to carry my briefcase. My earliest impression of this two-teacher establishment, this family-unique, was of children under my feet. Previously I had experienced good teacher/children relationships but never before had so many children come so close, all at the same time. When hearing them read I had previously put an arm out to draw them close. Here there was no need. They leaned on me, got in front of me and when I stepped back I trod on one of them. They were like Betty the goat.

On that first morning they clustered round me in the yard and when I opened the heavy half-door into the tiled porch children entered too. The floor was shining with holiday elbow grease, what I could see of it for moving feet around me. I felt like a whale surrounded by pilot fish all asking questions and telling me what to do, showing me the staff room, entering it with me and offering to put on the kettle and ring the bell and give out the hymn books. I was utterly hypnotised by them. They were organising me. They continued to do so, in part, for over twenty years.

There were only forty-eight children but there seemed to be four hundred. They followed the caretaker into the staff room and they came in with the infants' teacher, offering holiday news, admiring her clothes and begging to ring the bell. Every time I opened the staff room door there was a different pattern of them. They were like a shaken kaleidoscope, re-grouping every time I looked. I could have shut the door on them, looked round my new domain, searched for the Admittance Register and composed myself to greet the mothers of the four new entrants I was expecting, but it would have been an insult. My colleague did not seem to think that children-under-our-feet was unusual and I could not find their presence assuming or precocious. The school had had no head teacher for nine months but there was distinctly an atmosphere and it must be the product of the infants' teacher and the children. I found it delightful. I looked at her, smiling and relaxed by the open fire, a cup of weak tea in her hand, attractive and vivacious, with at least half a dozen children leaning on her, asking questions, telling news and slipping shy little glances in my direction.

I fumbled awkwardly among the files, looking for the Admittance

Register as the sound of parental footsteps neared the staff room door. In they came with the four new entrants, their siblings and several friends eager to show them the cloakroom pegs and initiate them into the ways of this child-orientated school. The mothers supplied me with birth dates and the other data required by law and then turned from me to the infants' teacher, chatting in an informal, friendly way. Here is someone who knows the way, I remember thinking. I would be wise to follow. So, like one of the refugees, I stood watching on the outside. New brooms sometimes sweep away the old, eliminate the past and lay new foundations. I cherished old things. We had torn down no walls at The Currer. There are plenty of new things to do without disturbing the past. I knew that things had been done at this school before me. The previous Head had been liked and respected. My new colleague was mature and gifted in our profession. There was already a unique atmosphere worth preserving and nothing to fear from a fellow teacher who was so popular. Trouble comes if one inherits an old battleaxe. No one, I thought, will complain about my staff and no one ever did.

A newly appointed head teacher is a newcomer for a long time. Many years later a report, following the visit of several County Inspectors, stated, 'The atmosphere in this school emanates from the head teacher.' They were wrong. It would have been more correct to read, 'The inherited atmosphere of this school has been preserved by the head teacher.'

Nine o'clock came and some enthusiastic infants rang the bell. We just grouped together, informally, round the piano which stood in the large infant classroom. The pianist was one of the eleven-year-old girls. I looked at the children, little and big, families like peas from one pod, neighbours side by side, an eleven-year-old sharing a hymnbook with a five-year-old. We sang and then they all looked at me and my headship had begun. They were waiting for me to say something. I made a few comments and each time I spoke one or other, or several at once, responded. I was used to children who listened in Assembly and did not interrupt. Everything I said brought a response and I jumped quickly from one thing to another to prevent myself being outnumbered. I said they'd have to help me remember names and they began at once. I hoped they'd had a good holiday and there was a definite move of the whole school towards me to tell about it. I looked helplessly at my colleague and decided that lessons should begin.

Few heads have enjoyed their first week of the appointment as much as I did. I thought that I had taught in a village school before but the four-teacher establishment I had just left was nothing like this amusing family. Joan called them her 'Giles Kids' and no wonder. What a lot of laughter we were to share in the many years that followed.

By the end of the first week I knew that we were going to laugh. TGIF, we used to say in college: Thank God It's Friday! I stayed later than usual, for the end-of-week clerical work was to do. There were no secretaries in those days. I quite enjoyed the administrative side and, having a finger on every button, I really knew what was going on. Years later, when the Authority provided clerical assistance, it was nice to have another friend but she took many of the jobs I liked to do myself.

On this first Friday I left late. The mills close early on Fridays now, but in 1960 they blew the 'Wow' long after the home-time bell. I had missed the bus I was aiming for. Whenever I do this my itchy feet take me to the next stop or further if time permits. There was no one at the next *en route*, but a queue formed immediately behind me. A workshop nearby must have opened its doors and spilled out the tired workers. No one spoke. It was a lovely September evening and I saw one of the infants appear over the railway bridge carrying a bulky shopping bag which all but trailed along the pavement.

'Mith Brown,' he called. Children seldom say 'Hello', they just call out a name and wait for you to reply.

'Hello, John, been shopping?' I asked.

'Well ...' the young man paused dramatically, playing to my audience and unaware of the amused smiles in the waiting queue.

'Bet yer don't knaw what'th in thith bag? Ah 'lectric light bulb went an' when me mam thold ah wather t'Mithuth Mitchell ah Janet'th potty wath in it an' nun ov ye ovverth'd fetch it, tho I did an' ah've gotten ve 'lectric light bulb and ve potty an ve fith an' chipth fer wer tea!' Regardless of the danger to the electric light bulb he shook the interesting bag and everyone in the queue burst out laughing.

Some months before I had agreed to be Assistant Guider in a County Cadet Unit which met monthly at the city home of the Guider. We met however at The Currer for the September meeting. Whilst it was in progress our fifteen-year-old Danish girl arrived in a state of some distress. She said she had forgotten to post a letter, had jumped off a moving bus and fallen. She was working as *au pair* within a very well-respected family in a neighbouring town but instead of running home for help she came to us. We got a friend to run the two of us to the hospital; an X-ray revealed a fracture and that was the end of her being of any use to a mother with several small children and a baby. It was decided that the girl had better stay with us until a booking could be made for her to return to Denmark. It was quite a traumatic month for the girl was highly-strung and quick-tempered but extraordinarily lovable and we had a lot of laughs as well as a few frustrated tears. She helped Margaret on the farm in a one-arm capacity and I took her up to stay with Jean two days before putting her on the boat at Grimsby. She was a very colourful character, but exhausted us. She needed us too much!

Joan was easy to work beside. She accepted my authority to administrate and I respected her longer experience and professional skill. She was an excellent teacher long before I joined her. She never shouted. 'No louder than "lovely",' my college lecturer in infant education used to say. 'I like this school,' one child said, on a temporary stay with an aunt whilst a new baby was born, 'there are no big shouts!' Visiting book representatives, workmen, even advisors never knew which one of us was head teacher.

There were things I naturally wanted to change. One was the venue of the mid-day meal and the seating arrangements. At twelve, the dinner children and the two of us donned coats and outdoor footwear and filed in an informal crocodile through the churchyard to the parish rooms, where Mrs Hartley had laid tables and dinner was waiting. I didn't object to the walk even though it was time-consuming to dress the children in wintertime, but I did object to the distance isolating us from our dinner lady. It was also the custom for the teachers to sit on a separate table from the children and for Mrs Hartley to eat standing up in the kitchen. Everyone's enjoyment of a school meal depends on teachers sitting with children and I very soon begged the authority to use the third classroom for dinners and make a small kitchen out of the end of the cloakroom. In the meantime we walked our brood daily through the churchyard and became familiar with the gravestones and the flora and fauna of the overgrowth. We did this long enough for an accumulation of memories of the Dickensian dinners in the dismal parish room. The plaster was peeling from the walls in many places and the trestle tables and forms were drab and ancient and little improved by the covering of check tablecloths.

Later we managed to order the dinners in tureens and sit in family groups with teachers and dinner lady in maternal roles at the head of three tables. Until then dinners were collected from the counter and our over-generous dinner lady filled each plate. Some could not eat such a large amount and leftovers had to be scraped into the pig bin. Well do I remember our very talkative Kathleen carrying her unemptied plate in front of the staff table, talking so much she did not see the child in front stop; she walked into his back and the plate of left-overs was plastered on her chest. With a gasp and a giggle she lisped, 'Mith Brown, ooh, thee what'th 'appened t' me dinner!'

Mrs Hartley was equally generous to the staff. Newly admitted David was passing our table one day when Joan had put aside the part of the meal she had found *de trop*. He tapped her plate, as I suppose his mother often did, and said, 'Eat that up!' It amused me to see Joan pick up her knife and fork and obey. What else could she do when we never had one rule for us and one for them.

Our return from the mid-day meal preceded our supervision of the children at play either in the schoolyard on in the Rec across the road. Joan and I used to sit together in the playground, or on the grass hillock in the field, or stand at the classroom window. This dinner-time and play-time chore, before the days of ancillary help, made us easy prey for children who wished to stay indoors on inclement days. We were more ready than most teachers to have them under our feet at break, more willing than most to forget play-time altogether when gales swept down the valley or the mad March wind made our brood too wild and excited. On the other hand how nice it was to extend the playtime on beautiful days whatever the season. Joan and I would kick off our shoes in the Rec and sit garlanded with daisy chains whilst six-year-old Jill teetered round the field wearing Joan's high-heeled shoes. The swing was continually in use, the trees always had human monkeys and children perpetually rolled down the 'ant hill', a misnomer, for no ant would have stayed there a minute.

The children were repeatedly told not to cross the road into the Rec without supervision but on that November day of my first year as headteacher, Roy and Ian decided to anticipate this and ran into the field whilst we were visiting the toilet and washing our hands. Feeling the Rec lonely and regretting their decision to test me out and see what I would do to boys who blatantly disobeyed, they decided to nip back quickly and find out another time. A line of more patient, obedient children lined the railings waiting to be watched across the road so there were plenty to witness what happened. The naughty boys did not hear the car creep over the canal bridge and the high wall, unfortunately, obscured sight of any vehicle smaller than a cattle wagon. They dashed carelessly into the path of the silent car and were thrown onto the verge. The playing children ran to join the Rec queue at the railings and all were too curious and shocked to even think of coming to tell us. They dumbly watched the driver of the car get out, lift two limp bodies into his car and drive off. Only then, did anyone come to tell us.

I was in the staff toilet and heard the commotion as forty children ran into school with the news. "Ss Brown!' they were shouting, "Ss Armstrong! Ian an' Roy a' dead. The've bin runned over!' I dashed out of a toilet quicker than I've ever done. Children were crying and grabbing our skirts and burying their heads into our laps. Out of the general chaos we sorted out the relevant details and allowed ourselves to be escorted outside to see the skid marks on the road. It was as if some UFO had swooped down, taken two of our children and left the tell-tale scorch marks to bear witness.

I think I spent the worst half-hour of my life. It was made only fractionally easier by being fully occupied pacifying crying children. Reason demanded I give the driver time to get to a hospital. I could not understand why a man, having knocked down two children, should drive off with them. On a lonely country lane, perhaps, but not just outside a school playground at dinnertime!

The minutes ticked by so slowly. Little village schools had no telephones in those days. The telephone kiosk was just across the main road, outside the post office. I was trembling when I entered the red box. There were two hospitals within a five-mile radius of the school. The first hospital I rang had had no recent admissions of children. I fumbled with the dial for the second, wondering whatever I would do if I got another negative answer. Yes, came the reply, two ten-year-old boys had just been admitted into Casualty, alive. My breath was released slowly. I explained the hardly believable truth. Whilst in my care the two boys had been knocked down by a car, picked up by the driver and whisked away. I asked for some reassurance that there was no serious injury but the hospital was noncommittal for the boys had not yet been seen by a doctor.

Only one parent was on the phone. She had to be told at once. I tried to soften the blow. If I'd had a car I could have picked up both mothers and dashed to the hospital. I ran all the half-mile to the second child's home to tell his mother. It was easier to do so than to phone but so much slower. When I felt I could leave her I ran back to school.

There was a police car outside the playground measuring the skid marks of the tyres and writing things down in his little book. He came inside. Over a cup of tea he told us that the driver of the car had been one of the local ambulance drivers and it had been instinctive to rush the children straight to hospital. I tried to excuse him for not calling to the row of watching children, 'Fetch a teacher!' Anyone else might have done but he was a professional, more competent than I and the feelings of a very new, very young headmistress were secondary. So I gave my statement to the arm of the law and filled in the necessary Accident Form naming two eleven-year-olds as witnesses and recorded the incident in the Log Book. The children dashed home to tell their parents all the gory details and I tidied the disarray and left the empty school. I caught the bus into town and the bus to my home village and walked along the five fields with heavy feet. The dogs and goats ran to meet me. It was almost dark.

Everything was normal. The cattle had come from the moor and were standing against the back of the barn and pressed against the yard gate. The mud was deep and well manured with their loose droppings for the new growth of the meadows, after the hay is taken, which we call 'fog', is full of water. I pushed my way past their steaming bodies and climbed the yard gate. In a short while I knew I could forget the stress of the awful afternoon and involve myself in helping to fodder the herd and feed the calves.

November brings a mass of wet leaves stripped from the sycamore. There is a dampness, a smell of wet bracken and fungus and decay. A wet mist clung to the dogs and when I opened the door they entered too, shook their wet coats in the front porch and left all their muddy footprints on the floor. Once inside the house the floodgates opened and I sat down and wept.

The two boys were detained in hospital for only a few days as is customary after concussion. Neither had suffered any serious injury. I was shocked into a greater vigilance over children in my charge. I have taken hundreds to remote places, climbed mountains, bathed on isolated beaches, walked incredible distances on dangerous footpaths. I have camped with them in gales and heat, I have taken them on trains, buses and boats, perpetually filled the Land Rover with a dozen at a time and, thank God, that incident outside the school yard is the nearest I ever came to disaster. With children, that is. On the farm we dice with danger nearly every day.

To Ian it was somewhat of an anticlimax to be discharged with nothing to show of the accident which so nearly cost him his life. He fabricated outrageously and told us they'd taken out his tonsils whilst he was in. A few months later he sprained his ankle badly on the football pitch and I had to carry him to the far outskirts of the village on my back. A head teacher without a car must be pretty strong.

I have had other children who have fabricated to impress, another who had an imaginary operation. His was even more outrageous. Simon's feet went every which way when he walked. I was guilty of reminding him too often. 'Walk straight,' I used to say. 'Your feet are all over the place. What a funny grown-up you will look, walking all cockeyed!' There is a limit to how much nagging a fellow can take. The summer holidays were over and we were back at school. It was the first Movement lesson of the autumn term and we were concentrating on footwork. To forestall any teacher's comment this young man informed me, 'My feet are all right now, Miss Brown. I've had an operation.'

'You have? When?' I asked.

'In the holiday,' was the bold reply. 'The doctor sent me to hospital an' now they are all right.'

I saw his mother a few days later and asked about the operation. 'Which operation?' was her immediate reaction. She wanted to scold but I begged her to let well alone. Simon now had to live up to his lie.

The need for winter headquarters for the Guide meeting became acute. It was a delicate situation for the church thought the accommodation it provided was adequate and told me that if we removed we would be at fault and a new church company formed. I had no wish to make the break so clean and had never failed to take the monthly church parade. It was not unpleasant walking to town, through the woodland, on one Sunday in four, but the dark nights were forcing us indoors and Margaret and I decided we would have to search for a permanent home for our busy family. We found one on the second floor of a building housing offices and shops. It was a mile out of town and few of the girls came from families with cars but the streets were busy with people in those days and quite safe. Raftered and reasonably spacious, this loft accommodation served us for over twenty years without an increase in rent.

I remember taking the Patrol Leaders for our first viewing. We walked the mile from town, jangling the key loaned to us by the manager of the local Co-op who owned the buildings. We needed a den, somewhere to learn proficiency in all our Guiding skills. Those who had played hostess to refugees for six weeks after camp had had an ordeal. A new interest must be found at once.

We opened the door on the unknown and climbed the dirty wooden steps to the first floor where there was a filthy, old-fashioned toilet. Then, with increasing excitement, we climbed to the next storey, the loft. There was a small antique kitchen to the right. The shallow yellow stone sink had been there forever and the ancient gas cooker looked as if it would have a struggle to work at all.

Finally we opened the door on the 30ft by 20ft loft. The principals and the queens were exposed, offering all sorts of rope ladder fun and the apex of the roof was timbered. There were two windows on either side and a solid fuel stove in the fireplace. The room had been previously used by some minor religious sect and was stacked with dusty forms and an old piano. The curtains were festooned with cobwebs and dust lay everywhere.

There was silence from the teenagers who saw only the dirty mess. Margaret and I saw the walls papered and the paintwork enamelled. We saw corners inhabited by busy patrols, with charts, notice boards, patrol boxes and stools. We saw rope ladders hanging from the beams, Orion, The Plough and Cassiopeia pasted on the roof timbers, and cushions in a campfire circle.

What stories those four walls could tell of the children who met there, sometimes several evenings a week, of their hopes and plans, of the games they played and the skills they learned. They became a 'happy breed', dedicated to every activity and service, be it party, stunt, competition, fund raising project or campfire hour. It was soon transformed with paper and paint and posters. There were patrol flags and mascots, totem poles and gaudy remains from Christmas parties, gory ones from Halloween and favourite gadgets and photographs from camp. New recruits joined at ten and could not bear to leave at sixteen. By that time I was a Sea Ranger Skipper and they stayed with me until they went to college or university or got engaged to be married.

And the background to everything was The Currer and its increasing number of animals and the constant struggle we had to find money to feed them and build sheds to house them. Lack of money breeds disasters. Cheap calves are more difficult to rear. Shortage of funds made us shy of laying in adequate stores for the winter. To buy when the need arises is all a poor man can do and in our case it always meant buying when the weather was at its worst. Margaret was constantly improvising, blocking up gaps to prevent draughts in the winter or tearing down the hessian sack curtains to prevent the cattle dying of claustrophobia when a warm spell came. She was always hunting for duckboards to erect quick partitions and always dismantling them and putting them somewhere else and we were forever moving the woodpile because we needed its floor space.

It was a continual struggle to keep wintering-out cattle alive. They clustered round the farmhouse for warmth and shelter, deepening and fouling the mud. Inside the sheds the bedding grew deep and where snow and rain blew in and where cattle were fed and watered, the bedding was soft and dangerous. Many a Christmas morning found us mucking out the sheds with four-pronged forks. Margaret and Father carried thousands of buckets of calf milk and water. Two and a half gallon buckets of liquid pig jock are heavy.

The suckling herd was fed and watered outside. Bales of hay were back-carried long distances to find a clean area each day. The fallen hayseeds reseeded the patch. Dangerously close cattle would be trying to steal from the bale before it was dropped. It is somewhat alarming to have a whole, hungry herd behind you. At weekends I used to let Margaret, who was less afraid, go first. Nearer to the ground than I am, she is not so easily toppled over. When the herd was higher up the hillside and we could take out the bales without having to force our way between them, we had to beware of the hungry mass suddenly stampeding down the hillside. The first bale was never released before danger arrived in the guise of a hundred animals whose only affection for us was cupboard love. 'Don't turn your back on 'em!' Father would yell. 'Face t' 'erd.' A formidable thing to do! They came so fast and slithered the last few yards through the mud and we would wave our arms about and shout aggressively and just when we thought only a prayer would save us from being trodden on, the herd would divide and our held breath be released. When frost hardened the earth there was always the danger that one would break a leg, fall and be trampled on, or fail to stop and go hurtling over the banking.

Shortage of money encourages a do-it-yourself attitude to everything. In winter the increasingly old tractor was wrapped up and put away and we relied on backs to carry. Father carried bales until he was very old indeed. Margaret has carried an incalculable number. She twice handles at least four thousand a year. One of our guests saw the mini-haystack walk through the yard one day and called to me, 'Jean, come quick. Look at Margaret! Look! She's carrying a bale on her back!'

I began to take a rucksack regularly to school to bring back the things Mother found too heavy to carry. I became well known on the buses as the woman who was forever struggling with long pieces of wood, zinc baths and buckets. I remember taking a half-grown dead pig in my rucksack, on the bus, to the vet's for a postmortem. We would frequently flounder through the snow with sacks of corn left in the village.

I was content, the first year, to reproduce the old and some of the goodly inheritance which was mine, I kept. Never did I tamper with the Christmas party. It was obvious that everyone but me knew about the party. They knew the games we had to play, the people we had to invite and I had no wish to do anything but agree to everything. Muriel must be asked, with her small daughter, because she had been a teacher at this school until falling numbers had made her redundant. Mrs Horner must come to help Mrs Hartley in the food department. Children are creatures of tradition. It is their joy and their security.

Joan and I were asked to organise the games at the Village Institute party, a job we enjoyed for several years and a pleasure we only terminated because it became increasingly difficult to get there without a car. The first Christmas there was a blanket of freezing smog which petrified the winter trees and made my double bus journey home a treacherously slow crawl. I alighted at the end of the field footpath unable to see a yard ahead. The school children who sang in the church choir begged me to attend the candlelight service. Margaret and I struggled to the first of twenty-one carol services through the sea of mud.

Now, when the animals are kept back from the house by fences and gates and have few reasons to come into the yard, and when there is a sheet of concrete around us which can be kept swept and dry, visitors cannot have any idea of the Mud Days. Our mud had to be struggled through to be believed. Those who have never lost a wellington and its welly-sock in twelve inches of well-manured, often rained-on mud, and have never felt it ooze grittily between bare toes, have no real appreciation of its malignance. The house stands on a small hillock and each year the mud grew deeper around us. In summer it never completely dried and in winter only the frost controlled it. It surrounded us like a moat, many yards wide and there was no escape from it. It slithered like an oil slick into the yard and we were constantly removing it with the barrow and muck shovel. It deepened at the edges of the concrete for we had been able to afford no more than an apron of it in front of the house. It slithered from the slope behind the laithe to lie deep against the dry stone wall. Water from it oozed between the stones and in through the back door of the laithe. A river of thin manure flowed through the barn, wetting the straw lying on the centre cobbles, between the wheel flags. Lastly it found its way out by the huge laithe porch doors to continually wet and discolour the concrete in front of the house door. When frost came this brown rivulet was halted and a golden glacier appeared, growing daily and presenting problems. Many a time have feet gone every which way and milk from a carried bucket has added white ice to the brown rink. Smog had frozen on the trees on that first Sunday before Christmas but had managed only the thinnest of crusts on the mud: certainly not one strong enough to take the weight of Margaret and me and our rucksacks full of Christmas presents to be left in school for some eager errand boys to take to the post office.

The church was packed. Few of the faces were known ones but, among the sea of Christmas strangers, little eyes twinkled and lips whispered, 'Miss Brown'. Next day the children came to school with polish and dusters; we took down the bunting and polished and scrubbed like an army of Mrs Mops. Something of value was lost when polished desks were replaced with Formica.

We needed to borrow more money and Father was too old to persuade the bank manager to increase the overdraft. I would not have known what to do but it was incredible how Father could solve his problems. Compared with some, the financial dilemma was easy. He sold the farm to the three of us, Harry, Margaret and me; we bought it with a mortgage from the building society and raised enough capital to keep it going. Less than five years after Grandmother died, less than two years after coming to The Currer, the most rightful owner of it sold it to his children. It was a demonstration of complete trust. Whatever we do with this little piece of Yorkshire's broad acres must always be a memorial to him. He farmed it with gratitude, not arrogance. It is ours for a little while to do the same.

In buying the place we sealed our fate and completely forgot the transaction until recently, when I was looking through the accounts of 1960.

So completely have we shared everything, who was the rightful owner was immaterial. Everything belonged to all. The responsibility of land, cattle and Harry was less heavy because we each carried an equal share of the load. That we were tied irrevocably, that we were owned by land rather than landowners, did not seem a burden. Had either Margaret or I wanted to opt out and go our separate ways there would have been a frightful mix-up to sort out but neither of us wanted more than we had got: she her farm, me my school and my Guide Company. The chains which bound us to The Currer and to the family were quite invisible. We never felt them tighten for we never pulled away. There has to be an extraordinary person at the head of a household to do what Father did and to know so surely that it was all right.

Chapter Eight

The seasons in the country have a tremendous impact and, in the years to follow, the pattern of them became part of a very pleasant way of life. Signs of spring came so much earlier in the valley than it did on the hillside. We used to look for the first snowdrops in the Remembrance Garden, at the foot of the churchyard, any time after 18 January.

Snow does not lie as long on the riverbank as it does here at 1,000 feet but snow in the schoolyard was something we all remember.

When it began to fall in great flakes of crystal the canniest of children would imagine a need to go to the toilet which meant crossing the small yard and provided the opportunity to see how deep the fall was. Eyes would perpetually leave the exercise books and wander to the window. Mine did, too. Should they notice this, they would take it as a willingness on my part for them to leave their desks and flock to the window just as they did when the swans flew in to land on the canal or, more recently, the helicopter swooped. I loved this gathering of children at the window, listening to their exclamations and interpretations. They would clamber on the sills, kneel on the desks, lean on the radiators and the cupboards and on me; they were very vocal and their language would be full of dialect. Later their written work would be more colourful and uninhibited. At playtime they would dash out without coats. We would have to call them in to button them up, and extend their play. Snow would fly in all directions, from thrown balls and sliding feet intent on making a treacherous ice rink in the playground. The bell to call them in meant a wet mess in the porch, steaming gloves and socks on the radiators, a pair of trousers hanging over a chair back before the fire and someone sitting with a towel round his waist. There would be a jumble of wellies in the porch pool, a helpful girl mopping it up and a sea of red faces waiting for me to start the next lesson.

On the first warm day we would walk up to the Hall to see the carpet of snowdrops and handle the already-bursting elderberry twigs and the swelling sticky buds of the horse chestnut. We would kneel in Parson's Walk to find the first half-inch of the bluebell shoots and walk up The Folly or along the wall enclosing the beech wood, heads tilted upwards to catch every movement of a newly awakened squirrel. Then, tip-toeing through the paddock, we would admire the newborn lambs and talk about the lambing and tupping, calving and farrowing. Finally we would romp through the gate onto the moor and make a dash for The Pinnacle.

When children used to run in from the Rec to tell me that one of Mr Baines's cows was calving and beg permission to ring him up and tell him, I used to view the line of watching children with some fear, for the miracle of birth is not always straightforward. I worried equally when children were told too soon about a new baby in the family. I knew from experience that not all human births are without tragedy. I have seen children's distress and perplexity over a miscarriage, a false pregnancy or a stillborn baby and beg parents not to be too hasty in announcing the news. Even if all goes well a long waiting time does not necessarily prepare a child for the arrival of a sibling.

Frequently I used to ring the bell early to bring in the watching children on the wall, inwardly quaking lest the miracle be not quite perfect. Most calves are born easily and naturally, in a field away from the herd and people. Some animals can halt the birth if there is an audience. If everything is going fine we stay away. The mother-to-be can cope best in privacy. But animal and human birth is not without pain and problems and sometimes things go absolutely wrong.

Scores of times I have heard Margaret get up during the night to peep into the laithe or a shed when a calving was expected. I have frequently heard her mutter on return, 'It's a wye,' or 'Your turn. Look when you get up. She's taking a long time,' and occasionally, 'I'm sending for the vet.'

There was a very bad calving during one March night in 1961, in the laithe adjacent to the house. It was a cold and draughty place bereft of the summer harvest. Water persistently found its way in from the back where the floor was below the field level; cold water from underground, wetting the bedding and chilling the atmosphere. High, cobwebbed and dark, the barn was our nearest neighbour. Its entrance was only a few feet from our door and it was an arena for all kinds of farce and drama and tragedy.

It wasn't an ideal place to keep hay for the entrance was low and determined the height of the load. It was high enough in the days of horse and hay cart but too low for today's machinery. The tractor and trailer came through but there was no room for the unskilled to manipulate and the lorries bringing straw had to park outside and the bales be carried in somewhat slowly. In

September, when the straw was delivered, I have seen the barn full to the door and a carelessly smoked cigarette would have made our neighbour an inferno too near for us to escape.

Vermin were hard to control when the barn was full of food. Cats did their job so well that we can count on one hand the number of mice which have entered the wrong door but, try as we might, we could never stop the occasional rat from finding its way into the underdrawing above the bedrooms. It always coincided with overnight guests whose sleep was less deep than ours. There was, I am sure, some amplification of the sound for, big though a rat might be, the sound of its journey across the ceiling was out of all proportion to its size. We were embarrassed as we woke to petrified screams from our guests. Time after time my sister would climb through the small manhole at the top of the stairs and investigate. I would balance precariously on stand steps below the hole, the upper part of me in the loft, handing Margaret a bucket of cement and directing a torch in the right direction for her to attempt to find the entrance hole. We were never successful and eventually admitted defeat. The purlins were so close to the eaves that it was impossible to find any breach in the wall. Eventually we resorted to leaving poison there. It was a last resort for poison presents problems of a different and thoroughly revolting variety.

Stray rats continued to find entry but now they seemed to get their timing differently. Instead of visiting us at the same time as our friends they tended to arrive about a week earlier. They feasted and died in the wall cavities amongst the random packing of four hundred-year-old stone. On the morning of the arrival of our guests the smell of decomposing rat would find its way into the house, either into the staircase, or at the entrance to our sitting room. Death has an unmistakable smell and when that smell invaded the sitting room we knew we hadn't a hope of eradicating it until time had elapsed and nature completed her work.

On this particular cold, March night, Cindy's slacks had dropped and we knew she would calve. The pelvic bones had fallen to make room for the birth and there should be a calf by morning. Margaret's night would be disturbed. She only called Father in an emergency. Rousing him always disturbed me and then all three of us would be up. Father was the best man of the three when things were going wrong and, on that occasion, they were very bad indeed.

After hours of straining, Cindy had only calved the forefeet of what was, undoubtedly, a very big calf. Our help was less than useless for we managed to calve the head and then met resistance from the enormous shoulders. There wasn't any way they were going to get through the available opening. The calf was going to be strangled in no time. Jed had left the house with Margaret much earlier. We called her to come in, again and again, and I rang for the vet. Our dogs bark furiously when anyone arrives and a stranger in the dead of a bleak March night might very easily get bitten. So Margaret called in Jed again but she did not come. There was no time to persist. There were two lives in danger so the dog was forgotten. Cold and defeated we paced the yard waiting for the headlights of the veterinary car. The whole head of the calf protruded but Cindy had ceased straining and though the bag round the nose had been broken, so the calf could breathe, it was slowly being strangled.

No Jed appeared to announce and deter the vet's arrival but we thought nothing of it for we were in danger of losing both cow and calf. Cindy had survived the lead poisoning. We did not want to lose her now, at a calving.

There is something comforting about the arrival of medical aid be it doctor or vet. Responsibility for life is suddenly in more competent hands but, even so, I hate a bad calving. The winch, used to drag out a dead or dying calf, too big for a small heifer to calve alone, seems to be a cruel piece of primitive machinery. It isn't, of course, and often it works miracles extracting the calf with the ease a dentist's tool takes out a tooth. On this occasion even the winch was useless. After hours of labour, our efforts and then the vet's professional skill, there were still only two front feet and a sagging lifeless head with swollen, protruding tongue. The calf was dead and the heifer would follow suit.

But the skill of the veterinary surgeon is superb. As the eastern skies began to pale ours performed the difficult operation of taking away the calf in pieces, difficult because of the grave danger of septicaemia. Ours was so proficient that, after a long period of intensive care, Cindy lived. There was no sign of Jed as we wearily crawled, almost fully dressed, into bed.

My alarm went almost immediately. In a sickly stupor I staggered into the barn. My eyes avoided the sack which covered the dismembered body of the calf. Few know how much a farmer loves his animals. They think he farms either for money or to produce food. He farms that animals might live. Money is a by-product that enables him and them to do so. Very little of it enters the farmhouse or the family purse.

I thought I might find Jed curled up in the straw or licking up the cleansings. There would be plenty of smells to attract home a scavenger like Jed who never went further than the village to meet the last bus and bring Margaret home. But only Cindy lay half buried in the straw, exhausted. I called for Jed and I wandered across the yard and did my morning check of the calf sheds. There was no dog. I picked my way carefully through the sleeping calves, whistling short 'come here' notes but no dog appeared.

Back in the house the kettle was boiling. I made a quick cup of coffee and put on my coat, picked up my briefcase and, at the foot of the stairs, called, 'Margaret! I'm going. I can't find Jed.'

I set off across the fields, looking everywhere, searching for a beloved friend. The real task must be left to Margaret for I had children waiting to be taught. For her it was to be a day of looking. Father did most of the chores and Margaret wandered the 170 acres searching every nook and cranny, every hollow of the moor, every bend of the streams, every thicket of hawthorn in the wood, not once but several times, again and again in an agony of fear and sorrow. She went up into the village leaving a trail of enquiries, asking everyone if they had seen our dog. Our collie seldom went out of sight. The road with its occasional midnight car was a long way from home. Our dog was devoted to Margaret, her shadow, almost. That she was nowhere to be found was scarcely believable.

Since our removal to The Currer Jed had always slept in the house, on the rug before the Aga, but Jed was not a house pet. She was essentially an outdoor dog, an animal of the wild with primitive instincts. Her pups were always born in inaccessible places in tunnels under the hay or in the cave under the fuel tank and she regurgitated food to feed them. If an old hen died and the stiff body was thrown out of the deep litter hut or if piglets were stillborn, Jed found them.

One of our neighbours in the village was having problems with leg paralysis amongst his hens and the dead ones were thrown out onto a pile. Perhaps on that disastrous March night, the scent of them, more easily detected on the sharp midnight air, attracted our dog and encouraged it to overstep the boundary and become a scavenger. Jed had lived a long time in the village. She was ten years old and canny and if she smelled dead hens I think she would investigate. Be it as it may the news came to us indirectly many weeks later than this farmer shot a dog prowling round his hen cotes in the middle of the night. He never confessed, but we believe it was Jed. We did not point an accusing finger. He was not to know that it was only our dog, a harmless collie bitch, accidentally let out of the house at night owing to a cruel calving. Had he still believed the dog was a killer he would have come, friend or no friend, to complain. Not knowing was almost unbearable for Margaret. Gradually she had to accept the fact that the dog was lost. For months she expected to come across Jed's body in some obscure hollow but she never did.

*   *   *   *   *

In March and November each year there were the eleven-plus examinations for grammar school entry. In the small family atmosphere of my school these brought more pleasure than pain. Preparation for the exam forged an intimate teacher/child relationship. The children in their final year spent a lot of time grouped round my desk or gathered in the staffroom, often loitering after school to finish off exercises or have fun with an intelligence test. Some of my most memorable moments were with the eleven-plus group searching for the right definition. 'What's a briefcase? Why is it called brief?' asked Jill one day and the whole group fell in hysterics when I said it was so named because a solicitor kept his briefs in it.

And I remember the day Roger stood beside me as we searched for the feminine of stag. Not a child knew. 'Try, Roger,' I encouraged. 'Be ...' I hinted slapping his firm behind with a clue-giving whack. I watched his unbelieving amazement before he answered. 'Is it arse?'

We used to say that the test day was a Coffee Morning. The date was always secret and I would make the only announcement necessary at Assembly.

'Today is a Coffee Morning,' and the crazy kids would cheer. For the handful sitting the test there was always mid-morning coffee and biscuits between the arithmetic and the English papers and the children thought this was great and we became known as the Coffee School. There were some lesser brethren who thought that C of E spelled coffee. We always had a pass rate of 100% because I told them they would either pass for the Grammar School or for the local Secondary School and that if they did not pass they would stay with us. No one ever did and unsuccessful candidates used to run home shouting, 'Ah've passed fer t' Secondary School.'

One child only found the exam unacceptable and cried throughout the November paper, muttering, 'It's pathetic,' and slobbering into a very wet handkerchief. He distracted other children but his own wet paper had enough right answers to ensure him a place at the Grammar School. I thought his behaviour had jeopardised other children's chances, so in the March test, he was sealed in the staff room with Margaret silently witnessing the tears. In the summer he went off very cheerfully to Grammar School education.

Spring excites us but no more than it does the calves. On the first warm day my father's grin would be from ear to ear as he opened the door on the baby herd. All of us wanted to watch. Like shy rabbits peeping out of the warren they hesitated on the threshold in unbelief. Then, suddenly appreciating their freedom, their ecstasy was complete and the charge of the Light Brigade was inferior.

Spring arrives in the valley long before it visits the hilltop but when it comes there is no mistaking the fact. The snowdrops in the valley have long faded and the daffies are dancing before the sap stirs in our sycamore. It is April before there are smells and sounds of spring on the pastures which were so recently the moors. But the very tardiness adds to the glory of it. Spring does not come slowly to The Currer as it comes in the valley, with a January bursting of some of the elderberry, the early bulb flowers, the colts-foot, wood anemone and dog myrtle. There are butterburr and celandine and winter aconite all in bloom near my school whilst winter stays at The Currer. Then, suddenly, it comes with a brilliant rush and it would seem that all the meadow flowers bloom at once.

It is April before the grass grows. The smell of it is quite unmistakable and is as intoxicating and as welcome as the smell of the sea must be to a sailor who has been long inland. It rushes in through the open door and infects the household with an activity bug and rids the house of winter dust and germs. The cattle leave the sheds early and eat the grass faster than it grows and should it be greener on the other side of the fence and they can find a breach in the boundary they are away. How often have Margaret and I hurried to bring them home from the neighbouring estate before I have dashed to school, leaving Margaret mending the boundary wall. Wanderlust gets into cattle when the grass grows and it is necessary to be insured for they can easily stray onto the golf course and that can cost the earth. A breach in the boundary is caused by walkers who do not follow the Country Code, by frost which attacks the dry stone walls, by drivers who venture on the unsurfaced road, flounder and take stones to fill the ruts to regain dry land and, very occasionally, by vandals who like to make a gap for some reason unknown to us.

Spring sets us singing and Aunt Janie used to air the songs she learned in childhood, 'Why, spring is come and don't you know, this is the time when daisies grow.' Too true. Spring carpets The Currer with as many daisies as there are stars in the heaven. At first the peewits seem to be the only birds returning. All at once anyone wandering across the horizon is beneath their swooping wings. Like the terns on Tir nan Orna they threaten and scold us from the air and walk in front of us, pretending lameness, to draw our attention from the vulnerable nest and the severely-at-risk babies. Then suddenly the air seems incredibly full of skylarks, until their song has become a background noise we do not notice.

Our swelling suckled herd was with us for many years and the normal, almost daily birth of the calves made us temporarily forget the abnormal one in the barn. A normal birth continues to be a source of wonder and awe and never becomes commonplace. Always there is the suspense and fear that things may go wrong. Never could a witness of such continual creation doubt the existence of a creative force, infinitely powerful. Nor can any genuine lover of the countryside, any naturalist, Christian or God-fearing man of whatever religion, condone the manufacture of any weapon which could end so wonderful a world. Deterrence is no excuse. Surely it is just another name for lack of faith, for hypocrisy.

Birth is most perfect in the springtime, when calves and lambs born outside can enjoy the warmth of long days and evening frolicking in the clover. That was the easiest time of day to count the herd, when feeding time brought the calves to suckle and tails were going madly.

Something known to the woman on Harris stirs us in springtime. We saw her, Margaret and I, one beautiful morning some years ago. We had risen at 5 a.m. and eaten within our little white tent outside Katie and Angus's croft at Luskentyre and we had scorned the new, neat road just recently built and cut across the island on the old road to the Bays which fringe the eastern shore. So sure had we been that the early morning mist had only been a harbinger of a beautiful day that we had set off early in shorts and anoraks and by 10 a.m. were well along the Golden Road. In the heat of the mid-morning sun we stopped for our elevenses and looked across the bay to Skye.

Down on the shore was a little house, closed and silent as if sleeping among the sheep and the lazy-beds. Suddenly, even as we watched, the door was flung open wide and the housewife began to throw out the dogs and the children, then the rugs and the furniture. We watched, feeling such an affinity with her as out came the newly washed blankets to be spread on the rocks. Then we could see her sweeping out the dust of winter, forcing it over the threshold. She opened the windows and let the air blow through. The same urge to spring clean excites us and our isolation from neighbours makes it possible for us to do so in an extrovert fashion.

Almost to the day the cuckoo returns to Jimmy's Wood. We welcome his arrival like good news. His song breaks the silence on St George's Day and is an accompaniment to all our activities. 'We've made it,' we say when we hear the first call. 'The winter is past and we are still here once more.'

It seemed important that Margaret should take a Camper's Licence and Ann decided to take hers at the same time. We all visited a site for it at Kettlewell and both were successful. The company was divided to make two camps possible. Margaret dealt with new problems in the shape of a very sick Guide who had to be brought home by ambulance for the doctor suspected, wrongly, that she had diphtheria. There was also one very homesick Guide but Margaret coped so admirably that the girl came to subsequent camps with great joy and came to see us, not long ago, to show photographs she and her husband had taken of their baby on a nostalgic return to Arran. 'My Guide uniform is still hanging in my wardrobe,' she confessed.

It is a constant source of pleasure to hear our grown, mature children say, 'The greatest influence on my life was Guiding.' 'The greatest fun was camping.'

Certainly the greatest outside influence in my life was the still-active Cloughie. Admittedly I made fewer visits to the Hall which had given birth to dreams and skills and creativity. My new school post necessitated that I pass twice daily but to call meant a broken bus journey. Any excuse, however, was good enough to alight at the green in front of the village church and follow the stream, past the home farm and over the stile into the wooded grounds. First to see the snowdrops which always laid a carpet of snow after the thaw, then the daffodils which littered the orchard where so much of my camping had been done. In the summer there were tents to collect, badge tests to organise and First Class hikes to plan. The autumn scattered horse chestnuts for the school nature table and the windfall apples in the orchard. Christmas needed no other excuse, for what was more natural than to want to see the annual display of the Nativity in the alcove of the billiard room with an authentic night sky as backcloth. I was no longer a child with an adolescent respect for a favourite adult. I was a friend visiting a colleague. My stile entry to the grounds brought me first to the drawing room window. Invariably, the good lady would be sitting in the bay enjoying a cup of tea and, seeing me, she'd beam her pleasure and let me in through the conservatory. Her housekeeper would bring me a cup of tea; the china would be exquisite and the silver teapot highly polished and valuable. If my visit coincided with her servant's day off, Cloughie would lead the way from the drawing room, through the stately dining room, along the dark corridor, past the great dinner gong and the old fashioned telephone, to the huge kitchen. There the good lady would command me to make a cuppa in an old kitchen teapot and she would raid the cake tins and get two cups without saucers. Armed with such inelegance we would retire to the beautiful drawing room and draw up to the fire. There was one memorable occasion when the cake was so light it crumbled and, with neither saucers nor plates there were going to be crumbs all over the floor. 'Here, use an envelope,' said Madam.

She wasn't a good listener, this very deaf friend of mine, but she was an interesting talker and a keen naturalist. From her I learned most of my knowledge of wild life, flora and fauna. She had a great love for all living things which contrasted oddly with the fact that, as a child, she had ridden with the hunt. She never removed the heads of big game which decorated the walls of the Hall, in a dozen places, for her ancestors had hunted in Africa. She was a strange mixture of Upstairs and Downstairs but if it came to the toss, she was every bit a lady. She could have survived in the open but in the house, without servants, she would not have known how to cope.

After the Kettlewell camp most of the company wanted to take Camper Badge and Margaret and I organised a weekend in the low pasture below The Currer. Practically every Guide came for testing and I arranged for a school friend to come as examiner. She had very high standards and took no account whatsoever of the weather. The tents were pitched one dry Friday evening and there was an atmosphere of excitement.

I wakened early to the call of the cuckoo. His dawn chorus lasts all day. In my subconscious state I had heard him shouting his ridiculous insults since daybreak. I peeped out of the tent and saw a stray calf nosing round the kitchen area. It was a black and white Friesian called Lucky, bought to replace a stillborn one and, being adopted, not nearly so dependent on being close to its mother. I remember thinking it was not the only lucky individual, that it was an incredibly beautiful morning and I was the luckiest of Guiders to have such a beautiful place to teach girls the fun and the skills of camping, that glorious game I played for nearly half a century.

The cobwebs on the drystone walls glistened with dew. Peewits and the curlew called and the grazing calf disturbed a flock of wood pigeons. A train hurried noisily along the valley floor. The rising sun had left a warning redness in the sky which belied the good weather forecast and I smelled rain before the day was out.

Hearing chattering in the tents I decided to get moving and take wakeful ones up to the silver birch spinney for kindling for the hike test fires they would have to light in the afternoon. A silver birch scrub stretches from the rough near the eastern boundary of The Currer as far as the Altar and beyond and the bracken grows high so that visiting children can play at walking through jungle country. Above the bracken, but still in the shade, are the most productive of the bilberry bushes. The bark and twigs of birch make good kindling. So, very early, we collected valuable materials for successful firelighting and returned to camp with ample fuel and dirty hands and faces. It was great early morning fun and thickening cloud didn't depress us.

All morning the tester posed her questions, inspected equipment and watched tents being pitched and gadgets made. We had a mid-day lunch sitting beneath the oak trees and afterwards assembled the fire billies and frying pans and the food each Guide must cook alone. And then the heavens opened. Never before, or since, has rain so quickly disorganised us. The tester had a one-track mind concerned only with whether or not fires could be lit and food cooked by campers in all weathers. No thought was given to the top priority of every camper, that of securing the shelter and of keeping dry. In this country, where continual rain is unlikely, no one starves to death if a meal is missed or eaten raw and sensible campers do not get wet on purpose. I begged for the test to be abandoned but the gallant examiner was insistent that good campers must find a way so the kids did their best, finding what shelter they could under walls and trees, protecting their fires with stones and their woodpiles with waterproofs. They lit their fires beneath the bell tent of a plastic mac and did their best whilst water ran from the intakes and made the low pasture a sponge. The struggle was disastrous and we had thirty very wet girls, half of whom were disappointed because the deluge had made their efforts unsuccessful. Campers must never be allowed to get so wet whilst tents stand empty. For what other reason do we take tents if it is not for shelter?

The rain continued to fall in unrelenting violence. It flowed in a steady stream through the farmyard and down the walled and ancient fold so many had chosen for shelter. The new stream was fed by innumerable tributaries and the campsite became waterlogged. Mud clung to the children's wellies, hands and faces adding another shade of grey to the already innumerable smoke smears. Torrential rain became the victor and thirty children hurried back to their tents with a jumble of dirty billy cans and a mess of uncooked food. I hurried up to the house and put a dixie of soup onto the Aga. Everyone followed and soaking anoraks and sou'westers made a revolting pile in the front porch. Inside children sat everywhere, huddling against the Aga, curling up before the sitting room fire, two in each armchair, sprawling on the rugs, whilst adults fought the gale to secure tents and put equipment under cover.

Being so near to home, we decided to send the Guides to sleep in their own beds. Incredible! Four hundred miles from home, battered by gales on a remote island with double the number of children and no one got wet and everyone was warm and fed. In the field below The Currer, because the 'Don't get wet' rule was ignored, we sent most of the children home for the night. Some parents had taken the opportunity this weekend provided to go away from home themselves, so their children and all the adults slept all over the house. There was a lot of laughter from the sleeping bags which so colourfully littered the floor. In the morning both sun and Guides reappeared.

It was in the spring of 1961 that a litter of pigs was ready to be sent to market. They were to go in two batches, half of them being somewhat smaller than the rest. It was therefore no disaster when one gilt from the first load escaped, leaping over the gate which penned them. 'It'll go wi' t' next lot,' Father said.

We had been rearing pigs at The Currer for some time. We had begun by buying eight-week-old weaners and then we started farrowing a couple of sows ourselves. I have vivid recollections of sows in my childhood and the journey we periodically made to a pig farmer in the valley who had a stud boar. Father and I used to go and fetch it with the horse and an old float. It was encouraged, protesting, into the low float, a wooden back inserted and a net tied over it. I was always very frightened but preferred to go for my fear of the animal in the float was less than my fear of being left behind with my imagination. I was always terribly afraid of my father being killed. And Margaret! I have taught many a lesson waiting for the phone to ring and set my mind at rest with the news that a dangerous job was completed without incident. Every battle to get an animal into the cattle crush is a potential danger. The 'friendly cow all red and white' in the poem I taught the children just does not exist. A mere human is regularly trodden on.

The last of the litter for the market were penned in the lean-to about a fortnight later and, amazingly, the agile, circus pig jumped the gate once more. This time the farmers did not give in easily. They forced the gilt back into the shed, the Land Rover trailer was backed into position and the trailer gate opened. But a pig that won't go, won't go. There was a snapping of gate wood like matchsticks, a complete disregard for the humans brandishing corrugated sheets and attempting to block the exit. The pig won, fortunately without crippling anyone and Father gasped, 'It's bahn t'stay.'

Sheila, the Sea Ranger Skipper, city girl from the south, mistook the term 'gilt' for 'guilt' and christened the pig Guilty. It seemed an apt name for one guilty of escapology. She had personality plus and we alternated between respect and desperation. When she littered in the barn and insisted on feeding her many babies on the farmhouse doorstep she was more gentle and tolerant than a human being but when roused or urged to do something she didn't want to she became immovably stubborn.

There was a memorable Saturday when I had a front room full of children learning knotting skills, prior to going to camp. I was teaching them how to make camp gadgets and, though the day was fair, we had been busy in the front room all afternoon. Father knocked on one of the mullions and called, "Ev yer sin t' sow?'

We had not put a foot in the farmyard all afternoon and could not help. Sometime later I decided it was time for tea and we crowded into the kitchen to cut some bread and make a meal. There was a distinct smell of pig in the kitchen and on the rug was a wad of chewed grass. The door into the washing kitchen was closed but my suspicions were roused.

There, contentedly sitting on her huge haunches, was our sow. She stared at us arrogantly, completely unashamed of the upturned bread crock, the semi-eaten contents and the pile which was responsible for the strong smell of pig.

Our humour out-laughed disgust. Beautifully clean, elephantine in size, she sat there with a look on her face which would have excited any cartoonist. The culprit stared at us as if to say, 'Just try throwing me out! I made it quite clear, some time ago, that I do as I like.'

The success of Guilty's numerous litters turned us into pig farmers with a herd of up to fifty pigs. They are the funniest, most appreciative of animals and they give untold pleasure. They are clean animals and the general public is ignorant of their traits and qualities. The end product of farming is not discussed in our household and we take unkindly to those who look at pigs and see them as food. Only once has Margaret ever found a comment on the end product amusing. She had bought forty week-old calves and two Guides arrived with their father. He leaned over the gate and looked at the beautiful babies, with little love for creation and only a selfish love of his Sunday dinners. He said, 'Just think, some day all that will be mutton!'

Guilty's end came sooner than it should have done for she was an excellent mother and a definite financial success, littering above a dozen babies every time. The small boars were, in those days, always castrated. Nowadays this is not often done and a good thing too for it was always a traumatic day. Any interference with their piglets and all our sows became dangerous. They lived in freedom, bedded in straw, often in the barn; they could go out and in at will and knew few restraints. We breed happy animals but their very freedom makes them more dangerous. Ours behave badly in a human-dominated situation. A Ministry TT or brucelosis test becomes a rodeo and all our heifers behave like broncos. A simple streptopen injection can be a fiasco as a sick animal suddenly becomes fighting fit and objects. Well-treated animals, whose dignity is preserved, behave appallingly under duress and we are often in danger of losing life or limb.

To handle Guilty's piglets with her anywhere in the vicinity was fatal. Indeed we handled no little pigs under the protective eye of mum. On this occasion the vet was sent for to castrate the small boars of two litters. Guilty had a litter, too, but her piglets were much younger and Father intended to call the vet a fortnight later. He and Margaret, therefore, separated the older little boars from their over-anxious mamas in good time. To do so needed time and a moderate amount of cunning if the old ladies were not to suspect interference. By the time the vet arrived the two huge sows with their small gilts were well out of earshot of the stable where the castration was to take place. We kept a heavy dolly-tub for the purpose. The little boars began to scream their heads off immediately they were handled. It was this screaming which always upset the sows if they could hear. To turn off the screaming the little boars were held head downwards in the empty dolly-tub. The silence was immediate, like turning off the fire alarm. Screaming pigs are not being hurt. They scream for no reason when handled. Their alarmed high notes could easily burst an eardrum.

Our vet, at that time, was a Hebridean from one of the islands we love so well. He completed the task with expertise and, when he was putting away his instruments in the car, he spotted Guilty's litter of smaller pigs. 'I'll do these as well,' he decided.

'Yer moan't,' said Father.

'No,' said Margaret, 'We'll send for you again.'

'Och, not at all,' said the vet. 'We'll do them chust now.'

'Not on your life,' protested Margaret. 'That sow's dangerous. I know before you begin. We'll send for you again and have the little pigs well away from her.'

Granted, Guilty never looked dangerous. Sprawled out almost on our doorstep, suckling a dozen babies, she looked the picture of docility. She was nowhere in sight. Her babies crossed the yard and the temptation was too much for the vet. 'We'll do them,' he said.

Against their better judgement, Margaret and Father opened the stable door. One piglet ran close to the vet who stooped down and picked it up. Suddenly, the infant began that appalling screaming no other infant can make. In an instant the enormous sow appeared from nowhere and, instead of dropping the piglet, the vet not only held on but up-lifted it out of reach of the angry mother. Up she stood, on her hind legs, an elephant indeed and in a split second he crashed heavily onto the concrete. She fastened her strong fangs right through his wellingtons and into his leg and tossed him about like an empty paper bag.

Margaret rushed in and Father, the most experienced, grabbed a dustbin lid and went into the fray like St George himself. In his unconsciousness the vet let go of the piglet and the screaming stopped. The sow heard the silence, saw the dustbin lid and Margaret and lost interest in the man on the floor. She trotted grumbling away. But she had done enough damage.

Before the ambulance arrived, our dazed and disbelieving friend returned to consciousness aware of a terrible headache and excruciating pain in his leg. He was taken to spend three weeks in hospital and the atmosphere at The Currer was one of shocked horror. I returned from school to find an agitated family waiting impatiently to ring the hospital for news. Next day I was horrified to see, on the newspaper placards, *vet savaged by sow*. In those days papers were sold by a woman who stood daily on the post office corner. I bought a paper from her and read the account whilst I waited for the village bus. It was many days before the news began to be reassuring.

In the summer Margaret and I returned to the island and we visited the vet's mother and father. His mother sat in a high backed chair surrounded by a multitude of Gaelic-speaking grandchildren. We were deeply aware that, had real tragedy befallen her son, our encounter with her would have been comparable to his encounter with our sow.

It would be wrong to leave you with this picture of aggression from an otherwise benign race of animal and to have you believe that this shattering experience in any way damaged our opinion of these most laughable of creatures. On the whole they are incredibly gentle and will put up with sleeping cats curled on their rumps, pups who sleep with their piglets and humans who step over them. But no animal with young can be trusted not to rise in defence and pigs have the most extraordinary equipment in their jaws for tearing humans apart which should never be ignored. It was Guilty's last litter. Perhaps it was as well.

Chapter Nine

E ach new day at my village school was an experience. I had inherited an excellence in singing I could not hope to maintain, being such an out of tune singer myself. For a few years the splendid influence of my predecessor kept the standard of singing high but it was inevitable that it should eventually deteriorate. I know when children are singing for joy but do not know if they are out of tune. So we sang for joy. My love of singing had been born around the campfire on islands and hilltops and in woodlands. I used to say to the children, 'This is one thing you can all do better than I can.'

Another thing they could all do better than I was Movement. The previous Head had gained quite a reputation with it but this had not been a feature of my first school where the children had done some good old-fashioned PE. I found I must learn a new skill from Joan and from the PE Advisor for the West Riding, Yvonne Easto, who was friend-extraordinary to the school for she and her husband lived in the village. Until her retirement she sent a continuous flow of visiting teachers to watch our Movement lessons.

My school was so small it had no hall. The largest of the three classrooms was big enough to be a hall but it was the home of the infant class and I would never have dreamed of releasing it for that purpose by removing the infants to the empty room at the east of the school. The County therefore rented use of the village institute which had an excellent floor. Twice a week, unless the weather was impossible, we made a journey there by taking the path through the churchyard, along the canal bank, over the swing bridge and up the Main Street. Only when mud on the towpath made shoes too dirty did we go all the way on the road. I did not willingly choose to take them through the culvert, dripping with seepage from the canal and echoing with the clatter of their shoes and the continual chatter of voices enjoying the novelty of distorting acoustics. There was an iron plate over a drain, halfway along the tunnel, which clanged when trodden on and every child delighted in making it wobble. The road was narrow, the footpath only really wide enough for single file and cars approached silently and drove too fast.

There was a third approach to the Main Street via the hump-backed bridge over the canal and the jumble of ancient cottages of Buckler Hill. We went this way if we needed anything from the shop on Newby Road but the best way always was along the canal bank watching the reflections of moored houseboats, collecting flowers and counting the ducklings and cygnets. All too frequently the stretch of canal above the culvert would be drained for repairs and then we had the fun of exploring the bed for household debris hurled in by villagers over the years. An ancient school desk with iron frame and pedestal stool lay there to excite speculation and puzzle us.

There are moments now, when I no longer make this frequent journey with my school children, when I smell the unmistakable atmosphere of a village hall and hear the ghostly clatter of fifty outdoor shoes on the bare wooden stairs to the cloakroom. Even on snowy days, the boys stripped to the waist and the girls to knickers and vests and all moved barefoot. For an hour they would be leaping and spinning in what could only be called dance. I know the smell of dust on the heaters of rooms whose windows are not frequently opened, of stacked chairs and cupboards full of crockery seldom used. I know the feel of trembling, barefooted children clustering round me eager to begin and the power of my voice exciting and urging and showering praise and encouragement. I know the bustle of re-dressing, the searching for gloves and scarves, the sorting out of similar underwear before the pegs are clear. Eventually we would open the door on the winter wind, the April showers, summer sun or November fog. I know the impossibility of keeping the line of children straight and orderly, of preventing wandering feet hopping on and off the pavement and tripping over improperly tied shoe laces. I know the excitement of seeing the first crocuses in Mrs Horner's garden and the weight of apples on the Idesons' tree. I know the rustle of autumn leaves underfoot and now, years later, I look back and am glad that I know.

Life beside the canal was colourful and we used it as an outside classroom for painting and sketching, for writing and measuring and for creative activity of all kinds. Kathleen, at ten, wrote:

The Hump Bridge

Large stones, chipped with age,
Built by sturdy people,
To form an arch across the water,
Beneath the lofty steeple.
Black moss fringes the hump.
But lovely the section
So bright in the sun
As I sit on the grass my work all done.
So cold and damp as an echoing cave.
An old piece of beauty from a bygone age,
Guarding the rippling road
On its winding way

To the wide open sea.
Over its old bent back
Runs a worn, cobbled path,
Where many feet have trod
On their way to worship God.

I loved to see my children sprawled out on the bank, with heads almost in the water and arms submerged to the muscle, hunting for freshwater creatures to take back to the fish tank on the nature table. With children who are now parents themselves, I gathered pounds and pounds of rosehips along the canal bank. In 1961 they were worth a penny a pound. Considering the size of the harvest, it was good pay and added extra money for Christmas presents to the pocket money in the children's purses. My earnings swelled the school fund which was counted in shillings and pence in those days compared to the hundreds of pounds it became twenty-one years later. Net bags were sent by the makers of rosehip syrup and the full ones were collected each week. Sharing out the money was a dinnertime maths lesson.

New boats on the canal were a recurring interest, and the swans, as they flew in past the school window, were a disturbance I never attempted to subdue. The canal provided drama in the sleepy little village. Several times, with a PE skipping rope, we rescued ewes from the water. More often we discovered the already dead carcase of a cow, hen or sheep.

The fear of the canal and its occasional toll did not escape us. All the children knew that one of the rising-fives had toppled from the wall where the canal narrows and crosses the culvert and drowned. A few years later, children were told that Keith had escaped a similar fate only because his brother had hauled him out in time.

'Whatever were you doing?' I whispered with my arm about him next morning when he, trembling, told me all about it.

'Ah wa' walkin' an' Ah go' reight 'ot an' Ah tried t' tek off me anorak an' Ah fell in,' he confessed.

*   *   *   *   *

It was a time of new beginnings, of an upsurge of confidence. Margaret and I were seeing new places and we felt that Harry should be doing so too and that our parents should see more of the country they lived in. A suggestion came from somewhere that they ought to have a change of environment and Father said, 'Something'll turn up.'

I decided to give 'something' a hand and wrote to a small coach firm at Grassington who operated a couple of tours a year for the country people of the locality. One tour was to Torquay. To Mother, Torquay sounded ideal and so it proved to be. In May 1961 the trio made their first venture south. They were a little apprehensive at first, but they had such an enjoyable experience there was no hesitation the next year about booking for Southsea.

It was the beginning of many excursions twice annually, seeing many places and meeting many people. Harry loved it. Mother thought Torquay was fairyland and Father beamed his pleasure at being able to give them both just what they wanted.

Of course the tours were early and late season which suited us and our pocket fine. The aunts used to come up for the week to make Margaret's meals which gave them a holiday feeling, too.

My mother envies people who can go on holiday simply by washing the family supper mugs, packing a case and turning off the electric. I don't think either Margaret or I have ever wished for that. I remember the night we caught the 3 a.m. Scottish Express with forty children bound for Tiree. We had no car to take us to the station in the middle of the night but a kind parent insisted on collecting us. Whilst forty excited children tried to sleep until 2 o'clock, Margaret and I, aching with the effort of bringing in the last loads of hay that evening, began the task of packing up breakfast for the whole party. We never went to bed.

At midnight Margaret left the sandwich packing and went to the sheds to check the herd and pigs. She returned with the news that the sow in the mistal had decided, not altogether unexpectedly, to give birth. 'Guess what,' said sister on return, 'Susan's farrowing!'

Our parents and Harry were all abed. Periodically Margaret left the vital packing to see how the old lady was getting on and when the piglets began to arrive I was left to complete our job alone. This done, I had my bath, put on my Guider's uniform, a large pinafore and wellies and went out to the mistal. 'Your turn,' I said to Margaret. Time was running out. She ran to the bathroom and, ill-dressed for the job, I remained in the farrowing pen. The smell of the new hay was sickening and the smell of warm pig equally nauseating. Usually I don't mind but the pre-camp feeling, especially in the dead of night, is tremulous to say the least, for large numbers of children under canvas, hundreds of miles away from home on forgotten islands, can only spell risk and responsibility.

Half a dozen small, satin-silky piglets had already arrived. To be a pig on The Currer is good fortune indeed. Here is almost unlimited freedom and undiluted happiness. Margaret went for her bath rather reluctantly. She is never quite sure of my capabilities in her sphere but if there was the remotest chance of a bath it had to be taken. I was left to lift away a continuous succession of babies. I was still in the mistal when the kind parent came and Margaret was still buttoning up her uniform. Only then did we wake Father to continue the vigil. We picked up our rucksacks and left the floodlit yard.

We had been invited to Denmark by our young Danish friend. I spent a week with her parents at Sønderborg before Margaret, Janet and Ann joined us. Ulla and Lone took us first to Roskilde and then to Hessel vig Enggård staying each time in the gardens of her relatives. We travelled in Guide uniform and camped. Briefly we crossed to Malmö in Sweden and to Flensburg in Germany and this was to be our only excursion abroad. People have repeatedly asked us why we have not ventured again on the Continent for with tents and a sleeping bag all things are within the resources of a relatively empty pocket. Time, distance and responsibility have been the reason. Increasingly it had been impossible for us to leave home too far behind as we were always aware that Father was an old man with a lot of cattle and a handicapped son. One of us must always be able to get back in a hurry. But the chief reason why we have never been abroad since is surely that there have been too many children in our lives. It seemed that our little extra bit in life was taking other people's children on holiday; it never became a chore and always remained a pleasure for another twenty years. So whilst all our friends explored the holiday spots of the world we were satisfied to head for the islands with our annual invasion.

Our one and only excursion to foreign fields was not without humour. There was one hilarious incident we are not particularly proud of but we are unlikely to forget. We learned that the British have a sense of humour which is different from a continental one.

We were at Roskilde, camping in the garden of Ulla's uncle and, having visited the cathedral during the day, we were being taken, in Guider's uniform, to visit the cinema. There was some delay and we were sitting on the harbour for an hour. We were close to the fjord at that most beautiful hour of the day when the sun is going down in splendour and sea and sky are scarlet. We would have been happy to miss the cinema altogether but our Danish friend was a very domineering young lady and we dared not interfere with her plans.

It had been a beautiful day and the still water of the fjord was lukewarm. A swarm of ladybirds had flown to the shore and, like a migration of lemmings, had hurled themselves into the sea. Thousands of them floated lifeless at the water's edge and cast a little sadness on the glorious evening. The harbour was fringed with sloping cobbles all along the edge of the fjord and Margaret's reflex to preserve life reacts more quickly than any one else's I know. One of the flying ladybirds, on its strange, suicidal journey, landed on Ulla's finger and, even as we watched, it hurled itself into the sea. It hit the water among its dead companions and began to struggle. Margaret had one thought: to lift it out, pop it in a match box and release it in the flower garden where we were camping. She climbed down the easy cobbled slope to within a foot of the water. Here the colour of the cobbles changed from dark green to a lighter one and before any of us had time to realise what was happening, Margaret had begun to slide. She slid under water as easily as she would have had she used the children's chute into deep water at the swimming baths. Ann and Janet closed their eyes in a fit of spontaneous uncontrollable laughter. I need my sister more than most people need a sibling; she is my other half more than most husbands. We need each other so much that the only thing which frightens us is being left to cope alone. There was no way I could stand on the shore, laughing and let Margaret drown. So, without analysing the situation and merely obeying reflexes which insisted that I give Margaret a hand, I climbed down the sets and held one out for her to take. I felt my feet slip and I entered the water as ignominiously as she had done. There is a lemming in all of us.

Janet's eyewitness report states that, on seeing Margaret disappear beneath the water, laughter blinded her for mere seconds. Opening her eyes she expected to see one swimmer with uniform hat but she saw two. Two fully dressed females in shirts and skirts and ties, wearing the felt, stiff berets of Guiders, with metal county roses catching the sun and sparkling above the water. We had to swim, side by side, to a jetty some yards away.

Our Danish friends and several members of a nearby Rowing Club viewed our misadventure with a complete lack of humour. They could not understand how we could climb out of the water, soaking wet, adorned with seaweed like female Neptunes and be unable to control our laughter. There we were, four of us, hysterical amid a circle of gloom. 'Take a taxi,' we were advised. Take a taxi indeed! What taxi man would have us dripping all over the upholstery! We covered up our plight with pac-a-macs and set off to walk briskly back to the tent. We stopped to empty the water from our shoes for the squelching was too great. In the tent we stripped completely and rescued strands of seaweed from our hair and clothes.

The film, when we eventually seated ourselves in front of the screen, was a noisy, very vulgar German farce which did not amuse us at all but the four of us kept dissolving into such fits of laughter that our Danish friends were delighted and convinced that the film was a huge success.

Our vivid young friend took us on a comprehensive tour of Denmark. We visited Odense, Helsingør and Copenhagen and saw places and buildings we had heard about, but the holiday did not give us a quarter of the joy and satisfaction we derived from being under canvas with children. So, though we look back on our one continental holiday with some pleasure there is no regret. What we put in its place was so much more rewarding.

*   *   *   *   *

I began my second year as headteacher with a larger 4th year. Two of their predecessors went to Grammar School and two to the very happy, local Secondary Modern. It was a year to enjoy thoroughly for the Top Juniors were as bright as buttons and one always remembers the first children most clearly. Following years tend to become a blur and when the children visit me I cannot say immediately to which year and which group they belong. I had inherited a happy school, an excellent infant teacher, a good teacher-child relationship, a bright top class, a lovely dinner lady and a reliable caretaker. A false step on my part would have spoilt it, but here were these grand children ready to put me on the right road. They overshadowed their seniors in number and were with me two years. I am unlikely to forget them even if time dims the memory of some of the others.

There was a lovely girl called Susan who played the piano for all our singing lessons and assemblies except for the one hour a week a pianist came into school. Kathleen's storytelling ability was superb. She could release me in an emergency and keep the class enthralled. There was Paul, artist and poet and David, farmer and charmer who later became a hairdresser. There were the twins, the one plump and kindly, my ever-present helper and the other clever but withdrawn. There was Margaret, the attractive one who always shared a joke by giving me a nudge with her elbow and Christopher whose occupancy of the staffroom had not been challenged since he was admitted at five, who wrote blood-thirsty war stories and used a thick black dash for words he knew he should not use. His work in Movement lessons was always military and his self-confidence left him never at a loss. Once we had borrowed scores of articles from abroad and had exhibited them around the classroom. Christopher was showing a visitor the temporary museum and I heard his comment. 'These are chop sticks,' he said and repeated slowly, 'chop sticks.' Then he laughed apologetically and said, 'My Chinese isn't very good.' One might have expected that he would join the army but he became an Anglican vicar. When he began visiting us at school, every Grammar School holiday, I sometimes left him in charge of the class whilst I went to the bank with dinner money and savings. One day I told him he could mark the sum books if the answers were correct but to leave for me any work which had been misunderstood. He put a comment in every book. Good. Very Good. Excellent. In one child's book the sums had been left for almost all were wrong. The comment read, 'Hard Luck'. Perhaps it was compassion which led him into the ministry.

There was John whose glasses made him look the academic he would never be and Michael who laughed at me one day. We were so busy the time had flown and when I looked at the clock I was ringing the dinner bell ten minutes late. 'Good gracious me!' I said. 'Just look at the time.'

'Yer allus saying that, Miss Brown,' Michael accused without bitterness.

There was, at the time, some industrial unrest amongst teachers.

'There's never enough time, Michael,' I complained. 'Mrs Armstrong and I are going on strike for more hours.'

'Aw 'eck,' said the boy. 'Ah fought i' wa' fer more money!'

There were two comparative newcomers: one quiet child named Ann and one extrovert named Ciona. Ciona stayed with us for less than a year and her parents moved at a time which fell between two entrance Eleven-Plus examinations. The tests had already been taken in the new area in which they were to live and the final test was still a month away in the West Riding. Provision would have been made for Ciona to sit the examination alone in her new school but we all felt that the upheaval of removal and admittance into a new school followed by an immediate Eleven Plus examination, alone, in a strange headteacher's room would seriously handicap even an intelligent child. Under stable conditions Ciona had every hope of gaining a Grammar School place.

So it was arranged that she would stay with us at The Currer, and travel with me daily to school until the West Riding examination was over. I wonder how many children's futures have been jeopardized by non-uniformity in testing procedures and dates.

It was a happy month. The ground was snow-covered and daily, in wellies, the headteacher and the pupil trudged over the white fields to the village bus and frequently in the early evening tobogganed down the Eightacre. Ciona was to teach me that teacher/pupil relationships need not be ruined by familiarity. She never took advantage of her strangely privileged position any more than did the countless other boys and girls who came to camp with me in the Hebrides. No harm is done when children see their teacher as an ordinary human being with home and family. It isn't all that healthy to think that the teachers live in the school, that the staffroom is their front room. 'Where's yer bafroom?' one child asked and another wondered, 'Where's yer lipstick drawer, 'S Armstrong?'

On the weekend of Father's sixty-fifth birthday I was in Whitby staying with my previous headmistress and her relatively new husband and we saw, on television, the Mechanics' Institute burning to the ground in one dreadful inferno. Harry would remember the date anyway but Father's retirement birthday fixes it in my less reliable memory. The chief landmark in our town went in a few hours and the people mourned it with great sadness. Everything had happened in the Mechanics. It had been the Village Hall of the townspeople and without it they were bereft.

A partnership was formed with Margaret and Harry working partners and me a sleeping one. The solicitor handed over the deed and Father was now back to square one, breaking his back for 170 acres of beloved countryside and a herd that he did not own. This time the circumstances were different. My father owned this land even then, was the revered master of it, the manager and director, whatever the piece of paper suggested otherwise. What's more, though he is no longer with us, my father still owns The Currer. Till we die it will be farmed with gratitude; it will be farmed with the utmost respect for living things; it will offer hospitality to all no matter the name, creed or colour and we have ensured that it goes to future generations of similar people.

At Easter we spent a week in Portsmouth, Margaret and I, at the home of the Sea Ranger Skipper who was such a frequent visitor at our house. She was preparing to emigrate to New Zealand in the August and we tried to cram as much as possible into the next few months. In return we invited her to accompany Ann and us on a tour of the Hebrides which we planned for the spring bank holiday. Sheila had bought a small Bukta tent and we copied the basic design with some material bought in the market at Arthur's wonderful stall. We bought a set of lightweight poles and made the prototype, the first of several such tents used in the course of the many years of lightweight camping with scores of teenagers. We called it the BP tent or the Little White Tent. Sheila and I set off a day before the others and visited a site at Machrie Bay on the Isle of Arran. We liked it so much we booked it for three weeks in the summer for the Guide Company, the County Cadets for which I was still Assistant Guider and the Sea Ranger Crew SRS *Spartan*.

Margaret and Ann caught up with us in Glasgow, the next day, and we went north to Oban. We were obsessed with the achieving of perfection in lightweight camping and had spent long hours reducing the weight of our packs. Over the years we were to reduce our load still further but even so our rucksacks and oilskins were weighty compared with the lightweight materials of today.

We had arranged, with the skipper of the *Island Queen* in Oban, to be ferried out to Croggan on the Isle of Mull. The Ordnance Survey map distinctly showed a pier there. The little motorboat was loaded with our packs and we set off, like Hiawatha, 'to the portals of the sunset'. It was a very beautiful evening and we enjoyed the sail immensely. When we arrived at the pier, however, we found that it was designed for coal puffers and cattle boats and that it had no landing stage for the *Island Queen*. There was no alternative but to climb the pier struts, like monkeys and haul up the rucksacks from the precarious slope which must surely have been a cattle ramp. The Sound of Mull looked incredibly deep below us. Had the skipper of the motor boat been a man he might have shown concern for four ladies who had not yet learned to wear trousers, let alone shorts, on back-packing holidays, but we were watched making our hazardous ascent by a weather-beaten lady who had probably made similar landings all her life. The lady skipper of the *Island Queen* batted not an eyelid as we swarmed up the barnacled struts and then looked down on her from what seemed a great height. When she turned the boat towards the mouth of Loch Spelve, and began her lonely return to Oban, her matter of fact nod of farewell left us momentarily spellbound.

We groped for footholds on the ramp and, still trembling a little, for I don't like heights, I went to a nearby cottage and collected a kettleful of water so that we could brew up.

We camped that night on the shores of Loch Buie and in the very early morning negotiated the rocky coastline to Carsaig Bay. We had planned to walk over the peninsula to Pennygael on Loch Scridain and pick up the bus going to Fionnphort and the Iona ferry as we thought it would be nice to go

to the Abbey service. We completely miscalculated the time it would take us
to cross the rough country between Loch Buie and Carsaig. Unwilling to be
beaten we asked a man outside the big house how long it would take us to
get to Pennygael and he said he was going there in the Land Rover, in a little
while, and would pick us up. Moreover, he would ring up the postmistress
at Pennygael and warn her to tell the driver of the bus to wait until we had
arrived. They are incredibly kind, these island people.

So, somewhere along the Pennygael road, we were picked up by the shepherd and taken to the road end. The story should have ended happily but no
bus came. When we could expect it no longer we lay down on the shore of
Loch Scridain and slept for a long time. We were very tired at the beginning
of a holiday. We found the mid-day sun warm and the smell of sea wrack
very soporific. The cry of the shore birds was a lullaby and hours of that first
day were lost in much-needed sleep. How frequently Margaret and I have
slept on some loch shore or curled up in the heather in the hills; how often
we have wakened sunburned on one side only. We could have hurried along
the road to Bunessan and Fionnphort; someone would have offered a lift; but
we had been to Iona before and were to go again, several times and there are
many places in which to worship God. One was in peace on the shore of Loch
Scridain.

We caught the returning bus and went to Tobermory to camp with the
midges among the trees overlooking the famous harbour. We asked the driver
why he had not waited, without malice for we had not felt deprived. 'Well,
and I wass waiting, chust,' he explained, 'and some ladies came running and
I thought it wass yourselves.'

So we left Mull and pitched the two little white tents on Tiree among friends
before sailing to Barra, camping first at Northbay and then at Tangasdale by
the little lochan of St Clair, near the Campbells who had been so kind to us in
1958. Then we returned to the mainland and spent our last night uncomfortably on the slate at Ballachulish before being picked up by the bus at Glencoe.
All future holidays, for many years, were to be with little white tents, and
even now that is how we would prefer to go. But there is no way we can
pack a bag, strap on the tent and leave our very old mother and Auntie Mary
and our increasingly disabled brother, so we bundle them all into the Range
Rover and head northwards to the islands. We do not look back and say, 'If
only we had.' We say, 'Thank goodness we did!' We may again, some day,
who knows.

A great yearning came over me the other day, for the little white tent.
There has been such a mushrooming of The Currer. The rooms are so big. We
walk miles every day inside it. Nothing is near to hand. I had a great yearning
for the limitations of the tent: so small it was that I could sit up in my sleeping
bag and touch all four walls. I could reach the water carrier and the kettle
and light the stove. I could forage in my rucksack and dress whilst the bacon
sizzled in the frying pan. Even to think about it is a tonic.

With the invention of the baler the old haymaking days were over.

Father now pulled the mower with the tractor and after days of turning and rowing with the tedding machine, a call was made to the baler and we would be nervous wrecks in case he could not come before the rain did. There always seemed to be dark clouds and a storm brewing and we would all be on edge for, whatever the harvest, it is necessary to the survival of the farmer. To us, grass is gold, be it grazing or hay. There is more harvest in grazing than in meadow. It occurs to me that people do not know that, yet they know how many inches a mown lawn produces each summer. Grazed fields produce much more food than harvested ones but they lie dormant in the winter and so something must be preserved. A man looked over the wall and was critical of the Eight-Acre. 'I remember when this field grew a crop of hay,' he said, belittling the short grass being grazed by a hundred yearlings.

'So do I,' said Margaret. 'That was in the days we had thirty milk cows.' He didn't understand. 'Do you also remember,' she asked, 'when the bracken over the wall was waist high and all that green hillside was bent and bilberry?' He did not. They have forgotten, those who have no backache still from the reclaiming.

One day the baler hurried to finish in front of a cloudburst. Margaret and I took off most of our clothes and stooked in immediately saturated underwear. We worked at speed and kept warm, and hid our trousers and woollies under a stook to put on dry at the end of the job. The downpour had eased before we finished and we stripped off the wet clothes, put on the dry and walked the mile home comfortably. If we could, we led the bales home practically non-stop, carrying on after dark. It was a bumpy lead for, though the meadows were level, the cart track across the moor was capable of bouncing off the load if it were not securely roped. This was a tedious job at the end of a hard day. I found the roping of the twilight loads the last one by the tractor headlights, extremely boring. It wasn't my job. Father and Margaret did the roping and knot tying and, to an increasingly cold onlooker, the job always seemed to take ages. But it was very necessary if the load were to sweep into the farmyard intact. The ropes were taken off before the tractor drew the load into the barn for it was a tight squeeze inside. The bales scraped the laithe porch walls on either side and the final course went in with only a couple of inches clearance. Any shifting of the load on the bumpy mile home meant a caught bale on the porch wall and the whole load deposited on our doorstep. We always held our breath whilst the load went in for the cobbled entry to the barn was steep and the flags had been laid for a horse-drawn haywain and not for the front two wheels of a tractor.

Sometimes a male cousin or a friend's husband would come and help. We welcomed this with gratitude but knew it would have to mean a special burst of energy on our parts to keep up with a newcomer, fresh and eager when we were jiggered. Sometimes it was easier just to keep going steadily than to compete with male strength throwing up the bales with an arrogance and vigour we could not match. It was a relief if the newcomer were cousin Freda's daughter Kathleen for then the last lap would not be too exhausting.

'Nowadays farming must be easier' is a misunderstanding on the part of the inexperienced. We have made hay with hand rake and fork, turning and shaking and cocking before leading it loose into the laithe. What is more back-breaking is handling thousands of heavy bales of new hay, lifting them with finger-cutting binder twine; stooking them, loading them, stacking them and finally carrying every one of them out again to feed them on the hillside in the winter. Machinery may have taken away some of the work but almost everywhere, for us, it has increased the weight we must carry and the speed at which we must do so. Overheads are too great and subsidies too small to allow a farmer to keep a few animals any more. When I was born, a farmer could make a living with a handful of cattle and afford to employ a labourer. Now, if his farm is not more productive, he will quickly be bankrupt. Our early life was spent caring for tame animals. One cow is a pet which knows the halter and does not mind being tethered. Now we have to worm over a hundred strong yearlings who have never been tethered and object wildly to being driven into the crush and forced to swallow the worm-killing liquid. We say a little prayer of thankfulness when the three-hour ordeal is over and thank God that we are still alive, bruised but not maimed.

It was always a trial that the haymaking and the packing for camp came together. The seasonal job of assembling equipment was not, as one might suppose, made easier by having the Sea Ranger Skipper living with us for the month before Arran. A resident guest means more work and more conversation. Sheila was preparing to emigrate and there was a great deal to talk about and plan. A replacement Skipper could not be found and I was being talked into taking the job myself. As if I hadn't enough to do already! Margaret and I were still sealing the skips in the early hours before the dew was off the hay. Margaret was left with the job of helping to manhandle the skips onto the railway van which used to come to the farm to collect the advance ton of canvas, poles, kitchen equipment and stores. This preceded us by two weeks and when it had gone there was a wonderful sense of freedom.

I managed the first week of the three-week camp on Arran alone, without Margaret. On the Friday Sheila left Arran and set off on her journey to the other side of the world, leaving me with SRS *Spartan* and my future title of Skipper. Margaret did not join us until the Monday which was a godsend for during the weekend we experienced the worst gales in our camping history. Fortunately it was a dry wind but it flattened all before it and ridge-poles broke like matchwood. When tents fell, everything blew away and there was utter chaos. Human poles held up canvas for over an hour before I decided to strike, a very difficult thing to do in the teeth of such a gale. Buckets, bowls, toilet rolls, were all caught by the wind. We were dodging tabletops and notice boards and only the little white tent and the flagpole survived. We sat on the canvas, a dozen at a time, to tame and roll it small enough for the bag. Rain would have made us less vulnerable and given things weight. The dry wind made everything a kite and I've never experienced anything like it since. We have never again lost so many ridgepoles in an hour as we did on Arran.

We spent the night, all forty of us, crammed like sardines in the too small loft above the byre. I spent much of the night stepping over bodies, uncovering faces, fearful that somebody would be smothered. Margaret came the next day with replacement poles from Steeton Hall and we repitched and enjoyed every minute of the next fortnight. The earth beneath us was peaty and perfection is sand so we never re-visited Arran with children but the hospitality, whatever the island, is the same.

We returned with my inheritance of the Sea Ranger Crew and many years of fun began.

Our return from camp usually heralded the arrival of Jean's children and this was the trigger to buy calves. Almost immediately Margaret and Father were off to the markets where the week-old calves were auctioned. Margaret loved this job. Going to the market to sell is not her favourite occupation but buying and rearing calves is.

The journey to the market towns had to be made by bus for we had no car. 'We don't need one,' we continually excused our lack of funds. We had learned, long ago, neither to need nor to want what we could not have.

They rarely bought only a handful of calves. Father's theory was that over-stocking would enrich the land. He believed it must be eaten bare, then limed and manured with bedding from the sheds and the droppings of grazing cattle. It must be reseeded with the feeding of thousands of winter bales, all over the pastures and the moor. It was a long-term policy but the only one, for we had no money to reclaim quickly. About forty calves must be bought within a fortnight and the two farmers went from one local market to another, buying a score or a dozen at a time until they had enough.

Rearing calves thirty years ago was trial and error. Disease was often brought home from the markets. Apparently healthy calves would begin to scour and the whole shed be in danger of infection. It was considered, and advised by the vet, better to starve the calves for the first twenty-four hours and give only a drink of water in which sherry, glucose and eggs had been beaten. Eggs and sugar were chosen for their nutritional value and sherry as a bribe. Sickly calves, straight from the gruelling experience of the market, the cattle wagon and the cruel separation from a suckling mother, would often refuse to co-operate and stubbornly reject the bucket. At the first taste of the sherry their tails would begin to wag; we would be immediately adopted, butted and followed. We used to administer this first tempting dose in a tonic water bottle. Twenty calves in one loose box always included a few broncos who were captured only with a struggle and forced to drink only when cornered and held. We used to back them against the stalls in the mistal and stand astride them, pinioning their heads between our legs. At the end of the session we were tired, wet and mucky but usually triumphant. Surely all calves would be alcoholics given the chance.

One year I remember feeding the dregs of the bottles to Bess's pups. They played around our feet when we were coping with a new batch of calves and performed irresistibly every time we bent to give them the last drops of advocaat. They couldn't wait. They were hinged in the middle so that not only the tail wagged but the whole rear end. Then they would climb the air with their front feet and lose their balance because their tails would not stop wagging and the two cannot be done together. By the end of the session they were quite tipsy. We are not drinking people and we always felt embarrassed buying half a gallon of cooking sherry to feed to calves. Out of the litter of addicts we kept two pups. Laddie and Lassie lived to be very old dogs but their mother outlived them by several years.

I was never unaware of the fact that my contribution to the struggle to survive was minimal compared with the eighteen-hour day Margaret and Father were devoting wholly to the farm. My evening help and my salary justified my share in the project but I know my back has not carried as many bales, that my strength has not been demanded quite so often, that I have not had so many dirty jobs or been cold and wet as frequently. Nevertheless I know what all these experiences are.

The extra responsibility of the Sea Ranger Crew took a great deal of time which I would have thought I did not have. Time can be stretched to include almost all one would like to do. We have laughed at the Hebridean saying that 'when God made time He made plenty of it' but it is true. You can pack into an already full life, more and more. It has also been said, 'If you want a job doing, ask a busy person.'

Almost immediately the crew of four became swollen with sixteen-year-old leavers from the Guide Company. We became fanatical about lightweight camping and I began to mass-produce two-man tents so that when the crew numbered nearly a score there was accommodation for everyone. The Rangers in the County held an annual Rimoca (river, mountain, cave) weekend camp and a wooden Maori souvenir came from Sheila in New Zealand to be used as a Lightweight Camping Challenge trophy. We won it nearly every time. SRS *Spartan* was enthusiastic about everything. There were to be Rimocas at Acaster Malbis and Jerusalem Farm, Grassington and Appletreewick. We are great lovers of the Yorkshire Dales and it was all tremendous fun.

Father never thought of his land as private property. Walkers were not told to 'get off'. He was more than happy to allow pony trials and camps, orienteering and sponsored walks and, for a few years, motorbike scrambles were held. These were eventually stopped because the tyres mutilated the fields and encouraged young lads to think they could practise here all the year round regardless of walkers, calving cows and nesting peewits. The last spectators also left an unacceptable amount of dangerous litter and when the Cycle Club applied again Father said no, regretfully, for he was a truly generous man.

The best thing to come out of the motorcycle scrambling was a disabled Scouter who took one of Bess's pups and became a friend who eventually taught the Rangers how to build canoes. The loss of one leg didn't prevent him from being an excellent canoeist and, as a teacher of woodwork at a city Grammar School, his help and encouragement were invaluable. He invited us to a canoe building, Scout weekend and then he came weekly until the *Sheila* and the *Arahina* were made. The Rangers met in the Guide Room and each week the unfinished canoes were hoisted among the rafters to await the next session.

There were critics who said there should be a change of leadership in the development of young people. Teacher could not also be friend and Guider and a different leader was desirable for the older girl. 'They are with you too long,' I was told. 'They need a change of outlook, a new approach.' There are always plenty of critics of success. Continuity is not, in itself, a bad thing. It takes a long time even to begin to influence young people and at the age when they have such energy and enthusiasm the most important thing is to be busy: to go to bed exhausted with healthy activity. It distresses me to see so many young people out of work at a time when physically they should be using that surplus of strength and 'get up and go'. My Sea Rangers were busy, happy and idealistic, dedicated to service to the community, daring and adventurous, extroverts, comedians and handymen. How I enjoyed them!

Chapter Ten

J ust recently I remarked to Joan, who retired with me after being my colleague and friend for twenty-one years, 'What would you most like to return to school for?'

'For Christmas,' was her quick reply. I repeated this to a visiting teacher who was groaning about the pressure of the next few weeks before Christmas comes this year.

'She must be mad!' I was told.

Not at all! We loved Christmas. We didn't over-do it by starting early. Three weeks were enough, we insisted.

An idea grew because I liked tying knots and lashing poles together and there was an abundant supply in the camp store. I began carrying the tent and gadget poles to school. I had long since lost all embarrassment struggling on buses with odd things. If people wanted to laugh, let them. Laughing is good for the soul.

With these poles we made the prototype of the life-size crib we were to make on every one of the following eighteen Christmases of my time in that small, so very happy school. Together, my class and I built a lean-to against the east window of the unused classroom. We built it with lashed poles and roofed it with PE mats and straw. We wove evergreens between the lattice-work and prickly sprays of bright green holly, laden with berries and twigs heavy with rosehips. We were generous with tiny particles of glitter and an edging of cotton wool snow.

We 'stained' the big east window with Nativity scenes made on black cartridge paper with a variety of coloured tissues and hung a star conspicuously in the east, proclaiming that, as St Francis had built his crib at Greccio, so we had built ours in remembrance of the Christ child, and we had built it big enough for a live Holy Family.

It was the beginning, simple and unpretentious, destined to grow into a more elaborate tradition, a part of our year we could not have changed even if we had wanted to for, come December, the children would begin to ask, 'When will we make the crib?' Only the location within the school varied in an effort to suit the need of each particular year.

Because cut sprays of holly and ivy droop if displayed too long and novelty dies when it becomes too familiar, we rarely built the Crib more than a week before the Christmas party and the end of the autumn term. Neither staff nor girls wore trousers in school, so the secret was out the moment I announced, 'Bring your wellies and your long trousers tomorrow.' Anticipation of the annual expedition to collect the greenery was always less than the fun of the real thing. The announcement would mobilise them into action. They would turn to each other and laugh and hug anyone who was near, remember previous years and promise hedge clippers and secateurs and other deadly instruments. There were offers of woolly lambs and more than one would want to bring a doll for the manger. One of the Hagars (there was always one in my class for there were eight in the first generation and goodness knows how many in the second) would obtain permission from home for us to go to the field where holly trees bordered the stream. In December the little brook was either a raging torrent or beautifully ringed with icicles.

I remember one of the second generation Hagars coming to school one day and leaving his three siblings at home with the current infectious disease. Joan knew perfectly well what was wrong with them but when Jonathan said, in a very deep voice, 'V'is only me vis mornin', 'S Armstrong. 'V'others ar'orl poorly,' she asked what was matter with them. 'Ah doan't knaw,' he replied, 'Ah fink it's egg cups.' It is a fact that, in Yorkshire, the receptacle for a boiled egg is a cup but all other such crockery are 'pots'.

The Hagars were my friends. They provided pot eggs and sacks for Sports Day. We had these at The Currer but it was the perogative of the Hagar children to bring them. They produced straw for the manger and, in later years, transport for the camp equipment. The last time it went to the station Jonathan was driving the lorry.

The project books, already full of stories, poems and Christmas shopping additions and party multiplications, of pictures, prayers, carols and customs, were laid aside as definitely inferior to the morning's more energetic activity. All were eager, even Tim who, one year, had been so busy thinking about what he was going to put into his Christmas book that he didn't listen to my instructions about a margin. Having finished the frontispiece he realised he hadn't been really attending and came to me to ask, 'Miss Brown, which side did yer seh Ah'd t'leave me virgin?'

Such a scrambling there was into duffel coats and anoraks, such a hunting for twin wellingtons and lost gloves, such an impatience with a teacher struggling to take Assembly and mark the register, collect the dinner money and answer the telephone; such a forgetfulness, on their part, to visit the toilet before trousered and jumpered and fully buttoned up; such a muttering of 'Aw 'eck' and a struggling to manipulate lavatory snecks and zip fasteners!

At last the winter-donned family would be ready for the climb up Priest Bank, narrow and winding and the clamber over the stile not far from the farmhouse. There would be an annual scamper across the pasture to the gate into the holly thicket. There would always be a handful of boys who were nuisance rather than help, who gloried in jumping the stream, dashing up the glen 'looking' for the reddest berries but succeeding only in acquiring the reddest cheeks, frost-shiny noses and ear lobes. There were always the daring ones who wanted the topmost boughs, those who leaned too alarmingly over the full and noisy stream for the choicest sprays and those who got too far into the holly bush and had to be hauled out. But there were enough sensible, diligent people who kept things moving smoothly, among them that incredible handful whose harvest was so big they had to have help with their overload, and then the lads who were out just for fun were harnessed into helping and somehow or other we would trail wearily and happily back to school. We would be dirty and scratched and tired but it was downhill all the way and I loved the walking holly bushes ahead of me, the happy tribe, the builders of our Nativity. Children feel atmosphere as the plants feel sun and rain but they do not remember. Real memory comes with increased age. It takes nothing at all to release, for me, the fragrance of those newly clipped branches, the clean smell of the stream, the human one of wet and muddy children and the warmth of the welcoming atmosphere of the school. To the existing smells of Christmas tree, of glue and paper, of drying clothes on the hot radiators and wellies placed too near the heat, we would add the new fragrance of holly and ivy. Our cut and scratched hands would hurt as we washed them, together, in the children's cloakroom before dinner, and I would eye the dirty roller towel with silent criticism.

Together the worker bees of our community and I would set the dinner tables and our hunger for the school dinner would be a pleasurable pain. Our enjoyment of it would be greater than usual and a lot of children would be guilty of talking with their mouths full.

If I have no vivid memories of the lesser Christmases of my childhood at the village school, will my children remember the rich environment of their seven Christmases? I cannot expect my children to remember their primary school Christmases simply because to me they are so vivid. It is for the 250 children I taught, who shared my twenty-one Decembers, that I write.

The infants decorated the Christmas tree but it was the top juniors who built the Crib. There were usually less than a dozen in the year and it was their privilege and pleasure.

'Can we 'elp?' the younger ones would always ask and would be given a minor job because the elevated positions, the ladder climbing and window-ledge perching, to secure the roof and walls and put on the thatch, was a job reserved only for those most senior in rank. How they loved staggering around with the caretaker's enormous stepladder; how they loved mounting the furniture in stockinged feet, lashing the poles and weaving in the branches. It took all afternoon. Infant faces peeped through the windows of the partition and surreptitiously the door would open and they would appear, a knot of silent, awed onlookers. We were too busy and lost in our creative activity to mind them or their parents when they were collected at home time. That bell meant nothing to us. We just kept on until the job was done so that the very next morning the Assembly could be round the Crib. Joan or, Winnie in later years when we added a third teacher to the staff, would iron the robes and make new crowns, bejewelled with Rowntrees Fruit Pastilles. The Crib must be complete with hay rack and docile animals, its lantern, its perching birds in the rafters, its manger with the Christ child and the little robin looking at Jesus. Each year was unique in lesser details only, but we loved tradition and sought only for perfection.

Against the backcloth of the Crib, different plays were produced, new songs were sung, new poems and stories heard. At playtime the children involved themselves in imaginative play in and around the Crib and one year the eleven-year-olds asked to perform a play they had produced themselves.

The part of Joseph was portrayed by Richard. He was all legs and bounce, clatter and untidiness. He generally propelled himself with kangaroo hops and he taught me that eleven-year-old boys really were the noisiest animals in my quite extensive experience. On that particular morning, however, he was quiet and sedate and he led a tired Mary to the over-full inn.

"Ev ye any room?' he asked in his most grown-up voice yet.

'Sorry. We're full,' said Roy, a bright boy who spoke with the authority of almost always knowing the answer. 'But yer can sleep in the stable if that would be all right.'

Mary and Joseph crept inside the Crib and the audience was silent, awed by the wonder of the Nativity. Mary stooped to pick up the already placed Christ child from the straw in the manger and cradled it on her lap. The innkeeper returned and the audience presumed it was morning.

'Ah've brought yer sum brekfust,' he announced and bent over the baby. 'Where did that cum from?' he said, obviously 'ad libbing'.

'Whear they all cum from, yer daft lump,' Joseph replied without humour. Only the two teachers found solemnity almost impossible.

In the early years, before we began to hold a Christmas Fayre and had to turn our attention to the making of saleable craftwork, we were obsessed with the making of family Christmas presents. Our small school became a factory, mass producing presents for an incredible number of relatives. This activity occupied every playtime which did not provide a frosty slide in the yard or snow in the Rec. Lunchtimes, too, were used and a constant stream of children flowed through the staffroom door with queries about needlework, waste paper baskets and calendars. David leaned on Joan one day during our dinner break appreciation of the open fire on the staff-room hearth.

'Can Ah finish me carpet?' he asked with a smile which wrinkled his nose.

'It's not a carpet,' she said. 'It's a mat for Mummy's dressing table.'

He frequently got things wrong but he tried.

One day Joan said, 'You'll have to pull up your socks, young man.' Life was unfair. How can anyone, however hard he tries, pull up ankle socks? On another occasion he saw the hopelessness of it all and admitted with an endearing smile, 'Ah doan't knaw, 'S Armstrong.' Then, as if to explain everything, he repeated, 'Ah nivver knaw.'

Perhaps this was because he frequently did not attend. One story time the infants were sitting in an informal group on the floor listening to a story of a small singing bird. David was dreamily looking out of the window so was asked, gently so as to return his concentration to the lesson, 'Who was singing, David?'

He looked round with surprise and said, "T'warn't me, 'S Armstrong. 'T'warn't me.'

In 1962, the first year of the Crib, there were scarcely more than fifty children on roll. We began each day of the final week with an Assembly before the live Holy Family and each child had at least one turn of dressing in eastern robes, of wearing a crown or a halo or the head gear we traditionally associate with Palestinian shepherds. Each day ended with the whole school in an informal group before the Crib and the flickering candles. The day would darken and we would be singing carols unaccompanied and probably untunefully. A five-year-old would find its way onto each of our knees, awed by loveliness.

During the final week everything happened round the Crib but, as far as the children were concerned, the most important event was the Christmas party. The morning was spent making paper hats and doilies for the table. Previous kitchen staff and past teachers came along to help. A Santa Claus would pay a visit and a good time was had by all. Of course I remember the children and their enjoyment of the traditional party, the fancy dress and the Grand Old Duke of York, the annual arrival of Father Christmas, the Musical Chairs and Spinning the Bottle. That game was a must and the eleven-year-old boys did not mind pecking the infant girls, or the teachers, though their aim had been most definitely for their contemporaries.

But most of all, I think, I remember the bonhomie of the staff after the children had gone, the darkness outside and the bright lights within and everyone busy clearing up the litter of wrapping paper, burst balloons and sweet papers, because the local shopkeepers invariably sent a bagful of toffees for a Scramble. If I value the happy hours spent with children in that

village school so do I also value the happy staff relationships and the togetherness of after-party, fête, rummage sale or Carol Service. After-party was best,
for when chores were almost completed, the dinner ladies, the caretaker
and the teachers gathered round the table for their share of the party tea.
There was always a great feeling of unity, a warmth and friendliness only
possible among people who share the same sense of humour. There was not
one Christmas in the twenty-one where this feeling of comradeship did not
exist.

There is nothing more familiar to me than the atmosphere of the last day
of a term and in particular the last day of the autumn one when the goodwill of the previous day's party overflowed into the next morning. There
was a chaos and a busyness unequalled. Every child turned out his desk,
scrubbed and polished it; every child parcelled up his Christmas presents,
exchanged cards and gifts. Every cupboard was turned out and every picture
and decoration stripped from the walls.

There were twice as many children, it seemed, and they were all over the
place, occupying odd moments of calm with toys and games brought from
home. Visitors would step over Tom, Dick and Harry running matchbox
cars along floorboard roads and wonder how all this disorder would be
resolved. But we had a faith born of experience and we knew that by home
time order would have been restored and that nothing would remain except
a full dustbin.

Junior and infant children mingled, careless of which room they played
in. The mature could be found doing baby jigsaws on the pretence that they
were checking the pieces but they deceived no one. Peace and order were
there even if they were not obvious to the stranger. In the midst of it all the
County Supplies van would arrive and the big boys would help carry in all
the requisitioned stock to clutter an already too-full staff-room. If I had bet
my last pound on stock being delivered on the last day of term I would never
have lost it.

The last day of the Christmas week was such a happy, peaceful day full
of children's seasonal offerings, the caretaker's wife's delicious scones and
mince pies and everyone's good wishes. When it was all over, the last child
gone and the school empty, I would make a cup of coffee and sit down to do
my clerical work, fill in the end of term forms and put an appropriate entry
into the Log Book. Darkness having then fallen I would not feel so conspicuous struggling with a six-foot Christmas tree on the two buses home.

'Nay, Missus, cun't thee a' getten one bigger?' the conductor would say.

After the activity of school, the Guide party and the carol singing at the
Blind Home, Christmas itself was always an anticlimax. The aunts came to
stay on Christmas Eve 1962. It was bitterly cold. We went to the midnight
service at the village church and sang a carol outside The Currer on our
return.

On Christmas Day, as on all other days, we carried out bales to feed
the herd. Until the hay was cleared from the barn there was no overnight

accommodation for the bulk of our cattle. Their thick hair was standing erect against the wind and the freezing temperatures.

The family came for Boxing Day; not the whole family for the cousins had left the mainstream. We would not have dared do differently, for Mother was devoted to family and at Christmas it was more important than ever. Aunt Elsie sat at the piano and we sang all the old-fashioned carols and the songs of the twenties, the light operas and musical comedies.

A very happy evening, it was, that 26th December 1962 and no one knew that snow was falling heavily outside. When we opened the door to let out the guests there was already a white blanket everywhere. A fine, driving blizzard swept across the yard covering the cars, whitening the porch windows and coming in under the door. As we opened it a thousand flakes rushed into the house. There are two kinds of snow. Wet big flakes you know are all show and no stamina and fine driving snow you know is here to stay. It all looked rather beautiful but the wind was nasty and there were no lights visible in the valley. A snow fog isolated us on the threshold of one of the severest winters we have known.

The road, which had opened up the way for visitors' cars and corn deliveries, now became a liability. Contrary to the laws of gravity, what comes down must go up and those who drive sit warmly in their seats, revving far too noisily, whilst we, the members of the so-called weaker sex, push and shove and shovel to reach the downhill on the other side of the Moor Gate. So did it happen on that memorable day and it was three months before the next car came down. That is not exactly true for our contractor friend came in a Land Rover, one day, and he literally drove over the closed Moor Gate, so deep and hard was the snow.

The exertion of the effort to get those three cars out at the top made us feel warm but when Father and the two of us re-entered the house we were saturated and numb. Mother and Harry were washing up after the party. There were still jobs to do which would last till morning. Sudden snow always takes us unawares. It finds a thousand entries into barns and sheds. A whiteness already covered the stacked bales in the barn for the east wind is expert at driving fine snow under the heavy Yorkshire slates. A sculptured drift had formed at the front door and others at the entrance to all the sheds. The wind had begun its winter artistry and with wicked determination Jack Frost was preparing for a long occupation.

The suckled herd huddled against the farmhouse, finding shelter under the west wall. They were already white and pathetic. We took out extra bales of hay, and dropped and loosened them in the relative shelter of the west wall. Mistaking every bale for a sail, the wind swept us before it without mercy. We had no piped water to the calf sheds and we re-filled the baths from the kitchen tap, letting in the wind every time we opened the door, filling buckets too full in our eagerness to get the job done and succeeding in spilling plenty of water down our wellington tops.

In the sitting room the logs burned brightly. The decorated tree caught the flickering firelight with its many baubles and strands of tinsel. Strings of cards from over a hundred friends festooned the walls. A sprig of mistletoe dropped from the centre light and sprays of holly crowned the pictures on the wall. Depleted bowls of nuts and tangerines, sugared almonds and chocolates littered the sideboard. Dogs and cats crawled from under the furniture, whither they had withdrawn while the relatives were here, and sprawled gratefully on the thick, woollen hearthrug.

The snow of 1963 was an epic which will be remembered for ever. It tested our endurance and our humour to the limit. Unlike 1947, we had plenty of hay and bedding straw but corn only ever lasts until the end of the month. The situation was different, too, in that we had no cows to milk commercially and no milk to deliver but as a teaching head there was no way that I could have been excused. In twenty-one years, sickness prevented my attending school for odd days on two or three occasions, the weather never.

Great drifts piled themselves up outside The Currer completely cutting us off from the outside world. I wrote letters with the home address of 'The Arctic' and when the first day of term arrived I set off in very early-morning darkness and struggled through drifts so deep that, at the end of the fields I had to remove the snow from my stocking tops. I wonder if the inventor of tights was a lady who had had similar experiences! In deep drifts it is disastrous to wear wellingtons for the snow wedges itself between welly and leg, and the boot is virtually impossible to remove.

The whole countryside was held in the grip of an abnormally keen frost. In the valley, where the snow did not lie so thickly, the river and the canal were soon frozen and the houses near my school were the first to be without water. The pipes in the village froze before the New Year came in but it was towards the middle of January before the polythene pipe bringing our own supply from the mains deserted us. When it did there was a state of things never experienced before.

Daily we needed hot water to mix milk for forty calves and a great deal of water is necessary for pigs and wintered-in yearlings. The pond was frozen too hard to break the ice but the overflow from it continued to run and where it plunged two feet to the stream the suckled herd could drink outside. We prayed that the flow would continue, for our only other source of perpetual water was the spring, that small hollow with its three little lifting areas of water. We could take water from there for our own drinking but no more. After 1963 we piped the spring water into a drinking sink and feel secure now when water from the mains deserts us, but the big freeze caught us unprepared. We were grateful that the water from the frozen pond continued to flow. It became an ice cave, treacherous to negotiate and quite beautiful with Jack Frost's artistry. The flow was slow and we used to place a bucket on the bridge which straddled it and patiently fill it a jugful at a time. The job was backbreaking and the tendency was to fill the bucket without looking, for the effort to unbend was too much. The noise of the small waterfall and the well-hooded ears lulled one into an unawareness and it was sometimes too late before we noticed an opportunist cow emptying the bucket as fast as we filled it. When we did, we behaved like comedians of the silent movies, waving and gesticulating and scrambling unsuccessfully up the icy bank and trying to shoo the thirsty animal away. But a bucket is empty when a cow lifts out its head no matter how definitely one protests.

Getting water from the spring twenty yards further along the road was a different matter. The bowl of water was no more than two inches deep and had to be lifted cupful by cupful for our own drinking. Because of an orange sediment which stained the pebbles in the hollow, the water was thought to contain iron and therefore to be health giving. Perhaps that was what gave us the necessary strength to endure that very long winter!

The road was completely blocked with ridge after ridge of deep white drifts, the final one completely covering the Moor Gate so no water could be carted from the village. We calculated that, during the forty-nine days of the frozen water pipe, between us we carried some 6,000 gallons of water and walked 250 miles to do so.

We carried the two camp bins into the kitchen and kept one full of drinking water and the other full of washing water from the stream. We were continually carrying this water upstairs to ladle it, little by little, into the water tank above the cistern. The space above the tank and the low bedroom ceiling is about four inches and we had to stand precariously on a shelf of the airing cupboard and tip it in with a small enamel jug. In this way we could keep the Aga going. It was our only means of cooking other than the Turm Sports meths stove we took on our wanderings. Keeping the Aga going was our number one priority.

Because of modern methods of road clearance there was not the chaos of 1947. The steep road to the town was seldom closed for more than a few hours. If I had to walk down the hill in the morning there was usually a bus to bring me up it at night and the buses along the valley to my village school kept running. They were not always on time but one eventually came. The five fields to the village at home were easier to negotiate than the road up the hill to the Moor Gate. On most mornings my previous day's track was obliterated by overnight snow and a wind change had re-shaped the drifts. I never left home without doing my smaller share of the lifting of water and it was always my first job on return.

The preservation of water became a perfected skill. We found innumerable ways of recycling it. The water we poured almost boiling into the hot water bottles at night was re-emptied into the cistern each morning. On Sunday evenings we ran an ungenerous depth of water into the bath and followed one another quickly so that the water had not cooled too much for the last person to take a dip. This was always Margaret, for the nature of her job made her the dirtiest.

We would then empty the dirty clothes onto the bathroom floor and put those which needed a steeping, into the bath. Next morning the grey water was wrung from the clothes, a little of it was used to wash the bathroom floor and the front porch but most of it was kept to flush the toilet. The outlet drain was so frozen the plug was decorative only. It was only by emptying a bucket of water down the loo daily that we were able to keep the sanitary arrangements working. We thought it was a miracle every time everything disappeared. It was not until the thaw that the truth was revealed. Sewage had been freezing like everything else and one day Margaret found a chaos at the septic tank the saga of which is unfit for publication.

We began to take meals before the front room fire and to forget what visitors were. Nobody came to The Currer in the long winter of 1963. On the half-term Sunday it was essential that I post some urgent letters. I scrambled over the drifts to the nearest letterbox. One of the villagers came out of her farmhouse kitchen to ask how we were surviving in such Arctic conditions and I saw, with wonder and reverence, her table laid for Sunday tea. I couldn't take my eyes from the white cloth and the plates of crisp lettuce and juicy, red tomatoes, the circles of cucumber and the brilliant yellow of the hard-boiled eggs. How long would it be before the table at The Currer would stand waiting for long overdue guests? This housewife was having a struggle too; but the farm is on the roadside so she is never isolated. She has a son who runs the farm and we share our long western boundary. He is a good neighbour whose cattle seldom stray onto our land. When ours get onto his it is usually into an empty field and we can get them back with the minimum of fuss. His life is singularly full of honest, daily work. He has inherited endurance from his now very aged mother. As an octogenarian she did more work than many of the local young folk put together. Now, at over ninety, she still hasn't fully retired. I often find her at the sink, washing dishes. When neighbours' cattle storm the boundary wall they are immediately surrounded by our herd and for half an hour there is chaos. Every animal is infected with the desire to stampede or meet head on in battle. Then men will appear and look along the wall for signs of their escape route.

'Where've the buggers got in?' they'll explode and we'll all join the chase, whistling at dogs and having a mad but finally victorious time. Puffing and blowing they'll accompany their efforts with derogatory remarks about 'the buggers' but once these are back through the gate we all lean on it and forget the chase. We have good neighbours.

The suckling herd stayed close to the buildings throughout the short days and the long nights. Fresh falls each day covered their droppings and it was not until the thaw that we discovered the mountain of manure which lay under the drifts around the house. Corn had to be bought to feed the calves and pigs and keep the cattle from becoming too thin. It was delivered to the Moor Gate, a quarter of a mile away, in 56 lb. bags and had to be carried home. The crusted drifts, which easily supported our unladen weight, collapsed under the extra half-hundredweight. Suddenly the crust would give and we would be floundering thigh deep, the icy surface capable of amputating a leg and the heavy weight threatening to dislocate a neck.

The school children revelled in the whiteness and depth and brilliance of it, rolling in it, hurling it at each other and building it into barricades and snowmen. The Rec was a museum of sculptures produced one handwork lesson and re-whitened every day with a fresh fall. We went on snow expeditions, climbing to the hilltops, measuring the depth of drifts and testing the strength of the ice coverings. The canal, the river and all the hill tarns and farm ponds were solid. Adventurous villagers crossed in safety and some got out skates.

Eventually even the children got sick of it. They longed for grass, for football and races and were fed up of wet clothes and red noses. The longing for running water became a pain which invaded our dreams and each morning the routine began with the chore of carrying gallons of water upstairs and pouring it half-pint at a time into the tank. A CCI who lived up on the moor above school often called in to exchange tales of woe. Her struggle compared with mine in the same way that mine compared with the hardship Margaret and Father had to suffer. They were always wet and sore, always had aching backs and frosted fingers and I felt a deserter, leaving them for the warmth of school.

If my lot was hard during those memorable months, it was minimal compared with the lot of Father and Margaret. Theirs was a continued outdoor struggle. Heavy buckets drag down shoulders and insides, gloves only become wet and freeze and are best left indoors so hands become swollen and numb. Each day sacks of corn had to be carried and bales loosened in the intakes.

When I piled more coal on the open fire in the staff-room and gathered the children about my feet for discussion or story, I thought of them struggling on the hilltop.

In 1963 the need for shelter was a crying one but in spite of the appalling conditions, the survival rate was a hundred per cent. The calves we had bought in August were healthy and the new calf sheds were secure and draught-proof. Over the years increasing age rusted, warped and loosened the corrugated tins. Repairs and patched-up sections of storm-damaged roofing were never again so perfect. The young cows were strong in 1963. Later, as they grew older, less severe winters were to cause havoc and we can look back on winters when death stalked the hill and every morning seemed to reveal a new tragedy.

As the terrible freeze-up dragged into March our store of hay in the laithe was depleted to such an extent that the suckling herd, to avoid weakening after so many months, was able to come inside. Twice a day they were let out to drink and their cloven hooves dragged out manure and bedding straw into the yard at our front door. The stream water was continually disturbed by drinking cattle. We were afraid of getting careless. Harry had already filled the teakettle with stream water by mistake. It tasted of manure. We were once asked how we knew. Oh, my goodness, we know all right. We cannot count the number of dirty tails which have been swished into our mouths whilst milking or the times an inconsiderate cow, loose with spring grass or autumn fog, has performed too close to us and faces and lips have received an unwelcome splattering.

We began to miss the weekly clothes wash, turning sheets and pillowcases and begging a bath in town from one or other of our friends. If no Friday night fall obliterated my track across the fields we would struggle to the bus with Mother and Harry so that they could go down to the aunts' for tea and they would take clean undies and have a bath there for still no thaw came.

'The first thing we will do when running water comes,' we announced with sincere intentions, 'is to have a bath and then spring clean the house!' but as each monotonous day passed the flesh became weaker and the will less determined.

The first of the spring calves was born in the near intake, behind a huge snow drift, one bleak Sunday afternoon at the beginning of March. We christened him Robin and Margaret carried a bale of straw to give him a warm bed for an hour or two before the thieving wind took it away. The knowledge that the March calves were being born, in some way, gave us hope.

When rain eventually came conditions worsened rapidly. We had believed that the thaw would be a blessing, that water would come flowing through the taps, green grass would spring up everywhere and the air become fragrant with instant spring. Nowt o' t' sort! Cold, icy rain fell on the snow, causing us to live on a glacier. Manure defrosted and became stinking sludge which not only seeped into the stream but also polluted the spring and we had no drinking water at all. We had to make a dangerous, sliding journey to the village to struggle home with a pathetically small quantity for human consumption only. All but the most essential uses ceased altogether and life became ridiculous.

Water came to the school long before it came to The Currer. We discovered later that our polythene pipe, which should be well buried, is very near the surface in the gateway of our neighbour's field. Now when frost threatens to persist Margaret carries a couple of bales of straw as a crude form of insulation. It seems to work, but there has never since been a year as cold as 1963.

It was essential that I looked respectable for a managers' meeting which fell during March. Joan said, 'Come and have tea with us and have a bath.' I did and for nineteen years thereafter I had tea with my infants' teacher before the termly managers' meeting, a ritual I remember with pleasure.

The grass appeared in the Rec long before it did at The Currer. I found Andrew leaping around the playing field when the first square yard yielded to the warmer morning sun. 'Hey, Miss Brown,' he yelled, "S green!'

I regularly carried bottles of water home from school in my rucksack. It was never enough. We tried to divert the glacial river from the road but the water continued to taste and inevitably we were all ill. One by one the members of the family vomited. We knew what was wrong, turned on the kitchen tap and prayed for water. I lasted until Friday. Sick and miserable, Margaret carried water from the village. The first day of spring was only a week away. I began to feel sick at school on that long awaited Friday when water at last began to trickle from the tap. It came a drop at a time, a thick brown sludge. I had expected, one day, to open the door of home to the joyous news, an active washing machine, a singing kettle. It wasn't like that. The first bowl took hours to fill and was undrinkable. Laden with bottles of clean water, frightened I wouldn't reach home before being sick, I staggered into the house to be told, not that water had come, but that a load of corn had been delivered to the Moor Gate and that I was needed to give a hand. I donned dirty clothes and helped Father and Margaret up and down the quarter of a mile of hill until the job was done and then I was well and truly sick.

When nice, clean, running water came we were all in no fit shape to enjoy it. The weekend was over before we had gathered any strength after the sickness. It was a lifesaver that the suckling herd could now crowd into the laithe each night. They will lie down happily on crisp January snow but February Fill Dyke did not come until March and when the fields are waterlogged cattle remain standing and weaken rapidly.

I had the first bath. If I had not had to go to school I think I could not have summoned the necessary energy. Little by little things became normal again and a lost routine was found. It took a long time to erase the scars of the long ordeal. Manure was a problem. Behind the farmhouse there had been shelter from the east wind and cattle had huddled there for weeks on end. When the temperature rose their three-month dung appeared. It held the thawing snow and became a manure slick which began to slither into the yard and in its semi-liquid state was difficult to handle and remove. The thaw also exposed the blocked drain to the septic tank.

But the peewits came. It wasn't long before we saw the cuckoo and eventually the swallows returned. The peewits are always the first to arrive and are Margaret's harbingers of the springtime. They are numerous on the meadows and pastures which were once moorland and how their flimsy nests and the minute, scurrying babies survive two hundred grazing cattle is an April miracle.

The spring calves were being born daily and Margaret and Father spent a great deal of their time counting and checking the herd. A morning check is always fraught with worry no matter how beautiful the day, how thick the mist in the valley or how confidently the larks are hovering and singing somewhere up against the blue. There is always a spring fear that disaster will have fallen in the night. A hard winter, a sudden rush of growth, a surplus of lush, wet grass and chaos can reign. Magnesium deficiency is sudden and often fatal, worm and foul a menace.

A pleasanter job was the evening check which I did frequently with Margaret whilst Father attended his garden. That wander over the hillside, just before dusk, was a joy. The herd gathered together at bedtime and it was the crazy hour for young calves. They would frolic like lambs or pyjama'd children and gallop madly all over the place for no reason. Then, instinctively knowing that the time was right, they would find their mothers and there would be a great banging of udders and a slobbering of froth and tails would wag everywhere.

Many of my contemporaries and some of the teenage children that I have known have experienced a period of agnosticism. They have found it difficult to believe in God. Wait, I would say; some day, when you have been present at birth and death, nursed sickness, witnessed health and a hundred little miracles of day and night and seasons and growth; when you've struggled and suffered, wept and lost, won and harvested you will find the hardest thing is not to believe. 'Prove to me there is a God,' they would say. 'Prove to me there is not,' I would reply and one day they would tell me. One would say, 'I remember standing before a storm on the coast of Skye and you said it was moments like that when you knew there was a God and I've never forgotten.' Another would say her awareness had begun one day on Tiree when we were standing in a worshipful horseshoe on a blue, blue day. Another would choose 'Amazing Grace' for a wedding hymn and in the words 'the hour I first believed' I knew that doubts had fled.

How poor are the rich who have never been country children. What hope is there for the poor in the inner cities? I think I have seen the stars on every clear night and every full moon that could find a window in the clouds to peep down onto the earth. Now I go into the dining room and say to our paying guests, 'The full moon is just coming up!' and no one moves. So I go into our sitting room and say it to my aged mother and Auntie Mary and Harry or disturb Margaret in the cattle sheds and they go to the window. They understand. I have seen thousands of sunsets but I have to drag most guests by the arm and force them onto the hill behind The Currer to see the valley flooded with gold and the sky painted a bold and glorious red. Not so my camping children who would leave every chore to bolt over the dune to see the sun set behind the island of Taransay.

Chapter Eleven

We needed more sheds. The winter had shouted this at us. A friend equipped himself with enough machinery to do contract work in the locality. What little equipment we had, to attempt to compete in an increasingly mechanised industry, was deteriorating fast. To spread muck from a hundred little heaps in the meadows was no longer economic. It was cheaper to get a contractor to do the work than to buy a dozen pieces of expensive machinery and, like as not, have to employ another hand to use it. This contractor became a good friend and it was he who brought us four 30 foot by 1 foot by 6 inch beams with which we were able to roof our first real cattle shed. With our own tractor and the hay trailer, we carried stone from the crumbling walls of the intakes and built parallel walls, east and west, on the other side of the yard entrance. Father was always the organiser. I became the builder, Margaret the cement mixer and the corrugated tin roofer, though rather than wait for cement I would sometimes mix it, and Father often added stones to the walls whilst I was at school. That first shed we built was the best because the roof timbers were so superb.

My head-teacher's hands became so mutilated that when I took the Sea Rangers on an educational visit to the Police Station and our fingerprints were taken for fun, mine appeared to have been worn away. 'Good God, woman,' the police sergeant muttered, 'what do you do?'

'I'm a headmistress,' I said.

He looked at me, laughed and said, 'Pull the other one.' Thereafter, every time I had occasion to go to the Police Station I was known.

We were justifiably proud of that shed. The beams were too heavy for us to handle but Les Pearce came with his fork lift and we manhandled them into place. Corrugated tins were delivered and Margaret roofed. Have you ever tried hammering springhead nails through heavy gauge corrugated tin? You'll need a very heavy hammer, your thumb will soon be black and you won't hear anything all evening. She is good on roofs, is Margaret. She doesn't mind the height as I do. If the tins bend under my weight my stomach turns over. I never thought I would be able to do it at all but when we started buying fibreglass sheets I had no option. We came home with a hundred, once, and only when we started to use them did we find that Margaret was not tall enough to nail them on. They were four feet wide and could not be stood upon. Even I could only just reach and the nail which had to go further-most away each time had to hold down four thicknesses. Have a go at that, too, and see how many human nails you blacken, lying horizontally and petrified, high above the earth!

Between this new shed and the calf sheds we planted apple trees and gooseberry and blackcurrant bushes and each year we extended the garden. Every March it was my job to dig the vegetable patch. I did most of the spade work, beginning one sunny weekend and working until dark each evening all the next week. Beautiful, it looked, rich brown, damp and level and very heavily manured. Father was the planter, tender and harvester. When the weeds beat him, Margaret spent long hours on her knees and when the peas needed stringing she would help. But the credit for the very productive garden must be laid at Father's feet.

I look back with nostalgia on those wonderful self-supportive days, when we could grow all we needed and when buying milk, butter and cream were unknown. The greatest joy of the garden was the opportunity to give. Only people who have, can give. The greatest tragedy of being out of work is that one can find oneself in the position of having nothing to share. I remember having an argument with a good friend whose very definite socialism and Christianity caused her to criticise the large car owned by the vicar. 'It should be bigger!' I said.

'Aw, Skipper,' she protested. 'A vicar shouldn't have a big car.'

'A vicar should have a mini-bus,' I insisted. Transport should be big enough to be of service to others. Similarly, a home should be big enough to accept guests, adopt elderly relatives, entertain friends; the table must seat more than the family and the hearth be big enough for many to get warm.

Father's garden produced much more than we needed and the best of everything he gave away. No one called at the farm and left empty-handed. If it were winter they would get eggs or a jar of cream or a pat of butter or some of Mother's homemade biscuits or jam. If it were the summer the produce from the garden was distributed liberally and over-generously. He would even give away the bilberries which took so long for us to gather. Yet our old man never had any money. His pocket was always empty and when he died all he had was one share in the corn merchant's which realised just £200 and only went half way to paying for his funeral. He never had any money to give but his produce, his home, his time, his advice and his assurance he gave abundantly.

My father could grow vegetables fit for the Palace and yet he was never fully appreciated, for a tidy garden wins the praise and our well-manured acre could grow weeds splendidly.

Whilst the spring calves were being born, the garden tended and the swathes of hay cut and turned, I was busy being a typical village head-mistress. I was teacher, secretary, dinner supervisor, odd-job-man, marriage guidance consultant, hostess, baby-sitter, Guider and friend. If a sheep fell into the canal the boys and I would fish it out. If a parent had to visit the hospital, her children and I would make tea and play Snakes and Ladders until after visiting hours. If a tramp appeared he was fed. Joan usually looked after the sick animals, especially the birds.

Together we went to funerals and nearly always, if there was a wedding in the village church, just over the playground wall, we would take the children to watch. I turned a blind eye when our dinner lady arrived late because she could not resist the temptation to steal in and sit on the back pew of the nave. Once, five-year-old Jennifer was beside us when the bride went in. Some time later our dinner lady came in with a rush, intent on making up with elbow grease for lack of punctuality. Jennifer intercepted her dash to the kitchen.

'Did yer see the bride come out, 'S Horner?'

'Yes,' said the hurrying lady's back.

'Did yer see the baby?' Jenny believed in instant miracles.

New babies were always brought to school, for the village teachers were hungry for cuddles and all new brothers and sisters had to be exhibited. One such baby was Colin, the fourth in a family which eventually became five. We were making posters for the spring rummage sale, due on 2nd April. 'That's ah Jackie's birthday,' Graham, the eldest, said.

'How old is she?' I wanted to know.

'She'll be three.'

'I can't believe it,' I said, amazed at the speed with which children grow.

'Yeh,' said her brother, 'An' ah lad's three weeks an' five days.'

Thereafter we always called Colin, Ah Lad.

One baby was a long time before it chose to arrive. Expected before the half-term break there was still no sign of it when we returned.

'We ... ll?' Joan asked the expectant brother, 'Have you nothing to tell me?'

'No,' answered Stephen. Then, 'Aw, d'yer mean about the baby, 'cos if it doesn't come before the weekend we're getting a new butcher.' Work that one out!

Alison spent the first weeks at school telling tales about other children. She walked through the staff-room door every few minutes if she knew we were inside. She prefixed every adverse report with, 'Yer don't knaw, you two.' Then would come the dreadful details 'John's peeping in ve girls' toilets!' 'David's in school when yer said we'd ter go out!' 'Lynne 'a'n't gor 'er coat on!'

Her brother had married and a baby was due. We were entertained with daily bulletins. Joan was waiting for the final announcement. 'If she says,

"You don't knaw, you two," I'll answer back sharply, "Well, Miss Brown might not, young lady, but I do!"'

Calves, babies, kittens, puppies! I took a kitten to school in the belief that a school cat would be a lovely pet, put an end to any mice problems and make the infrequent telephone call to the Pest Controller unnecessary. That gentleman would come after school and put a little pile of poison down all the likely holes, of which there are plenty in an old school. We were so near the canal and an occasional dead rat on the road made us wary. We were in the staff-room, one story-time, about a week after the rat man had been, when I suddenly saw this huge rat crawl out of the gas meter cupboard in the corner. It was obviously a very sick rat but nevertheless not a pleasant sight. The children were marvellous and we evacuated the room in no time. I shut the door firmly and sent for the caretaker.

Yes, we thought, a school cat would be an excellent idea. The poor, half-grown kitten was very frightened. It found a hole behind the radiators and it disappeared. We spent hours trying to get it out. Two days passed before we finally succeeded and I brought the poor thing home, a wiser person.

Now pups were a different matter. How I loved to take a hamper of puppies for a day's frolic among the children! Whereas a kitten runs away, a pup immediately makes human contact. I always found one or two good homes. One is not a village school head long before one knows everyone in the village and where each child lives. The knowledge comes from taking sick children home, visiting ill parents, providing families with pups and kittens and waving to mums at the kitchen sink and grandfathers in the garden while out on nature walks.

There are few occasions we enjoyed more than the annual rummage sale. The top class girls helped Joan to sort out the rummage while I attempted to keep the rest of the school occupied. The older boys spent the whole morning collecting jumble. Contributions were so tremendous in quantity and value no one could fail to have a good time. The girls, helping Joan, would be encouraging her to try things on and little piles would appear as the privileged pupils put away the articles they intended to buy when evening came. When our numbers nearly doubled the girls lost the enviable jobs to adults, which was a pity. Long live small schools! The smaller the group the more responsibility for meaningful work falls on each individual.

In the days of Roddy, Jill, Lynne and Christopher all children took an active part and we had great fun watching them buy. Jill's mother complained bitterly that her daughter annually bought back the things she had thrown out. The children seldom knew what belonged to them. Jill would re-buy and Julie would take off her cardigan in the heat of the evening and someone would sell it.

Someone brought a carpet beater. Few children know what it is like to beat the carpet on the line and see the clouds and clouds of dust fly out. 'I think I'll buy that,' I said, 'It looks a useful sort of thing.' I gave it an experimental swish and asked for a volunteer so that I could try it out. Andrew was game and I produced quite a noisy whack on his backside. The whole school had gathered to watch the fun and Andrew, always an actor if given an audience, pranced round the room yelping and holding the not very sore spot.

That evening I found Christopher's father diligently searching the stalls. 'Are you looking for something special?' I asked.

'Yes,' said the obedient father, 'I've been told to buy a carpet beater!'

Roddy bought clothes. Whilst his contemporaries clustered round the toy stall, bought jigsaws and books, old cameras and radios and gorged themselves on hot dogs, pies and peas from the kitchen, Roddy bought clothes, drab, ill-fitting ones, and wore them for weeks. Had his mother asked him to wear a coat with the sleeves too long and the pockets too low, I am sure he would have refused scornfully. He would have noticed that the collar was too big and that the buttons fastened the ladies' way. To all these imperfections he was blind and he wore rummage sale clothes with a certain swagger, turning with masculine clumsiness in front of us to exhibit his wonderfully cheap buys.

Lynne bought huge lampshades, umbrellas and high-heeled shoes, amassing her amazing pile until the last penny was spent and then waiting patiently for the give aways from the piles we were sweeping into the bag for the rag and bone man.

The hard winter was not long behind us and Margaret and I needed a tonic so we went to Jura. It lies peacefully alongside its busier neighbour, Islay, and has a fast diminishing population of people and an increasing number of deer.

We packed our rucksacks, strapped on the BP tent and caught the night train to Glasgow.

We sailed up the Kyles of Bute to Tarbert, Loch Fyne, and crossed the strip of mainland by which hangs the Mull of Kintyre, to the West Loch Tarbert pier and the Jura/Islay ferry. In those days it called at the twin islands in that order. It was the bluest of May days, the decks were scorching and the mountains very hazy and distant. A spring heat wave was on its way and we had not yet learned to wear shorts. We did not anticipate that the tar on the Jura road would bubble and that we would suffer sunburn. We had brought with us heavy tweed skirts and lined tailored trousers. We hitched up our skirts inelegantly on deck and seeped up the sun. The wooden seats were red hot and the sea shimmered as far as the eye could see.

We landed at Craighouses and sweated up the pier to the island shop, a ritual we performed annually to buy stores before we left the beaten track. On the small islands, the shop is always closed while the boat is unloaded. We were eventually told that the delivery van-cum-minibus-cum-taxi would be following the one road in about an hour and we decided to accompany it and get to the north of the island. We occupied the waiting hour watching barebacked men roll whisky barrels up the slope of the distillery. Their activity seemed piratical and foreign against the backcloth of deer hills. Eventually the delivery van meandered its way from house to house, emptying the post boxes, leaving stores and newspapers, picking up gossip and passengers and passing on messages. We were in no hurry.

We were dropped at Ardlussa and pitched our tent on the shore, an idyllic spot. Behind us were trees; in front were the sea and the distant hills of the mainland. Our few days there were utterly peaceful. We were alone and saw no one. The morning sun was old before we woke on those idyllic Ardlussa mornings. It was hot, the earth beneath us was warm and no one needed us. Eventually I would sit up in my sleeping bag, look out of the tent door which had been open all night and think dreamily about breakfast. It posed no problem. All I had to do was to put my hand under the tent wall and bring in the Turm Sports, kettle, frying pan and water carrier. From the cosiness of my bed I could light the stove, make the porridge and fry the bacon and the eggs. Margaret would waken; we would lean against the framed rucksacks which had been our pillows and eat facing the open door and the sea.

Eventually we would get up and, barefooted, Margaret would go to the stream to wash the dishes. Later we would take chocolate and apples and wander off over the deer hills happily being free. There were miles and miles of grass and heather and no people's voices, only the call of sea birds, the constant slap of waves on the shore and the splash of them against the rocks. The heat was May madness and the midges had not yet come from wherever they do. The curlew and the cuckoo never stopped calling. We found that we could bathe in peat streams without fear of being seen, that skin is water-proof and needs no towel. Soap and swimming costumes must take away the natural oils which turn water like good PVC. The heatwave scorched and blistered us relentlessly so that the cool, deep pools were a frequent tempta-tion we could not resist.

One day we headed north and sat for a long time watching the turbulence of the Corryvrekken. We took off our shoes to walk at the water's edge but the coldness was unbearable. It caused real pain. I don't think I've ever felt a colder sea.

We did not want to leave Jura without meeting people so, somewhat reluctantly, we packed our rucksacks and turned south looking for some-where to make a phone call home. At Lussagiven, having telephoned, we met an old man, Johnny Darroch, who invited us to pitch our tent on an apron of grass just outside his cottage. It seemed an excellent way to get to know the islanders so we accepted and within minutes had been drawn into the community. It happens to us on all Hebridean islands. We met the school teacher and were invited to spend an afternoon in school where there were just three children. I remember taking a photograph of the PE lesson with a five- a seven- and a ten-year-old, all boys, jumping over bamboo canes just as if they were in a class of forty. It made my village school look enormous.

I remember Lussagiven for the heady scent of bluebells and the sickly coconut-ice smell of the gorse bushes. They were so full of flower, you could not know that there were prickles underneath. In the exceptionally hot sunshine of Jura we could forget the winter.

Then came another opportunity to get a lift with the delivery van back to Craighouses. From somewhere south of the Jura pier we took a track along the shore, to a house at Crackaig. We called there to fill our water carrier and walked another mile along the edge of the sea searching for a suitable place to pitch our tent. The shore was a mass of driftwood and whenever we passed the cottage, at Crackaig, and every night when we went for a céilidh with Mr and Mrs Sandy Shaw, we deposited armfuls of kindling beside the door.

We were very sunburnt and swollen with the intense heat. We seemed to have all the wrong clothes. It was only May and there was still snow in the corries on the mainland mountains but Jura was an oven.

Eventually we walked south to the jetty and the ferry to Port Askaig. A boat left Islay, very early in the morning, for Colonsay so we pitched our tent on a postage stamp of grass within a stone's throw of the gangway. The small lawn overhung the shore and it wasn't the boat engines which woke us but the lapping of water under our tent. The tide was full; it had eroded the earth under our turf and made tunnels and caves through which it gurgled uncannily. We both woke up laughing and felt to see if we were wet. Not only could we hear, we could also feel the weight of the sea behind each wave.

And so we went to Colonsay, one of the most beautiful of islands. For a short time we lived with the sea birds on the shore at Tobar Bay. The violent heat had gone out of the sun, its gentler rays browned us and the swelling left our arms and legs. I say, 'Hurrah for small islands!' You can walk round them and see them all.

The Sea Ranger Crew took up so much of my time it seemed logical to hand over the Guide Company to Margaret and appoint Enid Shackleton, a County Cadet, as lieutenant. They were more than qualified to run the unit and worked very well together. We decided to spend the first week of summer camp together on Tiree after which the Rangers would sail to Barra for a week of lightweight camping. When we returned from Jura, we were pretty busy trying to prepare ourselves for this, to cope with the hay harvest and the end of summer term activities children enjoy so much.

On the outward journey to Tiree we lost our D'Abri, the big tent in which we all sat for meals. This could have spelt disaster, for the islands are windswept most of the time and only in hot weather did we ever eat out of doors. Food cooled too quickly and anyway the joy of the meal eaten gregariously was too good to miss.

The D'Abri must still be lying in its canvas sack at Tobermory, or Coll, or Castlebay, or Lochboisdale. MacBraynes never traced it, the insurance paid for it and the God of the Open Air looked after us until the Rangers left for Barra and the remaining children could get into the biggest of the other tents.

We count that camp as a success for many reasons but we never put the Minch between us again. When the time came for the Rangers to trek off alone they did not want to leave Tiree. People had told me I was a fool to try to take Guides and Rangers together; that the older girls would not want to be with the younger ones at all. They were wrong. The success of all future camps was the wide age range, the extended family.

But it was a good thing to do once. When the weather turned really nasty, which it did, Margaret had the fewer numbers which made life possible. I think, too, that it was essential that Margaret should be left to find out that she could cope just as well as I could.

The crew camped first at Traigh Vais, where the Atlantic crashes on the shore. The weather was foul. I had planned a telephone rendez-vous with Margaret and, at the appropriate time, one of the Seas and I fought our way to North Bay to the call box. I love the inevitable reminder in these remote call boxes. 'Make your call brief,' we are told. 'Someone may be waiting to make a call!' We had left half a dozen small white tents sheltering, somewhat unsuccessfully, among the sand dunes and it was quite the worst night I have known in the islands. We made our way blindly across the narrow strip and the wind from Eolligarry nearly lifted us from our feet. It brought stinging sand particles which reddened our eyes, matted our hair and hurled horizontal rain at us. Rain which found entry, in spite of sou'westers and PVC jackets and streamed down our bare legs. We were pretty vulnerable in small, homemade tents on the edge of the Atlantic but Margaret, with bigger numbers, had just lost two Icelandic tents on her Salum beach. Two of the ridges had succumbed to the weight of wind against sodden canvas. They had snapped like matchsticks. We were neither of us honest over the phone.

'Are you all right?' I wanted to know.

'Yes! We're fine and dry.' The latter was true. At all costs one must not get wet. We were both loud in our reassurance that all was well. I remember that in one of the tents Barbara sang and from all the other little white tents came the choruses. First came the campfire songs and then the hymns. Long after midnight they were still singing. The soft and lovely tunes fell like oil on troubled waters and the gale blew all night and spent itself so that in the morning we were able to lift our tents from that exposed and noisy shore and take them to Tangasdale, in the south-west, to the Campbells, whom we had met on the 1958 Trek. We were prepared to re-pitch on the machair, down by the lochan, but our friends insisted that we used an empty house. It is difficult to refuse an islander who is very worried about you in flimsy tents, when the sea is full of white horses and there is a red sky at dawn. We feel quite safe and really quite like hearing the rain thumping on the tent roof. Our friends would not listen to such nonsense. We had no option but to humour them, so we cheated and went indoors. Margaret fought the rest of the bad weather under canvas while we hung up our little white tents to dry in the living room and all twelve of us unrolled our sleeping bags in the bedroom in the roof. The floorboards were hard and we longed for the comfort of the machair but generosity such as belongs to the people of the Hebrides is not to be insulted.

We re-crossed the Minch on the overnight ferry arriving at Tiree at about 5 a.m. Margaret vows she has never seen it rain more heavily than when her children dashed from Johnny Kennedy's bus to run down the pier and join us on the RMS *Claymore*, the old one with the antique dining saloon. We spent the long sail back to Oban drying shirts and shorts on the radiators all over the boat and waiting our turn in the queue for breakfast. The saloon seated less than twenty and if you did not join the queue you got no breakfast. If you did and were a poor sailor you got no breakfast either for the narrowness of the passage induced claustrophobia and the throbbing of the engines combined with the smell of bacon and eggs sent a few landlubbers dashing to the deck.

The hardened sailors, with hungry tummies, used to wait very impatiently outside the saloon for the stewards to lay the tables, open the door and to allow in just the right number to fill the seats. If you were unlucky and found yourself left on the corridor side of the door you had to wait until everyone had eaten, the tables had been cleared and reset and you were almost ready to push the door in. A full breakfast of porridge, bacon and egg and toast could be bought for children for just half-a-crown. There came a day however when we could no longer afford cooked breakfasts, when there was no half price and only buffet service. The Good Old Days had gone! Margaret ran the Guide Company for some time before handing it back to me when farm responsibilities were too great but she stayed as assistant.

The early days of the Sea Ranger crew were great fun. I loved those sixteen- to twenty-year-olds as much as I did their younger sisters. I had known the Rangers longest for they had first been my school children and then my Guides. With them I could discuss politics and religion, morals, ideals and ambitions. They could enter wholeheartedly into every service project which came our way, accept every challenge, meet every danger with courage and every disaster with laughter. They would go anywhere, do anything and were constantly under our feet at The Currer.

We were too busy! A strong woman is stronger than most men but she is nowhere near as strong as a strong man. She has neither the height nor the muscle. Lack of money meant second-hand materials must be bought, rusty tools used, door snecks and gate hinges repaired with binder twine. 'A ferry guid friend,' is how John Lachie described it. As a repair it is second to none, in the garden it is essential and for sealing skips for camp equipment in advance to the Hebrides, it is indispensable!

The hard winter had made us afraid of the next. It had made us look seriously at our problems. We needed some overnight shelter for the suckled herd. We had built one new shed but we knew that it would only house the bullocks being fattened for market. The hard winter had accentuated the unsuitability of the kitchen where the sinks were. We had come to The Currer at a time when our parents ought to be retiring and we had saddled Mother with a wash kitchen which was higher than the cooking one. Every time she wanted to turn a tap she had to climb four steps and she couldn't be expected to do that for ever. The kitchen door opened north on the rear of the house, miles away from the yard and the buildings. There was no path round the back, no windows, no shelter and the wind swept up the valley and hurled itself against the blank back wall with no consideration for us. What happened, of course, was that Father and Margaret carried all their full buckets of water down four steps through the living kitchen and out of the front door.

Our old tractor had seen better days so we exchanged it for an American army jeep called Genevieve. I will never forget the day it was driven into the yard. It was so full of character, our first motorcar! It cost £40 and it was never licensed for the road. It would do anything, go anywhere, any weather. It would bring home a newly born calf from the moor with mamma walking beside. Logs could be brought up from the pasture below Jimmy's Wood for it tackled any gradient with ease. It could pull the side delivery rake and the hay trailer full of bales or building stones. It would take Mother and Harry to the Moor Gate when they wanted to go to town and collect Mother when she came back with heavy shopping bags.

They were often busy, Margaret in the driving seat and Harry beside her making innumerable overland journeys to take bales to feed cattle further away from the house, reclaiming more and more acres with bale seed and cattle droppings. Mother got used to seeing Genevieve crossing the moor with the back laden with bales and the whole herd following behind.

We wondered why we hadn't bought an army jeep before. No matter how she listed, Genevieve kept all four wheels on the ground. Each of them seemed to have eyes which knew every inch of our land and her little engine never failed us on a hill. We, who had always so loudly proclaimed that wheels were not for us, did a U turn. Had we thought that our indomitable parents would never grow old? That they would one day be unable to walk to the village we had conveniently ignored. To the back of our minds, too, we had pushed the thought that, with increasing age, Harry's physical handicap would be accentuated. We had been blinded by necessity.

*   *   *   *   *

There are always animals in general and animals in particular. No farm is without animal personalities but this farm has more than average because Margaret attracts waifs and strays. The very nature of our farming methods breeds a collection of animals with very distinct personalities. If one calf prefers warm water to drink, and will come to the back door when thirsty, its whim will be satisfied.

Farming is serious: at the end of the day animals must be sold but whilst they live at The Currer they are happy and free. They command our attention, need our service and dictate the time we rise, the time we go to bed and virtually what we do all day. They are our only permanent neighbours. They provide us with plenty of entertainment and, because they offer no sympathy, are a comfort when we are sad. They drive us to distraction, cause our language to be extreme, test our ingenuity and resourcefulness to the limit, very often challenge our strength and oppose our authority but never fail to gain our love and devotion.

The craziest animals must surely be the pigs. Pigs really laugh at you and so many of our most memorable incidents have been with them. Ours have never lived in concrete sweathouses. When we kept sows the piglets were almost always born in straw, on an earth floor, in one of the corrugated sheds we built for calves at the bottom of the orchard. That is unless someone was misguided enough to open the door at the precise moment when a mother-to-be felt that instinctive urge for privacy known to all creatures of the wild.

This happened several times. One summer afternoon a pig called Joanna disappeared and was later found on the furthest boundary. She was lying in a snug bed of bracken in a hollow she had made in the earth and she had sixteen piglets. It is no joke carrying food and water half a mile to a distant maternity ward until mamma discharges herself and comes home. Joanna was not the only pig with this trait. Sows make a better bed in the open than they do indoors but their truancy is not to be recommended, for nature provides for wastage in the wild. Only the fittest survive and a farmer depends on rearing the whole litter.

It frequently happened that a piglet received a hedge-tear rip from the sow's carelessness. The skin would be torn exposing a triangle of proud flesh to all the germs imaginable in the shed bedding. This happened to a piglet one Sunday and Margaret took it inside her jacket to the vet's surgery for the little fellow was strong and ought to survive. The vet was mildly amused that we should incur his fee for such a small animal with such a huge piece of skin missing. Straw and muck were all embedded in the wound.

There is nothing so endearing as a baby pig. Forgive the comparison but babies and piglets look very much alike and between the two, the piglet is the most beautiful when born. Only after a few feeds of breast milk does a baby achieve a skin as soft and as satiny as the piglet.

The vet carefully cleaned the two-inch patch, lifting out the bits of straw and dirt with patient hands and sensitive tweezers. Then he swabbed it with bacteria-killing disinfectant and stitched. He was noncommittal about its chances of survival but it lived and we never again took one so maimed to the vet. Each time a piglet was torn Margaret copied the vet's technique, gave it a jab of Streptopen and watched it join the litter nearly as good as new.

Pigs on the hearth were no uncommon sight. None survived broken limbs and few recovered from paralysis. Nevertheless, the survival rate was higher than average and, litters being frequently large, there was often a little runt who could not find a teat. Each baby immediately establishes a claim and allows no interference; sixteen teats and seventeen suckers means one to be fed by hand. When demand exceeded supply one little pig would run to the kitchen door and scream. Henry is remembered because his failure to find maternal comfort made him a right nuisance. He was continually under our feet, often in the stable looking for corn, in the front porch searching for dog biscuits and drinking from the cat's milk bowl whenever he could. One day the somewhat stout and middle-aged corn deliveryman put up with the little pest just long enough and then yelled at it to get out of the way. Unexpectedly he called it Henry and Henry it remained.

Sometimes it was mamma in trouble. One sow, I remember, had a bad heart and a big litter. Suddenly, with many mouths to feed, she had an attack and lost all her milk. It is possible to hand feed one little pig, or two or three, but impossible to take on a whole litter that have not even had those first important feeds of colostrum. The sow did not die, so we sent for the vet hoping he could give an injection which would bring back the milk. In the meantime little pigs were dying one after the other. In desperation the last three surviving pigs were brought in a box into the cloakroom and fed by hand. Two of those died and only Biddy remained. She lived in the house until she was four weeks old.

Pigs are not dirty. They know from birth to leave their droppings away from the bed and you can watch day-old sucklers trot off to a corner of the shed to make their small toilets.

Biddy was particularly clean and as dainty as a lady. Her skin was satin soft and blossom pink and she walked, as on high heels, on the daintiest of feet. She was fed from the bottle until she was as round as a cartoon pig or one of those depicted in 'The Three Little Pigs'. We had a laugh one day when Christopher was reading. He was five and a farmer's son who knew all about cattle, tups, pigs and market prices. He knew when, 't'cow 'ud cawve, when t' sow 'ud farrer, when t' sheep needed tuppin', whear proven came from an' 'ow much t' last litter fetched.' At school his face had that healthy glow of an outdoor boy and his hands were rough and chapped. He was reading 'The Three Little Pigs' and their escapade with the Big Bad Wolf and he turned the page on a picture of three beautiful pigs, as fat and pink as only a children's illustrator can make them. These well-known characters were just jumping into bed and this small farmer stared at them in disbelief and embarrassment. He looked at Joan, wide-eyed and said, 'Thu've got nuffin' on!'

Biddy lived in elegance in a three-sided box, full of straw, in the cloakroom and, on the many hours of freedom to trot around the kitchen, she never disgraced herself once. The bitch, Lassie, had littered in the stable and when the pups were old enough to play, we put Biddy in to join them. As the weeks went by it became increasingly obvious that she thought she was a pup. She acquired and retained a grunt, which was almost a bark, and she never associated with the other pigs. She was more interested in people, preferably ramblers. Walkers suspected that her interest was unfriendly and we often saw them running for the nearest gate or climbing a wall with Biddy in hot pursuit.

Some pigs have individual characters but some are remembered in the collective form for being exasperating or even downright destructive. Pigs are gregarious, sleeping as one, more often than not in a pile. Asleep, they form a tableau of extreme bliss. Stretched in abandonment they sleep smiling, always look full and immeasurably content. Margaret can walk over them and they will not move. Yet, one unfamiliar noise and they wake and flee as one. If disturbed whilst rooting they all dash away together and make a great commotion doing so. Many a time, coming home from school in semi- or full darkness, I have disturbed them. The silence of dusk can be profound with only the distant sound of traffic along the main road in the valley. A sudden upheaval of pigs would take me by surprise. Suddenly, they would bolt ahead, in front of me, kicking up grass and mud in a frenzy of idiotic grunts and charging home as if a whole army were in pursuit.

Should I encounter a brimming sow on the way home that was not so funny for she would be behind me in the darkness, not in front. Brimming sows will follow anyone. If he should run she will also, talking in a many syllabled language. Most certainly she cannot be shooed away, or driven and if one should try, with a slap on her rump, one effectively makes her a permanent statue. We have seen many walkers disappearing over the wall before we have had a chance to pen our demonstrative animal and send for the boar.

Litters born in the proper shed seem to inherit a civilised respectability. Those born away from home, in field or bracken-filled hollow, behave badly. They are proficient in finding holes in fences to escape from the farm altogether. One group found its way, repeatedly, down to the railway line. A phone call came with embarrassing regularity, summoning Margaret to retrieve a sow and fourteen piglets from a neighbour's farmyard. One litter crawled under the Moor Gate and out into the road. They trotted along to the next farm and like a gang of teenage vandals caused utter chaos in our top neighbour's corn store. On that occasion we did not think that pigs were funny at all.

In fact there are many times when we are not amused. After so many disastrous experiences it is surprising how slow we are to respond, especially when the invasion storms our own defences. One day, after an exhausting job, we were sitting in the front room, half asleep, drugged by an uninteresting television programme. Harry, who seldom sits for more than ten minutes at a time, makes a continuous clatter whether he be sweeping the front porch or washing the dishes but we are quick to tell the difference between this normal clatter and the sickening, frightening thud of him falling.

On this particular evening we listened for some time to scuffling and banging in the back porch. One minute we were ignoring the disturbance and the next Margaret and I were leaping out of our armchairs. We knew what had happened long before we got there.

The back porch is very small and was always so embarrassingly untidy that we seldom let visitors in that way. A cluttered bench ran along the back wall and there was a wide window ledge with a drum of louse powder and umpteen tonic water bottles used to dose calves with colic mixture. The bench held tins of nails and cans of paint and beneath were dirty wellingtons and a plate of cat food. A paper sack of tins and bottles stood in the corner ready to be taken, fortnightly, to the Moor Gate for the dustbin wagon. There was a mop bucket, invariably half full of water strongly smelling of disinfectant, waiting to be thrown out well away from the sycamore tree. Should pigs push a way in, chaos must follow.

We stood for one moment of horror. The culprits were wet with upturned water, wild-eyed and garrulous. The paper sack was torn to pieces, tins and bottles all over the floor. Bleach water was trickling into overturned wellingtons and the self-confined prisoners had, in their agitation, forgotten their rules of hygiene. The smell was far too atrocious to be erased by disinfectant.

At that moment, if we had not had such an over-riding sense of humour, I think we could have hated pigs and the wagon taking them to market could not have come soon enough. But the appreciation of the ridiculous is a trait which is inherent in us so that, when there is least cause, we laugh most.

One year our four litters were never in the yard. Each morning, early in the year, before the meadows were closed to the cattle so that the summer hay could grow, Margaret released the pigs and they disappeared and stayed away all day, causing no trouble at all. They seemed a model herd. They came home each evening looking perfectly angelic and lay exhausted in blissful, smiling sleep. Too late Margaret found them out!

The cattle were mostly near home, even during the day, for hay and straw were still being fed nearby and daily counting assured us that no walls were down and no animal was straying. However, the weather improved and the herd began to go further afield. There was a scent of spring grass in the morning air and with that comes a bovine wanderlust. So Margaret went to walk the boundary to make sure no gap had appeared during winter giving access to the green lane which runs along the top and the estate which borders it.

The boundary was safe but when Margaret came to the meadows she disturbed the herd of pigs. There was a commotion over the wall and a stampede. Margaret climbed over and found, not one meadow uprooted but every one of the eight fields patterned with broken sods like some giant child's jigsaw, tipped from a box and barely begun. No imagination could conjure up a mess as big as that.

We have spent a great deal of our lives on our knees. We have replaced sods after many campfires at The Currer and on far islands. The hard way had always been our way. This one was mainly Margaret's for she had to 'ger on wi' it' whilst I was at school. I helped at weekends but day after day, for weeks, frantically, for there was no time to lose if the sods were to be given a chance of normality before the hay harvest, Margaret crawled around the eight meadows on her knees. Unless the sods were back, a mowing machine could not cut the little grass there would be. The failure of his hay harvest is to a farmer a severe financial loss and it was one from which we would have little chance of surviving.

So Margaret firmly closed the gate when she went home. We will not make that same mistake twice. She did, more than once, think of a Hebridean friend who once stammered, 'P-p-p-pigs and Barb-b-bara Castle. Sho-o-ot 'em.' She could well agree with him about the pigs but about Mrs Castle she had reservations. She reckoned that a woman, even a female politician, would have tackled that job better than any male counterpart.

One day two sows went down for a wallow in the side mud of the duck pond. Wallowing is obviously as essential to them as a bath is to us but not for the same reasons. After coating themselves all over with mud they seek the shade and are soon snoring loudly. Harry will say, 'There is a dirty old woman just walking into the yard.' He is not referring to any human dropout.

On this particular day the two dirty old women trotted off back to their sty whilst I was building a new shed wall. Their enormous, grey backsides were just disappearing through the door when a family of picnickers came along the footpath. The youngsters were gambolling about, some distance from their parents, when they suddenly stopped, spellbound watching the two mud-covered bottoms slowly disappear into the darkness. Then they dashed back to their parents shouting, 'Hey, there're two elephants in there!'

We now had a whole row of calf sheds, built by Margaret and Father. They were very low, no more than seven feet high and when the winter manure had deepened even Margaret used to bump her head on the beams. Bedding was always a problem for bought-in straw is dear and we always had to be sparing of it, using it only where the animals slept. When this became dangerous, Margaret forked it out into a mountainous heap outside the door.

Before our contractor bought a forklift for the front of his tractor, the rest of the two feet of bedding had to be forked out in the spring and re-forked into the muck spreader. Margaret loved this job. The tractor men hated it for the sheds were too low for them and they were perpetually banging heads against beams.

One such tractor driver was big and broad, young and very strong. He was as rough as they come and Margaret could not keep up with him as together they threw out the muck. At one point this huge young man's fork disturbed a nest of mice. He paused, and he and Margaret leaned on their forks and watched whilst the courageous mother picked up one naked baby and disappeared with it into safety. The remaining babies wriggled in the nest, suddenly cold and vulnerable.

At a loss, the two workers continued to watch. Back came the indomitable mother to take a second baby away, scurrying past the big man's enormous boots. She did not stop until every baby was carried away. Her maternal instinct made her oblivious of the potential danger but the gentle giant was as soft as his lady companion. Both shook their heads in silent wonder and did not resume their mucking-out until the rescue was complete.

As the pig population grew we kept fewer hens. Leg paralysis claimed many. Father built brick sties in the Nissen hut to house the litters at night but the laithe was still the most versatile building of them all. From August to January it was full of hay. Seeds from it decorated the cobwebs clinging to the stable walls and the kitchen windows, attracting numerous wrens, blue-tits and house sparrows. From May to July the swallows occupied the barn rafters. Father was fanatical about the swallows, pining for them if they were late arriving and radiant when they came.

The mistal was kept free of hay but with no milking herd it was used for expectant or farrowing sows, for sickly calves, the goats or a litter of pups. Later, when we piped water from the house to the buildings, we mixed calf milk in the far corner and when we bought a corn roller we installed it in the mistal and thereafter the cobwebs were floured with corn. The spiders didn't seem to mind.

No milking was done there. Margaret milked the house-cow as the Hebrideans do. She would take the bucket to the cow and milk her in the field, on the moor, or in the yard, without tether and only her ration of corn to keep her docile.

The massive barn, as it emptied of hay, became full of animals and then the smell of them pervaded the house. In spring it had to be emptied of their manure and the sows took residence. It was no uncommon sight to see a mother laid out flat, suckling a litter almost on our doorstep. Genevieve was garaged just inside the porch doors and camp equipment was stored in the dark passage which once led into the wash kitchen. Sometimes, after a wet Camper Badge or Permit camp, sodden tents would festoon the interior from lines hanging from the principals and if Jean's children were here then the rope swing, on the loft, would be in use.

We have believed in using land and buildings for a multitude of purposes. After Maggie and Dick, the stable was never used for horses. We used it for corn, little runts and ducklings. When the hen population became just a handful of farmyard fowls they all roosted there and laid their eggs in an old bath we had in the corner.

Margaret, surely a descendant from the legendary Nightingale, is The Lady with the Torch who steals quietly round the sheds in the small hours, followed by a devoted dog. Her midnight prowls result in written messages to me instructing and determining my first, early morning jobs. Many are the times I have come downstairs and found Margaret asleep on the front room rug, her bed neglected because it was too detaining and a cow was calving or a small animal dying and she was catnapping. I have frequently found a piglet in a box by the Aga, or a pigeon. Once I even found a calf in such luxury on the rug in front of the stove. Margaret must be tolerated for she is farmer *extraordinaire*. Or is she? Most farmers love their animals far beyond the call of duty.

The canoes were finished and launched with ceremony. We opened the screens which divided my school into classrooms, laid a banquet and invited the County Commissioner to break a bottle of cider over the hulls. We kept the canoes in the cellar of one of my school children. Many of the village houses had a cellar leading directly on to the canal. This very old house had one which was also a boathouse, with a wide, permanently open door, ideal for the job. We acquired a third canoe and several life jackets and spent a good deal of the summer paddling, like a flotilla of Indian braves, up and down the cut.

There was no part of my life which was separate. Home, school, Guides, Rangers, friends, holidays were all intermingled so that one enriched the other. School was used for Guide occasions, camp equipment was used for school. Each gave to the other and took from The Currer and the harvest of everything was ploughed back in the community and the inheritance passed forward to the next generation. We did not see that one thing was leading to another, but just lived all of every day, enjoying 'the perfect present'. Everybody had an essential part to play and I take no credit for the fun we had for the youngsters were far more ingenious, far wittier than I was and I think I did less leading than most leaders.

I was not unaware that my life was more varied than Margaret's or that other people always seemed blind and ignorant of the way that she and Father were changing the face of The Currer. Most people notice if one decorates a room, sews a new outfit, or cultivates a garden. A few women have hit the headlines by keeping a few cattle on some outpost away from civilisation but the world, in general, has very little knowledge of farming and what Margaret does is too big for them to comprehend. Guests who now come to the farm are interested in our cats and the goats and the donkeys and think that Margaret exists to look after them. But that she is a stockman, with a herd of two hundred cattle to feed and inject, worm and supervise, buy and sell in the competitive Dales markets, seems to go by unnoticed. Others could always see that I was busy, but farming is nonsocial and no one understands its trials, its deprivations, struggle and success. They tend to go sentimental about individuals farming smallholdings and call it 'The Good Life'. They mistrust serious farming and label all real farmers 'rich' or 'beef barons'. Because Margaret's job was so big, no one ever noticed.

She met an old dear in town one filthy winter day on her way to the hairdresser's. 'You won't be able to do anything outside this weather!' the old dear said. Margaret sat in the hairdresser's chair, looked at her weather beaten face in the mirror and surveyed her cut and calloused hands. She repeated the old lady's recent comment to the young woman clipping her locks.

'Silly bugger!' the hairdresser said, most unexpectedly. It said it all and, as a phrase, has often been of great comfort to us for, remembering it when a very foolish or hurtful comment has been made, has made us smile and not retaliate.

Chapter Twelve

P aul had just had his tenth birthday and Julie would be eight in September. On Tiree we seemed to attract small boys from the locality. It seemed inconceivable that we should deprive Jean's Northumbrian children of the opportunity to camp on the machair. To go with Skipper and Flim to the Hebrides was fast becoming the dream of every girl over ten. I was not the attraction, just this wonderful adventure that I had to offer.

What was this magic? No one could explain. The children came home radiant but they could not paint a picture that others could understand. Walking alone on a deserted Harris shore, not long ago, I thought aloud, shouting above the din of the Atlantic, 'You lucky, lucky children! Some of you came here again and again, ten or eleven times.' And I was suddenly humble for if they had been lucky, what about me? How much more privileged had I been? Twenty-five years I took the children camping. A quarter of a century!

When we went to Tiree, in the summer of 1964, we took Julie and Paul and a brother of one of the Rangers. Immediately on our arrival the Tiree boys came with their sleeping bags and a new norm was set: one extended family, the ultimate secret of success. Mix age groups, and delinquency, promiscuity, lack of discipline, disappear for where the older ones have responsibility they grow to deserve the adoration of the younger ones and all is right with the world. It is the thread of commonsense which society has lost. Only in theory may it be considered advisable to have play groups for the under-fives, junior adventure centres, teenage discos, sixth form parties and visits abroad, under-thirty clubs, over-sixty outings, old people's homes and so on. All seem commendable but few people have stood back and seen what has happened to the family. If this is an age of juvenile delinquency and teenage promiscuity, defiance of parents, neglect of children and forgetfulness of the elderly, then surely the reason is obvious.

I see only one outcome of age group activities and that is selfishness.

Interdependence should be our aim, for independence is often just another word for 'I'm all right, Jack'. There were critics who said I would fail if I mixed Guides and Rangers. When they heard I was including small boys, island toddlers, an occasional bed-wetter, a disabled child, they were aghast. But our group was never happier than when May insisted that two-year-old Peter could come with us to Ballephuil or when we were sitting on the kitchen floor of Mary MacKay, wrinkled, toothless and, to children, as old as the hills. 'Where shall we go?' I would ask and the answer would be, 'To see Callum.' 'Who shall we invite to our campfire?' and the answer would always be none other than, 'Annie the Post'.

We have forgotten that education is being taught the art of living. How can the young learn about being healthy teenagers if they meet few? How can they mature if they do not enjoy many activities with those who have matured, and how can they learn to be parents if they are not frequently with their own? How can they learn to be needed old people if grandparents are not active members of the family?

So I blatantly ignored those who told me I was wrong to take younger children and we had a wonderful camp, the highlight of which was a céilidh and dance in Callum's barn when our children danced barefoot among the islanders and one of the Rangers carried a sleeping Julie back to camp long after midnight.

On the last day Janet joined us by flying from Glasgow. I took the children home; Margaret stayed with Janet and flew on to Barra. Having seen all the campers safely home, Ann and I caught the overnight bus back to Glasgow and flew direct to Barra. Life seemed extraordinarily carefree. Just Ann and me, after all those children. Margaret and Janet were waiting to watch the little plane land on Barra's beautiful cocklestrand, the Traigh Mhòr. The tide was covering the airstrip with a few inches of water when we came in and caused a great shower.

We retraced some of the steps of the Trek in 1958. It was a holiday reunion for the four of us. We were all in tune and, whilst sorry to leave Barra, we were intent on getting further north as quickly as we could. So when the RMS *Claymore* came from Tiree to Castlebay we boarded it for Lochboisdale, caught a bus and crossed all the causeways which make the Long Island, joining the Uists, Benbecula and Grimsay. We spent the night bivouacked at Sollas, on North Uist, which is one of the most peaceful places on earth. The stillness there can be profound and the spring tide seeping over the tufts of thrift can be as warm as a tepid bath.

We pitched our tent on an elevated hassock of bent and cotton grass. The sea birds had given us a noisy welcome but we slept soundly and did not awake until long after their dawn chorus. We were unaware of the deepening channels between the hassocks of sea-pinks as the tide came gently in, or of the morning mist which foretold a beautiful day. We did not wake until a lady, a total stranger, lifted the untied door flap and said, 'Would you be offended if I offered you aiggs for breakfast?' There is no limit to Hebridean kindness.

We fried the eggs in the cramped cosiness of the little white tent. I looked at our compass and it pointed to Harris.

We had heard about Harris from island-loving relatives and a photograph, in the current MacBrayne Brochure, of Luskentyre beaches, had been beckoning us since January. So we made our way to Lochmaddy and sailed to Tarbert, arriving in the heat of a scorching afternoon.

There was a bus at the pier and I showed the driver the photograph of Luskentyre and asked him if he was going anywhere near.

'Ach, whell,' he said, 'I'm going there, right enough.'

We announced our eccentricity by asking him to take our rucksacks.

It was a beautiful day and there were still several hours of it left so we had agreed to walk across the island. If we could do so unburdened all the better. The good man thought we were crazy but was quite happy to stow the heavy rucksacks on board.

We walked for the first time through Tarbert with its street of grey houses puffing peat smoke into a blue sky. We passed the little shops, the owners of which we were eventually to know so well, who all sold the same things from sheep dip and hardware to clothes, paint, wellingtons and groceries, and we took the steep road south.

We will never forget that first crossing of Harris on the old road with its central ribbon of sheep-clipped grass. The road wound in and out, up, over and down the bare rocks. Rain-washed, wind-eroded and sun-bleached, they threw off that August heat like the desert. There were more than any ten miles of that determined track, climbing steeply, dropping suddenly, skirting lilied lochans and worked peat bogs. We passed sheep and funeral cairns, saw the buzzard hover but met no people. After the lodge at Horsacleat we passed no other house till we came to the western shore. There were no trees and only sparse, deformed and unnourished heather. Compared with the fertile island of Tiree this was the moon, 'Nightmare country', I have heard it described.

But the wastes and desolation of the interior did not prepare us for the glory which awaited us on the shore. We were very sunburnt as we climbed the last stretch of road before the steady decline to the Atlantic and when we saw the western beaches we just sat and worshipped. Every step nearer to the shore, on the wonderful two miles down hill, intensifies the myriad colours of the sea. When the tide is in it is a dozen shades of turquoise, green, cobalt and midnight blue and the path of the peaty river can be seen as a ribbon of gold two miles across the bay, to the bar where the great rollers crash, foaming and noisy, in a white line against the backcloth of the sea and the island of Taransay. It excited us. Luskentyre; how we love that place!

We reached the shore, sore, rather tired but feeling great and took the branch road right and followed it over the rickety bridge. We found our rucksacks at the side of the cattle grid on the outskirts of the straggling township. We did not know that greater beauty lay ahead. The last two miles had seemed heaven enough so we left our kit where it had been tossed by the driver and wandered on to the first house, standing back from the road. It is not only courteous to ask permission to camp but it is an opportunity of meeting people well worth knowing. We would never presume to pitch without approval and our query has never failed to provide us with friends.

We bivouacked on the machair just below the cattle grid, took off our shoes, cooked and ate. In the cool of late evening we wandered happily to the end of the road. The ten crofters have scattered their houses along the shore. They blend against the backcloth of Ben Luskentyre as if they have been there always, but it is only comparatively recently that the crofters have been given back the fertile western fringe from which their ancestors had been ruthlessly evicted. The present inhabitants are descendants of those unfortunate people who refused to be shipped to Canada, carried their still smouldering beams across the island and rebuilt, on the rocky ledges of the eastern bays. For many years they scratched a bare existence from the sea, cultivating minute lazy beds, stripping soil from almost bare rocks and piling it in heaps to grow potatoes and corn.

Paradise lies at the end of the Luskentyre road, just below the MacDonalds'. A white, sandy broadway leads down to the beach. A continuous line of breakers fringes an often turbulent sea but it is always blue and, on most days, the hills of North Harris are etched on the skyline. John MacDonald was making hay the old way with scythe and fork and rake and beside the hay strip was a flat area of machair just right for camping Guides.

For the rest of our week on Harris we made it our job to meet people for we were already planning next year's camp. We had three blissful days swimming and climbing, talking to the crofters and buying tweed from Katie, who used a handloom made by a local Yorkshire firm. We could have stayed there forever but we wanted to encircle the island so we rolled our tents, packed our kit and set off for Northton.

A bus slowed up beside us. We stopped it and threw in our rucksacks. It was the same man, a Mr MacVicar. 'This time we'll come with you,' we said.

We began to wish we had done no such thing for it soon became apparent that it was a Communion bus, taking crofters to a Meeting over at Finsbay. All were dressed in sombre black, almost silent, clutching their prayer books. We were acutely embarrassed for we were in shorts and sleeveless blouses and hardly respectable. We were confused and tried to hide our knees beneath our rucksacks. In our disturbed state of mind we forgot to pay and we were standing at the Northton road end, watching the bus disappear, before we remembered. The back of the bus announced its owner, John Morrison, Northton and we lost no time in finding the house to pay our debt. In so doing we made very dear friends. Katie Ann made us a *strupak* and John solved all our camp transport problems.

Northton is a compact little township, much bigger than Luskentyre. It is always busy: cattle being driven, a travelling shop vending, a builder putting on a roof. It had not been difficult to find the Morrisons' hospitable house nor was it hard to talk to them even though we were strangely dressed. They found it amusing that we had come on the Communion bus and forgotten to pay. Their son Donald John took us out onto the machair in his van and left us on the second bay, just below Temple Hill, a mile from Northton. From there we discovered the rest of South Harris. From our little campsite we could see no other habitation but we were to visit Temple Hill a few years later when an archaeological team were uncovering a Stone Age Site of extraordinary interest. We could well believe that the island had changed but little in 4,000 years.

Next day we went out to Rodel on the Communion bus, suitably clad in skirts. On the east of the island we found rocky bays and harbours and the cliff-edge cottages of crofters who owned small boats and supplemented their diet with fish and their income with lobsters.

The new road which was built to link the eastern bays of Harris cost so much that it was aptly named the Golden Road. Some say this nickname was due to the amount of whisky consumed by the builders but one only has to walk along it to appreciate the expense which the construction of it must have entailed over the inhospitable terrain. We have walked the Golden Road on so many occasions with so many children we know its every rise and fall and bend, its every bay and lochan, and the names of its small townships fall like music on our ears. Drinishadder, Cluer, Scadabay, Grosebay, Lingabay, Plockrapool, Stocknish and Finsbay.

From Finsbay, in 1964, we decided to take the inland road back to Leverburgh and when a bus pulled up behind us on that deserted peat road we hopped in to find it absolutely empty. Our driver was again Mr MacVicar. He was just going out to his peat bog to put in an hour or two lifting. When he dropped us we had little over a mile still to go to Leverburgh.

'This time we will remember to pay you,' we laughed.

'Och, no,' he said, 'I wass chust going that way anyway!'

Almost immediately we came upon a woman working her peats. An old bicycle was propped against the road fence and she sweated at the task of lifting peats into small pyramids to dry. We sauntered over and offered to help. We were excitedly and graciously welcomed by the incredible lady whose only embarrassment was that she was not wearing her false teeth. Once she had retrieved them from a cranny in the wall she was happy and we all worked together for over an hour. 'Annie the Post' has been our friend ever since and the fun she had with generations of Guides gives us some of our most precious memories.

We climbed Temple Hill on a beautiful evening, finding late violets on the higher slopes but failing to reach the top. A sudden white mist placed itself on the summit like a clean nightcap and stayed there till morning. It did not come low enough to chill and envelop us and it took away none of the glory of the sunset and the gilding of the beaches which scallop the western coast of Harris.

We spent the last two nights of our stay on the shores of West Loch Tarbert on the outskirts of Ardhasaig. We were able to follow the Stornaway road until we crossed the border of Harris and Lewis. The North Harris Hills had beckoned us from Luskentyre and we could not leave the island without a journey into the heart of them. The next day, therefore, we took the Hushinish road through Bunaveneader and along the shores of Loch Meavaig to where the track leads up to Loch Uiskeval and the perpendicular cliffs of Ben Uiskeval. We were totally in love with this new island and immediately committed to taking children there.

The weather broke when we reached Mallaig. We spent one of the wettest of nights cramped into one tent on a lawn below a cottage on the Arisaig road. Close by, a small burn became a mighty torrent hurling itself into the sea beside our door. The dear lady of the house braved the storm to cry outside the tent that we must leave it immediately and come indoors. From the dry warmth of our sleeping bags we thanked her but refused the extraordinarily kind offer. 'Why?' she insisted, no doubt becoming saturated.

'Because we will get wet,' we answered. Few people believe a tent will keep you dry.

Calf buying began again. Even in the small radius around us there are four markets and a thousand new born calves change hands every week. They come from the dairy farms, for their birth is necessary to excite lactation and the world needs milk. I often wonder what the vegetarians who eat cheese and drink milk would do with these beautiful babies. They cannot be kept as pets, for it costs a great deal of money to feed them. If the world did not eat meat they would all have to be slaughtered at birth and some giant incinerator erected. Few things are more beautiful than a newborn calf. There is something appealing about the enormous eyes, the long eyelashes and the silky coat. The ones we buy have two very happy years pasturing on The Currer with not a care in the world, plenty of grass and winter shelter. The milk cow has a hard life perpetually carrying a yearly calf and an over-full udder because man has learned how to mass-produce milk. Beef cattle, which are grazed out of doors, know a freedom comparable to that of the wild.

The needs of these calves are met before our own. For them Margaret will lose any amount of sleep and not grumble. We have a lot of land to graze and a thin purse so from the beginning we never bought expensive calves but they were healthy, our two farmers were good at their job and it need not have been too difficult if Margaret had not been unable to resist the temptation to buy the odd one here and there that no one wanted. She has brought home many a calf bought for a pound because it was premature, a twin, or one deformed in some way. A calf with a bent foreleg is unwanted but the joint nearly always straightens. A bad eye or navel can be cured. She brought one home that had a big head like a mentally handicapped child. It caused us no trouble. She brought home one that no one else had dared to buy because it had a badly deformed mouth. One nostril and half the upper lip were missing. Margaret called it Smiler and even as she lifted it from the cattle wagon she wondered whether it would be able to eat grass and ruminate and if it would inhale water when it drank from the bucket. She had bought it for a song so that it would escape the butcher. She had no real faith that it would be able to cope but it never looked back.

Increasingly Margaret was doing the bigger share of the work and took a more equal share of the decision-making. She was twenty-five and as good as any man, a better farmer than most, utterly dedicated. We grumbled that when she came in, so did all the dogs and the cats and that they occupied the hearthrug and took away the heat from the fire. We never made our point successfully for she and her retinue still invade the sitting room in totality. She is acutely sensitive to the needs of animals. It makes her an excellent stockman. Her compassion for the non-productive creatures ensures that she will never be a roaring financial success. She exists to keep things alive in comfort and her only interest in the cheque she receives annually, when she sells, is that it will buy more and feed more and house them better. I think she is like most hill farmers in this respect. Money usually stays outside the farmhouse door and farmers continue to belt their coats with binder twine. Few enjoy luxuries, all brave the wildest weather because survival to them is a living animal not a potential pound note.

We live in a veritable aviary. Blackbirds and wrens scurry along the manger in front of us when we sweep it clean before feeding time. Robins and finches colour the yard whenever Margaret throws a handful of split maize. The starlings are noisy invaders who scatter the rest but the yard, but the handful, is big enough for all. Sparrows live in great numbers in the beams under the laithe porch and a fair number of crows and magpies come scavaging near the house.

A grey squirrel sometimes comes running along the wall of the back passage and darts up the sycamore. He is wary of the dogs but will risk anything, for a crust of bread.

If we can help it at all, we do not feed the fox and we try to shut our poultry up safely every night. The beautiful creature has got to live, so we do not condemn him if he lifts a duck from the field in the early dark but remember to chase the others home early next day. We know when he is about for there is an uproar from the dogs in the house and a stampede of them through the door when we open it.

Calf rearing methods have changed, but the housing conditions have remained the same. Our calves have always been kept on straw bedding, loose, in large sheds so that they can gallop about if they want to. Feeding time is easier when calves are in separate boxes or kennels but we have considered quality of life for the calf our first priority and have suffered the consequences.

As the season went by the bedding rose and we were perpetually bumping our heads on the low beams. Squashed and broken toes were a daily torture. We were perpetually being bowled over. Animals have no respect for you whatsoever. If a cow steps sideways and you are between her and the wall you have eight hundredweight pressing against your ribs and abdomen. If one steps on your toe, wow! I know why all farmers walk splather-footed.

Yet, ill-treated and disrespected, Father would rub his bumped head and bruised knuckles and glow with satisfaction.

New methods of feeding were introduced. A system of teats attached to plastic tubes leading to the bucket effectively slowed down the intake to a more normal rate. It wasn't easy directing heads to the right teat but it was considerably less hectic. Sometimes there would be eight calves drinking in a row. Later came the *ad lib* days when milk was available all the time. We began mixing large quantities in an old bath someone gave us. People were always giving us old baths! And we are always moving them, like the woodpile and the beds.

I always spent at least one day of the last week of the holiday in school unpacking the requisitioned stock which invariably arrived on the last day of term. I love new books and untouched reams of paper, pencils and new rubbers, boxes of rulers and scissors. It was always a pleasure to unpack them, quietly, by myself and get the classroom ready for the New Year to begin.

Should any child see me arrive I would not be alone long for the news would spread and small feet clatter through the porch and little people give big offers of help. I am ashamed to say that I tried to creep in unnoticed but if children came I always enjoyed them for they were full of holiday news and gossip. The caretaker, too, liked to come in for a natter and groan about this and that which had gone wrong and together we would fill in a few repair forms. Invariably the time for me to catch a bus would come before I had gone through my post and I would take the whole bundle of it home to deal with by the fire.

The first day of the autumn term the children all seemed very young, the singing in Assembly rather weak and we wondered how we could manage without those capable children who had left us for the Senior School. The school captains seemed to still have their baby teeth and the new entrants seemed smaller than ever. The dinner lady would bring in news from the village, the farmers' children would be full of the harvest. I always found it difficult to walk unnoticed through the infant classroom and at the beginning of a new year, with the first pages of new exercise books to exhibit, progress was impossible. I found it rather amusing that the greatest excitement in our infants' school life seemed to be receiving a spelling book.

*   *   *   *   *

It was imperative that we do something about The Currer kitchen. We had regretted having big sinks, sacks of milk powder, buckets and old coats in a room in which we had exposed such a lovely sixteenth-century fireplace. Storm lamps and cow halters hung from the beams and coconut matting covered the floor. The old-fashioned electric washing machine looked incongruous beside the teak sinks and dirty wellingtons were invariably flopping on the mat by the door.

We talked about building a new scullery, a lean-to behind the house. The unused privy could be utilised as an entrance porch which would open onto the raised terrace which ran round the house. This would be a hundred times more convenient than the present back door lost in the wilderness of field. There would be little more than the north wall to build, I argued, and that could be nearly all window. The teak sinks could be brought in and the room with the inglenook fireplace could be made into a sitting room.

I went to the Borough Architect with some plans I had drawn and the good man showed me how to put them onto linen, detail them professionally and make them acceptable to the Planning Committee. He gave me the forms and literature necessary for me to make an application for permission to build.

'Who's your builder?' he asked.

'Us,' I answered and the dear fellow did not look surprised or critical. This lack of red tape was a blessing to us at a time when we could not have afforded an architect or a builder and if we wanted something we had to do it ourselves.

Several autumn evenings found me with ruler and mapping pen. At week-ends we collected building stone from the wall nearest to the quarry from which Arthur Currer had taken stone for the house and waited for the plans to appear at the next Planning Committee meeting.

Early in 1965 I attended a County Ranger Meeting in a city school and was informed of a national plan to train selected Rangers for service so that, should local or national need arise, there would be groups of already trained personnel on call. It was a fine idea but the Rangers on this Headquarters List, in our locality at any rate, were not called and we had to search for service opportunities ourselves which is, perhaps, as it should be and service became a part of the everyday life of the Crew.

I was asked to accompany two other Ranger Guiders to a Cheshire Home, fifteen miles away, to discuss the training of a County Team. The journey was by bus over bleak moorland, white with snow. We offered the Cheshire Home an Easter week of undiluted hard labour with a team of Eight Rangers and three Guiders. We would be self-catering from a base camp in the kitchen garden. We would report for duty at 7 a.m. and finish about 10.30 p.m. Our offer was accepted and we returned to advertise for suitable applicants. It was decided to interview candidates at The Currer.

Mother, Father and Harry had been invited to cousin David's wedding on that particular Saturday. Going to a wedding, from a muddy farm in March, poses problems. On the morning of that day, we even wished we had a car to take them. We could always take the family to the Moor Gate in Genevieve but she was definitely unfit for licensing for the road.

I remember that Mother would not buy a new coat. She had bought a new winter one for cousin Stuart's February wedding and there was no way she could be persuaded to buy a lightweight, spring one more suitable for late March. Relatives argued that she could not possibly wear the heavy one but she was adamant. She did like new clothes and she seldom had many and would sometimes grumble that the only money we ever had walked about on the hillside eating grass. I've heard her say that if she died we'd have to put her into the spare room until the cattle were sold but she wouldn't ever buy a coat she hardly expected to wear again.

Six of the candidates for the eight places came from SRS *Spartan*. I had no part in the selection but few Rangers had had the experience that *Spartan* Rangers had. They were First Class and Queen's Guides with many years of camping experience in remote places. Familiarity with handicapped people had come after many hours of service at the Blind Home. They were used to Harry and one of them had a handicapped sister of her own. They were destined to become nurses, teachers and physiotherapists.

It was not going to be easy, working in a centrally heated home and eating and sleeping in tents in the icy kitchen garden. The very cold Saturday of the interview really tested endurance and I was very pleased when all my six were chosen. It is so much easier to lead a team of familiar teenagers.

During the interviews snow began to fall. The County Commissioner and her staff, who formed the selection committee, were advised to take their cars up to the Moor Gate. Only the County Camp Advisor returned with her small car over-full of drivers.

At the wedding Mother was grinning from ear to ear in her warm winter coat whilst other relatives shivered in the height of fashion. It's an ill wind, as the saying goes.

After the interviews, the buffet meal we had prepared was eaten noisily and somewhat hastily, for darkness was not far away. The Rangers buttoned up their topcoats and, heads down, disappeared into the blizzard, heading for the village and the bus to town.

The selection committee gathered round the piled-high logs burning in the sitting room and I went out to see Margaret, battling on alone outside. The sudden snow meant that more bales were needed to feed a herd prevented from grazing. She was wet and overworked but offered to take the VIPs up the hill in Genevieve.

There was a lot to discuss after the selection for there was little over a fortnight to Easter and quite a lot of training to be done. I felt to be pushing them out of the house too soon but snow was already deep and Margaret, peppered with flakes, was revving up the funny little vehicle which was quite happy in the Arctic.

I have a lasting vision of those important County dignitaries putting on their uniform berets at the correct angle and trying to maintain some decorum as they clambered, one after the other into the ex-army jeep. 'I feel like Montgomery,' said Mrs Ellershaw, Advisor for many years.

Genevieve thought nothing of climbing in six inches of wet snow with too many soldiers on board but the Camp Advisor's car objected in no uncertain terms. It had to be pushed nearly all of the way and its wheels kicked out so much slush and mud we looked as if we had been mudlarking.

The house was warm when we eventually got inside to peel off our saturated clothing and begin worrying about our seventy-year-old parents and our increasingly handicapped brother. After the reception they went to the aunts. Then Father took one on either arm and went to the bus for home. They waited in vain. Our bus is the first to stop. The steep road up the hillside becomes impassable very quickly and a bend in the one-in-five gradient adds insult to injury. But a car might manage it so Father left his two big responsibilities and went in search of a taxi. Precious time was being lost and soft snow was deepening.

Successful at last he manoeuvred Harry into the back seat beside Mother; the taxi driver engaged a low gear and started a steady ascent, but too much time had been lost; the steep hill, the nasty bend and the driving blizzard were inconquerable. There was nothing the driver could do but let his passengers alight and continue, on foot, for over a mile of treacherous road. It was a nightmare for all of them. This experience made us think seriously that, whatever we had previously proclaimed, we would have to have some road transport, sooner or later.

When the time came there were only seven Rangers in the team and I have nothing but praise for the way they tackled a difficult challenge. They brought such a ray of sunshine into that Cheshire Home and became so involved and dedicated that now, many years later, there can be no weakening of the link they forged. We did not realise at the time that we had made an unbreakable connection and we could not see into the future and the opportunities for service this would bring to hundreds of my Guides and school children or know that it would directly lead to the work that we do now. We were too busy then, just coping with 7 a.m. to 10.30 p.m. and the endurance and effort needed to do so.

There were the humdrum daily chores of cooking and washing up, bed making and cleaning. For a week, wherever you went, you would find a Ranger with a duster, a vacuum cleaner, a pile of sheets or a bedpan. There was a Ranger doing a pile of dirty washing, another ironing clean sheets and pillowcases. They were busy in kitchen, common room and bathroom. They washed, toileted and bathed the residents. They cleaned out their drawers, polished shoes and wrote letters. They did their shopping, took them out in wheelchairs into the crisp Easter sunshine and in the evenings entertained them with camp-fire songs and dances from 'Old Ma Bott's Concert Party'.

In their tents, on nights which were so cold that the water froze solid in the water carriers and exhaled air was clearly visible, Rangers talked of illness, disease and deformity and sometimes wept tears of pity and anger. They argued long into the night exchanging experiences and sharing conversations they had had with the handicapped. Listening to their subdued voices I knew that, though they would be very tired if they lost a lot of sleep, they had to talk out their fears and voice their frustration. From each other they learned case histories which shocked and saddened them and made them indignant of family neglect and intolerant of accidents caused through carelessness. Thus purged they eventually fell asleep and were to shake out of their sleeping bags next morning to report for duties in kitchen and bedroom and begin another day of bringing sunshine and happiness.

'Do you want your shoes cleaning?' I heard Dot say to Jim. Both his legs had been amputated. The funny request brought the laughter intended. Jim's droll little body shook with merriment and everyone in the common room was in hysterics.

Had the weather not been frosty the kitchen garden would have been an impossible site for there was no turf and last year's cabbages had to be uprooted before tents were pitched. Mild weather would have made it a sea of mud. We were never again to camp there and we never again invaded the Home with so many at once except on fête days when we would almost fill a marquee with sleeping bags. Thereafter, every holiday, we supplied a rota of two or three Rangers for just a few days at a time. For the next four years we never missed a holiday and Christmas and fête days continued *ad infinitum*.

The training camp and the continued service which followed knit us together in a very special way. It was responsible for the increasing number of Queen's Guides. The weekly meeting in the super little Headquarters was only part of a bigger whole. Every Saturday there were Guides at the Blind Home, every few days they were at The Currer. The farm was a big attraction and Margaret an important part of their experience. We were often hiking, often having weekend camps, and every year we had a fortnight in the Western Islands. It was not difficult to see why everyone was happy and why results were good. The product of many good opportunities cannot be small and the tradition new Guides inherited gave them a head start.

The go-ahead to build our kitchen had come just before Easter. Margaret and I had dug the foundations and begun building the wall, in the teeth of the biting nor'-wester.

I returned from the Service Camp to this excitement. We bought a very big window frame from the seconds store of local mass producers. My reputation as Hell Fire Jack is apt. I work long after my strength and daylight go. It became a joke that my final course of stone or brick was never straight and sometimes had to be removed next morning. Father would run his critical eye over it and accuse me of having gone on when light should have stopped play. Sometimes he would come out and steal the trowel and take my job; I would be restless and itch to get it back. Between chores Margaret mixed the cement and ferried the stones and we were all three involved when the big window frame had to go up.

We worked continually with our backs to the view of the valley and the rising hillside, blind to the beauty of anything except the growing wall and the varied colour of the stone. There came a level at which the two marble slabs which were to form the base of the larder could be laid and thereafter every time the wall rose a foot we could build in shelves. We worked quickly and with dedication and the weekend soon came when we were ready to put on the roof. Roofing is traditionally Margaret's job. I become the assistant and she the employer. This switching of roles from first to second in command has been, I am sure, the secret of our excellent partnership.

And now, at last, we could break a doorway through from the living kitchen. If we had measured correctly there should be a piece of what we call Brown Luck: only just enough room to make an entrance. We bought a couple of iron girders for the lintels and attacked the outside wall with heavy hammer and stone chisel. To remove the first stone took a great deal of patience. Hundreds of years ago they may have filled the wall cavity with random stone but they certainly knew how to wedge the stones of the face so that they were immovable. We persisted with that first stone for more than an hour, all of us taking turns to chisel away enough edge to loosen it enough to lift it out. The hammer missed the chisel on several occasions and we'd a few purple patches but a wash-kitchen which could not be entered from within was a pretty useless ornament so we persevered until the first stone came out and thereafter found it easier.

I have felt, for twenty years, that our efforts to take down that doorway were rather feeble and amateur. It seemed to me that a professional builder would have 'framed' much better and opened up that door in the two foot six wall in no time. But more recently we employed a builder to restore the back porch to its former use as a 'privy' and he had to break an entrance through from the sitting room. He had to attack the same north wall face as we did and it took him more than one day to do so: at £7.50 an hour! So now I don't feel so bad about the time it took us to insert those girders and take out the doorway.

The Brown Luck was there with not half an inch to spare. On the contrary, half an inch had to be taken from the standard door we bought at the seconds dump.

Suddenly we saw, for the first time, the view northwards. We had farmed the hillside for a quarter of a century and lived in The Currer for nearly seven years but suddenly there was a newness, a spaciousness, as if a door had been opened on the unfamiliar. Now, guests coming into the kitchen stray across the rug in front of the Aga and stand in awe at the door into the wash kitchen. They see this rather wonderful view and, if it is sunset hour and gold floods the valley, they are bewitched. If it is summer the patchwork of the hay fields changes daily, if it is late August the ridge of Ilkley Moor is purple with heather and if snow lies sometimes the black stone walls are gone and only scattered farm steadings and tree clusters punctuate the whiteness.

We had appointed a new caretaker at school, Derek Thorp, born in the same month of the same year as myself. He had been advised to take the light job of verger-caretaker after a severe and very premature thrombosis. He was told that he must do no strenuous work but he was often disobedient. The determination to live normally drove him to spend long hours making cupboards and furniture for the School House in which he lived. We were naturally anxious but we need not have worried so for, thirty years later, married with two children and many illnesses behind him, he is still active.

I did not ask him to hang doors in the new scullery or fit new cupboards, just to show me how to do it. He told me what tools to buy and how to cut timber and hardboard, set hinges and assemble drawers, but also did a lot of work beside me.

We left the room with the inglenook, denuded of its sinks, untouched until the autumn. There were more urgent things to do.

*   *   *   *   *

Building the canoes was a creative activity we had enjoyed. Now they must be used. At the first opportunity we were packing them with lightweight equipment for a weekend on the canal. Each canoe was a two-seater but more than six Rangers wanted to come. This did not matter for some could hike along the bank, opening bridges and changing frequently with those in the canoes.

Eleven miles from the cellar boathouse I was taking my turn on the bank when I spied an extraordinarily angry male swan coming towards us. Before we could collect our thoughts, the white monster dived on the canoes like a fighter plane. Paddles were dropped in an effort to shield faces from the powerful wings. I tried to fight the aggressive thing away with noise and arm waving, for I was scared. Brenda was in the canoe most at risk. She was alone, for her partner had jumped out to open the last bridge. Her bare arms and legs were exposed for the cockpits were spacious and we canoed without aprons. Brenda's white limbs were long and very vulnerable and the massive swan swooped on her again and again. I stepped into the shallows and grabbed the painter; her partner ran towards us with flailing paddle beating off the swan whilst I hauled on the canoe and brought it to the bank.

The field bordering the bank fell away over a low wall. We hauled Brenda out, rolled over the wall and dropped to safety leaving the swan still persecuting the canoe. The others took advantage of the drama to pull into the bank and hurl themselves over the wall beside us. Trembling with relief, we began to laugh. It wasn't really funny. We learned afterwards that the same swan had broken a soldier's arm a few days before.

It was imperative that we rescued the canoes before he punctured the PVC bows, letting our precious equipment and stores sink to the depths. We ran along the shelter of the wall to regain the canal well away from the attacker and assess the situation, but immediately we reappeared, albeit at a distance, the swan turned towards us with such a speed and ferocity that we all tumbled ignominiously and cowardly over the wall once more and sprinted back hoping to rescue the canoes.

The swan, however, had our measure. When we attempted to climb out of the field near the canoes he was already bearing down on us again and it was stalemate. We thought he might well understand our language, so we whispered our plans: half the group ran back along the wall and created a diversion whilst we, who had been left behind, nipped out, towed the three canoes to the bridge, lifted them out and hid them on the other side

We decided that enough was enough and were content with eleven miles. We gained permission to camp and bivouacked for the night. We felt we had

had an encounter with a demon and have a greater respect for swans and an understandable fear of the cob when the pen is nesting.

There is never any temptation to stay at home in preference to a holiday. However much we are in love with The Currer it is good to get away to some place where we can stop working. The Whitsun break found Margaret and me heading north with packed rucksacks and the BP tent. We were feeling particularly smart for I'd found a man in the city who sold superb waterproof anorak material. I bought yards and yards of cloth from that friendly man and his wife. They had a mentally handicapped daughter who sat smiling by the counter and she recognised me every time I went. Whilst Father was building the pig pens and Margaret the hay racks; whilst Mother was filling the cake tins with homemade goodies, and Harry was fetching the groceries from the village and sweeping the yard, I was treadling away on the sewing machine, clothing us all. The anoraks were lovely that year.

They really did look good beneath the used khaki rucksack. We were well dressed in those days. Now I am too busy to take out the sewing machine and my hands are too numb with rough work to wield a needle properly. We had light, good quality corduroy shorts. I found two gentleman's pairs in the school rummage sale; they were top quality but enormous in the beam and long in the leg. Their size made them easy to cut down and adapt. The anorak material was light, too, and we had good walking shoes and ankle socks.

One always feels good with bare legs. It's like getting out of the shower. One feels fit for anything. In Glasgow we paused to buy a map in one of the multistores and the assistant asked if we came from Norway. It tickled us no end.

At Oban it was bitterly cold and wet and there was little to do, whilst sailing, to keep warm. We braved the deck for only a short while and then curled up in the lounge, as close as we could to the radiators. 'What's the matter with us,' Margaret said, 'that we can sail to the islands sitting in the lounge? We must have grown old.' We were very tired, I think.

We were to get off at Coll. In 1965 the pier had not been built and passengers had to assemble below deck. We spent this waiting time struggling out of trousers into shorts, much to the horror of other passengers for outside a tempest raged. It takes a measure of discipline to bare legs in the warmth of a mail boat and prepare to meet the elements. Our golden rule was always that clothes must be kept dry and anything which hung below the oilskin jackets was better off bare. Legs will dry easily for skin is waterproof and unless exposure means you will die, trousers are a nuisance.

We were lowered into the little motorboat that ferried passengers to Coll. I remember asking one of the seamen on board how to pronounce the place we were heading for. He mistook my query, looked at me as if I were an imbecile and said, 'Coll!' So we entered Arinagour not knowing how to pronounce it and chuckling together at the silliness of life in general.

It really was one of the wettest of island arrivals. Rain streamed down our legs, making great puddles on the lone island road. A horizontal wind laid the marram grass and, finding no tree to torment, dashed towards the mainland. We needed to find shelter to pitch the tent and get inside out of the deluge. We reached the west quickly, for Coll is very small and narrow, and hurried to the house at Cliad to ask permission to camp.

We were literally hauled inside out of the rain and our exceptional hostess would not hear of our pitching a tent until we had been revitalised with some hot Scotch broth which was simmering on the hob. Our generous hostess tried her best to keep us but no one should go to remote places dependent on the hospitality of the people. We create a certain dependency by asking for a site and for water, but independence under canvas is important. So we eased our way out of Cliad and fought the wind down onto the machair. We could hear the mighty roar of the Atlantic but visibility was poor and we dropped into a hollow and struggled with the canvas as we might have struggled with sail in a storm at sea.

There were moments when we caught glimpses of a wild, green ocean, unbroken as far as Greenland and the Americas, but we were too occupied throwing our rucksacks inside, crawling in after them and lacing up the door on the turmoil. We took off our oilskin jackets and laid the ground sheet. We lifted sleeping bags and a towel from the rucksacks and draped the oilskins over the frames to dry. We towelled our legs, our hands and faces and although it was only mid-afternoon, we crawled into our sleeping bags and slept. The rain beating on the roof, as noisily as a battery of machine guns, did not keep us awake, nor the wind throwing itself against the canvas so that it billowed like a mainsail. When there are no other tents and no sleeping children in our care, we can sleep through anything.

We wakened briefly to sit up in bed, light the Turm Sports and make an evening meal. The sheer luxury of down-filled sleeping bags! I had made ours in the front porch of The Currer. The lit stove warms the limited space of the BP tent in no time. It is the height of comfort and luxury. Unfortunately it is necessary to don a still-wet oilskin and venture out into the night to check the guys and pay a call but the effort to do so is exhilarating.

We closed our ears to the noisy, inhospitable weather outside, burrowed deep into our sleeping bags and slept the clock round. The year of hyper-activity must certainly have exhausted us. Sometime during the night the tempest exhausted itself also and slept like we did. We awakened, long after the shore birds, to a blue, blue day; a day of daisied machair, fat cattle, basking seals and the blessedness of isolation. Walking barefoot where the quiet tide creeps up on the shore is a soul restorer, indeed.

The next day we were walking south towards Crossapol Bay and Caolis when a tractor and trailer pulled up beside us and we were offered a lift. There were already passengers, for the crofter had his wife and handicapped son with him and was going to the southern-most tip of the island to tend sheep at Caolis. We hopped aboard the strange taxi and were able to spend two hours exploring the extremity of a very lovely island. Our new friends insisted we return with them in the trailer and the good man made a detour to show us Traigh Feall, one of the most beautiful bays in Britain. His wife and Willie came across the shore with us. It was a holiday for them too and they could not bear to let us go. When we finally reached their home at Arileod, the wonderful day ended with a feast at their generous table.

Coll accepted us like all Hebridean Islands have and we ache to return. It supports a truly generous people and we loved it. One day we went to the school garden fête, where there were not more than a dozen pupils. I remember also a lady who treated us to her delicious scones and pancakes and, because at that time there was talk of putting a man onto the moon, told us about the green moonmen she sincerely believed lived there.

Then we sailed in the RMS *Claymore* to Tiree intending to spend a few days in Happy Valley, that dip in the machair where our children have had such fun, but this time we did not win. Calum Salum would not hear of it. There had been an unusual tragedy on the island; it had disturbed him deeply and there was no way he would allow us to sleep in our little white tent. Knowing we were coming he had had beds made up for us in Salum House and he would not be said nay. We spent the next few days cooking meals for himself and Big Neil and talking well into the night with our dear philosopher and friend. Big Neil was a man of few words but infinitely gentle. He could tighten up the ropes, which secured our skips for the homeward boat and train, until I thought they would snap but he loved the daisies and he told us about a sparrow which had fallen down the exhaust funnel of the tractor and what a time it had taken to pull things to pieces to get the little bird out alive.

There was an uneasiness about the summer camp on Harris. Repeatedly have I advised leaders never to take a group of children to a place they do not know intimately. The feeling that we did not know Harris enough persisted and the urge to go back to look at the site and talk to the people on whom forty children would depend, was irresistible.

So we boarded the *Claymore* for Lochboisdale and travelled up the Long Island by bus on a glorious evening. We saw the sun drop through the gold and paint it red and the splendour it created lasted long after it sank into the sea. We are worshippers of the sunset just as all our children have been. We pitched at Lochmaddy on a minute carpet of grass not far from the pier and next morning we sailed to Tarbert.

We spent every minute of the few days we had left exploring in the environs of the campsite and talking to the people in their homes. I find it amazing that a township of but ten crofts, at the end of nowhere, could calmly accept an invasion of forty mainland children, who would live in tents, run barefoot and cook outside. There was no indication that they thought there was anything unusual about us, no look of amazement as if we were people from another planet. Without question they were willing to provide us with milk and peat and they were helpful when we harassed them with queries about how to light the peat and how much heat it would give, for we knew only wood burning skills.

We walked along the shore at high tide and low tide and found the soft sands by the river which would be dangerous. We walked under Ben Luskentyre to find the raised beaches where winter storms always threw up driftwood and we climbed the hill to see what problems it posed. When we left the island, a few days later, we felt better prepared for the summer camp and were ready to go home and tackle the haymaking, the school trip, the packing for camp and the annual sports day.

A letter would come through the post every year from the Education Authority asking me to indicate the date of the school Sports Day. The letter was sent to all schools in the area, in an effort to make sure that the games fields were in good order for the most important day of the year.

There would be some annual amusement in the office on receipt of my reply that Sports Day would be the first glorious day in June. Village schools are a law unto themselves. They are accepted by the Authority with kindly amusement, and envied for the simplicity of their uncomplicated lives.

No child at my school asked, 'When is it Sports Day?' There was no mistaking that heyday of the summer when it arrived. Each child in the village woke to find the sun streaming in through the uncurtained bedroom windows and felt the warmth of it caressingly on the pillow. They opened windows on the noisy chorus of birds and let in the intoxicating smell of new-mown hay. There would be a buzzing of bumblebees on their early morning search among the clover and a blue canopy over all.

The dew, evaporating from the grass, would hang a mist over the river and already heat would begin to shimmer from the playground as I attempted to pass the barelegged and coatless children impeding my way with, 'Sports Day, in't it, 'S Brown?'

'We'll see,' I would reply, deceiving no one.

'Ah'll carry yer bag,' Peter would say, grabbing the well-worn article and elbowing everyone else out of the way.

'Ah'll do t' service, Miss Brown.'

Would-be champions would climb down the school steps clamouring to be allowed into the Rec to practise, exhausting themselves by running round and round the field and leaping over imaginary canes until the all-in bell went.

The girls would loosen their hair ribbons to tie legs together in an effort to become experts in the three-legged race and Susan and her playmate would push the chairs into position for the Assembly and carry out the hymnbooks.

Inside school was lovely and cool after the heat of the out-of-doors. Only a major catastrophe would postpone Sports Day on the first glorious day in June. Everyone knew exactly what to do.

One of the Hagars would say, 'Ah've t' fetch t' sacks.'

Another would affirm, 'Ah 'ev t' go 'ome fer t' eggs.'

'Ah'll 'ev t' go fer me shorts.'

'Ah want me pumps.'

'Aw 'eck, Ah'm doin' it barefoot.'

'Finish your sums first,' I always insisted without much hope. For a little while there would be a silence but minds would not be on mathematics so it was best to ring the bell and call it playtime.

'What about the squash?' I would empty my purse of enough silver and the girls would pelt off through the churchyard to the village shop. I would glance at the pile of sum books, show as much interest as the children had and leave them unchecked.

Over coffee, sitting in the schoolyard, we would write the children's names in a new exercise book knowing that, without exception, every child would take part. 'We'll do the high jump and the long jump before dinner.' It was useless to insist on written work with such a fever of energetic activity abroad.

When eagerness could be kept at bay no longer, when those who had dashed home for suitable gear had returned and the shoppers had emptied the change into my lap, the juniors would dance into the Rec, every muscle competitive.

Their approach to the long jump was always individual. Some ran so fast they forgot to jump at all, some barely left the earth and collapsed with a little giggle of embarrassment. Several screwed up their faces with such determination one was tricked into a belief that a record was about to be broken but performance fell short of the dramatic beginning. Others made a fair showing, walked away with no loss of face or dignity and a few would propel themselves through space regardless of danger to head and limb. Spectators would hold their breath and expect a crash landing but, oh, the wonderful relaxation of the young.

When we had determined, beyond all shadow of doubt, who were the three winners, we clustered round the jumping stand to test the high flyers. Many were content to be eliminated early, to disturb the rope before any real height had been reached, satisfied with having taken part. Some took too long a run and pushed away the rope with their chests as if it were the tape at the end of the 100 metres but many had no fear and reached incredible heights and we stopped breathing for each dramatic performance. Some went feet first achieving a passable western roll and Stephen surprised us all with a winning forward dive.

'You all right?' I gasped with relief as he bounced up again.

Our numbers had risen somewhat and we had been given a second dinner lady, Mrs Horner. She and Mrs Hartley would be clattering cutlery on the Formica-covered trestle tables and we would hear the van come bringing the school dinners. The infants would pour out of their classroom to wash their hands and the juniors would run in from the Rec, ravenously hungry.

'Remember las' year?'

'Ah think Steve'll win!'

'Ger away. It'll be a girl this time!'

'Ugh, don't be daft!'

'Get on with your dinner,' I would interrupt. 'You're wasting time and there's a lot to do.' There would be a brief uneasy silence.

'Who's scoring?'

''Ave yer go' t' whistle?'

'Do t' Dinner Ladies know wi've got squash?'

'Who's clearing tables, Miss Brown?'

'The noisy ones,' I would say and, for a little while there would be a hush and a whispering.

'Aw, we'll all 'elp,' someone would say. 'Ah'll do t' trolley.' This was always the favourite job.

'Me t' tables.'

'You sweep. Who'll do t' chairs?'

And the sun would come streaming in through the windows and everyone would be a friend.

During the dinner break chairs would be carried out into the Rec. Sports Day proper began with the running of the marathon twice round the field. What fun we used to get out of our village school Sports Day! We were mentally totting up the marks, trying to spot the champion long before the final results.

'Who's winning, Miss Brown?'

''Ow many points 'ave Ah got?'

''Eck! Ah wish Ah could skip.'

We would be noncommittal, secretive, tantalising, 'Wait and see,' would be our only, eye-twinkling answer.

''S Stephen, in't i'?'

'Goodness me. He can be beaten, I'm sure.'

The infants gave us the most pleasure, the five-year-olds who brazenly held onto their pot eggs, who crumpled up in a tangled mess when having only three legs between the two of them and who disappeared completely into the depths of Christopher's enormous sacks.

'Cor, Ah'll 'ev pain laughin'!' the older brothers and sisters would gasp as they ran illegally onto the field to disentangle Matthew, Mark and John, Susan, Sarah and Jane.

At last, dying of thirst, we would file into the playground for Sports Day squash. Bare feet tripped across the hot concrete, tee shirts were left on the rails and cold water splashed over faces in the cool porch before we were all ready to start again.

The girls preceded us to lay the obstacles, the hoops, balls, sacks and nets. Championships were won and lost in the obstacle race. It was a gamble which could topple the winner and bring up the outsider.

Then it would be all over and from the youngest to the oldest they would gather at my feet, lift expectant faces and await the results. Amid cheers and shouts and exuberance of every kind, the year's champion would be proclaimed.

Then lost socks would be found, tee shirts gleaned from the long grass and PE equipment humped across the road.

"Bye, Miss Brown. See yer.'

'See yer,' I would reply informally.

'Warn't it fun? Ah nearly won, di'nt Ah?'

We would be very tired but relaxed. For us there was none of the traumatic tension of most sports days. We never had to worry about the weather, never had to make decisions or concern ourselves with threatening clouds. Our weather was always assured for Sports Day was on the first glorious day in June.

We had to sell Harris to the Guides and Rangers, so besotted were they with Tiree. They did not want to be weaned. Children thrive on doing the same thing year after year. Initially they were against the thought of a new island but, as usual, they all decided to come with us and make the best of it. No one had heard of Harris as an island, only as a tweed. 'Where are you going?' the children were asked and the reply always brought the same response. 'To Paris! How lovely!'

No place could be more unlike Paris than the barren beautiful island the children were to grow to know and love over seventeen years of frequent returns. They were to learn to cook on peat with expertise and the wilderness of rock and sand, towering dune and mountain was to become an integral part of us all.

That first camp at Luskentyre was an experience we repeated over and over again. The island was so totally different from Tiree there could be no comparison. There were children all over the place and it was a joy when the cookhouse whistle blew to see them all come running back to the D'Abri,

Cookhouse Blows

Cookhouse blows!
    D'abri doors are open wide, wherever they are the children run;
From the clean shore, salt-crusted, browned and freckled by wind and sun,
Carrying the treasures on the tide, starfish, bone and delicate shell,
Encouraged to come more quickly by the tantilising smell.

Cookhouse blows!
    Hair flying, young cheeks reddened, they leap from rock strewn hill,
Their gentle fingers cradling bugloss, orchids and tormentil;
Skirting the lochan, water-lillied, climbing the lichen wall,
Healthily hungry, happy and strong they respond to the whistle's call.

Cookhouse blows!
    They come from the silver sand dunes, barefooted deeply tanned,
From dizzy heights they leap and fall, buried unharmed in a cloud of sand.
They race across the machair, from peaty bog and tumbling burn,
Into the joy of the D'abri impatiently waiting their turn.

Cookhouse blows!
   They leave the woman weaving, the crofter lifting his peats,
The shepherd shearing his yearlings, the Cailleach dyeing her fleece.
Those in the tent who are singing, put down their pipes and guitar
And arm in arm run to the D'abri. Hungry? Of course they are!

Cookhouse blows!
   Oh what enormous golden pies, mouth wateringly delicious.
Light potatoes, early lifted, carrots and peas, voted scrumptious;
Fruit crumble crisp from the oven, in custard sea, smooth and creamy;
Buscuits and cheese and coffee hot, a menu fit for a gourmet.

   Some may choose a small fire or stove of liquid gas,
But they've never known a peat fire, an oven turfed with grass.
They've never sat with fifty in warmth and friendship close.
The heart of our camp is the D'arbi when the cookhouse whistle blows!

D'arbi: Dining Tent
Cailleach: Old woman

The aunts began to accompany our parents and Harry on their annual coach
trips, and the five of them visited south coast resorts they never expected to
see.
   They were off on one such jaunt in 1965 when the Electricity Board were
putting a new line of poles across our moor. One afternoon, Margaret was up
checking cattle and she saw that they had dug one of the big holes and were
preparing to leave the erection of the pole until morning. 'You're not just
leaving the hole like that, are you?' she said with some astonishment.
   'Yeh!' they answered. 'Why?'
   Didn't they know that cattle are the most inquisitive of animals and we
had a hundred roaming the area? They would jostle each other about, each
wishing to see the big hole, like a group of playschool infants.
   'You'll have to fence it off before you go,' Margaret said with that tone of
authority she can use when she expects to be obeyed.
   The workmen said they would leave it safe and Margaret should have
stayed to watch them do so but she genuinely wanted to keep on good terms
with the men who would be on her land, digging holes, for quite some time.
So she came home and had barely reached the doorstep when a rambler came
running into the yard yelling that a bullock had caught its horns in some wire
and would be dead before we got there.
   We tried to keep our heads and grabbed a small hacksaw which was
hanging on the wall. For the life of us we could not remember where the wire
clippers were. We dashed up the hillside faster than we believed possible.
There was awful bawling on the hill and steam rising from a hundred
stampeding cattle.
   The workmen had fenced off the hole! To do so they had pushed four

metal pegs into the ground round the crater and they had rolled a coil of thin wire close by. They had freed the end of the coil and, leaving it still attached to the drum, had wound a single strand round the pegs. The disturbed coil became dangerous. A dozen strands sprang proud, as they always do. The bullock, in a playful mood, had poked its horns in to the loose wires and lifted the whole circlet over its head, then, annoyed at the unexpected collar, it had stampeded away from the coil and the twelve strands round its neck had pulled taut until finally the wire snapped but not before the animal was strangled almost to death. Wild eyed, sweating and crashing about it created a terrible stench of loose muck and sweat and saliva. The rest of the herd panicked and stampeded alongside, churning up the moor with their hooves and sweating so profusely that a steam rose from them as they thundered along. Any walker in their path would have been killed. We were in grave danger ourselves.

Had the choking bullock gone down before our arrival the whole herd would have turned on it. Fortunately it did not collapse until we arrived; somehow we fought off the herd and attacked the coils with the hacksaw, knowing that the collapse of the animal would either precede certain death or be the godsend which could give us the opportunity to save it if only we could get through the wires in time. I have seldom been more scared, sitting on a valuable animal which could not breathe, sawing dangerously near its throat whilst Margaret held the head. Suddenly the last wire was cut, an awful noise came from the dry throat and there was a bubbling around the distended nostrils.

Margaret stayed with the animal to fend off the herd and I dashed to the phone to ring the Electricity Board. Everything had happened so quickly the staff had not left the office. They insisted there was no blame attached to them as they had fenced the hole as requested. Men! Their arrogance leaves me flabbergasted. Usually benign, they make us very aggressive when they put us in danger.

A pylon was felled on the moor and left for a different team to dismantle. It was discovered by a jostling, curious herd and at the farmhouse we heard a sickening bawl of a cow in sudden pain. It is a bone-chilling sound which will wake us in the night or set us running in the day. It is an animal 999 call we always hear and never ignore. On this occasion we found a Hereford cow with a broken leg. We sent for the vet to bear witness as to the cause of the accident for compensation purposes but the poor, much-loved Sally had to be shot. Almost all accidents are negligence, many are ignorance, only a few unavoidable.

The green lane which divides us from the estate with its golf course, lake, nature trail, manor house and home farm has never been repaired since the electricity workers mutilated it in 1965. The three miles are unsurfaced but motorists are always trying to negotiate them. The going looks quite good at either end but then the road becomes deeply rutted and waterlogged and ordinary cars come to a full stop. Because there is usually no help available the stranded driver takes stones from our wall to build a causeway and get himself out of the mess. When he drives off in a temper he leaves a hole in our boundary wall.

Margaret has tried for years to persuade the Council to do something about it. All that is needed is a bollard or a chain across both ends of the road or a firm notice which says 'Impassable' but all she has achieved is one which says 'Unsuitable' and this does not deter the determined one little bit.

Occasionally we are there when it happens and we can speak our minds but then we have to help push out the stranded vehicle. This is not a pleasant task for we certainly will not allow the use of our top stones. When the haymaking or muck-spreading contractors are in sight they have been called to help and have always managed to extract a fee for their lost time but when we tried to do so it did not work.

Margaret and I were up repairing the boundary wall one Sunday afternoon. We had come up onto the moor in Genevieve and we were silently going about our own business when we heard a small car approaching. We knew what was going to happen. The little Mini stuck well and truly in the mud. The undercarriage was sitting on hard ground and the little wheels were spinning ineffectively in slime. The driver did not even try to step out. He spent a long time just pressing his foot on the accelerator sending mud in all directions. We pretended we hadn't seen him but eventually he put his head out of the window and yelled at us to pull him out with the jeep. It may have looked like a miniature Chitty Chitty Bang Bang but it could not fly and to get on the other side of the wall meant a round tour of a couple of miles through the village. The jeep wasn't licensed for the road so there was no way we could do so.

We left him to simmer for a time for we were really too busy repairing the wall some other motorist had vandalised but eventually we wandered over and offered to help. 'When the men are up here,' we said, 'They charge a pound. We'll do it for ten bob!'

He was not amused. I don't suppose we looked very glamorous up there, walling on a rather dull autumn Sunday. The car was very light. One on either side we could lift the undercarriage off its pinnacle. The man, warm and clean and very red in the face, never got out. 'Stop revving so much!' Margaret yelled but Toad was desperate and believed the only way out was to stamp on the accelerator regardless of the ladies outside pushing and shoving and slithering in the mud. Once the blighter began to move no doubt he was afraid to stop and perhaps that was his excuse for no backward glance, no thank you and no ten bob! Perhaps it was that he looked in the mirror and saw us. We were completely covered in mud and exhaust soot. It was caked in our hair and ears and our faces were unrecognisable, our hands blacker than Epaminondas.

As the nights lengthened in autumn we turned our attention to the emptied kitchen, with its inglenook fireplace and beehive oven. We began chipping off the plaster and exposing the whole wall. The lime and cow hair plaster was easily removed. The latter must have been applied when the fireplace had been built up and the room turned into a cowshed. It was two inches thick in places and a hammer and chisel were necessary to force it from the stone.

It took us four months to complete the conversion and we finished in time to decorate it with cards and holly and lighted tree at Christmas time. I thought there was no more beautiful room anywhere than the Snug. A hundred hours were spent on the wall, exposing it, and cleaning it with caustic soda and acid. We built up the outside doorway and it remained blocked for several years but what we do, we invariably undo. We are always blocking and unblocking doors just as we are always moving the woodpile.

The wall was in remarkable condition for all its four hundred years. It needed pointing but there was not one stone loose or too blackened by soot to be cleaned. Sadly, there was no hope of an open fire in the hearth for someone, many years ago when the last re-roofing had been done, had slated over the outlet.

We replastered the three remaining walls. How beautifully a professional plasterer works and how ham-fisted I was at the job. I try, and the finished work is passable but the journey there is often of cartoon quality. Plastering is a job I prefer to do without an audience! Too often I use my hands as well as the trowel. One wall, the brick one we had put up to reduce the size of the room when it was the kitchen, posed the biggest problem for it had never been plastered at all. I looked for a way to get round it. There are legitimate ways in which the professional reaches a goal and less authentic ways in which the amateur can achieve an effect. I made a large bookcase. I made it big enough to reach the ceiling and put a hardboard back on it so that when it was lifted against the wall it covered a multitude of sins. I also built a cupboard to encase the electricity meters. Once I start working in wood I cannot stop so I made a bench which began as a window seat and continued the length of one wall and three feet round the bend. It was a beautiful storage space. Comfortably cushioned, it seated many Guides for scores of campfires, slept many of them and was only undone a few years ago. I remember that, when the bookcase was growing on the floor, Mother came in and added a new prediction. Now she feared that the funeral would be held up whilst her do-it-yourself daughter insisted on making the coffin herself.

Janet came to help us stain the beams. Perched on a step ladder with the deep stain in a bucket and wielding a five-inch brush she got carried away with romantic thoughts, lost her balance and came down with a crash and a shower of brown stain all over herself, her hair, our floor and the walls. The liquid was dripping from her hair and running down her face until she resembled a monster from some horror film and all we could do was laugh. The humour in slapstick comedy has always evaded me. I just cannot see anything funny in custard pies being thrown at someone. No doubt it is because the real thing, which happens to us frequently, we find so enormously funny. We are repeatedly spread-eagled in mud, always spilling water and landing ignominiously in the duck pond. We always think it is funny. Perhaps it is as well, otherwise we'd have been in the asylum long ago.

We were extravagant. There was no pressing need for an additional sitting room when our finances were still in the red. Friends and neighbours were satisfied with only one. Granted, they did not have the hordes of visitors that we did, the scores of children, the camp-fires and barbecues and barn dances and an increasing number of Queens Guide Presentations but it was extravagant to have the concrete floor surfaced with black asphalt and to cover it with wafer-thin imitation parquet tiles. Perhaps the NUT had negotiated a rise.

There was one other thing we spent money on at the beginning of December which had become a necessity we could no longer avoid. Winter was coming and Mother was really too old to be struggling through snow to get to town for the groceries, although too young to hand over the job. Harry was finding it difficult to struggle three-quarters of a mile by road to the bus. The friend who had bought us the jeep told us there was an Austin Gypsy for sale, advertised at £80. We sent him to look at it and buy it if it were in reasonable condition. It looked quite like the Land Rover we could not afford, had three seats at the front and a van body behind. It was in need of a spray so we bought a can of paint and made it look respectable. We licensed it for the road, took out an insurance, filled it with petrol and felt rich. Father still had the driving licence he had periodically renewed for many years. He had learned to drive long before the era of driving tests but the only car he had driven regularly had been the little Austin which had delivered milk. He never got into the driving seat of the Gypsy, declaring he was too old to learn to cope with the increasing traffic and the faster flow but he legitimately sat beside Margaret and taught her to drive.

We could now pick up a bag of cement whenever we wished. We could bring calves home from market, take dogs to the vet and camp equipment to and from Steeton Hall. We could go up to the quarry for sand, to the builder's yard for plasterboards, nails and Calor gas. We wondered however we had managed before. We moved furniture, carried corn and bales and sacks of potatoes.

I will never forget the first Christmas of the Snug. We finished school in the warmth and togetherness of Crib, parties and carols. Two days before the twenty-fifth I was on my knees laying the mahogany tiles and they were beautiful. Mother had made a Readicut rug and the new paint smelled clean. The spruce fir I had brought from school on the bus, for the Gypsy was of no use to me, scented the air and its lights and baubles reflected in the polished floor. It was like something from the front of a Christmas card. We bought an imitation log electric fire and found frequent excuses to go into the room just to look.

Our friends said, 'Thought you weren't going to become drivers!' They wore smiles which said, 'I told you so!' They had never accepted our plea that we could not afford a car. All our lives only the bank manager has believed the state of our finances. The general public believes all farmers and businessmen are rich when in actual fact, farmers seldom take a personal salary. They feed themselves from the produce, rarely take a holiday and plough everything back into the land.

'It's a wise man who changes his mind,' we answered. 'We are not one bit afraid of a U-turn.'

Margaret passed her driving test and thereafter took the passenger seat and taught me. That summer we were able to take our parents, Harry and the cases to the coach when they went on holiday. It was over a year however before I passed my test. The older one gets the less easy it is to learn to drive. I failed three tests before I had success.

There is one memory which stands out from my year with only a provisional licence. We were driving round the town one evening when I was approaching the lights at a crossroads in the shopping centre. A learner driver was halted in the street ahead but the lights changed and I had to stop so Margaret and I had a front seat view of what was remarkably like a film of the Keystone Cops. The driver turned his wheel and passed in front of us to follow the road on our left but he never brought his wheel out of the lock and we saw him doing a U-turn. He lost his head, put his foot on the accelerator instead of the brake and narrowly missed the centre-of-the-road bollards, dodged on-coming traffic, mounted the pavement, crashed through a dry cleaner's plate glass window and disappeared down some wide steps leading into the shop basement.

I was trembling. There was traffic behind, the lights changed and I had to move. Safely round the corner I pulled into the side and dashed to the police station a hundred yards away, leaving my kid sister to cross the road to investigate the accident. I have felt a coward ever since. She is far braver than I am but miraculously neither the learner nor his instructor were hurt. Next day we passed the boarded-up cleaners and some wit had scrawled across the boarding, 'We clean clothes, not cars!'

One would have expected that every year things would get better. The land improved but the area around the homestead deteriorated. Mud encroached on us like an unwelcome neighbour. As more and more cattle collected at the yard gate, the last fifty yards of road were covered with six inches of mud in no time. Periodically Margaret would push tons of it down into the hollow when it was raining heavily and easy to move, but try as we might the mud remained a sea whose tide was perpetually incoming. The slick crept into the yard like some evil thing we could not get rid of. The postman refused to deliver our mail in winter unless we placed a box half-way up the hill. My shoes were perpetually muddy. I kept polish in school but I frequently had to wash them before I could use it. On the bus I felt so ashamed I tucked my feet well under the seat.

A quarter of a mile of road, all of it uphill, is a liability. When we made it we saw it as all beneficial. Now we had our own transport it suddenly became a monster which had to be dug out when snow fell. The removal of the east wall had left it exposed to sweeping snow and winter winds piled drifts mountains high every bit of the way. Things did not get easier!

The increasing suckled herd meant more calvings. Most were healthy but we had experiences all farmers have to contend with. I remember Meg who had post-natal attacks of neurosis, who would have killed each calf she bore, within minutes, if we had not been there. We tried to drive her home but failed. When birth seemed imminent we parked the jeep and waited. When the calf was born and she should have busied herself licking it clean she began to attack it with such malice we hastily put the baby into the jeep and took it home. We placed it safely behind bars in the mistal and went to collect its mother. Lifting a newborn calf which has not been licked is a messy business.

A story a friend told me tickled me no end. She is quite well-to-do but kind and practical and she was driving alone on a deserted country road when she witnessed a little drama she will not forget. A cow gave birth too close to the field gate onto the road down which my friend was travelling and the calf slithered out of the cow and down the slope, under the gate and into the highway. Somehow my friend managed to drag the calf under the gate to its mother. Just imagine!

We tried to rub Meg's calf clean with an old sack but the yellow slime must be licked and Meg would never co-operate. After her head had cleared she was always a perfect mother. She had a lot of milk and her calf was always the most beautiful one we had.

Difficult calvings are inevitably remembered more than healthy ones. Easy, natural ones were happening all the time in the days of the suckled herd. It is reassuring to know that, at the point when you cannot cope, a vet can be sent for but vets are like doctors and muck spreaders and shed-builders; they come and do their professional bit and then they go and leave ordinary people to cope. They give expert help and advice but they seldom work miracles and the farmer is left with future injections to give, poultices to apply for many days, tubes to push down a calf's oesophagus so that potion or a gallon of water may be poured down directly into the stomach.

Diagnosis is important but so too is the daily carrying out of professional instructions. 'Turn the cow over every few hours.' Try turning eight hundred-weight of sick animal over several times a day. However deep the straw there is an abundance of wet muck. A cow which is down excretes and urinates beneath it so that everything is warm and wet and flanks are always covered in manure. The animal will not help and every few hours comes a struggle you dread. A vet was sent for because of summer mastitis in a heifer carrying her first calf. She was wild and had never been tied or handled. 'Squeeze this tube up the teat every day and give this injection.' No one sees the struggle we have. The heifer will not go into the crush. She will not stay in the yard either. We dash around like some cartoon characters. Suddenly the heifer sees the fence and heads for it like a show jumper. Fortunately the fence is strong and she is no champion. Her front legs are over but the back ones are still on our side. 'Quick, Margaret!' I yell and with the heifer in a compromising position in goes the first injection.

On Boxing Day Ozzie was calving in the mistal. The calf was big and she was small and it soon became obvious that she was not going to calve it herself. We gave her all the help we could without success. So we sent for the vet whose work, like ours, does not stop for Christmas. There is something magic about a normal birth and something very sickening when things go wrong. On this occasion, a winch had to be used, for the heifer had ceased straining and lay exhausted on the straw.

Though the presence of the vet is reassuring I hate every minute of the struggle to save life. His hands are always gentle as he loops the wire over the protruding front feet of the calf and begins the slow, but powerful winching. Ozzie's eyes began to roll, her head, roped to the manger, fell back and she looked at us with such fear and pain we were in agony too, and cradled her head, stroked her neck and muttered soothing words of comfort. Usually the calf's head will be dragged free. The next hurdle is the broad shoulders and then the rest is easy but it is often an hour of fear and sweat before that happens. On Boxing Day the winching took a long time, the calf was dead and we did not feel one bit like a family party.

The professional appears when the penning is over. The vet sends his card warning us of a TT or a brucellosis test and when he comes the cattle are waiting for him. When the livestock removal wagon comes the cattle for market are ready to be loaded. These men have no idea of the palaver of herding animals on our land. It is grazed ranch fashion, and, when needed at home, the cattle are always as far away as possible. They seem to know intuitively when the vet and his needle are expected, they become as awkward as they know how and will not be driven home. So we have to be canny.

Now we are helped by the water hole being near the homestead. The medieval dewpond in the meadows has dried out and the cobblestones which line it have become overgrown with buttercups and hawkweed, daisies and clover. The moor pond, which watered the cattle until recently, has been so mutilated with the big herd that it has drained in summer and grass and rushes have made it little more than a mud bath in winter, too dangerous to leave unfenced. Lack of water on the hill ensures that the cattle come home, at some point, every day and when we see the herd coming for water, we open the yard gates and snatch an opportunity.

But in the sixties and seventies cattle could drink a long way from home and we had problems. It is easy enough to bring home a milking herd, for cows learn the routine, but a herd which is running virtually wild will not be driven easily. Success is never assured until the herd is in the yard with no escape except through the crush. I have seen the whole hundred turn and run in the opposite direction when almost at the gate and I have seen them turn and gallop off at the flush of a lark from the heather. Come a car or helicopter and there is a stampede indeed. One, following the pylon line, sent two hundred animals on the rampage and returned to make a second observation of the line. The pilot must have seen steam rising. Summer brings lots of walkers so we phoned to ask the authority to advise pilots of accidents which might be caused by stampeding cattle but the pilot said he had been on the other side of the valley all day. May we be forgiven if, on these occasions, we shout!

Nevertheless, if the vet is scheduled to arrive at eleven the herd must be penned at eleven and if the cattle wagon is to come at ten, the animals for sale must be ready. It is risky to leave the gathering until morning, for the appropriate hour comes quickly and there is no time for a replay.

It is not a bad idea to pray for heavy rain, or even a thunderstorm, for this brings the herd home in rapid time and with no assistance from us. The sky has only to turn yellow and a rumble, just one, be heard in the distance, and every man Jack of them comes home in a hurry. They tell us when there will be a downpour nearly as soon as the Met. Office. As Ministry tests, worming, subsidies, and occasional sales are the only reason we ever gather cattle the exercise is strange to them and the dogs get little practice. It is of no advantage to get help to drive them in. In early spring and autumn the cattle come home for shelter for the night and one can almost set the clock by their arrival and relax all day, so sure that they will come home. I remember one spring when we thought we had it made. The TT test was fixed for the beginning of my Easter holiday. It was a wet spring, bitterly cold and the herd came home every night to pack themselves tightly into the sheds and the April emptiness of the barn. The grass was poor and wet and we had to ration what little hay we had left. Several of the herd lost weight and the healthy sheen we like to see had disappeared. March and April kill more animals than mid-winter for their reserves are used and there is danger of a magnesium deficiency.

But the night before the test was warm and, for the first time that spring, the cattle didn't appear, so we set off to bring them home by fair means or foul. At the farthest extremity of our land they had broken through a gap where the winter frost had toppled a wall and they had found shelter among the heather on the rough ground near the Altar.

We had three options. We could try to drive the herd back over the fallen wall. A hundred cattle will climb through unbidden but not one will return if pressed to do so. The thing to do was to drive them the length of the rough and let them through the gate at the corner of the Eight-Acre, not a sensible job to do in the semi-dark when every foothold is insecure and not one animal willing. The third choice was to leave them cosily bedded in the heather and wait until daybreak. Margaret decided on that option and we walked home alone in the moonlight. It was a beautiful night. I could have slept out myself. The gateway at the corner of the Eight-Acre is notoriously boggy. We opened it in the semi-dark of a full moon and noted the standing water everywhere. Usually, in spring, the earth can drink whatever water falls, but that particular spring, water flooded every hollow.

We were up at five, drinking hot coffee and pulling on wellies. The new day was less attractive. A cold wind had risen and a cloud cover came with the dawn. The animals were therefore quite biddable and moved steadily towards home and their ration of hay. The passage of the herd through the gateway made havoc of it. Four hundred feet churned up the mud in the standing water until it was thick mire. The last, weaker members of the herd had a struggle to drag their way through. By this time the mud was eighteen inches deep and we urged the animals on quite noisily in case they stopped and, in so doing, stuck fast. The last, weak yearling hesitated and all our shouting at it to keep going was in vain. It floundered and went down. Defeat in a bullock is almost instantaneous. That one was down and he was not even going to try to get up.

Within seconds we were covered in mud, struggling to prevent him from falling over on his back in which position he would soon die. Happily the herd, like a troop of naughty children filled with remorse, went steadily home to the sheds where Father was imprisoning them. We knew we had no hope of getting that animal out without some artificial help. Sacks would do. Anything to lay on the mud so that we could roll the animal over and over until dry land was reached.

We rushed home behind the herd, grabbed some sacks and, as an afterthought, Margaret put some sherry into a tonic water bottle. We left Father to cope and hurried back up the hill. A great comfort has gone out of our lives with the replacing of hessian sacks with paper and plastic. They made excellent draught excluders when the wind blew unexpectedly from the north-east, bringing its donation of heavy snow. They made a warm coat for a cold animal, could be used as a towel to dry a wet one and excellently covered a box of new born piglets hurriedly carried to the kitchen to have their teeth clipped. Several could be used for races at the school sports and, if the original wore thin, a very good replacement tent bag could be made. I have seen my grandmother wear an apron made with one and one was always tied with string to make a sausage to stop draughts coming under the farmhouse door. In the days when hessian was stretched on the rug frame to make tabbed rugs out of old coats, sacks were often used. We thanked God for them daily and miss them sorely now they are no more.

Armed with spade and rope, sacks and sherry, we hurried back to the gateway where the unfortunate bullock sat in the mud completely resigned to a slow death. The winter was about to claim a victim. There was no bellowing, no struggle, just a hopelessness. I have seen old cats and dogs and people give up and stop trying but this was a young animal and, anyway, Margaret never gives up. Weak with poor, wet grass, chilled to the bone with a hard cruel winter which would not give way to spring, the yearling had decided that enough was enough and this present predicament was the last straw. We laid the sacks to form a carpet, rolled the stirk onto it and dug out its legs. Thus free we began to roll it unprotesting, over and over until we reached good turf.

We hoped that it would now scramble onto its feet but it really had given up. Margaret poured sherry down its throat. We were exhausted and covered in mud and with another sack we began towelling some warmth into the yearling. Sweat poured out of us. He didn't weigh very much so we lifted his hindquarters off the ground but they only buckled. In desperation we struggled to persuade the sack to go under his belly and lifted him clear of the ground. All four feet took a little of his weight but we dare not let go. All the long difficult journey home we supported him with the sack, one each side, taking most of his weight and all of his balance. It played havoc with the muscles in our biceps. Heaving and floundering and too exhausted to talk we moved at only a snail's pace and the clock hand approached eleven. The vet and we arrived almost simultaneously. We struggled into the stable with the poor and wretched creature. We covered it with straw and the vet gave it a jab.

Now the penned animals had to be let out of the sheds into the yard. Margaret waded through the mud and manure which had built up over the winter to a rich and smelly consistency more than a foot deep. It was so wet it was level and a hundred animals ploughing through it left no footprints for, even as they lifted out a hoof, the slime found its level again. I was watching her open the gate and the mud was higher than the first rung so she had to pull hard at the handle, an iron tube soldered onto the gate. I saw it happen. The handle had rusted and chose this moment to come off. Margaret, pulling with all her strength, suddenly left the gate with the handle and sneck in her hands and hit the wet mud behind her with a loud splash. She began to sink and could not for the life in her get up. I ran to the rescue but we could hardly do anything for laughing.

Eventually, having left her clothes in a pile in the yard in exchange for clean ones, we began the time-consuming task of passing animals through the crush.

We had a visit at this time from a neighbour who is classics master at the city public school. Raymond came in wellies, jeans and old anorak and offered to help turn the animal over. It is a messy job. There is always loose manure, warm which is even less acceptable, and Margaret's opinion of the man, and her respect, grew considerably when he offered to take the messy end. It was weeks before that animal stood alone but eventually it did.

The countryside is full of farmers struggling with a weak animal, hoping that it lives, not just for the money. At a farmers' meeting we attended the members were asked why they farmed. Was it because it was a way of life, a love of animals, a service to the nation or a means of earning a living? All the votes were for the first two options. 'Fiddlesticks,' said the financier, 'You farm to earn a living!' True, one must make a living or one cannot farm but the farmers at that meeting did not think that way.

'D'yer get many like this?' Margaret asked the dead animal remover when helping to lift one of her failures into the wagon, all skin and bone and having been lovingly nursed for a long time.

'Aw, aye,' said the man. 'They all struggle wi' em dahn till they're worth nowt. They'd fetch summat if they gev up at once but they all struggle on an' think they'll win.'

Chapter Thirteen

W hen spring really begins to come it wastes no time. The bought-in calves revel in their new-found freedom and gallop all over the place. Suddenly we were free to pack our bags and head for Scotland. 1966 was the last time Margaret and I went alone. We had no hope of getting to the islands for there was a boat strike. We booked places on the overnight bus to Glasgow with no definite idea of where we were going. Nowadays there are as many women back-packing as men but in the fifties and sixties we were different. I remember a lady turning round to stare at us in Edinburgh. She tripped on the kerb in front of me and, Princes Street being crowded, I was too near and several pedestrians and myself all tumbled in a heap. Perhaps because Glasgow is so close to the Highlands, we never felt conspicuous there in spite of shorts and enormous rucksacks.

We found a train leaving for Fort William and booked tickets for Spean Bridge. There was a lady in the compartment who told us that a war could be fought with midges. We were grateful that she was an observant woman for when we alighted at Spean Bridge we did so without our precious tent poles. They lived in a narrow white bag and were strapped to one rucksack, but packs are cumbersome in train compartments; the poles must have been released and thrown onto the rack. We did not notice our loss until we were climbing the steps to cross the line and the guard was waving his flag. We dropped our packs and leapt down the steps. The train was moving and we ran alongside shouting to the lady in our compartment. She was quick to catch on and threw out the poles. We waved our thanks and it was a while before we started laughing. Whatever would we have done without our poles? We had no money to bed-and-breakfast and were a long way from anywhere where we could buy replacements. We would most certainly have spent the night in the open.

Instead, we spent it beside a stream, hidden from the road by a cluster of fir trees, just below the monument on the road to the Great Glen. Having pitched and eaten we climbed the hill to a crofter's neat white cottage and asked permission to phone home. There was a beautiful moon.

We walked a long way from Spean Bridge with heavy packs and blistered by hot sunshine. From Invergarry we took the high road up above the loch, then across the moor and down to Loch Cluanie. We bathed swollen feet in the cool burn just before the road joins the Road to the Isles and would have pitched our tent if there had been anywhere to phone. Instead we took the road westwards; the evening was coming. We heard a Land Rover behind us; a Mountain Rescue squad offered us a lift and dropped us at Sheil Bridge. We could have gone all the way to Skye for the Kyle of Lochalsh ferry was running but we decided to see the mainland for a change.

There was a call box at Sheil Bridge and somewhere to camp and it was a beautiful evening. Twice only have we used a campsite. This one was deserted and extremely uncomfortable. The ground was as solid as tarmac. Next day we followed the narrow road round the loch as far as the Eilean Donan Castle. The road has since been widened but in 1966 work on it had only just begun and the Road to the Isles was indeed narrow and interesting. We left it at Dornie to turn north to Strome Ferry, in a heatwave. When we arrived at the ferry we were exhausted and gladly accepted a lift from the ferry to the village.

A need for coppers to visit Loch Carron 'Ladies' earned us a lift up to Gairloch. We asked for some small change and the driver of a caravanette offered us a back seat. The elderly couple were delightful and we had a very pleasant journey. The lift made it possible for us to get further north than we had dared to hope. We prefer to walk, even on the mainland, but distances are great and the lift was a boon. The campsite at Little Sands was practically empty. Whitsun is not a holiday in Scotland and the season has barely started in May. We found a sheltered, private site, very close to the sea. From the open door of our tent, when the very late darkness fell, we watched the return of the fishing fleet. It was such an isolated spot that we decided to stay a few days and explore the area around us free of the burden of our rucksacks. I remember bursting tar bubbles on the road as we used to do when we were children and swimming in the coldest loch we have ever tried, up on the moor between Gairloch and Poolewe.

Each day we took a new compass direction and our most memorable day was spent on Loch Maree. We were very nearly stranded many miles from camp. We had taken an early bus out to the Loch Maree Hotel and were told by the driver that he would return at three o'clock. This gave us about six hours to explore the locality and we did so with our usual zest. At 2 p.m. we were about two miles from the hotel, sitting at the water's edge, eating a packed meal, when we saw the bus hurry past. We couldn't believe it, leapt immediately to our feet and waved frantically but the driver never saw us. We decided that it must not have been our bus. An hour early, in a land where most things are late, was absurd. So we finished our meal at leisure and, as three o'clock approached, made our way onto the road, expecting the bus to come up behind us any moment. But it did not and when we reached the hotel we were told the bus had gone and learned that the hotel was a stop on the journey for passengers and drivers to eat.

We were not hitchhikers, but this was an occasion when we had to ask for a lift. We set off for Gairloch rather sore, physically and spiritually. We had already walked many miles for we had risen early. The heatwave had toasted us until we were russet and swollen. Several miles along the loch side we came across two gossiping lorry drivers, timber-men. Going in opposite directions, they had pulled up alongside and were leaning out of their cabs, having a good old natter and completely blocking the road. It is the only time we've ever asked for a lift. It was granted graciously and we clambered into the high cab and sat squashed onto one seat all the way back to Gairloch. We were extremely grateful. We arrived back before the Wild Cat closed. The little coffee bar sold us more tomato rolls that week than I care to admit. Now, when we are tucking into a tomato roll twenty-five years later, and I say to Margaret, 'What does this remind you of?' she says, 'The Wild Cat'. If it is a bacon roll she says, 'Mallaig'.

We walked 150 miles that holiday. Our wanderings on islands are full of people and the evenings find us at some céilidh round a crofter's peat fire. The Whitsun we spent on the mainland was singularly without encounter.

The train we caught home did not stop at our local station and we had to alight ten miles away, at three in the morning. It never occurred to us to ring home and get Father to run out with the Gypsy. We shook the sleep out of our eyes and set off to walk. Halfway home we passed through the village where I taught. Had I had my key we could have slept in school but I hadn't so we kept going, enjoying the early morning beauty of our much-loved homeland.

When we had roofed the new kitchen we had continued over the old curing house. On our return from Gairloch I cleaned out the rubble of stone, slate and rotten wood and put the camp equipment there. Every year we were adding more tents and billies and the passage store was too small. The curing house was to serve us admirably for many years.

We returned to Harris for a second year with the children. It seemed sensible to consolidate our relationship. We approached Harris via Tiree and Barra and travelled up the Long Island by bus, adding island after island to our list. The sand dunes were the main attraction. The fun the boys and girls had, leaping from those dunes and tobogganing down them on trays and plastic bags, is a story in itself. During our camps the smooth dunes were disturbed with thousands of bare footprints. If the wind obliterated them overnight they appeared again the next day. If one of my top class boys was not going on holiday I offered him the chance of going to camp and boys from Luskentyre and Lone Guides from all over Harris joined us so that our numbers topped fifty and our visits became a legend.

We soon learned that the Austin Gypsy was a very 'guid friend'. Harry became a permanent fixture in the passenger seat and new horizons appeared for him. For over twenty years our vehicle has never left the yard without him unless it has taken me to school or to a meeting. School children, friends and neighbours all began to know that when they clambered in Harry would be already there. It had only three seats but it wasn't long before we had fixed a back seat so that we could take all the family or pick up the aunts. It was a performance getting everyone in, but worth the effort.

Once I had passed my test, it took me some time to pluck up enough courage to drive off alone. For many weeks I continued to struggle onto the bus with a packed rucksack to go to the Guide meeting, and to walk back home. I never even thought of taking the Gypsy to school. Then one day, an early morning telephone call told us that the cattle were out. Margaret and I dashed up the hill with the three dogs, but had considerable difficulty getting the herd back. It daily took me a full hour to get to school by bus and there was no hope of getting to the end of the fields in time to catch it, even if Margaret got out the Gypsy. 'Tek it,' Father said. So I went alone for the first time and I was a nervous wreck by the time I drove up to the school gate amid the cheers of my school children. They clustered round the funny little vehicle competing with each other to carry my things. A hurdle had been leapt.

I have known so many teenagers. All of them have taken driving tests as soon as they have reached the minimum age to do so and most of them have passed first time and immediately driven with confidence. I was thirty-six and apart from the year we delivered milk in a small Austin in 1947, I had seldom been in a passenger seat. I used to travel a little with my headmistress in my pre-head teacher days but that was all. Neither Margaret nor I could really say we had any road experience. When we drove the jeep there was only open moor in front of us and no oncoming or overtaking vehicles and when we went anywhere we went by bus on the kerbside seat just watching the countryside go by. We were dreadfully ignorant of the high road and its innumerable hazards. I suppose we should have paid for professional instruction but the do-it-yourself habit dies hard and we were always so dreadfully hard up. I think the £80-worth of Austin Gypsy with its amateur coat of paint and makeshift back seat might have had nothing to do with my repeated failure to pass a test but the examiner always looked at her critically. She was to be Harry's lifesaver against boredom. My ten-year-old essay wish was granted. We had a car for Harry. We had just had to wait twenty-six years, that's all.

The passageway in the barn, now empty of camp equipment, took my insatiable fancy. There was obviously a built-up doorway from the front porch. I became convinced we needed a cloakroom so I built up the barn entrance to the passage and opened up the porch one. Light flooded into the small room, illuminating the gigantic, beautifully cut stones with which the passage wall had been made. For four hundred years that lovely stone wall had been wasted in the dimness of the barn. It had never been weathered and needed no cleaning and we could not dream of covering it so when we panelled the other three sides with tongued and grooved pine, we left it bare.

The cloakroom was a useful place for coats, freezer, buckets and calf milk. It also housed sick animals: Biddy-the-pig, MacRae-the-crow and Squeak-the-pigeon that Father always called Billy. The inhabitants of the cloakroom gave us pleasure even if we did a fair amount of grumbling at Margaret for bringing home any stray animal she could find.

Father loved birds, especially swallows, but they were creatures of the wild with whom he could only distantly relate so Margaret brought him a baby pigeon she found on the streets of town. It must have fallen out of the nest too early for it was incapable of fending for itself. A female St Francis is Margaret. She ignores all our protestations with the skill of long practice.

The pigeon squeaked like some child's toy and we so christened him, except Father who called all stray pigeons Billy. Only tired homing birds ever settled at The Currer and they stopped but briefly. Sparrows, wagtails, finches, tits, wrens, greenfinches, robins, starlings, blackbirds, magpies all lived here in great numbers but pigeons never stayed. They had bed and breakfast and then went on their way.

'Billy'll stay,' Father said hopefully.

Squeak made an awful noise in his constant demand for food. Having survived the first few days in the cloakroom he was brought into the porch during the day for he needed the sunlight. We lived in constant fear of leaving a door an open invitation to one of the cats to put an end to the little fellow. We dared not endanger Margaret's dependants. We grumbled about the birdlime all over the place and wondered what we were going to do, for a visit of Glasgow relations was approaching. But Squeak had it all organised. The day before their arrival he found an open window, flew up onto the roof and so liked that elevated position that he never came down. No one called him Squeak any more. He was Father's pigeon and his name was Billy. He needed a mate but other pigeons were all birds of passage. Some would stay a night on the roof and Margaret and Father would throw up tit-bit bribes but none stayed and Billy was a lonely soul. He turned to us for companionship and learned to peck at the window to ask for his breakfast.

Billy stayed with us all year. When spring came again he took off each morning, flew a circle of respect above our heads and then headed directly towards town. Every evening he returned to peck on the kitchen window for food. If he was late Father would be out looking for him. Then came the day he had another pigeon with him and we hoped he'd stay but they flew away and a little ray of sunshine went out of Father's every day.

MacRae, the one legged crow, lived only a short time in the cloakroom and then was transferred to the greenhouse. This was indeed luxury for the uncouth gentleman and he stayed with us a long time before he was able to fend for himself. When he finally flew away we all found ourselves looking at every crow to see if it had but one leg. Wild birds teach us to accept people, too, as birds of passage. As Kipling said, let 'all men count but none too much'.

Margaret rescued a bluetit one day from the jaws of one of the farm cats. In those days kittens could be born in the barn and we would not know until they emerged almost grown. We never knew how ThreeLegs lost one hind limb, but it did not stop him hunting. This little bluetit was the most beautiful creature and seemed happy to be released onto the windowsill in the kitchen, opened up its beak and did not cease its repertoire until it was exhausted. It was almost as if it had been resurrected from the dead and grateful to Margaret and the Almighty for life itself.

Seldom has any small creature given us so much pleasure. All morning it held us spellbound with its song of gratitude, then, finding the handle of an empty basket to use as a perch it tucked its head neatly under its wing and slept. But its tiny heart must have suffered too much stress, first beating irregularly with fear and then pulsating with an overspill of joy. Even as we watched the little thing sleeping, we saw it fall off the perch to lie quietly dead at the bottom of the basket. Though it had been with us but a few hours we were bereft.

Our land, by overstocking and manuring and liming, became so much more productive that the barn would not hold the hay harvest. We had more shed space to in-winter some of the animals and straw was needed for bedding and had to be bought in the autumn and stored. One way and another we decided we must have a Dutch barn. We planned it as we journeyed up to Perth by train in the May of 1967. We were joining Ann, now a physiotherapist in the hospital there, and she was driving us up to Harris.

The holiday seemed to be a breeding ground for plans. When we have decided we want something we are Mother's daughters and want it 'instant'. Nothing excites us more than a new idea. But one idea cannot be discussed the whole way to Perth and most of the time we slept. The motion of the train going north is very soporific and we have slept more journeys than I care to confess.

We stayed one night with Ann in Perth and then squeezed ourselves and our three packs into her small Mini and drove to KyleRhea. The new road was barely begun and the narrow road, in that almost-on-the-ground Mini, was rather hair-raising. The steep one on the south side of Loch Alsh was even more so. We were glad to get onto the ferry and cross to Skye.

We pitched the tent at Uig, that jumping-off place for the Outer Hebrides. Like Oban, its only attraction for us is the pier and the mail steamer. Next morning, we left the Mini in the car park and sailed for Harris. We couldn't keep away. Beautiful, beautiful island! It was good to feel wind on bare legs and to walk. We are essentially walkers, not motorists but we were on the brink of compromise.

We spent a lot of time with the islanders. Over a *strupak* with Katie and Angus Morrison, who live on the shore at Luskentyre, we asked if they could accommodate our family for bed and breakfast and Katie said yes, if Margaret and I slept in a tent on the shore.

'That's what we'll do next year,' we said.

On our return we were in a hurry to get started on the Dutch barn, for after Whitsuntide the haymaking followed quickly and camp would be there in no time. We went straight to our ex-army supply man. Billy's huge shed and yard always had just what we wanted. Sure enough we found twelve 20 foot by 12 inch by 6 inch beams which we reckoned would do for the uprights and a wealth of timber suitable for the horizontals. We arranged for his lorry to deliver them. Lying on the bank, behind The Currer, they looked far too long but height was essential. In any case there are things we will do and things we will avoid and one of the latter is to saw a bit off twelve very thick beams.

So we set to work to dig twelve deep holes. We dug when rain stopped play in the hayfield, after the camp equipment had gone north in advance, and we prayed as we dug that we would encounter no rock which needed blasting. That our prayers were answered is a miracle for we have later experience of how solid the rock is beneath our feet. The holes were just about ready when Paul, Julie and, this time, Vivienne, were deposited with us so that they could travel all the way with the campers. In the few days they had before camp, we mixed the cement for the holes and, with ropes and all hands on deck, we erected twelve poles. There was a definite slope on the bank and we had to dig the uphill holes the deepest to allow for this. Amateurs have to be very canny.

When we left for camp the poles stood like a circle of pre-historic standing stones and, to a passer-by, they would have been just such a mystery. The haymaking was finished, the barn was full and there was no space for the straw which would come but, when we left for Tiree, we were confident that we would be ready in time.

Taking Vivienne to camp was different from taking Julie who had been a baby to cuddle and adore. Julie slept with Margaret and me in the little white tent and she was pick-a-backed everywhere. Now she was ten and it was her fourth camp and she wanted to join a patrol so Vivienne went straight into an Icelandic tent with her and was independent from the start. It was pleasant to return to Tiree, so different from Harris, so near to the shore, with Calum and the MacInnes family and so many friends.

We had been camping on the islands for a decade and it was a way of life we loved. Children who had come on the first Tiree camp were with us as adults. We had shared a common experience of infinite value and this created an unbreakable bond of fellowship. It was always hard work but we were unbelievably happy, whatever the weather. I do not regret one minute and consider myself fortunate that, when I was ten, I was allowed to be a Guide and that 'Somebody Up There' introduced me to Cloughie who taught me to camp.

We returned full of enthusiasm for the Dutch barn. I had two weeks holiday left before the autumn term began. My cousin Freda's husband had been selling paint in a shop in town in a temporary building of corrugated tin. It was demolished to make way for road improvements and we had an unexpected source of tins. We transported them in the Gypsy.

Roofing a high Dutch barn is easy even if you have no head for heights like me. First you fill one side of the barn with bales of straw. You need not wait until all the loads have been delivered for the season. When you are about four feet from the top of the uprights you can start roofing in complete safety. You have a secure and soft platform from which to work. You do not need to climb ladders which bend and give in the wind or fear that you might plunge eighteen feet to the ground. All you have to worry about is the nail you accidentally let fall on the straw and fail to find, in case the springhead is eaten or trodden on in winter.

Chapter Fourteen

O ne of the joys of teaching in a village school was the relationship with the staff and the villagers. We were all friends. Annually we used to go and have tea at Mrs Hartley's, our dear dinner lady for many years. When our numbers increased, Mrs Horner was called in. I often had tea at her house, too, when I had to stay late. It was expected that I go to Joan's on the evening of the termly managers' meeting and when our caretaker married I often had tea with Derek and Liz in the schoolhouse next door.

Dorothy Hill and her sister Mary used to invite us all annually to a splendid banquet. They had presented the school with a trophy and they came to the end-of-year presentation to hand the children their prizes, certificates and trophies. We were all invited, teaching staff, dinner ladies, secretary and, if the staff were coming to The Currer for tea, the caretaker came too.

That I was headmistress was seldom acknowledged for we all had equal social status. Only when the 'can had to be carried' did I step out of line. I remember using the phone, one day, when Joan was sitting drinking coffee by the fire near enough for me to kick. 'Good morning,' I said. 'I'm the head-mistress.' And Joan, may she be forgiven, burst out laughing.

We laughed an awful lot in those days. I used to go to headteachers' meetings and hear discussions on appointing staff and, even when I had been Head of my school for twenty-one years, I had to admit that I had no experience of interviewing applicants. The caretaker was always the verger and although I was present when new ones were appointed I never had any real say in the matter. Caretakers lived in the house adjoining the school and were always our best friends. Dinner ladies stayed with us a long time. When one was ill I would find a supply in the village, Mrs Wass, and she was automatically appointed when one retired. The same thing happened with teaching staff. We needed a supply and Joan knew a friend who lived nearby who could fill the bill. Then, when we were told we could appoint a part-time member of staff, Winnie was offered the post. It eventually became a permanent one and Winnie introduced a friend, Liz, who admirably filled the part-time vacancy. Secretaries found their way onto the staff in much the same way. A poorly paid, part-time job will not attract people who have to spend the small wage on travelling, so it was inevitable that our secretary was always a parent.

Husbands lent a hand, caretakers' wives sent homemade goodies in to the staff-room. Winnie helped me with badge testing. She was a Brownie Guider and eventually a Commissioner and, when Cloughie handed over the Camper Badge tests to me, Winnie would occasionally be at the weekend camp. There was an interdependence in the staff-room and we liked it that way.

Few heads would have tolerated such an informal and uncontested filling of vacancies but I worked on the assumption that staff relationships were all-important in a small school. To the Local Authority we were an enigma but we had few problems to lay on their doorstep and we were undemanding in our needs so no one interfered.

Perhaps I was too undemanding. The world was rapidly changing from one of little choice to one of too much. I was increasingly worried that the values and virtues of simplicity were being exchanged for the pitfalls and temptations of plenty. I would visit other schools where money was being spent on carpets and equipment and where wall displays covered every available space; my conscience would prick and I would wonder if I were doing my job properly. Then my concern for the children faced with this new, encroaching environment of materials and noise, colour and choice, would win and I would stand by my faith in simple things. It seems to me that, nowadays, the poor little souls do not know where to turn for a little peace and solitude. Even the paper boys walk the early morning streets with headphones so that they can listen to constant pop, and they never hear the cuckoo.

In my new role I am constantly asked to give advice on rearing children. It always shocks for they expect a teacher to say, stimulate and excite and feed, explain and answer in detail and tell the truth about the birds and the bees. Poor little stimulated and excited children, full of squash and crisps and convenience foods, confused with misunderstood facts about life and religion! What children need is a kitten to fondle in a hay barn, a tree to climb and a job to do. They do not need more than one soft toy to cuddle, and pan lids and wooden spoons, sand and water will do.

I am sorry for these children. They are given freedom of choice too early and taught that it is everyone's personal privilege when it is no such thing. Children should not be able to choose what to wear and eat and how to behave. They should not dictate a routine but fit into it, for they must learn that adults can make very few choices. Almost everything we do affects someone else, and before any action we must assess its effects on family, friends and environment. Choice must be responsible, and children cannot carry that burden without stress.

One parent told me recently, her grandmother had had eight children. 'I cannot cope with my two hyperactive ones. I asked her how she'd managed.' Grandma had answered, 'When a new one was born I just put it between two of the others and we coped.' Children should be part of a family and not dictators of it. In their enthusiasm to 'do right' by their children, parents have begun to focus far too much attention on them. They can take a little healthy neglect without suffering, I assure you.

The summer of 1967 was a bumper one for bilberries. Margaret and I can collect more bilberries in less time than most people, as we are absolutely single-minded about fruit picking. We have been known to gather over 40lbs of bilberries in a season and that is many billions of berries! We pick as if life depends on quantity, squatting on the moor or under the silver birches at the Altar, ignoring flies and shigging bushes of all the berries the size of an aniseed ball. We leave the tiny berries for the birds. We use both hands equally for picking and soon these efficient tools are purple. If children accompany us they have purple lips and almost empty jars but we do not eat one and our bowl is always full.

Father's garden was very productive. Even though he gave so much away, there were more peas and gooseberries than we could eat so we bought a second hand ice-cream freezer to store the harvest. We even stored some of the blackberry crop which usually went wholly into jam.

Blackberrying is a different art. The year has turned towards the fall and the season of mists has crept up on us. The days have shortened and chilled and it is quiet in Jimmy's Wood and down the Marley Bank where the black-berries grow. We wear protective trousers and old jackets to fight the bramble strands. I love the smell of autumn, damp, fungoid, extraordinarily earthy. Bracken changes from green to a sea of gold and the oaks and birches yellow; the russet beech leaves become paper crisp and the berries on the hawthorn and the briar have been painted scarlet.

When we were small we collected blackberries in Horlicks jars; since we came to The Currer, by the bucketful. We bottled them in the war years, for jamming-sugar was in short supply. In the sixties and seventies we made a hundred pounds of jam a year to sell for Guide funds to buy tents. We picked from early morning, unwilling to return until our buckets were full, too scratched and weary to relish the evening job of cleaning them and stir-ring the contents of the jam pan. We put in hours and hours of work for a few pounds. We were always holding a coffee morning, a Christmas Fayre, beetle drives and afternoon teas. We battled our way through rummage sales and barbecues and sponsored walks, making the few pounds which, added together, amassed us £2,000-worth of camp equipment. Eventually we were independent of the Division stores kept at Steeton Hall.

In the spring of 1968 we had our first family holiday for eighteen years. We packed the fast-deteriorating Gypsy with the care and precision with which we packed for camp. Into the 'guid friend' went the family cases and our little white tent, a couple of sleeping bags, the Turm Sports, a kettle and a frying pan. We gave the Gypsy a new coat of paint and washed its windows. The days of preparing meticulously have gone, I do believe, for good.

We suffered a lot of criticism when friends and relatives heard we were taking our 72-year-old parents and our disabled brother to the Hebrides. For years they had thought we were mad to take so many children to such remote places. Now they heard we were going to take the old folks in a rickety old van, they knew we were insane. My mother's character is extraordinarily interesting. It can be predicted that she will always view change with pessimism yet when the one very debatable step was taken, to remove to The Currer, she said, 'Yes', and stood by her decision whatever people said. She loves holidays more than any of us, but she annually gets cold feet, fears we will never be ready and almost has a nervous breakdown before we are. She feels ill, thinks she is 'in for something', even that she might die before we get off. But, when we suggested going to Harris in the Gypsy she was all for it, even making amused remarks behind the backs of derogatory friends who prophesied that the Gypsy would break down.

'If we only get t' Skipton before it does,' said Mother, 'We'll book bed and breakfast there an' tell no one.'

That we were able to go on holiday together was because of the Blamires. I had taught two of their three children and taken them to camp. We were all at a wedding of one of the Sea Rangers. Whilst we waited for the bride, Phyllis and I were whispering and I mentioned a hope that we could have a holiday together and she whispered, 'You can. We'll look after the farm.' It was as easy as that. Since then there has been no shortage of Old Guides, Rangers and friends in the queue to look after The Currer for us whilst we escape to recharge our batteries.

Our holiday was a strange mixture of convention and camping. We piled into the hand-painted Gypsy, with its do-it-yourself back seat, crossing our fingers and laughing with Mother. She is wonderful to have on holiday. The enjoyment of a break from routine must be taught. Cabby Tom taught Mother and she in turn passed the knowledge on to us.

By breakfast-time we were only a few miles from Richmond. Afraid of the A roads we had plotted a course which followed the by-ways and we meandered along unharassed by traffic. We pulled onto a grassy verge and brewed-up, bag-packing fashion.

Similarly, lunch-time found us frying fish and chips in a hedgerow near Rothbury. This will do for us, Margaret and I thought, this compromise is acceptable. We will not waste time by crying for what we cannot have. Yet now, nearly a generation later, when we are still following the Romany trail on wheels, with Mother, Harry and Auntie Mary, if we are asked what we would do if we were free to go alone our answer is unhesitatingly, 'Take a rucksack and a tent, of course.'

By mid-afternoon we were dawdling up the coast road between Seahouses and Bamburgh. Suddenly the Gypsy began to rattle and lurch and the steering wheel in my hand was like a weight. I had not the slightest idea what was wrong. 'We've got a puncture,' Father said. Sure enough, we had a wheel as flat as only a pancake can be. It was our first puncture in a roadworthy vehicle and, miraculously, the garage in Seahouses was only a few minutes away. It seemed more judicious to have the tyre repaired at once than to unload the cases to expose the spare which was wedged under the homemade back seat. This first puncture, just minutes away from a garage, set a precedent for all future flat tyres. Each time we seem to have been parked outside a mechanically minded friend's house or such a friend has been visiting when a tyre has gone down in the farmyard. We have had two punctures on country lanes in the neighbourhood when friends have driven past and come to our assistance. If we have had to change the wheel ourselves we have been in a beauty spot with flasks of coffee unopened and we have been able to do the job whilst the family have enjoyed their morning elevenses. Our luck is consistent and we almost expect a miracle before it happens.

Nevertheless, the incident at Seahouses reminded us of our friends' pessimistic predictions and our confidence was a little shaken when, half an hour later, we arrived to spend our first night with Jean and Peter and the children, all of whom slept on the floor so that we could have beds. I remembered waking in Julie's and seeing Margaret already staring at the ceiling from the comfort of Vivienne's. For some time neither of us spoke for we were, after all, country cousins; sometime around mid-day we had to drive through Edinburgh and we were petrified. Margaret let out a sigh and muttered, 'We are wrong in our heads!' and we dissolved into laughter. It seems pathetic, in this age of motion and technology, that we should shake at the thought of driving through Edinburgh.

We headed north, inland to miss the A1 and passed through Edinburgh with a certain amount of stress but no incident. It was at Crieff that the Gypsy made heavy weather of pulling out of a car park and began to make ominous, underground sounds of distress. The bumping did not stop or get worse and we reached a garage in Aberfeldy without disaster.

The proprietor crawled underneath and said that he had found some important bolts loose. He admitted that the thread was almost bare and that they would doubtless come loose again. The Austin Gypsy was not a vehicle he saw frequently and he had no replacement bolts so all he could do was to tighten them and hope for the best. He had got rid of the bumping and we had a trouble-free journey to Spean Bridge.

When we had last been in Spean Bridge, Margaret and I had camped in a fir copse below the Monument and had telephoned from a small cottage nearby. I had written to the owner and reserved bed and breakfast accommodation for us all.

This shepherd and his wife were delightful. He had a young collie pup with quite the most intelligent face I have ever seen. We fell in love with the little cottage and we booked a night for the homeward run. In the morning we went to the garage, had the bolts checked and replacements ordered for our return. Then we took the same Road to the Isles we had walked a few years ago. I don't think we have ever been happier.

When we drove off the ferry onto Skye we paused to take a photograph of our brave little Gypsy, just to prove to the pessimists at home that we had almost made it. There is such a safe feeling about the islands; a security in knowing that someone will take care of you if something goes wrong. The new road had not then been completed to Portree. It has shortened and simplified the journey but I liked the old road, narrow and winding and so often on the shore. I don't ever want to drive fast through Skye. There is too much beauty. The new road has commercialised Skye so that it is now a pleasure to leave it behind and sail for unspoilt Harris. In the sixties Skye was relatively quiet and we liked it that way.

At Uig we drove onto the ferry and found that we were known by the members of the crew. It is impossible to travel unobserved with fifty children.

We have enjoyed few things as much as we enjoyed introducing the family to the Hebrides. Where is there a better place to stay than with Katie and Angus on the shore; where better to eat breakfast than at their table with the multicoloured waters of the bay only feet below the window and dinner watching the sun set in splendour over Taransay? Where better to pitch one's tent than on the daisied machair just above the sands? The holiday was a huge success. The OAPs enjoyed it as much as the children always did and Margaret and I were understandably over the moon for honestly, I don't think we can live without the Hebrides any more than we can without The Currer.

We did not, after all, spend another night with the shepherd and his wife for they had a sudden visit from family and recommended some friends who would accommodate us. This was one of those accidents for which we are very grateful. John and Cathie MacLennan were to become and remain friends; we visited their croft at Tigh na Coille innumerable times.

I cannot emphasise too much the importance of teaching children how to enjoy leisure. I believe in teaching children to enjoy it simply and inexpensively because I have never had any money to do it any other way. I do not think I am wrong. If a child I have taught to enjoy simplicity is now rich and can afford to cruise on the QEII I think he will enjoy it more because he knows how to stand on deck and commune with the stars, watch the sea birds or feel the wind.

We had many visits from school, to abbeys and museums, cinemas and theatres and places of local or historical interest. We wandered over building sites in the village and visited farms at lambing time but the school trip was seldom anything but a holiday. It was spent on the beaches of Flamborough, Whitby and Scarborough, St Anne's and Morecambe, Silecroft and Ravenglass. It was spent on the riverside at Bolton Abbey or Newton-by-Bowland, Grassington, on the moors at Haworth or Malham, in parkland at Studley Royal or Fountains Abbey, among the rocks at Bingley or Brimham and in the woods in St Ives or Hardcastle Crags.

These God-given days were nearly always in the sun, for our village coach proprietor would quickly alter the day if the chosen one dawned wet. The children would be disappointed and view the storm clouds with disgust, a trembling lip and sometimes tears but it was better to wait a couple of days rather than spoil an outing on an unworthy day.

Usually the day dawned fine and mild and there was great excitement. Almost everyone came early and carried a bag containing food and a change of clothes. We nearly always went near water and children have a habit of getting wet. Sometimes I would take a tent just for the fun of pitching it on the riverside or the seashore. I remember always taking a frying pan and sausages and my shorts so that I could kneel at the fire to fry them or stand in the water holding the Guide swimming rope which marked a boundary with inflated rubber rings.

We learned things about the children on the school trip we had not known: who could cope and who would cling. Some had to be watched for they were confident and apt to wander and some would stay so close we would be falling over them all day. Some would spend all their money early. Some would buy presents, some sweets, some useless souvenirs. We would supervise them in the village and seaside corner shops, to influence their unwise spending and make sure they were polite and well behaved. We learned that David was cute enough to buy sweets for profit-making resale on the journey home and that Catherine would give away money to anyone who asked.

We had one very wet day in Malham we could not avoid. We had arranged a hiking adventure and were equipped for bad weather, carrying a change of shorts and sweaters. Our transport was leaving us for the day and rejoining us in the late afternoon. Winnie accompanied us by car with the picnic hamper and to pick up the odd child whose unsuitable footgear began to inhibit and finally torture. It rained continually, heavily and without mercy all the way to the Cove and up the steep banking to the limestone pavement. 'Ee, M's Brown,' said one boy, 'Ah betcha watta's cumming down t'dry valley!'

There are few wetter terrains than limestone country. Water stands in pools everywhere and grass becomes as slippy as ice. Much to the children's amusement I went down several times. We had to keep walking so that our bodies generated enough heat to keep the water in our clothes warm. We laughed a lot and ran much of the way and most were still cheerful as we hurried across the moor. We paused only a moment where the river from the tarn sinks and, seeing Winnie's car and anticipating food, dashed for the road. Between sandwiches we played 'Tig'. Anything energetic to keep the water warm. There were only one or two Moaning Minnies in the car. Returning to Malham we used the public conveniences as changing rooms. There is nothing more comfortable than dry clothes after wet ones have been removed. Then we went into the information centre and watched a film until our bus returned. It was a happy day.

I remember one day when we had already cancelled a previous choice because of rain and I felt we could not ask our so-considerate gentleman to postpone the booking a second time. It wasn't exactly raining when we set off for Stump Cross caverns and Brimham Rocks but the forecast was pretty awful and we knew what was in store. The rain did not start until we had left the caverns but we arrived at the Rocks in a torrential downpour. No one seemed daunted, indeed the rain seemed to over-excite. The children seemed unable to walk sedately and ran from one spectacular rock formation to another in high spirits. Winnie and I had our work cut out to keep up with them and we all got wetter and wetter. It was the last time I took boys on such an expedition in long trousers. Their jeans became saturated. Once more in the bus the girls could dry their legs with towels but the boys in longs could only suffer.

There was a snack bar and a café on the moor and, although there were people in the self-service bar, the café, with its beautiful red carpet and immaculately laid tables, was empty. I explained to the proprietor that I had a bus load of wet children who would appreciate a bowl of soup and the dear lady told me to bring them in. They left their wet shoes in the doorway and tip-toed barefoot over the expensive carpet and seated themselves before the clean white tablecloths. Please behave beautifully, I prayed. They did. The more splendid the environment the better children respond. If I'd taken them into the transport café they would have wanted the jukebox and splashed their pop on the Formica tables. In the posh café they behaved impeccably.

Children did not change much over the thirty-one years I taught them. They are like chameleons, reflecting the environment, and behave as the adult with them expects. People say children are different today but I do not believe that it is true. I think that adults are different. They are more affluent, less work-worn, have more leisure and fewer children. They are more worldly, less God-fearing and less family orientated, therefore the children they rear behave differently but placed in any other background they would reflect it. I had occasion to ponder on this one day.

I do not often have meals in expensive restaurants, and neither do I often accept invitations to evening wedding receptions. It was to be expected that, in this unfamiliar atmosphere, I was trying, with some difficulty, to enjoy the excellent buffet.

Then quite unexpectedly, the lady opposite me leaned across the table and said, 'You used to teach our Peter,' and I was quite at ease.

'Our Peter' must be over thirty now but I was suddenly back in the first village school in which I had taught and I could see Peter, his stocky little figure, unruly hair, cheeky grin and perpetually dirty hands.

'Do you remember him?' his mother asked. Well, of course. Peter was eager, tough, grubbier than most, cleverer than many of his classmates. I'd not heard anything of him since he had won a scholarship to the Boys' Grammar School and I'd moved further up the dale.

Adele had had a birthday, I remembered, and had brought her cake to school to share with the class. It was heavy with fruit and rich with almond

paste and sugar icing. Anthony had just returned from an appendix operation and his face crumpled with disappointment. 'T' doctor sez Ah 'aven't t'
eat currants,' he said.

'Perhaps someone will do a deal,' I suggested. 'Swap the sugar icing for
your fruit cake.'

'Ah will,' offered six-year-old Peter, unselfishly for most children like
the sweet part best. With sticky fingers he separated the delectable almond
from the less inviting fruitcake. I watched him thoughtfully cramming his
denuded cake into his mouth until it was far too full and hoped that the
second piece would not follow too quickly.

But no, with his mouth still too full, Peter was attempting to push the
second slice into his pocket. It already housed bits of mutilated rubber,
pebbles and string for his conkers. The sticky cake proved disinclined to slide
into his pocket and I gasped, 'Peter what are you doing?'

'It's fer me Mam,' he said.

Those were less affluent times and children were not so casual with their
possessions, nor so sure their wants would be supplied. What about children
today, I wondered as I tucked into my plate of turkey salad, perfectly relaxed.
They are so outrageously honest about their parents. Did it make them less
respectful?

What about the five-year-old who proudly came to school displaying a
pair of shoes. He stood on the staffroom hearthrug, very conscious of the new
shine which would never again be repeated. 'Those look lovely,' Joan said.
'Who bought them?'

'Me Mam,' said the angel, fully aware of his new found smartness.

'Isn't she a good Mum,' said his teacher, wishing to direct his thoughts
from gain to gratitude.

'Yeh,' he admitted, then added for good measure, 'An' in't she fat?' Though
frankness indicates honesty it does not illustrate tact.

I wondered if Peter's careful preservation of the birthday cake for his
mother meant that he cared more than the child who told us, 'We've a right
mucky room in our house. There are cobwebs an' spiders all over the pelmet,'
or the one who said, 'Me muvver meks 'orrible custard!'

Did all children, I wondered, criticise their parents? Did they say, like one
did to her grandmother, 'You don't know. Only Miss Brown and the Vicar
and God know.' Are children really any different?

I got my answer a few days later. We went on an expedition to Beamish.
My children crowded into period cottages to watch bread being baked in
a Yorkist hot air oven and saw tabbed rugs on the floor and embroidered
texts on the walls. They saw the peggy tubs and rubbing boards and zinc
baths and they stroked the velvet mantles on the fire shelf. They poked their
noses into the outside privy and saw the twin circles on the scrubbed seat
and learned about the 'neet soil' men whose job it was to empty the buckets
below. They saw the old colliery and gasped with shocked realisation to hear
that eleven-year-old boys were still down the mines seventy years ago and

they fondled the pit ponies remembering, with compassion, their long prison sentences in the dark.

People talk so glibly about the 'Good Old Days' when, they say, children were so much better than they are today. I had been wondering since my encounter with Peter's mother. But the children were good all day and as we returned to the coach, across the muddy car park, David found a pound note. My children always immediately displayed their finds. 'Look,' he showed me, 'I've just found this.'

'We'd better take it to the office,' I said.

He trotted happily beside me. 'I nearly put my foot on it,' he said. 'Cor! It was just lying there. I couldn't believe my eyes.'

The girl at the reception desk was uninterested. 'No one will claim that,' she said as if pound notes were of very little value. 'A watch or a wallet, maybe, but a pound note? Never!'

'It's your lucky day,' I said to David.

We were late and I turned hurriedly towards the bus. The child grabbed my arm and begged, 'Please can I go to the shop?'

I was impatient. 'What do you want to go to the shop for? Everyone is waiting.'

'I want t' buy something fer me Mum,' he said. Children have not changed!

In the summer of 1968 Phyllis Blamires came to camp with us, bringing her youngest son. We went to Tiree and the camp was memorable for two reasons. It was easily the hottest, most perfect weather we have ever experienced in camp. For seventeen days there was never a cloud in the sky. The children lived in swimsuits and Julia slept outside. We were in and out of the water like mermaids. The heat was pleasant. There was no early morning nor evening invasion of midges for which the West of Scotland is famous. Everyone was brown but no one had sunstroke.

Equally important to us was the presence of our Division Commissioner's daughter, Joanna. Shortly before camp Hazel came to The Currer to a Queen's Guide Presentation. These were great occasions when twenty or more would gather round an extended table in the kitchen for a veritable feast of ham salad, trifles and the cakes and pastries for which Mother is so famous. In the evening fifty or more would squeeze into the sitting room to the delight of Mother, Father and Harry and sing campfire songs for a long time.

The singing of campfire songs was a tradition. Few could compete with my 'Song to Sing' children. Campfire singing was always spontaneous, even in competitions. Our repertoire was such that a non-stop programme could go on for hours. In my inadequate way I would start the ball rolling and then the initiative for new songs came from anywhere in the circle. The choice would be sensitive so that if the mood were lighthearted the songs would be noisy. Then nostalgia and tiredness would breed beauty and peace and be reflected in the choice of song. One competition judge accused us of having rehearsed, said our campfire singing was too polished to be spontaneous.

For nearly a generation we had sung on shores and hilltops and woodlands, in buses and boats and trains. We had sung packed like sardines in the Land Rover and round the fire at The Currer but we had not rehearsed.

At that particular Queen's Guide Presentation in 1968 Hazel joined our Magic Circle and before she left I suggested that Joanna, not one of my Guides, might like to come to camp. The offer was accepted and Joanna came to Tiree, became one of my Guides and then a Saturday Child for many years. She gave us a great deal of joy and helped Margaret with the calves with loyalty and devotion. That she enjoyed camp so much was one of the most important things that happened to us for she infected her mother with enthusiasm and when circumstances at home prevented Margaret from coming to camp, Hazel was to take her place and make it possible for me to carry on invading islands with children.

The children who went to market to buy calves with Margaret always named one calf after themselves and we soon had a calf called Joanna. It was a very small, premature Charolais cross which Margaret bought for a pound. Joanna was particularly difficult to rear for we were still feeding from buckets in those days and this calf had the habit of choking, would keel over several times a feed and have to be resuscitated. Each feed was an alarming occupation. But the little joker survived and became very beautiful and had a longer and more cosseted life than most for it had a lot of lost ground to make up.

At the beginning of the new year the Old Gypsy had to have its MoT test and failed. The garage man told us it was too old and it would be a waste of good money to repair it. It was a cold January day and already dark and Margaret and I stood hesitantly in the draughty workshop and said 'Goodbye' to our old friend. There was a bright red Austin Gypsy in the corner. Possibly it had belonged to the Post Office. Incredibly, there was a For Sale notice clipped to the windscreen.

'How much?' we asked.

'A hundred,' said the garage man. Well, we had to have a Gypsy of some sort for life without wheels was suddenly unacceptable. What would Mother and Harry do? How could we go on holiday? We were planning to return to Harris and to visit Tiree and the Uists on the way. How could we do that without a Gypsy? Surely the bright red van was there just for us. It wasn't luxurious, and had definitely seen better days quite a long time ago, but it was roadworthy and we bought it without any masculine help.

When we drove it home, a few days later, we got out the paint can and converted it to a friendly green and cream and I don't suppose many people noticed the change of number plate.

The winter of 68/69 was a killer. In spite of additions to our sheds, only when hay was depleted could we house all our cattle and even that was by overcrowding. This would not matter when spring came with warmer days, less chill nights and a flush of new grass. The suckling herd had thick coats and never really wanted to come inside. They were perfectly happy to drop their calves in the snow and to find shelter in the enclosures of the farmyard and behind the barn. We suffered the mess they made with relative silence for it is a cruel master who will shoo away animals in the bitterness of driving snow and freezing rain.

But 1969 gave us no respite. At half term I was recalled from the Cheshire Home to fight a blizzard but apart from that we were spared deep snow. We might have welcomed it instead of the icy sleet and the bare, waterlogged pastures. March is a bleached landscape at the best of times. Given a little warmth, March 1969 might have been lush for rain, warm rain, is needed to make the grass grow but the precipitation came in the form of freezing sleet and hailstones and it fell on frozen fields so that it stood in pools and ran in rivers down normally dry valleys. It came in constantly on the prevailing wind, driving into the sheds and dripping through any imperfections in the corrugated tins.

The cattle, wintering out, found no dry places on which to lie and stood dejectedly under the walls. The mud, our constant enemy, began to flow, to find its own level and become treacherous in the hollows. We were soon aware that conditions were actually worse than 1947 or 1963. Cattle stood with humped backs to the wind and began to go thin, not for want of food but through lack of appetite and will to live.

The first to go down was a black Aberdeen Angus called Mary. She had never been robust. She went down just behind the Dutch barn and could not be allowed to lie there in the deepening mud for the hollow she made would soon weep and hold a pool. Nothing can be left many minutes in mud without being held in a suction vice. Margaret ran to fetch a corrugated tin and she and Father rolled Mary aboard and strained until they thought their arms would leave their sockets and their tummy muscles tear, to drag the tin down the bank and into the yard. Still Mary would not get up. Risking dislocation and rupture the two of them somehow managed to heave the tin up the cobbled incline into the draughty emptiness of the barn. They built the remaining bales round Mary until she was snug within an enclosure and Margaret struggled a week to keep her alive.

There came a sudden hardening of the earth and enough snow fell to block the road so that when Mary died the removal wagon could not come to take her away. She weighed only a fraction of what she had a few weeks before. We thought we could bury her in the quarry as soon as the snow left so Margaret and I dragged her down the Five-Acre and left her at the foot of the rock face from where the stones had been taken to build The Currer. Such was the severity of the winter and the hunger and plight of the scavengers that, when we went to bury Mary, the carcass had been eaten bare. When the weather allowed burial there was only a skeleton to inter.

Ice was the problem. Its weight brought telephone wires almost to the ground and, locally, sheep were frozen to the earth. I was hurrying up the road, towards the end of March, on my way to school and I found a dead stirk in the stream near the summit. The belly was distended, the eyes glazed and staring. For a moment, I was paralysed with shock. It must have been approaching the water hole to drink and slid or been pushed down only a slight banking. A strong animal should have managed to struggle out and this was not a weakling. I think we were very angry.

We knew we must get the animals indoors. They had reached the point where they would not lie down at all. We threw out manure in a frenzy of effort to create a safe space to overcrowd animals into the sheds and scattered what little straw we could spare. Then, on the Sunday, Margaret and I went out to bring in the suckling herd. When we were about fifty yards from the water hole, we saw yet another young bullock fall in. The accident seemed to happen in slow motion. The animal did not even struggle, but we did! Both of us leapt into the water shouting and thumping the animal, forcing it to flounder and fight to get out. We succeeded but were both as wet as the bullock. We goaded it almost cruelly down the hill home, trying to invigorate some warmth into its chilled muscles. We drove it into a circle of bales and towelled it for a long time with hessian sacks but it died. Tears were not far away.

We penned the rest of the suckled herd in too small a space. We had no alternative and we lived in fear of what the overcrowding might mean with three generations of animals all together. There was one old cow, Jenny, who, when she finally lay down, would not get up again. She had a strong, eight-month-old calf still suckling. We sent for the vet, and turned her over two or three times a day, trying very hard to get her back on her feet. The bad weather persisted and the manure deepened around her and we were constantly forking it out. Margaret walked round the sheds two and three times during the night, afraid of accident. There came a morning when I did my early round and found a big, strong bullock smothered in the mêlée of animals snuggling round a still breathing Jenny. How very weary and disheartened we were. We again called the vet. We could not ignore the bedsores and there was no way we could raise her. 'She is never going to get up again,' the vet said. We knew he was right and that it was best to put her out of her misery.

The dead bullock was too heavy for us to move and we feared another tragedy so we sent for the good man who removes dead animals. Such was the severity of the winter that the man was far too busy and unable to pick up carcasses with his usual promptness. A dead animal can be left a few days but one which had to be killed would bring him immediately. Sure enough, he came with his gun that very afternoon.

The removal wagon picked up one stream victim from beside the road and one from the barn and then drew up beside the shed. We had turned out the remaining animals in anticipation of his errand but the calf would not go. All the men who remove dead animals are sensitive fellows who see too much death, remove too many skeletons, witness too many farmers' suffering, too many financial losses. This one went quietly into the shed where the dead bullock lay and Jenny waited a peaceful end.

'Aw, bloody hell!' he said. He was a rough young man with a lousy job to do. The calf was driven out of the shed and Jenny was shot and taken away.

Her calf decided there and then that it would not eat. It hung around the shed, forlorn and miserable. For days the poor thing mourned. Then, after several days of icy rain, it finally accepted the fact that its mother had gone, left the shed and joined the herd splashing, without enthusiasm, through the cart tracks level with standing water.

At night, when the herd came home, the calf did not and we blamed ourselves for having let it go. It had wintered well, still suckling until its mother went down. Margaret and I set out to find it. A cold, white sleet was falling and, wet though the earth was, the landscape was accepting it and the intakes and the moor whitened. The next day was to dawn warm and reassuring and the birds were to start to sing and begin their belated nest building activity but first we had to get through that last, soul-destroying day.

We found the stirk lying on its back in a river running down one of the naturally dry hollows of the moor. It would not get up. We were near to miserable, frustrated tears. We, too, had struggled long enough. We called a neighbouring farmer who came with his tractor and forklift. He lifted the calf clear of the water and began slowly to find the road home. Darkness was falling. We followed the tractor steadying the calf on the lift, and stroking its forehead, full of self-accusations at having allowed it out in the hope that it would eat outside instead of starve in the shed.

The calf was too weak to stand. A wild, beautiful thing it had been and now it was like a poorly stuffed child's toy which had been left out in the rain. In the warmth of the garage Margaret cosseted it with blankets, hay and hot water bottles to raise its temperature, without success. At our wits end, Margaret decided to bring the calf into the cloakroom, that last receiving house of all sick animals.

We dragged it in on an old plastic mat, scraping our knuckles on the hard concrete and completing the task only because, having started the job, there was no alternative but to finish it or leave the poor thing to die in the yard. All night Margaret tended it, refilling the bottles and slowly raising the temperature. She continued the intensive care next day whilst outside spring crept in fast. The larks sang their happiness and the daffodil shoots began to accelerate their upward thrust. Warm sunshine flooded the pastures and the sap began to rise.

In the warmth of the cloakroom condensation ran down the walls as the poor animal began to thaw and dry. Then, two days later, when we were just beginning to think it would recover, it died. Just like that! The cruel winter had taken another victim.

A late spring is always more of a miracle than an early one. We are tired with the ordeal of a bad winter but never fail to appreciate the sudden smell of grass and the accelerated bursting of the light green buds. There must be places in the world which look barer than the Yorkshire Dales in February and March but not many. The pastures of the hill farms are so well eaten that they look absolutely barren and bleached by the disappearing snow. The walls and the stone farmhouses, the trees and hedges alike look as grey as the earth. Then suddenly there is overnight greenness, enough to hold a shimmering of dew. Waiting for a late spring is like waiting for a meal. We are never past appreciating it when it finally comes.

By St George's Day spring is usually advanced enough for the prompt return of the cuckoo and we hear his complimentary call whenever we open the windows to let the fragrant breeze blow away the cobwebs. He tells us all day and every day that we have 'made it' once again. His congratulations are shouted at us every time we shake out the mats and hang out the curtains and blankets. We see him sitting on the pylon wires or flying steadily towards Jimmy's Wood. He knows we will never admit defeat.

Failure is relative and success a state of mind. Failure comes from expecting too much and placing the goal posts too far away. Success is an accumulation of small achievements. Acknowledge each one as it comes but don't add them together beforehand or you will have to wait too long for the results. A happy journey has many milestones, many conquered summits and many downhill runs.

Success is chiefly an ability to cope with failures and disasters and get to the end of awful days. Margaret's are days when cattle have had to be herded, forced into the wagon and sold at market: days of brucellosis and TT tests, even just copper injections or worming. Awful days include those when cattle have strayed, when one has been found dead and blown; days when the wind has been high and sheets have flown from roofs and chimneys been at risk; days when the water has frozen and many buckets have been to carry.

My awful days have been coping with problems laid at my feet by unhappy parents or difficult children. On these occasions I have lost sleep and wrestled to find a solution. Success is to flop into a chair and know that you have come to the end of that awful day having coped. Most people see success only in positive achievement, more often than not financial, and therefore it is so seldom obtainable that pessimism and despair overwhelm.

Happiness comes from recognising it in its negative form, not what did I win? but what did I not lose? I think that is why we have ridden on a wave of optimism. When things have gone well we have been grateful. When they haven't we have found satisfaction coping with the challenge. When things have been bad we have thanked God that they were not worse.

One day I was breaking up old wood for the fire. I picked up an ambitious armful of rotted floorboards and joists and walked towards the chopping block. Suddenly I tripped. The bundle fell beneath me, and my left arm shot out and prevented me from falling flat. My weight practically dislocated it and I was blinded by a spray of wet mud. When I opened my eyes and looked down at the pile of wood beneath me, there was a 3ins by 4ins joist with a six-inch nail protruding upwards just inches away from my chest. It stuck out like a bayonet. With horror I realised I had nearly met my Waterloo.

Major jobs, Subsidy roundups, TT and brucellosis testing were done during school holidays when I was at home to lend a hand. Dehorning sessions are annual events which rarely disturb the routine. This one certainly wasn't expected to trigger off such a chain of events.

There was a great deal of mud; its blessings were few and its disadvantages many, especially at night. However, calves to dehorn during daylight were penned, the path leading to the rear of the shed was dry and the morning's work went well. The vet arrived early, chatted amiably whilst he froze the sprouting hornbuds, brought us up to date with local and veterinary news whilst he clipped away the tiny horns and then relaxed with us over coffee in the farmhouse kitchen.

The job was done without any traumatic experience and he was free to go and we to get on with the never-ending job of feeding hungry mouths.

I turned to the preparation of some dinner for the family and Margaret, out of habit, went to the calf shed before beginning to bag her corn and distribute the hay.

To her dismay she found one calf bleeding profusely. Somewhat disturbed, she came to the house for linen to stem the flow and help coagulate the blood. When this failed she returned to mix some flour and water in a vain, old-fashioned effort to seal the wound. We rang the vet who said he thought it would now stop but that we must ring again if it did not.

By lunch time the calf had lost a lot of blood and was still bleeding. The tension was increased by an insistent banging in the adjoining shed, the home of our two sows at that time. One had farrowed a few days ago and the other was due to do so any time. A low partition separated the two large ladies, the one blissfully content, the other irritable and uneasy, heavy and uncomfortable; banging angrily to be let out to stretch her legs and find her own water.

'Oh, do shut up!' said Margaret with matching impatience, hurrying to let her out before the door was in smithereens. She was harassed and worried by the calf. She barely glanced at the contented litter and paid little attention to the door-basher who ploughed her way uncaringly through the mud, an element she enjoyed as much as a hippopotamus. Her huge belly left a meandering path which became a muddy stream as she zigzagged to the beck.

We ate lunch without interest and returned to the shed to find a wobbly and dejected calf, its ears down, its hair all matted with blood. Margaret again rang for the vet, knowing that only cauterisation would stop the bleeding and prevent a quite unnecessary death. In the meantime we bound up the wound with a pad and bandage of such dimensions that the calf could barely hold up its head. We barricaded it into a corner with bales of straw to protect it from inquisitive neighbours and we completely forgot about the sow. Our negligence was unforgivable for we've let out sows ill-advisedly before and had them farrowing in the wood. We thoroughly deserved all we got.

The vet returned in time to cauterise the wound and save the calf and we honestly thought that our troubles were over and that all we had to do was get on with the feeding. February days are short and darkness never very far away. It was not until dusk that Margaret discovered that the sow was missing.

Outside, the wind was rushing in from the east bringing with it flurries of sleet, a dampness and a cheerlessness which made the luxury of tea by the log fire very tempting and the thought of searching for an errant sow very distasteful.

Towards the end of winter the Dutch barn too is emptying of hay. When the bales, stacked to the roof, insulate the barn it can be the snuggest place on the farm. When the harvest is gone in March it is a colder place than out of doors for winds congregate inside. It is impossible to escape a draught and the corrugated tins drip rusty moisture. Around Christmas time some cattle had been kept in an empty corner of it so there was a depth of manure, sufficient for a determined pig to rout and churn into a poor hollow, far too messy and quite inadequate for her needs.

When we found our straying sow she had already produced her first son in a climate comparable to that of the North Pole. The first arrival was wet and shivering. Its mother, stupid and irrational, would not budge one inch from her exposed and highly unsatisfactory bed. One by one the little pigs were thrust into an unwelcoming world, shivering and vulnerable. Piglets have no warmth of their own at birth. They accept and have to make do with the temperature of their surroundings, needing either a sun-ray lamp or a sensible mother capable of making a proper bed in a sheltered spot, content to have her babies at home. These newest arrivals had neither. Their mother was stupid and the babies were very likely going to die unless my resourceful sister could do something.

In frantic haste she organised me. We carried bales of straw from the diminishing pile in the laithe. If the ridiculous sow would not go into her own shed, she argued, then a temporary shed must be built around her. The walls of this were easy but they afforded little comfort for the wind seemed to come from above.

With aching fingers we stretched a few lengths of netting over the top of the bales and secured it with binder twine. Finally we laid a layer of insulating straw on top. And all the while little pigs were arriving to the grunts and snorts of an irritable mother who clearly wanted to be left severely alone.

Having provided warmth we realised we had inadvertently excluded even the borrowed light from the yard lamp. There was no electricity in the Dutch barn as there was in the pig shed and there is a definite need for a light at a farrowing. I connected our long extension to the nearest power point and borrowed a bedside lamp, wondering if I would experience bed at all that night. The improvised light was an unstable contraption but it was preferable to paraffin with so much straw about and superior to a torch.

Heavy with tiredness and exasperation we left the cussed sow to get on with her mass production and returned to the neglected task of feeding. The sleet had turned to heavy rain. We could hear it incessantly beating on the tin roofs, hurtling down the drainpipes, exciting the normally placid stream, cleansing the concrete and deepening the mud. We felt it finding illegal entry down our necks, soaking our shirts and seeping into our underclothes.

'Have we to cut teeth first?' said Margaret. We were so wet it seemed sensible to complete all our jobs before going inside and getting changed. Cutting teeth is a job I hate. Not the actual cutting. That is simple. The sharp fangs are brittle, the point is easily clipped and doesn't hurt the piglet however much it screams. It's just that I'm scared of sows with litters and I don't mind admitting it. Normally I don't mind sows at all. They are placid and benevolent creatures, tolerant of humans and very slow. Motherhood makes them agile, suspicious and vicious. Overnight it turns them into ruthless killers, monsters not to be trifled with, who will respond with sudden fury to every squeal made by their offspring, and nothing can squeal louder or more unnecessarily than a piglet. In fear and trembling I accompanied my sister on her errand to steal half the litter and drop them one by one into the wooden, sack-covered box I was holding. When the box became too heavy and too alive in my arms, we both put a safe distance between us and the sow, and retired to the warmth and security of the kitchen.

None of nature's babies can compete with the piglet in the vocal field. For twenty minutes our kitchen sounded like a cell wherein were a hundred souls in torment and yet the illusion was created by single pigs in turn merely because of being handled. Immediately released each snuggled down contentedly in the hay of the box, twitching, pink and very beautiful.

But then they had to be stealthily replaced and the other half stolen. Only when the fourteenth piglet had been returned to Mum did we breathe a sigh of relief and thank God that the job was over once more.

We went indoors, stripped off our wet things before they had time to cool after our exertions and struggled into warm, clean clothes. What a day! The ten o'clock news was on. We carried our overdue tea to eat in the luxury of an armchair pulled close to the sitting room fire. Could our troubles be over? We were hypnotised by comfort and security into thinking that they were.

Then, very late at night, Margaret went on her near-midnight rambles to check that all was well. She returned almost at once demanding my immediate help. I struggled reluctantly into my damp jacket and Father's wellingtons which, being two sizes too big, slipped on easily. We hurried towards the Dutch barn where all hell seemed to be let loose.

'What's happening?' I asked the noisy darkness.

'She's going mad!' gasped Margaret.

The improvised shed was being destroyed. The sow was lifting each bale with apparent ease and shaking it in anger. Little pigs were screaming beneath the clumsiness of her careless feet and incredible weight. There was a tangle of wire netting and binder twine and steam, from the irate lady, was rising. There was indescribable chaos and I was petrified.

'What are we going to do?' I feared the answer. My sister will 'force her brain and nerve and sinew to serve her turn long after they are gone' 'and whatever she said, we had to do.

'We'll have to get her back to her own shed,' she said.

'We can't,' I stammered, knowing full well that I'd be forced to try. 'She'll kill us!'

'Hold that box!' It was thrown at me through the darkness. 'When it's full of pigs run to the shed.'

'What! Fourteen of them!'

'I'll keep one. Its screaming will make her follow me.'

'It'll make her kill you.'

'Oh, shut up. We've got t'do something.' She put the thirteenth pig in the box whilst the destructive mother continued to tear down bales and erase the 'shed'. 'Go on, run!'

'Be careful,' I shouted. 'She's dangerous! '

'Be careful yourself,' I could feel Margaret's growing exasperation with me. 'Run,' she said.

How do you run with thirteen pigs in a box and wearing your father's wellingtons? How do you traverse thirty yards of mud, frightened, weighted and blind? You do anything if you have to. Halfway to the shed I turned and hesitated. Margaret was following me with the little pig held as bait, screaming its head off and an angry mother was following, careering through the mud as clumsily as we were.

'Keep going!' she shouted but I'd hesitated too long. Both my too-big wellingtons were firmly sucked into the mud. I left them, and my Harris wool socks behind and ploughed on recklessly, barefoot, through the mud, fear greatly exceeding disgust.

The shed door was open. 'Empty the box and get out of the way,' Margaret ordered, dodging through the doorway, dropping the screaming pig and scrambling with me blindly to find the open door again.

Safely outside we leaned on each other trembling, listening anxiously until the sow's angry shouts became maternal baby-talk. With incredible speed she settled down, obviously glad to be home again. Silly thing! It had been her fault! Afraid of leaving too soon, Margaret rescued my unusable boots and we sat together in the pig trough contemplating my completely black feet and mud-caked trousers.

'Tell y' what,' said Margaret. 'Let's sell up and buy a bungalow. In a little garden.'

'With the path all tarmacked and with little flower beds and a garage with a Mini in it,' I contributed to the immediate dream of heaven.

'The neighbours wouldn't have us long,' laughed Margaret. 'What d'yer bet we'd soon be keeping a pig in the garage?'

Chapter Fifteen

In early May 1969 my mother's oldest brother Willie died, suddenly, of a heart attack, whilst on holiday in a caravan at Morecambe. It came as a dreadful shock. At the time I was refusing to go on an overnight hike with Rangers at the invitation of a group of Scouts. The activity seemed foolish considering the appalling April weather. The moorland chosen for the hike was still saturated, the night air was still very chill and, though I would not admit it, I was too exhausted with the awful winter and too upset by this sudden death in the family to miss a night's sleep walking over a moor. We would all get our 'deerth o' cowd'. I did not feel equal to coping with joint activities over which I had no control. If we wanted to go hiking with long-legged Scouts we could do so first in the daylight and we would not meet at the local pub. I saw this hike as the beginning of a new era and felt that acceptance on this one issue would lead to more and more commitments for which I was untrained and unready, so I dug in my heels and said, 'No'.

Eleven Rangers accepted my decision but four took no notice and went off with the walkers. All were very ashamed afterwards and horrified when I said they could not accompany us to camp on Harris, in the summer. Our simple, group rules had to be obeyed. The Movement stipulates that the Guider in charge must accompany Rangers on such an expedition. Parents had been notified.

Children must learn cause and effect. I remember Michael who was very spoilt and often naughty. 'What do your parents do when you don't do as you are told?' I asked him.

'They send me to bed,' he said, 'but I don't care because they say I can come back before I get to the top of the stairs!' Too many children are treated like that. Adults must stand by what they say or not say it at all. It is a measure of the success of the Movement that all four girls accepted their punishment and remained my friends. Two came to future camps. One became my Assistant Guider. The whole Company learned something of value. There grew a new awareness of the responsibility adults take when they lead other people's children. The happiness of a family or a community depends on individuals not being able to do just as they like. I have heard it said, again and again, that everyone has a right to personal choice, that the private lives of the clergy, doctors, teachers, youth leaders, and politicians are nobody's business. I disagree. I think that people in the public eye, those who lead or entertain, teach or administer justice should know they have a responsibility and, for them, the choice is to conform.

March and April had been tough and the beginning of May was a different kind of ordeal with unrest in the Crew and sadness within the family. A premature death is always unacceptable. We came away from Uncle Willie's funeral with little heart to prepare for our planned spring bank holiday a few days later. We went away more subdued than usual. We headed north to Brampton, a small Border country town, and we stayed the night at a modest hotel, a thing we have done infrequently. It seemed necessary for us to unwind in obscurity and, on arrival, we ordered tea to be brought to the bedroom. We felt withdrawn and unsociable and we spoke to no one.

Next morning we were composed and ready to enjoy our holiday. We avoided the A74 and drove via Dumfries and Annan to Glasgow. We stayed one night with relatives and talked about Uncle Willie, a much-needed opportunity to allow us to mourn enough to leave the immediate past behind and feel free to enjoy the next fortnight, recharge our batteries and soak up some welcome sunshine.

In the quiet warmth of a beautiful spring Sunday, we drove to Oban where we had reserved berths on the *Claymore*, the old non-drive-on ferry. Margaret and I rose early to drive the Gypsy onto crane slings so that it could be lifted onto the boat. The tension was seeping out of us as we steamed up the sound with Mull on the port and Ardnamurchan on the starboard bow. The old folks were sitting on deck, Harry was leaning over the rails and Coll was appearing on the westerly horizon.

We disembarked at Tiree and allowed the Gypsy to continue to Lochboisdale which must have been cheaper. We were always scraping pennies. Whilst we were on Tiree, staying with John Lachie and Effie MacInnes in their thatched cottage at Salum, we used their car. It is the only time either Margaret or I have ever driven one. It felt like a toy.

It was an utterly carefree few days. Father would go off with John Lachie to find the nesting eider ducks on the shore or chat for hours in Calum's kitchen. It gave him great pleasure to visit the home of Donald Campbell's parents at Cornaig Beg. Donald was no longer our vet but Father had respected him for the many years that he was. Father found the same affinity with the Hebridean crofters as we did. I remember visiting Marion MacLean, at Salum, very late one night, for a *strupak*. When we arrived the old lady was still painting the concrete floor of the nearby cottage. It was used as a holiday cottage for May and Hugh and their four boys had gone to Australia. She put the paintbrush in my hand telling me to finish it whilst she put on the kettle. Our stay on Tiree, as a whole family, was far too short.

We sailed towards Barra on a grey day, and from there to Lochboisdale. The cold evening was improving but the brightness in the west could not dispel the chill. The sight of the Gypsy, sitting waiting for us on the pier, was friendly indeed. We clambered into it with the eagerness of wanderers returning home. Seating was always a squeeze and the closeness was comforting and secure. We felt the warmth of a kettle being heated in the back of the van and when it boiled we brewed tea and buttered and cream-cheesed a whole loaf of fruit bread, whilst still parked on the pier.

Those were great days! The memory of holidays when Father was still with us brings a glow of pleasure nothing surpasses.

From Lochboisdale we motored north, crossing the causeways between the Uists, Benbecula and Grimsay and arrived, very late, at a delightful cottage on the machair at Sollas, that utterly peaceful place we have only ever known in calm and gentleness. Good weather was coming from the west and the new day dawned very beautifully. Our hostess, Mrs MacLean, made an excellent breakfast. She had been recommended by the kind lady who had, a few years ago, appeared at our tent door with the query, 'Would ye be offended if I offered you a few aiggs?' We had kept in touch and when we needed a bed and breakfast address she had been able to supply one.

From Lochmaddy we sailed north to Tarbert, Harris and spent another lovely week with Katie and Angus on the shore at Luskentyre. Mother was utterly in love with islands and Gypsy travelling and, as usual, she was planning how we could possibly include the aunts on next year's holiday. She always wanted 'Ah lassies' to go too. Whenever she had a good time she always wished that they had been with us. It did not matter. We had grown up with them as part of our extended family. Father did not mind 'yar lassies', coming either. He had appreciated their help and he knew their inclusion always made Mother happy and if she were content it was all right by him. All the way home across Skye she was wondering how we could manage to get them into the Gypsy. When we stayed with John and Cathie at Spean Bridge she was checking to see if there was enough accommodation for two more and, on the last night that we spent with Jean and Peter in Northumberland, she was mentally sorting out that Margaret and I could sleep on the floor too.

The suckling herd was growing and we decided to keep a bull. We actually kept two. One was a beautiful Hereford which Paul and Julie named Frank. This we sold and we kept an Aberdeen Angus called, more appropriately, Billy. I remember that we had to put his mother out to graze on our neighbour's pasture because we could not stop Billy suckling her.

Father assured us that beef bulls were quiet enough when they ran with the herd. In a way the old man was right for I cannot say that Billy caused us any trouble at all but he was a character. We only once asked him to do something he did not wish to do. Like some eastern deity, he roamed our broad acres at will and seemed a peace-loving fellow.

He was also a home-loving man who preferred our doorstep, the laithe porch and even the garage rather than the sheds and, summer or winter, when night fell, he was not far away. This posed a problem for whenever we went out in the dark we fell over him. Black as jet, he remained unseen until he was tripped over but he was quite complacent about our clumsiness. I was less so about our frequent, unexpected encounters in the dark. It is no small thing to fall over a boulder and find it is a huge black bull. Wherever we wanted to go he was blocking the way and when he condescended to use the sheds he lay against the barrier over which we fed the calves so that, in the darkness of the early morning feed, we had to lean over him or step over his broad beam. We never opposed him or moved him on so he began to assume the divine right of kings.

Our neighbour asked to use him once.

'Ah'll bring t' cow t' Moor Gate,' he said. 'Just bring t' bull t' top o' t' road.'

Our bull had never been asked to do anything in his life. City dwellers have no idea of the carry-on farmers sometimes have. Our friend Calum, of Salum, Tiree, was having trouble trying to get his cow to the bull and, being increasingly infirm, was attempting to take the cow in his van. He had fastened a rope to the gallivanting cow and, having passed it through the windscreen window, was gradually pulling the cow into the van through the rear door. When a passing cyclist asked what he was doing, he replied, 'I'm after taking the cow to the pull an' she canna ride the picycle!'

More recently we fell apart listening to an amazed friend tell how, on the Island of Harris, he had been asked to help take a heifer on a similar expedition and of the fiasco they had had because the heifer would only lie down. Life has its lighter moments.

I have taken a lot of cows to the bull and many of the occasions have been amusing but it is not one bit funny taking a bull to the cow. The herd was grazing peacefully in the Low Footpath and the Moor Gate was a quarter of a mile away. How do you drive a contented bull away from his harem and propel him across unfenced pasture? How do you impose your will on a monster who has always had his own way? The answer, if you are me, is that you leave most of the job to your more competent sister and, for a start, you forget all about driving and concentrate on bribery. She stands in front of him with a bucket of corn and then takes it away knowing that he will follow but with every reason to mistrust the frame of mind in which he will do so.

If it had been up to me to torment the enormous creature in such a way, George's cow would never have been in calf. Margaret is braver. She gradually coaxed Billy nearer and nearer to the Moor Gate, too dangerously near the snorting nostrils and inflamed eyes for comfort. Though polled he could easily have tossed and gored her and his anger made it quite plain that he would not think twice about doing so.

The mission was, however, successfully accomplished but thereafter my fear of the animal was more positive. I began to anticipate, which is a foolish thing to do. He was a complete stranger to halter or tether. What would happen if we had to put him in the crush? How were we to cope with a TT test? Would he be unmanageable in old age? My fears were silly, for he was very little trouble, just a stumbling block in the mistal door or a squatter in the garage whilst the Austin Gypsy remained outside.

The trouble came much later, not with the bull but because of him. We tried to isolate him from the yearling heifers. We were too busy to attack properly the crumbling walls, too poor to put up bull-proof fences and buy field gates. A lack of money causes problems the rich never encounter. I cannot adequately tell you how much Father and Margaret struggled for this reason, partly because the subject is too exhausting and partly because, as Margaret so often says, I have so often not been there. I have been at school whilst comedy, drama and tragedy have been enacted at home and I have been coping with those scores and scores of Guides whilst the evening chores were tackled by Margaret and Father.

They did try, but were unable to keep the bull from a few of the yearlings. It brought us eventual trouble for heifers were in-calf too young which can spell disaster.

We desperately needed another shed to house the out-wintering cattle. The last winter had left us shattered, so we again began the task of collecting stone with Genevieve, mixing cement and laying the foundations of wide walls and stout pillars to support beams, roof timbers and corrugated sheets. Out-wintering cattle, on this exposed hillside, is a risky business. The west wind blows in from the Irish Sea with little to moderate its speed. It brings slanting, stinging rain. Between us and the east coast the Pennine Range gradually falls to the Vale of York and the cold east wind from Scandinavia tears across the plain. Hardly a winter passes without dropping its snow generously on our hillside.

So, we hugged great boulders and built stout walls, adequately if not professionally. The haymaking season was upon us. The mowing and baling were now done by those good neighbours who lived below us. They had many acres of their own harvest to reap first and this baulked us. We could no longer rely on having the last load in before we left with the children. Indeed, if the season were late, we had sometimes not even started haytime before leaving with the tribe. Father was too old to leave alone with the hay and the calving cows, the pigs and the garden at its most demanding and productive time so we had problems. When the sun shines the hay must be made and our holiday-scorning neighbours could not be hurried or halted.

1969 was a late season. The winter had lasted too long and, when we saw there was no hope of having started the haymaking, Margaret decided she would spend only one week in camp. Hazel, Joanna's mother, was coming with us and maybe I could cope the final week alone.

It was a great pity that Margaret had to give up something she loved so much and could do so well. Though green with envy when ever we left her behind to hold the reins, she sacrificed her pleasure for the good of everybody.

We had a happy week before Margaret left us. She slept most of the way home so that she was refreshed enough to leap into the haymaking straight away. I was deeply sorry for her for she loved camping as much as I did. I was to learn the same sadness, much later. It is hard to give up a job before the ability to do it well has gone. Life is full of sacrifices but when one door closes another opens.

So there began a new era, camping with Hazel. At first without Margaret, I felt like a skipper without a mate but there was Ann who was always so good in an emergency and we had picked a winner in Hazel. For nearly ten years I was to thank God that her doctor husband would let her come with us for a fortnight in the Hebrides, every summer. Life without her help and humour would have been relatively colourless. She was good for the Company and the Crew. Skipper and Flim were different. We were rather odd, career women, whose good fortune it was to have the opportunity to give a great deal of happiness to a lot of children. They could not do without our strength, our know-how, our enthusiasm and our friendship but few would follow us and be what we were. Most would marry and they could have no better example for that role than Hazel. She was an extraordinary, ordinary housewife whose morals and priorities were right. She could look elegant doing the most menial of jobs and the youngsters all adored her. She had old-fashioned values and we have proved again and again that young people respect these and know that they are fundamental to happiness.

In Margaret I had a companion who could walk long distances, climb any hill and come down and have the energy to climb it a second time. We thought nothing of a forty-mile hike. In Hazel I had a companion who would man the fort whilst I went with the hikers and who would have a meal ready for our return.

Many loads of hay were in the barn when I returned and many were still to come so it was in at the deep end for me after only a couple of hours' sleep. We did not like the after-camp haymaking which was becoming a habit. The weather is less certain in August. There is too much danger of thunderstorms, too much dew on the ground and the nights are pulling in, but there was nothing we could do about it other than buy another tractor and all the necessary equipment and employ a man full-time on the farm. To contract out the haymaking seemed the best bet whichever way you looked at it but if you are paying the piper it is he who plays the tune.

One of the calves we most remembered was one Margaret bought for two pounds because it had two bent front legs. Now, it is not uncommon for a calf to be born with one bent front leg. It hops around on the weak ankle for a few days until it strengthens and all is well. We have never had one born here with two weak joints. But Margaret bought one at market and after a few days all was not as well as she had expected. Soon the calf could not walk at all and we christened it Craig after a quite severely handicapped boy we had at school. The authorities were just beginning to recognise the importance of trying to place handicapped children normally but Craig's mother had had to fight most of the way to persuade them to let her son be educated in a non-specialist school. A compromise was made. She was advised to bypass the larger one nearby and place Craig in a small, village school. So he came to us and, like the calf, he could not walk at all without falling all over the place. But his progress was positive. He disregarded the continually grazed knees and was humped about by the top class girls, dragged about by his contemporaries and pick-a-backed by his teachers until the wobbliness was less apparent. Indeed he was eventually one of the campers who walked to Rheinigidale, on Harris. I remember Linda and Viv carrying him up the Scriob on the return. In his last year at primary school he climbed the spiral staircase to the top of the village church tower. I will never forget his beam of satisfaction as, on the bottom, downward step of his achievement, he collapsed in an exhausted wobble and badly grazed both knees.

During his final year we fought to place him in the local senior school and won. From there he went on to polytechnic college.

'Call the calf Craig,' I said, for Craig was, at that time in the infants' class. But initially the calf only got worse. It ate too much and after a few days the bent front legs would not hold it up at all. It was fit, had a healthy coat, drank and ate hungrily but could not even stand.

'It's spastic,' we concluded. 'Never mind,' said Margaret, 'Harry walks and so will Craig!'

So, twice a day, she lifted the courageous little animal onto a bale of hay, massaged its legs and exercised them, and she kept up this bovine physiotherapy longer than anyone else would have done. Months later that calf walked. It always had funny legs but it could graze happily and was able to join the herd.

I remember Quackers, our lame duck, who never walked again. A calf has got to walk, there is no alternative, but a lame duck can be carried down to the pond every day and back to the shed every night. I remember the awful noise it made, either in gratitude or annoyance at the indignity of being carried. It lived for years. Then one day it was missing and Margaret was sure it must have been swept down the overflow from the pond which rushes under the road when we have had a period of rain. The small culvert was big enough to take a duck. Convinced it was trapped under the road, Margaret still searched the streams which riddled the Dyke Field. Two small boys were passing and they helped her futile search and prodded the far reaches of the culvert with her. I do know that if Margaret had located it we would have had to dig up the road. Margaret would never have left it there to die.

Then, one day, the two little boys came running across the fields, shouting that a classmate had taken a lame duck to school and they had all had a nature lesson. The little 'owner' had denied stealing the duck from our pond but his friends said he told lies. So Margaret went to David's home in the village and, sure enough, there was Quackers, pretty miserable, having missed the pond for several days. David later became a Saturday and all-holiday child. He was very fond of us and always said, 'Thank you for a lovely dinner,' and spent his pocket money on buying a bar of chocolate for Harry or a plant for Mother at Christmas-time.

Of the other handicapped children we had at school I remember, particularly, Lorraine. The school doctor noticed a curvature of the spine when she conducted the entrance medical examination and for a long time the brave child was subjected to a collar. She wore it cheerfully and led as normal a life as possible. When the family removed from the immediate locality we did not lose contact, for Lorraine remained one of Winnie's Brownies. She underwent an operation to insert a steel rod and lay in plaster for several weeks. Winnie was instrumental in gaining her a Girl Guide Association Award for Fortitude. We were all very proud.

Winnie was our third teacher when an increase in numbers came in 1970. We had a happy school relationship. She was a generous member of staff and a cheerful colleague. She was with me when we squeezed water out of the children's trousers at Brimham Rocks, and when so many children were travel-sick on a visit to the railway at Ravenglass. Without a cheerful companion the visit would have been a disaster.

I can see Winnie now, stooping over a five-year-old spending play-time in the classroom and nursing an aching ear. 'Oh dear,' said the teacher kindly, 'whatever makes you cry?'

The small Lisa lifted a tear-stained face and cradled the painful ear. Her bottom lip trembled. 'I've got diarrhoea,' she said. It was unforgivable for us to laugh.

Close on the heels of Uncle Willie's unexpected death came another. We could not believe it when the phone rang to tell us our lame Uncle Joe had just been rushed into hospital with a severe heart attack. A few hours later Mother had lost both her brothers. The youngest one, who had had polio when he was a baby, was only sixty. This second premature coronary in the family, in the autumn of 1969, shocked us all. His death transformed his very capable wife into an old lady. It was sad to see the terrible change. We had not appreciated that she needed his support so much. It was as if the guy ropes of her tent had snapped. The aunts made a determined bid at rescue but Aunt Elsie, who had played the piano so wonderfully for all our Christmas parties, went steadily downhill. We chauffeured her often to spend the weekend at the aunts and often brought her home for the day but when we took her back to her lonely house we felt really sorry for her.

For a while the realisation that our folks were growing old occupied our thoughts and goaded us into making some necessary adjustments. Our parents, twelve years senior to Uncle Joe, showed no sign of reaching the end of their road. Indeed, twenty years later Mother is still baking her cakes in the Aga and enjoying holidays in the Hebrides. But we were considerably shaken and determined not to put off doing things.

The most important insurance against old age is to have a downstairs loo. In a house like ours it was a long walk to the bathroom. No sooner had the idea occurred and the last tin had been nailed in the new shed than I was off to the stationer's to buy some linen. The idea was to reopen the north door from the snug, build a wall parallel to the west wall of the old curing house and make a vestibule and an L-shaped room to house a toilet and a shower. I indicated how the drains could be let into the main to the septic tank and brazenly went to the Borough Architect.

'Who's going to do the building?' our friends asked again. 'And the plumbing?'

'It'll have to be us. We can't afford anyone else.'

'Huh. Who do you think you are?' No one has any faith in us. When we complete things people walk past without comment. There is very little danger of our becoming bigheaded as long as Mother thinks we are 'ridic'lous' and other people just don't know or prefer not to see.

Whilst we waited for the application to pass slowly through official red tape, the turn of the year took us into the seventies. 1970 dawned inauspiciously. My days as Ranger Guider were coming to an end through no fault of mine. There were changes in the Movement over which I had no control. First there was a uniting of the three branches of the senior movement. We had to say 'Goodbye' to the nautical uniform and we were furious. We had loved the jaunty sailor hats and my tricorne and there was nothing, we thought, smarter than the white shirts and navy ties and neckerchiefs. More disastrous was the lowering of the age to fourteen at which girls could join the senior section. Most of my Rangers came from my own company after their sixteenth birthday, mature and capable of adult thinking and service of a high and valuable standard. They did not welcome the idea that younger girls could come. If Guides left my Company at fourteen the Unit would be the poorer and the Crew ruined. Fortunately we could ride the storm for quite a while before the idea caught on and then I opted out rather than sacrifice the Guide Company.

I had been Head of that small village school for ten years. For most people such a small headship would have been just a stepping-stone. Looking back, it seems that all the excitement in my life has been in the small, ordinary things which make up most people's lives and perhaps to read this is deadly boring. But life hasn't been at all boring. There have been no runs along the straight. It's all been up and down and nearly all a struggle.

The job for which I was paid gave me great joy but it was only a part of my life and of supreme importance was The Currer. It was the Talent the Great Master had left in our safe keeping and we had got to use it to the full. One day I watched Harry Secombe singing his way through a television series. There was an unrehearsed moment when an old lady slightly embarrassed him by suddenly leaning forward and saying, 'You've been given a very lovely voice.'

The tenor looked at a loss for words. Then, spontaneously, out came, 'Yes, and some day I'll have to give it back!' I like it. I see him standing there and his Master is saying, 'Well done! Thou good and faithful servant. I gave you a voice and you used it!' One day He will say to us, 'I gave you the Currer', and He must be able to say we used it.

The school children began to know The Currer. Suppose a parent was ill, her children would come for the day. A bereaved family, mother and two children, came almost every Saturday for months after the father died. One parent was very ill. She would bring her three children, every now and then, for a break from making meals and doing chores. She was determined to make a last bid for life and started taking afternoon lessons in the hope of gaining enough GCE passes to enter a teacher training college. The classes ended much later than school closed so the two boys would stay with me until she collected them. They would run up to the shop and buy baked beans and we'd cook them in the staffroom and have our tea. I regularly had tea in the staffroom with some child or other whose mother was on an unexpected errand or was hospital visiting and I've played many a game of snakes and ladders waiting for her return.

Sadly the brave mother lost her fight with cancer. She sent for me on the Saturday, just before the school term ended for Christmas. Her husband had come home with 'flu and suddenly she could not cope. A neighbour took the two-year-old and I helped the older boys decorate the tree and got them ready for the Institute Party. Next day I took the children to the Candlelight Service in the village church and a few days after Christmas I heard that the brave mother had been taken, in a coma, to hospital and had died.

Children were not allowed to write on walls or desks in school and I was understandably annoyed when, several weeks later, I found the eldest boy scrawling, in ink, all over his desk top. I shouted at him, fool that I was; 'How dare you!' I demanded. 'Get a cloth, this minute and wipe it off. You naughty boy!' He stood miserably beside the desk, in a trance which seemed to prevent him from moving and I walked towards him to point him in the direction of the cloakroom and the dishcloth. All over his desk he had written, 'I want my mother'.

I took the child in my arms and we both cried.

The children always seemed to have more problems than I had. There was one little fellow who seemed to think, with justification, that all the world was against him. To look at he was a real little toughie with dirty knees and real little football legs. For a while in the infants' class he learned normally and made average progress. Then, when his family fell apart, learning stopped and what he had learned he forgot.

A word of chastisement sent him running out of school. A difference of opinion in the playground and he was off. Visiting the toilet, one day, I heard a child in the adjacent lavatory swearing. 'Who's that in there?' I asked. He was off like a shot, tearing through the churchyard at breakneck speed. He found temporary sanctuary in a neighbour's house and, following hot on his heels, I had to prise him from under the sideboard to carry him screaming back to school. The poor, frightened little seven-year-old thought he hadn't got a friend in the world.

Teaching became difficult with him in the class. We dared not reprimand unless we were certain the door was locked. He was continually testing to see how far he could go and when he reached that limit and someone scolded him he could run like a hare on the riverbank.

The matter came to a head when he and two other boys were so naughty they had to be punished and the only safe thing I could think of was to take away their dinner-time play and make them sit separately in three corners of the staff-room. Two were ashamed and embarrassed, sitting there being ignored by teachers having their after-dinner cup of tea, but the little baddy was wriggling about and pulling funny faces behind my back until I threatened that I'd take down his dungarees and slap his leg hard. As this was an unheard-of punishment in school, I thought just the mention of it would settle him.

'You can't!' was the muttered answer.

I can wrestle with a determined bullock, a defiant pig or a noisy gander and can surely win a battle with a seven-year-old boy. 'Oh yes I can!' I promised, praying that I would not be put to the undignified test. I was not to be spared. He asked for it and I pounced. There was a struggle in which I got a few bruises before his outer pants were lowered and his bare leg loudly smacked, several times. Trembling, I held the crying child on my knee. I was almost weeping, too, tried to the very limit of my patience.

'How dare you do this to me,' I cried. 'Look, I'm trembling all over. Look at my hand, how sore it is. It hurts a lot more than your leg! Don't you ever make me do that again. You have to do as you are told like all children. You are not different. You are just like all the others and you have to behave properly!'

I continued to hold the child closely on my lap partly because holding him steadied both of us and partly because I dared not release him so sure was I that he would run. I was angry at having threatened something I did not want to do and afraid that I had lost.

When the dinner-break was over I whispered to Joan to lock the outside door and pull a desk across the one which connected our classrooms. When I released the boy he did not run as I had feared but in the middle of handwork he came to my desk and asked if I were staying on after school. His father was not at work and I suspected that he planned to bring Dad down to stand up for him. I had intended to leave early that day but I changed my mind. I might as well face the music at once if I were going to have to at all.

'Yes, I'm staying in school,' I said.

'Aw, well Ah'll stay an' 'elp yer,' he offered. At home time he announced that he was just going home to tell his dad and I thought, 'Here we go!'

A quarter of an hour later he returned with a bag of Love Hearts, those highly scented sweets which bear corny messages and make you feel sick after you've eaten too many.

'Ah've brought yer these,' he said.

I felt I must respond with an activity which would restore his dignity. 'I was going to clean the top cupboards,' I suggested, 'But I'm not keen on climbing so high on the stand steps.'

The seven-year-old smiled engagingly. 'Ah'll go up. 'S nowt,' he assured me. For an hour we worked together cleaning top cupboards which were not dirty, rearranging neat piles of heavy exercise books and eating too many Love Hearts.

'Ah'll help yer agen sometime,' said my colleague.

'You can help my sister on the farm, now and again, if you want to,' I said.

'Yep. Ah'll do that.' He was very matter of fact. 'Ta-ra.'

'See you,' I said.

'Yep. Ta-ra.'

'Ta-ra!' I called hearing his running footsteps echoing down the long empty school. Apparently I had won after all.

Things improved but not in the learning field. We began to suspect that this was because the bright child knew that to be dim brought him much more attention. He would pay any price for the extra individual treatment being a slow reader brought. We had forged a new relationship and he no longer behaved badly. Many children have called me 'Mum' by mistake and giggled at the slip of the tongue but this boy, who lived at home with only his father, was the only child who ever made the mistake of calling me 'Dad'.

Eventually he went to secondary school and he played truant several times during the first weeks. He missed the mini-bus and came straight to the village school instead. 'Heck, Ah missed it agen!' he'd say. 'Ah'll do me sums here instead.'

I used to let him stay a while and then I'd drive him back to his proper class in the neighbouring village. The headmaster thought I was aiding and abetting him and asked me to lock the door on him. No way! He soon became adjusted and the truancy stopped. At sixteen he came to see me to ask for a reference when he was seeking a job. He is now a successful panel beater with his own business. He came to see me not long ago bringing his small son.

Nowadays even the odd smack on the right occasion is not only frowned upon but is illegal. I so seldom had to resort to it but on the one or two occasions that I did I found it did no harm and actually served a very useful purpose as an ultimate. It is an eventuality every child instinctively expects. 'When I've gone far enough someone will stop me!' is a secure feeling. More often than not a warning: 'That's enough. Or else!' is sufficient to indicate where the 'electric fence' of social behaviour lies.

I hope that we tried, to the best of our ability, to teach the basic skills and that we succeeded, in some measure, in nurturing an awareness of acceptable behaviour. I remember Linda pushing between the school nurse and me, whilst we were talking, during one of the visits commonly referred to as 'Air Raids'. I intercepted her and prompted, 'What do you say, Linda, when you pass in front of someone?' The smile was angelic as she looked up at Nurse and said, 'Hello!' You can't win every time.

Seeing unacceptable behaviour in other people is the foundation on which to build the self-discipline which leads to good manners. Children can always see faults in other people but must be taught to see them in themselves.

We never had any graffiti in school, no scribblings in the lavatories. This was, I am sure, because staff and children used the same toilets. A family atmosphere provides few opportunities for delinquency.

We were on the way to the swimming baths and the bus used had been vandalised. I was less than a yard away from Gavin. Only the aisle separated us. Someone had scrawled obscene language all across the back of the seat in front of Gavin. Had it happened to me, when I was at school, I would have been embarrassed and gazed fixedly out of the window. Not so Gavin. Silently he read every word. His head followed every letter of the disgusting, four-letter rubbish. I could see him, out of the corner of my eye, leaning forward and taking it all in. Then he leaned across the aisle and gave me a nudge.

"Ave yer sin that, Miss Brown?' he asked. I nodded. He wrinkled his nose engagingly. 'I'nt it disgusting!' he said.

I loved eavesdropping on the way to the baths. The son of the local policeman was in serious conversation with a classmate whose father was one of the village farmers. 'Hey, what 'ud yer dad seh if yer wor a punk?' Mark asked.

"E'd kill me,' replied Simon.

'Yeh, mine would an' all,' said Mark.

There was a short silence. Then one of them said, "E wor a Teddy Boy.'

It says it all!

We had no graffiti and no vandalism, in twenty-one years. We did have one piece of mischief, I remember. A lovely new Rec gate disappeared on Mischief Night. Mrs Wass, who joined the dinner staff on Mrs Hartley's retirement, reported seeing it in the Cut. It was the crime of older children because it took all the top class to tow it to the bridge and carry it home and it took the caretaker and me to lift it back. I asked the Authority to get someone to turn one of the gudgeons upside down to prevent it happening again.

Mother was determined that the aunts should take their holidays with us and see the Hebrides. We began to do something we had never done before and have never had the opportunity to do since. We put aside a part of my salary. I opened a bank account for this purpose and we only took out of the monthly cheque sufficient to eat. Normally the rest went into the business but for a few months the rest went into the bank so that we could buy a vehicle with seven seats. We were interested in a Land Rover station wagon. A friend told us of an ex-army dealer near Bawtry. When we rang him he said he had a very old model but that there was an interested buyer. If we rang again, in a few days, he'd know better.

We waited nearly a fortnight and then we rang again to hear that the other fellow had not yet turned up to collect and it might be a good idea if we went over to have a look. On a bitterly cold February Sunday in 1970, Harry, Margaret and I drove over to Bawtry. The traffic was thin through the towns and we had no difficulty finding the way.

The dealer owned a spacious campus littered with Land Rovers and I'm sure he did not think we would be interested. He told us the vehicle in question was at the far end of the field and that we could go and look but that he still expected the other fellow to turn up within the next fortnight. Fully aware that we were on a wild goose chase and semi-regretting coming so far, we crossed the field.

The veteran was beautiful. She must have been one of the first station wagon models. We liked her squareness, her age and her very definite respectability. The asking price was £450 and she would have suited us fine. The seats looked comfortable and we could picture the seven of us heading north towards the Hebrides. Bed and breakfast for all had already been reserved on Mull and at Sollas on North Uist, and an arrangement had been made with Katie at Luskentyre. The aunts were coming with us come what may, and we had to have a station wagon. When we phoned the dealer a fortnight later the vehicle had been sold to the somewhat tardy buyer who had staked first claim.

We were desperate. We insisted the dealer move heaven and earth to find us what we wanted. In 1970 they were scarce and time was running out. March was slipping by and our holiday was booked for May. We continued to phone regularly and at last the dealer was confident that he would come away with one from a big ex-army sale which was being held somewhere. He was unlucky and we began to panic. 'We have four OAPs,' we said, 'and a disabled brother to take on holiday in just over a month. We've got to have transport!'

At last the dealer saw we were really in earnest. Within days he phoned to ask us to come and look at a B registration station wagon he had bought from the Northumbrian Fire Service.

We left Father with the chores and this time we took Mother as well as Harry. The newer model had less character and cost £200 more but it suited Mother better. In the older model we would have looked as if we were setting off for Brighton. The school children would have loved it, but I think Mother might have been embarrassed. This one was suitable in her eyes and that was everything.

We promised to return by train at the beginning of April. Auntie Mary and Harry went with us for the rail ride and our only worry was driving it home. Margaret, the better driver, took the wheel and found it similar to the Austin Gypsy. At the weekend the family thought it should have a trial run in the Dales. This time Margaret was left at home and the remaining six of us went up to Pateley Bridge, Gouthwaite and over the tops beyond Ramsgill and Lofthouse.

The vehicle had been bought primarily for its seating capacity and that fact was never forgotten. A family of seven went everywhere. Very soon its potential as a school bus became obvious and it carried more singing Guides than any other of its kind.

In their childhood Mother and her two sisters had been part of a unique family squeezed into a horse drawn coach, laughing and singing. I don't think we looked much different. Heads always turned to look when everyone piled out.

Margaret and I accepted graciously that the days of backpacking and walking were over. Perhaps for ever? Who knows? But the joy of the wanderlust was exchanged for the equal pleasure of taking all the family among the mountains and along the loch sides of our beloved Scotland. We sailed across the Minch to the islands we love nearly as dearly as the acres of The Currer.

The first station wagon holiday was a success and no one loved it more than Auntie Janie. The minute the Land Rover stopped, be it on loch side or shore, beside tumbling burn or waterfall, that seventy-two-year-old lady was jumping out. Mother was over the moon and Father smiling that special smile he gave whenever he had been able to give Mother all her own way. Auntie Janie did not miss one minute of that holiday.

Mull was very kind to us. There was only one rain cloud throughout our stay. We had sailed to Iona, seat of Scotland's Christianity, on the most perfect of days and, suddenly, when we were in the vicinity of the Abbey there was a short but heavy shower which sent us hurrying inside. Rain always leaves us in hysterics.

From Tobermory we sailed up the Sound of Gunna, out to Barra and finally to Lochboisdale, on South Uist. It was a stormy crossing, not wet but with a strong head wind. In the dining saloon we had difficulty in preventing our plates of fish and chips from skating all over the table.

We stayed two nights at Sollas where thousands of rabbits run ahead of you across the machair and where the sun sets over the Americas. Then we sailed from Lochmaddy to Tarbert, to spend the rest of our holiday at Luskentyre.

I remember taking the aunts back to their street house, feeling deeply sorry for them having to live in town when they were such country lovers. Secretly I toyed with the idea of using a section of the barn at The Currer and making a small retirement cottage for them. It was only an idea, unvoiced, and probably partly a selfish urge to build. I had the building bug. In the meantime I did their decorating and laughingly promised, 'When you find your dream cottage I'll do it up for you!'

There was, of course a building project already on the horizon. The plans for the Low Loo had been passed and the go-ahead given. But first there was the haymaking and the summer camp and the harvesting of Father's garden.

We returned to Tiree for the summer invasion of the Hebrides by the annual swarms of Yorkshire children. I am eternally glad that we did so. We went without Margaret for, able though he was, Father was really too old to leave and Hazel had not only enjoyed herself so much the previous year but she was also ideal. So we went together with a lot of children and it was unusually wet throughout the fortnight. Wet camps were always fun for the necessity to entertain ourselves artificially was always a challenge. We used Calum's barn more frequently for céilidhs and dancing and sometimes, in a downpour, we took the Calor gas inside and cooked meals under cover.

A few days after our arrival on the Salum shore, I hurried across the cold beach to collect the day's stores from Calum's shop and he was not there. I searched sheds and kitchen and called upstairs. A feeble voice answered. I ran up the steps and found our friend still in bed after having a severe nose-bleed in the night. His sheets and pillowcases were saturated with blood and I was reminded of the morning I found Grandmother Brown in such a predicament.

The limp old man was taken to the Eventide Home at Scarinish, the sleepy little village where the boat comes in. We were left to cope with the buying of all our stores from his shop and the manning of the counter when other people came to buy. I even milked his cow and Hazel delivered some of the Calor gas in the MacInnes's car. It was an experience we will not forget and the novelty of it coloured an otherwise wet camp.

Before the fortnight had passed Calum's condition had improved suffi-ciently for us to take every camper to the Home to sing for him. We had travelled to Tiree with a Thanks Badge, the Guide Association's official recog-nition of exceptional, prolonged service, to the Movement by a non-member. We had anticipated the need but not the circumstances of the presentation.

Dear old man, he had been the father figure of our early camping days, the secure presence we knew we could trust completely. The last we saw of him was at that presentation. It was deeply moving. Paul was already tall and his handshake that of a nearly grown man. Only a few entered the bedroom. The rest piled up outside the French window, row upon row, some kneeling, some standing, some on the shoulders of their seniors, all in uniform. They filled the whole window and the sun came out behind them. My happy chil-dren, singing with the gusto of a dawn chorus. How Calum loved it!

He recovered. Next spring we had a letter from him saying he was making excellent progress and had been planting his garden. Then suddenly we heard that he was dead. We couldn't believe it. He had been getting ready to attend a dinner at the Lodge Hotel. He was to be the speaker, a role he most certainly would have enjoyed but a sudden heart attack ruined every-one's evening. The island had lost an elder. We had lost one of our dearest friends and we felt as bereft as if he had been a member of the family. He had been a real Highland gentleman, kind, generous and with that peculiar island humour and wisdom that we have experienced so many times. It was many years before we returned to Tiree with the children. We felt vulner-able without his shop, his tap and the shelter of his barn for the wind almost perpetually blows and the horizontal rain and the storm clouds from the Atlantic can cause havoc with canvas. We felt, too, that we would miss his presence too painfully and that we should allow many tides to wash the shore of our footprints before we returned. It was seven years before the compulsion to do so was so great we just had to find a way.

That autumn we really got started on the building of the Low Loo. We wanted to get the drains dug before the frost came. Once again I appeared at school with broken nails. The station wagon found two new roles. With Margaret and Father it brought home the autumn calves; Margaret used it for all the cement, roof timbers, plaster boards and bathroom porcelain for our small extension.

Joan, my indispensable infant teacher, had a nosebleed similar to Calum's. For a few days she came to school reporting an evening attack. 'Every night at the same time, my nose bleeds,' she said. I was uneasy. Then, during assembly, she started to bleed very badly and we could not stop it. Winnie was sent for to drive Joan home. I rang the doctor and insisted he was there to meet them. He arranged for her to be taken immediately to hospital where they sorted her out and she has had no more trouble. At the time I was in danger of getting a hang-up about nosebleeds.

Another thing that happened was that Ann announced an autumn wedding, We were delighted to hear that she had found a strong, bearded Scot to give her the excuse she needed for settling permanently in Scotland. Working as she did in Perth, she was already adopting the accent and her love of the hills and the islands, of country dancing and song, determined that north of the border was the right place for her.

She asked Margaret to be her bridesmaid and it was at the wedding that we heard some more good news. The aunts came to the marriage service and, in the privacy of the pew, told us they had been to look at an old cottage on the outskirts of the town. Pleased with what they had found, they had said that they would buy it. All this had been done on the spur of the moment with no time to tell us.

Everything happened quickly. The owners moved out at once; someone heard that the aunts were moving, asked if they wanted to sell the street house and bought it. Margaret and I went into the empty house with a crowbar and sledgehammer as we had once gone into The Currer. We pulled out all the rotting cupboards, prised up old floorboards and tore out ancient fireplaces. Aunt Janie abdicated when she saw the mess and worried about whether they had done the right thing but Auntie Mary never faltered, making cups of coffee and sweeping up the mess throughout that very busy month. There were only four rooms and a small bathroom and it wasn't the marathon task The Currer had been. Nevertheless I know I spent more than two hundred hours in that little house, replacing the cupboards and floorboards, replastering and decorating. Margaret had to feed the calves without my help and then, tired out, she had to take Auntie Mary home and bring a filthy me back to The Currer.

All work on the Low Loo was abandoned. I would spend seven hours after school, every Saturday was a sixteen-hour day and Sunday never one of rest. The only time I took off was for the Guide meeting. It's good to have a deadline. Auntie Janie became enthusiastic as soon as the gloss paint began to go on and the man came to fit the new fireplace. The final extravagance was a black bitumen asphalt floor. I remember it the night before the carpet was laid. The black floor was all new and shiny.

I know, too, that I had no time to sit back and look at what we had done. The aunts took over and I leapt into the neglected preparations for Christmas.

Joan returned to school and the traditional routine we knew so well occupied our every minute. Christmas will never ever be the same as it was in those village headship days. In the village school we clung to old fashioned ways and values and methods, and when Advisors came in to school they stopped preaching new ideas, smiled benevolently and said, 'This school reminds me of the good old West Riding days,' and when they left whispered, 'I wish my child could come here.'

Stability is better than change for children. In a maze of new ways and new parents and different teachers they don't know where they are nor what is right. After ten years I was almost the institution that Joan was. I could not imagine a life without my school. It was so secure and manageable.

Frequently parents brought their troubles into the staffroom. I tried to prevent them from being too dramatic. Experience taught me that they usually wished they had said less. We could forget or at least see the unimportance of it in the long run but, when the moment of panic was over, the memory of what had been said was an embarrassment to them. There was often the funny side when children related a family tiff.

'Ah cun't cum t' school this morning, 'S Armstrong,' one five-year-old said, "cos me Mam 'it me Dad wiv ve fryin' pan. Not ve one we do bacon in, ve one we fry fish in.'

I remember only one parent who entered the staffroom angrily on my account. The poor man, whose wife was in hospital, was coping alone with four lively girls and was at his wits' end. I had asked one of his daughters to bring a note from home if she wasn't allowed to go to the baths. This small request was the last straw. He burst into the staffroom demanding, 'Where's that bloody Miss Brown?' We never held it against him.

I never thought of seeking promotion. I had found my niche and there I intended to stay until retirement. Pretty unadventurous, but only a fool would exchange such job satisfaction as was mine. The setting of the school was so beautiful. I have memories of glorious summer days when we had Assembly out of doors, beneath the trees in the Rec. We were often tempted to take desks into the yard for activity work. Sometimes we took out the dinner tables and picnicked in sunshine and we were always sketching or writing on the canal bank. I loved the bonhomie of the neighbours, the friendly passers by and the regulars in the bus shelter.

There are few disobedient children in a small school. Anyone who will not conform stands out like a sore thumb. Joan was a master of the art of getting children to do as they were told. A look, a word from her and the infants were happy to do her bidding. We used to say she could get children to do anything, even to look for me in impossible places. 'Where's 'S Brown?' they would ask.

'She's in a green jar in the cupboard,' she would answer and off they would trot, nearly all the way to the cupboard before turning with a frown of disbelief. Joan had no discipline problems except, she admitted to me one day, with her own grandson. He had been taking no notice of what she said and generally behaving as some children do at home and few do at school. She had become cross, shaken her finger at him and told him, in quite a dramatic way, that the children at school always obeyed at once, and that he must jolly well do the same, or else! She was quite proud of her performance. Certainly her grandson was spellbound. He had never heard anything like it before. There was a silence then he clapped his hands in glee. 'Do it again, Grandma,' he said.

Gradually the walls of the Low Loo grew. Windows were fitted and the pipe work begun. I followed this venture into plumbing with others. The job is not difficult with Yorkshire fittings easy and plastic pipes a blessing but I am never really relaxed on the job. There is a fear that somewhere along the line of copper piping, some connection to the loo or the shower, the taps or the tank, there will be a leak I won't know how to rectify. There can be no turning on of the water until the route is completed. Work must progress with only faith, and mine in my plumbing is somewhat shaky.

We bought a cheap loo, a seconds stainless steel washbasin and a very expensive shower and we coped. There was always Father to ask about the valves and the split pins. He spoke with authority and was very definite about what we needed, how and when. He would have liked to do every job himself but farming is a full day in a full week and, until he could no longer do so, he spent his time with Margaret.

Father was extremely sensitive to our weariness and was kinder than anyone to Margaret when she was exhausted with the dirty, physical work. If a job had to be finished however he never told us to, 'Gi' ower,' until it was done. He was quick to notice an animal which needed worming, a fence which needed repair, an area which must have some concrete or a draught which must be stopped. Brave man, he saw there was so much to do and time, for all of us, is perpetually running out. We do not believe it when we are young but we are certain when we are old. Opportunity does not come in equal shares and it came to my father with a vengeance when he was rather older than most but he wasn't ever going to let that deter him. His contemporaries had all retired a decade ago and were collecting their weekly allowance and spending the declining years with too much spare time on their hands but Father was trying to work like a young man, full of plans and ideas, interested in every detail, long after his hair had gone grey and almost disappeared. He never saw a ha'penny of his state pension, for improvements in land and house and cattle swallowed everything we had.

The years did little to him or Mother. Children loved him. Guides married and brought their children and whilst we talked at table, long after eating was over, recalling shared memories of the past and putting the wrongs of today's world right, Father would disappear to his armchair and be happy amusing the children. It was sad that we never gave our parents any grandchildren but we brought more home than most people. The sitting room would often bulge with fifty singing children and Mother, Father and Harry would be in the midst.

Father was an outspoken, benevolent philosopher to whom everyone wanted to talk. Mother lived in agony that he would be too critical of a guest whose ideas and attitudes were different. He never talked small talk, went headlong into serious discussion and he often embarrassed Mother by being so definite about major problems. Miners, fishermen, those who worked in factories all concerned him. He taught us not to accept government or religion as incapable of malpractice and hypocrisy. Mother trembled, quite unaware that she was even more definite in her likes and dislikes and far more extravagant with her language.

The aunts thought they were in Paradise. The little house had 'welcome' on the doormat. On hot days there was tea on the lawn. When frost glittered on the hillside the two of them were walking briskly up the valley to Newsholme Dene and Slippery Ford. Auntie Janie led her sister on daily missions to visit the sick and lonely everywhere. They radiated happiness from that little cottage. Hardly a day passed but they had someone to tea. Uncle Joe's frail widow often spent a weekend there. Few things gave me more pleasure than putting that little house in order for them to enjoy.

The herd increased, we built new sheds; the Guide Company grew, we bought more tents; the school population rose and we appointed Winnie full time. More boys wanted to go to camp. We ignored regulations and took them.

We had to be selective about this. We could not take every boy who wanted to come. Those who were already fixed to go on holiday with parents were refused. Michael was one of these. One afternoon, before I had left school with my bag of books to mark, he came running back into the staff room. "S Brown,' he said, 'please take me t' camp!' I was tempted. I hated to refuse any child the experience of the Hebrides. But Michael was already going on two holidays. His parents were separated and, in his case, that meant two trips to the sea, for both parents were equally determined to give him a good time. Had I said I would also take him to camp I knew of several more boys who were already going on holiday who would demand that I take them too.

'Michael, I'm sorry,' I said. 'It's a Guide Camp. I'm not supposed to take any boys at all. I just sneak in those whose parents can't afford a holiday.'

'I think I'm going to be sick,' he said and ran to the sink. A year later, heartbroken, I tried to convince myself that everything had been for the best. Michael would certainly have enjoyed camp but I had to be firm. So he went off on his two jaunts and then went to senior school. Had he come with us I would, most likely, have taken him in 1972 for when the number of boys was small each one came again and again. Instead he went on holiday with his mother at exactly the same time as we went to camp and, whilst away from home, was taken ill. He died a few days later of a brain abscess. It was the first news I heard, shortly after my return. I had deprived a boy no doctor could save of a happy camp, but spared myself and my children the agony of such a tragedy happening whilst he was with me. In my anguish I could only reassure myself that my early refusal had been for the best. His parents bought us a Sports Day Cup in memory of him. I never presented it without sadness.

That I was to continue the long camps with so many children was entirely due to the loyalty, energy and companionship of Hazel. Each year I went through agony waiting for her reassurance that she would come. It was no small thing to give up a fortnight every year for over a decade, to help a colleague face the isolation and the elements, and the job of feeding and caring for so many.

Holidays in the Land Rover with the family and aunts assumed the quality of tradition. With them we toured the Highlands before ending up on Harris. If we went up the east coast to Inverness you could be certain that the wheels would turn westwards. If we went to Plockton or Aultbea, we ended up crossing the Minch. If we went to Mull or Skye, sooner or later we would be heading for the Outer Isles.

In 1972 the Blamires were unable to caretake for us during our May holiday but one of our Guides had married a young gardener. The Sheriffs were in love with The Currer, too, and excited at the opportunity to be here alone. I had a shorter holiday than usual so the Land Rover left without me. Promising to join them in a few days' time, I waved the laden vehicle away and was about to re-enter the house and prepare for the afternoon arrival of the Sherriffs when a movement, on the ten-acre we call The Rough, caught my eye.

The cattle were out!

The coincidence is too frequent not to be uncanny. When there is most need for calm there is chaos. Oh Lord, I thought, how do I get the herd home alone? When our cattle get among the heather they are silly. Perhaps an over-indulgence of bilberry leaves is intoxicating. I crossed the Dyke Field, pulled down a yard of wall and spent the rest of the morning getting the wanderers home.

It is difficult to force animals through an unfamiliar opening especially when the spirit of adventure has really caught on, but the thing I remember most was that, after my eventual success, whilst I was rebuilding the mutilated wall, I dislodged a veritable boulder and crushed my foot alarmingly. In the split second between knowing it would fall and feeling it land on my foot I thought it might break my leg. I removed the monster, which gave me a limp for days, with such relief and thankfulness. I could have had a broken leg and the Sherriffs would never have found me. I would have had to drag my painful way through bracken and bog to end up in hospital. I sat amid the silver birches praising our God of the Open Air who looks after us.

During the winter of 1972/73 Uncle Joe's sixty-five-year-old widow failed perceptibly. The aunts and often ourselves rang daily. What a blessed invention is the phone. In late January Margaret took her home and noticed that she found even the few steps to the front door too much. 'I'm not taking this old lady home and leaving her alone again,' she told herself.

A few days later Aunt Elsie died in her sleep. Heart attacks and heartbreak are no respecter of age. We could not believe it. She had not complained. She was a young woman.

A new member joined the family. We already had three dogs. Bess, one of Jed's pups, was a beautiful curly-haired collie with mottled feet and big brown eyes. Laddie and Lassie were from a later litter but all were getting old. Twelve is a good age for any dog and Bess was already fourteen. Still, we did not need another dog. Two are quite sufficient. Three dogs are more than enough.

But one day Margaret had to go to the vet's for some worming liquid. A six-month-old mongrel, probably of collie, Labrador, corgi descent, was tied in the waiting room. His frightened, sad look was not suggestive of ill-treatment. 'What's the matter with him?' Margaret asked the girl assistant.

'Nothing,' she answered. 'He's been brought in to be put down. He keeps looking at me.'

He kept looking at Margaret. Wise dog. 'What's he being put down for?' she wanted to know. The vet came in.

'You can have him if you want,' he said. 'There's nothing wrong with him.'

'Hold on,' said Margaret. People were always ringing us asking for pups.

When she got home Father said, 'Fetch 'im. Somebody'll have 'im.'

So she brought him home and his name was Shep. 'Summat'll turn up,' said Father. 'Somebody'll 'ev it,' but no one did. If they had I do not think that Shep and Margaret could have been separated. We have had loyal, devoted dogs but none to compare with Shep. He never smiled but he never left Margaret no matter how the blizzard blew or the heavens opened. Useless as a cow dog he found his niche as bodyguard. The sad look never went but it was not so much misery as abject adoration. I am sure he knew she had saved his life. She could never have left him at home when we went on holiday for he knew when the cases were being packed and he would jump in the Land Rover and not get out. Of all dogs Shep belonged to Margaret. If I have been a Pied Piper Margaret has been a Saint Francis.

Chapter Sixteen

We began to reap the benefits of having our own bull. Little Aberdeen Angus calves were being born everywhere. There was a moment of panic when Billy's own mother had a calf; he was too interested in the cleansings and started to bellow and carry-on in quite an alarming way. We enjoyed every minute of the spring calves, and wandered up the hillside, every night, just to watch their evening capers. How silly and frisky young things can be. Pups take the biscuit but calves come a ready second.

Believing that all was well we became greedy. In 1973 the idea of two holidays was born. I think it originated out of selfishness. The aunts wanted to see more of Scotland and we desperately needed some time on the islands. We could briefly go to Arran in May and we could go to Harris in July, before camp. Why not?

The Sherriffs had gone to Scotland to live. Arnold had secured a job there but the Blamires, dear friends, said they'd love two periods at The Currer. With such enthusiasm we kidded ourselves into thinking we were doing them a good turn letting them have two 'holidays' on the farm and that it was our duty to go away and let them have fun!

But trouble began in early May when very young animals began to calve. A few yearling heifers had been served too early. We were going to have to pay a high price for not having been able to keep them apart. We had no serving dates and it is difficult to know when a cow is in-calf at the best of times. There are ways of telling. If she is a dairy cow and always on your doorstep you know if she doesn't come 'a-bulling' but when a suckling herd roams free you do not have any real guarantee until you begin to see them 'bagging up'.

In 1973 we began to see the smallest heifers with increasing udders. Here were we, preparing to go to Arran, not knowing when they would calve and leaving inexperienced people to cope. We were ready to leave one of us behind but the Blamires, blissfully unaware of the responsibility, would not hear of it. I think they were quite looking forward to babies being born. The fields were already full of them. Easy as pie!

Two heifers calved before we left. One caused no trouble at all. Our spirits rose, then plummeted, when we had a very bad calving and a dead calf. Worse than that, the heifer was badly torn and had to be stitched. Nor would she get up. Charlie MacLean from Tiree came to see us before we were leaving for Arran, and, together, the three of us struggled for a long time.

I took the Land Rover to school on the Thursday. That evening on the home side of the Moor Gate I pressed the starter and there was no response. I sat there pressing the starter over and over again. We were going on holiday, for goodness' sake. The Land Rover couldn't just pack up on us like that!

After twenty minutes I got out and began to run down the hill. At home there had been a chapter of events. Both the television and the washing machine refused to work. We really ought not to be going away. We were as near as we ever get to panic. What we needed were a few calm friends.

One arrived and unexpectedly made an offer of extraordinary generosity. Alan looked at Mother and Harry and the old man who had once again been struggling to force the unwilling heifer to rise, and he must have had great compassion and affection for us. When he heard that the Land Rover wouldn't start he said, 'Take my car, Jean. Take mine.'

We could not, of course, accept the offer. There weren't just five of us, there were seven, all adults, and a dog. We must use our transport as a home *en route*, cooking and eating in it. We were going to run it on beaches, take it on boats and utilise it in ways we could not use another person's car. But his kind offer lifted the panic off the boil; we phoned our neighbours, those magicians with spanner and screwdriver, and they sorted out the self-starter.

Next morning we left the dead television, the useless washing machine and the heifer who refused to get up. We were very shamefaced. Our first night was spent at relatives in Glasgow and from there we phoned home. The Blamires were in a panic. The pigs had taken an interest in the heifer which was down and, before they could be chased away they had disturbed the healing tear that the vet had stitched.

'I'll go home,' I said. 'I'll catch the next train.' It wasn't noble of me. I was always embarrassed by the fact that I now had a fortnight longer than Margaret, each year, in the Hebrides. If one of us had to go then it would have to be me.

But the Blamires wouldn't hear of it. 'Tell us what to do,' they said. It was very brave of them. We told them to drive in some fencing posts and enclose the heifer within pig netting so that at least that wouldn't happen again, and we sailed for Arran leaving them to deal with two more unfortunate calvings before our return. One calf was born with a very bent foreleg which never straightened; the other calf was born dead. There seemed a temporary hoodoo on the young members of the herd, as if someone had made a calf in wax and stuck pins all over it. They did not tell us until our return.

There was no point in not enjoying the holiday. So we sailed to Arran for a few days and then drove down the west coast to New Luce on the Mull of Galloway.

With another happy holiday behind us we returned to face the music and rescue our friends. We were full of praise for their endurance and for the admirable way in which they had coped but we fully understood when they said they just couldn't face another fortnight of the responsibility in July. We had been greedy and fate had reprimanded us.

The heifer finally got up and we milked her all summer. Incidentally she gave us another drama at a future calving. Her bag was full and her slacks were down but something was obviously wrong and, towards midnight, Margaret rang for the vet. There was no sign of a calf but after an internal examination he told us there were twins and that they seemed to be dead. I will never forget his expression as he withdrew first one dead calf and then another and then, 'Ye gods!' he exclaimed. 'There's another.'

It was all very tragic but there was a glimmer of a smile. The young vet, had he been gowned and bearded would have looked like Santa Claus, delving to the bottom of the bag. Three dead calves on the shed floor is a pathetic sight. We needed a success story to give us courage. The vet came to another bad calving which came hard on the heels of the triplets.

'The calf is far too big,' he said. 'I'll have to do a caesarian.' He put a halter on the cow and tied her to an upright in the shed. Then he gave just a local injection. She stood throughout the operation. An incision, about twelve inches long, was made and a live calf rolled into the vet's arms and onto the straw. The docile cow suddenly began straining and everything she had seemed to bulge through the opening in her side. With extraordinary calm, the vet took his needle and thread and began to push everything in again and stitch up the gap just as I do when I am putting a cover on an overful cushion. The calf we named Caesar.

The calf bed will often appear after an easy calving. When a calf slips out suddenly and brings the womb with it the vet is needed to put it back. Margaret once sent for him on the coldest of days when a late frost held the earth hard and painted the dead bracken white. The cow had calved on the Rough and her calf bed was out. Margaret felt so sorry for the young man as she led him a quarter of a mile down the field. He looked at the cow and began to peel off his clothes. She watched him hesitate before he finally took off his vest. He asked what day it was and decided he could not dirty his vest so early in the week and took that off too. A calf bed down can take ages to put back. Margaret, fully clothed, was frozen. Luckily this misfortune took hardly any time at all. With a look of surprise and relief the vet was able to put back his sweater much sooner than he had expected.

Two calves had been born dead, that spring of 1973, but many more were born alive and soon thirty or more frolicked on the hill. Then just before the rest of the family set off for Harris we had the last dead calf. We had plenty of milk for the house so Margaret decided to buy one and let the heifer foster it.

Father warned it might not be easy but Margaret asked a dealer friend to get her a little Friesian bull, quickly.

The heifer however immediately rejected him. She would not bear him in the pen, let alone feed him. Margaret had left the stillborn calf with her and now she skinned it and draped the smelly coat over the new calf. Now the heifer no longer minded him in the pen but she had no intention of feeding him. She could kick, and she did so, viciously, every time he went near her. The only thing to do was to put on a halter and tie it to an upright in the Dutch barn, high so that her head was up and her nostrils pointing to the roof. In this posture she could not kick so hard but she could swing her rear around to avoid the unwanted calf. To mesmerise her I enveloped myself around her head, nipping the skin between her nostrils and singing loudly and untunefully into her ear. Margaret braved the danger zone of her hind legs and pushed the hungry calf towards the dripping teats. It caught on at once and sucked enthusiastically whilst sister scratched the swishing tail roughly, to placate the animal and to say, in a language cows appreciate, that she was sorry we were treating her so badly.

After the first feed the calf would have followed the cow to the ends of the earth convinced that she was his mother, but she was not deceived. We kept her in the Dutch barn for a day or two, and every morning and night we had the feeding performance. My unpleasant renderings could be heard hypnotising her with campfire songs and Scottish melodies. Margaret was trampled on, pinioned against the gate, kicked and bruised and the date fixed for the family to go to Harris drew nearer.

We could not keep her indoors but to let her out added an hour to our day. The calf would follow her but she would not feed him so we had to bring her home protesting. We would get her within yards of the Dutch barn and she would turn tail and we would have to start the round up again. We were heartily sick of her. Once in captivity we kept her overnight and didn't release her until after the morning feed.

Two days before the family left, four little ducklings were hatched. Ducklings are much smaller than chickens and ducks are not such good mothers as hens. Cats and crows hovered about just waiting their time. I was being left with a whole bag of problems. We probably always have a whole bag of problems and they do not really increase when we have some other activity in the offing. It's just that normally Margaret takes them all in her stride and we only notice them in the peak hour.

I waved the family away with some trepidation. Joanna stayed with me on the first weekend. Like all modern teenagers she lay in bed late on the Sunday morning. I was up before seven and I noticed a solitary heifer in the Eightacre and knew Bonnie had isolated herself to calve.

I watched her through the binoculars. She began heading downhill, into the low pasture and disappeared. Suddenly, from nowhere, came a thunderstorm. Torrential summer rain bounced off the concrete and the tin roofs became noisy as the big drops beat furiously on the metal and hurried down the corrugations to fall in veritable waterfalls everywhere. With one accord the herd began to run home to the shelter of the sheds and thirty packed themselves tightly under the sycamore tree in front of the sitting room window. All except Bonnie, of course. Their steaming bodies sent up a cloud of enveloping mist. The saturated ground was steaming like some thermal spring.

I let the storm pass then Joanna and I went for Bonnie. She did not want to come but I wanted her under cover, where I could cope. We had lost too many calves already. Bonnie calved with no problem at all but there was no maternal response from the stupid animal. The calf was getting stronger and more able to fight for his rights provided I held onto her head and sang lustily.

Joanna returned home and the aunts came to make my meals and keep me company.

On Tuesday morning there was a disturbance of comic quality. Had the postman come a little later he would have driven away in hysterics. But he pulls into the yard at precisely seven o'clock and his arrival brought me hurrying downstairs in my red woollen dressing gown, intent on silencing the dogs and preventing them from knocking the plants off the windowsill. Why all our dogs have wanted to eat the postman I really do not know. He handed me my letters through an open window with a smile, and I paused before closing it, to breathe in some early morning air. There was a lot more noise outside than usual. I noticed it at once.

We live in a silence which is full of sounds. It can be heard, as silences usually can, but compared with most places we live in quietness. On that Tuesday morning there was just a light fluttering of the leaves on the sycamore, just an awareness that somewhere in the distance a train was speeding towards Scotland. The cuckoo was calling in Jimmy's Wood and there was another noise which should not have been there at all. Some tragedy seemed to be happening in the stable where the duck lived with her very small brood. No alarm is more heart-rending than that of a mother duck who has lost a baby and no creature on the farm is so small as a duckling.

The stable was not an ideal place to keep a duck and its offspring but animals have a habit of choosing for themselves where they live. The stable door was not a perfect fit. The lower half was skellered and left a two-inch gap big enough to need stuffing in winter-time to prevent the snow driving in; a gap big enough for field mice to escape the cats and amply big enough to allow one khaki duckling to fall through. Like a true Campbell he was piping his distress on the outside of the door. Neck outstretched, wings spread, feathers ruffled, Mamma was raising the roof the other side.

Feathered things frighten me and I give a wide berth to angry fowls. But something had to be done quickly, for Threelegs was visibly on the prowl. His intentions were obvious. Usually benign and friendly, he had become a hunter convinced he had found easy prey.

Barefoot and be-gowned I ran into the yard. 'All you have to do,' I told myself, 'is to open the stable door. Mother and baby will be reunited and Threelegs will have to wait for his breakfast.'

The duckling got in the way as I struggled with the unconventional bolt on the door. A cold wind found its way between the folds of my dressing gown, bits of spilt corn embedded themselves between my toes and I was far too slow for the impatient monster behind the door.

Finally the shaft slid out and the stable door sagged heavily on its hinges. I heaved it open, narrowly avoiding the panic-stricken bird hastening to protect her distressed prodigal. Two less adventurous ducklings fell off the step to join her and suddenly it was all over. The silence was almost tangible. In high, mute dudgeon Mother Duck marched off to the pond with three ducklings clinging to her still ruffled skirts.

I heaved a sigh of relief. It had, after all, been relatively easy and I would not think about the hovering crows and the greedy magpies, Ginger and Threelegs who lurk in the reeds by the waterside.

I watched the united little family wriggle under the yard gate, aware that I was very cold, improperly dressed, barefoot, and that I hadn't had my breakfast. Suddenly the awful truth dawned on me. I ran to the gate. There was Mother Duck with her three babies. Good Lord, there should be four! How could I be so stupid?

I ran back to the gaping door of the stable. The abandoned baby was wrapping itself against a corn sack, its tiny wings hugging the dusty hessian, its flailing legs trying to find a foothold. Its voice was hoarse and between it and me were many obstacles.

'It's just a small, frightened thing,' I reassured myself. 'There's no mother to attack. You've only got to pick it up and carry it to the stream. It's not a trapped sparrow fluttering against the windowpane. It's only a tiny duckling that can neither fly nor peck.'

But as I picked my way carefully over the feeding trough and the splatter of wet mash and bird droppings the wee thing disappeared behind the pile of corn sacks. Gingerly I began to move them. The suddenly exposed baby dashed for the stable door and the freedom of the yard.

I climbed carelessly over the sacks, and slipped dangerously on the greasy floor feeling, without revulsion, the unpleasant slime ooze between my toes. The duckling was still there. Not knowing where to go and having no Mamma to guide him, he had hesitated. The great outdoors must be pretty frightening to one so small. My presence was even more so. When he saw me he made a beeline for the gap under the mistal door and disappeared into the semi-darkness within.

With fumbling, sweating fingers I untied the string, lifted the latch, opened the door and switched on the electric light.

The two sows had boxed themselves lengthwise, gregariously filling the nearest cow stall. They were blissfully unconscious, deeply asleep.

Of the baby duckling there was no sign. I felt like Tom in search of Jerry. The mistal was only part of a huge barn and my task was impossible. That little Khaki Campbell's camouflage against the straw would be absolute.

There was only one thing to do. I could not find him but perhaps his mother would speak the right language to get a reply. With my dressing gown billowing in the wind, I flapped my way to the pond. The ridiculous mother, unable to count, could not believe it when I tried to shoo her and her three petite shadows back to the farmyard.

In her indignation she began to protest very loudly which was exactly the magic needed. I opened the mistal door and immediately there came the answering piping which told me the duckling was still alive and led me to its hideout.

But what a predicament he was in! Somehow or other he had crossed the mountain range of in-pig sows and had slithered down the final slope into a minute triangular cell walled by the manger, the stall and the enormous ham. Hearing his mother's voice he was valiantly trying to reclimb the hairy mountain, unaware that one movement of the pig and he would be well and truly squashed.

I almost gave him up for lost. I was no longer afraid of picking him up. I certainly wasn't afraid of the recumbent sows. Without litters they are docile ladies who lie in late. But I was scared of witnessing the end of the little fellow. I wanted to go away as I do when a cat catches a mouse or a dog streaks after a rabbit. I was a coward when it came to watching the little mountaineer meet his end.

But I must do something for Margaret had left me in charge. She'd never have gone to Harris if she could have seen me dithering in my dressing gown.

I stroked the nearest sow, scratching the rough skin behind its ear. How deeply sows sleep! They thrive on having fellow bed companions. They don't mind being trampled on. How often we have laughed at their smiling unconsciousness.

But a sudden noise or unfamiliar movement and there is an eruption of the whole herd. Quiet, purposeful pressure on my part and they would remain hypnotised by their own sleep. A wobble and I'd be in the middle of a scrum. I continued ear scratching whilst I wriggled my bare foot between one fat belly and the other. Having got it firmly wedged I let it take my weight as I leaned over the second sleeper whilst the intrepid hill climber teetered halfway up her backside screaming his head off.

If either pig moved I'd lose my balance and all would be lost but the rhythmic snoring continued. I reached out and captured the rascal in my right hand hoping that his incredible energy was spent.

The complacent sows never moved. I extricated my cramped foot from its vice, breathed again and slipped thankfully through the mistal door. The irate mother stood in the yard, her neck fully stretched, breathing fire and brimstone on all mankind and on me in particular. I dropped the weightless bit of fluff within a yard of her and fled.

The weather was hot and the herd came home regularly to drink, avoiding the warble flies by sheltering in the sheds. Where warble fly is concerned cattle show a glimmer of commonsense not usually attributed to their species.

Fortunately it is almost eradicated now. The only good it ever did us was to bring the herd home when Jimmy's mother refused to adopt him. As soon as I noticed she was inside I bolted the shed doors.

The cow's full udder was always leaking and the calf was dotty for milk. He would butt his way under her belly regardless of the kicks which came fast and furious until I had dragged her head high up the pole and begun my infernal singing. 'We'll all go mad,' I thought.

The fortnight on my own taught me that I could barely cope, that one man and his dog are not sufficient. Farming is teamwork. This probably accounts for the low divorce rate in farming and the high suicide rate. Most certainly the farmer's wife is needed and to be needed is more important than to be loved. A man alone with a farm is as handicapped as one man in a three-legged race. Margaret, much more competent than I am, can still chase a bullock round and round a shed and not get him through the door. When I am called and there are two of us, he goes meekly through.

On the Friday, at the end of the fortnight, I went into the shed to see if the herd had come down. It had. I looked for the heifer which had caused me so much trouble and there she was, placidly suckling her infant. The struggle was over.

The family returned bringing the most beautiful Hebridean collie bitch pup. Harry called her Miss World but we named her Floss. She was predominantly black with a white belly and a white streak down her face. Her lovely eyes were set in two brown patches. She was a Floss dog, very much like Father's dog in my childhood.

Everything had to be done at once. The haymaking the school prize giving, the packing for camp. We only ever had a few hours in bed. I was always typing reports at six o'clock in the morning.

As regularly as the arrival of the cuckoo there came that day when everyone assembled on the platform with kit bags and rucksacks and the annual migration to the machair was ready to begin the long journey north. I was exhausted. Hazel always looked as if she had just stepped out of an advertisement for Camay. She coped with all the collection of health forms and ticked off everyone's name. She was always the friend in need, the ray of sunshine who took the last-minute responsibility from my shoulders and let me sit down in peace whilst the moving train restored me for the hectic fortnight ahead. Friendship really is a thing of harmony.

There is a sub-category of the division which separates those who have camped and those who have never done so. There are those who have camped and those who have camped with us. An American Guide recognised the understanding and comradeship which had grown between us and wrote,

> For here I had an experience,
> Which for all my life I'll remember.

Hazel came to the 1973 camp with her husband and they stayed with Katie and Angus on the shore. The arrangement was a success because Ray was happy to come to camp nearly every day of the fortnight for his wife was no more happy away from the fun and the responsibility than I was if I chatted too long in Rachel's cottage and left seniors in charge.

It was an extraordinarily hot camp. We took the children to the Butt of Lewis, climbed the lighthouse and pretended we could see the Arctic Circle. We picnicked on the beach at Europie and it was such a temptation to allow the huge rollers to break over the children that we allowed them to wallow in shorts and shirts with no fear that clothes would not dry. Just to mention these happy days fills me with an inner effervescence and an incomparable nostalgia.

My association with Cloughie at Steeton Hall continued. She was approaching her mid-seventies but there was still no ruling which forcibly retired these founder members of the Movement. She was still running a Guide Company and taking them to camp. As the testing of Camper Badge and Patrol Permits shifted from her shoulders to mine so the venue of the testing came to The Currer.

It was no uncommon sight to see forty tents pitched outside the kitchen window and, at each end of the weekends, the yard full of cars, children and equipment. Nor was it unknown for Cloughie to be having tea in our kitchen instead of me sitting in state in her elegant drawing room. When she became too old to drive the car, her chauffeur used to bring her and he would sit down round the kitchen table too and Mother would revel in making a spread for My Lady and her family retainer.

Mother was several years older than Cloughie but when Cloughie was disabled by a slight stroke Mother used to help her on with her coat and fasten the buttons. I remember Father trying to overcome the embarrassment of seeing her fumbling by saying, 'Ah ye a bit flummoxed?'

'She won't know what that means,' Mother reprimanded.

'I do,' said the good lady in the deep tones of a born aristocrat.

'When will you come again?' Mother wanted to know.

I think my old friend was quite lonely in her big house where tradition built barriers.

'When ye'll 'ev me,' she said in broad Yorkshire.

School children used to love to come and camp in the paddock. 'How long do Ah boil me eggs?' David asked.

'About five minutes,' I shouted through the kitchen window. His fire wasn't very big. He looked at his watch and put on the pan of eggs covered with cold water. I can still remember his face when, five minutes later he took the eggs out of their lukewarm water and expected to eat them with his bread soldiers.

Just as Rat thought there was nothing quite so much fun as messing about with boats so I could find nothing more satisfying than messing about with tents. I loved the smell of them, the sandy grittiness of the sod cloths so frequently on the machair, the gaudy emblems stitched on by competent Patrol Leaders to identify individual Icelandics which otherwise all looked the same. I loved the stainless steel billies and the heavy, well-used, frying pans, the plastic plates and outsize ladles. Over them all hung the aroma of peat smoke.

After camp would come September and the nature walks along the canal bank to collect the nuts and berries and the autumn leaves dyed with a hundred shades of red and gold and brown. We would chase the fairy men blowing from the rosebay willow herb and spin the sycamore propellers and the ash keys. We would sample the blackberries growing in the hedges and bring a little of everything home and have a hedgerow harvest. We would reject the traditional festival with its abundance of orchard fruits and garden vegetables. We would emphasise a different harvest, one of fields, woodland and moor and we would decorate our assembly with wild flowers and delicate fronds.

Autumn days with children were not complete without the feel of October leaves, deep and rustling beneath our feet, up Parson's Walk and along the top road to The Folly gates. We gathered up the autumn as the squirrels did the beech nuts in the wood along Bradley Road, aware of bleak days to come desperate to soak up as many riches as we could before the November fog and rain blackened the countryside.

Out came the football boots and shirts; the cloakroom lost its summer emptiness and became cluttered with muddy footwear and heavy duffel coats. We became more eager for food, waiting with anticipation for the arrival of the mid-day meal. With what hungry speed the children and I set the cutlery on the desks. In their enthusiasm the girls found their feet could only run for the trolley of steaming food. I fear those enjoyable mid-day meals, in the family atmosphere of the village school, have disappeared. This is unfortunately an era of convenience. I think that, if authority had tried to abolish the traditional school dinner in my career, I would have hit the roof. During the thirty-one years of my teaching experience not one child ever brought sandwiches. It is part of a child's education to learn how to sit at table with an adult.

There came a very lean period in the cattle markets of the country. Calves were selling for ten pence. and some were given away in the local pubs just to get rid of them. Beef to the butcher was low and old cows were selling for a song. It was with great reluctance that we decided that the suckling herd would have to go. There is nothing nicer than spring calves even though there are many hazards nor is there anything to compare with a suckled calf. Like a breast-fed baby it thrives better and, because it is bred from a beef and not a diary cow, it is more profitable at the end of the day.

The first step had to be the sale of Billy. I was terribly afraid of this. He was very big and enjoyed his freedom as few bulls are ever allowed. Because we asked nothing of him and allowed his untethered right to do as he pleased, he was very docile. But there were moments when we knew perfectly well that he could be aggressive.

The old Irish cattle dealer was informed that we had a bull for sale. Billy stood placidly chewing his cud as if butter wouldn't melt in his mouth whilst he was inspected. A Land Rover and trailer were to be sent for him next day. I couldn't sleep for worrying about how they would get him into the box.

That night he obligingly chose to sleep in the barn, with his mother and a few more of the herd. Margaret closed the gates and we crossed our fingers. I went to school in an acute state of anxiety and could not teach well for thinking about the accident which I was sure would happen. Be Prepared is a good motto, but avoid wasting hours worrying about what may never happen. Father and Margaret are 'two very guid men'. They skilfully steered Billy's mother into the box and Billy followed meekly enough. Very obligingly, the old cow turned and walked back out again and the gates of the trailer were closed.

A few months later the old dealer was back on another errand. 'You know that Aberdeen Angus bull, Margaret?' he said, 'He was dangerous! No one could do anything at all with him. You were wise to get rid of him!' Deep down, hadn't we always known he was a funny customer?

The cheapness of the calves tempted us to buy many more than usual. There came the memorable day when Margaret and I quarrelled, a thing we so seldom do. We were so busy, both had too big a workload already and it made us touchy. Poor weather, deepening mud, shorter days all combined to increase the stress and I came home to be told that Margaret and Father had decided to go to market and buy another batch of calves.

'Over my dead body,' I remember saying and Margaret and I had a right 'set to'. She won, of course. She won't admit it but I think she usually does. In farm matters at any rate she has a right to her own way. The calves were bought and the extra work was done, as it usually is. Quarrels are few. We never go to bed until we are smiling at each other. Mother taught us that. 'Never let the sun go down on your wrath,' she always says.

We decided that there was no way this great number of calves could be left to a caretaker in May so Margaret elected to hold the fort, with Julie and Vivienne to help her, whilst I took the family north. There was an ulterior motive in all this for we were planning to take our old folks and Harry to camp! To take two seventy-seven-year-old parents and a middle-aged handicapped brother to sleep in tents was impossible but we saw the possibility of them all staying at Katie's, on the shore.

Unwittingly a step was taken that May which maybe led to what we do now. Life is a jigsaw and all the pieces fit. I saw an advertisement for a cottage on the shore at Skipness, on the Mull of Kintyre. 'Let's go self-catering,' I said.

With some apprehension we crossed the Mull of Kintyre from west to east with the setting sun behind us. The singing passengers had become silent. I was tired and ready to get from behind the wheel. The hilly, gorse-scattered interior gave way to a glistening sea as the ribbon of road began to follow the coastline north towards a village on the shore. We found our cottage overlooking the bay and Auntie Janie, that agile seventy-five-year-old, leapt out of the Land Rover like quicksilver. She and I ran up the garden path, turned the key in the door and went inside. It was beautiful, even perfect, recently modernised and decorated, with none of the wear and tear a season of holidaymakers brings.

Auntie Janie was making excited noises as she skipped into each small room and inspected each little corner. We hurried upstairs, threw open doors and fell in love with everything. We settled in remarkably quickly and we have been using holiday cottages ever since. Auntie Janie was totally in her element organising the buying and cooking and giving everyone jobs. We had a wonderful holiday. We all agreed that we'd go back the next year.

The Mull of Kintyre is a beautiful, remote part of Scotland with the feel of an island. About mid-week we took the boat from West Loch Tarbert to Jura. It seemed unthinkable that, living so near to the pier from which the Islay/ Jura boat sailed each day, we should not try to see Jean Shaw who had made us so welcome at Crackaig. Nothing had changed. The brief visit was too short. It was lovely to see Jean and to talk quietly with her about her husband Sandy who had died.

Holiday cottages are the ultimate in comfort and freedom. We had started a way of life which we were to continue but we had started it too late. If I were to live my life again I would start self-catering earlier, whilst there were seven of us.

On this occasion there were only six for Margaret was at home with Julie and Vivienne and there was no need for one of us to travel cramped in the back, wedged in by luggage. And in all the holiday cottages we have used there have never been enough beds; Margaret and I have nearly always been on the floor.

Almost immediately we were packing for Harris. Father, Mother and Harry were coming too, and Margaret, after all those years of staying behind, was returning. Everything was going our way. The Sherriffs were back home from a year in Scotland and were more than willing to come to The Currer.

The Land Rover left a few days ahead of me for Julie and Vivienne had to be picked up in Northumberland. We met up with each other just outside Sligachan, on Skye. Those Guides on the back seat yelled out that the green station wagon was behind us. We stopped the coach and I changed places with Margaret and drove the rest of the way to Uig for the Harris steamer.

It was wonderful to have Margaret and nothing spoilt the fortnight. It was one of the happiest experiences we have had and I am only so very grateful that Father and Mother were able to see, for themselves, the Yorkshire children at their very best. They knew them all, of course, but it was necessary to see them and us in camp. We could never really explain the fun and wonder of our magic circle on the shore. There were more than fifty children and we all joined a sponsored walk along green tracks among The Bays in aid of the Harris Association.

It was great to see the old folks sitting among the young on the Luskentyre beach. We thought we had solved another problem. Why hadn't we thought of it before? I have vivid memories of sea-wet children running from the waves to the old couple, splashing them with a shower of salty, Atlantic spray. I can see Father laughing and singing, 'I'm so happy, oh so happy, don't you envy me,' and Mother handing them towels and worrying in case they got cold.

We were all together for meals and for campfires. When we went to the Harris Games we tried to get Father into the OAPs race and when we went to Stornaway we all crowded into the bus. Having the Land Rover was a new experience. We could go to Tarbert. We could ferry a load of barelegged children halfway along the route and set them down to begin walking whilst we returned to pick up more who had already left camp. The shuttle service soon got everyone there.

We put Harry and Father out at the Leverburgh road end, where the signpost says five miles to Tarbert: Father who was seventy-seven and Harry without good walking legs! I returned to pick up another load, Mother among them, intending to drop a couple, pick up Father and Harry and go straight into Tarbert. We expected them to have walked about half a mile and for Harry to be on his knees but there was no sign of them. We were a bit worried but there they were, just coming out of the barber's. They teased that they had walked all the way, easy! They had only walked a few yards before being picked up. Now, every time we are driving to Tarbert, when we reach the Leverburgh road end Harry says, 'That's where we got out,' and immediately, 'That's where we got a lift.' I cannot count how many times he has said that.

We decided to extend the Dutch barn and make it twice the size. Our good neighbours brought us some telegraph poles and we bought more fibreglass sheeting. When the straw came we stood on the stack and roofed in safety as was our custom. I have seen us build a small stack, specially, under a roof needing repair.

There came a memorable day towards the end of the year when the bus put me down as usual at the end of the fields and I walked home in comfortable anticipation of tea by the fire. Margaret was in the farmyard with her usual heavy load and she set down the bale to make a comment, a thing she never does. If the bale is up only a passing jogger, causing havoc, will make her put it down. Joggers are the most selfish people on earth, and the most arrogant, especially male ones. They were not taught that in the vicinity of animals, you do not run. I have seen a lark flush and startle a hundred grazing cattle into stampede. We never approach a shed without speaking for a sudden rush of animals in an enclosed area is dangerous. A human can be killed or bovine legs broken in a pile-up.

Joggers, with their long white legs, mechanically moving arms, heavy breathing, smelling of sweat and angrily growling, 'Gerroff,' cause chaos. The dogs, dashing in pursuit, are further rebuffed. 'Call off yer bloody dog.'

Margaret drops her bale then and shouts, 'Stop running! Keep to the footpath! Walk!'

The geese on the pond rise from the water with outstretched wings and half-flying, half-running, flee screaming into the yard. The dogs go berserk. The jogger, in anger, loses the footpath and comes towards us. The pigs throw off the loose straw under which they have buried themselves in the Dutch barn and blindly follow the geese into the yard, tripping up an unsuspecting Harry sweeping the yard or Auntie Mary hanging out the clothes. The goats mount the bales, startled and frightened, and the donkeys gallop wildly in the paddock.

Regardless of putting more than himself in danger the jogger keeps running. One even kept going when the vet and we were putting heifers through the brucellosis test. Suddenly there came heavy breathing, the sound of running footsteps, a smell of sweat and we had two bucking broncos in the crush.

'What d'you think y'doing?' we yelled. 'Get on the footpath and stop running near the buildings.'

But nothing halts the jogger. Do they all swear? Bloody dogs! Bloody women! Bloody footpath! It is marked! Can they not read? Arrogant, running men that they are, they mutter that they'll have the dog put down. 'It's the law!' they pant. 'This is a footpath. By law I can run on it.'

Is there a law which prosecutes the runner who has caused an accident by running along the footpath which, for hundreds of years, has passed The Currer? Is there a law which makes him responsible if Harry, or any one of our many disabled visitors, is killed in the yard because startled donkeys bowl him over? A law which will provide compensation if we are trampled on by a stampede in the shed? If there is what good is that? We do not know the identity of the hit-and-run jogger. He has no number plate that we can note and he never stops. Urban man does not know how dangerous startled cattle are.

Whatever we are doing a jogger will cause us to stop doing it and turn all our efforts to accident prevention just as I have left my main story to digress and comment on the jogging menace. To return to that memorable Friday when Margaret put down her bale, let me remind you that I had just walked home from the bus in comfortable anticipation of tea by the fire.

'Can you stand a shock?' she asked without any twinkle in her eye to suggest she was joking.

'Why?' I was on the defensive. I'd had a hard day, too.

'Look at the gable end!'

Look at the gable end indeed! On the inside of this high wall of the barn which William Currer built onto the house before 1633, was the mistal and the loft. The wall, four feet thick at the base, was dry walled right to the peak and, suddenly, it was showing a bulge in the middle where the loft joists entered the wall. Had it just happened? Had the bend been there for some time and we had only now noticed it? Was it safe? What in the world could we do about it if it were not? If it collapsed there would be an awful mess which could not just be ignored. So far we had been lucky: no barn fires, no chimneystack falling through the roof.

We convinced ourselves that perhaps the wall had slipped when the hay had gone in and that it really was safe enough to 'sort out in the morning'. There isn't a lot one can do in the dark. I went to bed before Margaret had done her night rounds. At midnight she went out with the torch to check the herd.

She shone the big beam up the gable end and the torchlight exaggerated the bulge in a frightening manner. 'It'll never last till morning,' she was sure. She came indoors and hauled me out of my bed. 'It's going. Come quick an' 'elp me get the cattle out!' She doesn't pull me out of bed unless she's in a real panic.

It is not easy to force a few sleeping cattle out of a mistal in the early hours of the morning and to drive them an unfamiliar way to an unfamiliar shed. I got up in a rush and pulled on a few clothes over my pyjamas. Our welling-tons live outside, just in front of the door. If it rains and we have forgotten to lay them feet upwards on the slope, there is a lake inside.

A wind was blowing straight through my clothes. I was cold and bog-eyed and worried stiff. We forced the resisting animals out into the dark night and managed, after a bit of a palaver, to get them temporarily re-housed.

'Look at it!' Margaret shone the torch on the gable end. It looked a thou-sand times worse. We went to bed in fear that we would hear an almighty shutter. If we had, our lives would have been quite different. Would we have rebuilt it? Probably not! How could we? The roof would have gone too. We had no money to meet a contingency like that. Everything we have done since hung on the thread of a chance that the wall would last till morning.

At daybreak we rang our good neighbours and waited with impatience for them to finish their morning feed. Eventually we heard their tractor bringing railway sleepers. We dug deep holes along the side of the gable end and propped up the wall, wedging a long beam against it.

It was a first-aid exercise and one we could not have done ourselves. Then the marathon task began of collecting stone and building four-foot wide, ten-foot high castle buttresses against the wall. We enclosed the sleepers within the stonework, we used tons and tons of stone and were liberal with the cement. When we had finished the buttresses we went inside the mistal and built a second wall inside to hold up the loft. We did it with extreme caution, even though we first propped up the loft floor timbers with railway sleepers standing in deep holes dug in the mistal floor. We worked in constant fear that everything would collapse and tons of hay bury us.

The preservation of the barn was to be one of our history-making jobs. Our whole future, the future of the hillside, its preservation for posterity, our hope of living here always, everything we believe to be important, depended on the safeguarding of the laithe and it only cost us the price of some bags of cement.

I did not cancel meetings. As regularly as the sun rose on Thursday morning I took a Guide Meeting on Thursday night. But there came a day in February 1975 when I cancelled the meeting because of fog.

Two weeks earlier Auntie Janie had been taken ill in the night with a terrible chest pain. Auntie Mary had sent for the doctor; he'd stayed a long time and diagnosed angina. He told her she must stay in bed a few days and prescribed more pills. We were all very worried, for Auntie Janie was nearly as dear to us as our Mother. She had been the support needed by all families with disabled children. I cannot over-stress the need for relatives, friends or, in the last resort, the State when there is a disabled person in the house. Auntie Janie had given up her job to look after her parents and was therefore more on call than anyone. She did not make the steady recovery we expected. I stayed there over the weekend and we goaded ourselves into thinking she was a bit better. She began to get up for a few hours each day and we were sure she was on the mend. We tampered with our telephone bell and succeeded in putting it under my bed so that we would hear it ring if Auntie Mary should need us in the night. Two weeks went by.

Then came February fog of such density as is seldom experienced nowadays. I drove home from school on Thursday 27th February at a snail's pace. Reaching home safely, I put the Land Rover into the garage and told it that it could stay there. Having proceeded so dangerously in the semi-dark, wild horses would not drag me out again behind the wheel.

How I envy people who can just do as they want without having to phone round and tell everyone. It is often far more bother than it is worth. I had a problem trying to cancel the Guide Meeting. There were the masses I could contact by phone and the few I could not get hold of at all. I dared not take the risk that these few would be sensible and not go. There is responsibility in having young girls standing in the street outside a closed door.

Jill, one of my early Guides who had become my assistant and held the fort during my last months at university, now had two children of her own in the Company. When I phoned her, she offered to ferry me to the Headquarters if I could meet her in town. The fog was less dense on the low road, though visibility on the hill was nil. I groped my way along the field path to the village and ran all the way into town. Jill's little Mini was managing fine. A Land Rover is hopeless without a fog light as the headlights are too high and the driving seat too far from the ground. We sat in the car, talking, a long time outside the Guide Room but no one came. Those without phones were obviously not without sense. Jill re-started the engine.

On an impulse I said, 'Drop me at the aunts'. Auntie Janie has been ill. I'll stay there an hour. They won't be expecting me home just yet.' Jill left me outside their front gate.

I found Auntie Janie extremely uncomfortable. She was sitting in an armchair by the fire in a cosy red dressing gown but she was very restless. It was 7.30 p.m. but the doctor had just been. He wasn't satisfied with her progress, had promised to send the district nurse next day to take a blood sample and had altered her prescription.

There was such a restlessness in Auntie Janie. Auntie Mary looked so tired and the fog outside was such an isolator that I decided to stay the night and let Auntie Mary go into the spare room and get a good night's sleep. Auntie Janie found it very difficult to climb the stairs. She paused on each tread and counted. She smiled and said, 'I count to ten on each step.'

'This is awful,' I thought. 'This isn't the Auntie Janie I know.'

It was a long night. The not-very-old lady in the next bed didn't sleep much. She kept getting up and going along to the toilet. I couldn't sleep for worrying. I determined to phone home immediately I reached school and get Margaret to come up to the cottage so that Auntie Janie wasn't left alone whilst the new prescription was being collected.

By dawn the fog had completely disappeared, leaving a hard and bitter frost. It was cruelly cold.

'Don't get up today,' I said as I prepared to leave for school.

'I'll feel better today,' she answered. 'I might get up this afternoon. I want to be up when the district nurse comes to take a blood sample.' She was sitting up in bed so I rearranged the pillows and said I must be off to school. 'Don't miss the bus,' she said.

The bus into town was empty and cold and its journey unfamiliar. It connected with a bus going up the valley in the direction and within half a mile of my school. I could have waited for one which would go the whole way but I felt the walk would do me more good than the waiting. The air was sharp and the weak sun was doing little to dispel the frozen fog on the grass and the bare branches. My breath hung on the air as I hurried along the flat road over the railway crossing and then the hump-backed bridge that monks had built close on a thousand years ago. I just wanted to get to school and warmth and the telephone. A dead rabbit lay spattered on the tarmac, a pathetic victim of last night's fog. I felt a great sorrow for the unsuspecting wild things suddenly flattened by hurrying, inconsiderate man.

The tougher children had found a slide in the schoolyard. 'Watch me, Miss Brown!' they were calling. The infants tried to detain me as I hurried to the staffroom but I ignored their morning news.

The other teachers were already there sipping pre-school cups of tea. There were children in the staffroom too, bringing notes and dinner money. 'I'm just phoning home,' I explained without taking off my coat. 'I've been at the aunts'. Auntie Janie's not very well.'

The phone barely rang before it was lifted. 'My, you're an early bird this morning,' I laughed. 'Were you standing over it or something?'

'Don't laugh,' Margaret said. 'I was just picking it up to ring you. Auntie Janie's just died.'

I was stunned. I couldn't believe it. I was full of self-recrimination that I had left Auntie Mary alone. It was of course unwarranted; neither of us could have known. Winnie guided me, weeping, out of the back door of school and into her car. I cannot forget her kindness. I knew they would be able to cope without me. 'I'll not be back today,' I said. Margaret and Mother reached the cottage before me.

There was a long day ahead, full of tasks for which I had no previous experience. We had not been ready to let Auntie Janie go. She had not lived long enough in the little cottage. Four years packed with happiness and hospitality did not seem plenty. She had not had enough of the advantages of the station wagon nor the joys of holiday cottages. Damn, damn, my brain protested but there is nothing so final as death.

We took Auntie Mary home with us and she stayed six weeks. We put another bed into our bedroom, for the spare room seemed too far away. We pulled another armchair up to the fire and this continues to be her home for half of every week.

I had not intended to go to Skipness with the family in May. It was Margaret's turn. We were loath to leave our responsibilities in the spring until the suckling herd was well and truly phased out, so I had added no extra days to the spring bank holiday. They were to leave me at home and then we were all going to go to Camp, as we had done the year before. Auntie Janie's death altered things a little. The family had been shaken. April had taken away a little of the pain but Skipness might be too full of memories.

I decided to accompany them there, stay the weekend and then return on the train. With six of us in the Land Rover it would not seem quite so empty. We hoped to go via Arran, sailing to Skipness from Lochranza but the ferry wasn't running properly and we had to leave the queue and make a dash by land. Before we left the pier we noticed a man tarring his tin roof with, of all things, a floor wet-mop. It was the answer to a problem we had had: the knowledge of this so-easy way has saved Margaret hours and hours of tarring time! It's an ill wind that blows no one any good.

It was a happy time I had those too-few days at Skipness before returning home. It is a lovely place. The shingle shore is twice washed each day and glistens in the sun. There is an abundance of gorse, a pleasing scattering of stone houses, a castle and an interesting graveyard. There were many memories of Auntie Janie but they were all good ones. She had enjoyed every minute of that cottage a year before. There was a togetherness which created a peace; an awareness that time was a commodity none too ample. I think that Skipness was, for all of us, an act of remembrance, a service of thanksgiving.

Father was a joy to be with. Whilst Harry and the two ladies sat in deck chairs, he would sprawl out on the grass like a schoolboy. He and Margaret went for long walks among the cattle-dotted pastures, talking farming. They were inseparable friends. I remember the last day I spent there. We were down at the Skipness road end where a large house sits almost in the sea. Everyone was sunbathing, Margaret and I in shorts, Father laid out asleep on the grass, still wearing his flat cap, the ladies and Harry sitting with arms bared to the good heat. There was a smell of sea wrack and clover, a buzzing of nearby bees and a screeching of distant seagulls.

They drove me back to Lochgilphead; I took the bus to Glasgow and then the train home. At Skipton the ticket collector came to the compartment and pointed to the main A629. 'See all those ambulances dashing to the hospital,' he said, 'There's been a terrible crash. Loads of dead and injured.'

Along the main road was a flashing of warning lights. The road seemed full of police cars and ambulances. We learned later that a coach outing from Durham had met with terrible disaster.

It is well to remember that the line dividing harmony from unrest, peace from panic, happiness from sadness, health from handicap, life from death, is very tenuous. In seconds it can be broken or crossed. Cloughie, one day, was discussing cancer and said that if it happened to her she would like to be told. 'Whatever for?' I asked, believing that ignorance nurtures hope.

'So that I can get my soul in order,' was the abrupt reply.

'Good Heavens, woman,' I exploded. 'Get it in order now. Cancer might give you time but there are a hundred and one things which might give you no time at all.' On reflection perhaps, some of the serenity of cancer patients or any who know that they have only got a little time, stems from the fact that they have enough to get their souls in order, their priorities right and to put into words the things they want to say.

Margaret and I both attempt to do many extra jobs whilst the family is out of the way. Perhaps it is because we are embarrassed by how much we try to do and hide some of it from Mother. I told no one that I was going to hold a camper badge weekend and add to it a moneymaking coffee morning and afternoon tea. The family wasn't returning until Sunday evening and all evidence would be removed. If I'd told them they would have worried. Keeping quiet has, however, its disadvantages. There is always the accusation, 'You didn't tell me!' if the truth leaks out.

So the weekend they left Skipness, planning to stay Saturday night in Glasgow with relatives, I crossed off a number of jobs in a busy whirl of activity, most of it messing about with tents. There were children all over the place, a canvas village in the paddock, the intoxicating smell of burning hawthorn and frying sausages. I was never happier than indulging in this favourite activity and whilst the excellent campers put their tent gadgets in order and brailed their tents for parental inspection, I laid out the cups and saucers and put on the kettle ready to make a bit-on-the-side to reproof the tents.

In the midst of it all a car came with someone hoping to see Father. It was Jack Clay who had been the third member of the 1947 snow team. He had landed on Fête Day and missed the man he had come to see. He talked a lot about the snow experience we had both shared. 'Herbert was fifty,' he said. 'I'm that now!'

Age is a funny thing. It expects everyone else to look different. I look at my contemporaries, matronly, retired and grey and feel myself perpetually young. I find myself opening doors and carrying their luggage and treating them like old dears. They probably all feel the same. I'm sure Mother does. The person she is, is perpetually young. It's annoying to her that her body won't keep up with her intentions.

Because the swallows used the clothesline in front of the house we never took it down. We used to watch them from the other side of the pane. When the early morning sun caught the deep blue of their plumage they were exquisitely beautiful. Father loved them. I was sitting by the window, watching them preen themselves on the line, on that traumatic Sunday. All trace of the camper badge weekend had gone. The yard which had recently been a jumble of cars and kit, tents and campers, was empty. I was eating a solitary snack, thinking about the Land Rover gently ticking away the miles, heading for home.

Suddenly it was in the yard and Margaret was stepping out of it in a daze having taken the fast road and driven quicker than she had ever done before. Father was ill, in terrible pain. Margaret had wanted to drive into the hospital but the old man had insisted on coming straight home. He seemed to think it important to see his home again, to know that his family was reunited and that all was well.

So Margaret had agreed to bring him home first and telephone the doctor from The Currer. The pain had started twenty-four hours ago and had become increasingly severe all the way home. On arrival he was really too ill to appreciate more than that the journey was over safely and now he could just think about himself and how to get rid of the awful pain.

The doctor came quickly, diagnosed a very enlarged prostate gland and rang for an ambulance to take him to hospital. This was a new experience.

Although Auntie Janie's death had shocked us all it had not depleted the family at The Currer. That had remained intact, as indestructible as the atom had once seemed to be. As I accompanied Father to hospital in the ambulance, retracing the road along which they had all come home, I was frightened. Father was an old man. He had exceeded his three score years and ten by an additional eight. He was heading, I felt sure, for major surgery and he had had no recent check-up to give us any indication as to the condition of his heart and lungs.

'He's always led an active life,' I thought. 'He gave up smoking ages ago, regretting ever having started. He's just had a restful holiday, in sunshine, in such beauty as can only be found in quiet places. He has risen and slept at will, eaten only what he wanted, lazed long hours in the sunshine at Carrisdale and Bayvallich. No one can have had a more excellent pre-operation period!'

The ambulance man drove very slowly, fearing to jar a back which was giving the old man such agony. I could see Margaret following behind in the still-laden Land Rover. The journey seemed interminable.

The presence of the gentle nurses on our arrival, the lack of panic, the unique atmosphere of confidence, made everything seem secure and controlled. Within a very short time the terrible pain was relieved with a catheter and Father was his own, normal, optimistic self. The miracle of medicine leaves me spellbound. Shortly we were able to leave him in safe hands and rush home to tell Mother that the pain had gone.

The decision to operate was taken next day when his heart and lungs were found to be in good condition. During visiting hours we found him confident and calm, full of praise for the nursing staff, the doctors and the cook. He was interested in the X-rays and the tests he had been subjected to and we were extremely proud of him.

It was five o'clock next day before the news came that the operation was over and that he had returned to the ward. Two hours later, leaving Margaret with all the feeding to do herself, Mother and I were waiting impatiently at the ward entrance for visitors to be allowed through. We sat silently beside his bed, in the small room off the ward, for almost an hour, watching the steady drip and praying for a safe recovery. He looked very old without his teeth.

To whom do people pray, to whom do they turn when in trouble if they do not acknowledge a caring God? Is prayer instinctive in man or only to those who believe? I know that when we need help, as Margaret said when Father was so ill, we must weary whatever divinity there is with our constant calling.

On our return home, within the circle of our hearth, the four talked of Father's devotion to his family. There was never one time he went out alone for pleasure. No pub, no hobby, nothing had tempted him away from the pleasure of his home. He had given us everything he had with absolute trust. Our Old Man's faith in us was as strong as his faith in God. He took a risk few people should take, for human beings are not infallible and human life is insecure. It took us a long time to realise that and place our inheritance in more secure hands than human ones.

Father had taken his philosophy into hospital with him and was determined to get well. If what we have done and the road down which we have gone has been the right one, his time to leave the plough he had set his hand to had certainly not come. There was only one point in our history at which Father could die. He timed it exactly right, dear gallant old man. Somehow or other he had to pick himself up and battle on with a terminal illness for another four years, in order to meet his Maker at exactly the right moment to leave his daughters secure. Neither we nor he knew that, of course.

He was determined to obey all instructions, take all the prescribed tablets and get well as quickly as he could. The weather was glorious and Mother took her sunshiny presence every day and twice every weekend. She almost ran up the stairs to the ward. When we were not there, Father spent long hours thinking up things we could do for the nurses and the other patients. I remember that Mother baked four sets of biscuits, to fill a huge tin with an assortment to satisfy his whim that the nurses should have homemade cookies for their mid-morning coffee. He promised lifts home to visitors of other patients in the ward who had no transport. We often had to make a detour to drop off a grateful wife. 'Don't thank us,' we'd say, 'It's the old man who thinks up all these things.'

Home once more, watching his beloved swallows and issuing daily orders about his garden, he seemed rejuvenated in mind and, we hoped, in body. His life appeared to have been enriched by the new experience, in a place where, for a month, he had seen miracles wrought each day. He had seen joy and courage and dedication. Sermons are preached in many places other than the pulpit.

For a little while we thought that we would be able to continue with our summer plans. Hazel wasn't intending to come to camp for her summer was to be a busy one.

We asked the nurses and the doctors, 'Can we take this old man on holiday?'

'Take him anywhere he wants to go,' they said.

So we planned accordingly but, at the last minute, we reluctantly decided it could not be. The risk was too great. Fifty children were too demanding and the strain on all of us would tell. We cancelled the bookings and Margaret tried to grin and bear it. I wondered who on earth I was going to get to replace her. I need not have worried for, as soon as she knew, Hazel rang. 'I can come the first week and Pat Roberts will come the second,' she promised. How fervently I thanked God for them both. It seemed that whatever the ups and downs, camp in the Hebrides was to be continued *ad infinitum*.

The weather, during the second week, was very bad. The newly proofed tents did not leak but the gales, which tormented us daily, snapped the ridgepoles and ripped the canvas. We knew they would have to be replaced or camping in the Hebrides must come to an end. But gales are fun and wet camps a challenge. A unique and happy breed, these Yorkshire children wedded to the Hebrides.

Chapter Seventeen

L ess active physically, Father's brain began to work overtime and he organised us all to greater and more productive activity.

'We need a Jersey cow,' he decided.

Margaret contacted the old Irishman and asked him to buy her a Jersey heifer. The spring and autumn calving had presented us with no still-born calf to release a cow to provide the house-milk. We hated to fetch it from the village, bottled and tampered with. Jersey milk is rich in cream and we saw a future with plenty of butter and cream cakes.

The Irishman, with all the charm and courtesy of his fellow countrymen, arrived with Joanna and we fell immediately in love with the golden princess.

'Give me a hand whilst I milk her?' my sister said, shortly after tea. Margaret's cattle can easily be bribed with a bucket of corn and cows previously milked for the house had not been tied. They stood meekly over a bucket be it placed in the yard, laithe porch or barn. They were equally willing to be milked in paddock, meadow or moor.

Joanna was different. She mistrusted our intentions and was completely uninterested in a bucket of corn.

'Start as we mean to go on,' I suggested. 'Milk her in the mistal. Tie her. She'll have been tethered before.'

With great difficulty we persuaded that lovely animal into a position where we could slip a rope over her head and push the toggle through the loop. She stood back in the stall with her hind legs in the groop so that the halter tightened uncomfortably round her neck and her frightened eyes grew vacant.

'You want rid of some of this milk,' Margaret told her, gently touching the full udder and pulling up the up-turned bucket which served as a milking stool.

We learned at once that Joanna could kick. She not only knew how to upset the bucket, she knew how to place her foot fairly and squarely in it. I gripped the chine nerve which runs along the spine but, try as I might, I seemed unable to immobilise the legs. She gave no warning.

The up-skittled bucket and my sprawling sister were fast becoming routine. Every half pint of milk we managed to save, we emptied into a bowl on the cobwebbed windowsill. Much more ran in a grey stream down the groop.

Margaret began to accuse me of being ineffective, so I grabbed Joanna by the neck, forcing her head into the air, murmuring endearments into her ear and scratching the bump on her Jersey crown. The inevitable still happened. A short period of deceptive stillness, then WHAM, bucket and sister were sprawling on the floor.

'It's your fault,' she said accusingly in my direction. So we changed places. She endeavoured to prevent Joanna's kicks from being effective and I spent my time alternately emptying small drops into the bowl and picking myself up dirty from the floor. We spent a whole hour barely getting enough milk to colour the breakfast tea let alone cover the porridge. We were thoroughly disillusioned about Jersey cows.

Early next morning we hoped that there had been a miracle overnight and that Joanna would want relieving of her two gallons of milk. But no, there was a repeat performance in every detail. I was in a hurry, however. Whatever happened I must be at school on time.

In the evening we tried different tactics. For a little while they worked. I lifted the honey-coloured head on my shoulder and with my mouth close to her ear, I began to sing. Few people have appreciated my singing. Certainly Joanna found my singing arresting and distracting. My Gaelic rendering of the Eriskay Love Lilt filled the low beamed mistal, and Margaret fairly made the milk splash into the pail.

'Be quick,' I croaked, 'I can't keep this up for long.' The milk we poured through the muslin-lined sieve filled the bowl to the brim. We were heady with success and helpless with laughter.

Next morning I was as hoarse as a crow and Joanna was not to be deceived twice. The opera had taken her by surprise. She had had time to think about it and had decided we had taken advantage of her. We spent another frustrating session, more often than not on the floor and the school children sang, 'I love God's tiny creatures,' with no help from me.

We decided that we were getting nowhere and that, much as we hated the idea of resorting to a rope, there was no other way but to tie her legs together or sooner or later one of us was going to be maimed. This was easier said than done, for she had satin-smooth legs down which the rope slipped as easily as if she were wearing silk stockings. Tying and re-tying that rope was time-consuming and it took us close on an hour, each session, to extract our daily pinta.

We thought of the millions of people all lifting their bottles from the step with no more exertion than it takes to walk to the kitchen door; of the house-wives, everywhere, who transfer their pound of butter from the shop fridge to the supermarket trolley with only a fraction of the effort it took us to milk, sieve, skim the ripened cream, churn it into butter, salt and wash and pat it into shape, but we felt no envy. Joanna posed us a challenge.

As the days went by we could no longer leave her in the paddock. She had to be allowed to join the herd even though it often meant an extra hour, each night, finding her and forcing her home. When she was within sight of the homestead she suddenly got the message and began to gallop and leave us far behind. We dared not let her go in the evening for there was little enough time before school.

Great-Uncle Tom had once been heard to say, 'Ah luv yer, damn yer!' This was the emotion we felt for Joanna. Frustration and, believe it or not, a growing affection.

Then Nature took a hand. The lovely Jersey heifer had been reared on lowland pastures and the sudden, exciting emigration to a hill farm was a shock to her delicate nervous system. She foolishly ran up the hillside every morning to join the herd. The exertion, the Pennine air and her neurotic disposition made her sudden prey to a vigorous virus. The vet confirmed Margaret's diagnosis. Joanna had pneumonia.

She was shut in a warm but airy shed and nursed with loving devotion. She was too ill to kick when Margaret milked her twice daily. She stood, miserably wheezing, poor, gorgeous Joanna. Her milk yield dropped by a half and the whole household was in a state of anxiety. When the crisis was over and she was well again, she had become unafraid of us. When the wheezing stopped she was relaxed enough to sample the proffered corn. She soon became addicted to it and was a cunning thief who would have eaten until she killed herself if she had not been discovered in time.

The wet weather I had experienced in the Hebrides was not reflected on the mainland. The summer following Father's operation was the hottest we could remember. The earth became parched and the grass shrivelled. The watercourses began to dry up and the reservoirs to drop below the safety mark. We were building a stone wall at the low end of the Dutch barn ferrying stone from a flattened wall along the top of the first intake.

We were scantily clad in shorts and sleeveless shirts and we were roasting. We filled the trailer with as much stone as it would hold and then pulled it alongside the growing new wall, so that we could use the trailer as – a platform. I built the wall and Margaret mixed the cement and heaved it up to me.

We thought the weather would never break. We were praying for rain but there seemed none in sight. Then, one day, we were sweating on the job at the top of the first intake and talking about Father's operation, about faith and what life is all about. There is no better view than the one afforded by the wall at the top of the first intake. Richard Leach must have seen it and the monks of Rievaulx who built the intake walls in the fourteenth and fifteenth centuries. They too must have looked up the Aire Gap towards the flat top of Ingleborough, so often etched on the skyline fifty miles away.

With the sun still blistering down on us, we heard a great din. A cloud had appeared and it was easy to identify the source of the din. Rain was bouncing off the tin roofs of our sheds only a quarter of a mile away. It seemed a long time that we stood listening in thankfulness to the volley on the corrugated sheets before the deluge reached us. When it did we stood joyfully under the welcome downpour, glad to be saturated, then, beginning to feel decidedly uncomfortable, we jumped into the jeep and drove it blindly home. Its wind-screen wipers had long since ceased to function and it had no roof. There was a hole in the floor and friends often asked for a parachute before daring to get in.

One of the most backbreaking, blistering, time-consuming of the summer jobs is thistling. Out-wintering cattle poach the gateways and pigs root and wherever there is sixpenny worth of bare earth the thistles will grow.

We must expect this for Father said it was poor land which would not grow them. There was an old, blind Irishman, he said, who had gone to buy a farm with his son and told the young man to tie the horse to a thistle. When answered, 'But there are no thistles,' the shrewd old man had declined to buy the farm.

So we must expect a few but a plague of them will come if they are not kept under control. The mower at hay-time hews them down before they seed but those in the pastures tend to spread. So, every year, come July and August, Operation Thistles has priority over most things. Being away at school all day and not being as single-minded about them as Margaret, I've done but the mouse's share. She has hacked away, day after day, all day, with a long-handled cutter until even her calloused hands have blistered.

I seriously believe there must be a cure for some fatal disease to be found in thistles for why else would God make so many and why draw man's attention to them so?

Close on the heels of the thistling comes the dragging out of the ragwort, that poisonous plant which would be, perhaps, eliminated if others, in partic-ular the local councils, were as conscientious as Margaret. Alas, the road verges are yellow in August. I have seen Margaret stop the Land Rover, fill sacks from the banking and trespass onto other farmer's fields to pull it out before the errant seeds could blow over our wall. Eaten by cattle it is poisonous but fortunately most leave it severely alone. They do die of it, though, and, as it spreads like wildfire, Margaret is not having it on her land. Dragging it out by the roots is a hard and heavy job and she tackles it usually before breakfast. There have been times when we have taken as many as a score of sacks to the Council tip. I believe the seeds travel on the prevailing wind up the wide sweep of the Aire Gap.

It was not the common practice to have a September break in the school year but a temporary re-shuffling of holidays gave us one God-sent week. I bought a copy of Britain's Best Holidays and, incredibly, there was an advertisement for a holiday cottage just about two miles away from where Jean lived in Northumberland. It seemed an omen. Where could there be a safer place to go with a convalescent old man whose medication seemed to be far too dehydrating?

I phoned Jean immediately. The cottage belonged to a friend of hers. If it were still vacant she was to secure it. It was. But we had a problem. The Sherriffs could not come to caretake for us as Barbara's mother was in hospital. Margaret said, 'Let's go up onto the top road. If we walk towards the village perhaps we may see someone who could help.'

We saw the home of the man who, when young, had been the hired hand in Grandfather's day. He would be able to milk Joanna. The autumn calves had not been bought and the buying could be delayed. We wondered if he would be willing to go down to The Currer for a week. He shook his head. Old men prefer their own hearth, but his son and his wife and their four children might really enjoy it. Strange how, when you really want things, you can mostly make them happen.

So we headed northwards as quickly as we could. We had a very fragile old man in the front seat. We did not know how well he would travel but his face was wreathed in smiles and all holiday he was singing, 'I'm so happy, oh so happy, don't you envy me?'

It was nearly dark when we arrived at Fenwick where tea was waiting for us. It was comforting to relax by Jean's fire knowing that all week she would not be far away. She escorted us down to Fenham, over the railway crossing to the row of farm cottages. The curtains were not drawn in one and the reflection of flames danced around the walls. Inside everything was warm and cosy and exactly what we needed.

We have to get away! Our life is otherwise far too demanding. A new project is always just round the corner. Father found our next one. He loved Fenham because it was a real working farm growing grain and raising beef. He was fascinated with the piles of whole grain barley and the roller which flattened it to feed the herd. If we rolled our own barley, he argued, that would be a real saving.

As soon as he got home he phoned our neighbours who themselves had a roller and told them to get us a second-hand one at the earliest possibility. They located one almost immediately and we had a discussion where to put the bin. The loft was the ideal answer but a bin there would hold sixteen tons and the roller and Margaret would be underneath it. The new inner wall of stone was supporting it but we dared not take the risk without further reinforcement.

We had a lot of charred beams salvaged from a fire. We were always scavengers for wood. We had collected floorboards from the hospital when it was pulled down in favour of the new Airedale General, from the isolation hospital when scarlet fever and smallpox, typhoid and diphtheria became a thing of the past and from the building which had once been the town workhouse. We have timbers and doors from the village church of St Barnabas.

Wherever there was demolition in those building-crazy years, there we were, stepping over the debris looking for wood, and sinks and canteen kitchen equipment.

We took several loads of wood from the back street in front of the Drill Hall whilst volunteer cadets of the Duke of Wellington Territorial Regiment lined the pavement and watched. They just stood there, open-mouthed, whilst two women, one only five feet tall and one a headmistress, staggered under the weight of the thick timbers, clambered onto the Land Rover bonnet and hurled them onto the roof. They watched whilst we roped the charred spillikins and stared at our blackened hands and faces, our filthy shirts and trousers. They stood there, on the pavement, not three yards away, immaculate in uniform, rosy-cheeked and newly shaven and I could have rubbed all their noses in the soot. One would expect Margaret, because of her size and gender, to get many offers of help. I expect fewer for, perhaps I look like a headmistress and therefore unapproachable. Neither of us get many!

Margaret has often been mistaken for a child. The five-year-old in the cottage next to us at Fenham wanted to know, 'Are you a little boy or a girl?' She was still being offered half-fare on buses long after she was twenty. I remember one occasion we laughed all the way home.

Our Land Rover specialist lives about nine miles away by road but only six as the crow flies. It is very poorly serviced by an hourly bus which misses it by half a mile. One day we took the station wagon in for some fault and were asked to leave it overnight. There are three ways of getting home without wheels. One is to take the trolley bus into the city from which there is a frequent service for the ten-mile journey to the town and a half-hourly service to the village. Another is to walk half a mile and hope it is about the right time for the hourly bus to pass and that it will connect with the half-hourly one home. Alternatively one can walk the six miles. We opted for the last. We turned up our collars, put Shep on a piece of binder twine and set off home.

The road passes through two villages and apparently so does a bus. We saw it standing on the outskirts of the first village. We ran frantically towards it. I was first, for Margaret was tripping over Shep's improvised lead. I jumped aboard and held it up whilst Margaret and the dog clambered in. Breathlessly I blurted out, 'Two an' a dog.'

'Nay,' said the driver/conductor from his seat at the wheel. 'The little fella can't be more than thirteen.' We kept dissolving into hysterics all the way home.

We used the charred beams to reinforce, satisfactorily, the loft. We doubled the uprights on the cowstalls and we put in many extra cross beams. Then we wrote off for eight bin sides. They were ideal, eight foot by six foot and very heavy so we had to get our neighbours to help manhandle them onto the loft. We lined them with hardboard to seal joints and cracks and a hole was put in the floor to allow the grain to slip into the roller.

The first loads of barley went into the bin in remarkably short time. They cost over a thousand pounds but this was so considerably less than rolled barley that Father was tickled pink. At first it did not seem too hard a task to place on an already bending back but then Margaret began to fatten cattle instead of selling stores, feeding more and more corn. She began mixing in molasses and this was time-consuming. Rolling the day's corn took longer and longer and the dust began to settle on her chest so that she acquired a little cough which fixed her whereabouts like the clock the crocodile swallowed in Peter Pan. Lying in bed worrying about her because she had still not come to bed and the midnight chimes had long since gone, I was glad when I heard the cough come to the back door.

The cattle loved the rolled barley and fought to get the most. Margaret's life was often in danger. I have seen her enter the lions' den with a sack and have completely lost sight of her in the mêlée, and I have seen her literally walking on the backs of a row of eating animals to escape being trodden on. We were constantly striving to plan mangers which could be approached without actually entering the shed. Some we managed but the sheds had not been built with that in mind. Doors were in the wrong places. They housed more cattle than the mangers would cater for and we had to put in portable ones. To empty corn into these was a nightmare. Things were so bad that Margaret would come and tell Father, 'I've fed the bullocks,' or 'I've finished the bottom shed,' and 'I've done the corn.' After this he would relax and know the real danger was over. Father was always happiest if I were out with her. He alone knew how difficult her job was.

All winter I milked Joanna. In the velvety darkness of early morning and late evening I approached her door, calling her full name, its abbreviation, Jo, or any other endearment inspired by the weather or my mood.

She took her time. Within the darkness of the shed she responded slowly and I leaned on the door post waiting, inhaling the rich smell of penned cattle, listening to their heavy breathing and the groaning of their full bellies.

No bullock moved but within the darkness appeared the luminous circle of her nose and the bright, liquid blue of her eyes. She stepped carefully round her sleeping companions until she reached the door where she became animated with the smell of corn. She pushed past me quite disrespectfully and began to run towards the lighted rectangle of the mistal door, tossing her head with exaggerated impudence. She entered importantly, upsetting buckets and scattering the cats. They leapt on a bale of hay to wait patiently in the sure knowledge that, when the milking was done, I would fill their bowl with the froth before taking the bucket indoors.

Joanna's nose would disappear into the corn and I would secure the rope which tethered her to the stall that had separated cattle for four centuries. She had the softest udder in the county for, after washing, I applied a little expensive hand cream, she and I being ladies, of course.

She ate greedily and in complete silence and immobility. The rich Jersey milk thudded into the pail and the froth rose. When the corn was done, the arrogant, determined look came back into her eye and without the tether she'd have gone. Immediately it was released she would trample on me or anything to get out quickly. The taming of Joanna was as complete as it would ever be. She lived to rule the herd and us for many years.

I was, and still am, the early riser. But I go to bed first and Margaret will only very seldom wake me. If I wake and she is not there I get up and can be seen running across the yard in my nightgown shouting, 'Are you all right?' Nearly always she is cross for my shouting disturbs a sleeping herd. Just occasionally she is in a pickle and is very glad I have come. More infrequently, when a catastrophe such as a water pipe flying off a T-junction occurs, she comes to waken me. I can think of nothing worse than a burst water pipe thrusting a jet of cold water all over cattle and manure and us in the dead of night. Once the pond overflowed and we were fighting to prevent it from flooding the sheds till nearly dawn and many is the time we have been nailing loose tins down in the teeth of a northwesterly gale. Because we have grown so used to disturbed nights with sheds and tents, animals and Harry, Margaret and I can re-sleep the moment our heads touch the pillow. A valuable skill indeed!

It would have been futile to speculate on how many times we opened the door for Bess. There was a time when we thought she was going to die. She lay exhausted in her basket unable to give birth to a stillborn litter. Fearfully, Margaret carried her to the vet in the Land Rover. He performed a somewhat tardy caesarian section and handed her back unconscious. We were torn with anxiety but after a few days she was streaking across the moor again.

As the years went by she lost her hearing completely. She did not respond when we called nor warn us of visitors at the door and neither the noisy corn roller nor the vacuum cleaner brought any response. On the coldest of mornings she would bark for re-admittance yet stand with her back to the door. She never heard it open, or my calls. Still barefoot and in my dressing gown, I often stepped out into the rain or snow to nudge her rear and inform her that she had been answered.

Bess was retired honourably. Being less active she put on weight. She was almost a fixture on the rug before the Aga and rarely did more than stagger into the yard a couple of times a day. She seldom crossed it to the garden and only ventured farther afield when accompanying elderly members of the family whose pace more nearly matched her own. If she were foolish enough to follow Margaret and Shep and the young dog, Floss, she had to be carried home a sadder and wiser dog, deeply humiliated and annoyed.

The vet diagnosed a failing heart. Dutifully my sister embedded the red capsules in each evening meal and I swept them up with the vacuum cleaner next morning for she invariably spat them out believing she knew better than her physician.

The first time that Bess 'died' we assumed that she had had a heart attack and allowed her to pass away peacefully in her basket by the stove. For four days she lay unconscious, untroubled by the world still going on around her. Frequently we bent over her to see if she was still breathing. The slight heaving of her hair was almost imperceptible. But on the Sunday evening, when the old folks were seated round the fire watching Songs of Praise on the television, and I was marking children's essays at the kitchen table, Bess lifted her head and looked at me.

I called and Margaret came at once offering food and water and affection. Surprisingly when Auntie Mary put on her coat, on the following Sunday, Bess was well enough to accompany her. She did not fully recover. Her head was on one side and her gait was a little unbalanced so that when she walked she went a little off course and missed the stiles and gateways. She was a very old lady but her feeble bark was a Royal Command. Every one of us became her willing slave.

Operation Tents began in November with a vengeance. We had to have the sleeping tents replaced before next camp. The weather of 1975 had given them a beating and I dared not risk so many children on an island with imperfect shelter. So we began several months of concentrated moneymaking on a scale we had never attempted before. In October we had taken in the blackberry harvest and now we began selling over a hundred pounds of jam at coffee mornings and the Christmas Fayre along with homemade cakes and toffee.

I bought the ex-hire tents from Blacks with a down payment and as the funds to buy them came so the instalments were paid. That winter and spring of 1975/76 we made over a thousand pounds.

The Carol Service at school had become an annual institution. It was performed before a packed audience of parents and friends, on the Tuesday before Christmas and we all loved every minute of it. The tableau of Crib and children was a spectacle which brought tears to more eyes than mine. I am sure no children could sing more joyfully than ours. Most of them had lovely voices but we never separated the grunters from the nightingales so the tune was never quite pure. The infants were the principals in the Nativity. The naughtiest became angels and the least intelligent ended up as wise men.

The collection invariably went to the local Sue Ryder Home. Toys were bought for Santa's sack at the Brownies' annual Christmas Party for mentally handicapped children and each child brought fruit offerings enough to fill two large boxes with oranges, apples, bananas and dates, nuts, grapes and tangerines.

Mother used to make a hundred mince pies and after the singing the children would have a feast.

On the following day the older boys and girls would stay in school for tea and then we would all crowd onto the bus for town carrying one of the big boxes of fruit. We would join the Guides on the chartered bus taking us to the Cheshire Home for our Gala Performance and the following day Guides and school children would take the second fruit offering to the local Blind Home and sing some carols. I outrageously used children to bring joy to the handicapped that alone I could not.

By the following March Father was very weak. At first we did not think he would reach their Golden Wedding on 5th April but the occasion came and was celebrated gently with the quiet dropping-in of people who cared. A few days earlier, Father had been attacked by a dreadful shaking fit and we had to send for the doctor as an emergency. When the dreadful spasm was over Father complained about his terrible dehydration and lifted the loose skin from his hand. It remained standing when he released it. 'Look how dried up I am,' he said.

The doctor advised him to take the water pill only every other day. The weather must have been frosty, for the doctor had left his car at the top of the hill and Margaret drove him back to the Moor Gate. She commented on Father's deterioration and the doctor said, 'Well, the prostate gland was malignant. A man your father's age could live four years. It is impossible to forecast.'

No one had told us of the severity of the condition. Father had asked the doctor, one day, "Ave Ah got cancer?' and the reply had been, 'No.' Thank God for a doctor who does not always think the truth must be told. We decided to keep the information a secret, too. If there was the remotest possibility that Father could have four years then we would see that he did.

On the days he did not take the water pill he felt a different man. Hazel and her doctor husband called in with Golden Wedding congratulations and Father told Ray how much better he felt on the day without the pill. 'Ask your doctor if you can leave it alone altogether for a few days,' Ray said.

Next day I was off to the doctor like a shot. He was cautious but Father was dying and there was nothing to lose. 'Never take your eyes off his feet,' he said. 'If they begin to swell, give him a pill.'

There was an immediate improvement in Father's health. Easter was late that year. Margaret was persuaded to take a holiday, to go up to Tiree for ten days in Hugh's cottage at Salum. We knew now how much Father had done right up to his operation: Margaret's job had almost doubled. I tried to give more time to the farm but selfishly we wanted to eat our cake and still have it. Work and weather and worry take their toll. Margaret asked a couple of friends to accompany her, but they could not stay the whole time. Freda's daughter Kathleen and her boy friend said they would sail out to join her for the last few days.

There was an anxious night on the eve of her departure for Father appeared to have a sudden relapse. Margaret spent the night in a sleeping bag outside his bedroom door, fully determined not to go. Her case wasn't packed and she hadn't had a bath.

I got up early and stepped over the sleeping roll. Father was awake. 'How d' you feel?' I asked.

'Better t'day than yesterday,' he said.

'What about Margaret?'

'She mun go,' he insisted.

I roused her. The train wasn't until 10.30 a.m. 'Get a bath. I'll pack your case. You're going.'

I was petrified of being left alone to cope but I forced myself to pack

Margaret's lightweight bag. If she didn't go I knew I must cancel camp and the beautiful new tents would never be used. If I couldn't be left, neither could she. When the case was put into the Land Rover Father was pulling on his coat. The flat cap usually went on at breakfast and remained there all day. 'Ah'm goin' t' see 'er off,' he announced. His face was a picture. Just like it always was when he was giving Mother just what she wanted.

Miraculously there were no problems. For the first few days Margaret saw winter on the island then came a sudden heatwave and she was swimming in the Atlantic. She came home sunburnt and refreshed.

During her absence I had taken the family out on several excursions. This rejuvenated Father was happy to sit in the Land Rover and meander along the country lanes looking for the signs of spring. I think he sensed that things were going to be a bit easier. He wasn't dead yet. You could see him thinking, 'Now what can we do?'

On one outing we passed a polythene greenhouse. The outer skin of plastic had been stretched over a tunnel of curved tubing. 'That's what we want!' he said. I think we'd have given him the earth if he had wanted it.

I wrote immediately to Lakeland Plastics for the DIY equipment to make one and our neighbours brought up some bendable tubing. Susan and Jane were practising for camper badge on the lawn and their help was needed to stretch the polythene tightly over the framework. Father couldn't wait and was already planting his seeds in boxes in the house. We all went over to a garden centre and bought lots of tomato plants and two cucumber ones.

We decided to forget what the doctor had said. Father was alive and comparatively well, he was coping with an unsuccessful operation and was full of good ideas. The greenhouse occupied him all summer. We never again repeated the bumper harvest of the first year when we collected something like three hundred pounds of tomatoes and eighty-nine cucumbers. What a wonderful opportunity this afforded Father of his hobby of giving things away. He never took another water pill. The remainder he threw in the sea off Holy Island!

Someone asked, 'Do you think your father would have approved of what you have done since?' There are no doubts about that. Father only ever wanted to share all that he had with other people.

There seemed nothing to prevent us taking him on holiday for the planned two weeks at spring bank. We could only book the Fenham cottage for one week. The second we booked on the other side of the country at Silecroft in Cumbria. Everywhere spring was at her most breathtaking. The unspoilt country above Morecambe Bay was decorated with May blossom, the hedgerows weighted down with hawthorn 'snow'.

The Silecroft cottage saw the birth of a new idea. It had recently been extended and a sun porch overlooked the sea. Father spent a lot of time sitting in it thinking we ought to do something similar with the blank wall of our sitting room. With an extension like that, overlooking the yard, he would be able to see nearly all the activity of the farm. The kitchen window gave him a view of the yard but an extension on the sitting room would give a better one and, in comfort, he would also be able to see the road climbing to the Moor Gate, the sheds and even some of his greenhouse and garden.

I spent a lot of time there too whilst the others did the shopping in Silecroft and Millom. The road to the cottage was a mile of potholed track which Father found very uncomfortable, so if the expedition were a short one, we stayed in the sun porch and waited for the others to return. The double-glazed windows of that sun porch mirrored whatever was on the cliffs. Gorse bushes were reflected and thrown onto the opposite window like a string of islands on the horizon. They could easily have been a mirage of the Long Island from Barra Head to the Butt of Lewis. So I sat and wrote a fantasy for my school children. I could not stop scribbling. It was an activity I had never indulged in before.

What a hot summer camp it was! We had worked all winter for new tents but in 1976 we could have gone without them and just slept on the Harris shore, under the stars. Without tents, however, we could never have survived the midges the heatwave inflicted on us every morning and night, but not a drop of rain fell on us all fortnight. We took Craig with us, that indomitable, courageous boy.

There is no need to go to Tibet or the Andes. Just go to Rheinigidale, that most remote of Britain's villages, approachable only by sea or by a green, exciting track over the mountain wastes of North Harris. Half of our party stayed at the foot of the Scriob, that precipitous, zigzag pathway which falls hundreds of feet to the shores of Loch Trollamarig and represents the halfway mark of the amazing journey. The villagers send their children to school up the Scriob every Monday and await their end of week return quite calmly. Incredibly they also drive their cattle along the track to the bull or the sale. I could never survive that ordeal. The postman makes a delivery on alternate days whatever the season or the weather and the housewives shop in Tarbert and carry home their stores.

What a place to live! We went for the first time on a boiling hot day in 1976. On reaching the Rheinigidale harbour, I remember the Guides stripping to bras and pants to swim in the cold waters. The village was asleep. I remember there were children sitting on a doorstep staring in utter bewilderment at our extrovert Guides.

That 1976 camp was a moving experience. Had Father's condition continued to deteriorate, it would never have been, so it was a luxury I had never expected. The weather was utterly beautiful. Hazel and Linda, Julie and Vivienne helped to make it a camp to remember and Paul, now a teacher, went to The Currer to help Margaret with the hay and the loneliness of responsibility shouldered alone.

'Write about it,' was the clamour, 'You must have a story to tell!' More than that I had a song to sing in praise of beautiful islands and isolated shores, of the hospitality of the Hebridean crofters and the activity and joy of the Yorkshire girls and boys whose good fortune it was to return year after year. I had a story to write in appreciation of children, their tolerance, resourcefulness and, above all, their cheerfulness.

Immediately I returned from camp I started to write, every day, a few minutes in the dinner hour, on the bus, at school on Thursdays before the Guide meeting and the words tumbled spontaneously from a grateful pen into a dozen exercise books. Hell Fire Jack was writing 'A Song to Sing and a Tale to Tell'. I didn't have to think, just to write.

Margaret was my most valuable critic, my reliable second memory. When I went exhausted to bed she sat up reading the typed sheets. Writing was easy, but typing was an ordeal.

Father sent for the plasterer who had done the work at The Currer nearly twenty years ago. We sat down together and discussed Father's idea of an extension to the sitting room which would let in the sunshine and provide a Royal Box from which he could view his domain. This time we felt that we must let a professional builder do the job for the wall, much of which would have to be taken away, was three feet thick at the foundation. In any case the laws concerning planning and building permission had tightened. This was no longer a job we could do ourselves.

One memorable Thursday during the winter of 1977, snow began to fall in the early afternoon, steadily at first, then very heavily. The children were excited, prefabricating excuses to go to the toilet and see how deep it was. At playtime they went wild in the yard and I didn't care how wet they became for they were due to go home in an hour and their mothers could do the drying. Beautiful, thick, white snow, it was, falling evenly in enormous, multi-crystalled flakes. There was no wind in the valley but, even so, it was bitterly cold.

When I thought they were exhausted, I rang the bell and, red-cheeked and happy, they gathered round the fire in the staffroom for whatever story I happened to be reading. I loved those warm, intimate story half-hours with Kenneth Grahame, Arthur Ransome and Louisa M. Alcott. How the children loved Nevil Shute's *Pied Piper*, Slavomir Rawicz's *The Long Walk*, Grey Owl's *Sago and the Beaver People* and Marjorie Kinnon Rawling's *The Yearling*.

At home time I told the Guides there would be no meeting and after they had all gone sliding and snowballing home, I went through my list of all those I could contact by phone, cancelling the meeting.

I cleared up in a hurry, fearing we were in for a heavy fall. I am over-diligent if I think there may be a disturbance of routine. I made doubly sure that all was tidy and ready for another day, then I went into the staff room and made my tea. No visiting children disturbed my peace.

I miss those lovely Thursday teas. Some child or other always bullied me into needing some frozen fish cakes from the village shop. It was a diversion to be able to scamper out of school on the important errand of buying Miss Brown's tea. I would switch on the Baby Belling and the electric fire and, in the over-heated room, I would pull up my desk to type my stories, write my letters or add up the farm accounts. In a fug of warmth and comfort I would eat my tea, plan the meeting or pull out the sewing machine to make another tent. Volumes of material would drape the floor and the clatter of the treadle would blanket the sound of footsteps coming towards the door. A visiting teenager would peep round the door. More often than not the caretaker would supplement my fishcakes with newly baked scones from his wife's cooling tray.

But no intrusion came on that day of heavy snowfall and at five o'clock I decided to go an hour early and give myself plenty of time to get to the Guide room to send home any 'who cares about snow' individual with a 'You must be crazy to come out on a night like this!'

The Land Rover was well covered with snow and beastly cold inside. Never mind, I told myself, in only twenty minutes I'll be at the Guide Room, lighting the Calor gas stove and burning a purple pattern on my shins. I smiled to myself, remembering a conversation I once heard between two children. 'Your mother is lazy,' one kept saying and the other child was adamant that she was not. 'She is,' insisted the first child, 'her legs are all burnt!'

There was a line of slow-moving traffic along the main road and some kind soul allowed me to enter it. The road was white with compressed snow and the traffic going in my direction moved at a snail's pace whilst oncoming traffic was passing quite happily at 25 m.p.h.

The crawling traffic came to a standstill long before the car heater had produced any warmth. I turned off the engine, for Land Rovers are heavy on petrol and pulled a rug from the back seat to tuck round a quickly cooling body. We began to move again, to move and stop, move and stop. The ten-minute journey of five miles took three hours. I could have walked it in half the time. The driver of an oncoming car said there was a traffic jam on every road uphill out of town so traffic had accumulated on the low roads. Drivers trying to get out of town were sliding all over the place and many were abandoning their vehicles. It required real discipline not to pull out from the line of traffic and pass them all. There must have been a great deal of bottled up frustration in the cars in front of me.

Eventually reaching town at eight o'clock, there was no point at all in continuing to the Guide Room. Any reckless female who had scorned to be beaten by six inches of snow would have stamped it off her heels and gone long ago.

I parked the car and headed for the telephone. A man was just vacating the kiosk and I asked him if he had any idea what the road home was like. He looked at me as if I were a fool who should know that the steep road would be impossible. 'Huh,' he said. 'Yer 'aven't an 'ope.' Nevertheless I decided to phone Margaret and let her know what was happening. 'What'll I do,' I said, 'Shall I leave the Land Rover here and walk or keep going until I stop?'

'There's only about twelve inches of snow,' she answered, 'Keep going until you stop. I'll come and meet you.'

I drove to the bridge at the bottom of the hill and a car was just coming down. I stopped it and asked the driver what it was like further up.

'You might be lucky,' he said. 'They've all abandoned their cars and gone home. They're all over the place but if you don't meet anyone you just might do it.'

A lady was beginning the climb on foot. 'Do you want a lift?' I called. She couldn't believe her good luck. She clambered in; I made sure of the four-wheel drive and we sailed up the hill with no problem at all. It was a piece of cake! It had taken three hours to do five miles on the low road. It took only minutes to do the one mile uphill. I sped along the flat at the summit, past the school and along the road to the Moor Gate. Margaret was just appearing out of the blizzard. There was a mighty wind on top and driving snow. Margaret threw her muck shovel into the back and clambered into the Land Rover. 'What do we do now?' I said.

'It's all downhill,' she answered. 'Keep going.'

Within half a dozen yards we came to a standstill in a two-foot drift. Quite undaunted we jumped out and Margaret began digging away the drift with her shovel. The snow was coming so fast we were instantly covered. The wind was appalling and the frost was sealing the Land Rover doors. My shoes sank in two feet of snow and I had nothing but sheer nylons to protect my legs. After a ten-minute struggle we feared exposure and gave up. I don't think I have ever been so cold. We abandoned ship and fought our way home. Exposure is not a thing to be treated lightly. We have had more experience of snow than most people in what is generally presumed to be a temperate climate. We have to work out of doors in falling and deep lying snow and we remain above the snow line long after the valley has become green but I have never been so cold as I was that Thursday night.

It was a hard winter. Margaret worked the farm virtually single-handed. We had reduced our pig population to a litter of weaners bought periodically from the local market and kept freely among the cattle in the sheds. The profit on pigs was reduced to an unviable minimum but Father liked to have some pigs on the place and he liked to give away pork so we allowed him his opportunity to do so. We used a small litter to restock our freezer. We hated the freezer-stocking days. Mrs Horner, my longest-serving dinner lady, and her husband would come and help.

She was a wonderful lady. Anyone who is a loyal member of the staff for eighteen years becomes much more than a colleague. To the children she was an institution. She was far too kind to them, loving and generous to a fault. The children leaned on her as a second mum. If one were in hospital a gift was always sent, if one were in trouble her lap was always available. We all knew her value to the school community and, being a member of the village, there was not one of her neighbours who did not know her worth. Like the rest of us she was never ill.

The work began on the extension to our sitting room shortly after Christmas. First the plans were professionally drawn. Then, when permission was granted and the weather began to improve, the foundations were dug.

Suddenly there were workmen all over the house for we were determined to install central heating at the same time.

One of Father's great pleasures in this new life he was leading was making cups of tea and coffee for workmen. He had the kettle on for their arrival and thereafter was always ready to supply the odd cuppas and the tea for the lunchtime break. We joked that the workmen were treated as well as Margaret's pigs. Mother was constantly employed making biscuits. Our old folks were having a bomb of a time.

There was a day when I had to hunt up an old tent to curtain the huge hole in the wall but, even so, the front room became an ice-box. The octogenarians were squeezed against the Aga in a kitchen so cluttered with furniture that they had to overlook chairs in order to watch the BBC news. But amid the clutter Mother baked, Father made the meals and Margaret struggled with the feeding of the cattle, watching the store of hay dwindle and hoping spring would be early. Don't we always!

Each morning I left the clutter and turmoil to find a tangible peace in school. There was a calm there which was almost autumnal. I marvelled at the seemingly undisturbable security and stability we knew there. Turmoil there might be elsewhere but for me, it seemed, there were no staff problems, no angry parents, no delinquent children. It did not seem possible that anything could go wrong.

Indeed, over everything there hung this feeling that everything was well. We persuaded Margaret to go to Harris for Easter. Father seemed exceptionally fit. The professional work, in what Mother called 'the New-Do', was completed. A warm spell came and we were able to let the autumn calves out to grass. They galloped round and round the Five Acre, tails flying. 'You must certainly go, Margaret,' we all said. We were all 'riding along on a crest of a wave'. Nothing could go wrong.

I have never been to Scotland in the early spring as Margaret has. I haven't walked through the April snow at Spean Bridge to spend the night with John and Cathy at Tigh-na-Coille. I haven't sailed to Skye against a backcloth of white capped mountains nor seen a normally barren Harris even more bald than usual or the machair bare of the myriads of summer flowers. Neither have I returned through the Highlands and seen the sun sparkling on the winter silver birches.

In Margaret's absence Bess 'died' for the second time. The old dog seemed restless and kept continually walking round the table.

'Felix kept on walking,' my mother said.

'She seems blind,' my father worried.

Exhausted, at last, she lay on the carpet and did not move for several days. We put a piece of plastic beneath her but she made no mess. Neither did she eat or drink. Each morning I expected to have to lift out her stiff form for burial in some clean place in the open air. But a few days before Margaret returned Bess began to recover and we, who were quite besotted with the nineteen-year-old animal, were overjoyed. She was even more unsteady and when she gave a little bounce, now and again, for she was a happy dog, she toppled right over. Thereafter she spent almost all day asleep on the rug before the Aga. Her aged bark was to become my alarm clock. It demanded that I arise at once or risk finding a pool on the carpet or the kitchen lino. Each morning she went out and in like a yo-yo, disturbing my breakfast with her restlessness.

She became a living legend, a symbol of our own courage and tenacity and we were willing to accept her occupation of the rug, her early morning demands and her occasional incontinence. We marvelled at her lop-sidedness, her incredible determination not to die.

But the heart is an unpredictable organ in man and beast.

Whilst Margaret was away we worked like Trojans to get everything shipshape for her return. The weather was good and the cattle were out to grass and caused no trouble other than a daily check and a few extra bales to stop them from scouring or getting staggers with too much new grass. I was determined to have lots to show for my break from school and energetically stripped paper from the sitting room wall and redecorated. The carpet-fitter promised to lay a carpet in the 'New-do' before Margaret returned. Father was busy planting his greenhouse and looking after Bess. Auntie Mary came for Easter. Margaret phoned to say Harris was lovely with snow on the hills. Everything seemed fine.

Then, on Easter Monday, Joan rang with the awful news that Winnie's husband had had a major heart attack and was in intensive care. For days we lived in fear. To distract myself I plunged more frantically into getting the clearing up done in the yard. The scaffolding was still against the newly built extension. I took it down, barrowed away the building rubble and swept the apron of concrete in front of the house. I used the rubble to pitch some of the remaining un-concreted area of yard and all the time I was agitated about Winnie's young husband fighting for his life. Mercifully there was steady improvement. Winnie was going to need some time off school and a supply teacher would be needed but I decided to wait until we were settled in after the Easter break. Joan and I could manage for a few days, absorbing the extra children into our classes.

Margaret came home with her cobwebs all blown away. She was full of news about everyone in Harris. With Winnie's husband on the mend things seemed on course again. The next day was Sunday, the day before school reopened. Around coffee time, Joan's son, Ian, phoned to say his father had had a heart attack, waiting for a cup of tea to be brought to the bedroom, and had died instantly.

We could not believe it! We were only just recovering from the shock of Winnie's ordeal. This was much, much worse. To have two members of my three-teacher staff suffer similar experiences within six days of each other was shattering. As soon as we could, Margaret drove me over to Joan's. I have never felt more sorry for anyone. She had planed a summer retirement. Jimmy had recently retired and a happy life had seemed just round the corner. Fortunately her written resignation had not been posted. 'Wait,' I begged her. 'Hang on a week or two.'

Margaret and I called at Winnie's on the way home; we all had a cup of coffee and wept together. I don't think I have ever felt sorrier for one colleague who had to accept finality whilst the other could continue to hope.

I re-opened school next day alone, I think. I can't really remember. We had a part-time teacher, Liz. Perhaps she came. It was her practice just to come in the afternoon. Mrs Crossley, my clerical assistant, supported me as much as she was able. Winnie asked for leave of absence but Joan came straight back after the funeral. The children she loved were the best therapy.

Somehow we tried to pick ourselves up and maintain some normality for the sake of the children. At home, Margaret and I picked up our sledge hammers and attacked the pitched rubble in the yard. We had no interest but forced ourselves into carting enough stone from elsewhere to finish filling in the perpetual mud which bordered the concrete square. When the job was completed we were surveying it and persuading ourselves that it needed time to settle before we concreted it. 'We'll wait till the autumn,' we said with unusual procrastination.

But Father opened a window of his new Royal Box and pointed to the still-present cement mixer. It had been left by the builder and any day he would come to collect it. Father screwed up his eyes. 'Y'ad better get it concreted before t' mixer goes.' We nearly threw something at him!

'Yer beggar!' I said, shaking my fist. We were both laughing, but he was quite serious and what he said made sense. It was just that we were pretty whacked and the thought of several loads of limestone chippings and a ton or two of cement and scores of square yards of concrete to lay was unexciting.

Margaret did most of it. I was struggling with a depleted staff and a strange atmosphere at school. Day after day, with only my evening and weekend help, Margaret threw grit into the mixer and the yard area grew to three times its size.

One day a cousin's wife came and saw Margaret carrying water, shovelling in grit and barrowing concrete to the remote corner she was currently laying. 'Oh,' said the cousin's wife, 'Do you only do it a square at a time?' It was usually men who got our goat!

My! were we proud of that yard! The mud had all gone. It would last forever. Suddenly we felt extravagant. We ordered a load of ready mix and laid the entrance to the yard between the gable end of the barn and the bullock shed. That would be easy, we thought but to lay a whole load of quick-setting ready-mix, before it does so, is the hardest work I know. Not a minute has to be wasted, the heap won't go down quickly enough and there is a danger of a mountain, an immovable one, being left in the road.

No mud! It was a miracle. Gillian had come to school one day and she had written in her News Book. 'Me mam washed ah Harry's nappies and they fell in the cow muck.' Snap, I had said. Now when we hung out the washing there was no mud below.

The children wrote such funny things in their News Books. 'I was naughty in the launderette last night,' Helen confessed.

'When me mam goes to work at night I can hear a lady talking in our front room,' was one observation.

'My daddy is a twist,' wrote Margaret whose father worked in the textile industry.

Teaching children was far from boring. On cold days we would supervise the children in the playground from the warmth of the infant classroom window. We had a very small playground and almost all of it could be seen. A knock on the window immediately attracted attention. On these days a child would invariably be leaning on the radiator alongside us, sometimes reading to Joan, sometimes just talking.

'I know how sausages are made,' said four-year-old Duane after an afternoon of modelling. 'Vey mek 'em wiv plasticine.'

His observation was quite serious. He followed it with another but this time his eyes twinkled as if his knowledge amused him. 'An' do yer knaw what fish fingers a' med from? Birds' legs!' We did not correct him. Legs do not offend. If he'd associated them with Bird's Eyes he'd never have eaten them.

One bright little girl, Nicola, thought it was much more fun to talk to the teachers than go outside on cold days so, bursting with robust health, she said she hadn't to play outside, her mother had said so. We allowed her one indoor play-time but told her that she must bring a note from her mother. She handed in a note, next day, which said, 'Nikky 'as to stay in cos she is porly.' It was written in the five-year-old's hand but we decided to accept it, for the day promised to be fine and warmer than of late. Sure enough, when the mid-morning break came we all went outside. Nicola was preparing to do so too but we reminded her of the letter and said we were sorry but if Mummy said she must stay in then we couldn't let her play outside. She brought no more letters.

One very hot day Duane's mother came about half an hour after school to ask me if her five-year-old had taken his clothes off at school. Children often took off their shoes in the playground, their jumpers were peeled frequently and on hot days shirts would come off too. But we always insisted bare skin was covered when the children came into their classrooms for the going-home story.

'If he took his shirt off during play-time,' I said, 'he put it back on for story.'

'I'm not just talking about his shirt,' the irate mother said. 'He hadn't a stitch on when he came home! Not even his underpants!'

I went with her to retrace his steps. We found each discarded, separate article of clothing thrown by the wayside all the way home. I did not wait to see what happened after Mum opened the door and went inside.

Amanda was very determined that she would never admit that she really did like school. She took a long time to settle in and her favourite word was 'wotten'. School was wotten, the children were wotten, dinners and lessons were wotten and the teachers probably came into that category too though she never left Joan's side and spent all her spare time in the staffroom. She began to really enjoy school and laughed and sang and cavorted about in Movement. After a really good day we would say, 'What are you going to tell Mummy tonight?'

'It's wotten!' was the only answer mother ever got.

We taught various members of a Travelling family. When asked to bring a reply from home, Joe told us, 'Us Travellers don't write notes.' His five-year-old brother told us, 'Us w' baggin' an' 'awkin' on Sat'day, Miss Brown.'

'How did you do that?' I wanted to know.

'Well,' he replied, 'Yer knock on a door and say, Hoss muck, Missus, fifty pence a bag. Two bags fer a pound.'

Father seemed capable of living a fairly normal life provided certain adjustments were made. We decided that it might be an idea to hire a Dormobile for a return to Fenham. This quiet spot, overlooking Lindisfarne, was just right for us. With a travelling house for our day trips to Bamburgh, Pease Bay or Alnmouth we felt most of our problems would be solved. With the roof raised, the dinner cooking on the small stove, the comfortable seating round the table and our own, private toilet facilities, what could be more luxurious?

The five of us and Auntie Mary set off north as happy as sandboys. It was the Queen's Silver Jubilee and flags were flying all along the route. We felt like royalty ourselves. We had the freedom to pull into any lay-by and brew up.

Knowing that speed was no longer a necessity we abandoned the high road and meandered along the byways, through sleepy little villages with their waving bunting, across moorland and through forests. Let the conservationists worry about the south. The north country is almost all natural countryside.

We returned once more to the Fenham cottage with its view of Holy Island castle and its abundance of waterfowl on the mud flats. Each day we drove the odd few miles to a sandy beach. On the day of the Silver Jubilee we watched the London celebrations on Jean's colour TV, a luxury we had never been able to afford at The Currer.

There were some lovely hot days, and lying on the hot sand, listening to the breakers crashing on the shore, I did a lot of daydreaming. Frequently my thoughts flew back to Joan, so recently and so suddenly bereaved. How important it is to get every ounce out of life and to put everything you have into it, for it is an unforgiving minute and what you do not do you may never do.

From my bed on the hot sand I would frequently glance up at Mother and Father, side by side like two little robins in their brown, quilted anoraks. I was so glad that the doctor had not told Mother the severity of Father's illness so that she could behave quite normally. Never anticipate illness, the form it will take or how it will end. For us the years after Father's operation were infinitely happy.

I wondered about Joan and it occurred to me that she might like to accompany us to camp in the summer. We were returning to Tiree. I couldn't keep away with the children any longer. I knew there would be no Calum and therefore no shop and no barn. A shop we can do without but shelter on a windswept island is necessary even if it is never used. Water is necessary, too, and we had taken from Calum's tap.

Margaret's visit to May and Hugh's cottage had presented the solution. Supposing we rented it, we would have shelter, cramped admittedly, but adequate in an emergency. The water supply there was good and not too far to carry.

From the grass verge outside the Fenham cottage, I wrote to Joan asking her if she would like to come with us and occupy the cottage. It was the best medicine I could think of.

The last half of the summer term was coloured inevitably by the Silver Jubilee. On a memorable morning, Joan and I and a group of excited children, joined the coach taking representatives from all the local schools to the stadium at Elland Road, to see the Queen. Nothing, absolutely nothing I have ever done with children has thrilled me more than being with those tens of thousands of cheering boys and girls in the spectators' stand for their Jubilee tribute to Her Majesty. According to the media, the good lady had never had a greater, more amazing reception.

The arena was filled with children occupying themselves with activity. There were Scouts and Guides, Sea Cadets and Boys' Brigade. There were gymnasts and athletes. Every healthy activity performed by young people was demonstrated on that football pitch. But it was not the entertainment which moved me but the noise of those thousands of spectators yelling, 'We want the Queen! God save the Queen!' The spontaneity of it was overwhelming. For every few children there was a teacher and every teacher had been told to discourage chanting but nothing could have quelled the surge of vocal joy which swept through the arena. It was a tide of ecstasy which no one could have controlled.

Activity is a diet young people love. One cool, bright day, every year, was the schools cross-country run in which almost every child took part. The run was twice round a traditional circuit so that any who wished to drop out after the first lap could do so easily. I remember carrying a crying Craig off the track after one completion of the course, crying not because he had fallen so many times on the first lap but because I would not let him attempt the second. The courage of that child amazed me and so did his strength, angrily fighting my refusal to let him kill himself.

During the last week of the summer term we always held a survival test. The really keen competitors would equip themselves with a survival kit complete with plastic bag, cooking utensils and basic rations. The more bumptious of the boys bragged loudly for a whole week about their certain skill in firelighting and cooking. At playtimes and over the dinner table I heard them declare supreme confidence in their ability to cope. I did not stop them. A certain amount of self-confidence is a necessary part of character building. Bragging is a different matter but consequences put a curb on that for the higher you build your own pedestal the further you have to fall.

'Cor, 'S's easy.'

'Ah can light a fire. 'S nowt.'

The quieter children would be silent as befits anyone who does not really know. I allowed them to organise the afternoon themselves. Surreptitiously I packed my own rucksack with the things I knew they would forget.

"Eck, Ah've forgotten me tin-opener,' was an annual cry.

'Aw, blumming 'ummer, Ah 'an't gor any matches!' was another and always from someone who had been an arrogant so-and-so beforehand.

But first we had to find a suitable place somewhere along the canal bank, or the riverside. The whole expedition was great fun. The boys were hopeless at lighting fires and succeeded only in cooking burnt offerings but when the lesson on how hard it was to survive in the open had been learned, I would get down on my hands and knees so that no one was defeated and no one went home hungry.

Dirty, satisfied children and a tired, smoke-smelling headmistress. Summer madness indeed!

Hazel couldn't come to camp with us that year but Joan agreed to come to the cottage. I thought I would be all right and so I was but I'll never forget Margaret taking me down to the station with my rucksack and the hampers of food for the journey. The platform seemed to hold the town's entire population of children, waiting for me, depending on me, needing and trusting me. They seemed to fill the entire train and I had a moment of panic. Both Hazel and Margaret stood there to wave us off and when I bent to say goodbye I felt a deep, aching loneliness and knew that whatever I have done I have never done alone. As a loner I think I would not have been much use at all. For the first time in twenty-seven years I would be alone in the tent. That did not worry me at all. It was having only grown children and an inexperienced Joan to lean on in an emergency which troubled me.

And so I returned to Tiree with the invasion Calum so loved and alone in my tent I wrote:

> I have been away too long
> From this windswept isle,
> Yet incredibly, I know every contour
> Of the machair, every tuft
> Of marram grass.
> I feel at home!
>
> Every whitewashed house shelters
> Friends, long known and loved
> And where they empty stand,
> Silent and bereft,

I linger at peace with ghosts
Of those with whom I had affinity.
With every breath I love
These isolated shores.
With reverence I share the glory
Of this small earth where the sun
Is morning born and nightly welcomed
By a golden sea.

I know the well-kept crofts,
Firm-fenced and fertile,
Where John Lachie's suckling herd
Ripples with well fed curiosity.
I wander nibbled pastures knowing
Where the mushrooms grow.
I am no stranger to the bending wind
Which blows perpetually.

I know the sting of slanting rain
Borne on the white horses
From the Barra Isles.
But I know, too, the blue
Of infinite sea and sky.
I know the silver of wet sand at dawn
And the enormity of the moon
In the star-studded heaven.

Most of the children knew Joan for she had been their teacher and their mother or father's teacher, too. Having her as a willing friend who allowed them to use her civilised loo was a novelty indeed. The whole venture was such a success we decided to repeat it if, to use an island expression, we were spared. Without hesitation Joan decided to come again, happy to have been one of our Magic Circle. It only took one camp for the islands and the unique breed of children to be appreciated.

In the spring I had painstakingly typed the manuscript of *A Song to Sing and a Tale to Tell* and it had been read by Hazel. Copies had been sent to Harris and Tiree for their approval. Margaret had collected the Harris copy and now I collected the Tiree one. On return I set about presenting it to a publisher. I was to learn that infinite patience is needed and that three months is lost every time a publisher is willing to read. Time was something I had not got for the book had been virtually commissioned and I had a guaranteed sale of nearly a thousand copies. The families of the children were clamouring but there seemed nothing I could do to hurry things up. Had I received any adverse comments, any damning criticism, I would have given up trying but publishers returned my manuscript with best wishes and regretted that my subject didn't fit into their particular programme. Every time the heavy parcel was returned it came with a suggestion, like clues in a treasure hunt, and I kept following the trail, hopeful of a solution. I had a leading article accepted by the *Scots Magazine* which encouraged me to think my subject might not be uninteresting.

The harvest from the greenhouse was only disappointing when compared with the bumper one of 1976. Strong though plastic is, our thousand-feet elevation is not the best place to put an igloo greenhouse. Severe gales the following winter made us move it to a more sheltered position where it caught less sun. On warm days Father was outside leaning over the field gates, looking at his cattle, or pottering in his garden collecting the harvest in his flat cap. On cold days he had to be content leaning on the radiators in the New-do, watching Margaret at work and banging on the window to point out a stirk which needed worming or a gate which needed shutting. As an onlooker he nearly drove us insane, seeing a hundred and one jobs to do.

Mother gave him all the vegetables to peel, all the fruit to prepare for the freezer and he often cooked the dinner whilst she baked the cakes and pastries for which she is so famous. Surely she must have a place in the *Guinness Book of Records* for the number of hours she has spent over the baking bowl. Together they skimmed the milk and made the butter, salting it and moulding it into pats for freezing and together they entertained the continual stream of visitors which perpetually entered the door.

November fog came prematurely that year, descending in October and completely isolating us. I let Bess out one Tuesday morning. The fog was dense and the bullock sheds invisible. Leaves lay black and wet in the yard and doorway and water dripped from the sycamore with sinister regularity. Bess normally went in and out like a yo-yo and I would get exasperated after the fifth time of getting up. It was always her bark, one sharp cough, which attracted attention. Her early morning uneasiness over, she would curl up for the rest of the day.

I let her out that morning and, because I never heard her bark for re-entry, I forgot her and went to school through the blanket of fog. She was not missed until mid-afternoon when Margaret tidied the kitchen.

'Where's Bess?' she enquired with a sick feeling of premonition. No one knew. No one remembered letting her out but the door is frequently open. If I had let her out then she had been out seven or eight hours. Bess, for whom seven or eight minutes was long enough!

The fog had never lifted. It hung motionless and clinging, wetting everything, making the yard greasy and the gateways treacherous. To find Bess became the most important thing to do. Cattle waited for straw which never came whilst Margaret searched every nook and cranny in the yard and garage and buildings before following the lines of field walls, praying that the old dog would emerge, lost and bewildered. She followed the track of the full stream, searching the murky water for any sign of her friend. Returning from school, at dusk, I joined the search until well after dark.

'She'll have gone away to die,' said Father. Many animals do, but we hated the thought of her wet, decaying body exposed to the elements of winter and the scavengers of earth and air. We lay in bed, listening to torrential rain dispelling the fog and a wuthering wind trapped in the chimney. We mourned our dog and cursed a fate which decreed that she, who had been cosseted and loved, should die of exposure, alone.

The house seemed incredibly empty next morning. When Margaret's chores were done she set off again, determined to find the body. She did not weary of searching until the boundary was reached. Bess's limit was thought to be about thirty yards but we always under-estimated her.

In the lowest corner is a bramble patch, fed by an overgrown stream, choked with water flags in spring and ragged robin in summer. And there was Bess, saturated and very muddy. In her hair were strands of bramble and fronds of bracken and she was alive. Not expecting this Margaret cried, 'Oh Bess!' and a weak tail thumped the wet earth.

My sister ran to lift her and staggered up the deep cleft of Jimmy's Wood. Filthy with mud and sweat, she appeared below the sitting room window. Father alerted the others. Our dog had come home!

She drank and ate a large meal. The mud dried, leaving her coat more silky than it had been of late. Thirty-six hours of wind and rain had rejuvenated her.

'Watch it,' my mother said. 'You'll not get rid of your old folks easily either!'

Early in March 1978, Joan came to watch, with us, the second Sula film. It was a children's story, filmed on Tiree with young Lachlan Campbell in the main role. In terrible pain, Father watched the film through and then admitted his agony. The monster had struck again. We had genuinely begun to believe that the cancer had been caught in time, that age had been on his side and that the growth of malignant cells, at eighty-one, was improbable.

We rushed him to the hospital in the Land Rover, the last journey we made in that loyal vehicle for, during Father's stay in hospital, we exchanged it for a newer model. Once again Mother visited him every possible time, age handicapping her not at all. I could see the hospital from school and, on mad March days, I took the children along the canal bank to collect the early coltsfoot and butterburr, the hazel and willow catkins and to examine the still tight tree buds for the first sign of spring. I hoped Father, whose gaze never left the window, would be able to see us. 'Wave to my old man,' I used to say to the children and we'd all face the hospital and wave like mad.

Father survived another, minor operation, was fitted with a catheter and emerged a new man. His plumbing problems had all been solved mechanically and now even a cold day did not keep him indoors. He could go anywhere, do anything and at Easter Margaret and Joan went to Harris.

In May our kind, motherly dinner lady, Mrs Horner, became ill. She had felt out of sorts for some time but I remember being quite shocked when she was taken into hospital. Her competent daughter-in-law came in to supply for us during the dinner hour.

Before we left for our spring holiday, at the end of May, I visited her for the second time. Somehow you know when someone is really ill and I came away with a sick feeling in my stomach.

Once more we hired the Dormobile and went to Northumberland and I do believe we had one of the happiest holidays ever. One day, our much more mobile old man was missing and Margaret found him playing cricket with the farm children. We were able to spend a completely normal holiday. Margaret could sleep in each morning, utterly content. I would go to bed early and get up at dawn as is my custom, as would Father, and we'd talk about important things. Father never talked small talk. After the first sentence we would be in at the deep end.

He looked young and healthy and at peace. He was eighty-one years old and was suffering from a terminal illness and there we were, on holiday, as if there was nothing wrong at all. He sat in the Dormobile more frequently than in a deck chair but every time we passed and asked, 'Are you OK?' he would sing his reply, 'I'm so happy, oh so happy, don't you envy me?'

Auntie Mary and Harry would do the washing-up, Mother made the beds and Margaret and I made the picnic and loaded the van with the day's essentials. All the while Father could be seen, warm and brown in Harris tweed and flat cap, wandering up or down the narrow lane, leaning over the field gates to watch the cattle or investigating the hedgerows. Sometimes he would be in the farmyard watching a new litter of pigs or talking to the tractor driver. It was a perfect, perfect holiday.

When we returned we found Bess had missed us dreadfully. Margaret was full of self-reproach. Our old dogs were not used to travelling in cars. When we drove on the land they ran alongside and when we went into town we left them at home. Had Bess enjoyed travelling, infirm though she was, we would have taken her along with us. Instead we had to leave her behind and it nearly broke Margaret's heart to see how she had deteriorated. She nursed her with loving care and tried to make up for the two weeks she had been left. The old dog was twenty years old and more than ready to meet her Maker. She had a quiet few weeks of being loved and then, one day, she did not wake up. She lay unconscious for several days. When she died we buried her in the plantation of trees which John and Cathy had sent us from Spean Bridge.

Mrs Homer came back to her home, a very sick lady. Nearly every dinner hour I would hurry along the churchyard to spend half of it at her bedside, telling her the day's news. She was always pleased to see me and she always managed a smile. It was summer and the village was filled with the scent of flowers; children were barelegged, the boys took off their shirts and dashed round the Rec like a tribe of brown natives but a pall of sadness was hanging over us.

Mrs Horner was almost a member of the family. The heat distressed her. We were learning the awful truth and it angered us. Hers had been a life of service to others, it was about to end prematurely and there wasn't a thing any one of us could do about it.

The annual presentation of prizes, leaving books, trophies, Rose Bowl and swimming certificates normally took place on the last day of term but in 1978 the important day came on the Friday before the last week; I am so glad it did.

It was always a day of flowers. It would not surprise me to learn that Mrs Horner had originally been the lady behind the flower-buying custom. Only the parents of the leavers were invited to the simple ceremony so somebody must have been carrying on the tradition and prompting the buying of bouquets. The occasion was happy. The children received their prizes, the winner of the Rose Bowl was named and we were given flowers. It was a normal Prize Giving Day. The girls looked lovely in their summer dresses and the boys abnormally clean in their white shirts and colourful ties.

On an impulse I decided to take the prizewinners from my top junior class and my bouquet of flowers to Mrs Horner. Sometimes, when I went, I found her sitting beside her bed in her dressing gown. When we arrived on that hot summer afternoon she was in bed and the sun was streaming through the window. She loved all children and seeing these, the dearest of them all, smoothed the lines of pain from her face. She opened her arms and gathered them to her. My eyes were blinded by tears. 'Suffer little children to come unto me,' I thought. I will remember that tableau always.

They, not comprehending the terrible nature of her terminal illness, were unafraid to talk naturally and were glowing with pleasure as they showed her their books and cheered the cup winners.

'You're the best children in the world!' she said.

She was too ill for us to stay long but, in a small way, our visit had been a tribute we needed to pay, to reassure her of the special place she held in all our hearts. When life is coming to a close it is important to know that you are loved. The girls touched her lovingly, the boys looked a bit embarrassed and we all tip-toed out.

The following Friday school closed for the mid-summer holiday. When I counted my class in the morning, to mark the register, I had too many. Stephen or Gavin, Mark or David, or all of them were sitting there hoping that I would not notice. Mostly it was the boys who came back. Primary school teachers used to grumble that it was unfair of the senior school to break for the holidays before they did and thought that ex-pupils returning were a nuisance. I might have thought so too if my school had not been so small that the wave of them returning was but a ripple.

Silly things! They could have been enjoying a vacation. Whatever the season, if they were on holiday and we were not, they would be sitting on the Rec wall waiting for us to go out for rounders or football. A few tried to hide themselves in the swimming queue in the local bus shelter hoping that I was blind and quite a few were known to turn up at dinner time, being latch-key kids and perpetually hungry. But they were welcome. I loved to see them and to hear their news and see their reports.

The last day of the school term came with its bustle of cleaning. Cupboards were turned out, desks emptied and polished and then came the goodbyes. The leavers hung around prolonging the agonising moment. They seemed suddenly to get under my feet with their arms full of clobber and the long brown envelope in which was their report. Most of them never wanted to go. The ones who chased off as soon as the door was opened were, likely as not, holding back their tears. To ease the situation I used to walk into the cloakroom and finally into the yard so that, should they have an arm free, they could wave at me from along the churchyard. One or two would always come racing back, having found something had been left behind.

On that particular Friday in 1978 I had not quite succeeded in emptying the school and I had a pile of unfinished work to do in the staff-room, some correspondence to seal and stamp, a phone call to make, some unopened requisition stock to pile ready for an after-hay and after-camp day when I could come into school and put it away and of course there was the end of term entry to put in the Log Book.

I was to write, 'Someone has just come into school to tell me of the death of Mrs Horner a short while ago.'

I sat quietly in the staff-room a long time before I felt able to get up and complete my jobs and go home.

Chapter Eighteen

There was a rush to get in as much hay as possible before my departure. The weather had turned very humid and heavy and although a lot of grass had been cut the week before, with the good weather, the grass was now drying slowly. Our neighbours baled one field for us and we dragged the heavy bales to stooks and collected them on the trailer. Genevieve had been replaced with a short wheelbase Land Rover which did all our rough work on the land and towed the trailer.

Load by load we brought home the bales from that one field and the thought of leaving Margaret with seven more fields, alone with Father, Mother and Harry, was unthinkable. We made a final bid to take one more field. 'It needs another day,' she was told by the tractor man who was a perfectionist.

'The forecast is bad. Bale it,' Margaret insisted. 'Leave it a day and it'll be wet through again.'

'Bale it an' y'll nivver lift t' bales,' she was told. No farmer had any patience with me taking all those children on holiday when the hay had to be made. Hay is extremely precious and expensive to buy. The hay harvest represents thousands of pounds but just now all we could do was to 'ger on wi' it'. I could not cancel camp.

'Bale it,' Margaret insisted on the afternoon before my departure, 'We'll stack it in the meadow corner.' Very reluctantly, the tractor man complied. He was a farmer and he knew the hay was not ready to bale but he wasn't the piper playing the tune. As he baled Margaret and I began ferrying them to the corner and stacking them. They were very heavy and the hay from them, in winter, would not be the best quality but at least they were safe.

The baler left the field with its hundreds of green bundles and we struggled on, prepared, if necessary, to work through the night. Then, unexpectedly, though we should always know these things happen on the eve of our going away, the Land Rover broke down, alongside the slowly growing stack. We could not get it re-started. In desperation I ran all the way home to return with the station wagon. The trailer tow bar wouldn't fit it, so the only thing to do was to tow the whole thing, small Land Rover and the trailer. We continued until well after dark, Margaret in the station wagon, me being towed in the Land Rover and the trailer following on behind like some silly cartoon. When darkness really stopped play we went home vowing to get up early and finish the job. The meadows, in summertime, are never really dark for the heavens provide a canopy of stars and the distant main road to the city and the metropolis itself, ten miles away, throw up a brilliance which ensures only a semi-darkness. But when the cloud cover is thunderously low, as it was on that evening, and when humidity creates a mist in the valley, the artificial lights are dimmed and then darkness really isolates.

Packing the picnic baskets for nearly sixty people occupied both of us until well into morning and we were up before dawn. I went to the camp store where I knew there was an old Icelandic tent which could be used as a stack cover. The rest of the tents would be already sitting on the pier at Oban, waiting for me and my tribe. Watch it, I thought, there is no place for complacency. Accidents happen when one is very tired. In thirty homes sisters and brothers were tossing in their sleep and waking early with excitement and anticipation. Their rucksacks would be packed and their feet eager to run barefoot on Salum Bay. Just because there has never been an accident, I told myself, it doesn't mean there never will be. Watch it, woman, you are not infallible!

I humped the old tent back to the farmyard and threw it into the station wagon. Margaret was already starting up the engine. It wasn't quite light. We had only had about three hours sleep.

The bales were wet with mist and heavy. We were soon saturated. Our trousers and shirts clung to us coldly. I had to be at the station at 10 o'clock but at nine we were still in the field bringing in the last bales. Then came the frantic struggle with the improvised sheet. We tried to use the guy ropes to secure it but found it almost impossible to push the thick rope behind the baler twine of the new bales. It was 9.30 a.m. before we were unhooking the station wagon and dashing home. Margaret never paused. She immediately slung the picnic hampers into the vehicle as I struggled into uniform. I was fastening my shoelaces as we drove into town.

A sea of faces greeted me on the station platform. Could I possibly pull something out of the bag and lead another successful camp? Fortunately the need to do so was not immediate. Hazel was coming, bless her. She was ticking off names and collecting health forms. Margaret was coping with the picnic skips and parents were handling children's kit.

Hazel took one look at me and said, 'Are you all right?'

'I will be,' I answered.

I think I felt worse about leaving Margaret than I ever had. I was leaving her in a right bonnie pickle. I should have felt torn with anxiety but there wasn't anything at all that I could do about it. In the list of priorities the children came first; when there is only one road to take you have to take it.

Somehow everyone got on the train but Margaret. How great is my debt to her, dear, loyal sister. We waved to parents until we could see them no more and then I took off my uniform jacket and flopped into the seat beside Joan who was returning to the Salum cottage. I slipped my shoes off under the table in front of me and I could feel a lather of sweat and tiredness oozing out of me. Every bone in my body was aching.

Hazel settled the children and came to her seat. She took one look at me and said, 'I'll get us all a cup of coffee.' She took a child with her to the restaurant car and returned with three tightly capped cardboard cups of steaming coffee.

'Wait.' Hazel was determined to play fairy godmother. She hunted in her bag for chocolate biscuits. I smiled. 'She's a good friend,' I thought. 'Thank goodness she is back again this year.'

I made no effort to take off the lids from the coffee tubs. I seemed incapable of moving. Hazel leaned across the table, full of energy. She uncapped my coffee, the train gave a lurch and I caught the whole, scalding lot on my lap. I could feel the hot liquid penetrating my skirt and petticoat. Then, as it found bare skin, I leapt out of my stupor. There was a frightful commotion. Everyone was mopping up the table, the floor and me. There was nothing for it but to stagger to the luggage van and sift through the pile of rucksacks until mine was found. Then I sought the privacy of the loo to change my underclothes completely.

I remember thinking, 'Thank goodness Hazel tipped it on me!' At that particular moment, I could not have coped with the embarrassment of having poured it over her or Joan who both looked immaculate. I returned, took the dry, empty seat next to Hazel and we all laughed.

It was Hazel's last camp. She had always said that after a certain September birthday she would retire. She had given me many years of loyal service and, if I continued, I would miss her as much as Margaret. At that moment my own future seemed very uncertain. I concentrated all my efforts on making it a camp to remember. A year at a time was the way we must all live.

Margaret had had a very rough ride but was in calmer water when I returned. It is always infuriating when, after a hard struggle, help comes when the worst is over and the helper has no idea just how awful it has been. We had bought calves earlier than usual that year which made things harder than ever. The Shaw-Smiths on the hilltop helped her out with the leading. Without them hay would have been lost. We hope they know how much we valued their help, Margaret because she was in need and I because I had left her needing friends. They are good neighbours.

Then Father suddenly became very poorly. They decided not to tell me. What could I have done but worry? Margaret's nights had become broken when sleep had been needed most. I know what she must have gone through and I also know that when I returned to the calm after the storm I dismissed the enormity of my absence in the relief I felt to be home. Nothing mattered. Everyone was still alive. But Father knew and he wasn't going to let it happen again.

My gratitude to Margaret is a thing we do not talk about, a family thing we know and accept. Between us there have never been presents or greeting cards. We are interdependent and we know it. To express it would get the reaction, 'Don't be silly!'

It does not however embarrass me to sing the praises of my schoolchildren. Michael was a tall, blond boy. His creative writing gave me the reward necessary, now and again, to all teachers.

I admit that there is satisfaction in sewing with cheap materials, offcuts and remnants. There is a sense of achievement when a new garment is made out of an old one but, just now and again, it is necessary to work with Harris Tweed and for a teacher to occasionally mark an essay of the quality Michael produced. He was only nine when he wrote this;

> One day, a few years ago, we discovered a sprout in the ash pile where we put ash from the boiler. The sprout grew each year being watered by the rain and the sun shining down on it. So the sprout sighed and started to grow thinking all the time, 'I shall be big, I shall be tall, I shall be strong.'
>
> Now what this sprout said was probably going to be true because this sprout was a sycamore sprout and it grew and it grew until it became as it is now. The sycamore is still in the ash pile, of course, but not for long it won't. Soon it shall be dug up and put in a better place. We are moving but it won't go there.
>
> It shall go somewhere it can enjoy itself, where it can stand among buttercups in spring and where it can bask in the sun and see all the beautiful flowers in summer, where it can drop its keys in autumn and, last of all, stand bare all the long, cold winter.
>
> Then, when it grows people can see it and the tree will have a long lifetime just being proud of itself and looking at all the wonders of the earth.

His friend was a lively, diminutive boy and their relationship was interesting to me for they were absolutely in tune. Michael, the taller of the two, was a dreamer and Richard, head and shoulders shorter, was imaginative. Together they lived in a different world from the rest of the class. They were always to be found in deep discussion planning for future adventures which never materialised, or leaning over the wall making their elaborate plans. On a nature walk, in the crocodile going to the Institute for Movement or in the bus going to the swimming baths they were always deep in conversation. I eavesdropped, listening to all their ambitious plans which never came to fruition.

The two of them were going to hire a canal boat that summer. The idea had just come to them and they believed it possible. What the Swallows and Amazons could do, so could they. Together they discussed the food stores and menus they would need and the clothes they would wear and the route they would take. I was glad they were both going to Harris for I expected real disappointment when the canal trip fell through but it never seemed to matter to them. When one scheme was abandoned another took its place.

One idea was to make a film. Michael firmly believed that he would get a ciné camera for his birthday. With this hope in mind they wrote the script and sketched the wardrobe necessary for the characters. One of them wore a headband proclaiming himself the stage manager and the other one pronouncing himself the director. They chose the cast and asked me if I would accept a part. They had already offered the part of the princess to our attractive infants' teacher and I was curious to know what role they had for me who had no such qualifications.

Michael displayed the sketches of my wardrobe and it looked as if I were expected to wear some sort of wet suit and wings. 'Whatever am I?' I asked.

'Super Brown,' Richard explained. 'It's a good part.'

But, of course, Michael did not get a ciné camera for his birthday. Undaunted by that they planned to hire one and then they started thinking about something else.

The barn roof was causing us concern. Margaret was so sure it was going to fall she hardly ever walked under the beam in the laithe porch. Elsewhere the hay and straw reached the roof, holding it up in the autumn but leaving it frighteningly vulnerable in the new year. We decided, very reluctantly, that we would take it down. Owning a sixteenth-century barn was not easy; we had to send for the man responsible for the ancient buildings in the area. 'Do you have to take it down?' was his first reaction.

We admitted that the house would look awful without it. It would have to be developed, landscaped into a garden of some sort. The alternative was to re-roof it, which would cost £5,000 at least. The barn could never repay us for that. Borrowers we may be but we are not fools and to borrow on something which could only be ornamental is insane. It housed hay in the autumn, of course, but the dutch barn could house it adequately, instead. We could put up a new calf shed with the timber we already had and the pile of fibreglass sheets we had bought from Blackpool was still big enough for the roof. We could not get a grant and £5,000 would more than double our overdraft. No, we told Mr Saul, the barn would have to come down.

The good man crawled all over the hay prodding the massive beams, inspecting the cracks. 'It's not bad,' he pronounced. 'Try to find some excuse for preserving it if you possibly can at all.'

Not a hope! Father was ill, Margaret was over-worked, Mother in her eighties. Reluctantly we phoned our builder friend and told him to make time, in the spring, to take down the barn. Currer's Laithe! We must have been mad! How dared we? Whatever possessed us to think we had a right to pull down a building of such historical interest and make our sixteenth-century house look ridiculous? There had to be some messenger from heaven to stop us.

God was certainly colouring his world that October. In 1978 autumn lasted until the beginning of the month we normally associate with fog and mud. On 5th November, a beautiful Sunday, Margaret stayed at home and I took the family up to Buckden to see Julia Wood. I don't think there ever was such a beautiful day. The trees still retained their painted leaves and the effect was breathtaking. Father had a whale of a time; he was fond of Julia. She had married a farmer; they showed the old man their cattle and land and the sun poured down.

It was Father's last journey along the Dales lanes he loved so well. It was like a passing out parade or a procession of remembrance. He was as happy as anyone could be. He had lived all his life, except for the four years in Glasgow, in beautiful places and it seemed important to enjoy this inspection of his North Country lest it be his last. Winter was coming. Who could tell what it might bring. As long as I live I will remember that promenade along the winding lanes, in the fall of the year. A swan song, a wonderful last look at a beloved country. My father was a lucky man.

Then winter came with a vengeance. We were suddenly feeding more than the normal autumn supplement. Grazing, even on the rough, became impossible. The barn began to empty alarmingly.

Three fifteen-year-olds were approaching the final stage of Queen's Guide Award. Two successful candidates out of the three would take us over the fifty mark. Fifty Queen's Guides from one company in nearly thirty years was no small achievement and we felt it ought to be celebrated in fine style.

Parties were not really our line of business. We still do not know one wine from another and have never had a cocktail. I remember sitting beside a child at school dinner when a new dessert had been sent from the kitchen. She sampled it and said, 'It tastes like gin, Miss Brown. Don't you think so?'

'To be quite honest, Sharon,' I answered, 'I haven't the slightest idea. I've never tasted any gin.'

We have no experience of eating out, rarely enjoy a wedding, being most uncomfortable 'dressed', as the Hebrideans would say, and do not have a social life in the accepted sense of the word. But we could certainly organise Queen's Guide Presentations. We had had years of experience and we acknowledged each achievement with a show of festive spirit guaranteed to make the recipient feel the success and the responsibility the new title placed upon her whole future.

I chose the Saturday after school closed for Christmas, hoping that most of the fifty-one Queen's Guides would be able to attend. Those living away from home would be coming for Christmas, students would be down from college, teachers would have broken up for the holiday.

The onus on the three final candidates to qualify was great. Two only were needed to reach the fifty mark but for one to fail was unthinkable. They were three very determined girls and the final clause was passed one very frosty night sometime around the beginning of December. They phoned to tell me the minute they knew. Alison told me the good news and passed the phone to a very excited mother.

'There is a form to sign,' I told her. 'I'll put it in the post tomorrow.' 'We're so excited,' said Alison's mother. 'We'll come up now and collect it.'

We were very tired and busy and I tried to put her off. 'It's far too cold and frosty,' I said. 'There is no hurry. Don't bother.'

'Of course we'll come,' she persisted. 'We are over the moon.'

We had cattle to feed and it was already after eight. I put the kettle on so that it would be boiling for their arrival and hunted out the necessary forms.

The headlights appeared at the top of the road, and we delayed the feeding of cattle in order to be hospitable. We tried to match their excitement. We have had our share of hard-earned success and each time the effort to succeed has been so great that when the good news has arrived we have taken it with unexpected calmness and silence. Just a deep intake of breath, no shouting or champagne. But, in the presence of the Drivers we pulled something out of the bag and we all sat there beaming our pleasure.

Eventually they got up to go. The precious form was signed, the hard work all over. An icy blast came in when we opened the door. They got into their car, we waved them goodbye and reached for our dirty anoraks and wellies. The yard was like a skating rink. Before we got to the entrance there was a premonition, a sickness in the pit of the stomach.

Sure enough the car was floundering on the hill. There was an over-acceleration and a whizzing of heated tyres and no progress uphill. We knew just what was going to happen and how long it was going to take and how cold and exasperated we were going to be.

The Drivers were so apologetic we could not be cross. It took an hour and a half to get that car up the road and out of the gate. They were good days when we had no road and people left their cars at the top and walked. It was midnight before the final chores were finished.

We were so busy during the last week of term that I seldom opened personal post before the mid-morning break. One morning, that last week, I escaped from the busy classroom, put on some milk for coffee and opened my post. It was too cold to send the children out to play and the school buzzed with chatter and creative activity.

There was a letter from a small publisher I had written to, having read his advertisement, 'Let the fascination of islands sell your books'. The publisher operated from Shetland, and I was eager to see what he had to say. It was a friendly letter. He had read the synopsis of *A Song to Sing and a Tale to Tell* and urged me to write to a bigger publisher. A book of 60,000 words was too big for him to attempt but he added that he'd quite like to see the manuscript. If he liked it he could guarantee the sale of a few hundred books if I decided to publish it myself.

The 'do-it-yourself' bug nibbled at me again. For years the profits on cattle and teaching had been fed into the farm. They had been swallowed in lime and sheds, animals and house improvements. It may mean temporarily increasing the overdraft, but hundreds of books would be sold immediately and the publisher would sell the rest. I didn't want to make a fortune. All I wanted was that those whose children had camped with me should know the fun it had been.

Next morning I posted the heavy manuscript to the Shetland Isles and at the end of the week we left the Christmas decorations for the Golden Celebration.

Two hundred replies had come accepting the invitation. Almost all the Queen's Guides were available. We left the tree and the evergreens, kept the screens folded back and ferried folding chairs and trestle tables from the Institute, with all the cups and saucers we could find. There was to be a great multitude to feed and afterwards space must be cleared for everyone who came would have danced at the céilidhs in Calum's barn, and would want to do so again.

In umpteen homes preparations were in full swing. Cakes and pastries and gateaux were being made by helpful mothers. Marie had taken home the full leg of pork and a ham to be cooked in her father's bakery. Everywhere there was a preparing of salads and trifles, a whipping of many pints of cream and someone was painstakingly decorating the cake.

School closed on the Thursday and by Friday all the tablecloths were laid and two hundred places set with plates and cutlery. It was a miracle of pouring a gallon into a pint pot. I stood looking at my transformed school. It had been mine for nineteen years and I had used it, just as we had used The Currer. What good is a front room, musty with disuse, a spare bedroom without a guest in it, a library with the newness not worn from the books, or a stove with none of the marks of constant use?

What a night to remember that was, with so many of my favourite people. We ate and talked, danced and sang. That evening Margaret and Hazel and I felt loved.

Had Mr Right appeared, in the pre-Currer days, we might have married, Margaret and I, and had our own children and all this would never have happened. But he did not and we are not sorry. Our children were perpetually Peter Pans, never lost interest, never threw tantrums or showed moodiness. Our children were always having a good time, always laughing and singing, always grateful, never bored. For us they were always ready for adventure, always ready to serve, happy to be working. We never knew them sick or without appetite.

And so, under the rafters of my village school, Sheila, the daughter of my primary school headmaster, who had been my first Queen's Guide, presented the new Awards which brought our total past the fifty mark. We stood back and looked at our work, and knew that the harvest was good.

Margaret took Mother and Harry home and returned to pick me up, and Paul, Julie and Vivienne who had travelled all the way from Northumberland to be present. We collected the few remains of the feast and left everything else until morning.

Next day we went back to school to clear it, ready for the caretaker to do his Christmas cleaning. On every window ledge we found Christmas cards and envelopes whose individual scribble read 'Skipper'. We gathered them into a pile to read at The Currer.

We took down all the Christmas decorations and stuffed them into the dustbin. We stacked the borrowed furniture ready for return and unfolded the screens which separated the classrooms and went home. The unique occasion was over.

Together, in the afternoon, we went through the pile of Christmas cards, messages and donations. There was a sizeable amount. Obviously everyone expected me to go on camping. One large, imposing folder revealed a hand-made 50th Anniversary Card bearing the name of every Queen's Guide and another one was signed by everyone present. This one succeeded in leaving us all in tears. The simple verse said:

> Don't walk in front of me, I may not follow.
> Don't walk behind, I may not lead.
> Just walk beside me and be my friend.

I knew instinctively that it had been bought by Barbara, one of my first Tiree campers, mother of four lovely children. She and Arnie her husband had released us to go on holiday so many times. I knew, too, that she was right. The only way to do anything properly is side by side as, unwittingly, we had done.

In the heat of the summer, on rare occasions when we had time to think about it, we wondered what we would do if anyone should be ill whilst snow blocked our road and to feed cattle demanded endurance, strength and sheer guts to go out and face the freezing weather. Health was something we all had in plenty but we thought about it, now and again.

After the excitement, Christmas was quiet and rather nice. On Christmas Day Skye littered a nestful of pups in the barn. Skye was one of our most beautiful dogs, whiter than collies usually are and much more timid. The six pups were beautiful and brought sunshine on grey days. All young animals need the companionship of others of their kind to tangle with in tumbling play, whether they be pups, kittens, lambs or children. Skye's pups kept Margaret sane in the early months of 1979.

A few days after Christmas, the first snow fell and our world became white. Margaret and I carried out the bales to feed seventy cattle in the foot-path field and the five-acre. Mother began to re-stock the cake and biscuit tins and Auntie Mary went home to the little cottage to create some heat to keep her pipes from freezing. Harry bemoaned the fact that he could not go out and Auntie Mary went out when she shouldn't have done, slipped when mounting a bus and badly cut her shin. She needed frequent hospital treatment so she came back to The Currer where she could get transport and stayed with us for nearly two months.

More snow fell, temperatures dropped, the landscape was a picture and Father began his last slow journey home. For most people the last lap would be described as a downhill one, but we got the impression that Father was still climbing. For over eighty years his had been an upward trail, a hard climb, tackling each obstacle as it came along. There was no downward slipping, at the last moment, of mind or courage. He was getting a bit out of breath as he reached the top, that was all. For all of us it was a winter that demanded the best that we could give.

And now came the weather that we feared and the predicament we had dreaded: the winter with one of us ill and snow blocking the road. Why is it then that there are no dreadful memories of the January of 1979? I can only assume that, though physically we nearly reached exhaustion, spiritually we were never more at peace.

We thought, at first, that Father had caught a chill. We sent for the doctor and left our Land Rover at the Moor Gate so that he could exchange cars, come safely down to The Currer and get back out again.

'Stay in bed for a few days,' was his advice. 'Let's get this cold off your chest.'

School reopened and I left Margaret with all the outside work and Mother and Harry with all the housework and two invalids. Auntie Mary's leg proved painfully slow to heal. More than a fair share of the load of responsibility fell on Mother. She was up and down stairs constantly, caring for the man she loved, and worrying, too, about Margaret struggling with scores of bales and walking dangerously in front of hungry cattle.

Every day Father said, 'I feel better today than I did yesterday,' but I think we all knew that it was nearly 'time for man go home'. How we loved him.

Margaret struggled further up the field with her heavy bales so that the feeding cattle could be seen from the bedroom window. Most days, I left the Land Rover at the top of the road so that there was less danger of having to go without it and having no means of getting home in a hurry. Frequently we could be seen as black dots up the road digging away the most recent fall of snow, determined to keep the road open. The last car came down at Christmas and the road was never clear until March. Such was the severity of the winter and the lateness of the spring of 1979.

The first murmuring of premature retirement began, deep inside me. 'Will I have to take leave of absence?' I wondered, every day leaving school with fully marked books, all correspondence done and all my cupboards tidy.

The landscape was absolutely white as far as the distant horizon forty miles away. Ingleborough stood out against the blue like a table covered with white linen. Trees were snow-sprinkled and the cattle were hungry. Each night one of us slept in a sleeping bag on the floor beside Father's bed for Mother, the day-time nurse, must get some sleep. The doctor came again and said that Father must get up and sit in a chair. He hated his confinement in the bedroom. The heart of the family was downstairs and there was a limit as to how many times an old lady could climb the steps.

'If we leave Father up here,' we thought, 'he is going to die,' and we were not ready to accept it.

Auntie Mary went home for the weekend to air her house and Mother was persuaded to take an afternoon off and have tea there on the Saturday. Whilst she was out we manhandled one of our single beds downstairs and re-erected it in the sitting room. Sunshine was pouring through the windows of the New-do. We knew that Father could not walk down the steps so we took a sleeping bag and put his feet inside. When he stood up we lifted the bag above his shoulders and drew up the zip-fastener. Gripping the soft walls of the bag we carried our fragile old man downstairs without touching him and without him feeling insecure.

Father was much better downstairs. The bed had good castors and could be pushed nearer the fire or towards the window to suit his every need. He was restless, finding no physical comfort but spiritually he was at peace. Mentally he was as alert as a teenager and as wise as a sage. He talked a lot, never complaining but still telling us what to do. He was still the master of the house and the farm manager, still the advocate and counsellor.

Margaret and I slept on the sitting room floor. It was easier that way for we were able to get some sleep, a necessity in a cruelly hard winter. Weeks went by and still the snow lay deep and beautiful.

A telephone call came from Shetland to say that the manuscript had been read and was being returned. I was advised to keep presenting it to publishers until eventual success. It would be accepted sooner or later, I was told.

'I haven't time,' I said. 'My Father is dying and wants a decision. The Guides are clamouring.' The reunion had stirred memories. 'Go on, Skipper,' they were begging. 'We are all ready to buy.'

So I told the Shetland publisher that I wanted to take his offer of selling the surplus and that I was going to publish myself. 'I need a thousand copies,' I said. 'So what do I do?'

'Take it to a printer,' he said.

'Where?'

'The best,' he said, giving me a name which was only ten miles away. I was flabbergasted. A publisher in Shetland gives me an address of a printer in a town I visit every Tuesday when I take the school children to the swimming baths. It seemed an omen.

I immediately made an appointment with the printer. Snow lay deep over the Cringles. The plough had kept the road open by daily hurling the new snow higher and higher on the roadsides. Even in a Land Rover it was difficult to see beyond the snow walls to the frozen landscape. In 1979 sheep ate the bark from the trees which lined the route over Cringles, killing many that had decorated the hillside for decades.

Snow was falling as the Land Rover put the ten miles behind it. I walked into the office, clutching the heavy manuscript, and found a warm and luxurious welcome. I was treated with courtesy and respect. Printing terms were used which were foreign to me. I was offered different papers to feel, shown different bindings and book sizes and was told that the estimate for 1,200 copies would be sent to me within a few days. I went home to tell Father that the book would be in print before the summer was over.

We had hoped that Father would recover to welcome another cuckoo, but we became increasingly aware that it was not to be. He became more and more frail and restless. We learned to sleep and wake, sleep and wake all night through. The doctor could only come when we collected him from the Moor Gate.

One particularly bad morning, I climbed the road, a treacherous glacier of ice between three-foot walls of dug-out snow, and forced open the door of the Land Rover I had left on the top road. Every night I left it in the village fearing that the morning would dawn with a fresh fall which would prevent me getting out except on foot. The vehicle was always surrounded by new blown drifts which had to be dug away. Doors and windows had to be de-iced and I held my breath in fear that the engine would not start.

I had already had a month of this pantomime. Father seemed worse and it was my intention to ring the doctor and take him up to The Currer. Margaret was to see that the road was clear enough for our magnificent vehicle to get right down to the farm and back. I parked it on the road outside school, close against one of the buttresses which held up the school playground.

Children were sliding all over the yard, calling to me to watch their capers but I was in a hurry to get to the phone. I walked close to the railings for safety. Children were tumbling and laughing all around me. I stopped several times to pick up those who could not keep their feet before hurrying indoors to brush off my mantle of snow and pick up the phone.

The doctor would not hear of my coming out of school. He and his daughter would enjoy the winter walk. Winnie was interrupting me, dragging at my sleeve, insisting I put the phone down and come quickly. 'There has been an accident!' she said.

'Now what?' I groaned, following her into the classroom.

'A little car has slid into your Land Rover,' she said. The unhurt driver was coming across the yard to apologise.

'I couldn't help it,' the driver said. 'When I came over the canal bridge there was a car coming towards me and I braked to let him through. They wouldn't hold and I slid into the Land Rover. I don't think I've done much damage but I'll need help to get my car facing downhill again.'

We went out of the back door followed by the indoor children, others on the railings were yelling, "S 'agar's tractor, Miss Brown, Yah, look a'r'it!'

Look at it indeed! A local farmer had come over the bridge with tractor and muck spreader. Seeing the small accident, the little car at right angles to the Land Rover, he had found it necessary but impossible to stop. The weight of the tractor and its smelly cargo had forced the little car forward until it was beneath mine. The Land Rover had been trapped against the wall and, incredibly, the width of the buttress exactly fitted the rear passenger door. This had been bulged and would never open again in that condition but the rest of the vehicle seemed unharmed.

The poor little car, half under the Land Rover and half entangled in the tractor wheels, had collapsed like matchwood. There is something quite comical about grown men surveying the muddle they have got into, but the situation we were in at The Currer was not comical.

We must have been born lucky for, when the road was ashed and the tractor moved, and when the little car had been dragged away in pieces and my trusty vehicle had been pulled from being impaled on the buttress, I found I would be able to drive away safely even though no one would be able to use the rear passenger door. All day I kept breathing out, 'Phew!' and saying to myself, 'We are still mobile, never mind.'

Our nights with Father were very disturbed. Towards the end of January a very heavy fall of snow filled in the dug out road and drifted, ridge after ridge along the top road. I daily dug-out the Land Rover and scooped out the pile of snow which came in through the damaged door. The route to town was lined with stranded vehicles whilst glum-faced owners walked. There is a joviality about those who walk in snow and who do not habitually have a car. Those who have become dependent on one have lost their appreciation of winter. Land Rovers will always go providing snow is not so deep that the undercarriage wedges. All the way down to town I picked up grateful walkers whose smile, at being lifted, was only momentary. When all the seats were full we had no alternative but to pass the rest of the head-down walkers. Gone are the days when people wave and cajole and laugh their way through difficulties. I put a great deal of blame for society's current disease on the car.

The snowplough came up onto the top road and cruelly left its final pile in one huge snow wall at the last house. It totally prevented the Land Rover completing its journey home. All day the snow fell. I left school immediately it closed, reluctantly left the vehicle, nose to town, on the top road and climbed over this mountain of compressed snow. Beyond it, for fifty yards to the Moor Gate, the snow lay white, undisturbed and undulating. I could have taken the lazy driver of the snowplough by the collar and shaken him until his teeth rattled.

Our road was completely blocked. We accept the fact that we will always have to dig that out ourselves but we pay rates, like all other members of society, and expect the adopted roads to be cleared to the end. On reaching home I phoned the Council and reported the neglect. 'We have struggled a month,' I said, 'with a very sick man. We have a disabled brother and two old ladies. We have 150 cattle and will run out of hay in a few days. We have ordered seven tons to be brought by lorry tomorrow and the snowplough gave up before it reached the end of the road. What do you expect us to do? Please send up some men with shovels at once! Please!'

Council men are quite nice really.

Father had a very poor night alternately sitting in a chair and returning to his bed by the fire. I don't think we slept for more than ten minutes at a time. The sitting room light was permanently on and we were fully dressed all night.

At four o'clock Father roused us for the umpteenth time to sip a little lemonade. We got up to move a pillow and stoke up the fire. The dogs began to run to the door. Skye, in the barn with her pups, was barking furiously. They answered her noisily as a knock came to the door. In retrospect we marvel at the calm way we opened the door to two enormous men. I suppose we were tired and weary and that our intuition told us that no cut-throat robber would come on a night like that, struggling through the deep snow to a lighted house, early in February. I think it was Margaret who went to the door and welcomed them in. They were big, rough as they come, Council workers, seeking help. I put the kettle on. Mother, who is as unperturbed by our relative isolation as we are, wakened, thought, 'They'll be from the Council,' and went back to sleep. Auntie Mary wakened and thought, 'They'll murder everyone and then come for me,' and stayed awake.

I have no recollection of thinking there was anything unusual. Certainly we showed them no inhospitality. Perhaps it was their opening query, "Ev ye a tractor?' Perhaps it is because unlike most people, we do not expect to be molested. Perhaps if we lived in a street or avenue instead of a farmhouse surrounded by dogs we might feel differently. Two dogs had followed us from the sitting room. He's a foolish man who will face our dogs with evil intent.

The men had been sent to clear the road and lessen our predicament. Deep snow had filled the ditch at the side of the road and, unaware that it existed, the snow plough had buried itself in an unexpected crevasse. Seeing the light in the farmhouse they had come for help. They were sure we would be happy to get out of our warm beds and pull them out. They had alternately slithered and floundered all the way to the farm and I am quite sure they were pleased that we did not have a tractor. It absolved them from duty. They were free to put their feet under the table, drink steaming mugs of coffee and whisper their disgust at the prolonged snowfall. Their presence was, somehow, comforting. The long night with Father so ill was relieved and shortened with their subdued conversation. It was a hard and cruel winter for all of us.

Next day the snowplough was hauled out of the ditch and men with shovels dug to the end of the road, clearing the way for the load of hay. It came with its lifesaving fodder and deposited its load in one large stack, a quarter of a mile from the steadings. Next day being Saturday, we had a chance to dig out our road again. Taking a shovel I walked to the top of the hill and left it leaning on the stack whilst I collected the post.

I think I might then have been at my lowest ebb. We had dreaded illness and snow together and here we were in the throes of one of the worst winters with Father dying and no one but loyal, limping Auntie Mary to help us. We seemed isolated with our problems, struggling to cope with a hundred difficulties a day. Freda's son Stuart helped us dig out the road on one occasion but we dug it out so many times that winter that we seemed perpetually shovelling snow. We don't often feel as lousy and as alone as I did that morning. No one phoned. No one seemed to know or care. There seemed no one with more friends and relatives than us but where were they? Didn't anyone know the mess we were in? Had we time or strength to ferry this seven-ton load of bales down the hill, when we'd cleared the road? Would it be remotely possible to drive the cattle up? Certainly not the calves! A lot of the hay would have to go down on the little Land Rover which was quite capable of conking out any time.

Was it unreasonable for hackles to rise when villagers I passed *en route* to the post office grumbled at having to clear their short garden paths, when someone with one horse complained about the icy wind and those with lane side garages nattered about road conditions? My hackles rose that morning as they used to do when families going on holiday wondered what they would do with two children if the weather were wet, when the mother sighed and bemoaned the fact that she had all the packing to do; as when a housewife compares her weekly shopping, her ironing and washing, her decorating and dusting and cooking with ours and says she knows!

I shouldn't feel aggressive for we have only ourselves to blame that we live so far from the road, will never do things on a small scale, take so many children away, whatever the weather, stock our farm with a maximum of animals and build ourselves a mansion to repair and decorate.

I collected my post and opened it in the queue at the village shop. A few bills, a *Readers' Digest* competition and a letter from Paul, which said:

'Have a holiday, you and Margaret, at half-term and I'll come down and look after everything.'

A hundred and fifty cattle, innumerable pigs and poultry, a very ill old man, a handicapped brother and two elderly ladies and Paul was offering to come down and take over whilst we had a holiday! I felt tears of joy threaten to appear. Someone cared.

Returning to the Moor Gate, I dropped my full rucksack in the shelter of the haystack and began to dig with renewed strength. We could not accept his offer, of course. Wild horses would not have dragged us away from our responsibilities. It was enough just to receive the offer. I knew the letter would please Father and Margaret. 'One day we'll accept that offer,' she said.

Father seemed a little easier. Auntie Mary had gone home to attend to some detail for an hour or two on the Saturday afternoon. Whilst she was out, Father seemed intent on talking about the future.

'There are three things I want,' he said. 'I want the farm to go on.'

'That's OK, Dad,' I said. 'I'll give up school and Margaret and I will go on together.'

He cried very easily. 'I want the farm to go on,' he repeated. It was terribly important to him. He had given his whole life to The Currer. He had been retired for nearly twenty years in name only. He had farmed for the future, as if he were going to live forever. Now he was leaving and I believe he understood what we understand. He did not say, 'Look after your mother and Harry,' for these and all our other problems are transitory. He did not worry about us coping with those nor doubt our intention to do so. The problems of our lifetime we would handle as we had been taught. But the continuity of the farm was another thing altogether. We may have eternal life elsewhere but the farm would only know perpetuity on earth. Father thought ours was a very beautiful corner of the earth and his dearest wish was that the farm should go on. It was not the sentimental wish of a dying man, asking for the moon. Father was rational, mentally sound, and it was almost a command. 'I want the farm to go on.'

'Yes, Dad,' I reassured him. 'I have told you. I will give up school and Margaret and I will go on together.' Now, nine years later, we are sure that he meant more than that, that he wanted the farm to continue beyond our lifetime. It is a great joy that we can promise him that also.

'And I want you to be independent,' he said. 'Give up making hay. Keep more stock and buy the hay.' He knew how dependent we had to be on our neighbours and on the weather lasting throughout their hay-time and ours. 'Graze the land. Buy more calves and buy the hay. Be dependent on someone selling it, not making it.'

'I'll do that, Dad,' Margaret said.

'And another thing,' the old man said. 'I'd like your book to be published.'

'As soon as I get an estimate, I'll do that,' I promised.

A crowd of youngsters came that afternoon, Hazel's children, Joanna and Jonathan and a number of their friends, among them Mike who has become our electrician. Joanna, already a nurse, rearranged Father's pillows and made him more comfortable. He beamed his pleasure. He loved all youngsters and nurses brought a wetness to his eyes. He had a great respect for them. He insisted that the boys could watch the football on television but they had seen the stack of hay at the top of the road. Jonathan, on leave from the Army, asked, 'Do you want us to bring it down, Skipper?'

So they finished clearing the road enough for the Land Rover to make several trips and they brought enough loads to see us over the weekend. 'We'll come back and finish the job next week, Skipper,' they promised. Dear lads, Paul wasn't the only one who cared. Someone Up There was still looking after us.

The following day, Sunday, Father had a heart attack. The on-duty doctor was called, collected at the top of the hill and brought down our treacherously narrow road with its high walls of dug-out snow and deep wheel ruts. We had a poor night, sleeping, waking, sleeping, waking. At one point Father distinctly said, 'Don't worry. There are two of me.' A little later he said, 'Don't go to school tomorrow.'

This is it, I thought. Now is the time I must ask for leave of absence. When morning came I rang Winnie and told her I would not be coming and asked if she wanted me to get a supply teacher. She said there was no hurry. They could manage a few days and see what happened. I don't think we ever had more than three supply teachers in all the twenty-one years that I was there.

Our own doctor came at mid-day. Father seemed to be in considerable pain and the doctor prescribed some tablets to relieve it. Father was sitting in a chair beside his bed in the sunshine-filled room, very weak but wanting to talk. He held the doctor to him and asked after his daughter. Then he said, 'The only thing a man ever needs to know is that he is loved and respected by his family.'

Mother sat with him all afternoon whilst Margaret attended to the cattle and I ferried the doctor back to his car and continued into town to pick up the prescription. There were thirty pills. It seemed a life sentence. I couldn't wish for him to suffer so long. On returning I gave him one pill and it brought him sleep but his breathing made a distressing noise which we did not know how to interpret. We could not close our ears to the sound. We hoped it was not made in agony and we moved restlessly.

When it was very late we persuaded Mother to go to bed and we unrolled our sleeping bags but we could not sleep for the noise of Father's breathing. At midnight we phoned the doctor to satisfy ourselves that the noise Father was making was not one of distress but of unconsciousness. It was a different doctor, one who lived in the village, just a few minutes away. 'I'll come,' he said.

Cold and miserable I ventured out into the night. The Land Rover wheels made a breaking noise as they began to rotate, so crusted were they with ice and snow. It was a dark, quiet night. I sat impatiently waiting at the top of the road, alert for the first sign of approaching headlights. When he came he transferred himself to the Land Rover and we began the precipitous journey home.

As soon as the doctor heard the noise he said there was pneumonia. He assured us that Father was unconscious and not in pain. He gave him an injection and then Father was sleeping peacefully. After a while I took the doctor back up the hill and Margaret walked round her cattle and turned out the shed lights for the night.

There seemed no point in waking a very old lady to tell her we had sent for the doctor and that Father was sleeping very quietly and that all would be well until morning. Instead we made another cup of coffee and were drinking it relaxed before the fire, talking quietly for an hour, maybe more. I remember that the fire was burning very red as it always does when there is heavy frost. We were very tired but we wondered, frankly, if we would ever sleep the whole night through again, whether we would have lost the habit. For four years we had known broken nights and for the last six weeks we had barely slept at all. We were stiff with snow shovelling and bale carrying and our hands were cut and blistered with icy binder twine. We were about to say goodbye to the person we had needed most in this demanding life of ours.

Somewhere around two o'clock Father's breathing became noisy, stopped, started again. We had no time to call Mother. I remember saying, 'I think he's dying,' and I think I said, 'Goodbye, old man.' Very quietly he had slipped through 'the open door'.

When someone, or an animal, dies, there is no doubt in our minds that in death there is mystery and peace and an absence of fear. Later, because we are human, doubts occasionally invade but at that moment I really believed that there were two of my father. 'There are two of me,' he had said. I think there were. The body we buried was the physical one we knew but the spiritual one, the one which had been the friend, mentor, comforter, husband and father, had gone elsewhere and yet remained. We can feel his presence constantly for we are always finishing the work he left us to do.

For a long time we sat waiting, talking, thinking. Then we phoned the doctor who said, 'Go to bed. Call for the death certificate in the morning!' The dogs, which had slept by Father's bed for six weeks, were called from the front room. We picked up our sleeping bags, closed the door and went upstairs to Mother's bedroom. She was sleeping but stirred and we told her. 'He's looking very peaceful,' we said. Auntie Mary heard us, came into the bedroom and got into bed with Mother, and we all cried.

It was cold so we got into our sleeping bags and lay down on the hard bedroom floor wondering whether we would sleep. It never occurred to us to go to our soft cold beds. Miraculously we slept until long after daylight, until Harry, who is not an early riser, came into the bedroom and wondered why we were all together.

Sunshine poured into the sitting room so that the absence of a fire went unnoticed. There was no chill, only a peace, a hope and a certainty that if, as Grandfather Cabby Tom said, you do 'nowt right wrong' there is no need to fear dying. We were only full of gratitude remembering Father. He could not have done more. Without parental affection he had continued to be a loyal son, assuming responsibility when he had to, taking the mismanagement and debt on his own shoulders and struggling always to get the weight of it off his back. He had been a perfect husband and friend to Mother. Never once had he left his family for personal pleasure. No drinking or golf or football. He had been a good shepherd, getting on with the job God had given him to do and, if there is a God in Heaven, there too will be our father.

It does not pain me to record these intimate details of the winter in which my father died for, to us, they were very beautiful. It was a wholly happy time. Nothing had been left undone or unsaid. There was no feeling of guilt. We had done for him and he for us, everything that anybody could do.

I arranged to meet the undertaker's car at the top of the road. Had any one told me earlier that I would have had to help lift the empty coffin into the back of the Land Rover and, a little while later, take the full one slowly back up the hill, I would have been shocked and unbelieving. Father took his last journey over the land he had ploughed and reseeded, through the fields to the gate, in his own Land Rover. It was the way he would have chosen. Sentimental I may be but, to me, that short journey was triumphant. He had made it, my Father, done his bit, multiplied, ten-fold, the talents he had received from his Maker and earned his place in whatever eternity there is. Though it was only February, somewhere my father would hear the cuckoo.

I cried a bit on the return journey. To mourn is healthy and right. Father died without worldly possessions, having passed on all that he had long ago. I collected the death certificate and only when she saw the cause of death did Mother know the real nature of Father's illness. I am sure we had been right to withhold the knowledge. The last three and a half years had been so happy. It is easier to behave normally than to pretend and Margaret and I had been too busy to worry.

That night Margaret and I slept right through till morning. We had been well trained.

On Wednesday afternoon I returned to school and the children, who had been told why I was absent, welcomed me with open arms. One small infant gave me a bear hug and a big kiss. Instead of a story, I told the children about my father, about the farm and what he had done. I told them of his fortitude and goodness. I told them about the snow and how it continually blocked our road and I told them how sure I was that the promise and teachings of Jesus were true.

There is so very much to teach children. Let them experiment and find out for themselves, psychologists told us. I preferred to teach them everything I knew, which left them plenty to find out for themselves. I told them I would be away again on Friday for the funeral.

Dolores Shaw-Smith came down to The Currer with a shopping bag full of simple groceries. Mother was very touched. Dolores spent the afternoon carrying water for Margaret.

Once more I began leaving the Land Rover in the village in case more overnight snow penned me in. Thursday was a normal school day but we had arranged that I would drive right down to the farm, and pick up Mother, Harry, Auntie Mary and Margaret and that we would all go to the Chapel of Rest to pay our last respects to Father.

Mother was waiting impatiently, that brave, little old woman who had been Father's pride and joy for nearly sixty years, and Harry, the son he had bathed and shaved and cared for, for half a century. There was Auntie Mary, still limping, who had shared so much of our joy and sorrow and Margaret who was virtually alone now to farm the hundred and seventy acres of good pasture and tend animals galore. They all piled into the station wagon. It was the first time Mother had been out for over a month, the first time she had seen the dug-out road with its high walls of snow and the huge drifts at the gateway.

It was very cold. I switched on the heater to clear the moisture which perpetually iced on the windscreen. It did very little to take the chill out of old bones. There was a constant crunching of hard snow beneath the wheels.

The road to the neighbouring village is steep and we were nearing the top of the first climb when our Land Rover stopped pulling. We had plenty of petrol but the power had gone. The gears wouldn't work. I freewheeled to the bottom of the hill, backwards all the way, praying that the brakes wouldn't fail. I couldn't believe our faithful friend was letting us down. I eased myself out of the driving seat to let Margaret get to the controls but the Land Rover would not move for her either.

Our luck is an ever-present miracle. Had the vehicle stalled over the brow of the hill, that would have been a different thing altogether. But the good friend stopped within feet of a freewheel reverse being impossible. At the foot of the hill lived my cousin Freda's boy and he was at home, a rare thing at that hour of day. His transport was incapable of taking us home but it could easily take us to the Chapel of Rest which was our immediate aim.

There was only one passenger seat in the van. We guided Mother onto it, pushed Harry and Auntie Mary into the back and jumped in ourselves. It was not a dignified last journey to pay our respects but it was typical. We always have what Mother calls a 'carry-on'. It was cramped and uncomfortable on the floor and in the pit of our stomachs was the gnawing realisation that we had no means of getting our old and disabled family home.

The Chapel of Rest felt warm after the chill of the evening air. The sleeping man in the coffin looked very young and at peace. We would mourn for a short time but all memory would be a thanksgiving. The Master he had served, had come for him to enquire into the use he had made of his opportunities and I know that He said, 'Well, done, thou good and faithful servant. Enter thou into the joy of thy Lord.'

Later, in the warmth of Stuart's sitting room, we phoned David Simmonite, six miles away, and arranged for him to send a couple of lads to tow away the station wagon. We knew they would come in a Land Rover. The best we could do was to wait for them to come, and beg a lift home.

An hour and a half later the breakdown Land Rover came with two fresh-faced longhaired lads in dirty, greasy overalls. ''S gear box,' was the verdict. 'We'll tek it an' do it next week.'

'Do us a favour,' we begged. 'Only a Land Rover can take us home!' We squeezed the two old ladies into the front seat and Harry we lifted into the open back, on top of the rubble of tools and equipment, beside the crane. The other young man, Margaret and I climbed precariously on top of him, and the vehicle turned towards home. The young driver listened without comment as Mother told him what our errand had been and about the funeral tomorrow.

Our isolation looked more complete than ever from the top of our road. There is only semi-darkness when snow lies. The frost was very keen. The road through the village was covered in black ice, the top road was hard packed with snow, a solid white smoothness polished by many wheels. Our road to the farm was little more than a glacier.

The young man at the wheel said nothing. He was finding the journey similar to a bob-sleigh ride. The road was a roofless tunnel down which you slid without steering. Cramped and frozen we climbed out into the yard among the heaped drifts. Discoloured water from the barn had frozen to form a golden rink in front of the house. Margaret on one side and I on the other, we escorted each of our dependents the last, treacherous few yards into the house. We thanked the two lads and stood in the cold yard watching their headlights re-climb the hill. We were home! Our luck was holding. Or is it the peculiar slant of our philosophy which insists that whatever way the coin lands it is right for us.

'We won't be able to go to the funeral,' Mother said. Margaret and I could walk, but the others couldn't. I rang a friend, Tony Ainley, who lives on the moor above us, on the farm from which Father, Jack Clay and I sledged hay in 1947. He has a Range Rover and a kind heart.

'Are you going to Father's funeral tomorrow?' I asked. I knew he would be. I told him what had happened and asked if he could come and collect us. See, that was another problem solved!

Margaret and I went out to feed the cattle in the frosty dark. The farm must go on, Father had said. No doubt there'd be speculations. Neighbours would wonder how much he had left and would never believe that his assets amounted to a single share in Preston Farmers. Many would now expect us to sell. They would say that Margaret could not carry on alone, that the dreadful winter was an omen, a warning to us to get out while we were still in one piece. Would-be buyers would keep their ears and eyes open.

Don't worry, old man, we are going right on to the end of the road.

There is comfort in a school full of children and there is consolation in the smelly warmth of a cattle shed. Hour after hour we coped with the feeding of cattle, the carrying of water to sheds with frozen pipes, scattering bedding straw and re-filling the mangers.

It was long past midnight when Margaret came to bed. She sometimes wakens me with a message but I do not mind. What pleasure is there greater than looking at the clock in the middle of the night and realising that there are several more hours of sleep?

'I've a calf out of sorts,' she said. 'If you waken, tell me, and I'll get up and have another look at it.'

I wakened again at about half past two. Something must have disturbed me. The heap in the next bed was unconscious and it seemed unkind to wake her and turn her out into the night, torch in hand, to check a sick animal but I knew I would be in trouble if I did not. As she emerged from the blankets I noticed she had entered them only partially undressed. She pulled on trousers and sweater and covered her bed to keep it warm.

I heard her sleepy feet drag along the passage. She was going to miss Father a lot. I must keep awake until she gets back, I thought. She was not long. Normally she will just grunt, say, 'It's OK till morning. Check when you get up,' or some such acknowledgement of my loyalty.

This time she came to my bed, wide-awake with excitement and emotion. 'Jean,' she whispered, 'Our Land Rover is in the yard!' Opening the front door and stepping out into the snowbound night, she had noticed a blackness against the white. She thought it was an illusion caused by switching on the porch light. There were drifts in front of the stable and the garage. The perimeter of the yard was sculptured so that dark shadows were thrown about anywhere. But it was no illusion. There was our station wagon, the right number plate, the same rear passenger door damage caused by the school-yard buttress. In tears of gratitude she went to check the calf. There was no panic there. The Streptopen she had given must be working. She hurried back to bed choking with excitement and wonder. She sat on my bed telling me. We couldn't believe it!

I couldn't get to sleep for quite some time. How Father would have loved it! He loved young people. Wouldn't he have been just tickled pink at the thought of those two, long-haired, dirty mechanics, working until morning, then driving six miles in the snow to return the repaired Land Rover because Mother was over eighty, Harry handicapped and Auntie Mary still limping; because we were so vulnerable at The Currer, in snow, without transport and a funeral to attend. I could see my Father's smile, the liquid eyes and hear him tell the story to everyone. He leaned to the working, dirty members of society, who did not brag about their good deeds or about how much this and that had cost and the lads who calmly changed the gear box and completed the job in the small hours had done so unknown by their employer. When they returned it to us they did not wake us to announce that they had done so. Oh boy, would they have pleased my father!

Was it wrong to feel so happy on the morning of a funeral? Jesus said, 'In my Father's House are many mansions. If it were not so I would have told you.' When my Father died it was not difficult to believe. It is futile and impudent to accept some of His commandments and to try to justify disobedience of the others. Mankind has never accepted that, but there are individuals, irrespective of colour, or creed, or class, who have lived by the standards He set. Here and there those with two coats have given one away, or have turned the other cheek, been servants of all and have made use of all the talents given to them. Now and again you find a man who, having put his hand to the plough, labours to the end, a Good Shepherd, a Samaritan who will cross over the road, a man who will give and give and give again. My father was one of these. He was a Sower who spent his life sowing good seed, a man with great compassion. He had taught as someone surely must have taught him and he had won, this little, peace-loving man of ours. If there is a prize to be received then Father is receiving it.

The memory of Father's funeral will stay with us forever. A severe frost held the earth in such tension, walking was a hazard for young and old. Snow had not been cleared from the approach to the church but it had been well trampled over the past six Sundays of Arctic weather and was little less than a skating rink. Those who came were clinging to each other for support but, even so, more than eighty people made the dangerous journey from car to church door and the warmth within. Eighty people representing all walks of life, all levels of a social order Father had never believed in for he treated all as equal.

There were farmers, of course, and teachers, grown-up Guides and school-children's parents. There were corn men and cattle dealers, magistrates and mill owners, old age pensioners from the village, relatives and close friends. Rich and poor had come to acknowledge that Father had lived graciously and farmed with gratitude, not arrogance.

There was an abundance of flowers, predominantly daffodils. Father loved daffodils. There was a rich volume of sound. 'The Lord is my Shepherd, I'll not want,' we sang with pride and without tears. It was as if we were all cheering Father past the final post and giving him the standing ovation he deserved.

Margaret and I, having safely escorted our dependents to the first car behind the cortège, returned again and again to help the aged over the ice. We begged lifts for village pensioners who had come on foot and for whom the return climb would be dangerous. Finally we got into the cab behind the hearse for the journey to the cemetery in the valley.

Grouped on the church steps were many of our friends. Incredibly, as the cortège began to move, Hazel, in the forefront of the group, began to wave as if we were a wedding party setting off on honeymoon. We waved back and others responded. As the line of cars bearing the family mourners drew away everyone was waving. How Father would have smiled.

All these things I told my children when I returned to school on the following Monday. They listened intently for children love pathos, and wonder at the mysteries of life.

And still the frost held and the struggle to feed cattle and to survive on the hill continued. Of great comfort to us were the puppies of Skye's Christmas litter. Margaret said they were the drugs which kept her going during that long winter. There was a joyous frolicking in the barn. True to their promise, Jonathan and his friend came and ferried the whole load of hay from outside the Moor Gate and deposited it in the empty Dutch barn. Now the pups could scramble up the bales and tumble from the heights for the short time that it lasted. Another load was left on the top road. Raymond and Dolores, neighbours who live higher on the moor, came to help for Jonathan's leave was over.

Every week I went down to the white cemetery intending to take off the dead sprays and each time I found the flowers still living, held in some uncanny, almost immortal, beauty. If anyone had asked me, I would have said that frost was a killer. But the weather of 1979 was a preserver. Week after week I came home to report my job still undone. The children at school kept asking, 'Have the flowers died yet, Miss Brown?'

'If we need proof of immortality,' Margaret said, 'the flowers say it all.' Six weeks later I brought home some of the daffodils and pressed them in the family Bible. Their colour still remains.

It seemed as though the postman would never deliver the mail again. On my way to school, each morning, I collected it. At half-term there was yet another fall of snow followed by a load of hay. The sequence was becoming monotonous. We began, once more, at the bottom of the road, throwing shovelsful of snow, one weary one after the other. We were getting near the top of the hill when we saw two people come towards us, wielding shovels. It was Pat and Alan, she a Guider friend and he a teacher on half-term holiday. 'We've come to see how you are getting on and we've brought our shovels! '

The four of us threw out the snow with gusto; we reached the gate onto the road. 'Come and have lunch with us,' I said.

'We'll all go down in my car,' said Alan, viewing the newly cleared ribbon of road.

'No way,' we said, 'the car stays at the top.' But it is impossible to say nay to a man who wants to get into his car and drive it down, if he has just bought newfangled chains for the wheels and is therefore full of justifiable confidence.

Lunch was pleasant. It was the first time we had had guests since before Father died. These were the first friends to come since our bereavement. We talked long over the dinnertime meal. Then Mother and Harry went to get ready to have tea with Cousin Freda. Alan said, 'I'll take them as we go.'

When everyone was ready he opened the car door and Mother and Harry were guided inside. 'Thank you a thousand times,' we said and watched the full vehicle, with its brand new chains, drive to the foot of the hill and flounder. We always struggle a long time before we give in and go for the Land Rover. We dig and push and go for cinders but, in the end, we nearly always have to go for a tow rope and our four wheel drive wonder. After nearly an hour we admitted defeat. We unloaded Mother and Harry out of Alan's car and into the station wagon and put on the towrope. Slowly and painfully we climbed the hill. We did not embarrass the good man by saying, 'I told you so.' There are no kinder people than Pat and Alan. He once offered to lend us his car to go on holiday, remember!

Towards the end of February we phoned our builder friend who had promised to take off the barn roof in the spring. 'When the weather permits,' we reminded him, 'don't forget our roof!'

I received an estimate for the printing and binding of *A Song to Sing and a Tale to Tell*. My Shetland publisher said the price was too high and I had better try another printer, but I was convinced I had already got the right one. The firm was so near and I had been treated with such courtesy. So I returned, over the snow-covered moorland, to plead my case again and see if we could reduce the cost.

A change of paper made only a small difference. The main cost was in the typesetting and designing. It was suggested that I present the manuscript as camera-ready copy. I returned home with no idea whatsoever how to go about it.

I rang Tony Ainley who had not, after all, been needed to transport us to Father's funeral. He seemed the only person I knew who might remotely know a typesetter. 'Certainly, Jean, no hesitation. David Hanson.'

'I can't believe it!' I said. 'I taught the boy.'

'He and his wife work together. She was Irene Wormald.'

'Never! I taught her, she was one of my Guides and I took her to camp!' I was on the right trail. 'The printers have told me if I present them with camera-ready copy that is the cheapest way to publish.'

'I can do that for you,' Tony said, 'And nothing would give me more pleasure than to do so. Bring up the manuscript.'

Miracles are funny things and happen in all sorts of roundabout ways. A friend in need is a miracle. It is too much of a coincidence that the right fellow is always on hand. We even have punctures on the doorsteps of people who can change tyres and we run out of petrol outside petrol stations. Father's philosophy was always, 'Sumthing'll turn up.' Something does, far too often for it to be just chance.

This is an autobiography about ordinary people getting the maximum fun out of ordinary things. If it has any value at all on the bookshelf it is to say to other ordinary people that life isn't ordinary at all. It's a miracle from first to last and if you do not know how to find it so you have missed the most important truth of all.

Part Three

Come, come, light up the fire,
Come, come, join in the ring.
Here find dreams to inspire,
Stories to tell, music to sing.
Campfire Round

Chapter Nineteen

It began with a circular sent to several hundred smallholders and farmers in our area, by the Ministry of Agriculture, no more than three weeks after Father was buried. The letter stated that, owing to an acute shortage of holiday accommodation locally, the English Tourist Board had labelled this area as 'High Priority'. Anyone who had a barn, shed or cottage suitable for adaptation, was eligible for a 30 per cent grant. Anyone interested was invited to a meeting in a Haworth pub on a date at the end of March. I read and re-read the letter over my playtime coffee and decided to hide it from the prying eyes of Mother and wait for an evening opportunity to speak to Margaret.

We were still deep in snow. I had promised Father that I would give up my teaching but how could I? We desperately needed the money. I loved my job. Forty-nine was far too young to retire. Margaret needed me at home but only in an emergency. What was I supposed to do between emergencies? There would be an almighty mess when the barn came down. There were walls and fences to build, the road to repair and decorating to do. The cow was to milk and butter to churn, clothes to make and my Guiding was pretty nearly a full-time job. But it wouldn't be enough. I needed more challenge than that!

Something will turn up, Father would have said. Well, it had. That he had initiated it, Margaret was sure. No one else, she said, could have come up with such a mad scheme to keep us busy, and at The Currer, for the rest of our lives.

Sitting in the Dutch barn, among the dwindling bales of hay, we re-read the letter and argued the outcome. Suppose we took down the barn and, with the English Tourist Board's grant, rebuilt with the materials on hand? Suppose we added a small amount of holiday accommodation, a dining room, a bathroom and a couple of bedrooms, would we not have killed two birds with one stone? To the farmhouse we would have added another source of income with a job for me to do until I wished to retire and at the same time we would have added a retirement cottage to the farm, a small, manageable place for us to retire into when Margaret got too old to farm and we needed to employ a manager. What would be nicer, we argued, than a ground floor, purpose-built flat in which to end our days at The Currer?

The idea of bed and breakfast wasn't entirely new. It had crossed my mind once before. We convinced ourselves that we really ought to go to the meeting at the end of March. In the meantime we kept the arrival of the letter a secret.

The snow finally began to go, leaving the heavy drifts lining the walls until well into April and the fields everywhere became waterlogged. As soon as the road was clear we advertised the pups. They were three months old and had been ready to go for quite some time. I went into the newspaper office and was asked how many nights I wished the advertisement to appear.

'I thought the minimum was three,' I said.

'It's changed,' the girl replied. 'Now you can advertise one night only. Shall I say two nights and if all the pups have gone on the first night, ring me and I'll stop the second night.'

I remember my sarcastic laughter. 'You must be joking. We'll never ever get rid of six. We'll be left more than we can cope with!'

I was wrong. Before five o'clock on the first night every pup had found a home. We recorded nearly fifty calls. I hurriedly cancelled the second night and the newspaper girl said, 'I told you so.'

The last pup was collected on Friday, a dark, wet night. There were patches of white on the field edges and everywhere else was a quagmire. At about eight o'clock the phone rang. Those collecting the pup were just leaving home. Harry stood by the sitting-room window waiting for the headlights to flood the top road.

Half an hour later he shouted, 'A car's coming.' Then he said, 'It's not coming down the road, it is coming down the field!'

Sure enough the driver had not turned abruptly and followed the road. He had continued forward, left the track and had careered down the field before becoming engulfed in the bog. He had ploughed to a standstill in the middle of the first intake. If there is one thing worse than pushing people out of snow it is pushing them out of a knee-deep bog.

A young woman came to the door. 'Oh dear,' she said, 'My father's going mad up there. He's blowing his top an' swearing like anything. I daren't go back alone.'

She took the pup in her arms and we followed with some reluctance. We had struggled too much, too long, too hard and the stupid man in the warmth of his car, in the middle of a field was just the last straw.

We walked up the hill knowing full well we'd have to come back and get the little Land Rover and a towrope. Still, there is always a chance that two good pushes will do and there is always a problem of where to attach a tow rope to a modern car!

The girl's warning was unnecessary for the good man knew how to behave in front of us if not before his daughter. His language was moderate and his apologies sincere. We struggled for a little while but there was no way he would ever get out without the Land Rover. Cold, wet and very fed up we went home for the rescue vehicle and towed the car out of the mud. Then we went home to change our saturated clothes.

I went to Tony's studio, on the moor, walking across the fields from Cliff Farm through the drifts. I thoroughly enjoyed the publishing of *A Song to Sing and a Tale to Tell*. Jenny Sharp, one of my sixteen-year-old Guides, did the illustrations and it was fun to send off for the copyrights of the songs with which I preceded each chapter. I made frequent visits to the typesetter, chose the photographs to be included and the important one for the cover.

The Haworth moors were still holding their blanket of snow when we attended the Ministry of Agriculture meeting. The previous day we told Mother and Harry about the letter and our intention to attend. Strangely, as was the case in 1957, when Father proposed the removal to The Currer, Mother did not voice the words, 'It's ridic'lous.' Whenever she is presented with the Impossible, Mother can cope. For me to end my career and be at home all day would be fine by her. She didn't mind the barn coming down. She would happily sell an acre or two if it would make things easier financially.

Neither did Mother mind about a few holiday guests around in the summer time. They would come and go in a quite separate, newly built part of the house and only in the holiday season. She amicably agreed to go with Harry to Auntie Mary's for an evening by the fire whilst we went to the meeting.

That night was an innovation for Margaret and me. The first and, so far, last evening visit to a public house. When we arrived people were already flocking inside for a pre-meeting drink. We were embarrassed and pottered around in Haworth Main Street, looking at the bric-à-brac and pausing before the bookshops, whiling away the time until the meeting began.

One of the Guides, whose home was there, caught us window-shopping. 'It's Skipper and Flim!' she exclaimed. 'What are you doing here?' Laughing together, we realised how cold we were. We all linked arms, turned our backs on the biting wind and laughed at the absurdity of our lives.

At the appointed hour we crept self-consciously into the crowded assembly and when the meeting was over we picked up an application form for a grant-in-aid and tiptoed out.

I cannot remember the actual order of the events that followed. Our first step was to delay the builder from coming to take down the barn. I think we had to apply for planning permission and grant-in-aid at the same time. The local authority, however, replied to our application for planning permission absolutely negatively. 'No building on the Green Belt.' Full stop. We would be allowed to convert the existing barn, all of it, but forbidden to pull it down and rebuild.

Margaret phoned me at school with the devastating news. I said 'The barn is enormous. We don't want an hotel.'

At the first opportunity I rang the Ministry of Agriculture in my best headmistress manner. 'You started this,' I accused. 'You tell the Council. What do you all think we are? The barn is as big as a cathedral!'

'Other people,' said the tolerant man whose life was comfortably spent in some distant office, 'other people are crying because their barns are so small. Hardly big enough to interest the English Tourist Board.'

'But we don't want an hotel!' I said for the umpteenth time. 'We are only farmers, willing to do a few farmhouse breakfasts. Do you know how big our barn is? Well, it's too big!'

'My dear,' said the tolerant man, 'if you are going into this you are going into it.'

But the man was our friend after all. He said, 'Perhaps the English Tourist Board would agree to two self-catering cottages in half the area and bed and breakfast space in the other half.'

Self-catering cottages! The words were magic. We weren't hotel people, but tell me anyone else in the country who loved holiday cottages more than we did! If the Tourist Board would swallow that then nothing would stop our plans going ahead and the barn would not have to be pulled down. If anything would tip the balance towards the go-ahead, the knowledge that we would be able to preserve the barn would weigh heavily.

We became determined that the plans would pass through all the necessary red tape. We buried our heads in the sand, forgot that I would have to leave the school I loved, forgot that it would all have to be paid with a bank overdraft, forgot the bed and breakfast visitors and thought wholly about holiday cottages. The rest we would cope with, little by little but the two dream cottages were what kept us going through the long and difficult months ahead.

The first thing to do was to draw the plans. I did so again and again. We had one early, useful idea. Instead of two narrow cottages with a lot of wasted space and cost if two staircases were needed, we decided to make two cottage flats. This would give us a ground floor area we could adapt suitably for the disabled and the first floor one could be approached by outside, barn steps. Having once mentioned the disabled it followed that we bore them in mind in the bed and breakfast area, too. We then passed the plans on to a competent draughtsman friend who put them onto linen for the Council. He interpreted them to the inch, bless him. We had tried to reach perfection but in our ignorance we did not know what lay ahead and can therefore take little credit for the extraordinary precision of our planning. We asked our builder friend for an estimate and went to see the bank manager.

*   *   *   *   *

Shortly after Father's death we made another decision. 'Let's go to Tiree.' we said. Since Marian Maclean's death, we knew that her cottage had been modernised and was being let to holiday visitors. I rang Charlie, her son, and asked if it were free for a fortnight around our spring bank holiday. It was. What could be more perfect than two weeks of utter peace on Tiree?

Considering that we are such very poor singers it is extraordinary how meaningful song has always been to us. From my lips, perpetually, came the psalm of my choristers, those two quite beautiful girls, Saskia and Joanne, who so often sang for our school assemblies,

> Lead me, Lord, lead me in Thy righteousness,
> Make my way plain before Thy face,
> For it is Thou, Lord, Thou Lord only
> That makest me dwell in safety.

The church bells played it to me on the hour in the little village where I taught. The parish church echoed it whilst I did the family shopping in town. The Tiree waves seemed to say, 'Lead me Lord.' My way seemed to be appearing plain enough.

I think we knew then that what we were planning to do would snooker us completely. We were hell-bent on doing something to The Currer which would be irreversible. Life would never again be the same. We were holding the thing we loved most, The Currer, as security for a bank loan, and failure in our new venture would mean bankruptcy and a sale. Our recent bereavement had robbed us of the person we did everything for. Margaret farmed for Father. It was as simple as that. We cultivated the land, made green the heather slopes, bought and reared cattle for Father.

Suddenly this fundamental reason for working so hard was gone and we searched for some replacement and we floundered around for half a dozen years, trying to find the answer to that one.

On Tiree, in 1979, we had this strange feeling that we were being led, that Father was still telling us what to do to ensure the continuity of the farm. Perhaps he knew already, in his new dimension, the right way to achieve it.

We absorbed a great deal of good sense from the whitewashed cottage at Salum. The white walls appealed and we knew that we would not burden ourselves with wallpaper in our own two cottages. Most of the time we sat outside in the sunshine, utterly content. The evenings we spent with long-known friends. Alone, without the large family of children, we could just lie for hours on the machair or on the edge of one of the bays, finding shelter from a wind which perpetually blows over the Atlantic. Without the noise of children we could clearly hear the lark singing, the seagulls calling and the flip, flop of the long wave on the Salum shore.

On our return we waited in vain for the swallows. For the first time they did not nest in the barn. How terribly sad Father would have been. I became paranoiac about the cuckoo but he sang all spring.

We took down a shed we had erected against the dutch barn. If we were to lose the barn, we argued, we'd need a shed to replace it but if we were to convert the barn into holiday accommodation that lean-to would be far too near. So we carried the timbers into the orchard quadrangle, our choice for the new shed. Three sides were already there. It meant we lost the fruit trees and a few soft fruit bushes and raspberry canes but none were very productive for the sheds we had built around them had taken away the sun and the wealth of manure which had oozed out of them had resulted in a forest of overgrown weeds which annually strangled trees and bushes.

In memory of Father we spent a great deal of time on his garden in 1979. I dug every inch of the huge area and we planted it with more vegetables than our kitchen needed, as Father had, so that we had enough to give away. Margaret was always the one who did most of the weeding. Father and she had been known to be on their knees weeding the carrots and stringing the peas on the morning of the day we went on holiday. Mother would be furious.

Towards the end of the summer term I arranged for Linda, one of my camping team, to come and help me inspect the tents. Mother had invited two elderly spinsters for a week and Auntie Mary was staying, too. Margaret was free to spend some long hours on the garden, planting out the cabbages and cauliflowers, stringing the peas and weeding the beetroot and carrots. There was a lot of work in the huge greenhouse. The tomato plants were already heavy with fruit. The flowers had set well and the clusters were just beginning to show a lightening of their green which preceded ripening.

We had taken Father's advice about the hay and put the meadows down to pasture. The pressure of hay-time was gone so the garden received the extra attention it had missed in previous years. There is no healthier garden than a farm one for the abundance of bedding manure ensures that everything grows, vegetables and weeds galore. Lettuces flourished in the greenhouse, laying a pale green carpet at the south end. The re-siting of the greenhouse, after the gales, had trapped the rhubarb in a dark passageway between it and the shed and the result was a mass of red, juicy stalks climbing to find the sun.

On the Saturday morning I was up early to plan the camp equipment day. Early but not before the sun for it was July. Cattle are on the move soon after sunrise. I put the kettle on for my early morning cup of coffee and went to let out the ducks. The garden gate was open and my breathing stopped. I hurried through and found half the herd placidly ruminating on the lawn.

Contented cows, full and warm, chew their cud with elevated heads and noses in the air. It gives them a look of superiority and arrogance. What farmer does not feel good if his cattle are over-full before the sun is high, their bellies so extended that little rumbling noises are heard. It is a sign of a good summer with plenty of warm rain and sunshine.

But the sight of these ridiculous animals, sitting on the lawn on that early Saturday morning, spelt disaster. What a mess! They were dirty with loose manure, each foot had a sock of garden soil and each nose bore the telltale smear of rich loam. A few were garlanded with pea strands and all were wearing expressions of such impudent smugness I could have screamed.

And the garden? Ruined!

I ran back to the house very nearly in tears. I called up the stairs, 'Margaret. The cows have got into the garden!' There was no way I could persuade all those cows out alone.

We closed our eyes to the chaos and calmly forced each bloated animal to rise. The lawn was riddled with hoof prints, flattened with scores of heavy recumbent animals and splattered with manure. There was a smell of it and of bovine breath and sweat, of bruised plants and disturbed soil. We shook our heads at the tragedy of it all.

The cattle had already been full when they found the open gate. They had galloped among the vegetables, vandalizing rather than devouring. They had played high jump over the pea rows then charged through them dragging the strings and stakes and climbing plants all over the garden.

The greenhouse looked intact but the rhubarb had gone. We became suspicious. We opened the greenhouse door and it was at that point horror gave way to laughter. The break-in was narrow and concealed at the far end of the plastic cloche. The animals had had a circus. Without further damaging the polythene they had rampaged round and round. There was nothing left of the tomato plants or the lettuces and seedlings. They had all been ploughed back into the earth and, for good measure, the bare beds had been well manured: we stood in the doorway and bent ourselves double with laughter. The tragedy had become farce.

All that day Linda worked alone at the tents and Margaret and I tried to salvage what we could, replanting the pulled up vegetables wherever possible. That night there was an hour or two of gentle rain, and next day, which was Sunday, we went to a garden centre and bought some new plants but they were too late in the season and the eventual harvest was poor.

Sadly, that was the end of the garden. I mourn its loss every March when the urge to dig gets into me. I miss the spring weekends and evenings when I used to dig and dig until blisters came and burst and came again. The earth was rich with an ever-plentiful supply of manure. I did not vary my evening activity until the whole area was turned and raked and ready. The smell of the good brown earth was necessary to me in those dear, gone for the moment, days.

Now when we want soft fruits we drive to the strawberry fields and the raspberry farm and gather in stones, not pounds. We put about two hundred-weight of fruit into the freezers. The old order has changed in many respects but the fact that we will sweat for hours, on our knees in a strawberry field, and return with 120lbs. to prepare for immediate freezing proves that we are basically the same people.

In spite of the setback, the camp equipment was ready in time to be sent in advance to Harris for my first camp without Margaret or Hazel or Joan. I felt more vulnerable than ever before but reassured myself that the strong, young team I was taking with me was a good one.

My publisher was operating from Stornoway and he came to meet me at the Rodel Hotel, in South Harris. We had risen early, and walked the Golden

Road on a damp, cold day. Twenty miles later we arrived at the Rodel Hotel, wet, hungry and in extremely good spirits. The hotelier gave us the use of a small reception room hardly big enough for us all to squeeze into. The electric fire and our own heat filled the room with a human fug and our cagoules soon dried. I have never been prouder of the 'Song to Sing' children. They behaved just as I had painted them with my pen. It was a happy hour that the publisher spent with us, in tolerant proximity, talking and singing after walking twenty miles in the rain.

I handed him the proofs of my book, the unbound pages, the sketches and photographs and a copy of the cover sheet. We were all very excited.

Following Father's last commandments, the hay was bought in from a farmer on the York plain and the whole of The Currer acreage put to pasture. This meant we must increase the size of the herd so Margaret started the annual buying of calves, alone and in earnest. Feeding them was easier for we had adopted a new self-feed method. Margaret mixed gallons of the cold milk and poured it into huge plastic containers, positioned round the shed and fitted with a number of teats. The calves could avail themselves of the ad-lib supply as often as they wanted and they seemed to do well, very well in fact. We were sorry for them drinking cold milk instead of natural warmth but they did not seem to mind.

We remember the first load of hay we bought. Margaret and Stuart unloaded it and the bales were so heavy they nearly did themselves an injury. I had to write the cheque for it and we realised that buying hay was going to be a very costly job and we'd have to have more cattle, not just to eat the meadows but to pay for the extra cost of the hay. We began to get cold feet but we bought seventy calves and, as it were, put on warm socks, left our heads in the sand and kept going.

Because the hay had to go into the Dutch barn instead of the laithe, we were short of calf-rearing space and it was imperative that the orchard quadrangle was roofed at once. We gathered up all the fibreglass and corrugated tin we had spare and, using both, managed to roof the shed for nothing. We removed the calves into it at the first possible moment as load after load of hay and straw began to arrive. The laithe remained empty awaiting the slow ritual of Council Planning Regulations.

The same farmer still brings our hay. My favourite Yorkshire story came from him. He has a thriving haulage diversification. A customer, wishing to do business with him said, 'Just fax it to me.' 'Nay lad,' had been the apt reply, 'wiv nobbut just getten rid o't pigeon.'

My book came out in September and as most of them were already spoken for and the rest were sold very quickly, the £4,000 necessary to pay for the typesetting, printing and binding came back to within a hundred pounds. The local radio showed interest; Hazel and I were interviewed and I was asked to read farm stories of Bess and Joanna and, for a little while, I was asked to speak at various societies. The newspapers got the story of Yorkshire's happiest children. Being notorious lasted a few months and then we were forgotten.

We forgot about it, too, with plans and estimates and talk of grants and overdrafts. How could we gamble so outrageously with money we did not have, two women with already enough work to do and enough caring for relatives to put a considerable brake on our activities? We began with less than nothing for we already had an overdraft. We had not worried about that for the cattle, if sold, would have covered it.

What we had now begun was different. We were gambling with The Currer, an uncertainty. By the end of the year we would be deeply in debt. The cattle would cover only a fraction of it. My salary would soon disappear. The interest would be appalling and if we did not succeed we would have to sell up and go.

To gamble with such high stakes was alarming and that we survived the strain was wholly because surviving the physical strain took all our concentration and called for us to pull out of the bag everything we had.

Perhaps part of the reason we did not fear the proposed borrowing was the hope that the English Tourist Board would come up with a 30% grant. This was calculated on the estimate. What we did not know was the cost of a barn conversion cannot be estimated. The one arrived at was totally wrong! If we had known the actual cost we would have backed out of the deal at the beginning. We didn't know so we kept going and remained sane. Another reason we did not feel totally insecure was a confidence trick. Again we are only grateful that a mistake was made.

In October I received a letter from the Local Education Authority bearing excellent news. It stated, briefly, that over three hundred teachers must be axed from the payroll because of the state of the economy and the falling birthrate. It was hoped that enough people would take advantage of voluntary redundancy and early retirement. Anyone was eligible. For those over fifty superannuation would be unfrozen and an enhancement of pension paid to make up for the unworked years.

I couldn't believe it.

There had been no question about if and when I retired: I had no choice in the matter if we were to stay at The Currer. Here I was, on the verge of sending in my resignation, and some demi-god in the local government offered me it on a plate. It could not be true. It was 1979, I had done thirty years of service and was nearly fifty. Therefore I was eligible! It was the thought of a golden handshake and an enhanced pension which kept us clear-headed and I am very grateful to the Authority for the mistake they made.

Joan had always said, 'When you go, I go,' so both of us sent in an application for release. I was convinced that we were doing the right thing. The 400-year-old barn must be preserved. The Currer must remain intact. Easy money did not taste nice. We prefer to get where we are going with sheer hard slog but it was no time for false pride.

The corn roller would have to come out of the barn before we needed to fill the bin with a winter's supply of whole grain. The glass greenhouse had been redundant since the polythene igloo was put up. We decided to take down the glass frames and build a corn store. It must be rat and waterproof so we ferried stone from a fallen wall, a thing we would not dream of doing now, and started again the heavy job of mixing cement. Load after load of stone, bag after bag of cement! We found the building of the corn store rather hard work and worried, a bit, as to whether we were really fit enough for the marathon ahead and the new life beyond. The winter had been tough, the spring and summer full of plans, autumn was approaching and we were whacked. Too much Guiding and camping, too much school activity, too many calves to feed, too much muck to get out, sheds to move, the barn to clear. Teaching, meeting the Council, preparing projections for the Tourist Board, visiting their HQ in York ensured that we were approaching another winter in poor fettle.

We remembered Paul's letter, received in January, telling us he would cope whilst we had a holiday and we decided to put him to the test, take his offer and have a week in Northumberland. Mother wouldn't hear of it. I told her what we were planning whilst in the Land Rover on the way to Auntie Mary's and she was so noisily against the idea that I had to pull in to the kerb, let her protest and quickly back down on the idea.

'Well, let's go to Grange-over-Sands,' I said. I don't know why I suggested that for I had never been to Grange.

'We'll go to Grange,' she said.

'That's right,' I said. 'We'll see the Lake District in autumn. Why not!'

It was a compromise. I saw an advertisement in *The Teacher*, phoned immediately and within minutes had made a booking for our half-term holiday.

Paul accepted without hesitation. It was not an easy job he was undertaking; seventy small calves is no small responsibility. He came down from Newcastle at the weekend to be initiated. We were to leave on the Monday and return on the following Saturday, just five much-needed days.

But before leaving on the Monday there was scheduled the annual brucellosis test. The vet was coming at nine and we had already packed the Land Rover ready to go as soon as the last animal had been put through the crush.

Nothing is slower or muckier than a brucellosis test. The yearlings and the fat heifers all had to be put through the crush. On our farm it is too traumatic to try to separate the bullocks from the herd. They are not tested but it is easier to pen the whole hundred and let the bullocks go through the crush freely while detaining the heifers for the obligatory blood test. The blood drips but slowly into the individual test tubes and each many-lettered ear tag number has to be taken. Our cattle behave like bucking broncos in the crush. Nerves result in a rush of loose muck and as the blood is taken from the tail I leave you to guess what happens.

Such a last-minute-before-departure was typical. It was, however, the first time we left on the heels of a brucellosis test. We became increasingly dirty and the yard got muckier and muckier. The Land Rover stood waiting. Mother, Harry and Auntie Mary watched from the window. Gone, it seemed, were those halcyon days when we could enjoy a perfect packing of our kit.

Like the haymaking the progress of the brucellosis test only gets harder. The fewer the waiting animals the more unco-operative they become. The docile ones have always gone first. When only a dozen remain in the yard they cannot be described as waiting to be put through the crush so much as waiting to cause trouble. They are always the ones who have been driven as far as the crush entrance a few times already and have escaped. They career round the empty yard determined that they will never go into that crush and we are rushing after them. Our vet always enjoyed the last fiasco. With little boy enthusiasm he charged into the ring and threw himself into the spirit of the game. His eventual smile of triumph was almost wicked.

Calmly he re-lit his pipe and, catching sight of the two old ladies and Harry impatiently waiting behind the window and the holiday-packed Land Rover, he turned to us and smiled. Then he said, 'When do you get your bath?' (puff, puff) 'When you get there?'

Too true, young man. Some people are unexpectedly accurate. His comments have become a saying in the household whenever our needs have had to wait. The essential thing is to get into the vehicle, start the engine and get moving.

I love our household sayings. 'Let's blue' is one of our favourites. 'Let's blue,' said one of our small relatives, in the days when whites were dipped in the dolly blue tub at the end of a day's wash. Let's call it a day! We closed the crush gate and Mr Russell came in for his customary cup of black coffee. We peeled off our dirty clothes, pushed them in the washer, replaced them and jumped into the Land Rover. A bath was only a few hours away. We thought longingly of it.

We were leaving Paul with fifty yearlings, thirty-odd very strong bullocks nearly ready for market and seventy young calves only just weaned. He had one other responsibility. The plans for the conversion had been recently passed and all we needed now was the approval of the English Tourist Board. The date this inspection was to take place was during our absence. Whilst we were in Grange the all-important gentlemen would look round our empty, dilapidated barn with its wealth of manure, wet with the perpetual seepage of water from the hill.

We took one last look at the barn before leaving. We no longer mixed calf milk in the last stall of the mistal and what had been our calf dairy was neglected, stale and cobwebbed. Cobwebs also festooned the mistal space where the corn roller waited its removal to the newly built store. They hung in heavy streamers from the roof above which was the loft housing the empty corn bin. There was manure in the groop behind the stall in which Joanna was milked, bags of binder twine, buckets and a dusty pile of empty paper corn sacks. The gnarled stalls looked their incredible age. The bulge in the gable end appeared dangerous even with the retaining wall and the outside buttresses. On the west, mud encroached right up to the almost blank, meandering wall. The fork holes, no longer used for throwing in loose hay, had been walled to keep out the gale. The roof was bad. Here and there the missing slates let in the daylight. A railway sleeper, wedged on the roof of the inside passage, held up the cracked purlin above. The glass had gone from the mistal window and rain had rotted the frame.

The stable was worse. In one corner was an iron bath, deeply embedded in manure. Stalls which had once separated horses, and more recently calves, were crudely reinforced with wooden posts, slats and duckboards. There was a conglomeration of things which ought to be thrown away but which had been kept in case of sudden utility. Everywhere was littered with hen and rooster droppings for the rafters of the stable were the perches of our poultry. The ducks lived in one empty stall and ducks make a wet mess wherever they are!

Finally, draining from the laithe porch was this continual, deep brown ooze with which we were so familiar. The estimate we had sent in to the English Tourist Board was a mere £25,000. We had no faith that the inspector, in his wisdom and with his experience, would think that an elderly lady teacher and an undersized lady farmer, both with no money in the bank, were a sound investment. When he saw the barn, by gum, that would be the end of that!

The brucellosis test was over. We climbed wearily into the Land Rover and left everything in the hands of God and Paul. We headed north to snatch five days' peace in the Lake District.

I remember that the re-deployment of our time was illustrated by the fact that we arrived at our Grange refuge without milk or eggs. Whatever had happened to us? I remember with affection the dozen or so screw-top aluminium pill tins, labelled COFFEE, CUSTARD POWDER, CORNFLOUR, SUGAR, DRIED MILK and so on which we filled religiously every time we packed our rucksacks. I remember the pride with which we proclaimed the truth that we never forgot anything. I remember the FIRST AID KIT and SHOE CLEANING KIT. The absolute perfection right down to a tin mug because with boiling water in that, you can iron a creased garment.

What had happened to us that we left The Currer without milk and eggs? We had so much milk we churned butter to give away to friends. We whipped cream to enrich the sponges and trifles to such an extent that we were guilty of greed. Eggs, too, we had in such great numbers that we always had plenty to give away and yet we arrived in Grange without a drop of milk to make a cup of tea and no eggs for breakfast. I had packed a box of food, hurriedly going from cupboard to cupboard lifting down tins and packets in a most unprofessional manner. Among them was a tin of Ambrosia rice pudding. Margaret opened it and watered it down; we drained off the liquid and it gave us half a pint of passable milk. We might be negligent in some things but our ability to survive is seldom in question.

How utterly beautiful is the Lake District in autumn. The leaves turn suddenly in the last fortnight of October and the area is a wonderland of colour. It is no use going earlier and jostling with the thousands of tourists. Colour does not illuminate the mountains and the forests and take its reflection to dye the lakes until the October half-term. When nature empties her paint box the effect is perfection. I cannot understand why modern man designs so badly or why the young people of today choose to wear so much black.

There was plenty of thinking time in those five days in Cumbria. 'This is your last year at school,' I told myself. 'Your last Christmas is approaching.'

Grange persistently awoke memories of Ripon and college days. I think it was something to do with the gentleness of the climate, the street lighting and the well-kept gardens. The leisurely, country town atmosphere took me right back thirty years to the almost monastic life we led and I wallowed in sentimental nostalgia for those happy training years.

The excess of undergrowth and its autumnal smells of wet bracken and fungus, blackberries and fallen leaves, filled me with memories of Steeton Hall. I know exactly how many smells rise from the tennis court, hide in the woodland below the stables or congregate round the potting sheds.

We returned home refreshed to find that the man from the English Tourist Board had been unperturbed by the dilapidation in the barn. We had reached the point of no return.

Early November can be a wonderful time with children. The snickets and ginnels and Parsons' Walk are deep in fallen leaves. Conkers and beechnuts are to be found everywhere and children compete with the squirrels in their search for treasure. I gathered the golden leaves with as much excitement as the first time. There was a smell of fungus and wood smoke to delight me and I dared not think about giving it all up.

At great danger to life and limb, Margaret and I dismantled the corn bin. It meant handling the 6 foot by 8 foot floor sections with which it had been built. Our neighbours had helped when they had had to be hoisted onto the loft. When they had to be lowered, we managed ourselves. They were far too heavy for us and there were moments when we were convinced we were mad to try and tragedy seemed only seconds away. With ropes and bated breath we allowed them to slither off the loft. 'We'll have an accident one day,' we said as the last one thudded to the barn floor without taking us with it and crashing us into pulp.

For some time we allowed the heavy sections to lie on the barn floor, not moving the pile until Christmas when the manure had to be taken out. We did this with the Land Rover, the small trailer and a couple of muck forks. It was a job which could have been done quickly and easily by the contractor and his modern equipment but we had no faith in the estimate of how much the project would cost and agreed that whatever we could do ourselves we would have to do.

We were about to enter a period of poverty not previously experienced. Big money would have to be borrowed and spent but small money on ourselves would have to come to an abrupt end. Shoes, clothes and just the basics of living disappeared. Mother despaired of our growing shabbiness, the wearing thin of underwear, the disreputable state of our footgear, but we became stubbornly tightfisted. I had no longer time to sew and was unaccustomed to buying from the hanger and, in any case, could not thoil the price. On the other hand I spent hours at the sewing machine making things to sell at the school Christmas Fayre, keen to swell the School Fund before I left.

I put everything I had into what I believed would be my final Christmas with my children. Everything we did was more elaborate. The Crib was made more perfectly, new 'stained glass windows' covered the screen which divided the classrooms and was only opened to reveal and frame the Crib for the Carol Service. It was all very professional. The star actually moved across the sky in front of the Wise Men. The Holy Family had a life-sized papier mâché donkey and it gave me great joy to know that Joseph was really the selective mute child we had admitted when he was six.

We put added effort into the Christmas Party, inviting the Vicar to be Santa Claus. My last: I sighed, laughing with Joan as the children got in a muddle in The Grand Old Duke of York.

The top class went to see Scrooge at the Alhambra. I took eleven in the Land Rover. How we enjoyed it. It was dark when we came out and it was snowing heavily. The children clambered into the vehicle and I pulled out into the traffic. At a T-junction in the centre of the city, I stopped to wait my turn and my engine stalled. The lady behind had drawn so close to me that in restarting I leaned back on her number plate.

'She's run in t'yer, Miss Brown!' yelled the kids on the back seat. I had felt no lean back, no touching of another car. I drew out of the junction and the irate woman put on her horn, blasting me to stop. I pulled up in a safe place and got out. My goodness could that woman swear. She blasted me to Hell in no uncertain terms. The kids were all open-mouthed. If they had heard such language before they had certainly not heard it directed at their headmistress. I inspected the damage she insisted I had done. The number plate had been pushed back. The car was untouched. I gave her my name and address and told her to send me the bill. Her male passenger had got out of her car and walked away, presumably in embarrassment. He was out of earshot so she added on the abuse by saying, 'That man with me is a bloody policeman!' The kids had never had such entertainment. I am sure their parents would get a better account of that than the theatre production.

Similarly we put great effort into the Guide Christmas Fayre. We had decided to hold it at The Currer instead of in the Guide Rooms. These were lately often filled with smoke fumes from the tannery or the central heating or something in the other half of the rented building. There were times when it was so bad I reported it to our neighbours but nothing was done about it.

'Never mind,' I said, 'We'll have the Christmas Fayre at home.'

Why did I always have such wild ideas which brought such hard work? We were perpetually transporting furniture. All the tables had to be brought from the Guide Rooms to display our sales. Mother never accepted chaos calmly. Her tolerance of it must be unique for I, at least, brought it perpetually to her doorstep. If she had met an early grave I would have felt guilty that it was my fault, always turning the house upside down, but she is in her ninety-third year as I write this and heading happily for her century. We still surround her with our extraordinary activity and she still gets in a panic but the excess flow of adrenalin must increase longevity.

I did wonder whether I had been completely mad to arrange this. The upheaval it caused was nobody's business. A friend, Dorothy, who had been the school swimming teacher in the days when we had walked to the neighbouring village, came on the evening of preparation and witnessed the shambles. I am sure we moved every stick of furniture in the house to squeeze in the folding tables and still leave room for the hundred customers we hoped to have. When readiness seemed impossible things suddenly slid into place and we were ready, when the morning invasion began.

The last day of term found me ruthlessly burning the Christmas paraphernalia I had accumulated over the years, with a strange sense of finality. No new head, I was sure, would want my well-preserved star, stable animals, 'stained glass' paper coverings. No one would want my Christmas Fayre stall labels, my well-worn Child Education Nativity pictures and all the bits and pieces stored with reverence over the years. All went up in flames on the pile of crisp holly and faded crepe paper. I burned them unsentimentally, believing that way was best. Somehow the process of leaving had to be got through and it was no good being dramatic about it. Michael took the papier mâché donkey home. It was too life-like to burn. I turned my back on the funeral pyre of my Christmas collection and walked away.

Chapter Twenty

T he New Year came and we wondered, rather apprehensively, what it would bring. There must have been a period of frost for we heard that Cloughie had fallen in her kitchen quadrangle behind Steeton Hall and had broken her leg. I went several times to see her in hospital. She had a belief that she would die when she was eighty as all her family had. I think that if her attitude had been different she would have made a perfect recovery but her Guiding days were over and she virtually gave up. I am not going to do that. It takes too long.

All her life she had been a prisoner of her deafness but her extraordinary activity and her position of authority in the Guide Movement had compensated. She had been the teacher, the talker. In her sick bed as a listener she was nothing.

On several occasions, during the past few years, she had come to have tea at The Currer, but after her broken leg there were no more visits so sometimes I would take Mother to see her. She told the housekeeper to take Mother on a conducted tour of the house. I knew it well but Mother and Harry were fascinated. There was a rare collection of precious antiques and pictures, the value of which she was totally unaware. Mother trotted round that enormous house almost like a teenager.

We had still received no final go-ahead from the Council. Until it came no work could begin. The bank manager had agreed to loan us the money, holding house and land as security. We had not budgeted to have to hold a Fire Certificate. Plans had to be readjusted to allow for extra thicknesses of plaster and then another meeting of the Planning Committee had to re-look. Each time they found a minor fault and another month would go by.

We were not idle. We were tidying up everywhere. We had recently made the acquaintance of a young agricultural contractor with the skill and the equipment necessary for all our excavating work. John Sugden is one of the many 'horses for courses' which have punctuated our lives.

We had taken out the manure from the barn but modern regulations insist that rooms have a minimum height and it was necessary to lower the floor level. John was employed to take out tons of earth and boulders. We saw no harm in doing this in advance of the plans being passed.

Margaret was almost totally committed to rearing cattle, that winter. It was milder and less traumatic than the previous one but there were seventy calves instead of fifty and she was fattening bullocks. Every Saturday, it seemed, we were loading them from the Dutch barn and Margaret went her enforced and miserable way to the local cattle mart.

Every evening I pegged away at rugs made with Harris wool and Mother sat and crocheted blankets. Friends gave her wool and hand-made garments to unpick. In all she made over twenty. We turned cotton sheets into pillow-cases and curtains into cushion covers. The demands of the ETB and the Fire Service really began to alarm us. We could have kicked ourselves for being so negligent as to leave the Fire Certificate off the estimate. The ETB grant was fixed on the initial expectation and we could see it was going to be a hundred per cent too low.

I blessed the Education Office for their retirement offer. Then, just before the conversion plans were passed, I entertained the managers at my February meeting. The schools officer chatted with me for a while afterwards.

'Are you taking advantage of early retirement?' I asked. I knew many administrative jobs had been axed.

'I would if I could,' he laughed. 'Not a hope. My job won't become redundant. People are only being released if their job disappears. Headteachers won't get it either. You'll be hearing early next month. Three hundred jobs will go but they won't be headteachers and they won't be schools officers.'

I didn't really believe him. I had a perfectly genuine printout in my name, telling me every detail of what I would be personally offered. But I hadn't really believed that either. We'd just have to wait and see.

I did not have to wait long. Early in March came the letter saying that mine was a statutory job and as such would render me ineligible for redundancy. Joan had to wait until mid-summer to see if roll numbers merited a loss of staff. They did not.

I waved goodbye to a large sum of money remarkably cheerfully. On the one hand we never wanted success the easy way. If it came it would now be due legitimately to hard work, and not because we had a sudden windfall. On the other hand it was patently obvious that I couldn't afford to retire. We could not meet the extra bills, pay for the Fire Certificate, build the bigger septic tank etc. *ad infinitum* without my monthly salary.

I was suddenly burning with gratitude. I could not leave my school, my children or my staff. I couldn't possibly leave! My heart sang, 'Oh God, I am glad! Oh God, I am reprieved!'

It was a lovely, mild, March day. 'Let's go for a nature walk,' I said. I felt like singing Father's song of praise, 'I'm so happy, oh so happy. Don't you envy me?'

I'm sure the children wondered why their headmistress was so benevolent, why, with a child on either hand and others clinging to her skirts and the sleeves of her jacket, she glided weightlessly up The Folly, looking for the first wood anemones, dog-myrtle and celandine. Ten-year-old Ian had written, 'Oh celandine, oh celandine, I wish that you were truly mine!' The carpet of snowdrops was fading but I was head over heels in love with it. I wanted to hold the children to me and cry, 'I'm not leaving you,' but not one would have understood, for no one had guessed that I even might.

I can't remember a day when I have been happier. Saskia and Joanne came close. 'Lead me Lord,' we sang, 'Lead me in Thy righteousness. Make my way plain.'

A few days later the go-ahead came from the Council. I sent a letter to the ETB telling them we could begin and immediately received a reply saying they would be grateful if we would spend some of the grant before the end of the financial year. They would pay 30 per cent of everything we spent before the end of March.

We sent for our friend who we had originally expected to be the builder but a recent slight stroke had put an end to any such dangerous work. It hadn't, however, prevented him from being capable of sub-contracting the work. The initial negotiating with Council and fire service, plumber, joiner and electrician was his domain.

He came and we were horrified to find that none of these workmen had been approached. I think that he, like everyone else, had never believed that we were in earnest. 'I'll have to find a builder,' he said. It shocked us to learn that we had no builder for such a big and urgent project. Did everyone think we would caffle at the last minute?

The ETB had given us a completion date of 31st August 1980. We had less than six months and we had no builder, joiner, plumber or electrician. We had a man with a tractor who was knocking things to bits. There was no one lined up to work creatively. 'Leave it to me,' our friend Les insisted. We hate doing that and became impatient and irritable.

We did not know how to spend some of the grant money. Glancing through the local paper we found there was a carpet sale so we went and bought two full rolls of carpet. Then we went to a furniture store and ordered fifteen beds. Another sale advertisement took us to a mill shop where we bought a dozen duvets and a full roll of nylon sheeting. We were hysterical. We gave Les a down payment on a builder we did not have, sent the bills to the ETB and back came the 30 per cent. We manhandled the carpet rolls into the Snug and fell over them every time we went to the Low Loo for over eight months. We packed the duvets on the top of the wardrobes. I put six on top of Mother's.

Attending to Harry in the middle of the night, I heard sobs coming from Mother's room.

'Whatever's the matter?' I said.

'I can't stand those big white things!' she cried. Pour soul! She was eighty-three years old and all summer she was to live on a building site, in accommodation increasingly cluttered with furniture, fittings and kitchen-ware. She was to watch her daughters spend money they did not have, work endlessly, hardly sleep at all, in the certain knowledge that a life sentence of work lay ahead for all of us. In the middle of the night I took away the offending duvets, piled them on my bed and crawled into hers to comfort her and make reassurances I did not know if I could meet. Poor Mother! Thank goodness she enjoys most of our new and demanding life. We have a tremendous admiration for her.

'We've got to have a builder!' we screamed when Les told us he had approached the man who had built Father's sitting room extension, and had been refused because of too much work already.

'Calm down,' he said. 'His son-in-law finishes a job next week and may be interested. He's coming up to the farm on Sunday morning to have a look.'

The two men, on that memorable March Sunday, walked slowly into the barn. It looked ramshackle and derelict, empty and impossibly old. The roof timbers, naked of packed hay giving secondary support, looked ready to fall in a heap on the laithe floor. The empty loft revealed all too frighteningly the bowed gable end. The job looked impossible.

When the two men came out both looked noncommittal. Neither came to the house to speak to us. Les had brought the man in his car. They returned to it, got in and drove away. We watched from the window with sinking spirits. Why had we not found a builder ourselves, long ago? Men were impossible. They just never got moving. We find delegating responsibility so frustrating. We are far too impatient to wait for more capable people to move slowly. Watching the car drive up the hill we exploded. 'Well that's the end of that!' we said.

Half an hour later Les returned. 'I asked him if he would rebuild the gable end. He's having a word with a friend. If they want the job they will ring with an estimate.'

We could have screamed. We wanted builders who were prepared to do the whole job, to stay six months and never go away, who would do every bit of the job, not a couple of unknown men who just might do the gable end. We needed experts who could convert a ruin into accommodation which would match the age of the rest of the house. We wanted skilled craftsmen with an eye for beauty. We were looking for artists in their trade, men who would be obsessed, as we were, with creating a thing of beauty. We were looking for supermen, but like the Tar Baby we said nothing at all.

'I'll let you know if he rings,' Les said. It was perhaps a good job we did not get our teeth into that builder first. We'd probably have frightened the good man away. As it was Les phoned us within the hour. 'I've got an estimate on the gable end,' he said. 'Dougie saw his mate. They've a job to finish which will take a couple of days. They'll probably start on Thursday.'

Next morning he went to the slaters and ordered the roof to be taken off. We admitted, with a smile, he was more capable than we.

Dougie, Brian and their labourer, Trevor, turned up on Thursday morning before I went to school. Privately I wondered what sort of a job they had made of their last one and why they had nothing else lined up. We had no references, and they looked a very unlikely trio. They staggered from a dilapidated car, dragging a huge cylinder of Calor gas, a kettle and three mugs. They struggled with this impressive piece of equipment, up the cobbles and through the rotting barn doors and into the vast, sinister emptiness of the laithe.

'Good Lord!' I said to Margaret. 'What have we got?' It was pure comedy, like some funny advertisement for a particular brand of tea.

We went to introduce ourselves. The young lad, red-faced and bonny, smiled in happy ignorance of the magnitude of the job. The two builders, Little and Large, contemplated the Calor gas ring with dour, early morning expressions.

'You don't need that,' we assured them. 'Whenever you need hot water just come to the house. '

"S'orl right,' said Brian. 'We can manage.' He lit the gas and put on the kettle.

I turned away, got into the Land Rover and started the engine. As I pulled away from the yard I saw the three of them, grouped round the cylinder, sitting on up-turned buckets with both hands grasping their Yorkshire pint pots.

The incredible fact is that, for eight months, those two men and their boy labourer never missed a day or made a false move. Slowly and with great skill and expertise they transformed our ruin. Dougie, Brian and Trevor! They took away the Calor gas and enjoyed our hospitality, eating thousands of Mother's biscuits. Almost immediately we told them the whole job was theirs. I wonder how many people are so completely satisfied with their builders as we are with ours. We began to rely on them to answer all our problems.

And so, at the beginning of April our massive job was begun and did we have fun!

'We can't do owt until we've got Acroes,' they said. These are strong tubular supports used to hold up roof timbers whilst the wall support is temporarily taken away. Next morning, Margaret and I went into the city to hire them for several months, and only by the skin of my teeth did I arrive at school on time. From that day we began to ill-treat our dear Land Rover appallingly, daily overloading it with heavy and ungainly materials so that it creaked and sank onto its springs. How extraordinarily well it served us all that long fine spring and very wet summer.

Almost immediately there was a dreadful mess. The gable end was three feet thick at the base; most of it was dry stone and fell rather than was dismantled. Had it not been for the three buttresses we had built, it would have come down long ago. The 400-year-old rubble was nearly powder. The whole job of dismantling was made infinitely safer by the presence of the wall we had built in the mistal to hold up the loft, a wall so full of cement it needed a sledgehammer to destroy.

Decent stone from the outer face was lowered onto the loft for re-use. The random stone which had packed the cavity became a huge mountain in the yard. It began to block the entrance and John was sent for to remove it to the bottom of the yard. We lived with a mountain for a very long time.

We had used the barn passage as a cloakroom for many years. In it we kept a freezer which had to be re-housed in what had been the curing house. We had re-roofed this when we built the kitchen and we decided that it must be 'the freezer 'ole'. In Yorkshire every thing is an 'ole. There is the 'en 'ole, the duck 'ole, the back 'ole, the coal 'ole, the donkey 'ole, and we needed a freezer 'ole.

One Saturday, with Mother safely out of the way, we quietly and with determination took away the stones blocking the inside entrance to the curing house. They had been put there in 1958 when we had sealed off that bit of our ruin. It wasn't a difficult job. Within a few minutes the doorway was clear again. We had the door posts ready and the door just to hang. Mother protested, of course, but the deed had been done.

There was a tremendous demand on our time. If a job could be done by us then we had to do it. When the builders went home at teatime we moved in with pick, shovel and wheelbarrow to clear away the rubble. We had put up the buttresses and we could take them down. We dragged out the rotting window frames and worm-eaten lintels and threw them on the woodpile. We scattered rubble all the way down to the calf sheds. Surely with all this random stone we could conquer our biggest enemy, the mud.

The greenhouse had become a wreck. Once the polythene had been breached all the winds of heaven had followed in the footsteps of the cattle vandals. So we put a tin roof over it and called it the wood shed, filling it to capacity with demolition throwaways.

The gable end came down quickly and almost immediately began to grow again. Sills and lintels were needed. It was important to find old ones and we needed about thirty for the gable end and the rear of the barn, plus fifteen mullions and twelve sills and lintels for the front. No one had time to hunt for that number. 'We won't have new ones!' we were adamant. Brian brought home two sills he had found in the yard belonging to a demolition firm. 'Is that all?' we cried.

Demolition is now done by bulldozers. Street faces are tumbled with a single ram from a mechanical monster; everything falls in one shattered heap and the sills and lintels are broken and buried. There is no time to dismantle carefully and preserve. The two sills, each of which had cost the builder five pounds, were used at once and the walls kept rising.

On Thursday evening I drove home from the Guide Meeting, skirting the town. Even in the darkness it was not difficult to see what was happening.

Half the road had been cordoned off and red, flashing lights warned of daytime demolition. Several streets of old houses were being removed. The huge excavation vehicles were motionless on the street, waiting for the return of the labourers.

Early next morning I went that way to school, a detour from my normal route. There were three men already on the site. No more were needed. I strolled over to where they were grouped, discussing where best to begin on a long row of house fronts. The backs and roofs had already gone. Amongst the rubble were broken sills galore and one or two whole ones. I asked to buy the sills and lintels from the long, untouched face. 'Please,' I begged.

'The'll orl be brokken wi' bulldozer,' I was told.

'You can't,' I almost cried. 'I need about thirty.'

I could see their difficulty. They were employed to attack the ruin with tractor power. Modern methods had no reverence for antiquity. I looked at the long street face, awaiting only a few blows from the monster. What hope had I?

'I'll buy every one you don't break,' I said. I took a few five-pound notes out of my pocket. 'I'll pay you five pounds for each one and I'll pay you cash, tonight.'

''Ow many did yer seh yer wanted?' one man asked.

'Thirty,' I said. I could see him mentally adding up the total. 'Ah'll see what we can do. Yer'll 'ev ter teck 'em t'neet. Termorrer the'll be gone!'

I jumped back in the Land Rover. At school I rang Margaret to get John organised with the tractor and trailer. At lunchtime I went to the bank and got the thirty five-pound notes. As soon as school closed I hurried to the site. The street face had gone but at the roadside was a heap of heavy stone slabs. There were eighteen. John and the men were beginning to lift them onto the trailer. I hunted around for more. We totalled twenty-three that evening. The others we collected next day, three at a time in the poor ill-treated Land Rover. The men were careless of her age and faithfulness. Every time they threw in a sill I heard the springs complain and cringed for the scratched and torn inside. 'She'll die on us,' I feared. 'Then what will we do?'

Easter came and the weather was perfect, dry with long hours of sunshine. We spent many evenings levelling the laithe floor with pickaxes and spirit levels. We were down to a hard brown clay. It was like chipping dark chocolate. Les pegged out the pattern of walls and Paul and a young workman began digging trenches for the foundations. Vivienne came one weekend. We were all working in short sleeves. The weather was warm and blue and work was going on apace.

The slaters had taken off the Yorkshire stone slates and the roof timbers let in all the sunshine. They made an attractive pattern against the sky and sent interesting shadows within the barn. John went behind the barn and took away the hill which climbed up the back wall. Water stopped seeping through the dry stone and the trickle from the barn porch, which had perpetually discoloured the yard, disappeared. We crossed our fingers and hoped it had gone for good.

As soon as the rising gable end had consumed all the good stone retained for it on the loft we were free to take down the age-old wooden structure for which the barn had no further need. We began to dismantle the loft, carrying the floorboards through the back door of the mistal and into the Dutch barn, Margaret at one end and me at the other, not an uncommon sight. We call it our Laurel and Hardy act, two determined women, the wee one in front, the larger edition behind, struggling with length or weight or volume. We invariably end up in hysterics for her strides are shorter than mine and when the ground is uneven or the double bed must go round a bend or upstairs, we are not always in step.

We looked at the gnarled cow stalls, chose the best for preservation, for we are now reverent of age, and re-erected it and the loft within the Dutch barn. We felt we had rescued a good friend and were pleased we still had a place to put things out of reach of cattle.

Next we turned our attention to the stable, took out the rotting partitions, the bath, the sundry rusty tools and oil cans and the depth of duck and hen droppings. The poor, homeless biddies and the cockerel still roosted on the roof tree, denuded of slates. We did not disturb them.

Father's most recent pigeon, Featherlegs, still spent the night in the barn and the daytime on the apex of the latticed roof. One solitary, lonely bird. A few of his kind made a brief stop to keep him company but none stayed. They were birds of passage and our accommodation was not tempting. We wondered what was going to happen when glass was put in the window frames and his night shelter went!

One thing was becoming apparent. I could not keep my Guide Company if I were going to retain my school. Something had to go. If guests came (we were not wholly confident that they would), they would come in the summer and Guiding without camping was not for me. They also might want an evening meal and I couldn't just run out on this to take a Guide meeting. I thought it might break my heart. All those happy children, all those Queen's Guides, all those thirty summer camps, all those tents pitched on the machair, those campfire songs round the fire on an island shore, all the romance and glamour of the Hebrides. This was me.

Gradually, I began to run down the Company. Fifteen girls would be sixteen years old in the summer; almost half the unit. I enrolled no new recruits. I used the increasing smell of gas, mysteriously permeating the Guide HQ, to abandon our long tenancy. We began to hold the weekly meetings at The Currer. I suppose I blinded no one to the wind of change.

Numbers for camp were higher than ever before. A Guider friend, Pat Clark, wanted to come with a group from another company. Almost all my school leavers wanted to come. Faithful Linda, already married, would make our third adult. There were fifty-nine campers and, I knew, it was going to be the last camp of all. The thought was unbearable.

The good weather continued to hold into May and those good men got on with their job unerringly. Our respect for them grew. When the footings were all in, John took most of the mountain and laid it on the barn floor as hard core. He topped it with some quarry bottoms and we were ready to send for several loads of concrete. Suddenly, on the smooth floor, there began to grow innumerable breeze block walls. The barn, which had looked as big as a cathedral, looked small until the rooms had height and ceilings.

I began to call far more frequently at Steeton Hall. There seemed little left for Cloughie to live for. The decision to retire all those over sixty-five must have left many foundation members of the Movement, in their seventies, with a feeling of uselessness. Cloughie didn't seem to have anything to do, or any clothes now uniform was not to be worn. So I called more frequently to have a cup of tea and listen to her. Guiding had been her subject. Now she rarely mentioned it. She was more interested in our farm conversion than my Guide company. She talked at great length about the birds, the robin on the cellar steps, the mistle thrush nesting on the statue in front of the library window, the squirrel in the back yard. When diseased trees had to be felled in the front drive it was, to her, a disaster. She talked a lot of philosophy and religion and was still convinced that she would die in her eightieth year.

We had booked the cottage on Tiree for a fortnight at the end of May. We were almost on our knees but first we had to hold the Division Camper Badge in the Paddock. It was the first year Cloughie missed.

Tired almost to the point of exhaustion, we spring-cleaned the house ready to leave everything in the capable hands of Barbara and Arnold. The peace they always associated with The Currer was to be shattered with the continual noise of building and their view was ruined by the mountain which had begun to grow again in the yard. The whole place looked like a ruined abbey, likely to fall down any minute. I said so to Brian. 'It won't fall,' he promised. I looked at the 3 inch Acroes holding up the 12 inch by 6 inch by 18 inch principals and wished I had his confidence.

We had a wonderful time on Tiree in the brilliance of the sunshine we seem to get on every holiday, and in the small cottage of Marian MacLean an idea was born.

There would be another year at school, thank God. Why not bring the school children to Tiree in the spring, in school time, as a finale. There, in the twin cottages at Salum, thirty children would not be too many. They would love it. Everywhere I looked seemed perfect. No immediate neighbours, a daisied fenced-in playground and the shore only a stone's throw away. All we needed was a D'abri to eat in so that we had no crumbs on the carpet. It was a grand idea which would dull the pain of the last camp now only a couple of months away.

Whilst I adore taking children to the Hebrides and miss them when they are not under my feet, there is something to be said for the freedom their absence brings. It is pleasant to be able to visit friends and linger by their firesides without the stress of wondering what is happening in camp, and to wander the lovely shores without the weight of responsibility. More recently the pressure of work at home has built up enormously and we feel, more than ever, the need to sit long hours outside a crofter's cottage in the sun. There is nothing like hard work to ensure peace of mind. The harder the work the less anxious the mind, because manual labour obliterates mental stress. We don't need to go on holiday to relax, just to get away from the work and to sit down.

'Our bottoms are too big,' Margaret said. 'Poor things never get worn down!'

All holiday I was planning bringing the children, Joan, Jill Ideson, one of our dinner ladies, and me. And a cook Patrol from the Guide Company? Surely staffing a Hebridean camp for primary school children would be called an educational activity by the Head of the Senior School.

What a lifesaver of an idea! I have come to the conclusion that I cannot live without a project in front of me. Whenever we are feeling a bit off-colour we say, 'What we need is a project. Let's think of something new to plan.' Then we have renewed energy.

We returned, very sunburnt, to find that the Sherriffs had lost four of our cattle. They had counted and re-counted the herd and each time they were four short. They had scoured the countryside, phoned everyone they could think of and had had no luck.

Margaret knew almost immediately which four had disappeared and we started at once to search the hillside. I think it was the experience of searching for those stirks, in the climate of our advent into tourism, which made us aware of the unique quality of our hillside. We had always loved it but we had never analysed it. We had seen our little bit but never placed it properly within its environment. We had never before looked at it as holiday territory and we had never looked at it as a preserved piece of history: a medieval hillside with a scattering of sixteenth- and seventeenth-century farmhouses, a patchwork of intakes from the moor, a shower of rocks left by the glacier at the end of the Ice Age, a Druids' Altar, an ancient manor and extensive clusters of natural woodland. 'What a wonderful place to come on holiday,' we thought, widening our search onto the moorland and over to the old farms at Hainworth Shaw where the Roman Road appears and heads in our direction. At a farm on Back Shaw I found an old pupil and the four stray cattle but we had found much more than that during our four-day search. We had found that we wanted to know more about the Currers and the Parkers and Ferrands and the history which had almost stood still around us

Work had continued steadily. Walls were rising. A joiner and plumber were employed. Brian asked me to collect two concrete inner-wall lintels, from the builders. They cost more than £6 and I was horrified. 'How many of those will we need?' I wanted to know.

'Thirty more, at least.'

'That'll cost £200,' I moaned. 'Can't we make them?'

The builders showed us how to use one of the corn bin sides as a base and floorboards separated with bricks to make the moulds. Les brought us some rods to reinforce the concrete and on Saturday we were in business.

All afternoon Margaret and I mixed cement and filled the moulds; it was child's play. The thirty were made in no time. 'What the heck are we going into this bed and breakfast lark for?' we laughed. 'We can make £200 a day making concrete lintels!'

With the increase ten-fold of the work at home I had to watch my step at school. Often I had to leave close on the heels of the home-time bell but books had to be marked as always. I never forgot to do that but in my preoccupied state of mind I occasionally forgot where I had put them afterwards.

There was one child, Judith, with whom I had always a good relationship. She was clever, witty, mischievous and as tough as old rope. She had been a Guide for more than a year and had already had one camp on Harris. I was proud of the child. She had a way with the disabled and talked easily with old people. She was a tomboy, a popular member of the class.

One day she lost her maths book and reported this to me at the beginning of the lesson. 'Look for it,' was the only help I offered. 'It will be in your desk.'

I ignored the sigh of intolerance she emitted. She wasn't so stupid as to report it missing without first looking in her desk. Dutifully she went to turn the whole contents out again. Her disgusted shrug said it all.

Sometime later she came to tell me once again that her book wasn't in her desk. 'Look in the cupboard,' I said. 'Look in the staffroom. It must be somewhere.'

Playtime came and she was proposing to go out with the other children. 'Not until that book is found, Judith,' I said. I can't cope, I decided, with children who lose their books. I really was quite cross. However, by the end of playtime, the maths book had not appeared, and I decided we must all give Judith a hand. 'Turn out your desks,' I said. My desk needed doing, too. I lifted out the registers, and the logbook and a wad of requisition forms and Judith's maths book. How are the mighty fallen!

'Oh Judith, I am sorry,' I said. I was undeniably embarrassed. 'I've blamed you all morning and here's the book in my desk.' Up went her hackles and in went a deep breath. I could see that intolerance had turned to something far worse.

'What punishment is it to be?' I felt so sorry for her.

A gleam appeared in her eye. 'The ruler!' said the delightful child. Why do children, when they are playing Mother, smack continually and when they play teacher walk around with a ruler in their hand?

'Fetch it,' I said. We had the attention of the whole class. I had to preserve some dignity.

Judith walked to the ruler box, took a good one and came back to my desk. I held out my hand. I looked for the smile, the wavering of purpose, the acknowledgement that I was headmistress. There was none. She raised the ruler and a dropped pin could have been heard. Suddenly there was a resounding, blistering crack across my hand. Breathing had stopped. I had to wince and hold back stinging tears. At all costs I had to take my punishment like a man! "Eck!' I heard one boy breathe.

Judith returned the ruler, collected her book and the lesson continued. The children were good all day and I had an influx of helpers. After story time Judith fidgeted and was the last to go after dismissal. At the door she turned a little uneasily, winked and said, "Bye, Skipper!'

'Oh Judy!' I said and we both burst out laughing. 'The atmosphere in this school emanates from the headmistress' had been written on an Advisor's report. I wonder what she meant. However was I going to bear to leave those children?

It was necessary to begin packing the skips for the last real camp on the edge of the Luskentyre sand dunes, a place we had called our own for so many years. I packed with the same loving care I had the first skips bound for the Hebrides twenty-four years ago.

A pile of rubble had been left by the builders in the mistal cottage. One Saturday, about this time, I bucketed and barrowed it onto the mountain. It was a backbreaking job but the rewards were many. The empty, swept floor gave me pleasure. One huge boulder remained. I called for Margaret to help me remove it. 'We'll keep it,' I said. 'When I collapse you can use it for a head-stone. Save you the expense of a monumental mason!'

Oh, the cottage looked fine with the floor brushed and the mullioned window overlooking the valley. The mullions for the front of the house had been another miracle. Part of a mill near to school had been taken down gently. The windows had been surrounded with cut lengths of stone which our builders could easily make into mullions. I am amazed how things just came.

'Come and see the cottage,' we begged Mother. I thought it looked pala-tial. She walked across the swept floor and we waited for the praise we ought to know never comes.

'Well?' I said.

'Wor a muck 'ole!' she said. Yer gotta laugh!

With the equipment safely packed, Libby Hagar's father came with his wagon to take the skips to the station. I had taught all his four children. Libby and Rachel were coming to camp. Fifteen-year-old Jonathan, who had once thought the rest of his family had a disease called 'egg cups' drove the lorry expertly down our farm road and backed it up to the laithe porch.

In 1980 the skips went mid-week, three weeks in advance of our party. On the Sunday of the following weekend Pru came to see us. She'd married the previous autumn after a degree at St Andrews University and she and Richard had bought a cottage on the top road. They had done all the conversion work themselves and there was a bond between us, plaited with many strands. She was the youngest of a family of three, all girls, all Guides, all campers. Her father was a partner in the local coach company and supplied all our needs for multiple transport. Pru became a Queens Guide. At University she was Vivienne's college mother. Our paths had crossed frequently.

On this particular Sunday Pru came down alone for coffee and she did the usual tour of inspection to see how the building was progressing. 'We've just put a parquet tiled floor down in the dining half of our little kitchen,' she said. 'Would you like some?'

'What for?'

'For your dining room.' We were standing in it, just by the barn doors.

'We're putting black asphalt down, and carpet. We've already bought the carpet.'

'We got them from a farm up at Wyke,' she said. 'The man has a lot more. They only cost £1 a square yard.'

I began to think perhaps a few at the laithe porch entry might be a good idea, to take the mud from shoes and wheelchair tyres. Margaret went with Pru to look at the tiles. They were obviously the real thing. She came back and insisted we measure the whole ground floor. There were 160 square yards. We would need eight thousand tiles and it would cost £160, a great deal less than an asphalt floor.

'You must be joking,' I said. 'The man won't have eight thousand tiles!'

Margaret is as determined as I am if she gets an idea into her head. She phoned Pru who said there could well be eight thousand for the pile in the middle of the field had been big and the two hundred they had taken had not depleted it at all.

So we went to this isolated farmhouse at the end of a narrow, walled, Yorkshire lane, with Mother, Harry, Pru and Richard and we took £160.

We waited in the Land Rover whilst Richard went to talk to the man who was a demolition expert sensitive to the preservation of antiquity for, in his spare time, he was converting a sixteenth-century farmhouse.

He returned eventually. 'He'll sell the whole lot for £100,' he said. 'He wants the pile moving.' We counted out ten notes and handed them over. We actually paid £100 for goods lying in a wet hayfield, goods we hadn't seen or counted. We did an awful lot of presuming things would be all right in those mad conversion days. We bought the tiles without a qualm.

Pru was as excited as we were. The tiles were 9 inches by 3 inches, wet, dirty and with a thick bottom of brittle tar where they had previously stuck to a school or church floor. But they were an inch thick, heavy and hard. We stacked about 1,500 into the back of the Land Rover until there was barely room for us to squeeze in. Margaret was literally lying horizontally on top and every time I braked she felt each tile move beneath her. The springs sank further and further to the floor. Poor, faithful station wagon. We couldn't possibly afford a new one.

Where do you put ten thousand tiles? We made six journeys over the next few days. All the tiles had to be stacked, tent peg fashion, so that they would dry. If it was sunny we carried some outside. If rain threatened we were dashing to bring them in again. There were stacks of them all over the place, on newspapers all over the sitting room, in bedrooms and bathroom, all over the new cottage floors. We could hardly get into bed. There was secondhand furniture, pillows, duvets, curtains and cushions everywhere. We couldn't get to the wardrobes so we wore the same outfits all the time.

We began immediately the marathon task of chipping the tar from the back of each tile. During the first day we tried various methods, even burning the tar off but there was no easy way. Hammer and chisel it would have to be. Margaret found that sitting in the garage with the tile between her feet was best. I went for the method of using Father's vice in the curing house which was soon to become freezer room. Hour after hour we chipped away. If uninterrupted we could clean fifty an hour which meant that altogether we must have spent 160 hours during the next two months, alone, determined and completely dedicated to the removal of tar. We became the colour of the legendary Tar Baby. Dust was breathed in so that when we blew our noses the tissue was black and so was our saliva when we spat out the nasty taste. We hastily bought masks and sweated in discomfort. We have been mucky before but farmyard manure and mud are clean compared to tar. Only miners and chimney sweeps ever look as filthy as we did. The clothes we used were completely ruined. Perhaps if we'd been able to put in a sixteen-hour day and finish in a week we might have remained saner but Margaret is a full-time farmer and I was a headteacher and chipping tar had to be a hobby. More frequent baths never seemed to get us clean, our pillowslips became a dirty yellow, gloves did not prevent our nails becoming disgusting.

This last week of term was to have been my last at that lovely village school. How wonderful it was to know that there was at least a year more.

It was our custom, on the last day of term, to end with a prize giving, the distribution of books and trophies, certificates for swimming and full attendance. Someone, one year, had started the tradition of buying the teachers and domestic staff flowers and plants. Every year, thereafter, at the close of the ceremony, children disappeared into the kitchen and reappeared with huge bouquets. There was always a special one for Miss Dorothy Hill who came to present the prizes until she became too ill. Mrs Horner's daughter Pam stepped into the breach admirably for my last few years.

On the last day of term 1980 there was no whisper of flowers, no discreet arrival of the florist's van, no lovely smell from the kitchen, a place we always avoided on prize giving day. Surprises must be allowed to be such and not spoilt by pre-discovery.

My secretary said, 'I don't think anyone has remembered flowers this year.' We decided we could not take the risk. She was sent to the florist's to buy the one necessary bouquet for our VIP lady, just in case.

Then Michael came to me. Now a leaver, he had come to us unable to communicate. 'Please, Miss Brown,' he said. 'I want to give a speech at the prize giving.' Over twenty-one years in the school no such request had ever been made before. It is never difficult to get a child to shout three cheers but almost impossible to get one to make a speech, especially one with Michael's history.

'Of course you can!' I was enthusiastic. 'That would be a lovely thing to do.'

So when all the book prizes had been presented Michael duly walked to the front, tall, blond, and very serious. 'Before I leave this happy school,' he said, 'I want to thank all the teachers for what they have done and we want to give them some flowers.'

See, I thought. They haven't forgotten after all. Michael's faith was beginning to be infectious. He had plenty, but faith is not enough. For six years, at the end of each summer term, the present leavers had seen their predecessors leave the assembly and collect flowers from the kitchen without realising whose responsibility it was to first place them there. Michael firmly believed that there would be flowers in the kitchen. He nodded a prearranged signal to his diminutive friend Richard. The smaller boy bristled with importance and marched to the empty kitchen!

He returned with a puzzled frown on his face, passed through the audience of parents and children and hurried into the staffroom. Finding no flowers there either he was really flummoxed. His eyes wandered round the junior classroom for something, anything remotely like flowers. He was in luck. Pushed into an overflowing waste paper basket was a sizeable bunch of last year's heather. It was as dry as snuff and the flowers were still purple, but as Richard calmly walked among us, breaking sprigs to give to each member of staff, the dry flowers fell and sprinkled the floor like powder. He was quite unembarrassed by this. Each teacher accepted the bare spray with dignity. The child bearing the bouquet for Mrs Barwick stepped forward and the annual ceremony ended. I don't think there had ever been quite so much appreciative laughter in the staffroom.

It was necessary, before the end of July, for us to advertise next summer's accommodation. It seemed more than presumptuous when the barn still looked as if a bomb had been dropped on it. We were getting nearer and nearer the point of no return. The ball was rolling and we could not stop it.

For thirty years I had been almost completely involved with children. Yet we had had no accident. No one camp had been less enjoyable than the other twenty-nine. Nothing more unpleasant had happened than a party of drunks who had occupied our reserved seats on the late night train from Glasgow, nothing more serious than broken tent poles when we had weathered storms on land or seasickness galore when we had a rough sail. If children had proved difficult it was only because they had asthma, or an allergy.

Complacency is dangerous and leaving Margaret, Mother and Harry in July 1980 I trembled with a nervousness not previously experienced. At the front of my mind was fear that, at the last, I might bungle it, have an accident on the last lap, fall at the last fence. Was it remotely possible to have another clear round?

Almost we had disaster. Linda and her husband Dave travelled up a few days in advance expecting to be on Harris awaiting our arrival. They were travelling northwards, near Spean Bridge and a motor drawn caravan was coming towards them. A Dutchman, following the caravan, in a car built to drive on the right hand side of the road, suddenly pulled out to overtake. There was a head-on collision and Linda and Dave ended up in a field, miraculously unharmed. They rang me from the hospital where they were not detained and they spent the night with Cathie and John at Tigh-na-Coille.

There was little to distinguish that last wonderful camp from all the rest. With no one sensitive to the real truth, everyone else assumed that camping in the Hebrides had perpetuity: it was just another experience in sharing and working, laughing and singing and absorbing strength and peace from the great beauty which is there at Luskentyre.

Since we found Harris one thing has changed. The cemetery at Luskentyre has become full and a patch of the machair has been fenced in. No longer is it necessary to carry the coffins from the east. There are cars on Harris and the Council has put tarmac on the road, right to the new enclosure and there is a square of concrete where the funeral cars can park. I was asked, not many years ago, in a Fort William filling station, if I knew Donald Alec who lives at the end of the Luskentyre peninsula close to the new cemetery. Apparently a tourist had braked outside his house to enquire of Donald Alec, who was leaning against the west wall of his home overlooking what could surely only be paradise, 'Is this the end of the road?'

There is no humour to compare with the Hebridean variety.

'Aye, for some,' he was answered.

If the end of my road is anything like Luskentyre I will die joyfully.

Each morning I woke early. I must never forget, I thought, lying there in peace, the only one awake. I will come just as often to this place. I will need to, perhaps more than ever. Each year I must smell the Atlantic and the blue fragrance of peat smoke but it may be that I will never again look out on a circle of white tents and know that inside them lie the sleeping children who have brought me such pleasure. Perhaps there will be no more early rising to stir the embers. This known way of life must be remembered, this wriggling into underclothes kept warm because they have shared my sleeping bag, this putting on of shorts and shirt to step barefoot out into a new day and all the fun which only children can generate. I must never forget what it feels like to grip the warm sand of the fireplace with bare toes and singe the hairs of my legs stirring the porridge and frying the breakfast sausages. I must seal in my memory the buzz of activity in the store tent as bread is buttered and cutlery selected in the D'abri, the intermittent scamper of feet to the lats, the shaking out of sleeping bags and the chasing of postcards written yesterday which threaten to travel home independently by air. If there was a fear that I might forget 'cookhouse' being blown, the hurrying of everyone to the D'abri, the double line of more than a hundred sunburnt legs, it was unfounded. Something repeated several times a day, several weeks a year, for over forty years must surely be indelible however much it becomes a past experience. Never would I forget the daily horseshoe service to the God of mountain, field, woodland and sea. It would be impossible to forget the impatience of children waiting for the safety line to be untangled so that they could swim. With me always would be the feeling of chill when cold, wet children came too close to me as I stood knee deep in the ocean holding the anchored rope and its bobbing line of plastic containers marking the boundary of our temporary pool.

Dear God, I prayed. A hundred thousand thank yous. I have been singularly blessed.

One thing helped. That was the presence of Pat Clark, new to camping and the Hebrides. To her everything was novel. I looked back over the years like a veteran and she looked on the new experience with such delight and wonder she could not fail to give us all great pleasure.

I took her to see Mistress Morrison down on the shore, the lady we have reverently called Granny for so many years, whose company I think I would choose if I had one last wish before the end of the world. She, above all, would find some humour in the event.

Saying goodbye to her at the end of the 1980 camp I promised, 'I'll see you again next year, Granny.'

'Well, you can come,' she said, 'but I'll no' be here.'

'Of course you will!' I declared.

'No,' she insisted. 'I am old. I will be ninety in August. I'll not be here when you come back but I'm not going until after August.' Her eyes were full of fun.

'Oh, well I'm not coming back if you won't be here,' I laughed for the conversation was far from morbid.

'That is what the Plack Man said.' She was speaking of a well-respected Pakistani salesman from Stornoway. 'He said, "I'll be so sad if you're not here, I'll not be coming. But I'll come to your funeral," and I said, "Well, then, I'll not be dead. I'm having no Plack Man at my funeral!"' She is still alive and still the best tonic in the dispensary.

I allowed myself one moment of sentiment. On the last morning I chose a site on a dune overlooking the shore for our last service. Traditionally I read from St John, chapter 15 and I asked my school children to sing, 'Lead me, Lord, lead me in Thy righteousness. Make my way plain.'

In the evening we had our last campfire, our last presentations, our last gifts and goodbyes on the rock where the high tide reaches and the setting sun paints the sea.

The boat drew away from Tarbert. Behind us lay one of the happiest camps, one of the most peaceful fortnights. The end of an era. We had again walked the Rheinigidale Track and climbed Ben Luskentyre. We had heard the corncrake, been at the fank, listened to the pipes and the Gaelic. Will they remember, those many children I took so often? Perhaps!

It seems to me that I took most from those years and years of camping.

Important as that environment was to children, it was surely the one who was needed most who benefited most.

I am frightened for today's children. They are born and loved, sometimes fanatically, but they are not needed. Their help is not required in homes with so many gadgets. They do not have to scrub and clean and bake or help to earn the wage which feeds them. Because I was needed most so did I take most from the thirty years I camped with children. So, too, did the peace, the work, the laughter and the singing reward me most. I know it was good for all those children to experience great beauty and interdependence but what we learn in childhood needs continuity into adulthood. It is what we do as adults which matters most. Only when each one of them in turn experiences what I did, will real fulfillment be found.

I don't think I will ever know a peace greater than we found travelling across Skye, on the last homeward lap. It was a day when time and wind and waves seemed to stand still. Nothing stirred. We sat in the coach and Pat and I talked in depth about important things. When we reached Armadale everything was still, as in Sollas. Not a leaf stirred. It was the softest, gentlest atmosphere I have ever known, scented, warm, caressing. Michael was drooping with tiredness. I laid an anorak on the ground, rolled him onto it and put another on top. I think he was already asleep. The other boys clambered down under the pier, looking for shells and sea urchins.

There was tranquillity, an unawareness of time and worldliness and an absolute affinity with each other. We sailed to Mallaig and, as always, slept the night in the schoolroom. It was full of memories of many campers, in particular of Pru at the piano and Kathryn on the stage and the hall filled with their musical comedy hits. All over! What a pity!

The train journey home was uneventful and parents and Margaret were there to greet us and struggle with the baggage. My shoulders felt strange. No rucksack, no responsibility.

Margaret threw things into the back of the Land Rover and we went home to The Currer. It was early evening and cool indoors. A log fire was burning in the sitting room. Margaret put the kettle on and I sank into an armchair as I had after all the other camps. What a lot of them there had been over the last forty years; at Steeton Hall, in the Dales, the Lakes, Northumberland, on Arran and on islands, islands, islands. We had had children on sixteen of the Hebrides.

Suddenly, without warning the tears came. Mother was concerned as she was when I was eleven and cried because I had won a scholarship. Again she misunderstood the reason for the floods. They splashed onto my Guider's shirt like good rain and were tears of thankfulness. 'I am not crying because all is over,' I said. 'I am crying because all is over safely. All those wonderful years, all those children and no accident!'

I cannot explain why, or account for the fact that we got away with it when others of my profession, equally diligent, meet with disaster. My heart aches for them. Children swept from the rocks, lost in the mountains, buried on ski slopes, maimed and killed on the road every year. I take no credit for the fact that no child was lost whilst swimming, none fell from the pier or the Scriob on the Rheinigidale track. We escaped being bitten by adders on Ben Luskentyre, our boat never ran into difficulties, our bus never left the precipitous tracks, no one was badly burned however the sparks rose from the campfire. We were ever watchful, ever caring but it could have happened to us, and because it didn't the tears of thanksgiving flowed.

Now when we return to these places where we know every rock and dune and tuft of grass, I feel that, with Margaret and Hazel, I could do it all again, that the feeding and the caring and the entertaining would be no problem, that I would be strong enough, young and active enough. When I sit on the shore without my multitude of children I feel sure that if they were there I could cope. I am incurably bigheaded. The only thought which rests and satisfies me is the knowledge that I had a very good innings and that when I was out there was a new game to play.

Every week hundreds of borrowed pounds were being paid to the workmen. The bank manager kept cool but we began to panic. Sheds were empty of cattle, for it was August. Margaret said, 'I think I'll buy some pigs.' It is not very profitable to keep pigs but we were surrounded at that time by a lot of friends and workmen who were clamouring for a bit of 'home fed'.

We always put an idea into practice at once. The next day was Saturday and Margaret went to the local market where pigs were auctioned at noon. Before long a Land Rover came down the hill towing a large trailer. Margaret usually brought home litters of eight-week-old weaners in her own Land Rover. Obviously she had bought more than one litter. There was no sign of her. She must be detained in the office waiting to pay.

I opened the shed door and greeted the driver. 'She must have got some,' I said.

'T'whole bloody market!' the man replied.

Ye gods! He opened the trailer gates and out came a Heinz mixture of fifty-seven piglets! The different litters were all ready to fight each other. Margaret came home fully intending to give them all a tranquilliser but the fifty-seven screaming babies were all over the place. There seemed no way that we could possibly catch them individually, inject and mark them. Two litters fight each other but in such big numbers, charging around in deep straw, surely they would not know who to fight first. The bullock shed was big, their playground unexpectedly enormous, they could get out of each other's way and chaser was chased. It was a place for fun not aggression. Margaret decided she had no alternative but to leave them to get on with it.

We had no means of penning small groups separately so it was a free-for-all. When they had settled in their new home and could be let out they had to have the freedom of the yard and the fields. They overstepped their welcome by also demanding freedom of the building site and the barn. When they stampeded they resembled a herd of wild boar. They became a menace to the workmen. The cry would be 'Pigs!' and we would all dash into the building and attempt to chase them out of the numerous rooms, all without doors; the bedrooms, kitchen, bathrooms, snug. There were pigs and swearing workmen everywhere. The dogs would have a beano, buckets would be upskittled, bags of cement burst open. In and out of the rooms we would all go, screaming and shouting, several times a day. I am surprised the workmen stayed. No pigs had more fun than those fifty-seven.

When the mountain in the yard was gone we brushed the yard with a stiff brush and were delighted to find no damage had been done to that lovely concrete apron to our house. After our efforts to lay that concrete four years ago and our struggle with the loads of ready mix we could not bear anyone to deface it. Suddenly we were all tidy again, all swept. 'All done and dusted,' as Mother would say.

Dougie came and said he was ready to lay the drains. Whilst John was here why not let him dig the drains with his digger? Time was running out. It was John's employee who did it! The very next day he drove his tractor onto our beautiful yard and, following the directions Dougie gave him, he began to dig a criss-cross of trenches, two feet deep, all over the yard. The mud and boulders and all the rubble with which we had pitched the yard twenty years ago, was brought to the surface and heaped all over the place. Where there wasn't a trench there was a heap of rubble. Not one clean bit of our yard could be seen. We could have screamed when the horrible men began behind the barn and across the yard entrance similarly mutilating our ready mix surface. How dare they? Men, who do all these things with heavy plant, just love digging up our hand-laid concrete! 'Men!' we screamed. 'Who'd have one given!'

In all fairness these men could not help it but it devastated us. We had to bridge each trench with a wooden plank and there were eight bridges.

'For goodness' sake, let's go away from this,' we said. 'Let's have a holiday!'

So we picked up Auntie Dorothy and Auntie Mary who had a friend from Malton staying with her and we all set off for a day in Grange-over-Sands. There was the promise of a lovely day. Seven in the Land Rover meant one on a cushion in the back.

The sun shone and seven of us and a dog had a lovely day in Grange. We had our picnic on the grass verge of the car park outside Berner's Close. Then the old ladies walked along the promenade whilst Margaret, Harry and I went to Flooksburgh to buy enough flukes, the flat fish found in Morecambe Bay, to stock our freezer. A flurry of rain spattered the windscreen.

The same shower sent the old ladies scurrying into a shelter on the promenade. The lovely sunshine had disappeared and the journey home was in a thunderstorm. Torrential rain fell, mile after mile.

'If it is doing this at home,' we said, 'we'll be able to sail boats down the canals in the yard!' It was!

What a mess! Mud everywhere. Old ladies in holiday shoes! Bridges wet and very slippy! Mother had insisted on bringing everyone home for tea.

She wanted to show Auntie Mary's friend our home and everything looked awful. We made journey after precarious journey to steer five people, all unsteady on their feet, from the Land Rover, up the muddy slope to the farmhouse and across the eight 'Seven-Dwarf' bridges. The water level was rising fast. The thunderstorm had brought the cattle hurtling down the hill, they had crowded into the sheds and were coughing and steaming. The only happy souls were the fifty-seven sleeping pigs buried under the straw.

The deluge was continual but inside was a hive of activity as Mother immediately began frying flukes for tea. Next morning we spent hours, sitting barefoot on the edge of the trenches, bailing out hundreds of gallons of water so that the job of laying the drains could go ahead.

We were behind time. The project deadline was 31st August; I wrote to the ETB for a two-month extension.

I returned to school in early September, so very glad to have at least one more year. There was no reprieve, however, for the Guide Company. I called a meeting of the parents of the remaining Guides. I invited them to The Currer and showed them what was afoot. Even to those with little imagination it was obvious that there were going to be changes which would swallow up my leisure time. All were sad but no one pointed an accusing finger at me. All were generous enough to admit that Margaret and I had already done a fair whack.

There were two, Sarah and Libby, who were almost Queen's Guides. We decided we would not close the company until everything was complete. Every Saturday during the autumn Sarah, Libby and a few others came to help us paint chairs and doors, walls and windowpanes. The younger Guides joined other companies and at least three of them became Queen's Guides. A great and wonderful movement, Guiding can be. It lies at the heart of all that I have done. It taught me to keep old-fashioned ideals whilst following new ways. It taught resourcefulness, endurance and laughter and it gave me a repertoire of lovely songs to sing for every mood and season. It gave me the recipe for a Christian belief. It taught me to find beauty in every animal, plant, shore and dale and mountain and how to sing their praise. It did not, unfortunately, give me a tuneful voice but, there, one cannot have all.

It was a difficult year, that last one at my village school. I had had easier children to teach. There was a preponderance of boys with high spirits for football and an inaptitude for academic work.

I never seemed to get clean. Throughout September we battled on with the war against tar. The piles of clean, dry tiles grew. It was a race against time. The joiner and the plumber never left until the light had gone. When the joiner went we used his tools and his electric saw and converted bomb cases into kitchen cabinets. I found a firm selling doors, hardboard and Formica, cheap. We bought everything either second-hand or at sale price but even so the expense was appalling. Thank God for the bank manager and that we did not know what the interest would be!

There was absolutely nothing we could do but finish the job we had started and hope for the best, but we were too scared to buy any calves that year. Everyone became convinced that we were giving up farming. What a ridiculous idea! 'They can't continue without their father,' was the common impression. They didn't know he was just up there, nudging us on.

Few of our neighbours seemed interested in what was happening. Those who came close no doubt thought we had inherited the money. How we had the nerve to do what we did, with nowt, baffles us still.

'You must have known that guests would come,' say our friends when it is now so obvious that they do.

The truth is that we did not know. If they had come in the numbers predicted by the Tourist Board we would have very soon been bankrupt. We leaned over backwards in price and we bribed with as many extras as we could think of. We gave Christmas dinner free even to those in the self-catering cottages. Although we believed in ourselves we really did not know whether we were on a wild goose chase or not.

So we didn't buy calves and we went on cleaning tiles. There came an era, which is not over, of freeze. We habitually spent little on ourselves. Now we spent nothing. Mother continued crocheting blankets and making biscuits. Eight thousand, that woman made, and fed the family throughout the conversion. It must have been alarming for an octogenarian to see the house in such a state of flummox and her daughters so dirty and active but she did not grumble. We completely neglected our own needs, risked health and ate too little. We lifted objects which were too heavy, got up too early and went to bed too late. We were whitening walls before I went to school, we were too tired to wash and too excited to mind as the conversion neared completion and our dream house became a reality.

As plaster dried we whitened it; as new doors were hung we varnished or painted them. Sometimes we would work until two in the morning. We fixed tiles behind the showers and on the kitchen window ledges. We did everything: not perfectly, but adequately.

A friend used that word when she inspected the almost-finished holiday cottages. 'They're adequate,' she said. Praise never comes our way!

A retired teacher, Mr Bastow, came every week with lots of electric tools and did us a hundred and one jobs. We received extra-ordinary help from the Blamires.

At the beginning of October the workmen poured a leveller over the concrete floor in the bottom cottage and when it set we spread a layer of Synthaproof over one bedroom and allowed it to dry. We found the centre of the room and began to dip the cleaned parquet tiles into a shallow dish of Synthaproof and to lay them, one by one. We started early one Saturday morning. A room started must be finished that day for unwedged tiles would move. I spent the whole day on my knees, dipping and placing clean tiles and Margaret walked back and forth with full boxes. On the Sunday we did another bedroom. On Monday I went to school with two bent knees and an aching back. The next weekend we finished the mistal cottage.

On Thursday we borrowed a floor sander. The overnight price was considerably lower than the day-time fee. I collected it from the hirers after school. We spent the first couple of hours failing hopelessly: each time the sandpaper disintegrated into a hundred pieces. With eventual success came the fear that it would not last and we hardly dared stop the machine. So we took turns, Margaret feeding the herd whilst I walked fearfully up and down the cottage with the roaring, heavy monster. When her job was over we changed places. Progress was so slow. We expected clouds of dust but the hardwood tiles would give nothing away. I took another turn, then went to bed. Margaret worked until three o'clock and I got up at four. The machine had barely cooled. It had to be returned before eight to the hirer's seven miles away so I put new sandpaper in and started, once again, guiding the noisy monster over the lovely wood floor. For three months those parquet tiles occupied our thoughts and our time. For hours and days, for weeks and months their history became ours. Their life will exceed ours by hundreds of years. Future generations who treat and polish them will not still have bits of tar lodged in their lungs. They will not know what the huge wet pile looked like in the steaming hayfield, nor will they ever know of the manure which used to be deep where they now lie, or see again that golden seepage which perpetually oozed from the laithe porch doors and stained the concrete outside our door.

From four o'clock until six-thirty I pushed the heavy, unpredictable machine over the floor. Then Margaret came and took over whilst I had my breakfast. The floor was a lovely, smooth, off-white. The sander was hot as we humped it into the back of the Land Rover. The main road was chock-a-block and progress along it was so slow I feared I would be late for school.

This dual role was hard to play. I remembered once asking the children what punishment there must be for those who came late to school. 'They've t'write lines,' they answered. So late scholars wrote lines at my village school until tragedy befell one household. When a mother died father could never get his children to school on time and they could not be punished for that. But, whilst the law remained, there had been a day when my bus had not come and I was late for school. After the home time bell I wrote, 'I must not be late for school,' one hundred times and handed it to the form captains next morning.

A man came to the door of The Currer selling lino. We bought enough to cover bathroom and kitchen floors and laid it ourselves.

The first floor was ready for our carpets. Joanna came, with her November wedding imminent. She helped us to unroll enough to carpet the top cottage. It was a hilarious struggle: three women and a heavy roll of carpet. We manoeuvred it round the bends, through the doors and up the stairs. Laurel and Hardy had a helper. I don't think we could have managed that job alone.

A fitted carpet turns a shed into a mansion. We stayed up until the early hours, the job excited us so.

Margaret sent some of the fifty-seven pigs to the market and a lot of them to the abattoir. Albert Horner and Pam and her family came to help us deal with them, for all our friends and all the workmen wanted pork for Christmas. The Horners stayed in the cottage for we had struggled up with the beds and linen. It was nice to have such good friends christen The Loft. It was the 25th of October, the beginning of autumn half-term. We filled our own freezer and put a little money into the bank. It slowed only momentarily our rapid plunge into the depths of overdraft.

We couldn't afford to fail. A doctor friend once said fearfully, 'Jean, we bury our mistakes.' It put things a little into perspective for we were not gambling with human life, just with The Currer. If we failed we would have to sell. Profits from the farm would never even pay the interest. But we were not going to fail. To leave The Currer, except in a box, is unthinkable.

Once again we were on our knees laying the second half of the tiles to cover two ground floor bedrooms, a passage and the dining room. We did it all in the half-term week. We found kneeling increasingly hard. Whilst I laid the remaining tiles Margaret cleaned the cottage ones with white spirit and put on three coats of wood seal.

Joanna's wedding was on Saturday 1st November. We began laying the dining room tiles on Friday and no matter how late we worked we could not finish so we had to wedge a floorboard across the room. We were determined we would go to no wedding until the job had been finished for the dining room was the most important and to spoil things at the last minute would have been sad. We were up before dawn and we didn't eat or do anything except lay tiles. Mother got very agitated and Harry insisted we give up but we wouldn't be persuaded.

At last we finished the job and dashed to take baths which only partially made any difference. I was covered in Synthaproof, a jet black tar on which pumice stone, nail brush, or Vim had little effect and only time removed. I have such elegant friends and am a total disaster myself. There were still flecks of tar on my face and matted strands in my hair as I pulled on tights and glad rags and gloves to cover a multitude of sins.

As we pushed first Harry and then Mother into a dirty, ill-used vehicle I noticed Mother was carrying a scent spray with her. I laid it beside the hair-brush. Margaret opened the gate to let in the cattle when they came home at night and the rear Land Rover door to let in Shep.

At the bottom of the road we met cattle. Ours will not move. The only way is to get out and shoo. A Hebridean churchgoer was rebuked for trying to get hens out of church during a service. He was saying, believe it or not, 'Get out, ye puggers, get out!'

'You must not say that,' chided the minister. 'Ye must say, "Shoo!" and the puggers will go!'

So we say 'Shoo!' and wave our arms about for we are always late. We arrive at church with the bride or, if it is a funeral, with the hearse.

We were once on time. A ninety-year-old relative from a farming family at Bramhope was being buried. The cortège was late. I surreptitiously bent down in the pew to fasten my shoe laces and button my sleeve cuffs, thinking I would have had time to do them after all. The minutes ticked by and no funeral party arrived. The pianist played solemnly and the congregation was silent. A quarter of an hour passed.

With a smile showing only in her eyes, Mother leaned towards me in the pew. Our experienced farmer's wife whispered, 'Imagine t' panic at Bramhope!'

Joanna's was quite the nicest wedding we had been to for ages. After the service there was an interlude to allow guests to travel the several miles between church and reception. We negotiated the church steps with our two unsteady relatives and prepared to shove them both back into the Land Rover. Immediately we opened the door we knew something was wrong. There was the most terrible smell. Hadn't we just been putting a lot of pork into the freezers and doesn't pork always give dogs diarrhoea! Shep had had too many titbits over the past week and had disgraced himself for the first time in his life.

Never have we scrambled into a Land Rover more quickly. Never have we opened so many windows on such a cold November day. We buried our noses in Harris tweed coats and pulled away from the wedding, shivering.

'It stinks!' said Mother. 'What do we always have to bring the dog for?'

'We'll have to go home,' I said. There was pandemonium in the Land Rover.

'We'll all stink!' declared Mother.

'Shut up!' said Margaret.

'She's right,' said Harry. 'We shouldn't have brought the dog.'

'Oh, shut up!' said Margaret. The windows were all open. Villagers returning along the pavement after the marriage ceremony could hear everything we said.

'No way are we going late to that reception,' said Margaret.

We pulled up at the nearest public toilet and stole yards of toilet paper. Then we pulled up beside a field and I gathered grass whilst Margaret, who always gets the dirty job if there is one, did a reasonably good job on the scratched and mutilated metal floor. Thank God it wasn't carpeted. All the while Mother was using the scent spray and repeating that we shouldn't have brought the dog.

We left the offending mess under a huge stone on the grass verge. Never have we been in a more bonnie pickle. We tend to laugh in these situations and this was no exception. Poor Shep stood trembling by the kerb, his habitually doleful expression even more so.

'Never mind,' Margaret comforted him. 'It wasn't your fault!'

There were some eighty people at the reception and the queue to greet the bride and groom was mounting the steps to the great hall. We, as usual, were the last in the line. I remember that we smelled too heavily of scent spray. We toasted Joanna and Brian fully aware that closeness to us might well be rather unpleasant.

We received a letter from the ETB telling us that our conversion would be inspected in ten days' time. I hired a sander again and we repeated the all night shift work on the remaining half of the parquet tiles. I was back at school after the half-term break. Wintry conditions had arrived. The cattle came in and needed more feed. I told a friend who sold mowing machines that I would have to have a polisher and he said there was an old one in the shop and he would bring it. Mr Bastow helped lay the rest of the upstairs carpets. We manhandled beds into position and curtains were hung. Then, in the wee small hours of the night, Margaret and I brought the carpet, step by step, down the stairs. We paused at the bottom to admire the newly carpeted flight and Margaret said, 'Glory be, we've got an hotel!' It was 2 a.m. and we couldn't stop laughing.

What, pray, did we want with an hotel? Holiday cottages, yes, but an hotel, that was quite out of the question. Whatever had we done? I will never forget those minutes of awful truth, just the two of us in the silence of the very early morning, tired beyond the telling, suddenly laughing, hysterically.

We furnished the ground floor, emptying the family bedrooms and cupboards of the hoarded tables and bed linen. We collected thirteen dirty old ship's dining chairs from an ex-army store. Covered in dust and grime they looked a sorry buy but cleaned and polished they became transformed. We filled the cottage kitchens with crockery and cutlery and a display of pans from our own kitchen and on 11th November I came out of school to meet the inspector.

It was the same gentleman who had visited the barn when Paul was in charge. He had accepted that we could make it respectable at the price quoted. He had been right on the first count and hopelessly wrong on the second. Now he had come to see what had been done and quite honestly I thought he would be flabbergasted. It was, however, his job to witness conversions. To him they were quite daily experiences and he showed no surprise and offered no praise. He walked round without comment until he reached the cottage kitchens where he enquired whether or not we had included wooden spoons in the cutlery drawers. 'Most people forget,' he said. He refused a cup of tea and went on his way.

The long days of preparing for his visit had taken it out of us. There was a terrible anticlimax. We collected the crockery and cooking utensils and replaced them in our own kitchen drawers and then we shut and locked the doors between us and the new conversion and, apart from stoking the new central heating, we tried to forget about the whole thing. We didn't even want to go inside.

It shattered us to realise how unready we were to do the job we had worked so hard for. We are not landladies. Farmers, teachers, builders but not caterers, not hoteliers! Whatever had we done?

Margaret went to market and she bought two goats. We must have needed milk, for Joanna was in calf and going dry. Neither nanny was currently giving milk but our real need would come in the spring. I wanted to know if the goats were in kid.

'The owner said they were.' Margaret is very trusting.

'Goats are like sheep. They kid in spring.' She is supposed to be more knowledgable than I am in these matters and where she is concerned I am trusting, too.

On the Monday, I brought my staff home to tea. When we arrived Margaret had not yet returned home from the mart where she had been selling cattle. It was a beastly cold day. Wet snow had fallen on our hilltop and the road and pastures were covered with an inch of white, wet slush. I ushered my visitors into the house.

We were hardly over the threshold when Harry said, 'Auntie Mary says the goat's had kids.'

'I don't know,' Auntie Mary said. 'I went into the spare bedroom and the goats are by the stile and there looked to be kids!'

Stones sticking out of the snow can look like anything. 'It won't be kids,' I said.

Nevertheless, Joan wanted to go and look. So before we took off our coats she and I went out into the bleak November darkness. The goats were certainly not in the barn and yes, they were still behind the stile and yes, Auntie Mary was right. There were two very wet, very weak newly born kids! It goes on record, here, that we could not tell the white nanny was due to kid. Why, is it then, that all our guests are so sure that she, having had no opportunity to be so, is now always in kid?

The two babies, born in the November slush, were definitely a surprise. We carried them into the shed and later brought the nanny kid into the house for it was very cold and weak. It died and we were left with the billy.

'Don't get rid of it,' our cattle dealer said. 'Get it castrated and it will bring you luck. It is an old Irish belief that where there is a billy goat good luck abounds.' There is no way that we would now part with Billy for Luck is our Lady, all right.

Chapter Twenty-one

I think if it hadn't been for school and for Christmas I might have gone mad. The Autumn Fayre was a great success. I shared the money amongst the staff to spend as they wished on equipment for their classes.

The workload was exceptional for, thinking I would not need them again, I had burned all my treasured Christmas properties in one big bonfire the previous year. Now I had to pay the price and replace the loss. Children stayed with me every evening after school until we had done so. They brought sandwiches and thought life had never been better.

Every afternoon we closeted ourselves in the staffroom to read the Dickens masterpiece, *A Christmas Carol*. Everything was as it always was.

One lovely December morning we trooped out, properly clad, hurried up Priest Bank and over the stile and along the stream to the holly coppice for the ritual bringing home of the holly and the ivy. For nineteen years we had done just that. Knowing that there is an end in sight, one gives of one's best on the final stretch, one takes everything possible from a life that cannot possibly continue.

The boys and I went into town to buy a Christmas tree from the market. We had admitted a new boy from a broken home, a nice, popular little fellow who had found his new environment quite different from anything he had experienced. He came with us in the Land Rover. The tree we bought should have cost ten pounds, but the market salesman looked at my vehicle full of boys and the season of goodwill prevailed. He insisted on handing me back five pounds. All the children were delighted. All of them saw me put the note back into my purse. 'Thank you, thank you,' they all chorused.

Next morning I needed some glitter from the village post office. I sent for two girls to fetch it for me and noticed that the five pounds had disappeared from my purse. I knew I had not spent it and felt an unpleasant chill. My village children did not steal from me. In all the twenty-one years I was not aware that anything had ever been taken from my purse. I habitually left it lying around and sometimes even gave it to a child to take to the shop. The staffroom door was never locked.

I told the children that the money for their party was missing. The new boy said immediately that he had found it, yesterday, in the school yard.

'You must always tell if you find any money in the playground,' I said. 'What did you do with it?'

'I took it 'ome,' he said.

'Have you still got it?'

'Yeh.'

'Then just go home and get it,' I said and he did. I decided to make no issue out of it but money went missing in the spring term. Taking a chance, I took the boy aside, and asked if he had taken it. There were tears and recriminations but the money had been spent.

'Don't do that again,' I said. 'If you need money come and ask for it and I will give you some. You won't ever need much. I can probably spare it.' We shook hands on the deal. 'Don't steal it,' I said. 'Remember to ask and I'll give you it. OK?'

He agreed and he never stole any more money from me. Neither did he ever ask for any to be given.

We collected the stacking chairs from the Institute, piling dozens into the Land Rover. This was always the job of the big boys. A local junior boys' public school Carol Service was being held in the church. The road outside school was packed with well-polished limousines. I drove the dirty Land Rover from behind the school and the children cheered because we had to take the roundabout route, up Priest Bank and along the top road. Everyone waved like mad as we passed the Hagars' farm. One grandson, at least, was in the Land Rover.

We bruised ourselves, as always, trying to put a record number of stacking chairs into the vehicle and still squeeze holes in which to wedge the children for the return journey.

The value of a small village school is surely the constant need for everyone to do some physical and menial activity. I think children should begin working even before school age for they take to it like ducks to water. Farmers' children have more opportunities than most, of really purposeful work. The man who brought our last load of hay was telling us that his four-year-old was capable of being left in charge of feeding the farmyard hens. Walking across the yard, the other day, with a scoop of too few eggs, he had been heard to mutter to himself, 'Vose bluddy magpies!'

In a village school everyone was always sweeping the floor, cleaning the sinks and moving the furniture. In the 1930s, children used to learn all these skills at home but some are now not even taught to tidy up.

On the evening of the annual Carol Service I was sitting alone in the staffroom with my feet up preparing to enjoy a half-hour of bliss before staff and children returned. The tray of nearly a hundred mince pies rested on my desk covered with a tea towel. Mother, that cook *extraordinaire*, had made them all.

I think I had made that staffroom more my home than most headteachers. I had cooked so many meals in it, stayed so late at night. It wasn't just an office. During school hours it was often a classroom where groups could get on with projects, where children could have cookery lessons making pancakes on Pancake Tuesday and toffee on Plot Night. Sometimes it was a science laboratory where heat experiments were carried out. Often it housed a pet, sometimes a sick child. The armchairs were worn, the hearthrug well used. It was a place in which to be busy but that evening everything was ready and I sat with my feet up. The school entrance door was locked, the Crib was lit. I believed I could just sit there in glorious solitude!

It was a clear dry night. I heard talking in the playground and saw bicycle lamps flashing as a group of boys from the senior school rode illegally round the yard. The temptation to ignore them was great. With the staffroom door safely shut I could pretend I had never seen them and escape the duty of telling the culprits that they must not ride round the schoolyard.

But for over twenty years I had been afraid that a running child might topple over the small, unspiked railings and hurtle ten feet to the road. I trembled even more at the thought of a child wobbling on a bicycle. I went out into the classroom prepared to chase them off home for an hour, to tell them once again that it was forbidden, dangerous and insane to circle a sloping yard with such a low rail and a ten-foot drop. The Crib had attracted a boy to the window. He was sitting in the saddle, looking in. It was a boy I had taught. As an infant he had often been naughty, as a junior he had been lazy in lessons and had distracted other children. But he had been a likeable boy. In camp he had been no trouble at all. 'I've been here three days, Miss Brown and you've never been cross!' At the end of the fortnight he was saying, 'Fourteen days, Miss Brown, and you still haven't shouted at me!' The same boy had picked up a pound note in Beamsley Museum car park and then wanted to go and spend it on a present for his mother.

I went to the window to insist he went home for an hour but he forestalled all reprimand by beaming an irresistible smile and saying, 'Please can we come in? It's your Fan Club.' A charmer and no mistake!

So my moment of calm was gone. I unlocked the door and several lads trooped into the staffroom and took the easy chairs in that proprietorial way they had always had. I pulled up a high-backed, hard-seated one and prepared to listen to their pre-Christmas natter. 'Forbid them not,' I thought. 'Of such is the Kingdom of Heaven.'

There are many things I would like to do over again and one would be to experience another Carol Service round the Crib, to sit in the wings, in front of my beautiful children, amazed that five-year-old Rachel Roberts knew all the words. I would give anything to hear again the lusty singing on either side of our Nativity and feel the togetherness of staff, children and parents in the mêlée of mince pies and tea that followed. But the 'old order changes for the new' and there is nothing we can do about it.

'Don't think about it,' I schooled myself. 'Shut it out. Avoid the pain. Enjoy the present. No one can take away the twenty-one years you have known.' Increasingly I was thinking, 'Age will not weary *me*, nor the years condemn.' This comforting thought kept me sane.

On Christmas Eve we were startled to hear violins being played outside our farmhouse. We opened the door to let in the Shaw-Smiths from one of the outlying farms. The four boys played, the parents sang and it was lovely.

How isolated and alone we felt on Christmas Day, just the four of us and Auntie Mary. The place seemed eerily empty. There was an expectant silence as if the ministry of the house were just about to begin. This was nonsense for the walls and roof had already done four hundred years of service.

It was a lovely, peaceful Christmas Day with dinner of turkey and one of Mother's cloth-bagged Christmas puddings. It had been hanging with its brothers from the beams for more than a fortnight. We ate it in the kitchen from a depth of rum sauce. After dinner we watched a little television before a roaring log fire. What could we want for more? The year of super-activity was nearly over and, not knowing what the new one would bring, it was foolish to anticipate.

After our big dinner 'had gone down' as Mother would say, we parted company, some to wash the dishes, Margaret to the cattle and I spent the rest of Christmas afternoon putting two bunk benches into the alcoves of the Mistal Cottage dining room ready for the imminent arrival of the Sheriff family. It is the only Christmas Day in nearly sixty that I have spent with saw and hammer.

On Boxing Day Aunt Dorothy came and a friend of Auntie Mary's. We were able to leave the oldies by the sitting room fire. Margaret did the farm chores and I made up the cottage beds and fitted the kitchen with its permanent equipment. 'One cottage will be enough for the present,' we assured ourselves, for our pockets were well and truly empty.

So on the day after Boxing Day we had our first holiday neighbours. From the emptiness of the dining room we could hear the happy voices of the Sheriff children and that evening the phone rang. A Mrs Simmil was phoning from Gloucestershire wishing to book for herself, her husband and two teenage children for a fortnight in the summer! We had, when we had had time to think, presumed that our guests would be coming to Brontëland and staying one night only. In our ignorance and with our freezers full of pork, we thought we might be able to dish up the same menu every night. Suddenly the truth dawned that we would have to vary it at least fourteen times.

All week Mother baked cakes and pastries and on the morning of the New Year I went to the Institute near my school and borrowed several very narrow trestle tables and brought home the school dinner benches. We erected them in the dining room and managed to set places for fifty guests. It was a squeeze but we had invited that number for an official opening on 3rd January.

Paul, Julie and Vivienne came from Northumberland and almost everyone who had been involved. Builders, slaters, plumbers, joiners, electricians and tractor men; the architect, the brochure artist and Les Smith who had found these people for us and held everything together. They all came looking incredibly clean and smart with a smile on each face and a wife on one arm. There were the two Guides, Pru and Richard, the Bastows, the Blamires, the Belseys, the Winups, the Roberts, anybody and everybody who had given a hand, everyone young and old who had given their skill, their knowledge or their help.

It was not a new experience to feed so many at The Currer but to have everyone seated in one room was new. We have been frequently referred to as The Late Browns and we were, as Mother would say, at the last push up. People were arriving before we were quite ready. Farm chores had to be hurried and there was a last-minute panic to have the four-course meal ready. We seated workmen and friends alternately and there was soon a happy din. There was plenty of laughter and a lot of washing up afterwards.

The following day the Sheriffs went home. Some friends of Pru were going to Australia, had sold their house and needed a cottage for three weeks until their flight. We took all the Mistal Cottage equipment up to the Loft, ready for the emigrants due to arrive on the 6th. We had just removed the last article upstairs when the phone rang. A single gentleman, searching for a house in the area, needed temporary accommodation and would like to come and look at the Mistal next day.

He came at lunchtime. I had returned to school. Margaret rang and said the man wanted the cottage for about three months.

'When?' I asked.

'At about half-past five tonight!'

I dashed home from school. There was nothing for it but to undo all the good work and bring all the kitchen equipment back downstairs, the crockery, the pans, iron and ironing board, bread bin and waste bin. This was fast becoming ridiculous. We made a bed, switched on the heaters and lit the fire within minutes of his arrival.

Margaret saw him settled and he insisted on paying two weeks in advance. She came into the kitchen brandishing a cheque for £60.

'I nearly said the most stupid thing I've ever said in my life,' she laughed. 'Guess what! I nearly said, "That's the easiest money I've ever made!"' We were all in fits of laughter.

Then Margaret and I went straight to the late night opening of the Cash and Carry warehouse to buy a second set of kitchen implements.

The Loft Cottage looked lovely, ready once more in all its newness. The plain white walls had not a speck or blemish. We saw it perfect only one day, for the new arrivals came on the Wednesday. Instead of getting rid of all the things they didn't want to take to Australia, they brought everything here to sort. From a grossly overcrowded top cottage they packed what they wanted to send to the other side of the world. Then they sorted out what they wished to share among their relatives. The rest they put in ten large dustbin bags to take to the tip.

Consequently for the three weeks they were here the beautiful flat was little more than a junk room. Insult was added to injury on Sunday morning. Our emigrants had a roaring fire in the hearth and things were piled on furniture and floor and condensation was steaming down the windows for it was a frosty weekend. The potential Australians were happily playing Scrabble round the kitchen table, oblivious of rising water round their feet and deaf to a continuously filling toilet.

The young man below heard water dripping from above, saw it streaming down his walls and came running to us. Someone upstairs felt his stockinged feet wet and pandemonium reigned. The loo was overflowing and the bathroom floor and kitchen floors were awash. The sitting room carpet was soaking. We couldn't believe it! Our lovely, lovely cottage! All our months of effort, and everything flooded with water dripping onto the ground floor. The plumber was sent for and the mopping up began. It took days to dry out and the top kitchen lino never fitted perfectly again.

Bookings for the summer were coming in fast and furious. This was a miracle we could not believe. It was reassuring, however, when the bank statement came.

Margaret took a booking for a cottage for two weeks immediately following the exodus of our friends to Australia. Two girls, working evenings in Leeds, wanted self-catering accommodation. Mother was horrified. 'They must be strippers!' she worried. I remember Margaret ringing me at school to tell me 'the strippers' had come.

'Guess what they do?' she said. 'They play in the Sadlers Wells orchestra!' You've no idea how much that knowledge did for Mother.

The cottages remained booked throughout the first three months of the year and, by then, holidaymakers were on the way. I don't think that in seven years we have had more than half a dozen free weeks. After the 'strippers' came a family made homeless because the milk lorry had run into their house, and they were waiting for extensive repairs to be done.

Our first bed and breakfast did not come until February. Four booked for one night only and no evening meal. It should have been so easy. We, who had fed sixty regularly in camp without batting an eyelid, and fifty and more for many Queen's Guide presentations and celebrations galore, suddenly went to pieces. For this breakfast for four we had to take payment and the state of flummox was unbelievable. I think we used every pan, every hot plate, grill and oven, every fish slice and plate. We made more washing up than we do now, daily, for twenty and we declared, there and then, that 'carry-on' would have to stop. We pulled ourselves together and put panic behind us.

Our first evening meal was rather unusual. The booking was made by a local firm for an employee in the south who had to come up here for a meeting. His surname was that of a girl friend from Margaret's school days, who had gone to live in America years ago.

'I'm sure she had a brother called Edward,' Margaret said. She was right. We made our first evening meal for a friend's brother. The initiation was over easily. We got two more men from this lift-making firm. They stayed one night here to be briefed and then went twenty miles away to begin installing a lift. They found they could do the journey in half an hour and came back every night for three weeks.

On Pancake Tuesday one was phoning his wife from our kitchen and I heard him say, 'I'll have to go, love, my landlady has my dinner ready.' With a shock I realised that was what I had become. A landlady!

It was a very mild winter. The cottage residents had no snow problems and spring seemed about to come early. We had bought no autumn calves but now, with bookings coming in apace, we went to the bank manager and asked to borrow more money to buy some. 'No problem,' he said from his comfortable seat on our Deeds. It was a tightrope we were walking. One wobble and we might fall off.

Margaret went to market and bought quickly before we could get cold feet. She did not stop buying until she had seventy lovely calves. Spring calves are just what we want, we thought. They'll be out all summer. The Dutch barn was almost empty of hay and we had pathetically few bales of straw. We put most of the calves in the barn and the others in the bullock shed. We felt safe rearing calves; it was a known art. 'This is us,' I said, surrounded by bovine babies. 'What ever did we do that for?' 'That' being the converted barn and the yard full of cars.

The smell of those calves was a tonic. Sickly though it was it was more acceptable than the smell of paint and polish. Our trousers enjoyed a different kind of dirt. In the depths of the Dutch barn we could forget the earthquake which had changed our lives.

But we found that rearing seventy week-old calves and running a bed and breakfast farmhouse was well nigh impossible when the only help is a full-time teaching headmistress, a very elderly Mum and a handicapped brother. Calves need undivided attention and we did not know the new, secondary job well enough to feel relaxed in it. The calves were being fed with ad-lib cold milk and Margaret was mixing at least fifty gallons a day and doing all the breakfasts. Mother and Harry were doing all the washing up, she was doing the baking and Auntie Mary the ironing.

By Easter, which was late that year, the new calves had settled and were thriving. We put half of them in the shed we had re-erected in the orchard quadrangle. The roof span was pretty big and a wicked wind could easily have blown it away. It was so well sheltered, however, we thought little harm would ever come to it.

Auntie Mary and her friends had booked the Loft for Easter and Margaret took a booking for the Mistal. The lady wanted to come on Good Friday and go home mid-week but the cottage wasn't vacant until Saturday so Margaret said they could spend one night free in the bed and breakfast. We were prepared to do anything for money!

Our willingness to oblige was really appreciated in a letter of confirmation which we received a few days later. They would be very grateful indeed. Furthermore could they book evening meals throughout their stay. There would be, the letter said, 'myself and my husband and our two teenage children, my mother and my sister and her husband, our two Yorkshire terriers and our Alsatian.'

All our guest rooms quickly filled for Easter week and we soon accepted the fact that this enormous party would take all our family rooms and Mother, Harry, Margaret and I would be camping out in the sitting room. Seven evening meals on top of a full house lifted the total to twenty.

We had an elderly German gentleman and his son who came with a London teacher and I remember that everyone cosseted him. Certainly we ran circles round him attending to his every whim.

Easter was beautiful, all sunshine. We levered the family of seven into the cottage to make room for a family of friends from Glasgow. Morag Ann is a Luskentyre lass from Number Eight. We had persistently begged her to bring down her husband and three little girls. Morag Ann rolled up her sleeves and helped us. How we loved having them.

We thought summer had come. The yearlings were all out at grass. Neighbouring farmers had turned out their store cattle. It was the last week in April and daffodils were bursting into flower.

On Easter Tuesday the Germans were to leave and there was a sudden and unexpected drop in temperature and a glistening of frost. The German car would not start. It belonged to the older man but was always driven by his son who pressed the starter unsuccessfully before breakfast. A weak sun was trying to disperse the iciness so the car was left while breakfast was eaten. Then it was packed with suitcases and the son tried once more to start the engine. A crowd gathered. Everyone was keen to offer advice. The old man made an attempt to get into the car himself but was firmly pushed aside. There were too many cooks and not a good one amongst them.

They decided to push the car up the gradient in front of the Dutch barn and bump it off. There was plenty of male strength to do so. On the brow of the little hill, the old man managed to get into the driving seat, but the 'experts' prised him out from behind the wheel as if he were a naughty child. 'Just stand right out of the way,' he was told. 'We'll start the car.' Someone jumped in, everybody pushed but the car would not start.

So the 'experts' gathered in a circle to pool ideas.

'I suppose we'll have to tow it up the hill with the Land Rover,' whispered Margaret, who has had to do this many times.

But quietly, without anyone seeing him, the old German climbed into his car. He pressed the ignition and the car burst into life. Everyone turned. There was a stunned silence broken by the healthy sound of the engine. The old man put his head out of the window and shrugged his shoulders. 'It is my car!' he said.

Only Margaret and I found this irresistibly funny.

The cold persisted all day and we spent a lot of time trying to stop the draughts in the calf sheds. We had an insufficient store of straw bales to build insulating walls. The wind was uncannily cold. Something was brewing.

On Wednesday it began to snow in the evening, and by morning there was at least a foot. High winds had sculptured it round the house in drifts some eight feet high. It had blown into the calf sheds through every crack and cranny, and the shed roofs were sagging. Winter snow is light and a foot not very weighty but April/May snow is wet and heavy. The roof, sheltered from the wind, had found the enemy it could not beat and it was sagging under several tons. We looked at it without any faith at all.

The road was completely blocked. Waves of deep drifts folded themselves in ridge after ridge the whole quarter of a mile to the new cattle grid and right down the top road to the bus stop. The drift at the cattle grid was a veritable Mount Everest.

Our guests from Surrey had never seen anything like it. Two young teachers from Northumberland donned waterproofs and tackled the emergency. All day huge white flakes added several inches to the deep drifts. New guests cancelled their arrival. Those who should have left were snowbound. There was togetherness only snow could have created.

Margaret let the eighteen-month-old stores out to drink. All seventy of them careered down the field with a sort of snow madness and stampeded through the drifts at random. Exhausted, they found the journey back more difficult and floundered up to their bellies in snow.

'We're going to lose them,' shouted Margaret. 'Keep 'em going. If they stop we'll have to dig them out!' We spent a frightening hour getting them all back into an overcrowded shed. We were lucky. A farmer on the other side of the valley lost fifteen heavy bullocks. All over the Pennines sheep, lambs and cattle were unexpectedly buried.

There is little one can do until the snow stops except seal off draughts and feed the herd. We found some old tenting and sacks and did what we could but the real danger, the weight of heavy snow on the roof, we could do nothing about. There was nowhere to evacuate the babies to. We were helpless.

In the middle of the afternoon the two girls from Surrey came running to tell us that the shed roof had gone. The fibreglass sheets with which we had so recently covered the orchard quadrangle had given way. The Northumbrian teachers ran with us to the jumble of beams and sheets and calves floundering under the snow. Tom began dragging out frozen calves and carrying them to lay before the Aga in the kitchen and beside the central heating stove in the front porch. The parquet tiles received the frozen babies regardless of the wet manure clinging to cloven feet. Pools of water appeared all over.

For two days we remained completely isolated. All we did was to fight to save as many calves as possible. Some died almost immediately. Their inert little bodies were put in a sad pile and the fight continued to save the others.

Guests who had come to see York, Bolton Abbey and Brontë Country were as housebound as the storyteller in *Wuthering Heights*. At mid-day I just put loaves of bread and bowls of tomatoes and fruit on the dining room table. I closed my eyes to the many pairs of dripping wellies saturating the parquet tiles. We served the evening meal by carrying food through the snug rather than risk tripping over sick calves in the entrance porch and letting the smell of warm manure filter into the dining room. After each meal guests cluttered the washing up sinks in their eagerness to help.

The next day we began to dig out the road. Our guests thought we were beginning a task which could never be completed and anything less than a finished job was useless. We have dug the road out many more times than the number of winters and we know it is possible. It is useless to start until the snow abates and a night of wind can refill the track. We borrowed extra shovels from neighbours on the top road, and Pru and Richard came to help and invited us all to their cottage at coffee time.

'Thank God for the parquet tiles,' I told them. 'There are calves sitting on ours in the front porch down there and pools of water are standing on them in the dining room. A carpet would have been ruined already.'

Next day our guests were able to leave but the cold persisted. We managed to push, pull and force their cars up the road. I think they were quite sorry to go.

Pneumonia was inevitable. We lost all the calves we had brought into the house and many more besides.

The snow had thwarted some secret plans. Hazel and Pat had planned a big reunion of some one hundred of my campers. It was to have been held on the Friday of the snow and to have been at Pat's home which is deep in the country. So this great occasion had to be postponed for a week.

One of my first Guides, Jennifer Hartley, sent me a retirement card and said how sorry she was not to have been at the reunion. This let the cat out of the bag, which was a pity for the secret had been well kept. By the following Friday the roads had been cleared and we were able to have the most memorable evening.

There is nothing I like more than to be in the midst of my children be they round me in the playground, the staffroom or the Rec; in the D'abri, round the cooking fire, on the beach or the mountain top; in the train, on the boat, in the Land Rover, at The Currer, the Cheshire Home, or among the blind. Wherever, whenever my children and my children-grown are around me, I am having a good time. 'Let's do it again, every year,' Margaret said, and we do.

I remember walking through deep drifts to the camp store to choose the tents and the equipment needed to pack the skips for Tiree. We were taking almost half the school on this our final and best school trip, leaving on 6th May, and the equipment in advance had to be packed and sealed. I remember bringing a Land Rover-load of boys home with me to collect the things so that we could assemble them in school. The boys were delighted to find quite a depth of snow on the hill. I let them out at the top of Currer Lane so that they could slide and roll in it to their hearts' content. It seemed ludicrous to be taking eight-year-olds to a remote island apparently in deep midwinter.

How easy it was to drag skips from the store. They slid across the snow as easily as sledges. The cottages were occupied but no bed and breakfasts were booked. 'Keep it that way,' I said. Margaret almost did. There was only one booking during the fortnight I was away. Forty calves survived the snow without a backward look but the final death toll was thirty. This was the wobble on the tightrope when we nearly fell off. Margaret frequently went to the knacker's yard. Normally the proprietor will collect from the farm but such was the enormity of the disaster, and so taken by surprise were the farmers, that dead animals lay weeks in the fields awaiting collection. The calves were small and it was easiest to take them personally. Such a visit was horrific. The whole yard was strewn with victims of the snowstorm, piled high in one grotesque, green, odorous mess. Cattle in hundreds, sheep in thousands. It was a year we will never forget.

On the morning of 6th May, aware that I was leaving Margaret in a mess, we shepherded our excited children onto the train. I had thirty of the sixty village children. Dorothy Winup, our swimming teacher, and her husband were to join us at Oban and spend the week on Tiree with us. They did not arrive at the appointed time for their car had broken down and they appeared in the early morning having been brought by National Breakdown.

The weather was all set to become a heatwave and we were to come home very sunburnt. It's a strange world!

We fitted the twin cottages at Salum perfectly. There was just enough room for thirty-three sleeping bags and little in-between space. We pitched two Icelandic tents together in the paddock so that we could eat outside. In fact, the weather was so hot we often sitting out in the sun under the gable end. We bathed daily in the hot sunshine and the cold sea. On Tiree there are only three hills; we scrambled up them all. We ran races on the lovely white beaches and lost a game of football with the local cubs.

There was one nine-year-old who was homesick in a brave, 'I'll be OK, sniff,' kind of way who kept saying. 'It isn't a bit like this at home!' Sniff! Home was the Pennine hills and Tiree is as flat as a pancake, its frill of white beaches surrounded by the bluest of blue seas. Tiree is tree-less, not a bit like home!

I think I was very happy that week. I did not give room for one thought of the coming separation. One-third of these children would be leaving anyway and what one has had can never be taken away.

I know now and I think I knew then, that I enjoyed taking children on holiday more than I enjoyed the classroom. I never stopped teaching them and I hope I never neglected the three Rs but I acknowledged that there was so much more to teach, of the world, its natural and historical beauty, its physical and geographical differences. Children must be taught manners and relationships, helpfulness and self-confidence, how to fit socially and survive happily. I do not think the general public has ever known how much responsibility teachers have taken for teaching all these things out-of-school.

I lay on the hot sand of Gott Bay, feeling the sun burn me, listening to my children playing around me, against the background music of the sea and I knew there would have to be children at The Currer.

Each night thirty pyjama'd children squeezed into the cottage sitting room to sing and play games around the fire. I think we would have been quite happy to stay there all summer.

We returned via Edinburgh. I promised the children I would buy fish and chips. We walked the length of Princes Street but could find no chippy. Eventually Jill and I left the children standing on the pavement with Joan, near the station, and followed directions given by a resident. We seemed to run a mile before we found our quarry and the proprietor was shocked when he learned we wanted thirty-three portions.

Time was running out so I left Jill to wait for the stunned man to begin his marathon and I ran back to my flock and shepherded them on to the waiting train. We took our reserved seats, the clock ticked away and there was no sign of Jill. I began to get truly alarmed. The departure time was reached and there was the usual pre-departure activity. Doors were being shut, the platform cleared and the whistle lifted to blow. Always in an emergency I have risen with some plan, halted the inevitable with a sudden reaction. On this occasion I had absolutely no idea what to do.

Standing there on the Edinburgh platform, with one foot on the London train, I knew there was absolutely no way that I could stop that train. I could see the guard coming to push me onto it. And then I saw Jill, running with fish and chips for thirty-three; I screamed to the guard to wait and dragged her onto the train.

It is never easy, even now, to come home to a houseful of guests and to be in harness the moment we return, but it is never unexpected. I knew darn well that I was a landlady and that soon I would be a headmistress no more.

Surprisingly, I came home to a full house. Fortunately, a Calor gas cylinder explosion did not make seven people homeless until my return. We got this urgent message from an insurance company. Could we house all seven until their burnt-out home was repaired? We were overflowing. Sixteen breakfasts in the morning for Margaret to cope with alone, sixteen evening meals to do after a day's teaching.

At Spring Bank holiday, Dot, Peter and their children came up from Suffolk. Dot had been one of the Guides. They took a cottage and were here when a cousin found two kittens abandoned in his dairy. Knowing that we were short of cats at that time, he rang to see if we would adopt them and of course Margaret accepted. Dot's children never stopped playing with them. The result was we had two very petted kittens. Subsequent guests nursed the twins every evening, cottage holidaymakers tempted them with tit-bits and we lost control. The tiger kitten we called 'Tiger' and the ginger one we called 'Ginger' because we were too busy to be original.

Ginger liked to follow guests to their cars and on several occasions had to be evacuated from the front seat when guests were leaving. He followed us wherever we went and holiday-makers when they wandered off into the fields and we weren't a bit surprised when one day, almost fully grown, he disappeared.

Margaret searched everywhere. Believing it quite possible that he had become a stowaway we expected to hear from some departed guests in the south of England who had found Ginger among the luggage. Margaret rang the RSPCA, the Cat Protection Society and the vet and called on all our neighbours with no response. One family had repeatedly lifted Ginger out of their car during their stay. They left to visit Haworth before going home. We only thought this was relevant many months later.

Ginger had been gone so long we had forgotten him. Four months passed before the Cat Protection Society rang to say a lady on the Haworth Road had rescued a ginger tom after a road accident. The back legs were paralysed and the vet had said there was nothing he could do. Given time the paralysis might go or it might not. The lady did not feel she could cope with a sick cat but was unwilling to have it put down without trying to trace the owner. The caller from the Cat Protection Society wondered if Margaret had found her ginger tom.

We hadn't found our cat but we'd lost it months ago and we did not expect to find it in Haworth. However, Margaret went to look. I had visions of her bringing home a maimed stray to add to our responsibilities. 'Don't you dare bring home a cat that isn't ours,' I warned.

But the cat was, unmistakably, ours; Margaret brought it home and it recognised its brother, knew its cushion and after some weeks, the paralysis went and all ended well.

After the Spring Bank holiday of 1981 there were still six weeks of teaching left of the summer term. With the disaster among the calves, my imminent retirement made the financial outlook appear bleak indeed. If we could keep a full house we might still regain our balance and stay on the tightrope. We decided to gamble again and buy some stores, eleven strong Friesian bullocks for £200 each. It nearly gave us heart failure but somehow we had to succeed.

These Friesian bullocks arrived simultaneously with a new guest. A caddy phoned from a pub near the golf course where a tournament was to be held. We had several vacancies and were pleased to take him. His car came down the road at the same time as the cattle wagon. The new caddy had to leave his car outside the gate which was well and truly blocked. He came over to watch the cattle being unloaded. 'Och, I'm Wullie,' he announced. 'Wullie Aitcheson.' When he eventually pulled his car into the yard we noticed that 'Lee Trevino' was written all over it. Before long the house was overflowing with caddies and professionals and Mother was baking rock buns for Eamonn Darcy.

'Aren't you doing well! ' said our neighbours when they saw so many cars, Sunshine Coaches, hospital mini-buses and cars with foreign number plates.

'Put it this way,' we said. 'If cars do not come we will be bankrupt within a year!' Of course no one believed us. All the same it was true. We had to have customers and satisfied guests are a good recommendation. So we provided accommodation for a song in the belief that many songs might eventually pay.

I took a booking for three retired people for a fortnight. The lady asked the price and made a definite reservation. Ten minutes later she phoned again asking the price. 'I thought that's what you said,' she remarked. 'My son says that for that price the loo must be down the field.' We found that all our friends were eager to tell us that we charged too little. They all thought they knew best what to serve and how to treat people. They laughed when they heard we did not charge for cups of coffee and tea, whatever the time or however many times a day. They were emphatic that we should not let people into the kitchen, that they ought not to bring pets.

'You're running a business, now,' one friend said. What, may I ask, is farming? Have we not always been businesswomen?

We took little heed of them. We have learned to smile and appear to listen and then do it our way. If we fail we have only ourselves to blame. The lady found the loo was not in the field, enjoyed her stay and all three re-booked for the following year.

Linda Cooke, one of my Queen's Guides, brought twenty-three mentally handicapped teenagers for a week. Some of them were taking Duke of Edinburgh awards and camped in the Five Acre. They entertained forty day-guests, similarly handicapped, to a cheerful barbecue. An atmosphere was being created, not by us, maybe because of us, but certainly it was the people who came to the environment that we provided, who created the warmth and friendliness that has become a part of The Currer.

'I like the atmosphere,' is a frequent comment.

'This place has a ministry of its own,' said one Guider after a weekend training. Hadn't we always known that The Currer was not just a house, that it had a personality, a spell which had captivated us since we were children.

I monopolised the Land Rover, taking my children out at least once a week. We went to local places of natural and historical interest that we had always been too busy to visit. We went to Wycoller where I had an amazing experience. We had explored the village and the ruins of the Hall and been in the Aisle Barn. We were returning to the Land Rover walking with the Park Ranger. On the outskirts of the village I noticed a barn for sale and I asked the Park Ranger if we could look inside.

In every detail it was identical to the barn at The Currer. It was as if we had turned the clock back and were once again standing in the cobbled entrance with the flags for the cart wheels. There were identical cow stalls, gnarled and greasy, the broken mistal window, the hay loft above and I am sure it was the same manure under our feet and the same cobwebs everywhere. Above us were the same roof trees and principals, the same cracked timbers and shifted slates.

I was spellbound. There was a peculiar silence. I felt to be in a holy place and my knees began to give as if they wanted to pray. Children were looking at me. One said, "'S like your barn wor, Miss Brown.'

'It is,' I said. 'It is just like our barn was.' Whatever had we done? It made the knowledge that we could never undo what we had done, quite painful.

I could not rest until I had taken the family. Together we wallowed in sentiment. We have no regrets, but we have many precious memories and the barn at Wycoller stirred them. It can do so no more. We sent all our guests to look back into the history it shared with The Currer. One day some guests returned and told us that the Wycoller barn had fallen down and we were indescribably sad. Later the rubble was removed and the site cleared.

When asked what I wanted for a leaving present I said that a photograph of the school would please me most. The kitchen door was naked of paint and would spoil the picture so I bought a can and stayed late one night. Villagers had the unique experience of seeing their headteacher busily painting the back door.

The only times I ever thought about my coming retirement were when I was alone, driving to and from school. As I frequently ferried a cleaning lady, who was a neighbour and had a job in the village where I taught, I was seldom alone. When I had no one in the passenger seat I had to sing, or talk to myself to stop the choking in my throat and stem the tears. 'Lead me, Lord ... make my way plain.' What a consolation hymns are! And poetry, too. 'Age shall not weary [me] nor the years condemn.'

There was too much to do, too much to leave, too much to leave for. 'You will miss school,' I was told. Of course, but Joan was leaving with me and so were many of my children.

There was another curtain being drawn on the past that no one could do anything about. The fall that had broken Cloughie's leg in the winter of 1980 prevented her from making any more visits to The Currer. One stroke after another left her more and more disabled and I visited her more frequently. Eventually she was confined to a brass bedstead in the ornate drawing room and when I took Mother to see her, one day, she did not recognise her. Mrs Eddie, her devoted housekeeper, had become her nurse, too.

She had inherited great material wealth, that dying lady, whom I had loved for more than forty years. She had had little money. I remember that she had moaned that the wallpaper in the Blue Room had faded so and I told her to buy some more and I would put it up for her.

What material wealth she had inherited was unknown until the eventual sale. She only saw it as inherited opportunity. What was hers she had shared with hundreds of children. Her home and grounds had a ministry, too, and she had, to the very best of her ability, used it for the good of others. A friend had told her one day how lucky we all were to be able to share it and she had remarked that she had been the lucky one having it to share.

I had delivered milk in the slums of an industrial town and I knew that the mill workers who had made the mill owners rich, were themselves in poverty. But no blame for this could be laid at Cloughie's feet. She was unable to sell her entailed inheritance and distribute it to the poor to enable her to follow the Master but she had given it away, none the less, a thousand times in order to follow Him and teach a new generation a more positive and creative way of life. And at the end of all her giving it was still there accumulating in value.

I learned a lesson. You don't have to sell all and give to the poor. That is one way. But there is another. Given ten talents, you must not just give them away. You must use them! Cloughie had! So must we!

For a few weeks in June she continued to recognise me with a weak lifting of the hand and a gentle smile. There came a time when she did not know me at all. I called or phoned daily but there was never any change. She who was so ready and so well prepared to meet her Maker took so long to do so it distressed us all.

I suppose she had often been lonely. Isolated by deafness and wealth she had reached out to find friendship and I am eternally grateful that, at the end, she had Mrs Eddie, her devoted housekeeper.

I remember her funeral service. The church wasn't packed as it should have been. That tribute came a few months later when the bigger church in the town was overflowing in remembrance. The funeral service was simple. One of the present Guides of the Steeton Company had been chosen to read a passage from the Bible and, in the middle of it, she broke down and cried. It was very moving indeed. We were all crying and the poor Guide stayed in the pulpit trying to control her sobs. No one came to her rescue and the silence was poignant. Eventually the girl controlled her tears and continued reading. I think, in its unrehearsed simplicity, the little moment of great sadness was very appropriate.

Outside, after the cortège had left the church, we all stood around in groups, a little lost, for the leader who had inspired us all had gone and only the immediate family, so few and so distant, were invited to the cemetery.

Before leaving the circle of Guiding friends I couldn't help saying, 'Cloughie influenced my life more than any other.' Barbara Sheriff was among the group. I was walking away towards my Land Rover and I felt an arm being linked in mine.

'Did you tell her?' I was asked. I did not understand.

'Tell who?'

'Did you tell Cloughie what she had meant to you? Did you tell her?' The question was repeated and was important.

I thought back to the day I had had tea in the drawing room and had given my hostess a copy of my book. I know I told her, then, that she had been the inspiration behind all my work with children. 'If it hadn't been for you,' I had said, 'all those children would have missed the Hebrides!'

It had pleased her.

'Yes, I told her,' I said.

'I'm glad,' said Barbara, with an affectionate squeeze of my arm. 'Just for the record, in case anything unexpected happens, I'm telling you.'

I cried all the way back to school in the Land Rover and looked a sorry mess sitting with my children for their dinner.

The school staff, teachers, secretary and dinner ladies were annually invited to have a July tea with one of our school benefactors, Miss Dorothy Hill. For the first time I had to leave soon after I arrived for I had promised to pick up two youngsters walking the Pennine Way. I felt awful leaving my circle of friends sitting in the pleasant lounge, overlooking the valley.

'Heck,' I thought, 'what life is this?'

There was a last minute struggle to tie off all the loose ends and clean out all the cupboards. I remember tying them up with skipping ropes and daring anyone to open them again. People kept coming in to see Joan and me and to wish us a happy retirement. My friends who had already retired said I'd now be able to do all the things I had never had time for before. There seemed no point in disillusioning them.

I spent all the last Sunday spring-cleaning the staffroom. Our lady caretaker had been in hospital and was not allowed back to work before the end of term. Jill had assumed her duties but a retiring head must do her own spring-cleaning. When the back of the job had been broken I sat at my desk in the empty classroom and allowed myself one moment of self-pity. 'There won't be time later,' I thought and I wrote,

> How can I convey my thanks
> To you who have been my friends?
> Today I have spring-cleaned your school
> And sorted the conglomeration
> Of more than twenty years.
> It saddens me to know,
> From now on, my family
> Will grow old.
>
> I sit alone, happy but bereft.
> My cluttered desk is cleared and
> The emptiness is full of memories.
> I feel the presence of my children
> Hear their laughter and singing
> Their questions, hopes and fears
> And through a mist of tears
> I see them all.

Lucky woman, singularly blessed!
I have loved and been rewarded
A thousand, thousand times.
Your loyalty and respect
Have been gifts of value;
Bestow them generously
On the rich inheritor
Of my beloved kingdom.

The last week was a succession of breakfasts, letters, phone calls, bed making, children's little gifts, reports, visitors, cups of tea, evening meals and prize giving. Our presentation was an informal affair. I don't remember much. Michael came after the home-time bell had rung at the Secondary School. From one pocket he produced a rather dirty cheque. 'My mother and dad sent this,' he said. 'Because I had been so happy at this school.'

'Give it to Mrs Annan,' I said, for she had been responsible for all that.

He delved once more into his pocket and produced a very crumpled pound note. He tried to flatten it, smiled and said, 'An' this is from me.'

'Thank you,' I said, 'for the tremendous pleasure it was to teach you.'

Suddenly it was all over, the photographs, the leave-taking, the distribution of the reports, the thank yous and all. After everyone had gone Jill and I were alone. 'I'm not going to leave this school until it is spotless,' I said, rolling up my sleeves.

So together we swept the floor and put on a layer of polish and dusted the furniture. We scrubbed and Vimmed the sinks and disinfected the loos. We shook the mats and vacuumed the staffroom carpet. A village headship is a unique profession. Soon there will be no village schools and the way of life which was ours will be a small piece of history. The way we taught and the way we thought, our priorities and our values will be forgotten and something infinitely precious will be lost.

Seeing the Land Rover still there, long after five o'clock, children began to filter back into school. I realised that if I stayed much longer there would be dusty footprints all over the newly polished floor. There was quite a crowd round the desk as I wrote my last entry in the logbook. We all tiptoed out and I locked the door. I slipped the keys in my pocket for they were mine until 31st August. The children stood on the pavement and waved as I drove away to make my many evening meals.

A few days later it was the Royal Wedding. All the holidaymakers stayed at home. It was a great day. I climbed onto the lean-to laithe porch roof and flew the Union Flag from the jack staff. We had four Irish teachers staying. I remember these girls, from Dublin, saying, 'By the end of the day we'll be royalists, too.'

They taught in schools for the handicapped. Anne Sullivan was in a wheelchair following a serious road accident. One afternoon I squeezed myself into their small car and took them all to see my school. I was relieved to know that my floor had been polished.

We were sitting in the staffroom, having a cup of tea, when footsteps clattered on the wooden floor. Three elderly people came, jubilant to find the door open in holiday time. 'This was my school seventy years ago,' volunteered the old man. He wanted to talk about it. The school had always welcomed past students and teachers and, to the best of my ability, I had kept the tradition. Not for nothing had we been named The Coffee School.

People like to come on holiday to a farm for the relaxed atmosphere, the comfort, the view and the food. We have found that few, if any, want a farm experience. One in a hundred brings wellingtons. No one brings an old boiler suit except Richard who comes every Easter. Richard was born with Downs Syndrome more than thirty years ago. He brings wellingtons and is more capable of doing work than anyone else who comes. Whilst his parents go off sightseeing Richard has a wonderful time at The Currer, carrying bales and bedding down cattle, sweeping and painting. Almost everyone else is away at the first whisper of a 'load of hay coming today'. Young girls, particularly Polly, are more help than boys, with the exception of Denis and Gavin.

Parents send their children to help as if small hands can do farm work and feeding animals is child's play. Many stroke the goats and donkeys but never see the shed with a hundred cattle. We learned a lot about people during those first months. They do not know that cows only give milk if they have a calf. They think all black cows are bulls. They think that farming is a healthy life, that you do not work if the weather is bad and they think all farmers are rich. One lady looked at our one hundred three-month-old Hereford heifers and asked, 'Will all these be cows or can't you tell yet?'

Many of the questions they ask are not suitable for publication. In this very promiscuous world the facts of life have been very badly taught.

Our most memorable guests of the summer were a doctor, his wife and children from London who, on booking, confessed they had two problems. 'That's all right,' Margaret said. 'We are used to solving them.'

'We have a dog,' she was told.

'That's fine,' said Margaret. 'As long as it's not a Staffordshire bull terrier or a Rottweiler, we don't mind at all.'

'And we have two goats!'

'You must be kidding,' Margaret said.

But they were not and I'm telling you, those goats had a wonderful farm experience! They arrived in the back of a car. Their owners tethered them, took them for daily excursions and milked them morning and evening. One goat was so like our own nanny they used to butt each other none too playfully. One day our nanny saw her own reflection in the Mistal Cottage bedroom window, thought it was the unwelcome newcomer and charged at the pane. Glass and goat descended in the bedroom and the lady in a wheelchair who was renting it for the week found she had to sleep one night with a boarded-up window.

People came from all over the world: Australia and Japan, Italy and New Zealand, Alaska and South Africa, America and Scandinavia, Germany,

France and the Low Countries. Every night was a first performance, trying
to keep up a standard, greeting new people and waving off those who had
become friends overnight.

On 31st August I went into school, collected what personal post there was
for me, saw everything was in apple pie order and left before any children
had seen my arrival. I locked the front door, dropped the keys through the
letterbox and that was that.

Chapter Twenty-two

O ne day in September I walked over the moor to check the cattle and make sure the boundary wall was still the fortress it must be. I think Margaret had sent me on purpose to see for myself the over-growth of grass everywhere. If we have brought changes to The Currer house they are no more noticeable than those brought by Father to the land. He inherited a barren landscape and left a green one.

We had about seventy animals to sell and only forty of the spring calves had survived the snow. We had the eleven Friesian bullocks and twelve Hereford and Aberdeen Angus. We had even allowed a cousin to hire some grazing during the summer and still there was this tremendous over-growth of grass.

'We could mow the meadows.' I said when I came home. 'Perhaps we should buy some stores.'

We approached that very obliging bank manager sitting on our deeds and he said, 'Go ahead,' so we went to the nearest store market, bought a few and arranged with the man who does all our movement of cattle to bring them home. What's more my incredibly confident sister said to him, 'Do you think you could go on buying cheap stores until we reach sixty?' We were gambling again but there is only one way to pay off an overdraft and that is not by sitting afraid on the starting-line.

We had never bought stores before. They were a hotch potch of unknown animals who were strangers to each other, the sheds, the land and the crush through which they all must go for copper and blackleg injections. We were kicked and trodden on, and life was a nightmare.

They were delivered about six at a time every few days and they bellowed and kept the guests awake. One otherwise satisfied customer wrote in the Visitor's Book, 'Next time please give your cows sleeping tablets!'

The cattle were strangers and did not know where they belonged. They stormed the boundaries and joined the herds of our neighbours and we hardly knew what they looked like. We were too tired to cope with naughty 'children'.

We had bought on an impulse and now we needed to buy more hay and straw. We approached winter inadequately stocked with fodder and with insecure housing. We had repaired the orchard shed by putting in some more uprights to take the weight of the large expanse of roof but the repair was messy. No amount of bedding seemed to dry up the mud floor.

Margaret said, 'I think I'll ask John to help me build a new shed. We'll pull down the calf sheds and I'll ask him to lay me a concrete floor and put in some cheap telegraph poles.'

Speed was important for the winter was fast approaching. We have built sheds before in mud and rain, in times when we have thought we had little of that most valuable dimension. Now we had no time at all for our stream of guests continued. We needed help, amateur help, but Margaret asked John, who is a professional, and before we knew where we were and what was happening, plans were drawn for a palatial shed, grant-aided and Government approved. It was likely to cost a hundred times more than anything we would have put up so that, whatever the grant, we were going to hurtle deeper and deeper into the red! All the summer earnings would look a mere drop in the ocean.

Steeton Hall was to be auctioned. We went to look at the lots, all laid out ready for the hammer, arguably the most valuable collection in the area. There were hundreds of items ranging from antique children's toys to paintings of great worth. Burglar alarms, which had never been necessary when the house had been solely occupied by one deaf old lady and her elderly housekeeper, were hurriedly installed.

The big, auctioneer's marquee was erected on the gravel in front of a house which had seen thousands of tents in the last sixty years. The sale took three days and I joined those seated under the big canvas for the final day and I saw pictures sold for £36,000 and carpets, old and threadbare, sold for a fortune.

I remembered a day I had hopped over the stile; Madam waved from the window and indicated that I must come in by the side door.

There was the usual noisy barking of her terrier companion. 'Come in and look,' she said, linking her arm in mine as we went along the kitchen corridor, past the library door and the huge dinner gong outside the morning room and through the stately dining room to the drawing room where, in her favourite window seat, we always chatted and had tea.

'I've been spending me brass,' confessed the good Yorkshire lass.

She'd bought a new carpet for the big, beautiful room. It was very ordinary and inexpensive.

'It's lovely,' I said.

'Well, it cost the earth!' she complained.

'Never mind,' I said. 'Spend your brass.'

'I haven't got any,' she said which was probably true.

I sat in the marquee, reminiscing. There were some worn carpet squares from the billiard room I might have bid for but they went for an unreasonable sum of money. They were at least forty years old, I could prove it. I could have afforded the huge new one she had bought recently for it was knocked down at £10.

Of what value could all those separated lots really be compared to the value of that home intact? The total of all the parts was a very great sum of money but it was as nothing compared to the value of that house and its peculiar and wonderful ministry. I came away from the auction empty handed. It was the first time I had come away without something, a grain of wisdom, a new idea, a solution to a problem, a useful tip, a thought to ponder over, some apples from the orchard, a bunch of homegrown grapes or a recipe from Mrs Eddie's book.

About this time Margaret read a piece of wisdom. 'If you are tired out and broke, you need a holiday.'

We were both but we couldn't take a holiday for we were full of paying guests whose revenue we needed.

'Yes, you can,' said Janet, whom we'd taken on holiday so many times. 'Michael and I will come.' Dear Janet! Paul would come and look after our 120 stores. So why not?

I bought a guidebook of self-catering holidays in Wales and booked a cottage at Uwchmynydd, near Aberdaron at the end of the Lleyn peninsula.

Ten days before we were to go to Wales, Ellen, from Salum, Tiree, her husband Donny and their children came to stay with us for a few days. We just wanted to talk to Ellen but we had evening meals to make and, what was more, we had a wedding reception on the Saturday afternoon. We had promised the use of the whole house to Dorothy Winup who often helped us and whose daughter was marrying. Dorothy was catering and she had been bringing in food and wine all the Friday evening.

We had just bought an old, very large kitchen table, from the local second hand shop. It was a lovely piece of furniture which no one with a modern kitchen would want. The beautifully turned legs needed some firmer screws and a little wood glue. Donny decided to fix it for us before leaving on Saturday afternoon, so we went into town for the screws and glue and to take Ellen to the Damart Mill. Donny upturned the table and began his painstaking work; we all ate some sandwiches and dawdled over lunch.

Suddenly, in horror, I looked at the clock and gasped, 'Hey, do you realise, they'll all be going into church?'

There was panic. Donny and John were righting the table, Ellen and Julie were stowing bags into their car. I was lighting fires in the dining room and snug, Mother and Harry were washing the dishes and Margaret doing one of those quick 'side-ups' she is so famous for. Within a very short space of time the Hebrideans were driving out of the yard to the cheers and commands of, 'Come again,' and we were turning into the house to lift delicacies from the fridge, unwrap the ham and beef and unveil the turkey.

We opened the salads and trifles delivered that morning, took the cover from the wedding cake in the dining room and spread out the cakes and pastries in the most frantic rush I think we have ever had. Mother and Auntie Mary were too busy to be in any state of flummox at all. We have never raced with the clock quite so desperately.

We were pulling on clean dresses and aprons, pushing stray hairs into place, stoking fires, slicing ham, boiling every kettle we had.

And it was a lovely wedding!

We had thought that the house would be so clean for Ellen's visit and the wedding that we would only need to flick a duster and we would be ready to leave for Wales! It was wishful thinking.

Guests kept coming. The weather deteriorated and the cattle began to come home to the sheds. Everywhere was a shambles. John had pulled down the calf sheds and this had taken away all the south front of the orchard shed. The bought-in herd didn't know the routine and the forty calves we had reared ourselves were confused with the demolition and the foundation excavation. We couldn't fence off the building site, cattle roamed everywhere and we didn't know how to prevent them getting into the yard or falling down the holes. There had been no go-ahead from the Ministry so the work came to a standstill and we tried to improvise fencing but it was all a dreadful mess. Mud was deep everywhere, tractor ruts held the rainwater, the cattle seemed wild.

Cars picked up mud and brought it into the yard, guests and family walked it into the house. We were booked up fully for half-term.

Janet and Michael arrived whilst I was still making up beds. At mid-day we were in a panic trying to pack a few clothes. Mother must surely be one of the world's most proficient holiday-case packers, but such was the interrupted progress of the task, before we went to Wales, that when Mother opened her case at Uwchmynydd, she found she must have put in a pair of tights every time she resumed the task.

The minutes flew by. We had no lunch. We were packing food to take self-catering, in the most haphazard manner. We needed a picnic on the way. I remember filling the flasks and putting a fruity farmhouse loaf, some butter and a bread knife into the picnic bag.

When we finally jumped into the Land Rover there were only two hours of daylight left and it was raining. The cattle were coming home and Paul had not arrived. We met all hundred-odd of them coming down the road. They came to their usual standstill in front of us and there was nothing for it but to get out into the deluge and shoo them off. The tractor wheels had brought clods of mud onto the road and the five hundred cloven feet had done likewise. Water was pouring down from the spring at the top of the hill. Rivers were forming in the Intakes and the Eight-Acre. We never had a more inauspicious start. I clambered back into the Land Rover, wet and very muddy underfoot.

'We're off,' some optimist said. It is our custom, at this point, to sing cheerfully all the way up onto the top road. 'We're all going on a summer holiday,' we warble untunefully. 'We're going where the sun shines brightly, we're going where the sea is blue!' I don't think, on this particular occasion, we did anything of the sort. We crawled in low gear and subdued silence to the top of the hill and headed for Auntie Mary's cottage. She too was silent, obviously appalled by our lateness. We turned off her water and electricity and threw her cases into the already too-full Land Rover.

'God help us,' I thought.

In shocked silence we put miles behind us as quickly as we could before pulling into a lay-by. 'A cup of tea is what we want,' we said. 'After that, we'll be all right! ' We found flasks and the loaf of currant bread, the butter and the knife but no cups. No cups! There must be cups! There were no cups, nor anything remotely like a cup. Why can we not be like other people and screw a cup on the top of a flask? One would have been enough. One plastic mug, a tooth mug, a jam jar. Anything! There was nothing.

'We can't eat bread without something to wash it down,' said Auntie Mary.

'Whatever were you thinking of?' said Mother.

'You should have remembered,' said Harry.

'Shut up!' shouted Margaret.

'We've too much work!' complained Mother.

'Shut up!' I said.

We pulled out of the lay-by. 'There'll be a snack-bar caravan somewhere,' said Margaret. But there wasn't. Nor a wayside café. Mile after mile, rain streaming down the windscreen, five of us desperately in need of a cup of tea.

'It's the last time I'm coming on holiday,' Mother said. We all laughed. We'd heard it so many times before.

Does Lancashire possess no refreshment places for weary travellers, no transport cafés at all? We seemed to be travelling continually in towns and depressed areas where houses were for sale everywhere. We felt strangers in such urban areas.

Somewhere, approaching the Mersey, we saw a café, still open. It was already dark. One of us grabbed the dog whilst the other helped Harry out, then Mother, then Auntie Mary, all stiff with travelling, all blinded by head-lights, all struggling into plastic macs, Margaret and I, too busy to put on waterproofs, getting wet as usual.

I couldn't remember when we had last been in a café and I don't think we've ever been in one since. But we sat in that one, eating egg and chips as if that was what we always did. The cup of tea worked wonders. We were all together, all on holiday, warm, fed, what more could we want?

The whole operation had taken well over an hour. We piled everyone into the Land Rover. I got into the driving seat and Margaret took the map. Suddenly we realised we were heading down a motorway westwards on the wrong side of the river.

'Get off it,' said Margaret. 'There's a road and a flyover coming up. Pull off.' The rain was coming down in buckets. I saw the pull-off thankfully and turned safely off the motorway. Before me I could see a dip in the road and considerable flooding. It was deeper than I'd anticipated. I put my foot on the accelerator and suddenly a tidal wave broke over us. Margaret was furious. We both knew you do not accelerate through a lake! On the other side of this one was a T-junction access onto the flyover. I paused to give way and stalled. I pressed the starter. It was dead. Margaret said all sorts of things and we both got out. My tail was well and truly between my legs.

We braved the rain and partly lifted the bonnet. We must, at all costs, not let it pour onto the engine. 'We won't be able to start it anyway,' Margaret shouted above the noise of traffic and torrential rain on the bonnet.

Margaret is the mechanic. I handed her a cloth and made myself a human prop and rain shield whilst she wiped the plugs.

Whatever were we going to do? Margaret and I could cope with a night in a cold Land Rover but whatever were we going to do with the trio in the back?

'Get me the Damp Start!' Margaret said. She took the weight of the bonnet and I went into the cab.

'Will it go?' I was asked.

'No,' I said.

Margaret squirted the engine very liberally with Damp Start, we said a little prayer and got back into the car. Margaret took the driving seat. I felt an absolute disaster.

She pressed the starter and the engine leapt into song. Good old Margaret! Good old Land Rover! Good old Guardian Angel! Everybody laughed, and we sailed over the flyover and back along the motorway. We were soon driving gently along the North Wales coastline blinded by oncoming traffic. The trio in the back was no trouble at all. In fact we were singing, for a little while, until we got more and more tired and headlights and passing fast traffic became a nightmare.

We stopped at Colwyn Bay to stretch our legs. Whilst the trio went to the loo, Margaret and I studied the map. We had a hundred miles still to go. We were horrified and dared not tell the family. The two of us sat glued to the wet windscreen, changing frequently, tired out, afraid to let go. We were in no fit state to drive hundreds of miles on a wet dark night in unknown country. There was silence behind us.

About twenty miles from Aberdaron we asked our way from some drunken men outside a pub. There was a lot of excessive gesticulating and absurd instructions in slurred speech. 'And the besht of British luck!' said one, patting the bonnet. The humour in us is never far from the surface. We relaxed, laughing and turned up the narrow road. For twenty miles we seemed to be following a single track and the blackberry bushes on either side were so high we seemed to be perpetually in a tunnel. We hardly met a car. It was ten times better than the high road.

At last we found our cottage and opened the door on the warmest, most welcome cell on earth. The beds were made and there were electric blankets and thick, lamb's wool rugs.

We have guests who appear in our kitchen at 6.30 a.m. and say they are so used to getting up early that they cannot sleep in. We smile. They do not work as hard as we do! Boy, can we sleep in! I wake at 5.30 every morning. On the first day of my holiday I do not wake at all until the rest of the family stirs and Margaret who always rises shortly after me does not wake at all until she is shaken.

When we eventually wakened at Uwchmynydd we looked out on a landscape not unlike Barra. We loved it there, though winter seemed to have already come to the peninsula. We missed the beautiful beaches and the spectacular seas of the Hebrides but the people were lovely, and perhaps we will see them again one day.

Each evening we phoned home and repeatedly stressed to Paul that he must hurry John into starting without the full approval of the Ministry. We had built our other sheds at the last minute, too but without the tethering of red tape. They had served their purpose and given long years of excellent service. All we had asked for was a little timely help with the foundations. Someone who could mix and spread concrete quickly because we were in a hurry. Someone just to dig the holes with equipment and drop in the telegraph poles with more speed than we could. And what had we got? Just a quagmire outside while the wheels of officialdom slowly turned.

'It's got to be finished by the middle of November,' Margaret said. 'How long will it take?'

'Only three weeks, or so.' It took two months and was a mansion in which we could have served bed and breakfast. It increased our overdraft and, because we had said the one little word 'yes', there was nothing we could do about it. Once a few pounds have been spent, once something has been pulled down, once the first few stones have been laid you have only two options. You give up, write off what expense there has already been, live with the mess and have nothing, or you keep going until the end when you have a valuable and essential addition to your property and a whacking amount of loan interest to pay. The first is unthinkable so you opt for the second and face the fact that, whilst your colleagues all bask in retirement, you are probably going to be doing bed and breakfast for the rest of your days.

The problem of money seemed infinitely less than the problem of cattle. For years feeding cattle had been a dangerous activity. Now it was suicidal. Some of the hotchpotch of stores we had so hurriedly bought had not even been de-horned. We had too many cattle in every shed and lousy weather. The shed go-ahead had come but progress seemed incredibly slow. Every day the team, headed by John, worked long, long hours building this bovine mansion. We thought we would go mad.

And we had another problem. Soon after Father died a gypsy from the valley came to ask Margaret if she would let him graze two ponies on the moor. Whilst he was in the yard there was a sudden emergency in the shed. This young gypsy happened to be there just at the right moment to help Margaret and she was grateful. He promised to pay for the grazing at a time when we needed every ha'penny we could get. So she said he could graze his ponies and he paid regularly but kept adding another.

He was a courteous fellow, excellent with horses, and the ponies, increasing in number, were not really a problem until we started feeding cattle in the fields. This we had to do as much as possible for overcrowding in the shed made things so difficult. The horses got wind of this daily 'soup kitchen' and came galloping down every feed time. They effectively scattered the herd and promptly helped themselves. The gypsy was only paying for grazing and, anyway, we just could not cope with this fiasco every morning. We went down to his caravan and left a message. Only an old gypsy mother was there and I'm sure the message was not delivered. We battled on. It was a problem we couldn't do anything immediately about and must therefore, like the building of the shed, be tolerated.

December came. Our last guests for the year left on the morning of the 7th and, we wondered, 'Could this be a moment of calm?' The noise of the departing car could still be heard fading as it neared the cattle grid at the Moor Gate. We looked at each other, smiled and shrugged our shoulders in an exaggerated, 'Well, that's it!' It was a beautiful morning, very cold and icy, so cold that the sun could not take away the glitter from the sycamore and the silver birches standing sentinel in front of the farmhouse. There was a wonderful silence. We savoured it, listened to its many voices: the cattle breathing heavily in the nearby sheds, the goats placidly ruminating on the straw, a delighted hen announcing a newly laid breakfast.

Our last visitors had gone; a mother and her paraplegic son, disabled ten years ago in a road accident. All that remained were the tyre marks of his wheelchair clearly defined in the frosty rime standing proud of the previous night's scattering of snow. Our season was surely over, until Christmas, three weeks away.

Peace, we thought. Once again we are only farmers. No pre-Christmas demands of primary school headship, none of the wealth of Guiding activities surrounding bygone Christmases. We shrugged off the harness of responsibility, shivered and went inside to get warm. Peace, we repeated, our long-awaited moment of calm; time to recharge our batteries. Nothing to do but remake the vacated beds, wash up the breakfast things, stow away the crockery and cutlery, dust the dining room and shut the door. Two of us to turn the one hundred and twenty cattle from their cramped conditions to stretch their legs on the white hardness of the Five Acre. Two of us to carry the twenty-five bales necessary to satisfy their morning appetite. Nothing to do but feed the pigs and milk the goat and Joanna, and two of us to fend off the ponies, roll the barley and fill the sacks for evening and collect the eggs. Nothing to do but tidy the house, wash the sheets, answer the phone and make our lunch for which anything would do! Time, incredibly, to drink a cup of coffee sitting down; to drink it all, hot, without interruption.

The frosty beauty remained all day. You could smell it. If ever I have to live in a town I think my nose would feel the deprivation most. Not to smell the frostiness of winter and the flush of new grass which follows. To miss the daffodils at Steeton Hall, the bluebells in Jimmy's Wood, the manure being lifted from the sheds. To miss the heady perfume of felled fields of clover, the warm smell of maturing hay crisping in the sun and the sickliness of newly stacked bales in the Dutch barn. Not to know the smell of autumn, of wet leaves, fungus and blackberries by the stream, of wet bracken and wood smoke and muddy children after a football match.

The exhaled breath from their nostrils froze on the winter coats of all our multitude of animals. The cats stayed in the indoor warmth, before a generous log fire and what few vermin they permitted had a day of freedom to explore our domain without fear. The sky was blue and empty and all our world was beautiful.

An early night, we prophesied. No late night cuppas, no meat to lift from the arctic depths of the freezer, no porridge oatmeal to cover with water. Bed, glorious bed! No early rise to prepare breakfast for a departing guest; no rude awakening by the postman's knock and the chaos it causes amongst the dogs, for in frost and snow we have to collect our own post.

One wave rippled the smooth surface of the morning tide. Joanna was a greedy soul and Margaret always tied the corn store door securely with binder twine for our milk cow was also a thief. Sometime, somehow, Joanna got an overdose of corn. It could not have been from the corn bin; maybe the domineering old lady chased the hens from their ration, or fought away some of her colleagues. When it became obvious that the silly animal had overfed, Margaret did not worry too much. She reasoned that if the store door had been tied Joanna could not have found a lethal dose, just enough to make her acutely uncomfortable with bovine indigestion. She suffered for her greed in the draughty ruins of our Nissen hut, groaning miserably and neglecting to join the herd feeding from the bales we scattered in the Five Acre. Margaret monitored her condition frequently, completely puzzled as to know where she could have found so much corn.

The intense cold brought the herd early to the gate and the shed doors were opened. Joanna made no attempt to leave the sanctuary of the Nissen hut and Margaret went to drive her into the Dutch barn, still warm with the winter store of hay and straw. To drive her the necessary fifty yards was a slow, cold job. She put one foot before the other with agonising carefulness, stumbling in the gateway, breaking ice in the hollows.

The farmyard was easier terrain. 'Come on, old lady,' Margaret coaxed. 'You'll soon be in the barn. I'll give you a strong dose of magnesia and you'll live.' Slowly Joanna crossed the yard and began the last six-yard incline to the barn. The slope was covered with compressed snow, for we'd entered and re-entered for fifty bales of hay and straw. Three yards from safety Joanna's feet slid in four different directions and she went down. Not gracefully as befits the matriarch of the herd but extremely awkwardly, legs all akimbo, back twisted and neck outstretched. Margaret started to heave and strain to get her legs into more normal positions but Joanna was a big, heavy animal and though Margaret is phenomenally strong she is no professional weight lifter. So she came for me. It was about 4 p.m. and darkness was not far away. When straight the cow would get up. The hope of an evening by the fire gave us strength. Together we'd feed the herd and by seven most of the work would be done. Then we'd have a bath, curl up in an armchair or stretch out on the Harris wool rug and enjoy anything on the telly. Often critical, usually choosy, when we are tired television is like an aspirin and anything goes. But first we had to get Joanna up.

I pulled on my mucky wellingtons and followed Margaret to the barn. A short distance from the entrance lay the golden heap. Together we started to untangle her, folding the nearside legs beneath her, then struggling to drag the eight-hundredweight of back and belly over so that the far side legs could be folded likewise. We received no help whatsoever from our fallen beauty. She was prepared to die ignominiously.

'Now she'll get up,' we prayed, clouting her rear end with a flat hand and ordering her sharply to, 'Ge'rup.' But a cow that won't ge'rup is immovable. One tries for hours, for days, but until that animal tries to get up all is in vain. We found a sack, one of the old-fashioned hessian kind and struggled to roll her onto it. Thereafter, one on either side, we heaved on the sack, lifting her a few inches from the ground, kicking her back legs and yelling, 'Ge'rup yer fool, ge'rup.'

'She's frightened of slipping,' Margaret said so we threw ashes on the area round her and beneath her. We coaxed and commanded and almost wept but she remained seated and we alternately sweated with heaving and shivered with cold and frustration. How dare she! What gave her the Divine Right to ruin our peace?

Margaret administered a liberal dose of magnesia and Joanna's belly rumbled encouragingly. Only semi-darkness fell. Snow illuminates the landscape more than adequately and the thin covering glittered with frost.

'She'll die here,' said Margaret. So we made a bed of hay and rolled her onto it and carried bales of straw to make a south wall. We backed the Land Rover to protect her from the north and filled the gap below the undercarriage with bales to render it draught-proof. Then we covered the poor animal with hay and half the evening was gone.

Feeding the rest of the herd was punctuated by frequent inspection of Joanna. We were tired and very late. We had had no tea and our efforts had been in vain. Thoroughly weary we finally went into the house and fed ourselves before the roaring fire. We were sore and dirty and disinclined to watch TV. The ten o'clock news was depressing anyway and the weatherman forecast no change in the temperature. Every quarter of an hour Margaret went out to our almost buried, recumbent cow. 'No bed for me tonight,' she groaned. Where was our moment of calm? We are the world's two most optimistic women for we always believe that there is an end in sight, that after this there will be less pressure, less activity. Who are we kidding? As soon as one task is over, one problem solved, one busy day finished, another presents itself.

The moon had risen. Never was there a colder, more beautiful night. Our water supply would be frozen in no time. The snow-covered landscape was a picture on which the cattle sheds cast clean, dark shadows. An owl hooted in the hawthorn in George's pasture. To breathe was painful. The cold night air entered lungs with icy fingers. 'Thank goodness it's not snowing,' Margaret said. Things can always be worse.

I went to bed knowing full well that she would not follow. Fully clothed, she wrapped herself in a blanket and lay on the rug before the restoked fire. Floss, our Hebridean collie, left her basket and curled up beside her. Every twenty minutes or so, Margaret re-awakened and, donning the warmest of her jackets, went out to see the stubborn Jersey beneath the hay. The great fear was that she would try to get up and, in her sudden weakness and hampered by her improvised igloo, she would fail and fall. A leg is easily broken and a cow with a broken leg is shot. Also, an awkward fall, on a slope, may put a cow on its back and an animal in that position cannot right itself and quickly dies.

Around two o'clock in the morning Margaret went out for the umpteenth time and whilst bending low over the prostrate animal she heard a calf bellow in the Dutch barn. Joanna's almost fully-grown calf was still suckling and had decided to protest that it was long past suppertime. Immediately Joanna made an attempt to rise but she was too weak and wary. Margaret came flying indoors and, oblivious of the snowy state of her wellingtons, yelled up the staircase, 'Come quick, Joanna's trying to get up.' The urgency in her voice put speed into my efforts to drag some trousers over my nightdress. Then came my quilted dressing gown, odd woolly socks left by two departing guests, anorak and wellingtons.

The yard was like an ice rink, the moon a full-blown balloon lighting the entire landscape. There was the heap of heaving hay and my sister bruising her hands trying once more to force the hessian sack beneath the Jersey.

'Quick,' she shouted. 'Whilst she's still trying.' The sack was stiff and cold. Little beads of sweat bejewelled Joanna's golden coat where the hay had protected her. She was trying, bless her! We mustered the strength we thought we had lost but her legs seemed all in the wrong place to take her weight, like some newborn Bambi. Fearing to let go the sack we kicked a bale beneath her belly to prevent her from going down again.

'She's not framing properly,' Margaret said. 'She's frightened she'll slip. You're not holding her properly!' Joanna began to take the weight and we tried to alter the position of her feet. She rocked from side to side and would have fallen on us if we had let go the sack.

'Move the bale,' Margaret shouted. She's just like Father was, shouting instructions, never giving in. I'm used to her shouting at me when we are struggling with an animal. We were like two drunken men holding up a colleague. The tendency, in such a situation, is to laugh. You can feel a shaking welling up inside and you know that your sister feels the same and whatever you do you must neither of you laugh or your strength will go and you and she and the cow will all end up in a pile.

Suddenly Joanna took the first exploratory step, found her feet gripping on the ashed surface, heard again the bellow of her calf and, as if nothing was amiss, walked confidently into the barn. It was quite unexpected, this sudden entry into her five star hotel. There was not one word of thanks, no look of appreciation of Margaret's selfless devotion, just a disappearing rear end in the dim warmth of the barn.

We resigned ourselves to the knowledge that, until the shed was finished, life was going to be very difficult indeed. In freezing wind and sleet, John and his team battled on regardless, intent on finishing the shed for Christmas. It was a mansion, indeed, but like all beautiful things it was created slowly, or so it seemed to us in our desperate need and mentally adding up the work hours and fearing the eventual cost.

The problem of the horses became acute. I went down to the gypsy encampment once more but still there was only the old lady. Every time we fed the cattle the horses came at a gallop, scattered the herd and helped themselves to the feast.

To rivet the bolts on the girder framework of the shed and manhandle the big sheets of corrugated tin must have been torment. The wind increased and snow fell heavily. The road became a mass of disturbed ice as tractors churned it up and the night temperatures froze it solid. Only a pick or an ice axe would have cleared the road. It was quite impossible to normal traffic and all the Christmas post had to be collected from the village.

With the last tin John succumbed to a vigorous bout of influenza and the shed was abandoned minus the gable end and the south front Yorkshire boarding. The conglomeration of over one hundred stores peered over the temporary partition between the orchard shed and the new one with the same exasperated interest with which prospective humans view the progress of their purpose-built bungalow. We had been forced to use hay space for cattle and now we had almost none. We ordered a load to be stacked on the common ground two hundred yards outside the moor gate, a third of a mile away from the steadings. We carried it just within the moor gate, forcing the cattle to climb the hill every morning to eat it and hoping that they would drink before returning, for the piped water was frozen. Every time we threw out hay the blasted horses scattered the cattle and when we drove them home the horses walked over the snow-filled cattle grid into the village, to encamp beside the depleted stack.

Two days before Christmas the road was nearly impassable even by the Land Rover. I bounced and choked to the top of the hill, in falling snow and thickening fog, knowing that I might not get out again for many days. I was making my final visit to the Cash and Carry warehouse to buy food for the numerous Christmas guests. Every bedroom had been booked.

I remember that I was in wellingtons and cagoule and that the lighted warmth of the enormous food store and the background music of Christmas carols did not excite me at all. This different Christmas was too close to the preceding ones. The absolute break with the old life was too new. Like a torn ligament, it kept me awake at night. Me! who could normally sleep on a clothesline. I had lost weight.

I met Winnie unexpectedly in the Cash and Carry. She looked incredibly clean and smart and I felt shabby, dirty and unkempt. I was conscious of my wellingtons, calloused hands and heavy heart. I had asked my loyal staff to a Christmas dinner on the house but they had been unable to accept and the weather had put its final seal on everything. Winnie, so clean and so full of Christmas, so stirring of memories, depressed me. I cried all the way back from the city, blinded by snow and fog and selfish tears of longing for the lost Christmases with children. They splashed unheeded on my worn anorak as I drove the dangerous miles to pick up Auntie Mary and two of her friends.

We climbed the well-known hill from town in four-wheel drive. It was snowing heavily. The new fall had obliterated the tractor ruts and lost the road but, having helped to build it, I know it too well and can follow its meanderings even if they are hidden.

Safely home I helped the near eighty-year-old ladies into the house and proceeded to carry £300 of stores inside. A sack of potatoes, an eighteen-pound turkey, a tray of tomatoes, five hundred white baps and all the fats and carbohydrates essential for the festive enjoyment of twenty-five people.

That evening all the potential guests cancelled. I put the turkey into the freezer and took out a plump chicken. I locked the dividing door between the front porch and the decorated dining room, quite relieved that we did not have to put on a show but very aware that there would be no financial rewards with which to pay the quarterly interest or the demanding VAT man.

The roof of the shed was on but the gable ends and the two feet below the southern eaves were open to the driving snow. Nevertheless Margaret decided to put the fat bullocks in. We shovelled out the drifted snow and, in the teeth of an arctic easterly, fought to nail up fibreglass sheets from the pile made when calf sheds were taken down. The dimensions of the shed were spacious. Now it regularly holds forty cattle and to block out the wind at each gable end and all along the south wall was no small undertaking. I don't think we have ever done a colder job in all our lives. We struggled with fibreglass sheets against the knife-edged wind until we cried. Snow can be very beautiful but in 1981 the white Christmas was blanketed in freezing fog, coating everything with ice and fringing every edge with a filigree which in sunshine would have been exquisite, but which against the depressing greyness was sinister.

We struggled until we could not hold the hammer any more and we cried and nursed our mutilated fingers, holding them under our armpits and frequently plunging them in almost cold water, tempted but afraid to lay them on the warm Aga. The water pipes froze, the manure froze, the straw we laid for bedding froze, the long hair of the cattle froze. They stood outside, with their backs against the wind waiting for us to prepare the unfinished luxury accommodation.

No matter how many precious bales of straw we threw on the new floor, the cold concrete, recently scraped of snow, offered poor comfort. Just before darkness fell, we let thirty bullocks into the shed, thus relieving the gross over-crowding and emptying the Dutch barn. On Christmas Eve, one of John's employees was able to bring the remaining bales, and place them more conveniently in the barn.

This brought the horses onto our doorstep and we were near the end of our tether. Ice had thickened outside the shed and on Christmas Eve morning we dared not let the cattle out of the sheds to drink or to feed. We knew, that if we did, the horses would scatter the cattle and one at least would have a broken leg. It was late evening when we finished. Weary and sore we settled before a cheerful log fire.

'Listen,' someone said. Out in the yard there were carollers. Dolores and Raymond, from a neighbouring farm up on the moor, had come again with their four boys and their violins to give us a truly old-fashioned Christmas Eve.

Increasingly am I aware that I am writing about a way of life which lingers with us but which has disappeared into the history books for most folks. Recently I made our twenty-five guests a Yorkshire ginger pudding. 'That was delicious,' said one lady and I knew instinctively that she was going to ask for the recipe. 'Did you make it in the microwave?' When she heard that we did not possess such a thing she did not ask for a recipe.

Here and there only, in small pockets, where farmers' wives are middle-aged or elderly, the old life, a good life still exists. It does for us and lest our way be forgotten by the new generation, I can't stop my pen recording.

Our old-fashioned carolling neighbours came in to bring their seasonal good wishes and to sample Mother's mince pies. They had walked through the snow and their dripping wellingtons, twelve of them, filled the porch.

We have spent some funny Christmas Days. The horses began galloping backwards and forwards over the cattle grid. Having lost the plentiful source of hay by the roadside they started troubling people in the village. They were in the gardens and everywhere.

There was nothing to do but send for the police. Our man came without any grumbling that it was Christmas Day and 'good men and true' should be at home enjoying festive fare. Together we carried a stout beam to the top of the road, shooed the horses outside our land and barred their return.

'Don't worry,' said the policeman. 'We'll find the gypsies and ask them to collect the horses. We won't impound them.' It was, after all, the season of goodwill.

It pleases me to remember that, at nearly eighty-six, my mother was still able to cope with Christmas dinner and all subsequent meals that day. Now, seven years later she despairs because she cannot 'set to' and feed the family and forgets that she could until recently. She can still make a pound and a half of flour into pastry but thinks she does nothing!

All the rest of the day we fed hay indoors. To feed in the new shed was so easy. Margaret could run down the trough with an evenly emptying sack of corn and, within seconds, thirty bullocks were fed. It took twenty times longer in the orchard shed. 'You know what we need,' she said with a smile.

'I know,' I replied. 'We need another, even bigger, shed. When is all this going to end?'

That Christmas Day we carried more than thirty, two and a half gallon buckets of water each rather than let out the cattle. Anyone in the village would have been justified in removing the bar and chasing the horses back. They never did and the police must have been successful in finding the gypsies. We never saw them nor their horses again.

Somewhere around ten o'clock, we dropped, exhausted, onto the hearth. Our OAPs had drawn so close to the fire there was no room to draw up a chair. The floor is often our roost. Our clothes began to smell of cattle and Auntie Mary's friends got a taste of what farming is all about.

One Sunday, when the new year was only a few days old, I had arranged to take a few of my former girl pupils to the Cheshire Home. I told them that I would pick them up in the village car park, not far from the school. When I arrived there were half a dozen boys, just larking around, hoping to be there when I came. They crowded round the Land Rover begging to be allowed to come with me. I told them to go home and ask their parents, tell them where I was going and that they would be coming home, to The Currer, for tea. They all returned with permission, but I was afraid more doors would open and more children spill onto the pavement, so I hurriedly piled everyone in and left.

It was just like old times with singing children in the Land Rover. We had a splendid time with our disabled friends and darkness was falling when the loyal vehicle began to climb the last hill home. Suddenly there was an ominous bumping and an awkward pulling on the steering wheel. I stopped the engine and we all jumped out onto the pavement. One wheel was absolutely flat. The tyre barely supported the hub above the tarmac.

'Yer've gor a puncture!' yelled the kids.

A car drew up behind. It was, unbelievably, the father of one of the children.

'I thought this Pied Piper could only be you,' he said. I had taught three of his children. What's more I had taken him to the kindergarten of the Grammar School when I had been a teenager and he a five-year-old. He changed the wheel for me. Call that a piece of Miss Brown-luck. There are not many occasions when we have had a puncture and not been in the vicinity of a friend.

John returned to put up the Yorkshire boarding and the fibreglass sheets went back to the pile. The shed was the most labour-saving thing which had ever happened to us.

Chapter Twenty-three

A young woman rang and booked the Mistal cottage for a week at the end of January. I warned her that the weather might be bad and asked if she had a car. 'No,' she admitted. I told her it was over half a mile to the bus but she was adamant that it was no problem. 'We will arrive on the 9 p.m. train. We're getting married in Brighton the day before. It's our honeymoon.' We were getting used to surprises but, frankly, we did wonder why our particular holiday cottage had been chosen for this purpose in deep mid-winter. We turned on every heater until the place was so cosy I could have hibernated there.

I arranged to pick up the young couple at the railway station and parked the station wagon outside the lighted entrance. It was bitterly cold. There was industrial unrest; some trains were affected by strike action and others running very late. I sat outside the station, in the draughty Land Rover, for nearly an hour before the arrival of a train. There were not many people on the one that eventually came. I looked carefully for a young couple obviously newly wed, smart and immaculate in new, going-away outfits. None came. No one came to the Land Rover and the last passenger disappeared into the night.

I was fed up! It was ten o'clock and I was frozen. The porter on the plat-form, fifty yards below me, seemed to be putting out lights. It did not look as if another train were expected at all. I decided I must brave the icy wind and ask him so I jumped out and walked down the ramp. The platform was already nearly in darkness but one couple still remained there, trying to bring some order to a pair of haversacks and a few plastic bags.

They were the most extraordinary couple. If it had been Christmas Eve I would have thought I was seeing a vision and looked for a donkey. The girl was beautiful with a gentle expression and long straight hair. Her dress reached her ankles and was gaudily appliquéd with red and orange motifs.

She looked extremely fragile, like some porcelain figure for the mantleshelf.

Her husband could have come from some eastern temple of meditation. He, too, was beautiful, bearded and long silky-haired. He had fine features and long, sensitive hands. My memory is not always accurate but I seem to see him with moccasins on his feet and a shaggy, imitation sheepskin coat, long and fringed.

I looked at them amazed but knew for certain that they were my honeymoon couple. Whatever will Mother say? It was all I could think! Of course I greeted them as if they were just the people one ordinarily expects on a cold January evening. I picked up some of their plastic bags and led them to the Land Rover.

Her skirt will be filthy in no time I thought, aware that Currer mud is no respecter of persons. Straight from Brighton, whatever would they do if overnight snow left us isolated and only those with stout wellingtons could cope? 'Whatever are we going to do with this pair?' I thought and 'Whatever is Mother going to say when I take two hippies home?'

But they weren't hippies. They were the most delightfully artistic people, hoping to start a studio in the north. She was a potter and he a woodcarver. They had been saving money, had married in church, and thought the north would be a more suitable place to settle. They began house-hunting at once. Whenever we went out we took them and left them in front of the estate agents and every day I wished they looked the near-normal people they really were. Before the end of the week they had bought a house.

Every evening they came and sat cross-legged on our sitting room carpet like Red Indians round a camp-fire, drinking our hot chocolate and eating Mother's biscuits and she loved them.

One day, Margaret was planning to go to market to buy pigs and this quite inadequately dressed couple wanted to accompany her. She saw many amused smiles when she had to load the piglets with such unexpected friends.

Meeting new people was a constant source of interest and amusement. Harry regularly followed one or other of us into the dining room to listen and to join in the conversation. We began asking guests for at least one evening supper in the farmhouse sitting room. It pleases me to remember that in the early days, when Mother was eighty-six, we served one traditional farmhouse high tea every week with every one of the many cakes and pastries made by her.

At Easter we had a full house and one of our guests accidentally mentioned that he worked for the BBC. It became the mystery of the week. Everyone wanted to know in what capacity he worked there. On the Wednesday of Easter week, he and his wife and daughter stayed in after dinner to watch the first episode of a drama series. At the end of the half hour our guest's name was emblazoned on the screen as 'Director'. The news spread like wildfire. Mother was impressed.

Next evening, when the director and another man were repairing a fault in the Land Rover for us, the rest of the guests gathered in our sitting room for a céilidh and Mother took the director's wife by the arm and said, confidentially, 'Did you know that a man in there directed a film which was on television last night?' She could not understand why there was so much sudden laughter.

All our guests were going home on the Saturday following Easter. Mother was going to Auntie Mary's to tea. We did not see that we needed to make a meal at all. Bliss was only an hour or two away. We would eat sandwiches by the fire and forget our new profession.

But before the last guests had gone there was a phone call from a neighbour to say that some of our cattle had joined his herd. This was awful news. He had a bull running with his cattle and, if that wasn't enough, his land is below us and as there is no gate between us, a wall always has to be knocked down. It is hard to persuade animals to walk uphill and go through an opening they have never seen before.

The remaining guests decided the experience was too good to miss and we all scrambled down the precipitous hillside. There is a profusion of blackberry and hawthorn, a mass of bluebell and foxglove. Bracken was appearing among the boulders and the stream needed ditching. The whole episode was fraught with difficulties and frustrations.

It was almost one o'clock before we had brought our strays home. The phone had rung in our absence. Eric, one of the disabled residents from White Windows, had telephoned to say that he and another disabled friend of his had ordered a taxi and were coming over and could they have a meal with us. I had to get fish out of the freezer and hurriedly make some pastry for a fruit pie. Instead of our sandwiches before the fire we had to sit up to the table and try to prevent our heads sagging onto our plates.

We bought no calves. There were more than enough bought-in stores to graze our pastures efficiently. In spite of a winter at The Currer, the hotchpotch herd remained wild.

There was no time to do all the things which had made the old life so enjoyable. No time to dig the garden on spring evenings, to milk Joanna, to churn butter, to sit at the sewing machine making clothes for the family, but the quality of life at The Currer was as good as ever. What we had lost on the roundabouts we had gained on the swings.

One Saturday, at the market, Margaret bought when we could least afford to spend money on non-productive assets. We could not afford to buy calves yet Margaret made a successful bid for a baby donkey and a small Shetland pony.

The donkey was the most adorable shaggy animal, almost white, not fully-grown, very longhaired and thin. It looked like a child's knitted toy, and we called him Jasper. The Shetland pony was wild, fit and jet-black. We called him Dick in memory of our milk horse but he was too difficult a customer to stay here long. He kicked, he chased cattle, he was impossible to handle. For trying to do so Margaret had to have several stitches.

Eventually he found there was a filly on the farm below us and that he could jump walls. On one occasion he decided to re-jump the wall and Margaret, at the same time, and why she wasn't severely wounded is a mystery. A friend who used to deliver straw said he would buy the errant pony from us and we took his offer. Jasper cried so much that Margaret went hurrying up to the knacker's yard where, in a field, he had a donkey grazing. I don't think knacker's men like to put down donkeys. He accepted Margaret's twenty-five pounds and Chocolate was brought home as companion for the lonesome baby.

The donkeys have been with us many years now and because there are only two of them, they are named, have become pets and their history is recordable. Our guests know them, take their photographs and think that our farm consists of three goats, a few pigs and two donkeys. People are rarely there when we give one hundred copper injections or worm one hundred wild beasts. They do not come to the sheds at feeding time and, because we have fenced the road and they have no longer to get out of their cars to shoo them away, I am quite sure our huge herd goes relatively unnoticed.

The donkeys can never go unnoticed because they make such an infernal din. In the middle of the night Jasper will sing his ghastly song and it surprises me that the alarm has never been raised.

One townee guest knew what had happened! She heard the horrible noise in the night and asked Margaret if we had a fox in the neighbourhood. The answer to that is an affirmative. The fox seldom misbehaves in our vicinity for the dogs bark like mad when they even smell one near and we make sure that the ducks and hens are predator-proof before nightfall.

'One came last night,' said our guest.

'Did you see it?' asked Margaret, interested as always in our wildlife.

'No,' said our wise friend, 'He bit the donkey, though.' She was absolutely serious. 'He'd never have made a noise like that otherwise!'

Jasper is like Mother, who cannot bear to be alone. If Chocolate is out of sight, he begins to wail and to run frantically in search of his friend.

A young manageress of a nearby factory walked out of the dining room door unaware that the brown donkey had just passed through the yard. She accidentally timed her exit to coincide with the lifting of Jasper's head and his sudden realisation that he was alone. She had reached the halfway between house and car when this white monster, mane and tail flying, began to gallop across the yard braying eccentrically. I have never seen a young manageress run so quickly back into the house.

The constant braying of the donkeys is eventually not heard. Like the noise of a busy road or a passing train, it begins to fall on deaf ears. One summer's day Margaret suddenly realised she had not recently heard the frequent evidence of the inseparable pair. The donkeys had disappeared from the horizon, they had jumped the wall somewhere and had gone.

Margaret rang the police and our neighbours and searched beyond the boundary but the donkeys could not be found.

Then some new, unexpected guests came in from the Brontë village and said they had seen a strange white animal's head look at them from over a wall on their way to The Currer. 'Could it have been a donkey?' we asked.

They did not think so but I put Mother and Harry into the all-purpose vehicle; we followed all possible routes and we found the donkeys a mile away from home. The farmer on whose land they were happily grazing said that the police had found them on the road and opened a gate to let them in.

The problem was how to get them home. Our donkeys have never been haltered and led. We have always been too busy to train them. They have been allowed too much freedom and fed too generously so that they are fit and strong and wilful.

Our guests were over-eager to help. They disappear when a load of hay must be manhandled into the Dutch barn but to fetch home the straying donkeys appealed to them. We set off, a dozen of us, in two cars so that for the two road crossings we would be able to block, virtually, any escape route. The donkeys were very high-spirited. They knew us, of course and wanted to be petted and Chocolate did not mind, so much, a rope being put round his neck but when they saw they had an audience and that they were expected to go in one direction only, they became very stroppy indeed. Margaret was alternately pulling a donkey which would not budge however much I clouted it from behind and then running faster than her legs could go being dragged by a race horse. Jasper did everything that Chocolate did. We knew that if we could get the one home the other would follow.

Our guests hurried ahead to be ready to turn the strays whenever the path turned or forked and to open the necessary gates.

The drivers of our back-up cars drove to the final road crossing and when they saw the comic procession approaching at a stop-pull, gallop-hang-on, they halted the traffic and we reached the Altar Lane with only broken nails and bruises. It is of vital importance to make sure that the two donkeys do not get out. We are not amused if one hundred cattle find an escape and trail all over the village or the estate but we are confident we can cope. We have no such confidence about the donkeys.

May came. We didn't know what to do about a holiday. We couldn't afford one but we couldn't rid ourselves of the accumulated tiredness. The yard was a mess after the drain-digging episode but we had no hope of doing it ourselves. We decided it would have to be done and brought back Dougie and a workmate to lay concrete for us before the stream of visitors began to flow continuously again.

'We'll have to have a holiday,' we kept saying as bookings began to fill each week. Whoever could we ask to come for a fortnight? We have a guardian angel, remember. In anticipation of his ability to care for us we confidently booked the Tiree cottage for a fortnight. It was outrageously arrogant of us to think someone would just 'turn up' as Father used to say.

We were beginning to despair of one doing so as the time to go drew near. We began to wish we had refused bookings. Barbara and Arnold were to come into one of the cottages to look after the farm but they could not do both jobs.

In a panic I took out my very full address book; we began at A and went steadily through the book. We paused at the address of one of the Queen's Guides who had been an excellent cook. Believing her never to have grown any older we argued that she must have been taught by her mother and decided, on the spur of the moment, to phone. Sandra answered. 'Hello Skipper,' she said. I confessed it was her mother I had been ringing and was told that her mother and father had emigrated to South Africa.

'So much for that good idea,' I said. I explained and found that Sandra had not, of course, remained a child. She had grown up, was eighteen and waiting to start a nursing career. She was keeping house for her brother and I knew her to be one of the most competent youngsters I had ever come across. She had been the only one in fifty-five Queen's Guides to cater for her own presentation and had done so excellently.

Now, hearing we wanted to go to the cottage on Tiree, she said, 'I'll come, Skipper.' Dear children, to whom I gave so much time and so much fun! There they all are, in a line, ready to help me.

So we returned to the Hebrides, the only place where we could properly convalesce; to that island so frequently in the sun. The great golden god was there before us ready to pour his heat and brilliance on the white beaches, the blue ocean and the Brown family. What a place in which to idle long hours listening to the sea birds and the flop-flop of the waves on Salum Bay. What a paradise in which to give thanks, to reaffirm promises and acknowledge one's faith. What a place to think and talk, plan and make assessments, to look objectively and critically at what we have done. What a place to worship and believe.

I am no longer teacher and Guider though I am proud to have been both. I am still a philosopher and need thinking time. I used to have an hour of travelling time each morning and evening to sit and try to understand the great mysteries of life, to solve my problems and choose my way. Now I have none so the long hours we sit on empty shores are doubly valuable.

Before, I was meeting children daily without their parents. Now I frequently see the whole family and it worries me to realise that the verb 'to teach' is being defined as 'to allow to choose'. The new generation is not being taught, as we were taught, and as I taught. It is being allowed choice and parents, teachers and society in general believe this to be a good thing. I, who surely have the right to do so, challenge the wisdom in all this. I see children, with parents, being asked what they want to eat, to wear, to do and I see the selfish product and, too often, the insecurity and the weakness which result.

I was not allowed to choose. I was taught, continually, what my elders thought was the best, the right, the only way to behave. I was never given a say in what the family should eat, what clothes were made or bought. I was continually taught by those in the Guide Movement who were my leaders. I was expected to be a certain type of person, obeying an exact law and keeping a solemn promise and, I think, I turned out to be more of an individual than most of those who were brought up less strictly.

The majority of society's problems are because people believe they have a right to choose. Whether or not they have babies, whether or not they leave spouse and children to go off with another, whether or not they care for their elderly parents, whether they are responsible or irresponsible, careful or careless, polite or rude, honest or dishonest, loyal or unfaithful. They are encouraged to believe they can do what they want in their private lives. No longer are children taught there is only one way and that it is straight and narrow. They are allowed to go at any speed they want along a wide and dangerous motorway and I am sorry for them.

I think I mourned a little, lying in the sun on the Tiree beaches, the fact that I could no longer bring children there to teach them that there is one right way to put up a tent and tie a knot and to say 'Thank you'; to teach them how to be inventive and happy and how to share and be interdependent.

When we weren't lying in the sun, Margaret and I were doing quite a bit of walking along the shores planning the next move. Away from home we looked objectively at our problems and sorted things out between us.

The new shed was a blessing but we still had too much to do. The man from the Ministry had been right when he said, 'If you are going into this, my dear, you are going into it.' Because there was no short supply of guests we had to make alterations to be able to combine the two jobs without having to employ labour. Far better to have yet another shed than employ someone to do Margaret's job. She wants to be the farmer.

But we didn't need it yet, unless we bought calves in the autumn, and how could we give twenty-four hour surveillance to newborn calves with an evening meal for twenty people already committed? In January bookings had rushed in. We had thought, in our ignorance, that if we were too busy with a farming job we could just refuse a booking or say, 'No evening meals tonight.' But people booked many months in advance. We already knew that July and August were absolutely full and that most of the June and September vacancies were gone. This long-term commitment was something we had not bargained for.

One thing was certain, only bed and breakfast guests would pay the interest on the conversion overdraft. We had been farmers long enough to know that cattle never would.

Margaret said, 'The answer is to buy three-month-old, weaned calves. A hundred of them, in one batch, all the same age so that we inject and worm and sell them all at once.'

For Harry, the 'common day' had become tremendously interesting. Who was coming, where were they sleeping, how long were they staying and where did they come from? He was far more interested in how many for the evening meal, what was I serving and had they enjoyed it than he would ever be in cattle. We were glad for Harry.

I think we would have resented the eighteen-hour day if we had not had such extraordinary guests. To slave and give cheap accommodation to the rich and selfish would not have been our cup of tea, nor are we intent on dying of over-work for untidy young people who do not tell us they are unmarried and put us in the embarrassing situation of wondering whether we have fuddled the booking and should have reserved two rooms. Unwittingly we had been selective. We had, without being fully aware of it, pointed our compass needle in the right direction. We had made provision for the handicapped and advertised in RADAR.

It is a fallacy to think that all disabled people are angels. But just as only a certain type of person lives in the country, or works with children, or is employed looking after animals, only those among the disabled who are game for a farmhouse holiday, come to The Currer. They are the most able-minded, fun-loving, outgoing, game-for-anything of all our guests. They create the atmosphere in the dining room so that the Lathams return, year after year, just to be here the week that Angie and Ian are. The Camerons were both injured in car accidents. They come in their car with their dog and the dinner table becomes a magic circle of laughter and intellectual argument and discussion. Each day they heave their wheelchairs into the back seat of their car and enjoy the Dales far more independently than most.

The courage of people who live from a wheelchair and their resourcefulness continually amazes me. John makes The Currer his overnight stepping stone on his way alone from the Isle of Man. A button motivates a mechanical arm which heaves his wheelchair onto the roof of his car. He is far more daring than I am, travelling solo to the South of France.

Our Easter becomes booked a year in advance because the Barbault family from Lyon and Anna and Marianne want to be here at the same time as Sally whose multiple sclerosis does not prevent her from teaching everyone lace-making and writing about adventurous wheelchair routes to be found in the Dales, or being a single-handed yachtsman. Almost all our guests know Jonathan who, unable to speak or walk or use his hands, can still write letters to the Queen and the Prime Minister and will easily win a game of chess. Similarly they know Richard, who lives in the kitchen helping us with our chores and daily serving meals. His wit is extraordinary. Entering the kitchen, one day, and seeing the conglomeration of cooking ingredients and utensils on the large table he leaned on it, grinned from ear to ear and remarked, 'Good Game!' It is truly a good game we play. Tom and Judy think so, and Jack and Elsie, Stan and Barbara, Jill and Moss.

The politeness of mentally handicapped children cannot go unnoticed. Normal children will push past us as we greet their parents, career round the room, run up the ramp and bounce on the bed. They are not taught to imitate their parents and say hello properly. They fuss about food and leave the table between courses. Their less mentally able contemporaries, whether they come with parents or with school parties, shake hands, show affection, behave beautifully, say thank you graciously. They make their beds, respect property, remain at table and eat everything. Perhaps it is because of Mary and Sheila, Jackie and Sylvia, Jenny and Chris who teach them.

It does not matter to us how hard we work when the Entwhistles are here, he with his cerebral palsy and his MBE, she running around on two forty-year-old artificial legs. Their beautiful daughter comes, too, with her disabled accountant husband and the dining room rocks with laughter. This is partly due to the fact that, if the Entwhistles are here so are the McGinties, Coxes, Warners and Holmeses. They re-book immediately for next year and, if Joe and Pauline are coming the following week, they prolong their stay over the weekend.

Both in wheelchairs, Joe and Pauline have been married well over twenty years. Each is an artist. It is such a privilege to know them. How neat and tidy and organised the disabled are. How beautifully Joe and Pauline have illustrated this book.

I said to Joe one day, when I watched him packing everything so meticulously into his car, 'You know something I don't, Joe. You know you can cope.'

'I know I can cope when I can't cope, Jean,' he replied. Disablement is being unable to cope therefore Joe is not disabled, surely.

If we satisfied a need by installing the ramps and correctly positioning the doors, the need was not just for those in wheelchairs but equally needy are the carers, Alma and Brenda, Geoff and Richard, Michael and Sheila, Stan and Mary, who gallantly bring their loved ones on holiday. They are the finest people in the world and there are hundreds of them, keeping going year after year, unnoticed.

A Mr and Mrs Churchill came from America. It was the summer when Chris Wilkinson came with her family. She is in a wheelchair because of MS but that hasn't stopped her from flying alone to Australia to visit her son. It was the July that Robert came, whose wheelchair was also his bed and we had to hurriedly remove a less interesting one from the bedroom to make room for his extraordinary contraption. There was much laughter in the house and the Churchills wrote in the Visitors' Book, 'Thank you for showing us that life's little problems can be "No problem at all".'

As one German lady said, wisely, 'A response is an echo.' There are plenty of echoes when David and Selwyn come. Selwyn is severely handicapped with cerebral palsy. When his parents died it was necessary for him to go into a home. From there he advertised locally, 'Is there anyone out there willing to befriend me?' Out there was David and when they come to The Currer the dining room becomes a Music Hall and the applause is stupendous.

Slowly, perhaps too slowly for my eagerness, the Guide Movement became attracted to The Currer and camps in the fields and Pack Holidays in the cottages appeared on our calendar. Winter weekends brought Guide and Guider trainings, the dining room began to seat thirty and their happy voices and familiar uniforms excited me as of old. Nothing is nicer than having to wait for the singing of one of the Guide Movement's score of lovely Graces before entering the dining room with laden trays. Regardless of the lateness of the hour nothing is more compelling than to join them in their Campfire Hour, either sitting in the snug or in our family sitting room with Mother always in their midst.

So, whenever the question surfaces in our mind as to the sense of our decision to diversify, the answer is not difficult to find.

We returned from Tiree as brown as if we had been to the Greek Islands and almost immediately the phone rang and the new leavers from my little school were asking me a favour. Could they come and camp for a week immediately on leaving school? Nine of them! So tents were pitched in the paddock and my own children were under my feet again. Joan came with her grandson and we all had fun. My school children continued to come camping until they outgrew the novelty. Then they began arriving to see me in cars, frightening the life out of me, too many careless young people in a car with a newly tested driver

Almost imperceptibly there were pigeons at The Currer. For twenty years we had tried to tempt them to stay. Our success had progressed no farther than Billy, who had stayed two years and Featherlegs who had survived the conversion because the joiner had made a nesting box under the laithe porch.

Suddenly there were pigeons everywhere and the pendulum swung quite the other way. We think the new guttering on the barn gave them shelter. They began to make a dreadful mess on the roof and to sit on the window-sills. In spring they came through any open window and tried nesting on the wardrobes. We were always swilling the lean-to roof and cleaning out the guttering. We even tried a strawberry net to deter them. Then Margaret began feeding them the old corn in the new sheds and that did the trick. We are amazed that their number does not grow out of hand. I suppose the cats are to thank for that.

We did not buy calves in the autumn of 1982. Instead we rang a calf rearer and asked the price of weaned calves. We were told each bull calf would cost £160. We were used to paying about £30 a calf so we left the idea on the shelf and concentrated on selling the Friesian bullocks and the hotchpotch of stores we had bought last September, slowly, a few at a time, as they were ready. It was painfully tedious, too many visits to the market, too many round-ups and too many times to load cattle into the wagon. Prices were reasonable. Perhaps we could buy weaned calves in the spring.

When we had re-roofed the barn we had not been able to afford to do the house one at the same time but there suddenly came the opportunity to do so. The Council was offering substantial grants on very old buildings and we jumped at the opportunity. The chimney needed strengthening and I remember panicking one night, when the roof was off and a wind got up. I could not sleep for fear that the chimney would topple. Soon after midnight Margaret and I evacuated Mother and ourselves to the spare room. Blankets and spare duvets were piled on the bed. We transferred them to the floor and all got into the one bed. Mother said it was like sleeping in Ashley Mill.

The chimney did not fall. When the snug was re-roofed the inglenook chimney was left open and a stack built so that we could light a fire in the centuries-old fireplace. We had a grin from ear to ear.

The grant was a godsend. It insisted that we also put in new window frames and we were required to point the walls. To do this we had to take down the lean-to shed we had hastily constructed to house the coke. We removed it one weekend ready for the builder on the Monday morning and had, thereafter no place to put the coke. At about ten o'clock on the Sunday morning I suddenly said that we were crazy not to use the cellar we had closed twenty-five years ago. 'Let's go and look,' Margaret said. We broke off what we were doing, pulled away the wood shuttering the cellar window and peered into the unknown. There was water, eighteen inches of it. We knew we had to get the water out before we could assess the possibility.

'We need a pump or something,' I said.

'We could bucket it out,' Margaret answered.

'OK. Where's a bucket?' I volunteered.

We almost ran to find a couple of two and a half gallon black plastic ones. Beneath the window, not fully submerged, were the stone uprights which had supported a stone slab. Being the taller of the two, I crawled in through the window and lowered myself into the darkness. The water was quite clear and there was no smell. We knew it was perpetually there for we had periodically tested it by throwing in a stone or measuring the depth with a clothes prop. It if wasn't stagnant it must be flowing in and out. I filled a bucket, raised it above my head and passed it to Margaret. Balanced on the stone upright there was more than a chance that I might fall in.

For three hours we bucketed out water. I thought we would never stand up straight again. When the water level went below welly tops I could stand on terra firma but the lift was higher and Margaret's lean-in more precarious. There was great excitement as the black hole of the well appeared and finally I was lowering the bucket into the well to empty it.

Margaret jumped in to join me. We listened. We could hear water trickling into the well, steadily, musically. We ran up the steps and, where the doorway into the kitchen, from the cellar head, had been blocked we could hear Mother and Auntie Mary preparing Sunday lunch.

After the meal there was already an inch or two of water on the floor of the cellar. We again emptied the well. It wasn't deep. The domed cellar was too beautiful not to have some utility. We feared to tell Mother but when we did she accepted the good sense in being able to bring cinders from within the house instead of from without, as we had always done.

On Monday the builder came to point the back wall and we showed him the nine inches of water once more in the cellar and then spent all day bucketing it out again and trying to unblock the drain. He recommended a pump, so I ordered one from the plumber. Two days, it would be, he said. So

I phoned our electrician, who said he would come on Thursday and put it in and on Friday we opened up the cellar head and ordered some coke.

We worked hard, that summer. We thought we had always worked hard! So we had but not like this; up at six o'clock, bed after midnight, never a pause to sit, never a proper meal. Guests came crowding to The Currer. Harry slept in a bed in an alcove of the New-do in the sitting room and Margaret slept on the sitting room floor. At weekends Aunt Mary slept in my bed in Mother's room and I slept on the floor. Once we made a mistake over the bookings and we all slept in the sitting room, Mother also.

Harry was working harder than he had ever worked. He was on his feet all day. He did all the drying of the dishes and was at the sink often at midnight. He is still an essential cog in the wheel that we cannot do without. Mother, then eighty-six, was continually baking, folding and airing sheets, wiping tables, putting away groceries, drying cutlery and playing hostess. Not one disabled person comes ungreeted by Mother. She entertains them whilst she bakes in the kitchen or in the evening in the sitting room, and all the disabled children come to kiss her.

An extraordinary piece of good luck came our way. Our young electrician said, 'Do you want a stainless steel sink, Skipper?' We already had double stainless sinks I had bought for £2 when men had pulled down the isolation hospital some years ago, but they were too small and hadn't a splash back. I had made one with blockboard and Formica but we had suspicions about how much water managed to get behind it.

But it was a job we could well do without, in the height of the season and guests all over the place, so we did nothing. Several weeks later Mike said, 'Did you look at those sinks, Skipper? They are still there. They've been there for months.' 'There' was outside a nearby college. It had been closed and the huge kitchens were being dismantled. We were passing one day and we drove behind just to see. Sure enough about half a dozen huge double sinks lined the driveway. Only one was suitable, having both sinks side by side.

We hovered over the suitable one, admiring the deep, shiny tanks; Margaret paced out the length with her feet and I did a rough estimation with my hands and we came to the conclusion that it would fit the kitchen. This was presumptuous for we had no idea how big our wash kitchen was. We had built it but we have many things to remember and the length of the kitchen was not one of them. I phoned the Authority and asked if it was for sale.

No immediate answer could be given. Where possible the sinks were being re-housed in other schools. That sink might be one they would use, maybe not. I was told to ring in a fortnight. I did but no decision had been made. Finally I was given the good news that I could buy it. I rang Brian and asked him if he could collect it for me in his pick-up. It was in two pieces, a huge stainless steel draining board and sinks and an ungainly, solid frame to sit it on.

'Yeh,' he said, 'Ah'll cum t'morrer.' And still we did not measure it. I suppose we wanted it so much we were prepared to pull down a kitchen wall or something. Brian never asked if it was the right size either. Nor did he question whether we had checked to see if the solid frame would even go through a door.

'You couldn't, by any chance, fit it for us?' we asked. Once upon a time we would have done it ourselves but the exchange of sinks would have to be lightning quick. Out and in between two washing-up sessions.

'Ah'll cum t'morrer.' (We've a wonderful builder!) 'After dinner.'

So after the breakfast dishes were washed, Margaret and I tore out the old sinks. We pulled out the cupboards from underneath, uncoupled the taps from the pipes and successfully ensured that there was no way we could undo what we had done and hastily reassemble the lot. Hell Fire Jacks, that's what we are!

Brian came. To bring either of the two pieces through the front door was impossible. Their length and rigidity meant there was no way the front porch could be negotiated. So we came in through the laithe porch doors into the dining room where there was plenty of room to do a right wheel. Then we forced it through the snug door scraping off paint everywhere, did another right wheel to line us with the steps into the kitchen. We bruised two more door posts. There was plenty of room to turn in the kitchen but when we forced our way into the wash kitchen we had to raise it on end, open the larder doors, pinion ourselves against the walls and take the skin off our knuckles to get it in. We fed it into the larder till we could line it up with the wall. Then we lowered it beneath the window. It fitted too snugly for comfort for we knew the draining board was bigger.

We returned to the yard for the expanse of stainless steel and repeated our journey with bated breath. I climbed into the larder with one end whilst Margaret and Brian eased it over the frame and we all lowered it until it nested. There was not an eighth of an inch to spare. It was the same length as the room exactly, touching both side walls.

'Yer beggar!' I said. 'Call that nowt!'

The Land Rover was due its MOT test. Poor, loyal station wagon. We had treated it so cruelly. It didn't die on us. It groaned but it didn't collapse. The mechanic said however that its ailments would be too costly. We should replace it.

'I wonder what a second-hand Range Rover costs,' Margaret said and rang Simmonites, who had serviced our vehicles since the days of Genevieve and the Gypsy. We learned that an old Range Rover cost as much as a slightly newer station wagon and considerably less than a friend's new car.

'We'll think about it,' Margaret said but Mother said if we were buying greater comfort for her then it would have to be instant. We laughed at her as we had done when we read of the old lady in the bank who was being advised to invest her money for a longer term in order to get a better return. 'Young man,' she had said, 'at my age you don't even buy green bananas.'

On our next visit to the Cash and Carry we called at the Land Rover showroom. The men were 'doing up' an M registration Range Rover. We decided it would do and asked them to spray it white. We measured its height and width and length and when we reached home we got straight out of the Land Rover and went to the stone wall of the corn shed and measured out sufficient ground for a DIY garage. With the help of a reverend gentleman guest we cemented in three full-length upright railway sleepers, and nailed up two of the redundant corn bin sides. We took some beams from the wood-pile and some fibre glass sheets from the heap we seem perpetually to have and, hey presto, we had a garage which cost only one bag of cement and four hinges for the doors.

We exchanged the old vehicle for the new just before we were due to go to Grange for an autumn holiday. Margaret drove the new-looking white Range Rover into the garage and it fitted like a glove. We were very proud of it. She ordered the corn bin to be refilled prior to our holiday. The enormous van came and the auger blew whole grain into the bin making the usual cloud of dust. We had left a four-inch gap between the top of the wall and the roof. It had been like that for years and it had been very convenient when we had had to slip in more beams to support the new garage roof. Now that the space adjacent was enclosed this cloud of dust could not escape and when we opened the garage doors we found a layer of corn completely encased our beautiful new acquisition. We were horrified, scraped a peephole in the windscreen and went down to a garage with an efficient mechanical car wash.

Since then Mother, Harry and the dogs and nearly always Auntie Mary have been in the Range Rover whenever it has left the garage. The trouble with the bank manager sitting safely on our deeds is that he is not as afraid to lend as we are to borrow. We will borrow to buy a second hand vehicle but not a new one, we will borrow to rent a cheap holiday cottage but not to stay in an hotel. We will certainly not borrow for a meal out, a hairdo, a pair of shoes if we already have one pair or to get a new outfit unless it can be made by hand.

The cheap holiday cottage we deem essential if we are to survive. We were not sure whether even we might crack under too much work. So we were determined to take advantage of Paul, Barbara and Sandra who were so generous in allowing us to disappear for a little while. The cottage we booked that year at Grange-over-Sands was not ideal. Margaret had to sleep on the floor of the sitting room; but we were happy enough.

On the first Thursday we went to Morecambe and had trouble with the Range Rover all the way. We had never had trouble with an ancient Gypsy, nor an ill-treated Land Rover but the Queen of the four wheel drive let us down. We had the humiliating experience of being towed back to Grange by the AA. Next morning the garage man told us they had no spare part for a Range Rover. We rang our good friends the Land Rover people and I arranged to return by train to collect the part.

It was raining. We have had so few rainy days on holiday. I left the family having coffee in a café on the main street. The rain was pouring down the windows and Mother looked old in her cheap, seldom-used, plastic mac. She had wanted the comfort of the Range Rover so much I could have cried.

I hurried down to the station. I dared not sleep on the journey home in case I went sailing on to Leeds. The spare part was being delivered to The Currer. I walked from the station in the rain and up the steep path from Park Wood Bottom. The trees up the wood were already bare. I continued along the fields to the lighted house in the middle of nowhere which was my home. In spite of the rain, the night was clear and thousands of lights danced in the valley. I felt a stranger walking into the impeccably tidy house. The evening meal was over and the cattle had been fed. I had a cup of coffee, collected the spare part and was taken back to the station in somebody's car. It was after midnight before I arrived back in Grange. I entered the cottage lounge apprehensively. I had left an old woman in an ancient plastic mac and I feared what I would find but my teen-age Mum was smiling, cheeks aglow with the fire, happy and ready to enjoy the rest of her holiday from the middle back seat of her royal carriage.

On our return the sale of fat and store cattle continued slowly and the herd decreased. Margaret was at the local market selling store cattle and became engaged in a conversation with a man she had seen often, bidding against her for calves. It transpired that he was a calf rearer.

'Could you rear me a hundred, more or less the same age?' she asked. 'Hereford heifers for instance? To be delivered in June? Three-month-old and weaned?'

Yes, he could do that. No problem. Farmers are so trusting. It was a gamble, a deal made at a chance meeting. No written agreement, no deposit, and Margaret only five feet tall, a woman at that. Of course we had to ask the bank manager. He's not a bad fellow, a 'very guid friend' in fact.

November 25 was a wet, mucky day. The Aga man was coming and we asked him if, at the same time, he would vacuum out the flue. The evening meal was a get-together for over twenty Guiders. They were all my friends, my recent colleagues. In such circumstances I admit to being a show-off. I planned melon and a choice of two soups. I chose roast pork and chicken with lots of stuffing and oodles of apple sauce. I had selected four vegetables and there would be both boiled and roast potatoes. There would follow trifles and flans, cheese and biscuits, coffee and a plate of After Eight. It was quite unnecessary. One soup, pork alone and one sweet would have been enough.

The trouble began early. Margaret found an almost fat bullock limping in the shed. After a struggle in which we, too, ended up limping, we managed to get the right bullock out of the shed and steer it into the crush.

'It's not foul,' Margaret said. Foul is easily treated with a dose or two of Streptopen. Now a bullock which is lame is in pain, and Margaret did not hesitate to send for the vet.

By the time he arrived it was mid-day and the lame bullock, having once been persuaded into the crush, was definitely not in favour of a repeat. But three are better than two and we cornered him and forced him into the crush. It took two of us to prevent him from climbing out again whilst the vet investigated the abscess and released the pus. He plunged the hoof into a bucket of salt water and told us to do so often and to keep the foot clean. Then he gave an injection and went. We took the lame bullock into the Dutch barn where it created havoc among the bales; in spite of the sore foot it careered round and round the barn, bellowing and storming. And how, pray, can you keep it clean? You try with a torn sheet and two odd socks but cattle like putting their feet into mud and manure and, had we kept the animal on our sitting room carpet, the foot would have been dirty in no time.

We eventually went indoors. I looked at my hands and wondered however they would be clean enough to make trifles.

Indoors the Aga man was slowly completing the job he had come to do. It was five o'clock before he started to vacuum the flue. I was nearly having the nervous breakdown we so often promise ourselves.

Margaret, sooted to the elbows, was standing on the Aga wielding a long flue brush, and a film of soot covered the Aga top and the kitchen table. If I licked my lips I could taste it.

'How long will you be?' I pleaded.

At six o'clock, looking like a chimney sweep, the man was assembling his tools and Margaret was dashing out to let in the cattle. I was left alone to prepare a four-course meal for over twenty.

Suddenly Margaret came dashing in to the phone, wellies plastered with mud. 'You'll have to help me,' she said. 'I've one with pneumonia.'

She rang the vet for the second time that day and I struggled into my dirty clothes and pulled all my pans off the hob. Sure enough, one large animal was panting away. We extricated it from the rest and took it to join the lame bullock in the Dutch barn. Margaret ran to feed her hundred cattle. It cannot be done quickly, neither can a vet be hurried for he is not one bit influenced by the fact that a bevy of Guiders will soon arrive.

In the kitchen there was panic. Two soups! Was I mad? Pork and chicken! Four vegetables! A choice of dessert! And no Margaret. I could only be likened to the man who spins plates on canes keeping a score of them spinning at once. I dashed from one pan to another, to another, from one oven to another oven, from dining room to kitchen to pan to oven to room. It is just possible to cook a meal alone but not to properly greet old friends at the same time, to hug them and take their coats and stoke up the fire and, every so often, answer a persistent phone. But all can be done, after a fashion as Mother would say, because all my friends are tolerant and think they know what Margaret has to do because they have read about ladies who have bought smallholdings, have watched *The Good Life* on TV and are quite prepared to chat happily in the snug for as long as it takes.

What none of them appreciates is that Margaret did not buy a smallholding in the country and assume a new way of life. Her three goats and two donkeys do not make a farm any more than one swallow makes a summer. Margaret was born a farmer, not a part-time dabbler with a family of pets. She is a professional with often two hundred head of cattle. Farmers throughout the country tolerate the intrusion, now and again, of amateurs opting out of the Rat Race. They do not resemble these in any way or at least only as a deep sea fisherman resembles a weekend angler or a mountaineer resembles a rambler.

What is not remotely possible is to serve that meal, the moment it is perfect, without Margaret to teem the vegetables. It does not matter what she looks like as long as she's there. She came on this occasion as on every other. She is the only person who puts on an apron to cover dirty clothes instead of to protect clean ones!

The second Christmas was looming and with it came the first Currer goose. Dorothy, whose daughter held her wedding feast at The Currer, brought it. It was found in a distressed condition hanging in a sack on a lamppost. Some thief must have seen a possible Christmas dinner and then decided against it. He little knew he had abandoned the grey goose to a life of luxury in Margaret's kingdom. Of course Margaret will not allow loneliness and very soon bought a gander we called Gandhi; from those two has grown the flock of geese now responsible for waking light sleepers with their early morning capers.

A family of nine booked in for the Christmas week. They would use the Mistal cottage and several other bedrooms and have all meals in the house. Ten other guests booked in and I bought an eighteen-pound turkey. Mother made two Christmas puddings the size of footballs and they hung with lesser brethren from the kitchen beams. We were all set for a splendid festive season. Then four people cancelled.

Christmas Eve arrived and the family of nine came in penny numbers from different parts of the country. Only eight of them appeared to join the six other guests for the evening meal and something was decidedly lacking in the festive spirit. When I served the main course there were two more empty seats and for the dessert only two of the nine remained. I was worried.

The grandparents of the family had arrived last and before they had left home they had received a phone call to say that their son-in-law's father had been rushed into intensive care, and everyone was wondering what to do. Within half an hour they had decided, some to go to London and the others to go home as their Christmas was ruined. So was ours. I had an eighteen-pound turkey for six guests and a real struggle to rescue a seasonal atmosphere. We put pounds of turkey into the freezer and grew heartily sick of it as the weeks went by.

In the middle of March Margaret, a diminutive figure beside the tall auctioneer, rented her top land to a neighbour for six months and privately sold the hay on the meadows to John.

The flow of guests never ceased. It was the spring of the 1983 General Election and it came to pass that the very young agent for the Conservative candidate booked at The Currer for two days and stayed four months. The laughter, the teasing and the wit which flourished in the dining room has never been equalled. It could have been a very difficult time had any of our guests taken politics seriously but no-one admitted to being a Tory and everyone professed to be SDP or Scottish Nationalists, or followers of Marx or the Raving Loonies. The truth was never told and a friendly, ridiculous atmosphere prevailed. There was a preponderance of learned young men in the house at the time. There was a manager from a local industry and a computer expert. There was the new clerk of the County Court and Fred, who was employed by a developer to represent the house buyers. Fred came three days a week for three years. 'Where are we putting Fred?' was every Monday morning's problem.

The young agent, not yet twenty, took all the teasing with incredible good humour though he was not allowed to eat anything red, was advised against tomatoes, must definitely reject rhubarb and, 'Good Lord, Jon, don't touch the beetroot!'

'Leave politics alone, Jon,' everyone said. 'Play the piano.'

That he could do extremely well and the whole house was filled with the strains of classical music.

One March visitor has her place of importance in the history of The Currer. She stepped back into my life after nearly forty years. She came to stay in the Loft and it was a happy reunion for she had taught me domestic science and needlework at the Grammar School. She too had found a ruin and hers had been in a cleft in the Lakeland hills. It had claimed her even as The Currer had claimed us. In a way we did not realise then, she was to be teacher again. It is strange how people occasionally drift into your life and unexpectedly solve your problems. Years later the solution to her problem became the answer to ours.

At the beginning of March we had our first Camper's Reunion at The Currer. We had promised ourselves this after the wonderful evening at Pat's in 1981. Over fifty came and an annual event was inaugurated. There is no evening in the year more pleasant than the one when we once again get round the campfire and remember. There was an over-abundance of food so we invited a busload of residents from the Cheshire Home and, with reunion fever at its height, we organised a mini-reunion of my College Year. For over thirty years I had been the year correspondent keeping the students of my generation in touch with College.

The things we can do with this place lead us to believe it is haunted with some benevolent spirit, be it one of the monks from Rievaulx or one of the Currers or Father, we cannot say. It has been said that it is not the world but the people living in it. With regard to The Currer the house offers something more than the people. Our good luck, our opportunity, our serenity come from elsewhere.

Chapter Twenty-four

T here is no holiday cottage at Luskentyre but across the sands at Seilebost John Fergusson's cottage is now let to summer visitors. We had booked it for a fortnight. Sandra had become a nurse but out of the hundreds of our campers had stepped Dot who had been one of the Sea Rangers frequently at the Cheshire Home.

With her family and a friend, Jill, she came from Suffolk to The Currer in May to release us to go to Harris. What a hot, sunny holiday it proved to be! We had almost every breakfast sitting outside the cottage.

On one memorable day I walked alone from Angus and Katie's cottage on the shore at Luskentyre, right round the sandy headland and under the towering dunes. It was a beautiful, blue afternoon and, somewhat emotionally, I was reliving the wonderful days, the joy of which will never leave me. It was as if I could see again my children come leaping over the dunes in the ecstasy of their youth, rolling, careering, tumbling down the sandy slopes and galloping into the sea.

I met three people, arm in arm and heads into the wind which was following me. They must have thought me slightly crazy. 'What a wonderful day,' I gasped.

'A bit windy,' one of them answered, 'and there's nobody for miles!'

'Oh, but there were,' I rejoiced. 'There were hundreds of children and their bare footprints littered the beach and they came leaping over the sand dunes all bare-legged and brown!'

'Really,' said one of the trio and they headed quickly into the wind which took me away from them and carried me and my memories to the water's edge.

Early one morning, Margaret and I left the oldies at Seilebost and we walked the Rheinigidale track from the Kyles Scalpay road. Shep was with

471

us. It was his last long walk. Now Margaret and I walked it mostly in awed silence. She broke it once or twice to repeat, 'How dare you bring a swarm of children here?'

From the dizzy heights of the Scriob our eyes followed the zigzag path plunging to the shores of Loch Trollamarig. 'You must have been wrong in your head,' she said.

Now, without the children, when the beach is deserted for miles, when the hills are silent and the sea is empty as far as the horizon I gasp a little at the thought of so many barefooted sand urchins scrambling in dangerous places. It was after our walk to Rheinigidale, over the green track laboriously built, repaired and used by the villagers of that most remote of all Britain's communities, that Margaret was ill. It had nothing to do with the strenuous walk, I am sure, and everything to do with the too-big plateful of baked beans on toast we had on our return but it was, perhaps, the first hint of something amiss. Margaret had the most violent indigestion all night. She could not move for it and sat propped up in bed, burping continually and wracked in pain. I was worried, then frightened, then desperate. At six o'clock I went to the telephone kiosk and phoned the doctor.

'Give her bi-carb,' he said. 'It sounds as if she has a problem. Give her lots of bi-carb and if it does no good phone me again and I'll come at once.'

It worked and we didn't send for the doctor, but it was a long time before Margaret could move naturally. She slept propped up for days and anxiety became a little part of my make-up. I had never seen anyone with such bad indigestion and thereafter Margaret often sat up in bed burping.

Angus had a four-month-old pup he wanted to give Margaret but we had left two dogs at home. Shep always came away with us and was never any trouble at all. The two bitches would never leave The Currer. Skye was far too shy. When guests came in to see Mother Skye dived under the sideboard.

The first time we had to take her to the vet she was too frightened to get out of the Land Rover and our nice vet came to the car instead to give her the necessary injections. Three things happened. Skye got her injections all right but the vet got bitten and I got covered with diarrhoea. Thereafter the vet gave Margaret the boosters and Skye was inoculated at home. Mother's dog she was, the most gentle of loving creatures.

Neither Skye nor Floss would ever cross The Currer boundary. Shep would have followed us through the streets of London. Harry had called Floss 'Miss World' and she was undeniably the most beautiful, her coat like silk and with liquid brown eyes, and she loved us. If one of us curled up on the hearthrug, she would crawl into some curve of our relaxed body. The mere mention of her name produced a wagging tail.

One dog is not enough. If it dies you are without. Two dogs are enough. We would never have kept Skye from the litter if she had not been so impossibly timid. We had three dogs, one more than enough but Shep was old. He had only just made the Rheinigidale track and Angus had this pup which he wanted to give Margaret and which wanted to be all over her.

There were two things which swayed us in favour of Lusky besides Shep's age. Floss had already had one operation for mammary tumour and she had more little lumps all over her belly. She would not be with us always. But the main reason I stood by Margaret and persuaded Mother to agree to the pup travelling home with us was because I had had a shock over Margaret's illness and I was prepared to agree to anything. Margaret really should not have had indigestion as bad as that and Lord help me if I lose my sister!

So when we left Luskentyre, Lusky was with us, enjoying every bit of the journey home. He, like Harry and Mother, is a permanent fixture in the Range Rover, sitting alert in the back: no trouble until he sees another dog when his barking nearly bursts our ear drums; docile until some stranger opens the back door. Then Lusky bites.

Dogs are all different. Lusky is more different than most and we really have very little influence on him at all. Praise does not excite him. Margaret insists it is because he learned the Gaelic and just won't try to learn English. It could be that he is deaf but he hears the postman's van long before I do.

Right from the start Lusky herded everything, from pigeons, ducks, geese, hens, goats and donkeys to pigs, cattle and cars. Only cattle are his responsibility but you try to tell him so. He thinks everything which moves, including joggers and wheelchairs, must do what he says. He often ignores us completely. He is invaluable with the bringing home of the herd for he is unafraid to nip and can move a hundred animals in one direction but he believes his way is right even if it differs from ours and if we vary our routine, open a different door or gate, we have to grab him by the long hair and hold on. He also has a habit inherited from the wild. When the herd is going through the shed door or field gate, Lusky takes the last one and separates it. In the wild this would be his kill but Lusky is only having his bit of fun and winding us up.

Really, Lusky is a veterinary miracle. A few weeks after we brought the pup home he began to drag his back legs on the floor and the vet said he had a very bad hip displacia. But his skill gave Lusky an almost normal use of his hind legs except when he needs to jump into the Range Rover or over a wall. His collie coat is so long it can easily be grabbed by one or other of us and he does not consider a heave to be undignified.

The first indication that he was a liability came when a neighbour said Lusky had burst his tyre. 'Impossible,' we said.

Then our young electrician was seen changing a tyre up by the moor gate. 'Your dog did it,' he condemned.

A man came to help us unload two huge wagons of straw. He too had a puncture and blamed the dog; we felt uneasy and paid £30 for a new tyre. Then we paid for a guest's burst tyre and for another puncture our electrician had and we began to take the matter seriously. The number of cars coming to The Currer could well cost us £1,000 a week. We tried to keep Lusky in the house when visitors were setting off for the day but someone would accidentally let him out. We chained him but you can't keep a dog chained all day.

So we decided he'd have to have his upper fangs filed down. Unfortunately the lower fangs were just as efficient and we had to have those filed, too. Since then we have had no burst tyres.

Our first batch of three-month-old, weaned Hereford heifers arrived even before we returned from Harris. Paul had put plenty of bedding straw in the new shed and when we drew into the yard we found the cattle wagon had been before us. We were back home with a vengeance, forty calves to feed, forty to vaccinate, forty ear tag numbers to take. For three consecutive weeks the cattle wagon brought more until we had 103.

A June election came and a triumphant Jon. Not everyone at The Currer shared his political persuasion. Gandhi was a socialist and he and Jon hated one another. Gandhi lay in wait for Jon's car every day. The boy was so afraid he used to park his car as near the door as he could and slither over the passenger seat to avoid the outstretched neck and hissed abuse.

They are amazing creatures, ducks and geese and swans. They protect each other in an incredibly human way. They know when one of their kind is in distress, caught in binder twine or lost behind the stack netting and they won't leave their friend but flap and screech to cause a diversion or hasten help.

When the vixen has cubs in the spring the dog fox gets quite brazen in his search for food and takes far greater risks, approaching the pond area in daylight to snatch a duck. He invariably causes a commotion and the dogs pile in. Startled, one day, he dropped the duck he had almost beheaded. Margaret was there in a flash. The duck was alive but the skin had been torn right round its neck and the muscles and arteries were exposed contracting and pumping erratically.

She picked it up and dashed for the house. The proud flesh was all covered with dirt and blood, grass and straw. She puffed wound powder all over it and looked critically at the skin which had wrinkled like a child's sock. 'Not a hope,' she despaired, taking a needle and some bright green cotton and dragging the two torn edges of skin together. Next morning she expected to find it dead but the duck lived. We have only two white ones among the mass of Khaki Campbell and even Margaret does not know which one of the two she stitched.

So 103 calves came to The Currer all looking alike, all costing the earth. We went to our complacent bank manager and asked him to allow us to build one more shed to replace the one so badly damaged in the orchard by the snow of 1981. 'Yes,' he said. Did he not notice how down-at-heel, how shabbily dressed we were, how rough our hands and how broken our nails? Could he not see how tight our belts were?

Every night the calves had to be rounded up from the low pastures. One day, the herd of babies got real spooky, a thing cattle can do when darkness isn't very far away. Margaret brought up the baby herd and did not know that the two donkeys were in the shed. The first calves were spilling through the door when Jasper began to bray. A hundred and three calves turned tail and galloped back to the wood. Margaret shooed out the culprits and shut the gate on them. Then she and the dogs started the routine all over again. I was watching from the window, ready to give a hand, if necessary, but the calves came meekly back and began to file past the septic tank. It is a modern one, with a tippler which periodically clanks noisily the other way. Just as the herd passed the tank the tippler did its work and whoops! the whole 103 stampeded down the Five-Acre at a tremendous pelt, almost up-skittling Margaret. I ran out to help but, believe me, we were just helpless with laughter. Children, calves, pups, piglets, they are all the same. Daft as they come!

Our diversification seemed self-perpetuating. As guests left they paid a deposit on a return visit the following year. If our health remained we were more secure than we had ever been. Margaret kept quiet about her problems; we sent for John and he started planning. In for a penny, we thought. Tomorrow must not be waited for. If sleeping berths are needed that night it was no use to do as the drunken steward suggested and 'sort it all out in the morning!' 'Buy now and pay later!' is not a recommended way of life but it had to be ours.

There was a wonderful security in this avalanche of guests. When the holidaymakers dwindled H. Samuel sent shop-fitters, BandQ electricians, Omeda joiners. An opera singer wanted a cottage for a month, an *Observer* photographer had local assignments, actors needed accommodation whilst they performed in the city. Whilst this source of income continued we could afford to 'buy now and pay later'.

The shed builders came and we lived on a building site once more.

We escaped for a somewhat uneasy fortnight at Grange. We had found The Studio, a small, very compact bungalow close to the railway and not far from the end of the promenade. It suited us like the Little White Tent. It was so small Margaret and I had to sleep in sleeping bags on the minute dining room floor. We could have a bath and listen, at the same time, to Robin Day on *Question Time* and we loved it dearly.

Margaret went home for a night, mid-weekend, for we had a changeover of supply staff and we had never left so many calves before. They were eight-months old and strong but the new shed being built scattered the housing of them. We kept many in an almost empty Dutch barn. We couldn't buy in a store of hay. There was literally nowhere to put it.

The shed was finished for Christmas, the weather was fair, the guests came and stayed and were pleasant. January gave us a month of snow and the joiners staying at The Currer, working in the locality, made a sledge and came careering down the road, three and four of them at a time. Eventually it got too much like an Olympic bob sleigh run and they realised they might end up in the cemetery so they gave us the huge sledge to pull bales across the yard.

Guests with cars in the winter time are a liability for they often need pulling out. One day I remember well, a guest could not start his car.

'Have you any jump leads?' he asked. The answer being, 'Yes,' he wanted to borrow the Range Rover. It was a bitterly cold day. I ran out, not sufficiently clad for the weather and drove the Range Rover alongside. The man was adamant that he could cope without my help. His wife was sitting snugly in the driver's seat of his car and I was not needed. In fact he dismissed me very positively, saying it was cold and he knew just what to do.

I had left the Range Rover alongside but he preferred to have it head on so he got in, reversed and drew forward until the two vehicles were almost touching. He left it in gear, as I would have done, turned off the engine and raised the two bonnets. He connected the jump leads, told his wife what to do, jumped into the Range Rover and started the engine. He forgot he had left it in gear and he drove the huge vehicle right into his own car, smashing the headlamps, buckling the bumper and demolishing the radiator. I can only imagine what his wife said. There was no damage, or scratch even, to our Range Rover.

Without doubt a guardian angel lives here. I am not suggesting that our guardian angel had anything to do with the poor man's car but that it must have had something to do with an incident in March when we had a party from Bromham mental hospital for the weekend. On the Sunday it was decided that two of the patients were not fit to go out sightseeing in the Dales. Groups with handicapped people are usually on a one-to-one basis so two staff stayed behind, with part of the first-aid box.

At lunchtime Harry choked over his meat. We thought he was dying and rushed for the help which God had left behind. One of the men ran to the first-aid box and produced an aspirator.

'Our patients often choke,' he said as he quickly took a mass of fluid from Harry's oesophagus and our brother started breathing again. 'You'd better send for the doctor,' said the human angel, unwilling to take full responsibility. Harry still had quite a bad pain. Our doctor came at the double, literally turned Harry upside down and dislodged another big piece of meat. It was impossible to say whether the meat had caused the pain or the pain had caused the choking so Harry was dashed to the Intensive Care Unit. Our fifty-seven-year-old spastic brother had never been in hospital before.

Mother and I sat in the ICU waiting room in a sea of misery. How would he cope? One thing about Harry was that he never batted an eyelid on the many occasions he has been rushed to hospital to have stitches. He falls as relaxed as a judo player but if there is a sharp edge of furniture there is a gaping hole in him and blood all over the place. He copes like the duck and heals as well. He really is the most uncomplaining member of society.

We were proud of Father's performance in hospital but Harry's really took the biscuit. The only trouble he caused was that he continually dislodged the cardiograph in the ICU. They found nothing wrong so they sent him to the general ward for observation and he enjoyed it as he would a holiday in an hotel. Because they could not understand his speech we were allowed to go any time and when we went he could not stop talking. He knew everyone, he liked the food, he enjoyed the novelty. Mother had expected to stay with him, 'As if he were a kiddy,' she said and she wasn't needed at all.

We were putting on our coats to visit him again when the phone rang. Margaret answered it. 'Currer Laithe Farm,' she said.

A voice with a speech impediment said, 'Do you do bed and breakfast?'

'Yes we do,' said Margaret, 'and we do evening meals. When were you thinking of?'

'Could you fetch me now?' Margaret had thought she was talking to someone with a handicap and now she thought she was talking to someone who had had too much to drink. She became immediately wary.

I know my teasing brother. 'Is it Harry?' I said and, would you believe it, Margaret said, 'Harry who?'

So we picked Harry up. His hospital stories lasted a year and are still toted out every so often.

Shortly after this the phone rang and the caller asked if we had accommodation for two gentlemen for a week in April. The chart showed a full house but an empty Loft cottage. 'Yes,' I said, 'if the gentlemen will use the cottage and come into the dining room for breakfast.'

The caller seemed to think this ideal. 'Give me names and an address, please,' I said, just like I do to every caller.

'It's for Anthony Quayle and John Quentin,' she said. She gave me a Compass Theatre address.

'Thank you,' I said. 'I'll make the booking and send you a brochure.' I did not believe what I had heard. I did not want to make a fool of myself so I rang the Leeds Grand and asked what was showing on that particular week and was told. 'And who is appearing?' I queried. 'Anthony Quayle,' was the answer.

I think it was one of the loveliest experiences we have had. Each day the two men would come down late and eat breakfast in the Laithe Porch entrance, talking about famous people as friends and colleagues, and the little Jack Russell would be always at the great man's feet. Then John Quentin would don tweeds, Anthony Quayle would put on the red and black lumber jacket which matched his bright red socks and men and dog would make a daily pilgrimage to the Druids' Altar.

His beautiful voice frequently said nice things to Mother and Harry and thanked us warmly for his late night soup. I can see him now, standing in the yard watching Margaret lift Lusky and allow Shep to jump into the Range Rover. We were taking John Quentin to Shipley for the bus to Harrogate and would not return until our shopping was done. So first of all Mother was enthroned, then Harry, then the picnic box with flasks and sandwiches, then John Quentin, then me and last of all the dogs.

Anthony Quayle was smiling as he watched the frenzied operation, for his friend was in a hurry and we were late.

'And the dogs go, too,' he said, obviously amused. He was worried about Margaret carrying bales. 'I don't see any men, Margaret.'

She did not wish to offend and replied very gently, 'I don't think we need them.'

'If you don't need them,' he laughed, 'to hell with them!''

Shortly after his stay he was knighted and we received a delightful letter acknowledging our congratulations and signed, Tony Quayle.

In May Dot came once again with her family and Jill, to release us to go to Tiree. We were taking Shep and leaving Lusky but when Jill's dog, Hudson, arrived he and Lusky hated each other and obviously we were going to have to take two dogs. Dot had enough problems. One of her sons, Thomas, had been seriously ill. We couldn't leave fighting dogs for her to cope with but, 'No way,' said Mother, 'are we taking two dogs to Tiree!' We did, of course but it was a traumatic departure.

Just occasionally Margaret and I can be seen standing in the yard, staring almost rudely at a couple of holiday-makers who get into their car without any encumbrances. No OAPs, no disabled, no wheelchairs, no picnic hamper, no rugs and hot water bottles and no dogs. They don't even open the gate because we realise we are staring and in embarrassment we dash to open it. They don't have to stop when they see a heifer has jumped over the wall into George's or leave the family nattering and, in best shoes, plough through bog, mire and nettles to chase it out.

We stare for a moment but we do not want to be alone. Our interpretation of carefree is to take our responsibilities with us but I give myself one morning of solitude each holiday, just to talk to me. One gorgeous morning I took the dogs along Salum Bay and sat for an hour below Bella's cottage.

There is no heartache, no soul searching, no recriminations or regret that the road along which we were led took an unexpected turning. Our lives have been a jigsaw. So far it is unfinished but each piece matches the whole. All the individual shapes have been linked together to make one. Wherever I go there are memories of children and family because where I have been they have been. I cannot return to Ripon or the Lakes, the Dales, Northumberland or the Hebrides without my retinue of ghosts and a sound of singing in my ears.

It seemed as if I knew Salum Bay in every detail. The tide was low and the band of green pebbles extended all the way to Calum's. I thought I knew every one of them. I was barefoot and in shorts and I could almost believe that I was carrying an enormous cardboard box, filled with supplies bought at Calum's, and that, hidden by the marram grass, was the camp in Happy Valley with its busy children, a continual movement of brown legs and arms, pulling out sleeping bags to air in the sun.

Looking back along the bay I could see Salum House and Donald Brown's red fishing boat beached by the tide. At a distance it was easy to believe that Calum was still there. I could almost see him leaning against the garden wall, in his navy fisherman's jersey, his grey hair and his eyebrows bushier than most. There were children all round him, begging him to come to the campfire. Then the children were gone and it was my father who stood beside him and they were both laughing.

My goodness, the Hebridean sea looked blue from my perch on the edge of the bay. Nothing, the world over, could be bluer than Salum Bay. There were seals still splashing about in the water, but no children. But there used to be! Because we turned when the road we were travelling did, hundreds of children have been deprived of the happiness I was privileged to give by invading the islands with their summer numbers. They came like midges but brought no irritation, only joy. Because Happy Valley knows an emptiness so also there is an emptiness, a small one, in the lives of the people who so loved our céilidhs and campfires.

Alone on the shore, with no regrets, some of the tiredness was seeping out of me into the sand. I was grateful for the sun and the opportunity just to lie there. I could see the new cottage belonging to John Lachie and his wife, Effie. It replaces the thatched Tiree croft we loved so well but does not look a stranger for it is low and white, also.

I lay listening to the waves plop-plop on the shore, thinking about the evening we had spent with Effie the night before. It had laid a ghost. It seemed that the island could provide all that I needed to get things into perspective and accept my loss. My heart had cried, now and again, for the loss of my school and the closed door on so many teaching years. Effie had asked us to accompany her to the Tiree School prize giving and I'd wondered if some old wounds would open. Would there be an uncontrollable lump in my throat, would it bring back too many memories?

We had been among the last to arrive and, as frequently happens in church or lecture theatre, there were only seats on the front row of adults, immediately behind the children. 'Watch it,' I had told myself.

The children could so easily have been my own. Dressed for a prize giving, each one of them looked beautiful. They behaved just like my children. That they recited and sang in Gaelic made no difference. I saw the teachers, some of whom I knew, sitting quietly at the end of the class row, controlling individual children with a look, a frown or a gently restraining hand. I saw each teacher respond when a group from the class rose to perform and from a seat give instructions silently. Eyes, lips, hands all controlling, unobtrusively conducting. I knew it all.

Around me, fascinating me not a little, were displays and murals done by the children, graphs and nail pictures, written work, prayers and poems I could have believed my own children had composed. Against the wall was a red, plastic centimetre strip to measure the children's height. It was all that was needed to bring back a flood of happy memories.

Sitting on the hot sand, below Bella's cottage, I realised I did not have to return to my own school. I just needed to see my children frequently, which I did and I buried all heartache in the sand.

A few days later we travelled home and, although it was nearly midsummer, the last few hours were in darkness for the boat did not berth in

Oban until five o'clock. Travelling in the darkness I always lose my identity and feel to be in Limbo. I never know who I am and nothing feels real but the moving vehicle taking us determinedly along the road we must go. On Tiree I knew what I had been: a Pied Piper, a privileged person, able to bring great happiness, rich in friends and health and opportunities for adventure under the great arc of the sky, our god the great God of the Open Air.

We entered The Currer in silence, wishing to waken no one; the familiarity of it ensured that I know who I am now and I don't mind at all.

Immediately came the new batch of 104 calves. They looked very small compared with the hefty heifers we would soon have to sell. The thought appalled Margaret. How does one set about selling over one hundred cattle at once? Even their sale would not clear the overdraft so go they must. There was a preoccupied look on Margaret's face and I knew she was worrying. She hates markets and the transporting of cattle even if she will admit that the cattle love a bit of excitement.

I have already pondered over the ignorance of our guests and our friends about the size of our herd. Where it is and how it is managed remains a mystery to them. They have no conception of the numbers. So those who happen to be here at the beginning of September get a shock! Margaret and I go up onto the hill at dusk, when the herd assembles for the night, and we bring down over a hundred big bellowing animals to the farmhouse paddock. It is more like the Wild West than anything for miles around.

Amazed faces appear at the bedroom windows as four hundred feet thunder past at the double. There is a snorting and a bellowing and Urban Man runs to lean over the farmyard gate whilst the stream of cattle rushes like a black torrent into the low pasture. Bewildered, amazed, fascinated, Urban Man is speechless.

Margaret and I are up very early for the herd must be brought back into the paddock and driven past the open door of the shed, slowly if possible, so that the best can be turned in and the leaner let go. Always is the fear that they stampede and we fail to trap the forty we need.

If we are lucky we have more than half the cattle in the shed and now we must single out those not ready to sell but the wagon is already coming down the hill and there is little time. A few brave holidaymakers come to the gate and offer to help. We station them with sticks in the paddock. The Dutch barn gate is opened wide and twenty heifers are driven in. This is the easiest job of all for the barn is full of hay and the cattle know, for they have trespassed there when a gate has been accidentally left open. They enter as quickly as children rush into the sweet shop.

The wagon is reversed to the barn entrance and the back ramp lowered and gated. Now, will they go in? Usually, yes. Cattle are so immensely curious. Pigs refuse but cattle go in. Some decide that, having looked, they'll come out again but the man is a professional; the first load goes away safely and we double-bolt and tie the shed doors. Twenty must be there when the lorry returns.

Then we go in and make breakfast for our guests. We are trembling. We hate round-ups and we hate selling.

The second load goes and the worst is over for me, though not for Margaret who hates the markets. We are glad ours are heifers, mostly going to suckling herds.

The first time that Margaret had to sell one hundred within a month, in 1984, the market price was so low on the day she took the first forty that she brought them all back. Most of the farmers did likewise. Imagine all that round-up palaver and no sale! On Saturday we rounded up the whole herd again and Margaret took sixteen to another market and brought all sixteen back. We were devastated. We saw our planned stay at The Studio in Grange being cancelled.

Another load of straw was delivered. Jack said, 'Yer cattle look all right.'

Jokingly I said, 'Do you know anyone who wants to buy a hundred?'

'Ah might,' he answered.

Next day he rang and suggested he brought over his neighbour. They came, the man offered a fair price, was accepted, Jack came five times with his cattle wagon and we breathed again.

So we went to Grange and wandered round National Trust country. We were always dependent on the willingness of one friend or other being able to supply. Dorothy Winup and her family were next to assume this responsible role. We never undervalue the courage of our friends to come and take over. Dorothy is essential, too, when putting a hundred beasts through the crush requires a third man to fill the syringe, fire the wormer gun or write down ear tag numbers.

Another Christmas came and went. We had a crowded house and no cancellations. Two turkeys were needed. One I put into the oven at 4 a.m. Three large puddings were lifted from the beams and the kitchen smelt like Bob Cratchett's. The family had cold beef sandwiches for Christmas dinner and Mother cried. Guests from all over the world crowded into the dining room in festive spirit.

'Christmas is too hard,' we acknowledged. Poor Mother was almost ninety, still working and watching her daughters slaving away. 'One day we'll close for Christmas,' we promised, 'and we'll eat our sandwiches in some Dales beauty spot and be utterly selfish.'

The mammary tumours on Floss's belly were frightening. We waited and waited for there was no guarantee that another operation would be any more successful and we loved her so. When the vet decided to operate we were uneasy and when she died under anaesthetic we knew it was for the best. I remember that Margaret sent me down to the surgery to bring Floss back home. Be it dog or calf or goat, Margaret thinks it only fair to let those of its kind know, for animals do mourn and are not continually searching if they know. So Floss was left with the other dogs who understood and therefore did not fret and then we buried our friend in the edge of the plantation where her predecessors lie.

We limped into spring. Harry was looking really rough. Margaret was sitting up regularly in bed with indigestion. Neither complained. The February half-term was busy, the house was full of guests.

I took Harry to the doctor's because he complained of a nastiness in his mouth. We had sent some pigs to the abattoir and I collected them on the Saturday and the Horners came. We had the usual awful day putting pork into the freezer and Harry looked ashen.

That evening he complained of a very severe pain in his chest. We rang the doctor on duty who said to keep Harry upright until the pain went and to ring again if necessary. In the morning Harry looked so white that we sent for the duty doctor. I think he was quite shocked to see his pallor and he took a blood sample. It was Sunday.

We have fed a lot of people on Sundays since we began taking guests. I suppose this was no exception. I don't think it was the Sunday that Thora Hird reprimanded us. We had just served the evening meal and she had been presenting an hour of hymn singing. The lovely tunes and words of comfort had helped us through the chore which we always have to do at such speed because something always prevents us from starting early enough.

We flopped into an armchair for a brief moment thinking 'What the heck are we doing this for? How come we got into this feed-the-masses lark?'

Thora Hird's programme was over and her head and shoulders filled the screen. She waited until we sank into the depths of our armchairs and then she spoke to us in particular. I am quite sure she could see us for she looked at Margaret and then at me and said, 'I'll leave you with a thought.' There was a definite emphasis on *you* and an uncanny look in her eye. She waited until she was sure we were listening before continuing. 'And the Disciples said, "Shall we send these people away so that they can buy food?" But Jesus said, "No, you feed them!"' I don't think we have ever laughed more!

Our own doctor came around coffee time and said Harry must go straight into hospital for a blood transfusion. We asked if we could take him in the Range Rover.

Whilst the doctor phoned the hospital we catapulted into necessary jobs. Margaret had hastened to finish the big washing up, started after feeding the cattle before the doctor came. Then she went to let out the cattle whilst I carried the laden trays of clean crockery back into the dining room to re-set the table.

Thank God most of our guests make their own beds. I hastily covered the neglected ones, then thrust a turkey into the oven and scooped up the morning out-post whilst Margaret drove the Range Rover out of the garage. She bundled Harry in with his overnight case and I issued my orders to Mother and Auntie Mary who is always there whenever we need her. There were instructions about evening vacancies, what to say in answer to the phone, what to do with the washerful of sheets just going into spin, how much pastry Mother should make, what sort of biscuits were needed, Auntie

Mary would see to the ironing, and what to do with the turkey should it be done before our return.

A hundred cattle impeded our journey up the hill. They will not budge. They even start licking the car. All the barking of dogs and the screaming of women in the cab will not move them on.

We always have to get out and shoo, one walking in front of the Range Rover all the way through the herd.

Hospital staff can work quickly in an emergency. Within minutes of our arrival, Harry was in bed and life-saving blood was bringing back his colour. We waited uneasily in the Day Room, watching the red drip from the upturned bottle.

A lady doctor came to us. 'Are you with Mr Brown?' she asked.

'Yes,' we answered. 'He's our brother.'

'Where does he live?'

'He lives with us.' We gave our address.

'Then you will be the next of kin?'

We hesitated, 'I suppose so,' I said, 'but Mother is still alive. She's nearly ninety.'

'Where does she live?'

'She lives with us,' we said.

The lady doctor gave us a look of concern we've never seen directed at us before. She leaned forward with a kindly gesture of understanding and asked, 'Are you managing to cope?'

We kept straight faces but laughter was very near the surface. 'Yes,' we said. 'We are coping!'

And Harry was coping, too. Once again he thoroughly enjoyed the four days he spent in hospital. He made friends with everyone. He was properly checked out and told he had a hiatus hernia. He never grumbles though this causes him no end of bother. Few people know how hard he has to struggle. He came out of hospital the day before the annual Guide reunion and let himself in for an overdose of admiring females.

We meet extraordinary people every day and no twenty-four hours is without incident, but there are so many of them and they pass so quickly. For a day, a week, a month and sometimes even for a year, they are family and we discuss, put the world to rights, laugh, sympathise and confide. Then they are gone, we cannot remember who they were, from whence they came, what day they left, where they went or even the colour of their skin. It's a sobering thought.

Our lives are a kaleidoscope with an ever-changing pattern of people and we are glad that some return again and again so that they become more than ships which pass in the night. Frankie, Philip, Kislingburys, Pat and Oliver and Sewing Machine John. Vinces, Braggs, Tindales, the Johnsons and the Scales. Mrs Weak Tea, the three ladies from Bromham and the four from Kent and dear Mr Van from Belgium whose visits date back to our beginning and whose Maurice Chevalier charm has captured our hearts.

Strangely, some of our guests are remembered because they did not stay; the young wife with her so beautifully dressed little girls who thought the farmhouse would be in a village and could not stay because it was not, and the Roland Rat film crew who thought it was too bleak. There was a couple who would not stay because they found that we had dogs. Do they really expect farmers to have no dogs? 'Have you cats?' say those allergic. There are, sadly, those who will not stay when they see a wheelchair. They go before they have the rich experience of meeting the owner of it. These unfortunate people have a greater handicap for disablement is a physical, emotional, mental or financial inability to cope with a situation. If you cannot cope with meeting someone who is disabled that, too, is disablement.

One constant factor in our varied lives is the nightly production of food. We only serve a traditional menu and those whose eating habits have changed from roast beef and Yorkshire pudding to pizzas and curries must go elsewhere.

'We come for the food,' someone told Mother and she replied, 'We don't serve anything fancy, you know. Only farmyard food.' I have this vision of Margaret walking into the dining room with a bale of hay!

Could it be that the change of eating habits is to blame for the breaking up of the extended family? Brought up on broth and dumplings, which did not shorten my mother's life, she could not possibly have joined the household of a daughter who ate what she calls 'muckment' pre-prepared from the supermarket.

People booking accommodation at a Yorkshire farmhouse, of course, expect traditional fare unless they come from France and have been sent here by their firm. Poor Henri! After a while he complained, 'Seex weeks and no spaghetti!'

'I'm sorry, Henri,' I apologised. 'We're farmers and don't even know how to cook it.'

The bottom cottage was vacant. 'Buy some and cook it yourself in the cottage kitchen.' I said.

So Henri bought a packet of spaghetti and several other ingredients and disappeared into the Mistal kitchen. In a while I looked in on him and found chaos. He had not bargained for the fact that spaghetti swells and had put enough in the pan for a dozen. It had grown and leapt out of the pan and mutilated the stove. It was only partly cooked and most of what he put on his plate he left. He also left the washing up. Nevertheless I said, 'Any time you want to do that, Henri, you may.' He lived on farmhouse food for the rest of his stay!

We were returning to Harris and on our way north we were hoping to arrive at Berwick Church in time for Vivienne's wedding. Whether we would be on time depended on a very early start. By six we must be on our way.

We never get off absolutely on time but we were on our way by 6.30, assured of having plenty of time to go slowly and enjoy the lovely countryside. We drove gently up the A19 with no traffic problems and then, two miles from the Tyne Tunnel, we came to a standstill. There was traffic in front as far as the eye could see and almost at once we were hemmed in from behind and there we had to stay whilst the minutes and the hour ticked by. We had our coffee break and still there was hardly any movement ahead of us. Inch by inch we crawled a little nearer our destination. We lost all hope of getting to the wedding. Margaret and I were not even dressed for it. We had walked out of the farmhouse in the trousers and shirts we had worn to do the last jobs, many of which had been dirty ones. Our wedding finery was neatly folded in a plastic bag to put on somewhere after lunch.

At last the long line of traffic began to move but we had little hope of getting to Berwick so we drove only a little faster than usual. The nearer we got, however, the more possible it seemed. If we didn't stop at all, not for lunch or loos or change of clothes, if there were no more hold-ups and no puncture, then we just might manage it.

There was no way that I could go to the wedding of one of Jean's children dressed as I was. Margaret was driving so I wriggled out of trousers and pulled on tights and shoes. Then I struggled with my shirt and exchanged it for underskirt and dress. In most Range Rovers the spaciousness of the seats would make such an operation relatively easy but we are cluttered with picnic hamper and flasks, hot water bottles, rugs, medicines and wheelchair cushions and maps, binoculars and overnight bags. The roof rack is full and the dogs in the back have to share their space with the wheelchairs.

So my exchange of clothes was not as simple as Margaret's or as quick, for she is small and very agile and slim. I am sure on-coming drivers raised their eyebrows and the one on our tail would have a wicked look in his eye.

At the next lay-by Margaret and I changed seats and I drew back into the slow lane whilst Margaret began her quick change. My goodness was it quick. Removing her shirt she realised that, in the haste of our 4 a.m. rise it had been the only top article of clothing she had put on. There were exclamations of disgust from the old ladies on the back seat who have never had to rush quite so much as we have. Margaret's little squeal of surprise was still amusing me during the wedding ceremony.

Because the church was the very first thing we saw when we entered Berwick we were actually on time. The bride had arrived and was arranging the beautiful dress her mother had made. We always do manage it but it would be nice if we could do things properly like everybody else!

That time on Harris was the last time we saw Granny Morrison for, two years later, she had gone to live in Glasgow with her daughter. At ninety-five she was still the most amusing, the most wise, the most outrageous of anyone I know. We spent as much time as we possibly could with her. Where age is kept alert by meaningful activity it is a precious thing and one cannot afford to miss a minute of its company. We felt that way about Granny and we feel that way about Mother, too. When I think of all that wisdom, all that experience, all that humour and tolerance and understanding being isolated or buried in an old folk's home instead of active within family and community, I grieve and so should society.

One day we had to wait a long time for Granny to return from a visit to the island of Scalpay. She had prolonged her visit and then called at the Harris House, the island home for the elderly without relatives. When she arrived she was full of fun. She had been telling an old man that she thought the Lord had said one person should live forever and it must be she. 'Ach, but you'll be thinking that it is you,' she had said.

The old man's humour matched hers. 'Well, no, Catherine,' he had replied, 'I'm thinking the Lord has forgotten the both of us!'

I have been told that, shortly before Granny died at nearly ninety-nine, her son took her for an outing to the coast. 'Ah, well,' she had chuckled. 'I wasn't expecting to be here. I was expecting to be dead!' It was a privilege to know such a person. Her humour has surely gone with her to make Heaven a better place for me if ever I get there too.

The shock of coming home to The Currer is cruel now, though it used to be a lovely experience when the barn was full of hay. Now the yard is full of strangers' cars and we have no escape. By bedtime I might admit that I like my job but the initial reaction to homecoming is far from that. I regret to admit that in the first hour we don't like anything except the lovely clean house. We certainly don't like the presence of holidaymakers. We don't like the evening meal we have to prepare or the pile of folded wet washing because it always rains on the day we come home. We like our dearest friends, the time-honoured supply staff, but we don't like the long list of phone messages or the pile of unopened post or the full chart for the next twenty weeks.

Mother and Auntie Mary withdraw into the sitting room to sulk in the armchairs. Only Harry enjoys it all. But everyone is deceived because we cheerfully introduce 'ourselves to the new guests, appreciate and applaud our dearest friends, shower our sincere gratitude, listen with apparent interest, privately wishing everyone and everything was in that place Mother calls Ummanick. But, by nightfall we begin to admit we can like what we have to do.

June fills the house with children and the Lathams and Olive and Manny from Texas who enjoy them so. Handicapped children are so good and, after dinner, they sing round the piano and everyone has a wonderful time.

August brings the Condons from Belgium, and the Barbaults from France, eleven-year-old Denis and little Emilie and the Whites from that other foreign country, the South of England.

Margaret was struggling, not that anyone knew. When we have a moment of calm, I'll do something, she promised herself but the moment never came. All my friends retired and began to enjoy their leisure whilst Harry continued to sleep in the front room, Auntie Mary in my bed and Margaret and I on the floor.

All for The Currer! What would become of it? We have no children. There was no-one behind us ready to step in, no-one to whom The Currer meant anything permanent. All acknowledged its beauty, its history, its ministry. Many saw a little, some even experienced a little, of the work it involved and all thought that little was a lot.

But to us The Currer was a permanent thing and we had no plans how to keep it so; the people kept a'coming and the job went on.

Again the cattle were sold to the man on the York plain. It was easy at a time when something had to be so and it was a sensible thing to do that summer when Margaret was struggling. Eventually, she knew, she would revert to selling at the market but we both felt to be waiting for something to happen. Like Father we were waiting for 'something to turn up'.

Chapter Twenty-five

There has grown in us an urgent need to spend two weeks in Grange-over-Sands, when the leaves begin to turn and autumn comes. It does not seem unreasonable that those who live at the end of a dark road, in a hollow among fields, close to the heather and the bilberries, for those whose every job is one of survival and utility, to like so much to spend a spell among street lights and gardens. It's nice to walk along an almost deserted promenade, to shop down a short Main Street, out of season, when guest houses have vacancies and the railway station is falling asleep. It gives great pleasure to see a man sweep the day's leaf-fall from his drive because he has nothing else to do but beautify his patch, and we take our dogs for a walk like everybody else. We can say to ourselves, 'Summer is gone and when we go home the pace will be slower.' That it isn't, makes very little difference. The two-week belief that it will be is a tonic.

Before this tourism lark we used to spend a great deal of October gathering blackberries to make jam. Now there is little time but the Lake District offers an opportunity to restock the freezers with pounds and pounds of blackberries and Mary, who owns The Studio, will keep them in her freezer till we go home. If the season is late there are damsons, too, and a sack of apples can be bought at the farm at Winster.

How I love the autumn. It is ridiculous how dry and warm and sunny is the weather when we are at Grange so that we can push Mother and Harry in wheelchairs along the promenade and open our coffee flasks where seats overlook the flower pots. Harry loves the wheelchair. He does not mind how bumpy the ground is, how tipped and shaken he is, or how dark it is.

We are not embarrassed by the good weather which haunts us in both the Hebrides and the Lake District and I feel like Lusky, smelling my way along the hedgerows in search of memories. Autumn leaves and fruits and the smell of water take me back to the nature walks of my teaching days with village children. I remember children deep in fallen leaves, hunting for conkers and beech nuts, puffing the fairy men from the rosebay willow herb with blackberried lips and pocketing the burrs to throw on the backs of unsuspecting teachers.

I remember collecting the windfalls at Steeton Hall. The smell of autumn will never fail to bring back memories, damp and fungoid, of the Hall grounds I knew so well. When the leaves blew from the drive into the corners of the stable yard we knew that the camping season was over. One Saturday, when the trees were a glory of red and yellow and brown, we would foregather in the stable to mend the tents and pack them away for another year and the russeting of the beech, the gilding of the horse chestnut, the yellowing of the sycamore, birch and lime would haunt us in the barer days of foggy November. The rapid metamorphosis of the Virginia creeper from green to brilliant red would amaze us as we stitched away.

In the autumnal peace of the Lake District come back memories of October in college when I walked the well-known paths to Studley Royal where the ducks shuffled among the leaves and had to hunt for the food I scattered. I remember the monastic peace of Fountains Abbey where, a few centuries ago, there must have been such industry and I remember the nearness of the willow herb and jauntiness of the bridges as I walked back to college over the seven arches of the Skell.

It seems that the two years in college were the only ones of freedom. It came over me in a sudden illumination last time I went to Reunion. Here, I thought, was utter peace, infinite freedom, no responsibilities. As I walk the lanes of the Southern Lakes it is in the knowledge that the peace does not free us from having to cook an evening meal at The Studio or from ringing home to make sure that 'nowt is amiss'. In Ripon my evening meal was made and the washing of the dirty dishes done by somebody else.

Nostalgia for college days suffuses me. Glorious selfish days, gone for ever, long ago!

Wandering in the mini-Scotland, in the comfort of the Range Rover, memories return of bigger and deeper lochs and higher and barer mountains. 'This is a Spean Bridge morning,' Margaret will say as we gently drive up the Greenodd to Coniston road with the Langdales in the windscreen. At every bend in the road we meet walkers with rucksacks. Most of them are wearing far too many clothes! How they must sweat, on dry days, so totally encased in nylon waterproofs! We have a brief reminder, too, of my school days when we visit my former teacher in Deepdale, in her house built of slate, and have tea beside her log fire in the beamed sitting room. We know her beautiful home will go to the National Trust when she dies.

Our 1985 visit to Grange obliterated, for a time, our anxiety over Margaret. She had an appointment to see the doctor on the Monday we returned. She went alone and later announced the verdict. Urgent hysterectomy. How often had I heard Margaret, humping heavy bales, wrestling with stroppy cattle and lifting sacks of corn, say, 'I can't have a hysterectomy. That's one thing I can't possibly have. Not with my job!' But we had both known that one was inevitable though we had not admitted it aloud. Now there was no escape.

'I nearly did,' Margaret said. 'You don't know how near I was to not telling all and walking out of the surgery.'

Margaret must have an operation which would prevent her doing her job for at least three months. Don't be silly! A hysterectomy would prevent Margaret doing her job for treble that time. You're a farmer, too, I told myself. What does Margaret do that you can't do? Plenty, my conscience told me. But little by little we had sorted things so that even Margaret would never again have to do the dangerous things she had once done. She'd given up rolling corn and mixing in the beef Promol. The two new sheds made feeding safe and quick. We had no pigs and decided to play a waiting game. The coming of winter would slow the flow of guests. These were all reassuring facts and I closed my mind to the less comforting thoughts such as one hundred to feed, every bale to carry and the harsh winter. Only Margaret and I can know how bleak and hard it can be. Memories of 1947 and 1963 and 1979 would not leave me.

Almost immediately Margaret was called for an X-ray and was given 10th December as the date she must go to hospital. So we had a month. A winter month!

I think we repaired the whole 800 metres of boundary fencing along the Altar Lane. We took the Range Rover up with fencing posts and barbed wire to do a job which must have two agile people to wield the heavy mallet. Should the cattle cross the boundary one person, the less competent at that, could not get them back alone. We could not rest until the outer fences and walls were safe.

We had bought a second-hand luggage rack for the Range Rover, a monstrous wire tray, one foot deep and standing three inches above the roof. It enabled us to carry anything but it totally prevented us from driving into the garage. Built beside the corn store, it could be no higher than it was without lifting that roof, too. This was a major reconstruction job but Margaret dug her heels in, saying she thought it out of the question that the Range Rover should winter outside. Therefore she insisted that the roof must be heightened and that it should be done before she went into hospital. I wonder how many women struggle on a tin roof in December sleet before major surgery. It was a lousy, cold job, crouched in an elevated position, in the path of an unrelenting wind, struggling to hammer spring head nails through two thicknesses of corrugated tin and fibre glass sheets.

Having completed it, she decided we should get half a load of pre-mix concrete and lay a decent floor. We did, and in spite of the cold weather the mixture began to set. I insisted on doing the lion's share of the heavy job and pushed the rapidly setting concrete with a muck pusher. The result was that Margaret had a very bad cold and I had a crippling pain in my back. I was doing most of the cattle feeding as a trial run for doing it all and I began quietly to worry about my back. Strangely, and fortunately, it did not hurt too much when I was working but when I lay down in bed, wow! There were nights when I couldn't sleep flat at all and secretly came downstairs and slept in an armchair.

The day before Margaret went into hospital I carried cement down the cellar steps for Margaret to jam into two suspicious looking holes. Any visitor coming that way would be most unwelcome. Few vermin escape the cats and those which do find easier food supplies in the corn store. If there is a worse job than raising a garage roof it just might be struggling over a mountain of coke, straddling a mediaeval well and blocking up potential vermin holes!

Margaret's cold was definitely worse. I covered my back with Fiery Jack. We were a decrepit pair. Next day, before we left for the hospital, Margaret phoned the ward and told them that she had this dreadful cold. Margaret doesn't get colds. It was very embarrassing to admit she was streaming!

'Never mind,' she was told. 'Just come.' So we all climbed into the Range Rover, Mother, Harry, umpteen rugs and hot water bottles and the dogs; we left Margaret on the ward and came home. Mother and Harry took it calmly. I was petrified. What if there was something seriously wrong with Margaret? However would I manage?

We had once been small, struggling farmers with an unpretentious house, a small overdraft and a regular wage. Headship was a responsible job but behind me had been the whole Education Authority. Behind me as a Guider was the whole Guide Movement. Alone, there was no future for any one of us at The Currer. Father had always had things sorted. We had not. We had sought legal advice but it had not been forthcoming. We had pushed our problems aside thinking that something would turn up.

We had barely reached home when Margaret rang to say they had done preliminary blood tests and the operation would be next day. It was therefore a shock to hear her on the phone at tea-time saying, 'Fetch me home. My blood test says I've a bad cold and they won't operate!'

So my first experience of feeding cattle alone was with Margaret in the house taking Paracetamol. She did all the household chores, fed the bed and breakfast guests, blew her nose and took her tablets.

Christmas came. On its Eve we had twenty-two guests. Mother began making the Yorkshire puddings whilst Margaret was in town, doing last minute shopping. 'Goodness,' she said, having put most of the ingredients in the bowl, 'I've no milk.' Margaret was bringing twenty pints so the bowl had to wait and, when the time came, I was the one who added the milk and whisked for the required length of time. Then I put twelve puddings in the Aga and twelve in the Baby Belling.

I summoned our guests to the table. The lighted Christmas tree, the candles and the holly all proclaimed the festive night. The meal must be good. I looked in the oven and the Yorkshire puddings were a complete and utter failure. Twenty-four solid, half inch thick buns stuck to the tins.

I rushed to make a second batch. I couldn't get them in the oven quickly enough. I chatted to the guests. I talked all the nonsense I could think of and suddenly said, 'Whoops, here's me talking when I should be serving the meal.' I deliberately put another log on the fire and swept the hearth. 'I'll just wash my hands,' I said. 'Then I'll bring the soup.' I'm very good with delaying tactics.

Margaret said, 'They're up,' when I went back into the kitchen. 'Just taste these disasters,' she said. 'Mother used coconut instead of flour!'

When I served the main course, putting two big roasts of beef on the long table with twenty-four Yorkshire puddings, Karen Nightingale, who has been our guest several times, said, 'Yorkshire puddings, I don't know how you do it. They are perfect every time.'

'Practice, Karen,' I said. 'Just practice.'

I got up at four o'clock to put in the first of the two large turkeys; Dorothy and her whole family were coming, adding eleven to our number but helping to cook and wash up. I had prepared it the night before. 'Don't open your eyes properly,' I told myself. 'Just float like you used to do when tent pegs needed a mallet and guys needed slackening.' I was back in oblivion as soon as I touched the pillow.

And after the twelve days of Christmas came the letter telling Margaret to go back into hospital on January 14th.

The 13th dawned cloudy and grey but the 104 almost yearling heifers did not seem to mind. They went out happily to fend for what winter grass they could find. Apparently the search was unprofitable close to home. They ventured over to the meadows on the boundary, completely out of sight.

A gale began to blow up over the Irish sea and the Pennine Ridge could not hold it. It skimmed the summits of Ingleborough, Whernside and Pennyghent, leapt over Malham Cove and came streaking down the Aire Valley. When it reached The Currer it was impossible to walk into it. Like tall ships we had to tack against it. Inevitably it brought torrential, horizontal rain and when the cattle should have turned for home they dared not leave the shelter of the meadows to fight their way into the wind. The rain brought premature darkness and we didn't have one member of the bovine herd.

There was nothing for it but to get out the Range Rover and go overland in search of them. The moor was awash and the track deep in water. The four-wheel-drive vehicle slid all over the place. Behind the first wall of the meadows 104 animals, streaming with sweat, were packed like sardines. They were so close together they had worn away all the grass under their feet. There was no western gate in the wall of that field and, try as we might, we could not drive them through into the next field with its gate onto the moor.

'We'll have to pull a wall down right in the corner,' Margaret said. So in the most northwesterly corner we dismantled one. The northern wall of the meadow continued westwards and we knew that if we could persuade them to go through it they would have the shelter of that wall all along the foot of the moor and into the intakes. We forced the first animals through the gap. They lowered their heads into the lesser wind and the single file was so long the first animals were nearly home when the last went through the gap. It was quite dark and we crossed the boggy moor with the headlights full on.

Next day we took Margaret into hospital again. It was an appalling day and I decided not to let the cattle out. The piped drinking water had been playing up. It was air-locking and if both troughs were emptied by drinking cattle, the trough in the bottom shed did not re-fill without a lot of bother. I ought to have let the cattle out temporarily to drink from the pond but I dared not open the huge, metal shed door into the gale force wind. It will either kill you as it blows open or kill you as it blows shut. I fed the cattle, bedded them down and then tinkered a long time trying to get the air-lock out. I kept turning the mains on and off trying to get rid of it and start water flowing into the bottom shed. I dared not leave Margaret's cattle without water on the very first day she was in hospital and the gale would not spend itself. Corrugated sheets threatened to leave the Dutch barn and I was wary of walking in the path they might take. I was far too harassed to think about Margaret. I went into the Dutch barn with a torch and tried to pile bales of straw against the flapping tins and tie some with binder twine. I thought the whole shed was about to become airborne. 'Glory be,' I said. 'Damn the air in the water pipe.'

I sought the hosepipe and attached it to the cottage kitchen tap. Unfortunately it would not reach the bath we had in the small, sheltered quadrangle into which a rear door of the bottom shed opened. The bath was brimming with water from a fall pipe from the roof. If I let some of the cattle out they would empty it in no time. I took a dustbin, dropped the end of the hosepipe into it and turned on the cottage tap. Thereafter I continually buck- eted water from the bin to the bath and went on letting cattle out a few at a time. About halfway through, when I knew I had carried more than twenty buckets, the bin stopped filling. I dashed into the cottage knowing full well what had happened. The force of water had blown off the hose but the nozzle remained on the tap and was cruelly pouring water all over the kitchen floor. I paddled through a depth of it to stop the tap. Then I took a broom and liter- ally swept a lake out through the door with an anger bordering on tears.

I reduced the pressure from the mains and the job slowed. It was nearly midnight when I finished.

Overnight the wind calmed and next day I let the cattle out after their feed. Margaret had said that I must go up to the meadow and widen the gap permanently so that the cattle always had a sheltered exit from the field. It would take my mind from worrying. There was a weak January sunshine and quite a stiff, drying wind.

I took the dogs. Margaret was worried about Shep in case he would fret. It was difficult to tell. He always looked sad even if he was having a good time. Recently he had been prescribed heart pills by the vet. I was petrified in case he would die whilst in my care.

I had forgotten to shut one of the yard gates and when I returned there were cattle in the Dutch barn, making a mess of the hay, a black mass of vandals with no sense of shame. I chased them round and round; the entrance was big enough but they had no intention of going out. Even Margaret finds it almost impossible to get invading cattle out alone. The dogs only excite the cattle more. If there are two of us it's as easy as pie. Nearly always one, alone, must get a gate and swing it on the inside with binder twine so that they cannot dash repeatedly past the open entrance. 'Out,' I yelled. Margaret says that if you are alone the only way is to swear which is maybe why most of the farmers we know use only one swear word, a noun almost always used to describe cattle!

'I'll never leave the gate open again,' I vowed, but I did. Twice more I galloped round the Dutch barn, yelling and brandishing a stick. I was gormless and incompetent. God help me without my sister!

At five o'clock I went into the house and phoned the hospital. Margaret was back in the ward. I did not ask if we could visit for fear of being refused. I fed the cattle quicker than ever before and Mother and I leapt into the Range Rover and drove to the hospital. She was conscious but sleeping. She looked very ill and I worried myself sick.

I needn't have done for Margaret is a survivor, I should know that by now. John came the following day and took out the muck, lying three feet deep in the two sheds. Even with modern equipment it takes two days. It was comforting to have a tractor man near at hand and I asked for help over the air-lock in the water taps.

When the sheds are empty of manure the concrete strikes cold. The snow we always expect in January was gentle. Only a covering whitened the ground and was hardened by frost. The tractor man and I threw many bales of straw on the clean floor to combat the cold before we let in the cattle. I could not feed them before going to the hospital. I just couldn't get on top of the work.

Margaret was already looking much better. 'Bring me some goat milk,' she said and thereafter, whenever I milked the goat, I said, 'Come on, your milk is for Margaret.' I chilled it in the freezer, put it in a flask and took it daily. Margaret insists it was the goat milk which effected the complete recovery. She steadily improved and when the ward was too full to admit more, she and two more were sent into the maternity ward. 'I hope no-one sees me here,' she laughed.

John thought he'd located the trouble in the water pipe to be in the section I had laid which lay buried under the concrete of the yard so he dug it up, rerouted the pipe and there was little improvement. Months later we found that the tap supplying the tank had not been fully turned on so that the tank had emptied quicker than it had filled. All that had been needed was the tap turning full on. The yard had been mutilated for nothing.

Margaret's confidence was boosted by the fact that, for the first few days, she was nursed by Joan Blamires, one of the first of our Guides and, in the maternity ward, by Judith Kisby, one of the last. They are all over the place, our children, ready to help. It's like being Miss Dove.

It was more important to Margaret than to most that she should make a full recovery to do again the job to which she was born. She asked the doctor, 'How soon will I be able to carry half a hundredweight?'

'Whatever will you want to do that for?' he answered. I don't think he had ever heard of women carrying corn or lifting walling stones. A nurse, however, told her that, with today's surgical skills, everything she had done before she would do again. We collected her at five o'clock, ten days after her admission. She phoned at mid-day to say they would not let her go until teatime. I rushed around all afternoon preparing for her return and accidentally left a yard gate untied. There is no need to narrate again what happened.

A few days after Margaret came home snow really fell and everywhere looked beautiful. I suddenly realised my back was better. Walkers who had stayed indoors because of the wind were out enjoying the snow. Someone opened the gate into the wood and wedged it open in a drift. All the 104 cattle walked through it, balanced precariously on the cliff edge and slithered down the precipitous slopes, crashing their way through briar, bramble and hawthorn and there was no way I could get them out alone.

Margaret, four days out of hospital, insisted on helping me. 'Don't be a fool,' I warned but to fetch help meant delay and maybe fatal accidents in the wood.

'I'm only going to make a noise and wave a stick,' she said, so we walked slowly down the snow-covered Five-Acre. Margaret steadied herself along the fence and shouted loudly and the dogs and I scrambled around the wooded valley forcing the cattle slowly towards the gate. Once they hit the path, nine times out of ten they will follow it. They did and all 104 filed through the gate. I don't think Margaret and I have ever walked more slowly up the Five Acre.

The snow gave them their next opportunity to disgrace us. There was not enough of it to keep them inside so, after the Sunday morning feed, I let them out. There was little to eat but they were already full and in the right mood for a bit of fun. If we have any snow at all it drifts at the Moor Gate and the first thing it does is to fill the cattle grid pit solid enough for people and animals to walk over.

On that Sunday, one week after Margaret came out of hospital, she was sitting in the New-do and she saw the whole line of cattle cross the cattle grid into the village. She had been sitting there, obeying doctor's orders and never giving a thought to the snow in the cattle grid.

I was carrying bales down to the sheds when Margaret started hammering on the window and pointing to the top of the road. We both jumped in the Range Rover and drove up there. A game had already begun. Seeing open garden gates, like Goldilocks, they were sampling each one, galloping round the house and the garden having fun. Can you imagine it? Over a hundred hefty, black heifers using each lawn as a circus ring.

The mystery was that there seemed to be nobody about, no irate house-holder, no proud gardener, angry husband, shouting wife or screaming children and no-one to help me! The cattle pushed and shoved their way precariously near greenhouses and kitchen windows. They scrambled through hedges, spilling themselves on the next door flower beds and manuring everything. Where was everyone? Glued to the telly, asleep by the fire, off for a Sunday run, out with the dog? The lane with its many houses was deserted. Margaret got out of the Range Rover and shouted whilst I ran in and out of gardens like a fool. The infantry found George's farmyard and gave us the opportunity to get in front of them and park so that most of the road was blocked. Margaret defended one gap and I did the other and George chased the 'buggers' out. Hooray, we had got them heading for home.

On the south side of the road are two acres of common land below a cliff. All the villagers call it The Crag and you can really lose control of cattle there. I drove the Range Rover forward to block the way at the point where the crag begins and Margaret took up her stand. The cattle were tearing up one side of the cliff, across the top and down the other side and pelting back towards a shouting, stick-waving Margaret.

This time the herd found the open gate of one of the two farms which sit on top of The Crag. Alone in the field I was wondering if I would ever get these stupid animals out when a young woman came to my rescue and she and I eventually drove all 104 back over the cattle grid. I was extremely grateful to that plucky young woman. As Anthony Quayle said, 'If you don't need them, to Hell with them!'

I don't know what the villagers made of the footprints all over their lawns and their licked kitchen windows. I collected the Range Rover and we went home. I dragged a gate, hitched it to the tow bar and pulled it up the road to gate the cattle grid and put an end to all that nonsense.

Shortly after Margaret came out of hospital, Shep died. Old age does not need much to take man or dog to the happy hunting ground. It was my job to carry him to the plantation and bury him but of all our dogs Shep belonged to Margaret.

Jack, an elderly and frequent visitor, who suffered from multiple sclerosis, phoned to ask if we had room for him for a couple of weeks. I put him off saying the road was impassable. A few days later he phoned again, said he was 'proper stalled' and could we lift him into our Range Rover and leave his three-wheeled invalid jalopy at the Moor Gate? What could we say?

My better half had no lift in her, so we had a problem. But there is always a friend, usually a woman, who will come. Together Dorothy and I manhan-dled Jack onto our front seat and left his mini-car in a snowdrift. 'It'll never start again after a fortnight there,' I thought but when Freda's daughter Kathleen and I bundled Jack back, at the end of his stay it was as gallant as its owner and at the first press on the starter it leapt into song. Margaret made all Jack's meals and did the family catering. When she paid a necessary final visit to the specialist he said, 'You're doing well, try lifting. Begin with a cup.'

Every morning I would find Margaret on the floor repeatedly doing exercises with the determination of one who is going to win, whatever the price.

The next few months remain a blank in my memory. The Visitors' Book is full so life must have proceeded normally, the only exception being that Margaret and I had changed roles. I suppose we were marking time and in doing so perhaps we had brief moments when we stood staring at our home and its location, wondering what would happen to it. The council proposed to move the boundary of the Green Belt to within yards of our west wall. Over the years hundreds of houses had been built to join the village to the town. What had got into people that they wanted so many houses in which to live alone? Pensioners, single parents, spinsters, bachelors, divorcees all unwilling to share; teenage children wanting to leave home; and houses, houses, everywhere. Whatever could we do to protect our home and the 170 acres of beauty from the oncoming tide of developers? The Council's proposal was defeated and the Green Belt was not moved but it might be only a matter of time. We might hold out but we would grow old. Someone, sometime, would surely turn The Currer into money and we couldn't see what we could do to prevent them.

In May Mother had a lot of pain in her shoulder and the doctor said, 'A little arthritis, my dear,' and gave her some pills. On Baugh Bay, Tiree, at the end of the month, she was determined to walk a long way along the water's edge, linked to Auntie Mary. Harry was in the wheelchair and we pressed Mother to thumb a lift but she would not. She hung on to Auntie Mary and when she got back to the Range Rover the pain in her shoulder was worse.

Next morning she could not press on the bed edge to stand. She instantly became a very old lady who could do nothing alone. She could not dress, or stand, or lower herself alone.

In desperation we took her to the Tiree doctor who said it wasn't arthritis, it was a rotary cuff lesion. He immobilised her arm and told her to go to a physiotherapist on return. The Tiree cottage has only beds for four and a bed settee. It was no use one of us being in the sitting room so I spent the fortnight on the hard floor at the foot of Mother's bed.

On our return Mother went dutifully to see one of my ex-Guides who is a physiotherapist. The rotary cuff lesion healed and there was no more talk of arthritis. Mother started baking again, making a pound and a half of pastry every other day, drying all the cutlery, folding all the serviettes and jumping in and out of the Range Rover and the bath like a teenager.

On 3rd August she celebrated her ninetieth birthday. Every bed in the house was full of guests so we were far too busy to have a party. She had never had a birthday party on any one of the preceding eighty-nine years so, she maintained, there was no call for one now. We secretly told a few people that we would have an open house all day for any who would like to pay their respects, and scores of people, relatives, friends, Guides, neighbours, some of the children I had taught and all our many guests showered her with good wishes and flowers. The vet brought a huge bouquet from the practice.

Several elderly guests came each year from Kent. They called themselves the Crazy Gang. They were all disabled ladies who brought unbelievable cheer into the house. Two of them, Gladys and Jean, had been anticipating Mother's ninetieth for two years and had been embroidering a collage depicting oast houses on a Kentish landscape. The result was beautiful.

Two cakes were required to give everyone a piece. It was a great occasion and Mother sailed into her nineties in tremendous style. She can tick us off right, left and centre but her graciousness, to all the many The Currer has magnetised, is without equal.

We were riding on cloud nine. We were coping with everything except providing for the long-term future of The Currer. Our now ninety-year-old mother, nearly thirty years ago, had said, 'We'll go t'Currer!' and given us quite a responsibility. Only a few people can shrug their shoulders and let the future take care of itself. We couldn't. The Currer was too important to us. We'd worked too hard and sacrificed too much. Somehow or other we had to get a preservation order, soon, before anything happened to any of us. We thought of Margaret Watson in Deepdale. It was worth a try.

Chapter Twenty-six

U nbeknown to anyone I went down to East Riddlesden Hall. I knew that in 1571, Arthur Currer had bought Leach Farm from the Paslewes of East Riddlesden for the princely sum of £30 and eventually bequeathed to Leach Farm the name Currer. This was the only thread of evidence we then had of any known history.

I asked for some leaflets to display on our notice board to encourage our guests to visit the Hall. East Riddlesden is a small manor house given to the National Trust in 1934 by the Briggs family. It had been bought by a developer wishing to build a lot of houses, prepared to pull down the Hall to create more space and even to use the stone in the new houses. The Briggs, a local family of means, were incensed and immediately stepped in, bought the Hall and handed it to the National Trust. We have a photograph of a funeral of one of the Briggs family, directed by the livery stables belonging to my great-grandfather.

I came home with leaflets and a handbook and we tried to learn as much as we could about a Trust to which we did not even belong. We read how to join, how to bequeath, how to covenant a property and land. We read what properties belonged to the Trust and which were covenanted, but we didn't do anything positive apart from thinking.

The hay was all bought and the loads of straw were coming daily. We could think about nothing but the continual task of feeding people and calves and the struggling to get the stack cover on before the rain came!

Then men, working on the pylons, left a gate open. Men! Margaret told one once that she would not marry a man for love n' money.

This gate was between our land and George's. A second gate, from this foreign field, onto the road, was also open. Had the cattle found the open door in the morning they would have had a feast in George's field for the hay was off a month ago and the fog well grown. But they did not discover the gap until evening and they were already full so they just acted daft, galloped all over the long grass and out onto the road, sampling anything and everything. They explored gardens and nibbled hedges. The villagers were alert this time and came out in force to drive them back into George's field and to phone us.

A few of our male guests said they would come and help. I am sure they were not prepared for over a hundred stampeding animals. The cattle were playful and silly and we tried a long time to get them back through the gate onto our land with no success. So we reopened the gate onto the road and our own Moor Gate and drove them that-a-way. Success depends on shouting like our male counterparts. We said a lot of things about those pylon men. Not nice things at all. The very next morning one heifer came home alone and Margaret saw that it was ill. There was very obvious swelling of the head and throat and its belly was empty. More than that, everything which should have been white was red, the saliva dripping from its mouth, the whites of its eyes and the liquid running profusely from the tear duct. The white skin where the hair was white on head and belly was red and its urine looked like sherry.

Margaret sent immediately for the vet. 'It can't eat or drink and just look at it!' she said.

The vet said it had been poisoned, most likely by St John's wort. He gave it an anti-histamine injection and, by putting a pipe down its throat, managed to get half a bucket of water into it. Deterioration was rapid. Within an hour Margaret was again on the phone to the vet who came hurrying up to give cortisone. 'If there's no improvement in two hours,' he said, 'send for Mitchell's.'

At the end of two hours there was stalemate. The heifer was no better, no worse. Margaret does not easily send for the gun. If there is any hope at all she waits. The deadline was past and in the morning the heifer was not dead. Just red and swollen and unable to eat.

I was dispatched to look for St John's wort. We did not think we would find this on our land. The coincidence of the open gate suggested that a poisonous plant had been eaten elsewhere. Even so, we searched our acres, George's field, the Crag and all the gardens down the top road. For the rest of summer we searched but never found.

The heifer was, at last, able to eat and drink; the swelling went and the colour began to fade but the vet told us the poor animal must never again go out in bright sunlight and we had to confine it mostly to barracks. The Electricity Board accepted the blame and we got compensation for having to feed it indoors and for being unable to sell at the right time. We were never compensated for all the extra hours Margaret spent tending it.

We decided not to sell all the animals privately but to take to market those ready, and to wait for those that needed another month or two. The heifer was one of them. So Margaret returned to the dreaded task of selling at market. No one way is best all of the time. I began going with her. When she shows animals in the ring they are taller than she is.

We could never go on like this for ever, we knew, just going from one big job to another, never planning ahead, always procrastinating about the future, never doing what was really important and getting older all the time. So we had the audacity to write to the solicitor of the National Trust and ask him how one ensured the preservation of land and farmhouses. I think it was the most preposterous, presumptive and outrageous thing we ever did.

We were going to Grange and the Lake District is full of National Trust properties and covenanted acres. We spent the whole fortnight talking to the farmers renting traditional farmhouses in beautiful places. They were ordinary folk like us with the same problems, countrymen with the same inner peace, and many of their wives were also offering bed and breakfast accommodation.

How comfortable it must feel, we pondered, to know that the land underfoot and the roof overhead is safe, preserved in perpetuity. We had this vision of The Currer of the future with its walls all repaired and everything cared for. We wandered around in cloud-cuckoo-land. We chuckled to ourselves, shook our heads in wonderment, leaned over the railings on Grange promenade, thinking buoyant thoughts, watching the sun silver the pools and gild the mud flats all across Morecambe Bay.

The sun shone throughout our stay. In a trance we gathered blackberries and bought apples in the Lyth Valley. Every time we saw a National Trust sign there was an excitement inside us. I think both of us were so intoxicated by the romance of the whole idea we lost sight of reality. Our feet, usually so firmly on the ground, were three feet above it.

A farmer told us to call at the Ambleside Headquarters and talk to the agent there. We'll never forget sitting in his shabby office listening to him bring us firmly back to earth. The National Trust not only had to be very selective, it also had to be realistic. Natural beauty was important and historical interest, but so were hedges and walls, so was viability and the condition of proposed properties. We thought of our many fallen walls.

'Put it this way,' said the agent, 'a property where walls and hedges are in repair looks better, doesn't it?'

We were presumptuous no longer. With extraordinary courtesy the good man escorted us to our Range Rover and was introduced to the rest of our family. He was waving when we drove the car out of the car park. I think we were laughing. At ourselves, of course.

'Guess what,' said Margaret. 'I think we are going to have to build all those walls ourselves!' Everything we have ever wanted we have had to do.

We drove back to The Studio and packed our bags for home. We sensed a challenge. We forgot Margaret had just had an operation and we instantly began to plan. It is typical of us that we decide in the morning and are knocking off the plaster by teatime.

Our first job, we agreed, was in the snug. We had restored the fireplace but we had reduced the size of the room. The brick-dividing wall must come down and the mullions must go back in the windows. Some insensitive person had removed them from the north face, probably when the chimney was walled up and cattle stalls put in. The sills and lintels and the upright sides of the windows were original, possibly 1571, lovely hewn stone. We would have to find mullions of the same period and we hadn't a clue where to look.

Our builder began taking down the brick wall and we removed the spare beds and lumber from the silly room. We not only needed the mullions for three windows, we really needed a whole new window to lighten the place. If we found the five necessary mullions it would be a miracle. To find more was beyond hope. A friend had recently sold her seventeenth-century house and I knew she had a few mullions because I had once, jokingly, asked to buy. I thought the new owners might be foolish enough to sell and I was right. They had already done so, to the milkman or some such person!

We couldn't go anywhere without looking for mullions and our builder searched the demolition yards. We remembered that Arthur Currer's father lived at Marley Hall. A new Hall had been built by the Savilles in 1626 and the old Hall was a ruin. We decided to go down and look, but the ruin was practically razed to the ground. If there were mullions there we would have to dig for them. Grass, nettles and trees ran riot. What had once been a Hall was only a mound.

Margaret rang our neighbours, those two competent farmers who excellently farm the land below us and maintain the 1626 Marley Hall. It is still a Hall whereas The Currer is only a farmhouse. The Currer laithe is part of the house. The occupants were farmers who needed to tend animals and to approach them through an adjoining door with the farmhouse. The Savilles built Marley Hall to stand separate from the barn and an old photograph shows that it was originally bigger than it is now. One wing was demolished, possibly a century ago.

Margaret was investigating every remote possibility of mullions. When she rang they were sorry, they didn't think they had any but there might be some at the old paper mill. We had never heard such even existed. It was a ruin lost in a tangle of bramble and undergrowth, less than a mile away. The men came with us to look but it was too modern to provide anything we needed.

So, instead of talking mullions we inevitably began talking cattle. We paused at the lane entrance to the farmyard and Margaret and the men leaned against the north wall and I leaned against the south one not eight feet away and market prices, trends and local farming gossip bemused us for a while.

I dropped out of the discussion for the wall on which the others were leaning began to fascinate me. It wasn't made entirely of random stone like the walls are hereabouts. It was most certainly a conglomeration of hewn stone, elaborately chiselled! Here and there long, shaped pillars had been used as throughs.

'Hold on,' I interrupted. 'There are mullions in that wall!'

Cattle and the dissatisfaction with the current prices were forgotten. We all turned our full attention to the extraordinary wall. It must have been built with window stone when the west wing of the Hall had been demolished.

'Yer know, ah've nivver sin them afore,' said one of the men who had lived there thirty years and more.

We could see the mullion ends of the throughs. The men began to pull down their wall and as they did so there appeared sill and lintel stones and the matching sides, all the corner pieces and some door jambs. We joined in and almost the whole wall at the farmyard entrance was window stone of exactly the right period. Our delight was indescribable. The men were as flabbergasted as we were.

Isn't it a fact that everywhere not covered with concrete and bricks can be read as a history book? What a tale could be read in that wall. It is only right that I should record our chapter of it for posterity.

We hired a large, low trailer to ferry the heavy stone up to The Currer. We took away somewhere in the region of two tons. Brian was amazed. He just couldn't believe his luck. He is not an ordinary builder. His hands knew how to reassemble the pieces. He was able to lighten the room with an identical, matching new window, to put back all the lost mullions, and use all the jamb stones. We were, in fact, two mullions short but a return journey to Marley was fruitful. We found what we needed in the garden wall.

This was an omen surely, a positive sign that our wish to preserve was justifiable.

There was little I could do until the builder completed his historic task. Margaret went out and surveyed the long wall which should have bordered the south boundary of the two fields we call the Footpaths. It had fallen flat for most of the way and what still stood was a shambles. We had abandoned all hope of rebuilding and had fenced it instead, crudely, when we let the top land in the summer of our depleted herd. We had believed that building The Currer walls was a job too big, too long, too tedious and too impossible for us to do.

'I'll show that man at Ambleside that I can put up walls,' Margaret muttered. 'And I'll prove that what you could do before a hysterectomy you can do after!'

I could not bear to see her working alone. The pressure of guests dwindled to workmen needing local accommodation. Mother and Harry and Auntie Mary were all well. We walled together, not too far apart for me to lift up Margaret's top stones. We may be daft but we are not stupid!

We did not use all our waking hours walling. There was another job I must do of equal importance. I must return to the City Archives and delve. A college friend was staying for a few days and we went together and found that a more competent historian than I had already extensively researched the history of Leach Farm and had assembled a family tree of the Currers and of the inter-relationships of the yeoman farmers of this hillside. It was too good to be true for the historian saved me hours of work. I brought home innumerable books from the library and searched the registers in the Parish Church and the Electoral Rolls of the nineteenth century.

We can only speculate as to why Arthur Currer, of Morton, bought this place from the Paslewes of East Riddlesden. The indenture dated 1571, the fourteenth year of Elizabeth I, says that he did, that he paid £30 for it, that it was in the tenure of Richard Leach and that he was granted permission to cut wood and stone to build a house.

The Paslewes had received lands hereabouts from Henry VIII in 1540 at the Dissolution of the Monasteries. The monks of Rievaulx had farmed the area and intakes from the moor had been walled and drained.

The Currer family belonged to the local élite. Arthur's grandfather was at Kildwick Hall and his father was at Marley. His mother was one of the Maudes from Holling Hall.

Our most exciting find was the Will of William of Marley who died in 1604. The beauty of its language fascinated us. Finding William's Will, in archives kept in York, made us more determined than ever to preserve what we could of our inheritance for posterity and to record what we have done, not with arrogance I hope.

We could not, initially, read the Will. A man in Bradford Archives department partially succeeded but it was a guest, staying here with a group of historians, who finally interpreted it. The Will made a provision for his wife, Isobel, to be allowed to remove to the messuage Arthur had bought in 1571 and in 1605 there is an indenture confirming that Isobel and her son William came to the hill top, to the house described as 'lately in the occupancy of Richard Leach' and currently called Leach Farm.

Twenty-eight years later, his mother having died, William released the property to Richard Sunderland, a wealthy descendant of the Paslewes whose sons were rich London merchants. This release describes the property as including 'one barn, newly builded and one fold to the same'.

So we knew that Currer's laithe was built just prior to 1633. Why such a big barn was needed we do not know. From then on only tenants ever lived here until we came in 1958. For nearly sixty years the property regularly changed hands. It was bought and sold, backwards and forwards, between the élite until in 1690 it was sold by descendants of the Currers to a descendant of the Paslewes, Robert Parker of Browsholme, resident of Marley Hall, for £509 15s. 0d. He was an extrovert, chiselling his initials into rocks on the boundaries and walls. We think he built the newer wing of the house.

If I have any complaints about this busy life we lead it is that, whatever our Hebridean friends say, there just isn't enough thinking time. Research needs commitment and with so much work to do in the snug and Christmas coming on apace there was too little opportunity to ponder on the perplexities of life.

I remember fleetingly thinking that this press-button generation must be quite wrong to believe it owes the past and future nothing at all. Perhaps there are just too many, too close, too irresponsible. Perhaps in a crowd it is reasonable to feel insignificant, to grab selfishly and think, 'What the heck! We're here today and gone tomorrow. It'll be all the same in a hundred years.' Will it? Do our lives barely disturb the water?

Certainly I didn't feel that way in December 1986. Four centuries of people came alarmingly alive. Their ordinary, unassuming lives had been part of a whole scheme. When we disturb the surface by being alive at all the ripple we generate circles wider and wider and multiplies to infinity. We are part of time and makers of history. We were very conscious of that as we struggled to get the improvements in the snug finished.

When the builder went we whitened the walls and prepared to lay the carpet before Christmas. We had bought a new one from a saleroom in an outlying village on the border of Lancashire and had scoured the city markets for curtain materials. On the night before Christmas Eve the curtains were all made and ready to hang and the roll of carpet was waiting to be laid. The new curtain rails had been screwed onto painted wood ready to nail above the mullioned windows.

Margaret and I fed the cattle and went together to complete the job in time for many guests to arrive next day.

'We'll just nail up the curtain rods,' I said, giving Margaret the end of one and lifting the other end to its correct position. The nails were already through the wood. I handed Margaret the hammer and she beat one into the wall. She passed the hammer back to me and I clouted the nail on my end. It went straight through a water pipe and a spurt shot across the room to shower the inglenook and threaten to flood the whole room. We dashed to turn off the mains supply and reduced the whole house and farm buildings to a state of no water at all. Surely other people must have catastrophies, too? I suppose it's what makes life fun!

Is it just a coincidence that our obliging electrician has a brother who is a good plumber and is equally tolerant? He did not seem one bit worried to be called out late at night to repair the damage. Margaret and I got on our hands and knees and mopped up the deluge and we turned on some electric fires to dry up the saturated floor. The carpet was down before the first guests arrived next day.

Christmas interrupted our frantic efforts but immediately it was over we were off again. The Currer had seen these two women behaving like this before. Houses which have stood four hundred years on a quiet hillside must have souls and eyes and memories. Walls which have witnessed centuries of births and deaths, festivity and tragedy cannot be just stones and mortar. If The Currer has any heart or pulse it must have quickened to see our activity during the spring of 1987.

The earth remained hard all January and most of February with only a thin sprinkling of snow. On the white hillside two determined women began putting up walls, hour after hour, day after day, often before breakfast, always after dark. We were obsessed. From almost nothing, we built walls. From heaps and tumbled chaos, from grass-covered mounds we built walls. We levered out stones with crow bars and pick axes and a black ribbon grew alongside the footpath. With morning light the first thing either of us did was to look out of the window and gloat on the lengthening line.

I do not like to think how much work we did that spring. We laughed and said that if our guests stood still we would paint them. We painted or creosoted everything. We whitened and varnished. We lopped down nettles and tidied woodpiles, we tarred all the corrugated tin and tightened all the fences. Inside we painted and papered and spring-cleaned. We took photographs and hung pictures and we felt sure someone would wonder what was afoot. In mad March days we piled all the oldies into the Range Rover and had a picnic in the meadows and put up yards and yards of wall. Before sunrise I was typing, sorting out the historical details and drawing maps. We were demented, surely?

We lost our identity. We began to have an affinity with the monks and the Leaches, the Currers, Parkers and Ferrands and for a little while didn't quite know to which century we belonged. We didn't live in the modern world at all. We never watched TV or listened to the news or read a paper. We ate spasmodically, bathed only occasionally, dressed in the same clothes, day after day; two silly women with an addiction for walls and an obsession with a hillside.

Easter came. The good weather was a kind friend, and nobody at all knew what we were up to.

Not even the Watts. They had been our nearest neighbours, at Jackfield, for over twelve years. We had not known them well for their mullioned house is not in our line of view or on any connecting track. Neither were they farmers. Out of the blue, at the end of January, Betty phoned to tell us they had sold the house and were homeless, until the people who had sold to them finished building a new house. She asked if we had a cottage free. We hadn't. The people in the top flat were house hunting but had got no further than that. Then unexpectedly the man came down to say they had been offered a flat in Ilkley and could they give notice? So the Watts came, for two weeks, they said, but they were still here in June. They had three large teenage children, a Jack Russell, a hamster and a budgie. They lived in the cottage until Easter, then they came into two bedrooms. As the season went by and we were already full we gave them one room and a tent and even sent them to Dorothy's for a few days. It was a laugh a minute. Betty is the most good-humoured lady I know. In her circumstances I think I would have gone round the bend.

If they wondered why we were being so fanatical about our spring-cleaning they made no comment. Perhaps no-one really noticed that walls were going up. There were so many down and people are not observant. We have a lifetime's work still ahead of us. A wanderer will comment that our walls, in many places, have as many ups and downs as castle walls. We'll get round to them all, someday.

For several years we had spent too much time indoors, with and for people we did not know very well. To be working on the hillside, facing it, or with backs to it overlooking the valley, was a foretaste of Heaven! To be handling stone, tidying the field edges and building on a firm foundation was just wonderful. We were intoxicated with the clean frosty air and we didn't care a hoot how long we worked.

We would come tearing home at six o'clock with the arrival of the first cars and the evening meal for eighteen would be on the table at seven o'clock. We loved every minute of it. Winter passed and the first flowers appeared and soft, green leaves broke from the buds in Jimmy's Wood and on the sycamore. 'It's so beautiful,' we kept telling ourselves, as the mist swirled in the valley and found its way up from Marley. 'It's glorious,' we praised as the sun went down in splendour over Ingleborough.

One day, in late April, we saw the cuckoo and thereafter heard him calling his impertinences all day and every day. Two agents from the National Trust were coming on 12th May to look at the land and the house to see if it had the qualities necessary for preservation. On the 11th Margaret and I walked the route we planned to take these gentlemen. It was a simply beautiful spring morning. The cuckoo never ceased praising it. There were larks and peewits and little birds everywhere.

We walked down to Jackfield and through the glen called Jimmy's Wood very aware of the bluebells, the violets, the first suggestion that there would soon be May blossom. We saw that the brown, bare sticks all over the place were really saplings of innumerable trees. We walked the boundary and scanned the distant horizons in a state of excited bliss.

We returned to the dry, swept yard; the sun was reflected from gloss paint and tarred tins. 'We've not done bad!' we said. We went indoors. It smelt of the newly emulsioned rooms and the polish on the parquet floor, of Mother's baking and the flowers on the dining room table. Sunlight sparkled on the glass all day and the view from whatever window stretched for miles.

Then on the morning of the 12th we woke early, ready to greet the big day, and it was pouring down. Rain was streaming down the windows in a pall of sadness. A nasty wind sobbed in the chimney and groaned in the sycamore. We could not believe it. There were no views, no colours and, when we went outside, no sound of birdsong, no lark or cuckoo and only the smell of wet grass and manure and saturated cattle. Water flowed down the yard culminating in a soggy pool in the gateway. The dry entrance to the cattle sheds had become an inch of mud to slither on. Water was coming down the lane like a deluge, streams flowed out of the mist hanging on the Eight Acre. A place that had seemed Heaven yesterday was isolated in greyness. We were devastated.

Our two guests arrived with all the courtesy of their profession. They wore clean wellingtons and hooded cagoules. We brought them in to meet the family and have coffee. We took them round the house putting on electric lights everywhere, for unseasonal darkness hung over all. Only the log fires, well stoked, brought any feeling of cheer. Then we put on our holiday cagoules, the ones I had made years ago, and our own less clean wellingtons and we all went out into the grey day.

There was too much silence. Hooded as we were we couldn't even hear each other talk. Occasionally the noise of traffic or a passing train in the valley penetrated the mist. We slithered our way down the clay path in the wood and braced ourselves to brave the wind. We scrambled through the heather and bilberry to the Altar path and the meadow walls looked neglected and the daisies were all closed. The hundred cattle evaded us. The few we saw looked miserable. We tried to salvage our inherent cheerfulness, to laugh in the face of terrible disappointment. 'How are the mighty fallen!' We tried to smile but we were sick, heartsluffed, as Mother would say.

We felt such fools! We felt like saying, 'Sorry to have troubled you. It's a pity you had to get wet!' We returned to the farmhouse and Margaret and I came in to prepare a lunch and the two men toured the outside of the house and the farm buildings. We think, when it is dry weather, that we have beaten the mud. It's a tale! There's mud all right! Plenty of it when there's a cloudburst!

Our guests stayed for lunch. They had an old-fashioned courtesy not often found in gentlemen these days but of course they were noncommittal and in our shame and embarrassment we did not press them for an opinion.

I don't think there has ever been a time when we were so deflated, when we couldn't laugh at ourselves. There wasn't a laugh in us. We are used to a certain degree of failure and when one road is blocked we climb a wall and find another; if one nail hits a knot and bends we just find another place to knock it in. But we had none of that left in us at all. We just lay down in front of the fire and slept all afternoon. It was the emptiest day we have ever spent.

In the next few days we had to try and pull ourselves together and get ready to go to Harris but we had no heart for it at all. If we had had no guests or cattle the spotless house would have remained so and we could just have packed our bags and gone. But life and jobs go on and the kitchen table accumulated kitchen paraphernalia and the sinks overflowed with dirty dishes and sheets were taken from the washing machine countless times.

A courteous letter of thanks for our hospitality came from the two agents saying that our application would be presented to numerous committees in the next few months in accordance with practice and we would be informed of decisions. One carrot was fed to us, just a little one, just a vague suggestion that they had been impressed by how much work we had done.

Only some of the lack of interest we felt in everything disappeared as we drove towards Scotland. We were tired. At the foot of Loch Lomond we pulled into a car park overlooking the water and had some sandwiches and made a flask of tea. Margaret let the dogs out and noticed that our petrol tank pipe was leaking. She searched the Range Rover for an empty ice-cream carton to catch it and I dashed into the nearest hotel to phone for the AA. It was a busy, water-sporty hotel with pushing people and loud music and I hated it. I felt shabby and worn out. No-one would help me with change for the slot or with a directory. There was no old world courtesy among the younger generation but there was from the nice, competent AA man who did us an excellent first-aid repair. I sincerely hope he had a safe journey home for we had inhaled far too many petrol fumes for safety.

Margaret had only driven a little way along Loch Lomond when she asked to hand over the driving. 'I'm falling asleep,' she said. If we had only had the sense to get out and walk a mile in the fresh air. But we were late; we had lost two hours. In any case we did not associate our tiredness with petrol fumes.

I took the wheel and long before the end of the loch was reached Margaret saw me veering towards the centre of the narrow road and alerted me. I saw a red car approaching and corrected my position but the red car had swerved and, fearing he had gone into the ditch, I braked an emergency stop. The car had passed safely but the car behind me could not stop and ran into my nearside back end. There was virtually no damage to the Range Rover, tough, reliable vehicle that it is, but the front, off-side wing of the car was dented and the headlight smashed. We were all shaking. We drove together to Crianlarich and reported to the police but it was unnecessary. No one was hurt and there was no roadside damage to other people's property.

Margaret was sure the petrol fumes had been soporific. If they were, the sharp fresh air on Loch Lomond side and the shock roused us and we were wide awake as we drove, in darkness, through the Pass of Glencoe, to Fort William, Spean Bridge and our bed and breakfast at Invergloy. We were extremely conscious of our vulnerability. If there had been an accident? If all of us had been killed and no proper provision made for The Currer? What if …? We could not sleep. Margaret and I, who can sleep anywhere, could not do so. What if, in our fatigue, we had killed someone?

We arrived on Harris in poor fettle and everything went right. If the sun god had deserted us on that important day at The Currer he was there to greet our island arrival. I think it must have been one of Mother's best holidays. Her health and spirits were never better and it helped to lift ours, just to see her sitting in front of the Seilebost cottage in almost perpetual sunshine.

She was sitting there one day when two elderly, very sunburnt cyclists got off their bicycles and came towards her. The view from the cottage is out of this world. They asked Mother for water to make a cup of tea. 'We can make yer a cup o'tea if you like,' she said but the two elderly men were prepared with picnic stove and were looking forward to brewing up on the shore.

'Yer live in a luvly place,' one man said.

'We don't live 'ere,' Mother replied. 'We're on 'oliday. Where d'you cum from?'

'Ah don't think yer'll knaw it,' the man said. 'We cum from 'Arden, near Bingley. '

'We just live over t'wall from yer,' Mother laughed. Later we saw the two men admiring the view of the seascape from Horgabost. We opened the Range Rover window and Mother called out, 'Call that nowt!'

The summer of 1987 was surely longer than usual. The days dragged by, full of guests and meals and loads of hay and straw and cattle sales. One day a friend came with her very well-behaved children. Father had a saying which said, 'One child is worth half a man and two children are worth nothing at all.'

Too true! One child is a help and more than one are a hindrance. These normally well-behaved children had brought a friend, maybe two. I only recollect that they started chasing each other in and out of the sheds in what might seem a harmless game except that the route included a run along a manger. They left both doors open so that animals could join in the game. Several did and when the chasing children next flew through the open door onto the manger passage the trespassing animals either jumped into the shed or tried to get through the iron bars. The distance between them is not much more than one head and not wide enough for a belly to pass. One smaller heifer got halfway through and stuck. The children screamed and came running for us. The open door at both ends was evidence. The permanently wedged animal was the result. We pushed and pulled and the children cried and their mother was silent and the heifer's tongue began to loll and its eyes bulged and we could not budge it. We had no saw good enough to hack through the iron bar.

'John will have,' Margaret said. 'If he's at home.' So she rushed inside and rang for John who said, 'It will be quicker to ring for the Fire Brigade.'

So Margaret did and within minutes two fire engines and twelve helmeted firemen arrived. The children were still crying and the animal was gasping for breath. It was freed at once and forced onto its feet amid a great deal of laughter from the men. Neither the children nor their mother joined in. Farms are not playgrounds.

The summer of 1987 slipped by in an agony of waiting. We had told no one of what we had done. If relatives and friends thought we looked a bit washed out there were plenty of other reasons why we might be so. We avoided all mention of anything remotely connected with the National Trust and when a friend came, who is a volunteer at East Riddlesden Hall, little knives felt to be sticking in all over.

Skye was ill. The mammary tumours which had killed Floss appeared on the belly of 'Mother's dog' and we felt a sickness inside knowing full well which way the wind would blow. Skye survived two operations but we lost her after all, just a week or two before we went to Grange. We wait a long time to be sure a heart has stopped beating. Our ginger cat died on the window ledge, of meningitis. For a long time its breathing was imperceptible. When she went to bed Margaret said to Harry, 'Ginger's died, Harry.' But next morning the body was still warm.

Skye's stiff little body only looked asleep as we buried it in the plantation.

We mourned Skye more intensely than usual. I think we were all feeling a bit sad about everything.

On the morning that we were to leave for Grange, that autumn, guests came running to tell us that Harry had fallen in the bathroom. We leapt up the stairs but, as he wasn't bleeding, we yanked him onto his feet, saw him downstairs and sat him at the table for breakfast. We had far too much to do if we were to be ready for Dorothy and Joy who were coming to relieve us at mid-day.

After breakfast he tried to rise to help with the washing up but muscles had seized in his chest and he could not move for pain. 'Stay where you are,' was the only sympathy the poor man got as we flew round making beds and packing the roof rack. 'Don't move. It'll pass.'

Auntie Mary packed the lunch we were intending to eat at the first convenient lay-by. Harry couldn't get out of the chair to change into clean clothes. We stripped him, threw his dirties into the washer and tried to ignore his groaning when we pulled on the clean ones. Dorothy and Joy were struggling through the door with their cases and all their paraphernalia. Their dogs were barking like mad in their car and ours were going beserk in ours and Mother was moaning it was definitely the last time we were going on holiday. I was saying we weren't going on holiday at all until we'd been to the hospital and Margaret was explaining to Dorothy that whatever happened we weren't coming back.

'We'll go to Auntie Mary's,' I heard her say.

We tried to get Harry on his feet to take him to the Range Rover. The wheelchairs were on top, under the rack cover. In any case we couldn't get Harry on his feet so I rang for an ambulance.

Harry tells everyone of the year he and I set off on holiday in an ambulance. Margaret, Mother and Auntie Mary followed with the laden Range Rover and lunch was eaten in the hospital car park whilst Harry had his X-ray. When we learned he had not broken any ribs and had only severe bruising, he was helped into the Range Rover and we made a non-stop dash to Grange. The hospital supplied him with plenty of paracetamol to dull the pain which he suffered for days. He could not get in and out of bed alone. We were up and down all night throughout our holiday. We avoided all National Trust properties like the plague. I don't think we had ever been so on edge.

And then we found Jess. We were buying apples at the Winster farm in the Lyth Valley and Lusky was barking at their dog and we said we had only one dog now. 'You don't know anyone with any pups for sale, do you?' I asked. It was just a chance remark.

'The bitch up at Hubbersty has seven,' the lady said. 'We're having one of the bitches. Do you want me to ring?'

We went up to Hubbersty and one of the month-old pups had not been spoken for so we said we would come back to the Lyth Valley in a month and that is how we found Jess.

We collected her on a wet mid-November day and she was sick all the way home. Margaret assured us that we had not picked up a pup who would permanently suffer from car sickness but Jess slobbered for months. We tried everything from canine to human travel sickness pills, music in the car and our untuneful singing. But still she slobbered and was drooling when we got to the Moor Gate and sick before we got home. Then Margaret bought a dangler to hang below the chassis and conduct the static electricity. From that day on Jess was an eager traveller just like Mother, Harry and Lusky.

We had intended to keep her outside. All our previous pups had been reared in the barns and Jess had been born in one but it was November and cold and we needed some warmth, some distraction from the necessity to wait for committee after committee to decide. So Jess came in and we could not take our eyes from her.

She did not herd, like Lusky did; she ignored hens and ducks and geese, balls and cars. She did not seem one bit interested in the job she had come to do. Then suddenly, the in-bred instinct to herd appeared and Jess is the best dog we have had since Jed.

We had waited for 20th November for so long we did not know how to greet it. Unlike May, one might expect it to be dreary but it was a pleasant day with weak winter sunshine. It had taken us nearly sixty years to set the stage and our contribution was small compared with that of the Currers who built the farmstead and the monks who built the walls and tilled the land four hundred years and more ago. In fact the God of Nature had done most and it had taken Him millions of years.

We were up early to put the final layer of polish onto the furniture. Mother, at the incredible age of ninety-one, was making her usual cakes and pastries. Auntie Mary was crossing her fingers in her own small cottage on the other side of the town. The weekday guests left. Only one young man remained, John, a quantity surveyor on the new Aire Valley trunk road being built in the valley. Harry, at sixty, born two years before Grandfather bid for The Currer and bought it for £1,050, finished the washing up and joined Mother who, her cakes being in the oven, was tackling the polishing of brasses from the numerous hearths and mantlepieces.

We completed the farm chores early. Outwardly we were calm but there was no ignoring the stress, no satisfactory way of easing the tension. Our Mr McVety was coming at four o'clock and we were ready! We were sitting, actually waiting, beside a huge log fire in the most uncomfortable silence our hearth has ever known.

Harry stationed himself on the sixteenth-century chest watching for the first sign of our expected guest's car as it came over the cattle grid. The weak November sun hovered on the southwestern horizon, spotlighting Ingleborough and flooding the whole landscape with unbelievable glamour. 'Please come,' we prayed. 'Please come and see the beauty.' But the sun dropped behind Mount Pleasant and the whole valley became sombre and grey. 'It isn't fair,' we moaned, 'it isn't fair!'

But when have we ever depended on the road being easy? We have seldom prayed for good weather. We have never wanted to win the easy way. In any case, whether the decision had gone for us or against us did not depend on the fact that the almost supernatural beauty had changed, with the setting of the sun, to a November semi-darkness. The final decision had been taken at a meeting several days ago and Mr McVety was just coming to tell us what it was.

The car came and we did not need the sun. The atmosphere created by our guest's arrival was warm and easy. Flames from the hawthorn logs leapt up the chimney. There is no mistaking genuine, old-fashioned friendliness and courtesy. He was sorry we had had to wait so long but if we were willing to give the covenants on our land and house, the National Trust would be pleased to accept them and preserve The Currer in perpetuity. Security had become ours because, whatever problems life would continue to bring, they would be only transitory, as we are ourselves.

Our one permanent problem had been solved in the most perfect way. Our signatures would be needed but not until spring.

We pulled the occasional table, laden with Mother's cakes and pastries, up to the fire and we all had tea. We switched on the lights but did not draw the curtains. Every star in Heaven was twinkling its delight and the valley was ablaze with the illuminations of the twentieth century. We talked a long time over tea. If there has been one moment in our lives when we could sit down and relax and savour the extraordinary way in which things have turned out, this surely was it. When our guest went the tide of contentment he had brought stayed on our shore and lapped warmly round us all.

What was there to do but sit round the fire and be happy? Not a lot. Even the meal was over. Much of our life is now spent making evening meals for people from all over the world but, on this rare occasion, our one guest required only bed and breakfast. There were just five cups and saucers and tea plates, a tray which had held the open sandwiches and a stand on which I had displayed Mother's tempting cakes and pastries. She and Harry could wash them easily!

There were twenty-three huge store heifers to feed in the corn mangers we had placed just over the fence at the bottom of the paddock and later, much later, there was the routine feed of 105 nine-month-old calves. Compared with most of our evenings it was child's play.

Mother stood up and went to the phone to ring Auntie Mary and tell her our news. Margaret and I donned our dirty trousers and jackets and went outside. The ground near the mangers had become a sea of mud. It was tenacious of our wellingtons, especially when we had the added weight of a shoulder-high bale of hay, but the heifers did not seem to mind. They approached the long manger at a gallop, eager for their nightly feast of corn which Margaret emptied into the trough. We carried their second course precariously through the mud to scatter on the dry ground before the field plunges to Jack Field's farmhouse with its Knights Templar cross on the roof peak of the gable end.

There is a spectacular view of the valley from that point. In the darkness the illuminations of the A650 and its overload of traffic and of houses scattered on the hillside make an interesting kaleidoscope of flickering light. In the daytime the great sweep of the Aire Gap points towards Ingleborough, fifty miles away. We completed the spreading of the fodder leisurely enough to appreciate the scene below us. We must do more standing and staring. We must not work quite so hard. We must always have time to be aware of the beauty of the place in which we live.

We turned towards the lighted sixteenth-century farmhouse. The whole evening, until the nine o'clock feed of the cattle in the shed, lay empty ahead of us. What bliss! There was not a pin acrook in the house, the washing up would be done and Mother and Harry would be waiting for us and wanting to talk over the day's excitement. It was all we could think and talk about ourselves. We felt we had come 'a long and distant journey to the portals of the sunset.'

A chill wind blew from the Brontë moorlands and carried us quickly round the gable end and into the farmyard. Our new pup Jess was sitting on the doorstep. 'We're coming in, Jess,' we said. 'We are going to sit by the fire for two hours. Imagine that!'

Why, tell me, after all these years of living at The Currer, do we still not know that the pleasure of the front room is not for us? Why do we dare to anticipate its undisputed comforts and so regularly believe our troubles are behind us?

We entered the kitchen together, Margaret, Jess and I. Harry was sitting on the floor, looking somewhat dazed and blood was pouring from an open wound on his head. Mother, for all her great age, was valiantly trying to get him onto his feet, knowing full well that it is an impossibility. The wash kitchen was in disorder, the dishes half done, cups and saucers undried on the draining board. In falling Harry had upskittled things on the Welsh dresser. There was blood all over him and over the carpet. The pup clambered over him in great excitement.

We are not strangers to this. A disabled, mobile person is much more of a liability than one safely sitting in a wheelchair. There was no alternative but to get him to hospital as quickly as we could. It was all too obvious that he needed stitching up.

Two people are needed to do all the things we have to do. We yanked Harry into a chair, found a clean pad and made quite a professional job with a triangular bandage. Margaret put the car rugs to warm on the Aga, I filled a hot water bottle and set a tray for John, adding a note telling him he'd have to put the kettle on himself. Mother lifted down warm jackets, put on her boots and fussed around Harry. Margaret drove out the Range Rover. Lusky, our Hebridean collie, heard the engine and left the geese he had successfully penned in the bullock shed. If we are driving out there is no way he will be left behind. There is a family joke that acknowledges the Range Rover never draws out of the yard without Harry, Mother and Lusky. 'There are three things I cannot do without,' says Harry. 'My two sisters and the Range Rover.'

We helped Mother into her comfortable middle back seat, enfolded her in car rugs and handed her the hot water bottle. Old ladies cannot be left alone in isolated farmhouses. We had no idea how long we would be.

Not much more than an hour had passed since our afternoon guest, with his quiet, courteous reassurances, had left. Margaret and I stepped out of our farm togs, pulled on clean trousers and jumped aboard. Yer gotta laugh! Why not? Harry did not seem in any danger of dying. He was laughing as much as we were.

We were still laughing three hours later when we returned from the hospital. The accident department had seemed relatively empty and all four of us had installed ourselves in the waiting area. I'd searched my pockets and found a few coins so that Margaret and I could share a hot cup of mediocre coffee. We'd been told that the staff were very busy. Indeed there was a lot of rushing about. A one-inch open wound in Harry's scalp was a minor accident.

'How did he do it?' I was eventually asked. I had no idea. It was Mother who had been there. So the old lady was brought from the waiting room. She explained in detail just how she had called Harry to be quick.

'Come on, Harry,' she had said, 't' pots are stawk'ning.' He had turned too quickly for his feet and had toppled over. Mother loves to be involved, especially with Harry. It offends her maternal instinct that we have to do so many things for him.

'Isn't it typical?' we laughed all the way home. Something nice, more than that, something incredible, happens to us and we have no moment to enjoy it.

Mirth is comfort indeed. From whom did we inherit it? To have to come home at half past ten, to a cold, dark farmhouse, to re-wash the dishes and scrub the carpet of its pool of blood; to stoke up the dying fire with logs from the pile across the yard, make several journeys to the cellar for coke for the three hungry stoves, empty the Range Rover of its rugs and hot water bottle, dash upstairs to put on Mother's electric blanket and then, finally, take off warm clean clothes and put on cold, dirty ones and go out together to feed the 105 bawling, hungry, almost fully grown calves, and still laugh!

Certainly we did not inherit that fund of laughter from Grandfather Brown. I don't think we inherited it at all. I think we created the ability to laugh ourselves and it has grown with us over the years and been a good friend.

The cattle were in no laughing mood. It was approaching midnight and they jostled with each other in greediness. We had to leap smartly out of their way to avoid being crushed. We floundered across the deepening manure with bales of bedding straw. 'It's time the muck was taken out,' Margaret said. How lovely it looks, that sea of strewn straw in each shed and the long rows of suddenly contented heifers with their heads buried in the manger hay.

It was morning. We sealed the door firmly on the ducks to foil the fox and, leaving our dirty wellingtons on the doorstep, we went indoors. Pulling off our cagoules we scattered the front porch, as always, with a confetti of straw. We made a cup of tea and joined Mother and Harry before the glowing embers.

It was too late to talk. The morning chores were not far enough away. Bed was essential but the effort to get there seemed unforthcoming so we sat silently, each thinking our own thoughts.

The tidiness of late afternoon had gone. A cat stretched on the hearthrug. Jess and Lusky lay before the Aga. Bits of straw littered the carpet and ashes had fallen on the hearth. Harry was eating Auntie Mary's biscuits oblivious of the large plaster on his head. Even Mother was quiet and she is garrulous at bedtime.

Margaret said, 'Nothing has changed. Has it?'

I roused from my weariness to answer, 'But wasn't that what everything was about? That nothing would change! We only ever want things as they are!'

And they were all laughing with me, Mother, Harry and Margaret, and Father, not far away, just 'through the open door'.